OFFICIAL REPORT

OF THE

FIFTEENTH INTERNATIONAL

CHRISTIAN ENDEAVOR CONVENTION

HELD IN

CENTRAL HALL, TENT WILLISTON, TENT ENDEAVOR, AND THE

CHURCHES,

WASINGTON D.C., JULY 8 – 13, 1896.

First Fruits Press
Wilmore, Kentucky
c2015

First Fruits Press
The Academic Open Press of Asbury Theological Seminary
204 N. Lexington Ave., Wilmore, KY 40390
859-858-2236
first.fruits@asburyseminary.edu
asbury.to/firstfruits

OFFICIAL REPORT

OF THE

FIFTEENTH INTERNATIONAL

CHRISTIAN ENDEAVOR CONVENTION,

HELD IN

CENTRAL HALL, TENT WILLISTON, TENT WASHINGTON, TENT ENDEAVOR,
AND THE CHURCHES,

WASHINGTON, D. C., JULY 8–13, 1896.

PUBLISHING DEPARTMENT,
UNITED SOCIETY OF CHRISTIAN ENDEAVOR,
646 WASHINGTON ST., BOSTON, MASS., U. S. A.
1896.

FIFTEENTH INTERNATIONAL CONVENTION

OF THE

YOUNG PEOPLE'S SOCIETIES

OF

CHRISTIAN ENDEAVOR.

WASHINGTON, D. C., JULY 8 – 13, 1896.

PRAISE God for the great Washington Christian Endeavor Convention!

It was decidedly the best of all our fifteen feasts of tabernacles; a gathering of power and promise.

The following pages present a picture of its scenes and an account of its events. Let us first take a review of its prominent characteristics.

Foremost — as was hoped would be the case — is its spirituality. "Not by might, nor by power, but by my Spirit, saith the Lord," was appropriately the "committee of '96's" motto. An unusual number of eminent evangelists gave earnest service throughout the Convention, — Rev. J. Wilbur Chapman, D.D., Rev. B. Fay Mills, Mr. C. N. Hunt, Rev. H. M. Wharton, D.D., Rev. Ford C. Ottman, Rev. F. M. Lamb, Commander Booth-Tucker, Mr. Ira D. Sankey, Rev. Ralph Gillam, and others. Boisterousness and frivolity were conspicuously absent. Over all the meetings brooded the earnest devotion and prayerful consecration that are more and more largely characteristic of Christian Endeavor. Not a few conversions were made in some of these meetings. Thousands were quickened to a higher spiritual life.

Though held in a city of unsurpassed attractiveness to the patriot,

3

the student, the lover of beauty in art and nature, the Convention did not suffer in attendance from sightseeing; but this pleasant occupation was reserved for the spaces in the programme prepared for it. And when the delegates did set out to see Washington, they saw it wisely and well; and to do this is to receive no slight education.

Not even the worst the Weather Bureau could do in the way of rain and wind beating down Tent Williston, and in the way of heat, served to dampen or wither the quiet enthusiasm. Discomforts were routed with a song. Hindrances were overleaped by zeal.

Some familiar Convention features were absent, or less marked than usual. We seem to have said farewell to the State "yell;" may it be forever! While the singing in the tents, and especially from the glorious choirs, was unsurpassed, the singing on the streets was slight. Washington was too interesting, and too hot. The "buzzer" was almost never used; the speakers kept to time.

There were some notable innovations, which deserve to become permanent. One of these is the holding of separate evangelistic services for men only and for women only. These meetings, at which some remarkable addresses were made, produced a decided and powerful effect.

Then there were the stereopticon lectures. There is no reason why we should not have an eye convention, as well as an ear convention and a mouth convention.

The meetings for citizens of the Convention city were held while the Endeavorers were attending their State rallies. It has always seemed a little selfish, though necessary, to bar from the sessions the people who have done so much to make them possible.

There were two magnificent mass-meetings, each devoted to a single theme of surpassing and immediate interest to the Christian world, — the session that considered the Armenians, and the Sabbath observance rally. Profoundly pathetic and appealing as was the Armenian meeting, and certain to result in immense blessing to our persecuted Christian brothers and sisters across the sea, we feel that the Sabbath observance rally, less dramatic, less thronged, though finely attended, will be productive of results more far-reaching and profound than any other session of the entire Convention.

The daily Bible-studies, under a competent leader, were another new feature, and one whose success at Washington certainly calls for its continuance in the Conventions to come. These great gatherings, based as they always have been on God's word and doing highest honor to it, should give definite and practical help and stimulus toward its study.

For the first time, in addition to the Junior rally, — and such a glorious Junior rally was never held, — an entire morning was devoted to a Junior workers' conference. Undoubtedly, from the standpoint of a practical worker, this was among the best sessions of the Convention.

It was a new idea to hold denominational missionary rallies, in addition to those denominational rallies which have heretofore met with success. These missionary rallies were superb successes, and they, too, will certainly receive an encore. And, by the way, the Washington Convention marks a distinct advance step in Christian Endeavor progress in several important denominations, while no loss of influence and favor is to be observed in any of them. Our glorious fellowship is ever widening and deepening.

The attendance, while stupendous,—over thirty-one thousand,—did not reach the enormous enrolment made by last year's gathering, held at Boston. This is easily accounted for by the hard times, the fear of Washington heat, the fact that a very large number of Endeavorers are saving up for San Francisco, '97, the enormous number of Endeavorers that live in and near Boston, and the fact that last year's Convention was held at a point so near Washington. Probably for a year we shall be relieved of the foolish cry: "See how vast, unwieldy, and unprofitable these monster gatherings are becoming! Let us split them up into sectional conventions or restrict the attendance to a limited number." On the other hand, what would have been said, ten years ago, if one had dared to prophesy that a purely religious convention would ever draw together, from great distances and all States and Provinces, and from foreign lands, and from all denominations, more than thirty thousand zealous young soldiers of the cross?

Last year were held the great patriotic rallies on Boston Common, at Bunker Hill, the Old South and Old North Churches, and under the Washington elm. This year the Capitol grounds furnished an arena for a popular patriotic demonstration such as the world has never seen. When before were fifty thousand people, mostly young men and young women, brought together at the capital of a great nation, not for a political jollification, not to honor a statesman or inaugurate an administration, but solely to emphasize their profound conviction that God should rule in the State, and that congresses and parliaments belong to Christ the Lord? That event will become historic, and to become a participant in it was alone well worth the journey to Washington.

We had in our national capital a model Convention city. Its scores of great hotels; its excellent street car service; its wide streets, so superb in their smooth asphalt, so stately with their shadowy elms; its spacious churches; its hospitable homes; its grand public edifices, museums, colleges, galleries, monuments, and statues; its crowding associations with all portions of our splendid history,—these things won all hearts, and thrilled us all with a new pride in our dear land. And our brothers that own the sway of England's noble queen could enjoy it all as heartily as we.

We had in the Committee of '96 a model Convention committee, backed up by a noble set of workers. Though coincidence with the Democratic national convention at Chicago prevented as wide publicity as would otherwise have been given to the Convention's history, the press was never so well served as by the splendid Convention press committee. The reception of delegates and their entertainment were cordial and in every way admirable. The hall committee's work was rendered exceedingly difficult by the overthrow of Tent Williston, but was heroically performed.   Never were the ushers better managed, nor has this important branch of Convention work ever been so well performed.   The decorations were numerous, and in unusually good taste.   The music, under the chairmanship of Mr. Chas. S. Clark and those mighty men of the baton, Messrs. Foster, Excell, and Bilhorn, with the help of the Hampton octette, Ira D. Sankey, Rev. F. M. Lamb, the men's choir, and others, was remarkably fine.   All the other committees did their work to universal acceptance.

And while the whole Christian Endeavor world is now speaking the praises of Washington and the noble Committee of '96, not one word too much will be uttered, for the city and committee are worthy of all honor.   At this time, particularly, reference must be made to that great host of workers, who, at immense sacrifice of time, money, pleasure, convenience, and self-interest, did such royal service for the great Convention, — the untitled and possibly unnoticed lay members of the Washington Christian Endeavor Societies.   To them, more than to any other human beings, belongs the credit for the success of the Convention.   They were invaluable.   For months they have given their lives to this work, toiling early and late on the various committees.   No political or other secular gathering ever could receive such service.   How shall we worthily praise the four thousand members of the chorus, — their songs are yet in our hearts, — the army of reception and entertainment committee members, who labored arduously day and night for the delegates; the fine corps of ushers and splendid press-committee workers, whose service money could not have bought; the tireless messengers, the faithful laborers at railway stations, church and committee headquarters, or the other multitudes who did glorious service in humble places?   We can not praise them rightly ; we can but appreciate them, and say how our hearts have been inspired and encouraged by their Christ-like example.   They ask no reward ; yet, nevertheless, high reward will be theirs at the hands of " the Father who seeth in secret."

Especial mention should be made of the remarkable evenness of the programme and the high excellence of the addresses, though an unusual number of the best speakers may be said to be the discoveries of this Convention.   From session after session the delegates came, declaring with fervor, " The grandest meeting of the Convention ! " " No, mine was ! " some one from another tent would cry.   " No, mine ! " a third would insist.   And especially noticeable, too, was the fact that nearly every speaker could be clearly heard.

The evangelistic meetings were often pentecostal in fervor and power.   In some instances the delegates, crowded out of the missions, held evangelistic meetings on their own account.   The first meeting of the World's Christian Endeavor Union was full of high promise.   It will not be long, certainly, before our International Convention is held in London, the metropolis of the world.   The large number of missionaries and missionary secretaries present gave the Convention a distinct uplift. The mission boards are utilizing, as never before, the immense power of these Christian Endeavor societies. Throughout the great gathering there were countless evidences of the fact that Christian Endeavor is constantly growing in the esteem of the evangelical denominations. The State rallies were far more carefully planned and enthusiastically carried out than ever before. Their programmes were miniature conventions. Never was there so good a representation of State officers. The reception given to them by the United Society was a most delightful occasion, and their all-day conference with the trustees was one of the most important milestones in Christian Endeavor history.

THE OPENING SESSIONS — WEDNESDAY EVENING.

FOR DEEPER SPIRITUAL LIFE.

The heavens opened. The showers came down. The clouds poured out their floods upon Washington throughout Wednesday. The outlook for the opening meetings was ominous. Many shook their heads and prophesied failures, but nevertheless they went to the churches themselves. And so did more than twenty thousand others. Almost every church was filled, and some overflowed. To a man the delegations, nearly all of which reached the city before Wednesday night, turned out to these opening meetings.

Then came the greater showers. The windows of heaven opened. There was a glorious downpour of spiritual refreshment such as has never before been seen at similar Convention meetings. A myriad of lives were enriched by the deep, quiet, and searching services of these opening sessions. Assuredly, the Convention's beginning was a fitting success.

"The Deepening of the Spiritual Life " was the topic of twenty of the meetings. Men whom God has honored gave his messages to the throngs of eager delegates listening with open hearts. In each meeting at least two addresses were given on the topic. To report a tenth part of these life-making speeches is beyond the scope of these columns. The words are written on the hearts of multitudes of young people, who will interpret them in lives that acknowledge the pre-eminence of spiritual things.

The speakers were of many denominations and from many places. The United Kingdom sent these noble sons with royal words : Rev. W. H. Towers, Rev. Arnold Streuli, and Rev. Joseph Brown Morgan, all of England ; Rev. W. D. Reid, Rev. Egerton R. Young, Rev. W. F. Wilson, and Rt. Rev. Maurice S. Baldwin, D.D., of Canada.

A large number of the addresses were by familiar and popular Christian Endeavor workers, whose words were of especial weight because of this. Some of these were Rev. J. T. McCrory, D.D., Rev. Smith Baker, D.D., Rev. Kerr B. Tupper, D.D., Rev. J. E. Pounds, D.D., Rev. Clarence A. Barbour, Rev. W. G. Fennell, Mr. Amos R. Wells, Rev. William Rader, Rev. J. Clement French, D.D., Rev. Leander S. Keyser, Mr. W. H. Strong, and Rev. James L. Hill, D.D.

As is the habit of Christian Endeavor, the pastors were given a first place at these meetings, and they predominated as speakers, as is shown by this list of names, which itself tells eloquently of the power of the words spoken : Rev. J. L. Withrow, D.D., LL.D., Rev. James A. Worden, D.D., Rev. Louis A. Banks, D.D., Rev. F. P. Ramsay, Rev. J. W. Fifield, Rev. Cortland Myers, Rev. W. H. Robinson, D.D., Rev. J. L. Campbell, D.D., Rev. C. L. Work, D.D., Rev. Rufus W.

Hufford, D.D., Rev. William J. Harsha, D.D., Rev. C. S. Mason, Bishop W. B. Derrick, D.D., Rev. P. Thomas Stanford, D.D., Rev. J. W. Hamilton, D.D., Rev. L. R. Dyott, Rev. R. F. Coyle, D.D., Rev. Franklin Hamilton, Rev. J. E. Mason, Rev. P. P. Watson, Bishop Samuel Fallows, D.D., LL.D., Bishop Alexander Walters, D.D., and Bishop B. W. Arnett, D.D.

In the Epiphany Episcopal Church the meeting was presided over by the pastor, Rev. R. H. McKim, D.D., and addressed by two Episcopal Christian Endeavor workers, Rev. Albert E. George, South Boston, and Rt. Rev. Maurice S. Baldwin, D.D., Lord Bishop of London, Ont., while a Massachusetts Episcopal Endeavorer, Rev. C. W. Palmer, had charge of the "quiet hour."

And those "quiet hours"! What times of silent searching, heart communion, and deep consecration they were! The desires for complete personal holiness, for the full enthronement of Jesus over the life, and for the exaltation of the Holy Spirit, generated in these precious moments, only the all-seeing Master himself can know. Evangelists Rev. Ralph Gillam, Rev. Ford C. Ottman, Mr. C. N. Hunt, and Rev. A. D. Thaeler, Mr. Charles B. Holdrege, Rev. W. F. McCauley, Rev. A. F. McGregor, Rev. Charles Roads, Rev. Charles A. Oliver, Mr. Arthur W. Kelly, Rev. T. G. Langdale, Mr. William T. Ellis, Rev. E. T. Root, Rev. S. Edward Young, Rev. Joseph Brown Turner, and Mr. Harry A. Kimports directed these solemn services. In the "quiet hour" many delegates learned afresh the Scripture, "Be still, and know that I am God."

A popular innovation at these opening Wednesday evening services was the introduction of two stereopticon missionary lectures. Audiences that crowded two churches to their fullest limit greeted the lecturers, Rev. Frank S. Dobbins and Rev. George E. Lovejoy, whose topics were, respectively, "The Land of the Rising Sun" and "The Crescent Against the Cross."

In all of these services, with one or two exceptions, the pastors of the churches in which the meetings assembled presided, and made addresses of welcome. At these meetings, too, the uniformed ushers did their first regular Convention work, as did also the chorus. It is needless to say that they did it well. The special music in many meetings was a helpful and delightful feature. Each church honored its guests by appropriate decorations, and these were often elaborate and significant. Since most of the churches were State headquarters, State colors and welcome banners were frequently to be seen.

Yes, Wednesday night was a night of great meetings, enriched by showers of blessing.

New York Avenue Presbyterian Church.

The spacious auditorium of the New York Avenue Presbyterian Church was well filled, there being few empty seats in the main body of the church, and the galleries were also occupied. While

the audience was being seated a strong male voice started a favorite
Endeavor hymn, which was taken up by the audience with well-sustained power and several verses were sung. The pastor of the church,
Rev. Wallace Radcliffe, D. D., presided over the meeting. Prayer was
offered by Dr. Radcliffe, and then he read a selection from the Scriptures, after which another hymn was sung, and with a few appropriate
words Dr. Radcliffe introduced Rev. Cortland Myers, of Brooklyn, N. Y.

Address of Rev. Cortland Myers, Brooklyn, N. Y.

When they tell me that in my own city and across the river in New York
City there are a million people who do not attend church upon the Sabbath
Day, it is an inspiration to come here to the City of Washington, and that inspiration is significant at such an hour as this, when we are gathered here in
such large numbers on such a stormy night, to speak about and to think about
this most important subject—The Deepening of the Spiritual Life.

About a mile from my own home was an old mill. One of the delights of
those happy hours was a journey to that mill. The anticipation always fought
with the reality, and the reality always won the victory. And I can now hear
the music of those forces, the roar of the old wheels and the buzz-saw. I recall
that there were certain hours in the history of that mill when it could not run
at all. But when the mountain stream was running down the hillside and the
larger stream flowing unto the mill-pond, the old miller could raise the gates,
and the water flowed ; but when those mountain streams were dry, there was
no music and no whistle, and the wheels did not turn and the saw did not buzz.
What was the trouble? What was needed? Water on the hillsides ; water
from the mountain tops. The old mill-pond was dependent upon that stream,
and the stream was dependent upon the water from the hills, and the water in
the hills dependent ·upon the streams from the mountain, and the mountain
dependent upon the clouds in the upper world.

The deepening of the spiritual life is from above, and that deepening has its
issue in power. We are not to deepen the stream of spiritual life by cutting a
channel or enlarging the channel. That is making merely a canal, and a canal
is a poor sort of a substitute for a stream by which we are going to run a mill,
by which we are going to receive the power. You are not going to deepen the
spiritual world by cutting a channel. No. The forces as they come from the
upper world will make their own appropriate and far better channel. The
spiritual life is not deepened by any process of the convent or of living the life
of a monk or a nun, dressed in sackcloth or living in ashes.

The Lord Jesus left us in this world, and we are not to be taken out of it
until we are to be transferred to heaven : we are in the world but not of it. If
you are to be just exactly what your heavenly Father wants you to be, your
spiritual life is not to be deepened by any external process, not by any method
or formula ; you can pass through all sorts of ceremony, and not have one
single atom added to your spiritual life. Why, I remember·recently of standing in the congregation of a church where the formal worship of God was going
on, and of noticing a young woman who, when prayers were offered, went
through her prayers as perfectly as they were ever uttered by any one in the
whole world ; yet I noticed at the same time that she was taking in every one
in the whole congregation, and I wondered if there were any additions being
made to her spiritual life in that hour of worship. I presume she thought
there were.

I do not believe it is within human power to produce faith in the human
heart. I believe though it is within human power to crowd out the bad by the
presence of the good. If you have a glass full of water, why, you are not going
to put any beer into it ! Now, there is something of the same principle that
must come into your own attitude towards this subject of which we are speaking to-night. Your spiritual life is to be deepened by the crowding-out process.

That is God's process. That which is untrue is best taken care of by crowding in all that which is true.

Now, it is a beautiful thing to see a true Christian character, but I declare to God that the most beautiful thing to be seen in the Christian life is the issue of this deepening of the spiritual life into power, not to get out of the world, but to move the world, and to move it for God. We are to be men and women, filled with the power of the Holy Ghost, to move the world on up towards God until at last it is bound with golden chains fast to his feet. What did they wait in the old city of Jerusalem for? Will you tell me? What did Peter wait for, and James and Thomas, and the rest of them wait for in the old City? Peter waited until that quick and hasty temper of his had been dispelled by the grace of the Spirit. We need to-day, more than we need anything else in this wide world, a deepening of the spiritual life, which is the divine energy moving through man. The weakest thing on earth is the man or woman who says he is Christian and is not moved by the Holy Ghost. The mightiest force on earth is the weakest man or woman who says "I am Christian, and I am moved by the divine energy, which is the Holy Spirit himself." That is the way this world is to be brought to the feet of our Master, and that is the process which God has marked out for you, to do your work in your Endeavor Societies.

The next speaker was one of the Presbyterian pastors of Chicago, and was heartily received.

Address of Rev. W. H. Robinson, D.D., of Englewood, Ill.

I speak this evening to those who have pondered the oracles of God, and who have worked in God's garden weeding and planting; not to babes in Christ, but to those hungry to be fed with meat. You are here because you feel a pressure toward loftier aspiration and discontented with common measures of spiritual life. You are asking for some diviner terms than the flat earth usually affords by which to mount to eternal life.

The spiritual life should rule the bodily. Man's living body is tenanted by a living spirit. He has a life within a life. There are those who are bursting with animal life at every pore, while their spiritual life makes no sign. They have wound such thick veils of flesh around the spirit that its light never shines through. The body, even, seems in some to have absorbed the shrunken spirit as the worm draws in the withered leaf and makes it earth.

On the other hand the inner life sometimes flames through the outer and transfigures it. Through the unconscious skin of Moses' face his secret Sinai fellowship with God forced rays of light that never was on sea or land. The faces of the Sanhedrim and its false witnesses, opaque with passion and heavy with lies, fronted in Stephen the incipient transfiguration of a face that seemed another morn risen on mid-noon — perfectly angelic.

Put a light inside a marble vase and the stone grows beautifully translucent. The spirit of man is the candle of the Lord and should shine through the texture of the countenance. Leddon, in his "Elements of Religion," a book worth reading, says of John Keble, author of "The Christian Year," that, "his face was like an illuminated clock." Through the time and tear-stained dial and across the weather-worn hands shone the light of a great peace within. Such men you call spiritually minded, they have a profound and powerful spiritual life. You want to be like them. You want to deepen your spiritual life. But men are full of vagaries, false ecstasies, and strange contradictions. "Blank does make a beautiful prayer, but he will lie," said a man to me. I fear it was true. Such a man seems to be religious. He seems to have spiritual life. His nature is like the tree of the tropics. The tenderest bird notes are heard in the foliage. Has not the spirit then alighted like a heavenly dove, and made its nest and rest? The leaves are stirred with rustling music. Does not the spirit, like some heavenly wind, breathe across these branches? Blossoms exhale their fragrance like swinging censers. What but the very breath divine can disengage such gusts of perfume? Is not this spirituality? But down below is the oozy ground where the cobra flashes his fangs and the centipede mixes his poison. The contact with the skies is good, but alas for the contact with the common earth of daily life! It is Balaam incarnate again. The language of the Mount is beautiful, but the life on the meadow is evil and teaches Israel to sin.

When, then, we seek to deepen our spiritual life, our very first anxiety must be to know what spiritual life is in its true essence. The thing to deepen is what? Thank God, the answer is clear. Ideal spiritual life is the life effected by the Holy Spirit. God has sent forth the spirit of his Son into men's hearts, and the spiritual life effected thereby in the inmost soul and its fruit in the outward life are clearly and definitely described.

When the spirit of God comes into our souls he produces certain thoughts and emotions. These are very definite. One of them is that we feel that God is our Father. God hath sent forth the spirit of his Son into our hearts, whereby we cry "Abba!" that is, "Father." Jesus' especial revelation was of God as a father, and the spirit sent by Jesus fills the soul with the cry which appropriates that truth.

Another effect of the spirit in the soul is to fill it with intense prayer, such profound desire for God and holiness and salvation from sin as can not be expressed in words. All deep emotions defy language. It is with feelings as with waters. The shallows murmur but the deep are dumb.

But there is no such thing as a spiritual life in the soul which does not manifest itself in the outward life. And there is no mistaking the manifestation. The fruits of the spirit are manifest, and are these: love, joy, peace, long-suffering, gentleness, meekness, patience.

And the connection between these two, the inner and the outer, is clear. He who feels that God is his loving father overflows upon men as from an inner fountain of love and joy and peace. The strength and joy of his inner life project themselves forth upon others in long-suffering, gentleness, meekness, patience. There is a beautiful correspondence between a tree and its roots. If the ground beneath a maple or elm could be made transparent, or if the X-ray could photograph the unseen roots as well as the seen tree, there would be two trees in sight—a tree of roots below and a tree of branches above, and the two wonderfully corresponding to each other down to finest filaments. If you find yourself gifted in prayer, and cross to your brother, or successful on the lookout committee and unhelpful in the home, set yourself to remembering that the spiritual life is symmetrical. If the tree of branches does not equal the tree of roots then some worm of death or some leak from an unsuspected gas-pipe is slaying the secret vitality. Learn to distinguish between the accompaniment of spiritual life, and spiritual life itself, yea, even between the accompaniments of the Holy Spirit and that Spirit itself.

Dost thou then really desire a deeper spiritual life? Enter into thy closet and pray to thy Father which seeth in secret. That Father is more willing to give thee the Holy Spirit than earthly parents are to give good gifts to their asking offspring. And co-operate with the spirit by your own effort. Say low to your own soul, "O my soul, thou art ensphered by the earthly and perishing. But thou thyself art the child of God." This sonship is begotten in thee of the Holy Spirit. Even now thou art a temple of the Holy Ghost. Thou wouldst not scratch the polish on a church pew or pulpit or cut the cushions—mar not in any wise that physical structure which is the temple of the living God. Thou art living in the spirit. Walk in the spirit more and more. Deepen thine own spiritual life with fear and trembling, for the spirit is deepening that life within thee. Use both prayer and care, grace and grit, tenacity and trust.

Is this then the conclusion of the whole matter? I think it is not. Is there any simpler and more living unity which fires and fuses all the details of the spiritual life, integrating them into its living self? I think there is. When we give thoughts and meetings and prayer to "deepening the spiritual life" we have some ideal more or less dim or clear before us. What is it? This is it. There can be no question what it should be. There was One whose spiritual life needed no deepening. It was already as deep as God. He was conceived of the Holy Spirit. He was an Holy thing from his birth. At his baptism the Holy Spirit came upon him not in the tongue form of a divided flame, but in the dove form of organic completeness. He was led into the wilderness by the good spirit to be tempted by the bad. He returned in the power of the spirit into Galilee. Through that eternal spirit he offered himself to God. His spiritual life needed no change in any dimension. The depth and breadth and length of it were equal. Its size and symmetry were perfect. His spiritual mindedness was absolute. Here is the touchstone, a corrective and short method for the whole legion of false notions of spirituality and spiritual life. Chemical analysis is the long method for telling what is healthy in atmosphere or food. The short method is by the senses of smell or taste. The long method for right and wrong is casuistry and systems of rectitude. The short method is conscience. So, books on holy living and holy dying, or on the Imitation of Christ, or even a wide and scattering study of the Bible, are the long methods toward the spiritual life. The short method is the living Christ within the soul to whom we calmly turn and say, " Did you do it, Lord Jesus?" " Would you do it if you were I?"

With this living Christ in the soul we see that spiritual life is not in the thinness of ascetic fastings. It is not in a diet of locusts with side dishes of unfarmed honey, for the Son of Man came eating and drinking. It is not in covenants or exclusive withdrawal into the wilderness of a "retreat." For Jesus was the companion of publicans and sinners. It is not in the prolonged eloquence of Isaiah's prophecies, for Jesus uttered none such. It is not in the despairing rush of Elijah into the wilderness and the morbid despondency that says, " I am not fit to live." For these things are not in the four biographies of Jesus. Oh! I would save all endeavoring souls, if I might, from egotistic strainings after the ethereal and hallowed Christs of poetic portrait painters, by creating within you the ever-shifting yet ever-constant image of Jesus Christ, perpetually changing in expression and attitude, so as to furnish the right ideal for each shifting hour. There are lovers here who need not even snatch a secret glance at the beloved picture to recall the face. They see it everywhere by day in its likeness or contrast to other faces. It is the background for other faces or is superimposed upon them. It lives before them in the night-time, dark, splendid, speaking in the silence, and holds them from their sleep. And there are friends, there are husbands and wives who have so loved and studied each other that in any newly rising set of circumstances each knows with instinctive and infallible certainty how the other would feel or act. And when death has separated one from the other the sainted form is present and sways the other's life from hour to hour. Sometimes the dear face appears with the warm curves of youth, and again with the lines that acid care has chiseled through the years. Sometimes the form is robed in the heavy clothes of toil, sometimes in the glory of anniversary apparel. Sometimes its unheard voice is sweet as first love, and again clarion like a soldier's horn. But it is ever the same face and form and voice. From a rejected huge block of marble, Angelo so carved David with his sling in hand that, from one viewpoint of the Florence Academy of Fine Arts, he appears the youthful boy he was; from another, his face seems changed to the almost mature determination of the antagonist of Goliath. Yet it is the same statue. So I would have you familiar with the composite Christ. I would have you see him amid all sceneries, whether upon the gray mountain top of prayer, beside the rushing river of John's baptism, on the pebbly shore of Galilee, or within the brightness of Hermon's cloud.

I would have you see him and all human surroundings, whether compassed about by the raving mob of Nazareth, or entrancing the crowd curved close to the circling waves of Gennesaret's bay ; whether answering the sharp questions of temple priests, or using gracious words to synagogue students ; alone with the Sychar woman at noon and with Nicodemus at night, or in the centre of palm branches that quavered in the breath of royal hosannas and in the midst of the same voices rested enough to cry, " Crucify! crucify!"

I would have you see him in all ages of his life, whether the grotto babe of Bethlehem, the high-hearted boy of twelve in his father's sacred house, the muscular young workman in the Nazareth shop, the embrowned and travel-stained man, the expiring sufferer of the last hours, or the ageless conqueror of the sealed and guarded tomb. I would have you see him in all bodily conditions,— held helpless at Mary's breast, or smiting soldiers with a look; weary at the well or walking on the waves; asleep on the pillow at the stern of the ship while others waked, or awake in the garden while the three others were asleep; striding tensely forward to the cross when his hour was come, or exhausted upon that cross where, from each spiked hand, blood-drop after blood-drop fell to join its fellow in the little pool that was making itself upon the ground, and pale and cold at last when death and silence, too, enamored of his voice, locked its mute music in their rugged cell till in the triumph of eternal youth he broke the lock, and the mute music of " Mary !" sounded in a woman's ears.

All hail, then, to you who have decided to become disciples of the inner and spiritual life of Christ. You must set your spiritual nature to rule your bodily. Appetites and passions must be subjected to the soul's welfare and used in the service of the soul. Then this general spiritual mind must make its condition most definite by seeking, praying for the Holy Spirit, and cultivating the sense of God's fatherhood and a better and purer bodily condition, culminating in a resurrection body like Christ's. And the spiritual life will become so intense as to be unspeakable in contents. Even also test your spiritual life by its fruits in a temper that is long-suffering, gentle, and patient. And that you may not be lost in maze and labyrinth of searching, consider and behold Jesus Christ, whose spiritual life was perfect. Have the vision of him, and have him within your soul more and more. Go away from this Convention with this one great secret resolve in your very soul: I will have the complete Christ within my soul, that I may completely incarnate him in my life. To carry out this resolve you will need to take some such pledge as this, and keep it ever before your soul eye : —

O Christ, trusting in thy Holy Spirit to help my memory, reason, and imagination, study thy life in all its connections, I promise not to study one of the four gospels more than the others. I promise not to study thy life of communion with God and thy prayers more than thy outward conduct among thy fellow men. I also promise never to study a feature or detail of thy life without trying vividly to see them in the very act. And I also promise never to leave my studying without the definite prayer, " O Lord, put this under me." And, finally, I promise to struggle to reproduce each feature of thy life in my own.

At the close of the two addresses a most impressive " quiet hour " was conducted by Mr. Charles B. Holdrege, of Chicago, Ill.

Mount Vernon Place M. E. South Church.

The meeting was largely attended by visiting delegates from North Carolina, South Carolina, and Georgia, with a goodly sprinkling of Washingtonians, who thus had their first glimpse of the sessions of a Christian Endeavor Convention. The Mt. Vernon Church choir of the Convention chorus had a chance to show what it could do in the musical line, and under the very efficient leadership of Mr. Page L. Zimmerman.

The pastor, Rev. Isaac W. Canter, D.D., was the presiding officer, and Miss Florence Ball, also of Mt. Vernon, played the big organ.

There was a preliminary song service, and then Dr. Canter called upon Rev. Rumsey Smithson, D.D., presiding elder of the Washington Methodist Church, South, to offer the opening prayer.

The 103d Psalm was read responsively, and then Dr. Canter formally, but none the less beautifully, welcomed the Southern Endeavorers to the church and the city.

Another Gospel hymn was sung, and then the first speaker, Rev. W. D. Reid, of Montreal, Canada, President of the Quebec Provincial Union of Christian Endeavor, was introduced.

Address of Rev. W. D. Reid, Montreal, P. Q.

The subject of which I have been asked to speak is an exceedingly solemn one ; it reaches down and brings us face to face with the awful issues of eternal life or eternal death. In considering what is meant by spirituality, we must beware of the fatal error of mistaking for spirituality loyalty to religious institutions or organizations. Many are exceedingly loyal to some particular institution, and they imagine that because of this they are deeply spiritual. This is strikingly exemplified in the history of the Jews. What loyalty they exhibited toward their temple, their Sabbath, their ordinances ! When the Romans, under Vespasian, invaded Judea, the Jews would die, and often did, by the score, rather than desecrate the Sabbath in self-defence. Yet they were the men whom Christ denounced as hypocrites, devoid of spiritual life. It shows me that it is possible to have wonderful loyalty and love for our institutions and yet have no spiritual life. The devil often deceives men by causing them to believe that loyalty to institutions means religion. Again, spirituality must not be considered as synonymous with enthusiasm, with Christian activity. You have read of the young man in the Bible called Jehu. He showed unparalleled zeal in the work of the Lord, slaughtered the priests of Baal without mercy. Yea ! he almost vanquished the outward form of idolatry, but, alas ! in after days he proved that with all his zeal no spiritual life had been there. Let every Endeavorer make no mistake here, and see that he is not mistaking Christian activity for spirituality. Spirituality should not be mistaken for morality, which may be defined as that rule of conduct regulating man's duty to himself and his fellow beings. Loyalty to religious institutions, zeal in the cause of humanity and morality, as a general rule are the results of spiritual life ; but do not mistake them for the genuine article. Spirituality depends entirely upon the relationship existing between the individual soul and its God. Deepening of the spiritual life depends upon several laws ; the dwelling in your hearts of a hungering and thirsting for righteousness and the desire to become more like God. You must also believe that a deeper life is possible for you. In the accomplishment of any object it is a great stimulus for one to have confidence in his ability to reach the point aimed at. Another principle is, be sure that you have been born again. Remember that before any spirituality can be developed in you there must be a new spiritual birth. Just as well attempt to grow a field of grain where no seed has been sown as to imagine that you can develop spirituality when your heart has never been renewed by the grace of God. You must become a Christian if you wish to experience a deeper life. You can not afford to tamper with conscience. You dare not question the dictates of God's spirit in even the smallest matters. Wherever the finger of conscience points you must be ready to go. You must listen for the faintest whisper and obey. Another principle is a recognition of the great truth that you are not your own ; that you belong, body, soul, and spirit, to the Lord Jesus Christ. Among the evidences of the deeper life are purification of character, stability to character, an intense earnestness to character, and stimulus to activity. It will show itself on a death-bed. I have stood by the death-bed of the infidel, who passed into the unseen world in black despair. I have watched the death-struggle of the agnostic as he passed through the vale with a faltering " don't know " upon his lips. I have talked to the nominal Christian while the grim monster tightened his grip upon the vitals, and with awestruck whisper and blanched face he said he hoped that all would be well. I have listened to the clear, urging note of triumph of a Paul, who shouted in victory as he passed through the dark waters,

" I know in whom I have believed." Death has lost its sting and the grave its victory.

After singing " Christ and the Church," Dr. Canter introduced Rev. L. A. Banks, D.D., of Brooklyn, N. Y., pastor of the Hanson Place M. E. Church.

Address of Rev. Louis Albert Banks, D.D., Brooklyn, N. Y.

Under the old dispensation it was expressly stated that " a dwarf " should not be permitted to " come nigh to offer the bread of his God." This had special reference to the priests who were allowed to eat bread, but were limited in their privileges because of their blemish. Under the Gospel we are all priests unto God ; and we are constantly having illustrated before us the fulfillment of that old requirement, for not a day passes but we see Christian priests shut out from the joy and honor of " offering the bread of their God," because they are spiritually dwarfed.

It is impossible that one should be dwarfed in any way and not suffer for it. One of the penalties of ignorance, for instance, is that the unlearned man must forego the keen delight of imparting knowledge. The heaviest penalty of poverty is that one so situated may not experience that highest type of joy which comes from relieving distress ; so the saddest penalty of a dwarfed nature is that it is shut out from the noble joy which enlarged and affluent souls share in bestowing the bread of life upon the hungry.

Perhaps the most interesting discovery which Mr. Stanley made in " Darkest Africa " was the race of small dwarfs which he found there. No wonder the daring explorer grows eloquent and romantic as he meditates upon their history, for he declares that for more than three thousand years this little race of pygmies have lived there under the shadow of the Mountains of the Moon. He thinks them to be the oldest types of primeval man, and believes they are descended from the outcasts of the earliest ages, the Ishmaels of the primitive race, forever shunning the haunts of the workers, deprived of the joy and delight of the home-earth, eternally exiled by their vice, to live the life of human beasts in morass, and fen, and jungle wild. These little people are the most ancient race who still possess the dwelling-places of their ancestors. Herodotus, the father of history, tells about them. But old as they are, they have made no progress in physical development, intellectual culture, or moral refinement. Their bodies are only from two to four feet high, and they live in little round brush huts, that look like a village of children's playhouses. But little as their bodies are, their souls seem smaller still. They have been so shut away from the sunshine, in the dark forest, that their bodies have not only been dwarfed, but their minds and souls have grovelled in the dirt.

But, alas! one does not need to go to Darkest Africa to find intellectual and moral pygmies. The dwarfs are all about us. They exist in the very midst of our brightest modern civilization. There are multitudes of people who are well developed and well fed, physically and intellectually, and whom men, looking on, suppose to be towering giants, who are in heart and soul the most insignificant dwarfs.

There are many things that may dwarf a soul, but perhaps the most common and potent cause of all is the living in a close material atmosphere. If you would know the glad exultation of a pure atmosphere and a wide horizon, you must pay the price of a climb to the mountain top ; so souls only grow large as they come into fellowship with lofty spiritual natures. Education, books, pictures, music, travel, enlarge men; but the great enlargement must come from the consciousness of God in the world. All narrow walls are broken down in his presence. If we look back over the history of the world, we will find that the men and women who have been the spiritual athletes and giants in their time have been those who lived in a horizon that was broadened and enlarged by their faith in God. The consciousness of God is the most potent power known to humanity in deepening the spiritual life and in enlarging the spiritual nature.

How clearly this is illustrated in the history of Moses! Many other shepherds there were, doubtless, who followed their flocks on the slopes of Mount Horeb, but Moses only found Jehovah there. This consciousness of God made it possible for him to live in an atmosphere strong enough where he was able to make that sublime choice and refuse to be called the son of Pharaoh's daughter, having respect unto " the recompense of the reward."

It was this same atmosphere, luminous with the presence of God, which Daniel and the three Hebrew worthies breathed, and on which they grew to be giants, so that a young captive from Jerusalem became a far larger and more important character than the king in Babylon.

It was the same consciousness of the ever-present God, that made Joseph, in his dungeon, a grander personage than Pharaoh on the throne in Egypt ; and which finally made the dungeon too small to hold him, and made him a ruler among the people who had held him in bondage.

You see the same truth illustrated in the story of Nehemiah. A helpless, weeping servant he seems at first, in the Persian palace ; but as time goes on, and his prayers to the God of his fathers are answered, and he comes under divine direction into a place of responsibility and power, he grows into a strong, self-reliant, daring man; and when they undertake to scare him away from his work by the threat of the assault of Sanballat, we are not astonished to hear his brave words: " Should such a man as I flee?" And if we turn to that sublime life of Jesus Christ which must ever be our final appeal in spiritual things, we shall certainly see that its supreme characteristic is the consciousness of God which pervades it. Whether he was alone on the mountain at night in prayer, preaching to the multitude, or pursuing his ministry going about doing good, working miracles of healing, or stilling the tempest at the terror-stricken cry of his affrighted disciples, the presence of God was like an atmosphere in which Jesus lived and wrought.

The same great spiritual forces are working in the world to-day. It is just as true now as ever, that the men who live in a close material atmosphere, and give themselves up to eating and drinking, become spiritual dwarfs ; and, on the other hand, it is just as true as it ever was, that the man who lives in communion with God, living in glad consciousness of God's presence and leadership, is enlarged in spiritual stature, and becomes affluent with the bread of heaven to bestow on all who need.

Such a soul becomes rich in spiritual resources. The desire to be rich, to have an abundance, to have more than we need for immediate requirements, seems to be in all healthy natures. It is one of the chief mainsprings of human action. While it is true that some of the early Pilgrims came to this country seeking freedom, and ever and anon since, there have been those from different lands who have sought here an asylum from tyranny and oppression, yet it can not be disputed that the overwhelming majority of the people who have crossed the ocean and spread abroad until they have covered the continent, felling the forests, bridging the rivers, irrigating the desert, until the whole land blossoms with fertility, have come from a desire to get rich or at least to obtain a more abundant life. Men are not to be blamed for desiring to obtain wealth. That desire is inherent in human nature. But many are to be blamed in that they choose the very poorest quality of riches. It may be a good thing to be rich in lands, and steamships, and stocks, and securities, and gold ; but it is an infinitely better thing to be rich in love, and hope, and faith, and noble character. A recent writer illustrates the superiority of spiritual wealth to that of material riches, which the world seeks and appreciates, by calling attention to the Hebrews in the wilderness, and the marvelous wealth which they had in the promise of God to give each one of them an omer of manna every day. This daily portion of manna was worth at least twenty-five cents an omer. The supply lasted for forty years, and the aggregate value of it was not less than four thousand dollars, for each of the three million of the wanderers, or twelve billion dollars in all. And this writer points out that if the Hebrews had been able to take with them out of Egypt twelve billion dollars in gold, they would not have been as rich as that simple promise of God made them. They had no trouble in hunting for food, or in transporting it, or in storing it.   God sent a full supply fresh every morning and they had only to go out and gather it.   God is as good to us as he was to them.   His promises are just as valuable now as when he led Moses and his followers through the Red Sea, sweetened the waters of Marah, and gave them manna in the desert.

Mere earthly wealth oftentimes walls in the soul and narrows its horizon, and causes it to be beggared in its instincts in the midst of abundance.   It is related of one of the wealthiest of New Yorkers in modern times, a man whose millions were multiplied many times over, that he was very miserable during the last years of his life because he was haunted with the fear that he would die in the poor-house.   Poor man ! though he was rich in outward show, he had a dwarfed soul, and in his real self he was a pauper.   He could not have felt this way about it if he had recognized that God had given him his abundance ; but feeling that he had gathered it himself, it was very natural that he should fear he might lose it again.   Many a man in narrow quarters, with sublime faith and confidence in God, is richer and larger than the prince in his palace.

The soul that lives only for this world, and through the senses, can not help being narrowed and embittered by the disappointments and hurts of life which ought to sweeten and enlarge the nature.   A friend brought me from " The Bad Lands," in North Dakota, a very interesting cane cut from a Diamond Willow tree.   This is a very interesting willow that does not seem to grow anywhere else except in that strange region.   The Diamond Willow, when it first begins to grow, sends up a very thrifty, promising shoot, and gives many early tokens of development into a large and sightly tree ; but, like many men and women, it does not live up to its promises.   For as soon as the little twigs and branches begin to die down, it seems to set all the sap and life of the tree to work, building little diamond-shaped tombs about the spot where each branch died, and it so devotes itself to this work that it is a very scrubby little dwarfed tree at best.

A great many men and women are like my Diamond Willow cane.   They have lived in such a narrow spirit, and have so turned their thoughts in upon themselves, that they are only stunted wooden calendars of the different epochs in their lives, where enthusiasm or ambition died out, and the dates where they ceased growing.   Disappointments and sorrows and griefs, that would have enlarged and enriched their natures if they had lived in a freer and nobler atmosphere, have only served to stunt them and keep them little.   How different is the story of the great pine-tree, or the fragrant balsam fir which only grow the higher because some of their lower branches are broken.   It is only by catching the inspiration of the upper air, as does the pine, that the misfortunes of life shall enlarge instead of dwarfing us.   If we are conscious that we are "the sons of the Most High," we shall be able to get strength out of weakness and trial, as did Paul, and Christ.   But the soul that only lives for the world and the senses can not help but be narrowed and embittered by the disappointments and defeats of life, which ought to sweeten and enlarge the character.   The lofty-souled pine, and not the stunted Diamond Willow, is the true type of a noble life.   How sweetly Ada Bowles sings our message !—

"World-worn and sad I one day stood
Within the shadow of a wood,
Whose lacing limbs, entangled, spread
Their netted curtains o'er my head.
I sighed : ' O balmy, breathing pines,
Must you, too, feel the vexing lines
That limit growth, that strangle life,
And make of effort endless strife ?
Your branches die, all brown and bare
With battling for the upper air.
Those broken boughs so closely prest
Your hard imprisonment attest.'

" Then fell the answer sweet and low :
' We grow as love would have us grow;
Our heaven-aspiring height attain
By crowded ranks and wrestling strain,
The lower life but gives its grace
To find a higher, freer place.

The hinder'd sap must yet return,
Must still with life's strong purpose burn,
To heal of broken boughs the smart,
To send its life through the heart,
Enlarging girth, extending root.
And breathing from each tender shoot,
Till, in close fellowship we rise.
To meet the blue of bending skies.
And thus, through ministries of good,
Is grown the monarch of the wood.'
Sing on, O pines, your song of peace,
Sing on till every doubt shall cease,
That I may trust the perfect plan
That works by love in tree and man."

The earnestness that gradually grew over the congregation while Rev. Mr. Reid and Dr. Banks were speaking continued into the "quiet hour," which was conducted by Rev. A. D. Thaeler, of Winston, N. C.

At the Eastern Church.

The large auditorium was crowded with Endeavorers and their friends. The delegation of Mississippi and delegates from Oklahoma quartered at the church were present.

The meeting opened with the anthem, "Wake the Song of Jubilee," by the choir. Rev. Thomas C. Easton, D.D., pastor of the Eastern Church, offered the opening prayer. A psalm was read, and " Scatter Sunshine " was sung by choir and audience. Rev. Mr. Campbell, of Pennsylvania, offered prayer, asking for the unity of the church and that great blessings should flow from the present Convention. After the song, "Sweet Peace," Dr. Easton welcomed the delegates in the name of the Eastern Church, the Young People's Society of Christian Endeavor, and in the name of Christ, expressing the wish that a mighty wave of salvation from this Convention might sweep over the country.

Rev. J. A. Worden, D.D., of Philadelphia, Pa., the first speaker of the evening, was introduced. He spoke of the unity of thought, aim, and effort of the denominations and cited the Apostles' Creed as an evidence of the unity. He asked the audience to recite the creed in concert, and then called attention to the fact that the belief expressed in the creed was a bond which in reality made all one. He wished it were possible that each denomination would come to the rescue of the ones which were hard pressed, and then the church of God would be rightly bound together and would successfully press forward.

The audience sang " Loyal Soldiers," and " Sunshine in My Soul."

The Rev. H. M. Wharton, D.D., was detained by sickness, and in his stead Rev. James Campbell, of Pennsylvania, was introduced. The likeness of married couples as age increases was used to illustrate the necessity of our growing to be like Christ. There are depths in Christ's life which we have never fathomed. To understand the Christ life we must be guided by certain laws and regulations. The speaker stated how deeply his mother's teaching impressed upon his mind the necessity of going to the old Book when in trouble. You can not live without prayer any more than a bird without wings. Faith also must be present and strengthened by communion with God and by study of his Word.

Rev. T. A. Wigginton, President of Mississippi Christian Endeavor Union, led in prayer.

The " quiet hour " was conducted by Rev. S. Edward Young, pastor of the Central Presbyterian Church of Newark, N. J.

Memorial Lutheran Church.

The prettily decorated church was well filled, and the badges of many cities and States were noticeable. The meeting was presided over by Rev. J. G. Butler, D.D., pastor of the church, who opened the exercises with a feeling address and a powerful prayer in behalf of the increase of spiritual fervor in all hearts. At its conclusion, he announced the invocation hymn as being particularly appropriate for rendition at such an initial meeting, and, led by the choir, the entire assemblage sung the meaning stanzas with expression that showed how earnestly their hearts prompted their lips.

After the reading of the fifteenth and sixteenth chapters of John by Dr. Butler, prayer was offered by Rev. Dr. Stahl, of Philadelphia, in which he pleaded that the Holy Ghost might ever dwell in all their hearts.

Dr. Butler then introduced Rev. Rufus W. Hufford, D.D., of Reading, Pa., as the first speaker.

Address of Rev. R. W. Hufford, D.D., Reading, Pa.

I want to say in the first place that whatever subjects may come before us during this Convention there will not be any other of more importance than this, and in my judgment there will not be any other of more importance come before us at any time anywhere than this subject of the deepening of the spiritual life. I would like to emphasize this thought, so that whatever else you may hear you may call up this subject and think about it. If you do not hear anything else here to-night, remember the subject. We are in danger of losing sight of just this thing. There is so much work that presses upon our hands, there are so many things that demand our attention, that we are in danger of losing sight of the very thing that needs to be done for us and in us. I trust that we shall receive such an inspiration that all the services, all the singing, all the praying we shall hear and into which we shall enter, may be the means of deepening our spiritual life. It would accomplish very great good if it would do that and nothing more. It would be worth while simply to have our spiritual life deepened, and to accomplish that we have come together here to-night.

It would not be a bad year's work in our churches if we should not take in a new member at all but deepen the spiritual life of all the members of our churches. It would be a great year's work. It would not be a year thrown away.

What do we mean by that deepening of the spiritual life? To deepen the spiritual life is to make the individual more a Christian ; it is to make him love spiritual things more and worldly things less ; to make him value his Bible more, and to use it more and understand it better ; to make him feel his relation to God as his Father, and talking with him to realize the fact that he is guiding by the Holy Spirit, and this is a very important work. We need our spiritual life deepened for the sake of our Christian comfort and satisfaction, for our enjoyment and the happiness of our souls. But the man who is always talking about being happy, who is yearning for happiness, and wants to bend everything to the seeking of happiness, who will tell you everthing about his miseries, and magnifies them in his talk, is not the idea of a Christian at all. It is not so selfish as that. It is right for us to think the Christian should receive a great deal of comfort. There are far too many who lack this happiness and comfort because they lack the depth of spirit to make it possible. They are trying to fill the aching void in a way in which it can never be filled. They are trying to find in worldly ambition that satisfaction of the soul which they can never get in any other way than by communion with God, trusting him and obeying him. It is a very sad thing to see how many persons who profess to be followers of Christ, are trying to find happiness in some other way than the right way. There is no sadder thing than to see people here and there, all over the world, trying this thing and that thing, to satisfy the soul. It is as bad as the prodigal son trying to satisfy himself with the husks which the swine ate. The soul may forget its duties for a little time, and may forget God, and what it owes to God ; it may forget Christ the Saviour and what he has done for it. But it sees this is not happiness. The reaction comes and instead of happiness there is a great deal more unhappiness than there was before.

I would say further that one needs this deepening of the religious life for the credit of the church to which he belongs. Some of these things I have briefly referred to are not to the credit of the church. The reputation of the church depends almost entirely upon the lives of those who belong to it. The Christian is the world's Bible. The world may not read the Bible that lies here before us. It may hear little about it. It may know little about it. But the world reads the Christian's life and the world notices what he is. " Ye are our epistles written in our hearts, known and read of all men." Wherever there are Christian people to-night and wherever they may be any day, they will be read by the world. The lives they live will be scrutinized carefully. The church will stand. It will have a reputation enviable or unenviable. Therefore, it is necessary for the credit of the church and its power in the community that its spiritual life should be deepened.

I remember hearing a man who now occupies a very useful position in the city of New York say that he himself had been guilty of forgery and of theft. He was a skilful forger and had forged a considerable amount of paper at the very time he came under the influence of God's spirit, and when he knelt down to pray he was met with just this question, "What are you going to do? How about this forged paper that is already out in the community? If you profess to be a Christian, you must tell the truth now, and that means that you must give yourself up." The temptation to give up and go back to his old life came to him. But now it meant to him arrest and imprisonment for years. But God gave him strength to resist and he persisted in praying, and he declared then and there that he had found the way of life. He determined to submit his soul to the spirit of God, and then and there he made a complete surrender of his spirit to the control of the Almighty. But the next day he went to see one of those men whose name he had forged, and told him the whole story ; what he had done before and what he was trying to do now. That man said, " You need have no fear from me. I wish, oh, I wish I had what you say you have now ! " The business man was a professed Christian talking to a veritable thief and gambler and was ready to say, " I would be willing to give much for what you have now." There is a great need of that in the churches to-day. They are in a condition in which its members are not really ready to say they are Christians. They have no real knowledge of the forgiveness of their sins ; so little knowledge in fact that they hesitate to say they are Christians. We ought to be ready and willing to give an answer clear and distinct, and the only way to do that is to deepen the spiritual life; and until we can understand the meaning of God's word, until what we profess has become a reality, we can never do this. It is to the discredit of the church when the professed followers of Christ lack this spiritual experience, this knowledge of the service of the Master, the reading of his Bible. The Christian should have some of the experience of the Psalmist,—" Thy word is a lamp unto my feet, and a light unto my path." It would make the church mean a great deal more. It would help draw the line between the world and the church, and would show that the church is under the control of the living God.

Dr. Butler said, in introducing the next speaker, "This blessed Christian Endeavor work not only emphasizes denominational loyalty, and cultivates international friendship, but it reaches around the world. We shall now hear an address by Rev. Arnold Streuli, of Manchester, England."

Address of Rev. Arnold Streuli, Manchester, England.

My dear friends,—I can not express the pleasure it gives me to speak at this Convention, as the first public act that I am permitted to perform on my visit to the United States. I have seen many things that have made me wonder at and admire your great country, but I must say that, notwithstanding all the wonder that I felt when I looked upon your great buildings in New York, the beautiful streets of Philadelphia, and the magnificent architecture of your own great city, amongst all these things there is nothing that inspires me as this wonderful Convention.

The genius of Christianity is to work from centre to circumference. We stand here to-night to declare that we seek not a mere superficial religion, but one which reaches deep down to the secrets of the heart. Perhaps there never was a day when Christianity was so popular as now ; but its popularity may be its peril. In these days men too often mistake the demands which Christ makes upon the human heart, and therefore I rejoice with you and with all the Christian Endeavorers who meet here in this city to-night that we open our Convention with this particular topic.

God never saves men in crowds. It is we who are to talk to the masses. God never speaks to save the masses. Christ did not die so much for the world as for every individual man in the world. He loved man and he gave himself for man. You are to God what no other person can be. There are no two of us whose circumstances, whose dispositions are the same. In God's sight we are especially definite, separated one from the other. God knows us each from the other and seeks us out in the great company of our fellow human beings, and for that very reason, because our circumstances are so different, our dispositions so different. Every one of us can feel that in a very special sense we needed Christ to die for us individually ; and therefore we need to consecrate ourselves to him individually.

Again, each one of us has a work to do for God which no other person can do. There is a part in this mighty work for every individual amongst us. Each life is commissioned by God to fulfil a particular purpose and therefore Christian consecration must be individual. You remember in that wonderful book, when we have a glimpse of the days that are to come, that the reward of the righteous is described under the form of a white stone and on the stone is a name which no man can read save him who receives it ; so that we learn that our reward from God will one day be this—that we have learned the secret of our lives with him. The secret of the Lord is with them that fear him, and our reward will be in that day to receive a name from him which no other shall know, the meaning of which no other shall understand but God and ourselves. Is there a sweeter, more encouraging, more inspiring thought than this, our individual relationship with Jesus Christ?

It is a great thing to know a great man. One of the greatest privileges of the Christian is to know such a man as the apostle Paul or Saint John. And many will almost immediately recognize these men by some expression. Something or other will tell us that these are the men we have read about during our pilgrimage here below. I may know Martin Luther, I may know John Wesley, but I know Christ, and more than that I know he knows me. "I know my sheep and am known of mine."

It is this individual relationship with Jesus Christ which makes a life a heaven below. There is something of the spirit of homesickness which we Christians need realize when we come into close touch with Jesus Christ. "As the hart panteth after the water brooks, so panteth my soul after thee, O God."

Heart longing for heart, and as I long for God so God longs for me. For the Father himself loved us, and therefore we must say with Augustine, "O God, thou art our home, and we can never rest until we rest with thee." Christ claims you. He longs for you individually. See how often Christ sought to impress this upon men when he was here; how he spoke to Nicodemus, the woman at the well, the poor woman who suffered from the issue of blood and tried to come into the crowd yet had to be singled out and saved individually. There may be things in me which separate me from others, but Christ loves those characteristics if consecrated to him. Jesus loved Martha and Mary and Lazarus. He loves variety in character.

There is a saying of our Lord Jesus Christ which used to trouble me for many years : " If any man come to me and hate not his father and mother, and wife, and children, and brethren, and sisters, yea, and his own life also, he can not be my disciple." " Whosoever he be of you that forsaketh not all that he hath, he can not be my disciple." Do we not despise the man who loves wife and children more than duty? Do we not honor the man who will do his duty at any cost? We come to the unlike feature of Christianity instead of the cruel code of moral duties which other religions present. To us is given not the tablets of stone, but the warm heart of Jesus Christ, and Christ is duty personified; and as we follow him we follow duty, and being true to Christ we dare not allow anything, either love of wife or children, brother or sister, or our own lives, to come before our devotion to Jesus Christ.

I remember a remarkable picture which some of you may have seen. In the foreground you see a young girl who is brought before the Roman judge on account of her loyalty to the Saviour. All around her are friends who are pleading with her to forsake Christ and cleave to her lover. The lover himself is bending over her and pleading with her for his sake to give up her love for Christ. For once the hard features of the judge seem to relax. In the background you can see the lions raging, preparing to receive her body; for if she loves Christ the more, she is to be thrown to them. " If any man love father or mother more than me he is not worthy of me, he can not be my disciple." She dare not, she dare not yield, and she is thrown to the waiting lions. But, borne down upon the breeze, we almost catch an echo of the song that swells around the great white throne. " These are they which came out of great tribulation and have washed their robes and made them white in the blood of the Lamb." Do you say she loved her dear ones less because she loved Christ? She loved more, though she must despise them on account of her devotion to Christ.

We can understand one another in the difficulties we sometimes experience as to this Christian consecration, namely, this whole-hearted surrender, to give up ambitions, to surrender aspirations of worldly success, to give up loves that come between us and Jesus Christ. How can we do it? We can do it. " I can do all things through Christ, which strengtheneth me." Christ first, Christ last, Christ all in all. Jesus said, " If a man will come after me, let him deny himself and take up his cross daily and follow me." If you love the world as much as you ever did there is no cross in your religion. Be sure of that; you are not his disciple. You can not be. But is this hardship to make us afraid? God forbid! There is heroism left in the descendants of the Puritans still, amongst those who know they have the blood of martyrs. There is still that fire of the spirit which shall consume every barrier, which shall make the way of every Christian soldier plain. Come what may, rather let the difficulties fan our devotion into a stronger, brighter flame. And circumstances, let them be what they may, they shall only bind us more closely to Christ. O brethren, let this devotion to Christ and his cause characterize our work as Endeavorers.

In conclusion, I want to say a word, if I may, in regard to continuity in Christian consecration. There are many people of only one experience. They always go back to the day of their conversion and never seem to get a step further than that. As though their poor lives are an adequate result of what should be the result of the work which Christ has done for men on Calvary! We are as nothing compared to the glory that is to be revealed. Paul said,

" Forgetting those things which are behind, and reaching forth to those things which are before, I press toward the mark for the prize of the high calling of God which is in Christ Jesus." He was never satisfied, and again and again the apostle pointed out that there was an inheritance reserved for us.

We have often been told that our Christian life is a matter of growth. We dare not, we can not stand still. Onward, upward, higher and higher day by day. Is your consecration continual? Is there not a danger lest in our monthly consecration meetings we shall simply go back into the old place month after month? That is not the meaning of the Christian Endeavor consecration meeting. It is rather that we should, month by month, if not day by day, take our alpenstock and mount higher and higher. Is your consecration continual? Is it a matter of growth day by day? — conquest and victory one after the other as long as we live? God grant that your consecration may be of this individual character — entire self-surrender, and continuous in its growth!

> Oh, let me know the power of thy resurrection!
> Oh, let me show thy risen life in calm and clear reflection!
> Oh, let me soar where thou, my Saviour Christ, art gone before!
> In mind and heart let me be always where thou art!

The "quiet hour" was in charge of the Rev. A. F. McGregor, B.A., of Woodstock, Can., President of the Ontario Provincial Christian Endeavor Union. He referred in his opening remarks to the meeting of the officers of the United Society with the State and Provincial presidents held throughout the day, as a fine instance of the spiritualization of a business meeting. The benefits of prayer were great and manifest. Christ taught us to pray by his example and precepts. A season of silent prayer followed; " Nearer, my God, to Thee," and "My Jesus, I Love Thee," were sung; a number of brief testimonies were given from the pews, and the pastor of the church, the Rev. Dr. Butler, closed the meeting with an earnest prayer and the benediction.

Gunton Temple Memorial Church.

The Endeavorers of the Gunton Temple Memorial Church, in addition to their fine house of worship, at the corner of 14th and R streets, have a chapel just across the street; consequently, they entertained their visitors at the latter building, reserving the church and its charms for the general meetings. The elaborate green and gold of the interior last evening was touched up just enough here and there with bits of red, white, and blue to relieve the otherwise somber appearance of the church, and to render it one of the handsomest auditoriums presented to the Endeavorers. The pulpit was banked with flowers, while just over the reading-desk was draped " Old Glory." In the enforced absence of the pastor, Dr. Patch, Rev. Howard Wilbur Ennis, pastor of the Western Presbyterian Church of Washington, the presiding officer, opened the programme by announcing the hymn, " Sunshine in My Soul," which was sung by the audience, led by a piano, played by Miss Nellie King, the organist of the church. Prayer was offered by the Rev. J. W. Fifield, pastor of the Warren Avenue Congregational Church, Chicago, who thanked God for one very noticeable feature of the Convention, — the total absence of any railroad accidents; and then asking a blessing on the officers of the United Society, the local officers, and on everybody present, concluded with the Lord's Prayer, repeated by all present. A hymn preceded the reading of the Scriptures, 2d Epistle to the Philippians, by Rev. Ralph Gillam, of Malden, Mass., and then "Hear Us, O Saviour!" was sung.

The first speaker was Rev. J. W. Fifield.

Address of Rev. J. W. Fifield, Chicago, Ill.

God be thanked, Mr. Chairman and fellow Endeavorers, for this great Convention. For twelve months we have felt the mighty heart-beat of that great gathering at Boston and have looked toward this with hope and prayer that it might prove mightier still. The Christian Endeavor forces are God's recruiting army for the spiritual conquest of the world. As in Palestine, once a year, the children of Abraham gathered to Jerusalem, the capital of the country, that they might stand before God and receive new visions of possibility and new messages of duty, so we, the new children of the covenant, are gathered here in Washington, the capital of our nation. This is the Passover feast for the young people of the world. By as much as this country and the sister countries about us are greater than Palestine, as our mountains tower above her foot-hills, our great plains throw their ripening harvests beyond her valleys; as our cities throb with power and flash with glory undreamed of in Palestine, so should this gathering receive such showers of blessing and strength as never fell on the people gathered on the sacred hills of Zion and Moriah.

Through the valleys and over the mountains we have sung our way; we have come loaded with lunch-baskets, banners, and Bibles. We have been jammed and pounded into the magnificent brevity of sleeping-cars until, like hungry bears in the spring, we come forth to devour the feast that is spread. Possibly some, because of delightful acquaintances found along the way, or the splendor of this queenly city, have already forgotten their mission here, and the opening services should bring all face to face with the great issues before us. To-night, my friends, we are not here as tourists, although we shall enjoy the national buildings and the halls where our legislators hook and stamp each other. Some of us are here with big eyes to see where some of our laws have come from. We have been whiffing mountain air and pure ozone from the prairies and we want to learn what foulness here could give them birth. Yet ours is a higher mission than to mouse around in the political garbage box to find some decayed corruption that is sent abroad beneath the label of American citizenship. The motto which hangs out before the mind of each Christian Endeavor youth reads: "For Christ, Church, and Country." Each one of these great words will be lifted up until it will unfold like a banner of victory, and beneath our triple ensign the millions of American youth propose to stand. Later on there will be something said about the church and country, but to-night we gather about that first great word, the one above all others, the one whose we are and whom we serve, even our Lord Jesus Christ. How fitting that in the beginning from all these places of sacred worship we humbly and fervently salute Almighty God! Oh, that we may come here as channels through which to you may flow the love and devotion of our home work and also from this gathering that there may come great tidal waves that will surge back with us and fill with a new power and life the dried places and shallow streams where we toil! From the great ocean of thy infinite deep, O God, send uplifting currents! O Holy Spirit of power, which dwelt in Christ and urged him ever to holiest endeavor, come and dwell in each one here! Come to us as the sun, which, breaking through the dark folds of night and the ice fields of spring, quickens into a new life each leafless tree and buried seed. Come to us as the wind, which laps up the pool and leaves the clean highway for travel. Come, if need be, even as fire, until the hay and stubble are consumed and we build imperishably on the everlasting foundation.

We are asked to speak to the theme, "Deepening of the Spiritual Life," and we will try and place what we desire to say in the answers to three questions.

First, Does the spiritual life need deepening? It requires not a careful study to learn that something is wrong in the spiritual world. Few chapters are now added to the Acts of the Apostles. Out of an upper room, with souls aglow with prayer, and the Holy Spirit dwelling in flames upon them, went a humble, unlearned band. But they shook Jerusalem; their voices rolled like great thunders through the hollow and meaningless worship of their time; they were saved and at once became saviors, and the church grew and multiplied and God added daily to himself through their faith and work. Times have greatly changed. We have no upper room for prayer now. Our greatest room is the basement, where we hold socials and serve ice cream and cake. We do have a prayer-meeting, but in it we repeat poetry and have long, cold pauses. We are learning splendidly how to stop. We believe that silence is golden. The favorite psalm for the modern church is the twenty-third, and especially that verse which says, " He maketh me to *lie down*." The old apostolic life that prayed and fasted, that stood true to weak causes, although stoned and beaten and imprisoned, has been left back in the heroic and conquering days of Christianity. We are told that Peter preached one sermon and saved three thousand people. Now it requires three thousand sermons to save one person. We are told that the disciples went everywhere preaching the word of God. They still go everywhere, they bend over the card-table, swing in the waltz, occupy chief seats at the theatre, make money in questionable ways; but as for preaching the word of God, that is given to the minister, who reads essays about stars and flowers, and delivers courses of addresses about the word "Selah." No wonder that the church stands powerless before a devil-tormented world. Much of our Christian work is a sad travesty on sacred things. The Christian Endeavor Society learns that it should go fishing for men. It equips itself with elaborate tackle. It secures a fish pole like unto a telegraph pole. It chooses a line as comely as a street-car cable. The hook is like a scant hook with which lumbermen skid logs. Then, using a few old platitudes and dried and withered services for bait, it is ready. When the society are all present, amid the singing of " Throw Out the Life Line," the janitor lowers a rear window and, heaving out the preparation to the street, they practically say, " There, swallow that or you are lost." Philip stopped the Ethiopian in the desert; Andrew went to his brother Peter; Jesus talked with the woman at the well. The great uplifting epochs of church-life have been when the disciples went everywhere preaching the word of God. And one great demonstration of the need of a deeper spiritual life is the purposeless, lax, and unstriving condition of the church now.

Only a deep spiritual life will be felt in the times in which we are living. If it required consecration and holy impulse to reach men eighteen centuries ago, how much more does it require it now? Without the help of God we are powerless before the rushing, busy age. As carpenters pound wedges into timber with mauls, so do we need to pound ideas into people.

Second, How may the spiritual life be deepened? The whole philosophy of the larger Christian life is found in Mark's Gospel, where it is recorded of Christ that, " He ordained twelve, that they should be with him, and that he might send them forth to preach and have power." Here is the mountain spring from which the great stream flowed. Being in the school of Christ until we have the presence of Christ, the guidance of Christ, and the power of Christ. This is the order in which they always come. First presence, then guidance, and then power. In the presence of Christ the disciples learned his spirit and method. They saw him prosperous but not proud, disappointed but not dismayed, abused but not abusing. In Christ lay the spirit of victory. The mightiest force in all the world is a heroic and sympathetic soul. It would overcome the thrones of the Cæsars, and all the mighty traditions and strength of the past would be driftwood tossed before a steamer on its way. The hope and joy of Christ that looked from the night towards a new day, and from hardship and pain to the rest at the steps of God's throne, found lodgment in the disciples. They saw this man at work. He fed the hungry and ministered with loving hands to those in pain. He established his kingdom by saving men one by one. He seemed to think other things of little value when a soul was in sin and he could lead it to God. The spirit and method of Jesus Christ can only be secured by staying in his company. To be with Christ is to grow Christ-like.

You know the power that lay in the apostles' lives. With such humble men God flayed the mountains. Along such simple wires God flashed the message of his love. Through such clay and broken conduct pipes God poured the ocean of his fulness into the valley places and desert regions of men. They had taken time to be with Jesus; they were willing to be guided by Jesus. They received the power of Jesus. Oh that we might so stand in the presence of Christ, that like the disciples we might be with him until his likeness would be fixed in us and we might go forth and reproduce him!

Third, What might a deeper spiritual life accomplish? I do not know. God's power is hard to measure. God in the hearts of a few people at Pentecost made Jerusalem ring with the gospel and carried it out along the highways of Judea and Galilee. God in the hearts of a few in Germany drove papal bigotry to the Tiber. God in the hearts of a few scholars in England placed the Bible in the hands of the common people, until Tyndale's words came true that the plow boy of Saxony knew more of the Scripture than the pope himself. It has beaten the fetters from the negro and spread before him books for study. It has lifted woman from the place of a slave and made her the queen of a home. It has made the words "mother, home, and heaven" the sweetest in all the vocabulary of mankind. God's unhindered power in a human heart —who can measure it? It has given the world a Spurgeon, a Phillips Brooks, and a Moody. It has sent missionaries to the heathen and opened the purses of the rich in great philanthropies. Oh, if all who bear the name of Christ were only given over to his service, what might not be done! What a revival would spread! The empty pews of churches would be filled not with a dense vacancy but a crowded throng. I think we would have money sufficient to pay the indebtedness of our missionary boards. "The trouble does not come from hard times but a soft religion." When it means something to belong to the church, the church will mean something in the world. Christ said the gates of hell should not prevail against it. But those gates need to be shut and spiked. Why leave them forever open? Why let indecent literature flood us? Why let the saloon blight and blast and damn? Why let Sabbath desecration run over the moral law, breaking it into more fragments than when Moses shattered the ten commandments by the altar of the Golden Calf? Why let the heathen millions go unevangelized while thousands at home are never urged to accept Christ? We need a deeper spiritual life, one that places our eyes on the great duties and issues of life. We need to be with Christ and learn his spirit and method. We need his guidance and power and then together like a great and mighty army commence to take the world for God. Oh, children of God's right hand, enlist! Put on the whole armor! Take the keen, flashing sword, and drawing it from the scabbard let it blaze in the light! And may this Convention equip us as never before for the splendid triumphs of the gospel!

The next speaker represented the Southern Presbyterians,— the Rev. F. P. Ramsay, of Augusta, Ky.

Address of Rev. F. P. Ramsay, Augusta, Kentucky.

I. What is the Spiritual Life?

1. It is to be distinguished from (*a*) the business, the social, and even the religious life. Two men may follow the same business, doing the same things according to the same rules, and with the same success, as two partners in the same business; and one of them may be living a spiritual life and the other not. Two men may be twin brothers, appear always together in the same social intercourse, and, by any merely social standard, behave equally well; and the one may be living a spiritual life and the other not. So also may those two men be members of the same church, teachers in its Sabbath school, and workers in its Endeavor Society, being equally active in the same religious work, living, in one sense, a religious life, and each the same religious life; and

yet the one may be living a spiritual life and the other not. But let me not be misunderstood. These forms of activity are not separate from spiritual activity, in such a sense that a man lives a spiritual life outside of his business, or of his social intercourse, or of his religious work; for if one is living a right spiritual life, this spiritual will lay hold of one's business activities and social intercourse and religious work as directions in which to put itself forth. The spiritual life will embody itself in these forms of living. But these may exist, and in a high degree of beauty and efficiency, in those who have no spiritual life at all. (*b*) In a somewhat different sense, the spiritual life is to be distinguished from the physical and the intellectual life. For two men may live the same life as animals, and very much the same life as minds, and be spiritually in contrast. That man is compounded of three substances, matter. mind, and spirit, I do not say, and doubt the philosophical correctness of this theory; but certainly on one side man lies against the visible and material world, and on the other against the unseen and spiritual world. The mind may be said to come in contact with the material and outward through the senses of the body, and in contact with the spiritual and inward through the sensibilities of the spirit. Outwardly, man is a physical organism; inwardly he is a discerning spirit. In the body he lives with things in the spirit, with persons. Without he has to do with animals, within he has to do with spirits. And accordingly the spiritual life is not primarily in the physical being nor even in the mental nature, but back, within, on the spiritual side, on that side of man in which he lies in contact with the invisible and spiritual world. (*c*) Once more, as by spiritual life we mean right spiritual life, as over against wrong activity on the spiritual side of our being, we must contrast the spiritual life with the fleshly or carnal life. The right and the wrong spiritual life agree in this, that each is the man's life lived with spiritual beings; for man can not live spiritually alone, any more than he can live physically alone. As outwardly he must be in contact with material things, so inwardly he must be in intercourse with spiritual persons. And a man lives a right spiritual life when he lives in communion with righteous spirits; and he lives a wrong spiritual life when he lives in communion with sinful spirits.

II. Turning our attention, then, away from business and social activities, and even from religious activities, passing from the physical through the intellectual on to the spiritual side of our being, and then contrasting what is alone worthy the name of spiritual life with the activity of the human spirit in communion with the evil in the spiritual world, the truly spiritual life with the enslaving of the human spirit to carnality, we now come to our question, *How to Deepen the Spiritual Life.* And I sum up all that I have to say on how to deepen the spiritual life in one word, *Live* it.

1. Since the spiritual life is living in communion with the righteous Spirit, (*a*) we must live in communion with God, who is the righteous Spirit; (*b*) we must live in communion with Jesus Christ, who is God revealed to sinners. Jesus Christ is God in touch with man, God within the reach and grasp of man, God become a fellow to man, so that fellowship between him and man is possible and easy. In other words, we do not deepen the spiritual by contemplation of the Infinite in abstract thought, but rather by communion with God as he is made known to us in Christ. Transcendentalism is not spirituality. (*c*) And we must live in communion with the Holy Spirit, who is Christ within. In the Biblical record Christ is two thousand years away; but through the Holy Spirit he becomes present. Christ sitteth on his throne beyond the stars; but through the Holy Spirit he is here with us all the days. The Holy Spirit taketh Christ from before our eyes, and putteth him behind our eyes, within the sensibilities of our spirits. It is in this inward, immediate and vital touch of the Spirit of Christ that spiritual life originates; and spiritual life deepens just in proportion as this the Holy Spirit pervades, permeates, and vitalizes the human spirit. This life does not begin or continue as ceremony, which is materiality; nor as thought, which is intellectuality; but as life, as spiritual vitality. It is not by doing, or by thinking, that we live, but by living. And spiritual life is the life

of the Holy Spirit in the human spirit, is the Spirit of Christ and the spirit of man living in communion.

2. In the second place, since this life is communion with the Holy Spirit, it must be, on the part of the human spirit, a life of obedience, of love, and of faith. (*a*) It must be a life of obedience. The human spirit in close contact with the Divine Spirit must be in an attitude of reverential awe, the attitude of obedience; for the creature can not be in harmony with the Creator while disobedient to him. And here much is gained by distinguishing, if we do not press the distinction too far, between obedience to the conscience and obedience to the Holy Spirit. For this is obedience to Another, and that may be but obedience to myself; this is reverence for God, this may be only self-respect. The habit of listening constantly to the Holy Spirit rather than to the conscience, to the Holy Spirit speaking to us through the auditory nerve of our spirit, the conscience, rather than to the vibrations of the nerve itself, conscious submission to the Holy Spirit, a constant sensitiveness and yielding to his guiding touch, this is living spiritually. (*b*) Or it must be a life of love. For all right ethical life is love. Obedience to the spirit of Christ can not but be love to Christ expressing itself, and the love of Christ towards others expressing itself For love is life become conscious of direction. (*c*) Or it must be a life of faith. And how does one despair of himself when contemplating this spiritual life! It is not in me to live this life. It must be Christ living in me. It must come from my surrender, from the mastery of my spirit by God's spirit. But as my life must be willing action, it must come from the willing surrender of love, which is faith. But this faith is not one act never repeated, but it is one action never interrupted. The human spirit begins to live in beginning to trust Christ under the persuasion of his Spirit ; and it continues to live in continuing thus to trust; and it deepens this life in deepening this faith. By instant and sensitive obedience, by serving and seeking love, by trustful, surrendering faith, we live the spiritual life ; and by fuller obedience and tenderer love and completer faith of our human spirit toward the divine, we deepen our spiritual life.

3. And in the last place, we deepen our spiritual, we increase the fulness of our inner communion with God, by living this spiritual life out into all forms of our living. (*a*) There must be no double life tolerated within our own spirit. Submission to the Holy Spirit is contradictory of submission to Satan or to the flesh, or to self. (*b*) We must have our spiritual life to permeate and dominate our intellectual life. The spiritual must dictate what to read and what to think about, and our intellectual activity must be in the service of the spirit. Whether we pursue science or art, we must do it with spiritual consciousness. (*c*) And then this spiritualized intelligence must dominate our physical life. The preservation of health and the purgation of passion, the choice of amusements and the regulation of such merely animal functions as eating and drinking, all must be baptized in spirituality. (*d*) Or, in a different direction, we must make our whole religious life spiritual. Reading the Bible, meditation, prayer, all forms of private and public worship, and all forms of benevolent, church, and evangelistic work, may become mechanical habit instead of conscious spirit. Or they may rise no higher than conscientiousness, observing certain rules and doing certain duties ; whereas they should be the free spirit putting itself forth in warm and living love. (*e*) We must make also our whole social life spiritual. Spiritual life is communion with spiritual persons. In social life we meet many that are not spiritual, and much of our intercourse with those who are spiritual is not with them as spiritual. Therefore we must beware lest in such social life we, at least momentarily, lose consciousness of the Spirit of Christ. By ever looking at these people with his eyes and talking with them with his lips and working or playing with them with his mind, not forgetting his presence or letting cease a conscious sympathy with him, we shall be able to lift the social into the spiritual. (*f*) And also our whole business life we must make spiritual. Here meet together all the dangers that we have named in connection with the religious and the social life. For it is so easy in business to become mechanical, to become a machine instead of a conscious person ; it is so easy to become

merely conscientious, obedient to rule, instead of freely loving; it is so easy to fix the attention on the business instead of on Him for whom we do all our work; and it is so easy to think of the people about us and forget the Christ within us. It is most perilous to engage in making money, but it is spiritual to engage in making money for Christ. Let us do all in the Spirit of Christ, in conscious communion with him of aim and action.

And we may sum up this whole address in the oft-quoted text, "Work out your own salvation with fear and trembling, for it is God which worketh in you;" only we should correctly translate it, "Work out your own salvation, with reverence and awe, because it is God who worketh in you."

At the close of the last address in the Gunton Presbyterian Church, there was a "quiet hour," which was led by Rev. Ralph Gillam, the evangelist, which was indeed a quiet hour.

Kendall Baptist Church.

A large reception was given to the delegates of Kansas at the Kendall Baptist Church. The stained glass windows of the church were decorated with bunting, while from the chandeliers were stretched strips of red, white, and blue to the altar. The organ was draped artistically with Christian Endeavor and United States flags. Above the organ the motto, "The earth is the Lord's, and the fulness thereof," was written in blue letters. To the right of the altar was the writing and resting room, which had been elegantly furnished with plush chairs and sofas, while the two lights were draped and connected with bunting. The reception-room was at the entrance, and was covered with a United States flag. Just inside the door was the entertainment booth, and not ten feet away the registration stand. The room in the tower, which was used for the State's officers, was one of the most comfortable spots in the church.

The Rev. Theron Outwater, the pastor, presided at the meeting, and after welcoming the visitors, introduced the Rev. C. S. Mason, of Los Angeles, Cal., the first speaker of the evening.

Address of Rev. C. S. Mason, Los Angeles, Cal.

The Lord Jesus Christ is the author of all life, physical, mental, spiritual. We get spiritual life by looking to Jesus Christ. As Moses lifted up the serpent in the wilderness, even so must the Son of man be lifted, that whosoever believed on him should not perish, but have everlasting life. The deeper we are rooted and grounded in love, that love shed abroad in the heart by the Holy Ghost, the sweeter, brighter, deeper, and more profound will our spiritual life be. We are transformed by beholding, meditating, thinking. Thoughts of the world oft show the impress of the world, whereas, if I think of Christ, I get the impress of Christ. Let us think of him. Christ was tender, loving, sympathizing, long-suffering, forgiving. Have we his spirit? The fruit of the spirit is love, joy, peace, long-suffering, gentleness, faith, meekness, temperance. Jesus was courteous, patient. When reviled, he reviled not again. When persecuted, he opened not his mouth. He was social, honest, brave, business-like, prayerful, in fellowship with God the Father. As we contemplate him can we not say,

> "I love thee, Lord,
>   But with no love of mine.
> I love thee, Lord,
>   But all the love is thine."

We see Christ in the garden, and we enter into his suffering; but we have the assurance if we suffer with him here, we shall be glorified with him there.

Changed from strength to strength, from power to power, from glory to glory, until now we awake in the King's likeness.

The next speaker, Prof. Amos R. Wells, managing editor of *The Golden Rule*, was enthusiastically received and made a deep impression by his address, which was one of the very strongest and most uplifting of any during the entire Convention. After Prof. Wells' address, the Rev. Chas. A. Oliver, of York, Pa., conducted a "quiet hour."

Vermont Avenue Christian Church.

Promptly at eight o'clock, the hour set for beginning the Endeavor services at the Vermont Avenue Christian Church, Rev. Dr. F. D. Power, pastor of the church, announced the opening of the exercises with the singing of the old, familiar hymn, " Praise God, from Whom All Blessings Flow." At that hour the church was well filled. Nearly all of the Indiana delegates were present, and their numbers were augmented by their friends and the regular parishioners of the church. Before the exercises were half over every seat was taken, and a number were compelled to go away disappointed.

Rev. Dr. Power, in opening the exercises, referred to the joyous expectation with which the Christian Endeavorers had looked forward to this Convention.

Owing to the unavoidable detention of Rev. Dr. Tupper, of Philadelphia, who was to have delivered the first address, the Rt. Rev. Samuel Fallows, D.D., LL.D., of Chicago, Ill., one of the trustees of the United Society of Christian Endeavor, representing the Reformed Episcopal denomination, made an impressive address.

After the singing of several hymns, Rev. Dr. J. E. Pounds, pastor of the Central Episcopal Church of Indianapolis, was introduced.

Address of Rev. J. E. Pounds, D.D., Indianapolis, Ind.

The subject, " Deepening the Spiritual Life," practically covers all the ground of the work of Christ and the Church in the human soul, as well as the influence of the indwelling spirit, so I shall by no means attempt to speak of all the essential things, nor of the most important things, of the subject, but shall confine myself to a few thoughts suggested by Paul in Galatians ii. 20: " I am crucified with Christ; nevertheless I live; yet not I, but Christ liveth in me: and the life which I now live in the flesh I live by the faith of the Son of God, who loved me and gave himself for me." This is the apostle's statement of his own spiritual life. Please notice in it these points: first, the preparation for it, "I am crucified; " second, the pattern spiritual life, " Christ liveth in me; " third, the province of its development, "in the flesh; " fourth, the power by which it is sustained, " I live by the faith of the Son of God; " fifth, the purpose which inspired his faith and desire to follow the Son of God, " who loved me and gave himself for me "—the preparation, pattern, province, power, and purpose of the spiritual life.

First, the preparation, " I am crucified with Christ." This is essential. Life is born of death, sanctity of sacrifice, and yet humanity has ever shrunk from the cross, though it is man's greatest blessing. During the ministry of our Saviour he was never without human companionship except on the morning when he needed help to carry the cross up the mountain, and though men were ashamed to be by his side, yet the walk that morning was the noblest and the most heroic the world has ever witnessed. From the cruel court of Pilate to Calvary's summit is as far as from selfish pleasure to self-sacrifice, as far as from human anger to divine love, as far as from the injustice of earth to the righteousness of heaven, as far as from the spirit of Satan to the spirit of God's dear Son. And the cross is after all a paradox, for while it seems a hindrance to a journey, it is really a help. He who bears the cross will be borne by it, for no one of humanity's children has ever climbed as high as Calvary's summit unless he bore the cross; all others have fallen by the way. He that would follow Jesus must take up the cross. When we pray for the holy light, we must be willing to be made holy, willing to bear the cross, that we may reach the summit of the mountain, for God will give us strength. Humility ever comes through humiliation, patience is born of pain, sympathy of sorrow, love and charity for humanity of the chastening of God. Christian pleasure can only commence at Calvary, and service of humanity is the lead by which depth of spiritual life is sounded. I sometimes hear an Endeavorer say, "I am enjoying my religion," and I am always tempted to ask, "Well, how are your neighbors enjoying it? Are they any happier since you got religion?"

Second, the pattern spiritual life, "Christ liveth in me." The ideal Christian life is, first of all, real, vital; it is life to begin with. The Endeavor Society undertakes to do nothing for a man until he is regenerated, except to pray and labor for his conversion. "Christ liveth in me." Christianity is the union of Christ and humanity. The first lesson I learned in chemistry was that there is a difference between a union and a mixture. You may mix sand and water as thoroughly as you will, and it will be sand and water still; but bring hydrogen and oxygen together in proper proportions and they will unite and form water, an entirely new substance, having properties different from both. Christianity is the union of Christ and humanity. The Christian is a new creature, produced by the union of the Son of God with a son of man. "Christ liveth in me."

Very much of the criticism we hear against Christianity is because of the acts of those who are not Christians at all, for a man may be brought very near to Christ — may know considerable about him — may even preach eloquently concerning him — without having ever united with him. A man said to me, concerning a brother whose life was depraved, "Well, Christianity has failed in his case." "Failed! No," I said, "it hasn't even been tried." The vine is not condemned by the barrenness of a branch which is not in the vine.

We hear very much talk to-day about Christian union, and very much of it is talk, but some are really in earnest and speak of church union. It is an open question if this is desirable. A combination of the various sects would certainly make a mixture, but not a union. There can be no union until there is unity. Having Christ within us, we should let him occupy more and more of our lives. Paul's idea was that Christ should completely predominate, and such an idea must tend to the deepening of the spiritual life.

Third, the province of the spiritual development. While in the flesh this world is not a barren wilderness, but a rich valley, fruitful of every element necessary to the growth of spiritual life, and every struggle necessary to maintain it against the enemy will give us renewed strength. We get by giving. "He that loseth his life shall find it." Christianity is produced paradoxically; it increases by subtraction and multiplies by division. To give is to live, and to deny is to die. He who is most in the world for service will be the least in it for sin. The monastery — that saddest of mistakes — shuts out the possibility of growth, struggle, service, sympathy, and shuts in the means of deterioration, selfishness, lust, and laziness.

As the life grows the senses become keen; they become keen by exercise. One of the best evidences of spiritual attainment is keen spiritual sensibility. Peter puts it in this way: "He that lacketh these things"—that is, courage, virtue, etc., which were to be added to faith —" is blind, and can not see afar off." It is a sad thing to be blind. The blind are so prone to stumble! Some people very often say, "I can not see any harm in the play, or the theatre, or in taking a bicycle run on Sunday." Can not see any harm! Possibly they are a little blind, or at least near-sighted; can not see afar off. And then spiritual decay affects the hearing. They can not hear the poor ask for bread; they can not hear the cry of the heathen in foreign lands.

When a man dies spiritually I think the feet grow cold first. It is hard to go to church; and then he can not see any good in attending all the regular and mid-week services. He is blind as well as lame, for he never sees anything to do. But even a blind man can be seen, and though he can not see any harm in attending the play and in not attending the services of the church, the world can see him at the one place and not at the other, and that will do harm.

It is said that some people go to church just to be seen, especially about the time spring bonnets get ripe. The practice is very generally condemned, but I believe that Endeavorers ought to go to church to be seen. What a blessing it would be to the children if they could see their parents in the Sunday school! A church-going people will be a church-growing people.

Fourth, the power that sustains the spiritual life, "I live by the faith of the Son of God." That is not food; it is the means by which we appropriate food. The virtue is not in the faith, but in the Son of God. Faith keeps the Christian united to God, as the branch is to the vine.

The Word is the bread of life. We received it by faith. The reason God's Word is powerful is because it has the bread of life within it. The work of the church is very simple. The commission is simple. It is to make learners; that is all — disciples of all.

To prayerfully read God's word every day is the Endeavorer's panacea for all the ills the spiritual flesh is heir to. The Word will sustain life because it has the principle, the germ, of life within it. The word of God is called seed, because seed encloses life. Jesus said, "My words are life." That is the reason the truth of God will sustain when all the wisdom, teaching, and planning of men fail.

Man plans, and God commands. Michael Angelo made of the dust of the earth an image like that which God made in Eden. The material was the same, the plan, the form, were the same, but Angelo's image lacked the life which God breathed into his. The same is true of every plan formed by men for the well-being of the world. They may be well thought out and very beautiful, but, like man, they are but the dust of the earth, though arranged in curious form.

The truth contained in God's Word, when taken into our lives, will nourish us, because it has life. Truth in the abstract is like coal in the mine, it is stored up for the use of man; truth in the concrete is like coal in the bin, it is prepared for the use of man; but truth in the life, truth in the Christian life, is like coal in the fire-box of the engine, which furnishes the power not only to turn the wheels of the mighty engine, but to draw the train grandly on. And the truth of God in Christian lives is not only moving them onward, but is drawing the train of human progress grandly upward toward the City of Righteousness, wherein dwelleth peace.

And then simplicity of faith tends to deepen spiritual life. "The faith of the Son of God." Not belief in many things, but in one person. The more you concentrate, the deeper it will be. A personal trust in the personal Christ is the essence of Christianity. Do not try to believe too much, for as you multiply the planks in your religious platform, the danger increases that some will be unsafe; and the man who is compelled to give up anything that he has held as vital to Christian faith has my profoundest sympathy, for it will shake his confidence in all that remains. I say I pity him. He is trying to be honest with himself, and the foundation on which he stands is going to pieces. How could he develop a calm, deep, spiritual life? But the faith of the Son of God, who is the same, yesterday, to-day, and forever, the faith of the Son of God is the faith that saves and sanctifies.

Fifth, and last of all, the purpose that inspired Paul's life, as though he would say, "My effort is to please Him who loved me and gave himself for me." It was a potent and adequate motive. To expect deep spiritual life from superficial motives is to expect the effect to be greater than the cause. And what low motives we sometimes present to people to become Christians — a fine church building, good social standing, business advantage to a professional man, are offered as inducements to join the church. Beggarly motives beget beggarly services. Only the fact that Christ loved me and gave himself for me will inspire my heart and direct my life.

The love of Christ has magic power. You may send lecturers to the South Sea Islander, and inform him on scientific questions; may instruct him in the laws of health and hygiene; you may tell him how far it is to the sun and the stars; that it is finally decided that Bacon wrote Shakespeare; you may tell him that the law of evolution has made him a very much greater and better man than his father;—he will be a cannibal still. But let the humble missionary go and kindly say, "The Son of God loved you, and gave himself for you," and the savage heart is softened. He will get up from the ground and clothe himself; he will provide an humble home for his wife and children; will build a family altar, and on the first day of the week sit quietly down beside his former foe, and read of the Son of God who loved him and gave himself for him.

The cross of Christ is the wisdom of God and the power of God. Think what the cross did for John, the apostle. It found him when he was vicious enough to contend for a chief place in the kingdom of God, and cruel enough to desire fire from heaven to consume his enemies; but how humble and gentle it made him! Tradition tells us that he spent the years of his old age at Ephesus, pastor of a church. Too feeble to walk, loving hands carried him into the assembly-room to break bread. He was the hero of many battles. He had defied the Sanhedrim to the death; had expounded the Gospel in many cities, and had suffered imprisonment many times. His voice was too feeble to say more than a single sentence, but on each Sunday morning, speaking these words, he summed up all that he had learned of Christ's will and the Christian's duty,— "Little children, love one another."

If Christ by loving and giving himself could made a John the Saintly out of a son of thunder, he can give us deep spiritual life if we but have unswerving, grateful love for him.

Mr. W. H. McClain, of St. Louis, Mo., was to have conducted a "quiet hour," but he was absent, and the time was filled in by individual extemporaneous prayer. A feature of the exercises was the visit of a number of delegates from Michigan. They came in the rain, singing a hymn.

Hamline Methodist Episcopal Church.

The singing of "Praise God, from Whom All Blessings Flow," by the choir and congregation, standing, opened the services at Hamline Methodist Episcopal Church. Nearly every seat in the body of the church was occupied, the larger part of the congregation being visiting Endeavorers. Each wore the Convention badge, while the insignia of the different States were also very much in evidence. Earnestness and fervor marked the services throughout, the continuous and general uttering of "Amen" being conspicuous during the prayers and addresses.

Promptly at eight o'clock the services began with the singing mentioned, and at its conclusion Rev. W. R. Stricklen, pastor of Hamline Church, announced that Rev. Chas. Roads, pastor of St. Paul's M. E. Church, Philadelphia, would conduct the opening religious exercises. Rev. Mr. Roads called for the hymn, "Come, Thou Almighty, Kindly Help Us!" Next he invoked divine blessing, after which "Though Troubles Assail, Though Dangers Affright," was sung.

Rev. W. F. Wilson, of Toronto, Canada, was introduced as the first speaker. Rev. Mr. Wilson is a man of striking personality and effective voice. In opening, he stated that he came from the protection of another flag than the stars and stripes, and added, "You Endeavorers of Washington have taken your visitors by storm with your kindness and love."

Address of the Rev. W. F. Wilson, Toronto, Canada.

> Assembled here with one accord,
>   Calmly we wait the promised grace,
> The purchase of our dying Lord.
>   Come, Holy Ghost, and fill this place !

Meeting within the confines of this great city is the largest religious gathering ever convened on this continent.

We have come over all the seas, and represent nearly every color and tongue found among the tribes of earth—and why? Not for mere pleasure, or to secure some office, neither to make money nor win applause ; and yet, we have a specific object in view, having one volume in our hand, feeling one spirit in our heart, and inspired with an overmastering desire to know more of Christ and be more like Christ, that we may do more for Christ. Is this our desire? It is our need.

> " Come, Holy Spirit, Heavenly Dove,
>   With all thy quickening powers;
> Come, shed abroad a Saviour's love,
>   And that shall kindle ours ! "

This subject is natural to Christians for discussion. The command of Christ to his new-born church was, "Tarry ye in Jerusalem until ye be endued with power;" and you remember he spent his last hours on earth in talking with men whom he had chosen, taught, and inspired, that they should be baptized with the Holy Ghost, transforming them into torch-bearers of the truth, and enabling them to witness and preach with such divine unction that thousands were daily added to the followers of the cross.

Yes, we need this power as pastors in the study of the Word, in the deepening of our spiritual life, and in the proclamation of the unsearchable riches of Christ, to a sin-smitten world.

We need this power as teachers, evangelists, editors, parents, and toilers in every sphere of Christian work, so that our efforts may be a benediction to the physical, intellectual, and spiritual life of all with whom we have to do.

I know the church is splendidly equipped for service. She has magnificent machinery, wrought out by the genius of Paul, Calvin, Luther, Wesley, Raikes, Booth, Clark, and other great leaders of the legions of Christ. She has matchless scholars, faultless orators, and generous supporters on every hand. Her opportunities were never as world-wide as they are to-day, and yet she is not succeeding as she ought; ignorance, superstition, cruelty, and sin still hold sway over large portions of this Christ-redeemed world—and why? Because we, as workers, lack that power that made Elijah, Daniel, Peter, Knox, Livingston, and Spurgeon irresistible for God.

First, no national distinctions can prevent us from enjoying the fulness and richness there is in Christ. Paul the Hebrew, Luther the German, Duff the Scotchman, Father Mathew the Irishman, Carey the Englishman, and Summerfield the American, all enjoyed this priceless power.

Glorious adaptation — every life, family, tribe, and nation on this planet may rise up into this satisfying experience that comes through fellowship with Christ.

Second, no educational distinctions need prevent us from enjoying this baptism of power. The religion of Christ is profound enough to engage the thought of a Newton, yet simple enough for the little child who whispers out its trust in Daniel Webster's prayer : —

> " Now I lay me down to sleep,
> I pray the Lord my soul to keep;
> And if I die before I wake,
> I pray the Lord my soul to take."

A few weeks ago Gladstone, the matchless scholar, statesman, and orator, bowed with his gardener at the same altar, and drank of the same divine stream, blending their voices in prayer and praise to the glory of Him who came and redeemed their souls.

Third, no ecclesiastical distinctions can keep us from fellowship; Jesus Christ, the Son of man, came to the sons of men. I am thankful for the broad sympathetic spirit and co-operation of all the churches in the last decade of this glorious century, but I am looking to our great Christian Endeavor Society, under the direction of God's Holy Spirit, co-operating with the other young people's societies of the world, to bring about the long-prayed-for hour when there shall be in spirit, one Lord, one faith, and one baptism. How is this power secured? How is any power secured? By complying with the conditions that surround it.

Thus the scholar enters the realm of literature, holding converse with the kings and queens of thought, by the mastery of the twenty-six letters of the alphabet. Thus the musician enters the sphere of music by the mastery of the seven notes. So with the Christian, acting in harmony with the conditions revealed in the Word, and by the spirit of God enjoys that blessed state and experience that enables him to say, " I live not, but Christ liveth in me."

We must desire this power. Our Saviour said, " Blessed are they who do hunger and thirst after righteousness, for they shall be filled ; " and thus Paul exclaimed, " That I may know Him and the power of his resurrection! " We want a longing, not merely to have love for God, but to have the love of God shed abroad in our hearts. Thus wanted the apostles at Pentecost and found joy in the consciousness of an indwelling Christ.

A young man, a member of my church, who wanted this power, attended the convention in Boston last year, and received such a baptism at one of the consecration services that he has been marvelously used of God during the year in the salvation of precious souls. So it is,— obedience and prayer will secure this blessing. God's plan is " seek and ye shall find, ask and ye shall receive, that your joy may be full." To our desire we must add capacity to receive and determination to keep this heaven-given gift.

This baptism of power touches our faculties and swings them into harmony with God. It vitalizes our conscience, bringing conviction of sin ; it vitalizes our will, bringing repentance for sin ; it vitalizes our intellect, producing faith in Christ ; and vitalizes our affections, causing love, joy, and peace to spring up in our hearts by the Holy Ghost.

This power must be continuously used. Oh, what unused forces and latent energies lie dormant in the Church of Christ ! Tongues that should speak are dumb, hands that should serve are closed, hearts that should love are cold, and lives that should shine are dimmed. If we were illumined by the Holy Ghost, we should see the height of Christ as he declares, " And I, if I be lifted up from the earth, will draw all men unto me."

We should see the depth of Christ as he proclaims the sublime truths of the Sermon on the Mount. We should see his breadth as, with world-wide vision, he exclaims, " Our Father ! "

We should see his length, as he issues his final marching orders : " Go ye into all the world and preach the gospel to every creature. I am with you always, even to the end."

Yes, we should use this power, and thus help to bring the kingdoms of this world to a knowledge of our God and of his Christ.

Who can describe the blessing and benefits conferred by this power? It gives us a testimony, personal, definite, and convincing, so that with Paul we can say, " We know whom we have believed."

Each one in his own sphere must pay his own tribute to Christ. Elizabeth Fry did on the streets of London. Jerry McAuley did in the slums of New York. Fanny Crosby, blind, yet patient, writes her song of trust. Bella Cooke, afflicted for forty years, yet patient, thus gives her testimony to the sustaining grace of God.

Oh for a baptism of this power, this abiding, steadying, satisfying grace! Jesus can give it, for our Captain is able to save to the uttermost.

As Joseph was nerved in the dungeon of Pharaoh, and Paul was strengthened in Imperial Rome, so shall we be in our work "For Christ and the Church," if our faith be strong in the blood, principles, plans, and promise of Christ.

The next speaker was the Rev. Wm. J. Harsha, D.D., of New York City.

Address of the Rev. William Justin Harsha, D.D., New York City.

I have been thinking much of one of the pleas God makes to his children,— a plea which contains an actual reprimand and an implied promise. It is recorded by Isaiah in his forty-eighth chapter, at the eighteenth verse: "Oh that thou hadst hearkened to my commandments! Then had thy peace been as a river." The best way I know of to deepen the spiritual life is to dredge the river bed through which God promises to set aflow the full and satisfying currents of his life and his peace. Exhaustive expositions of Scripture, theories of the higher life, even explanation of the baptism, enduement, and filling of the Spirit,—valuable though these be,—will not accomplish what we want so long as we leave hidden rocks and lurking sand-bars in that course through which the river yearns to run. Let us look at this promise of God from this standpoint, and may the Holy Spirit teach us what we must get out of the way in order that he may come fully in.

There are three important words which we should consider carefully.

1. *Peace.* If we are to dredge the river, we must get out of the way at once and for all time any false conceptions about peace itself which we have been entertaining. Nothing stops the inflow of the divine life more effectually than false notions.

There are some young people who think that peace means a sort of Christian Nirvana, a state of abstraction, absorption in the Infinite, or self-surrender to nothingness in general and nothing in particular. It means to them quietness in all circumstances, passivity in prayer-meeting, and a superior disdain of sociables. It is a matter of light on the cheeks and in the eyes. It is "looking pleasant," as the photographer tells one to do at the supreme moment when the bulb of the camera is to be squeezed.

One must cultivate this by long thought. One must go and sit under an imaginary Bo-tree and stare continuously at one object. It is a sort of semi-consciousness of external things which enables one to bear the trials of life,— to be a "fakir" in society and business. It is best and purest when it gives a rather egotistical cast to the countenance. Thus some think, and it is no wonder that they fall into despondency after a time. They come to suppose that Christian peace has to do with old age; it is associated with grandma's lace cap or grandpa's spectacles. Young people should not expect it,—they have not been under the Bo-tree long enough.

All this is a grave mistake. We live in a practical age and the promises of God apply to practical people. If the divine peace is not for young people with much upon their hands and hearts, God's Word has no meaning. A great deal of practical business is to come before this Convention. We are to discuss Christian citizenship in all its multiform and important bearings. We are to consider the best methods of evangelism at home and abroad, and absorb inspiration for an active participation in it. The purification of municipal life and city politics, the furthering of temperance reform and Sabbath observance, are to be presented by specialists in the several departments, and we are to be surcharged with energy to assist in all branches of the great work. Well, then, if peace consist in mere self-abnegation and abstraction to external forces, it has no place in our programme. It is out of its proper environment in these stirring times. This conception of it is clearly erroneous. Peace is consistent and co-existent with the intensest activity. A river may run through the busiest cities without losing its deep steadiness and gentle murmur. Our Lord Jesus was called "the Prince of peace" (Isa. ix. 6), and yet he was the most practical of workers.

A life of active philanthropy may give joy to the heart and cause a certain quiet satisfaction to descend upon the soul, but this may not be genuine peace. Faithfulness at the services of the church and attendance upon Christian Endeavor gatherings tend to produce peace, but in themselves they are not of its real essence. Conventions such as this inaugurated to-night conduce to the desired end; but we should never confuse the means with the end. Let us never forget that peace is the gift of the risen Christ. "My peace I *give* unto you."

The saintly Dr. Watts said, in his old age, "I thank God that I can lie down with comfort at night, not being solicitous whether I wake in this world or in another." Dr. James Hamilton wrote, "Peace is love reposing. It is love on the green pastures; it is love beside the still waters. It is that great calm which comes over the conscience when it sees the atonement sufficient and the Saviour willing. It is the soul which Christ has pacified spread out in serenity and simple faith, and the Lord God, merciful and gracious, smiling over it."

Yes, this is true peace.

2. *River.* This is the second word in God's sweet promise which we need to consider carefully. What a beautiful figure does the word present to our imaginations! "Peace as a river." Among the quieter objects of nature none is more suggestive of God's power and wisdom, of God's loving presence in the world which he has made, than the river which winds in and out among the hills, steals quietly through clattering towns, kisses fields and pastures into fruitfulness and verdure, and smilingly bares its breast to be scarred by the countless keels of the world's commerce. Hence the figure of the text gives us at once an idea of what peace is and what it does. It is the inflow of the divine life, bringing the divine quietness, patience, and power, and resulting in spiritual beauty and faithfulness. Straight into, and straight through, the heart and life the river runs. Men come and go, but God's peace flows on forever. It is not compared to a stagnant pool, for peace is not mere quietness and abstraction, as we have seen. It is not likened to a clear lake, nor a deep reservoir enclosed in the distant hills, shut off from the homes and haunts of men; for peace is not mere intellectual elevation and absence from the distressing cares of life. It is not compared to the mighty sea. which sometimes sleeps and seems to afford a figure of depth and calm. The sea is treacherous and unstable. If for a day or a week it sleep and smile, it is at other times tossed by the hurricane and waves upon the snarling rocks which line its shores. "The *wicked* are like the troubled sea when it cannot rest, whose waters cast up mire and dirt." But "peace is like a river" in the hearts of those who receive its gentle, cooling, constant, unruffled waters. We have, hence, but to apply our ideas of a river to peace to discover the practical lessons we need to learn.

A proper river grows broader and deeper as it progresses toward the sea. One of the Hebrew words translated "river" in the Bible means literally " a strong place," indicating the mighty power of its current and its ever-increasing depth.

It tends by its very onflow to wear a more ample channel for itself. God's promise has in it, therefore, a thought of progressional expansion. Our peace shall grow broader and deeper as we go on in the Christian life. "Behold, I will *extend* peace to her like a river, and like a *flowing* stream." (Isa. lxvi. 12.) A stream that truly flows becomes stronger and sweeter as it goes. . Our peace should not be like the Humboldt River, that loses itself in the alkali marshes of the sink, or like the Rhine, which, after sweeping between hills crowned with lordly ruins, finally grows languid and sluggish in the ditches of Holland; or like the Sabbatic River of South Palestine, which runs certain days of the week and rests on others. Nay, let our peace be like the noble Thames, or the mighty Mississippi, which run on with increasing power and weight. Let our path be like that of the just, which is comparable to the shining light of the morning, "which shineth more and more unto the perfect day," the meridian splendour of noon. Let the inflow of the divine life be like the river which Ezekiel saw,— at first, possibly, reaching only to the ankles, but growing until it comes to the knees; growing still until it reaches the loins and " afterward " becoming "waters to swim in, a river that could not be passed over!" (Ezek. xlvii. 5.) Oh that our spiritual life may be deepened after this fashion! Such "quietness and assurance" are far better than mere clattering joy, mere sparkling hilarity, mere effervescing enthusiasm and "feeling." The foam-touched ripples of a mountain stream may be beautiful to look at ; but what the thirsty country needs is the deep, still torrent of the great river. This is also what our hearts need. There may be sorrows and trials, "nevertheless afterward " there flows into us the river that " has risen," and there grow beside us the "peaceable fruits of righteousness."

Some of you came from the banks of the Missouri or other western rivers, and you have seen, as I have, the extensive works called "riprapping" carried on by the government, or by private corporations, to prevent the waters eating away the banks and inundating the fields. There have been heavy rains in the mountains, or the snows have suddenly melted and a mighty freshet comes tearing down the stream. The soil composing the banks is loose and loamy, and some protection must be afforded where the bends occur and the cities are built.

Then the men set to work, and great nets of boughs and branches of trees are built, and these are made stable by rocks and bags of sand, and so the "rip-rap " is formed and the waters are kept in their course.

I hope you will not think me unduly fanciful if I use this as an illustration of what needs to be done in the spiritual life. We are constantly in danger of losing spiritual power through the broadening of our energies and the dissipation of our forces. A proper overflow of blessing to others is necessary, as I have said ; yet the river is not to run entirely out of its channel and waste itself fruitlessly, and even harmfully. The love of Christ is to "constrain " us — keep us within limits. Let us not be afraid of being "narrow " in this sense. A river is powerful only when properly narrow, — otherwise it becomes a bog and a stench. Let us learn to apply spiritual power upon the places where it is needed. Surrender to God's will is the key-thought just here. One of the subtle ways in which our peace is destroyed is through fretting anxiety to do more than God wants us to do. "Thou art careful and troubled about many things." Keep in the channel of the Father's will. Live in such close touch with him through the Spirit that you will know when to be idle for his sake. Sometimes we attempt too much. Sometimes we need to sit with folded hands.

Those who dwell near sandy rivers or near harbors formed by river-mouths know what an amount of careful piering and dredging is necessary to keep the channel clear.

Let us learn a lesson from the pains taken by the engineers. If we find a place in our spiritual life where sudden bars are apt to form, disturbing or retarding the flow of peace, let us at once protect the spot by special prayer. This is the key-thought here. Piers of prayer in all eddies and places of danger! There is nothing like prayer to keep the channels clear and the river flowing. Stated prayer, family prayer, closet prayer, ejaculatory prayer, are all availing. I like the thought of ejaculatory prayer, especially prayer that is like the *jaculum*, or "dart," which the warrior sends flying from the string in sudden danger and is able to watch until it reaches the mark. Oh that we may cultivate constant communion with God through Christ in the Spirit, and then shall our peace be deep and calm and strong — like a river unobstructed in all its course !

The " quiet hour " was an impressive service conducted by Rev. Chas. Roads, of Philadelphia.

Metropolitan African M. E. Church.

The Metropolitan A. M. E. Church was the scene of one of the most interesting services held by the Christian Endeavorers. There was a large attendance in the handsome edifice, which was most tastefully decorated with bunting and American flags, this work having been designed by Miss Jennie M. Spears, president of the society of Christian Endeavor of the church, and executed by her associates.

On the platform were the following distinguished clergymen : Bishop W. J. Gaines, D.D., Bishop W. B. Derrick, D.D., Bishop J. H. Armstrong, Rev. Dr. H. T. Johnson, Rev. Dr. L. J. Coppin, Rev. D. W. Jones, Rev. E. G. Hubert, Rev. William Rader, Rev. T. G. Langdale, Rev. Dr. J. T. Jennefer, Rev. W. R. Arnold, Rev. M. C. Brooks, Rev. Mr. Edwards, Rev. Mr. Jenkins, Rev. Mr. Tyce, Rev. Dr. Beckett, and Rev. James Allan Johnson, pastor of the church.

The meeting was opened with prayer by Bishop Gaines, and by singing by the choir of 125 voices, under the leadership of Prof. J. T. Layton, chorister of the church. The feature of the musical programme was a solo," God Is Love," by Miss Helen Adams. Bishop Wm. B. Derrick, of New York, delivered a stirring address.

Address of Bishop William Benjamin Derrick, D.D.

Life may be defined as follows: animation, vivacity, briskness, vigor, energy, spirit.

In this paper we will speak of life from a spiritual standpoint, as the object of Christian Endeavor Societies is to infuse a deeper spirituality throughout Christendom.

As the believer sinks into spiritual life he becomes more and more dissatisfied with self; his hunger and thirst increase and become eager for the body and blood of Christ, and, with increased desire, for the sincere milk of the Word. As it is a well-known fact that when people are hungry they will find time for their meals, and a good appetite does not think three meals a day too much, so with the believer,—as he grows deeper into spiritual life, he is not satisfied with one spiritual meal a day. No, but, like Daniel, he sits three times a day with his window open toward Jerusalem, feasting on the spiritual manna, in the meantime exclaiming, "The Lord is my shepherd, I shall not want . . . . He prepareth a table for me in the midst of my enemies. My cup runneth over."

As he goes to this spiritual feast he does not forget to pray all the way, and to feed his soul on the hope of hearing some good news from heaven and from Jesus, the faithful, loving friend whom he has there. His light is attended with the warmth of love, and is not satisfied simply to be acquainted with the way to heaven, but he walks constantly therein with joy and gladness, regardless of the storms and hurricanes which confront the believer on his passage to the skies.

Again, as the life deepens and expands in the spiritual atmosphere, it becomes more acquainted with the way to obtain the precious love,—to consider the free mercy of God, and to believe implicitly in the pardoning love of Jesus, who died, the just for the unjust, to bring us unto God. "For we all with open face beholding as in a glass the glory of the Lord are changed into the same image from glory to glory, by the Spirit of the Lord." (2 Cor. iii. 18.) He is frequently, yes, constantly, supplicating at the Throne of Grace; applying his faith with all the attention of his mind and all the fervor of his heart; exclaiming, "I know in whom I believe, and am persuaded that he is able to keep that which I have committed against that day;" and positively setting his affection on Christ, whom he cannot see, and for his sake upon fellow-believers, whom he does see; always devoting much time to private meditation,—for himself and others,—thus holding unbroken communion with God and absent members of the mystic body of Christ. By this he gathers strength, which affords him powerful resistance, so when tempted he yields not to the temptation, but continues his pleadings for consolation in Christ, comfort of love, bowels of mercy, and for complete fulfilment of the joy as is promised in the Word of Divine Truth, that believers may become more and more like unto his Lord and Master, having the same love, being of one accord and of one mind — discarding anything which is done through strife and vainglory, but accepting all that is done in lowliness of mind and sincerity of heart.

Such a state of mind and heart is the strongest evidence of a genuine spirituality, which causes its possessor to exclaim, " May the eyes of my understanding be opened to behold the beauties of thy law and the suitableness, freeness, and fulness of the redemption which was bought not with corruptible things, such as silver and gold, but with the precious blood of Christ, which is applied by the Spirit through faith."

As the believer contemplates, his soul glows with joy and gladness, becoming more ardent and burning and powerful, until it brings him on his knees, and in that supplicating posture he pours out his soul:—

> " Let me love thee more and more
> Till this fleeting life is o'er,
> Till my soul is lost in love
> In that brighter world above."

To grow deeper in spiritual life we would suggest the following rules of conduct : —

(*a*). Heartily repent of our sins, original and actual.

(*b*). Believe the Gospel of Christ in sincerity and truth.

(*c*). In the power which true faith gives, — for all things commanded are possible to him that believeth, — walking with humble confidence the way of God's commandments before God and man.

(*d*). By continuing to take up the cross and to receive the pure milk of God's Word, growing in grace and in the knowledge of Jesus Christ.

These simple rules will lead the believer in the path and cause him to grow in peace and joy all the days of his life; and when rolling years shall be lost in eternity, he will continue to grow in bliss and heavenly glory. The Lord will be his sun, and his crown, and he shall be forever with the Lord, where the perfection of spiritual life is attained; where the fulness and grandeur of the King of kings will burst on our vision, and the bliss of the redeemed shall be realized, and we shall join in the saints' triumphant song, " Hallelujah, for the Lord God omnipotent reigneth," in that land where the mansions are tinged with the electric light of immortality and are bathed in endless sunshine throughout the realm of eternal morning.

Angels and redeemed spirits are its citizens, whose lot is neither poverty, nor riches, but one of joy, happiness, and calm repose, innocent and tractable, bearing in their hands palm branches, symbols of their wondrous victory ; and who are living with God in the heaven of heavens, and shall continue throughout the endless ages of eternity with no bar of sickness, no distance of time or place, no gulf of death or the grave, to part us more. We shall meet in the bosom of Jesus, the fountain and author of divine love. Oh that blessed " meeting " which shall put us " beyond the smiling and the weeping ! "

Oh that blessed meeting, which shall end the "meeting and the parting," where we shall behold the Sun of righteousness without a cloud, and forever bask in the beams of his glory. Is not this a glorious prospect ? One which is enough to incite us to grow daily deeper and deeper into spiritual life until the poet's dream be realized in us :—

> " Consecrate me now to thy service, Lord,
> By the power of grace divine;
> Let my soul look up with a steadfast hope,
> And my will be lost in thine."

Thus bidding defiance to sin and the grave, we join the cry of the Spirit and the Bride, " Come, Lord Jesus, come quickly."

The next speaker was heartily received.

Address of Rev. Wm. Rader, San Francisco, Cal.

According to Paul, man is a trinity, composed of body, soul, and spirit. The body is the physical house; the soul, the seat and source of life, the animating principle of the physical organism; the spirit, that restless something which laughs and cries, which throbs with emotion, worships God, and, facing eternity, refuses to die forever.

It is this spirit that paints pictures, and writes the lasting literature of the world. Never satisfied, it is forever reaching out after more life and love. It is the development of this spiritual nature of which I speak. The average man is higher than he is deep; he is more parapet than foundation, more dome than corner-stone. Height is more popular because more conspicuous than depth. By depth is meant the moral resources of our nature, the reserved force of character, that latent and unseen capital which lies hidden in the personality. Depth is character. Character is not intention. If it were, then the world would be full of angels. Character is not motive. Motive is character in the wheat, character is motive in the flour.

A man is manly in the degree that he is able to translate intention into life. Character is related to motive as the sea is related to the wave. The wave is powerful, because it is reinforced by the strength of the ocean, and it is able to beat down the crag along the coast, because the pulse of the sea beats in its surf.

The depth of the man spiritually includes all his available manhood; it embraces all that is potentially good within him, all that reserved force which is latent in his moral nature.

It is a duty we owe to ourselves to make the most of our spiritual nature. Few people are as good as they might be. There are few perfect bodies, and there are fewer perfect minds, but people neglect the development and enrichment of their spiritual nature far more than their physical or mental faculties. Self-development is personal responsibility. Laziness is as bad as dissipation. The man who refuses to cultivate his best nature is as great a criminal before God as he who wastes his force and dissipates his strength. Indifference is as bad as intemperance. If we have a party for Prohibition we should also have a party for Stimulation. The spiritual nature may be deepened by our own hand. This is a solemn and responsible task, which faces every human being. For the most part we are responsible for the depth and richness of our own spirituality.

Circumstances deepen life; sorrow stirs and awakens the soul. It sometimes disturbs nature, as dynamite moves the solid rock. " Sorrow is bread, and tears are medicine." The great grief mellows us and drives us nearer God. There are flowers that must be crushed before they expend their fragrance.

John Milton wrote his grandest words when God curtained his eyes. Dante in the solemn splendor of his grief became a genius. John Bunyan became great in the shadows of Bedford jail. Tennyson constructed that marvelous tribute more lasting and magnificent than any material monument, "In Memoriam," because his college friend had passed away suddenly into the world beyond. When Jennie Lind sang in Castle Garden, N.Y., Goldschmidt, hearing her wondrous voice, remarked, "If I could marry that woman and break her heart, she would sing like a nightingale." He did marry her, he did break her heart, and the voice of the English Nightingale will never die.

Joy deepens the spiritual life. We must not suppose that people who are sad are necessarily good, and that because one has been profoundly moved by a great sorrow, his spiritual nature is deepened. A great joy sometimes lifts the soul to the very throne of God.

There are people, and they are many, who never know the inspiration of real happiness. They pass through the world and never feel the soft and inspiring touch of a great joy. Their best nature is never found; it never will be found except by a great happiness. There is nothing so orthodox as laughter; there is nothing so deepening and enriching as a stainless pleasure. If sorrow may be likened to dynamite, then joy may be described by the delicate but powerful strength of a sunbeam. Yonder on the mountains the sun is melting the snows, which form themselves in refreshing streams, move on to the valley with health and vigor, giving life, which is the sunbeam striking down deep into the heart of the snows.

To be spiritual is to be natural. Do not suppose that spirituality means a certain tone of voice or cast of countenance or attitude of worship. The spiritual is always natural, always rational, and everywhere at ease. Don't permit your religious life to make you awkward, morally awkward; be yourself, and if you are not like other people, if you are sincere and honest you will express the most attractive type of real spirituality.

Science asks, " Whence came the spiritual in man? " The story of its birth has never been told. The wisdom of the world stands mute before the mystery of this fact, as children on the shore watch the ship emerge from the dense fog, and, passing in magnificent action before them, they see it disappear again in the fog-bank beyond. Thus evolution and eschatology alike are shrouded in mist, and the honest thinker must stand before these phenomena in the agnosticism of Paul, and say, " Now we see through a glass darkly, but then face to face; now we know in part, but then we shall know even as we are known." One thing we know,—that the spiritual within us is to live forever. How majestic that thought! Webster said it was the greatest thought which entered the portals of his brain. We are to live again! " Now are we the sons of God, but it doth not yet appear what we shall be." When all things are destroyed, when the moon is blood, and the earth shall melt with fervent heat, the spirit, that passionate and immortal self, shall stand on the summit of the destroyed years and reach out for the living God. Our duty is to yield it up blameless, and not our spirits only, but our bodies and souls blameless to the God who gave it, for the eternal life is but the mortal life, writ in larger type.

The " quiet hour" was introduced by the solo, " Calvary," after which Rev. T. G. Langdale, of South Dakota, using the words of Luke viii. 18, " Take heed *how* ye hear," called the attention of the Endeavorers to the need of approaching the meetings of the Convention with the distinct purpose in mind of deepening their own and others' spiritual lives — in order to hear in the right way the things that God has for them.

After singing a verse of " Nearer, My God, to Thee," the benediction was pronounced by Bishop Arnett.

John Wesley African M. E. Zion Church.

There were three speakers at the John Wesley African M. E. Zion Church, where a good-sized audience assembled in spite of the rain. In the absence of the pastor, Dr. R. A. Fisher, Rev. J. B. Colbert presided. The service was opened by singing " Onward, Christian Soldiers," which was followed with a Scripture reading by Rev. J. E. Mason, of Rochester, N. Y., and prayer by Rev. P. P. Watson, of Beaufort, S. C. Mr. W. H. Strong, of Detroit, president of the Michigan State Christian Endeavor Union, was the first speaker.

Address of Mr. W. H. Strong, Detroit, Mich.

The things which are seen are temporal. The things which are not seen are eternal.

Nearly two thousand years ago, in Corinth, the beautiful metropolis of southern Greece, was a church in the midst of the city. Not only was the city fair to look upon, but full of the bustle of business, the excitement of pleasure, the cankerous wickedness of self-seeking wealth. It was a spiritually minded church, full of thoughts pointing to heaven and of temptations luring toward hell. To this church Paul wrote at least two letters, and in the second he said that the real things are the inside things, and that outward show, whether it be in church life, in business, or in society, is passing and temporary. History and daily life alike voice the same eternal antagonism. Thirty and five years ago our ears were deafened with the roar of war; the factors seemed to be men, money, and muskets; it seemed as if old John Brown had gone defeated to his grave, but the end was not so wrought out. What kept the nation together? Not facts, but faith. Not arithmetic, but the Bible. Not preference, nor prejudice, but an abiding sense that right was right, since God was God; and all the past tells the same story, — that fact is always the coward, faith has always won the day.

I would turn aside a moment for just a word of caution. We are tempted to think of the unseen as something awful and uncanny; ghost stories have frightened us; the very term " Holy Ghost " is misleading to many minds. Spirituality is not spiritualism. Religion has been fringed with superstition, but that type of spiritualism which conceives spirits in the heavenly land as turning tables or thumping doors to surprise an audience is sometimes entertaining, but never helpful.

The spiritual life is the real life. Spirituality is not a place, but an attitude. Spirituality is never selfishness.

There is a battle of the standards not only in finance, but in the soul of every man. So was it in Corinth; so it is to-day. Flesh and spirit, self-indulgence and self-sacrifice. An act may be spiritual. Spirituality looks up and out; it looks up to God and out for men. Spirituality is not simply religious meditation; it is not the babbling brook of psalm and hymn singing ; it is not like a pond in a park, made to look at, but it is a great living current, directing us ever forward. I would repeat, spirituality is self-surrender. How are we to deepen it? As Jesus deepened the spiritual life of the woman at Jacob's well,— first, by removing our prejudice and having our eyes open to see the truth; second, by lifting up our ideals of life and finding that sin and not the weight of the bucket is the heaviest load.

We deepen water in a stream by dredging it out, digging away the dirt, stone, or sand-bar. We narrow the channel to give strength to the current. We mark the channel with stakes and buoys, and obey them. We build dams to stop the waste of worldliness, the draining-away of force. We want depth in the river and "everything shall live whither the river cometh." Whatever the sphere in which we work, wherever the home in which we live, whatever the end we seek in our lives, all shall live if the river of life is in our hearts, — a deep, strong, mighty, overflowing current, bearing the world's burdens and ours to the foot of the throne of God.

The next speaker was the Rev. J. E. Mason, D.D., Rochester, N. Y.

Address of Rev. J. E. Mason, D.D., Rochester, N. Y.

We are exhorted by the Scriptures to set our affections on things above and not on things on earth; to lay up for ourselves treasures in heaven. Of these things we acknowledge the truth, but it is to be feared that many go further, or at most resolve within themselves that they will become spiritual-minded when this world and its concerns are fading from their view and the next is opening upon them. I would describe spiritual-mindedness as consisting in a following of God's will instead of our own; as a subjection of the body to the spirit, a deliberate seeking after things eternal instead of things temporal, and this under all circumstances of our daily life. He who intends deepening his spiritual life will be a man of prayer, for prayer alone can fix his thoughts on the world unseen. He will live in habits of self-denial, for not otherwise will he gain the mastery over those fleshly lusts and appetites which war against the soul. He will cultivate a spirit of awe and reverence for holy things, as knowing that irreverence is the first step to unbelief. He will never be unduly anxious to speak much openly on subjects connected with religion, as knowing the danger to himself lest his professions should outrun his performances, and danger to others, lest, from his example, they should get into a careless way of speaking of holy things. His light will shine before men because they who watch him will see that he is diligently discharging the duties of that state of life to which it has pleased God to call him, but there will be no ostentation or display; rather, he will live in his own thoughts and be so cautious of exposing them to that world which he has renounced that to casual observers there will seem to be nothing peculiar about him. The great mass of Christians, it is to be feared, owe what they have of religion to accident more than any other cause. They do certain things because it is the way of the world to do them; they abstain from others because the habits of society seem to require it. To the spiritual-minded man God will be everything and the world nothing. The first and chiefest aid to spiritual-mindedness is that of God the Holy Ghost. He dwelleth in us, is ever ready to assist us, cleanses and purifies the heart. He renews us where everything has been decayed by the fraud and malice of the devil or by our own carnal will and failures. How diligently, therefore, should we listen to his voice; how carefully should we attend to it when heard; how wakeful should we be lest by thought or word or action we should grieve him, or quench the fire which he has kindled within us! The next great aid which has been provided for those who are aiming at deepening the spiritual life is to be found in the privileges which the church offers us. As she sees Christ in all things, so she will lead us to do the same. With her daily round of prayer and praise, it should prepare us while still on earth for the never-ending services of heaven and the unceasing adoration of our Lord. To the better accomplishment of this purpose let us constantly ask the questions, "What lack I yet?" "How far am I walking worthy of the Lord unto all pleasing?" In order to judge accurately of that standard of perfection which God is pleased to set forth as the model for our imitation, we must refer, not to the opinions and language of the world about us, but to his own Word. He has set forth his eternal Son, the head of the church, as the example which the members of his body are to follow. No lower standard, no, not that of the purest saint or the highest angel, will be sufficient. In seeking to deepen your spiritual life you must be guided not by the state of your religious feelings, but by a strict review and unshrinking self-examination, whether or not you can trace in yourselves a steady development in the true light of the spirit, a gradual maturing and ripening of the full fruit of holiness. There is no criterion so little to be trusted, in estimating our Christian status, as arguments drawn from the state of our religious feelings. Religion does not consist in excitement, but in action. No man who is in earnest but will have some natural fervor, — a fervor which must be trained. not repressed,— but stiil this fervor will vary in intensity in different constitutions; and, therefore, it is conceivable that a man may discharge his daily duties to God without his being sensible to himself of any very lively emotions about him. His heart and feeling may appear to himself cold, and yet this may not arise from unbelief, but from his natural temperament of mind. We are never to fancy that we have attained to that degree of righteousness that is sufficient. To halt, to look back, or to slumber, are but so many tokens of impending ruin. Let us beware of mistaking words and professions for Christian faith, and of confounding good feeling with good works. We are Christ's soldiers and are fighting under his banner. Our duty is not only not to lose heart, but to press forward and gain more ground continually.

The last speaker to take up the general topic was Rev. Mr. Watson, of South Carolina.

Address of Rev. P. P. Watson, Beaufort, S. C.

The closing of the nineteenth century witnesses an effort that is almost universal in our schools and colleges, looking forward to the building-up of a strong, vigorous manhood and womanhood, laying deep the foundations for mental, moral, and spiritual life. The life of Christ, his association with and his relation to his disciples, gives emphasis to the possibility and the necessity of a progress in the deepening of the spiritual life. It is plain to us that there are many who have received Christ, but are not working for Christ as they should. They seem to be in possession of certain gifts and graces that, if used, would tell on the lives and consciences of men; but there is a want of enthusiasm, and this demonstrates the want of a deeper consecration and sanctification for the services of the Lord. He who would enjoy the benefits of a deeper spiritual life must throw open the windows of his soul and let the beams of Christ, the Sun of righteousness, fall thereon. This being done, our will is lost in the will of God; our bodies are yielded up, and becoming emptied of self, God fills us with his Spirit. This state brings us into communion with God, and communion is one of the essential means for the deepening of spiritual life. Another means for the deepening of the spiritual life is the inspired Word of God,— appropriating it by a spiritual assimilation to the wants of the soul. The history of the Christian church from the days of the apostles to the present time is a history of the glorious achievements of men and women whose hearts have been touched, whose lips have been purified, whose intellects have been consecrated, and whose souls have been surcharged with holy fire. This deepening of the spiritual life works wonders in the soul. It brings man into a closer relation with God. He understands more thoroughly his duties to God, and delights more in the services of God.

God with us, and success will come ; God with us, and the windows of heaven will be opened and showers of blessings will come down upon us; God with us, and we shall leave an impression upon this city, her business and commercial enterprises, her homes, her schools, her colleges, and her churches, that shall enhance the peace and prosperity of her inhabitants. God with us, and the nation's capital shall feel a spiritual shock, unparalleled in her history, that shall bless her and magnify her among the cities of the world.

In the absence of Rev. Wm. Shaw, of Atlanta, Ga., the Rev. J. B. Colbert conducted the " quiet hour " with which the meeting closed.

Calvary Baptist Church.

An immense congregation filled every seat in the Calvary Baptist Church. They packed against the walls and filled the aisles and stairways. Dr. Samuel H. Greene, the pastor, announced that there was nearly as much more room in the " adult room " as in the church proper, and if those who were standing would go into that room, speakers would be provided for them, and music would be conducted by Mr. Judd. This was immediately taken advantage of, and, without seeming to affect the size of the crowd in the church, the adult room was quickly filled, there being no more room than in the church.

The music of the main meeting was directed by Mr. P. H. Bristow. The singing was heartily entered into by the entire congregation. Rev. Dr. Greene presided and conducted the exercises, offering prayer.

The first speaker was Rev. J. T. McCrory, D. D., of Pittsburg, president of the Pennsylvania Christian Endeavor Union. The speaker referred to Peter's efforts to deepen the spiritual life, summing it all up in the word " grow."

Dr. McCrory emphasized the importance of Christian Endeavorers keeping their pledges by reading their Bibles every day. God would help the young people to grow.

Rev. Dr. Smith Baker, of Boston, Mass., was the second and last speaker.

Address of Rev. Smith Baker, D.D., East Boston, Mass.

The material is a type of the spiritual. The laws of the lower represent the laws of the higher. The wise men of the Old Testament constantly refer to them. "Go to the ant, thou sluggard; learn her ways, and be wise." "The spider layeth hold with her hands and is in kings' palaces." No other teacher is so fruitful in this method as our Lord. "Consider the lilies, how they grow." "The kingdom of heaven is like unto a grain of mustard seed." "A sower went forth to sow." And without some kind of a material illustration he did not speak to them. There are but few so instructive, complete. and beautiful types of the nature and growth of the Christian life as that of the healthy tree. The tree has an unseen and an outward life; so has the Christian. The tree has trunk and branches, without which its inner life could not be manifested; so the spiritual life has its great fundamental doctrines and moral precepts which give it strength and without which it would be only a changing sentiment.

This is the importance of our subject, "The Deepening of the Spiritual Life." The strength of the tree depends upon its roots, the beauty of the tree depends upon its roots, and the usefulness of the tree depends upon its roots. How is the unseen life of the roots to be cultivated?

The first thing for the deepening of the life of the tree is nutrition. The soil must be rich in that which feeds the sap of the tree. Thus in the deepening of the spiritual life the love of Christ is not enough. The Christian life must be rooted in the truth or it will be but a transient emotion without strength or fruit.

The Bible is that truth; it is the soil in which the faith of the soul is to grow. All other soil is desert land for the spiritual life. There is no nutrition for the divine life in heathen mythologies or ancient philosophies or modern science. As well try to satisfy the hungry body with historical facts, or the healthy eye with moonlight, or the natural affections with paper dolls or marble statues, as to seek to satisfy the soul with anything less than the revealed Word of God.

Mere intelligence can not unlock the spiritual mysteries. Secular education can not feed the soul any more than agates, and pearls, and beautiful stones can feed the roots of a tree. Secular education must fall before the cross, be baptized with the spirit and warmed with the love of Christ, before it can deepen the spiritual life.

The Bible is the basis of the Christian religion. The Bible is the life of the Protestant church. The Bible is the spiritual life of the world. A man, in order to get the spirit of Shakespeare, or of Browning, must not only hear them read once in a while, or read a few verses of them now and then, but he must read and read and study them over and over before the thought which moved the poet shall become clear and real to him. We must get into the words before the sentiment can fill us. Thus with the Bible; it must be read and studied and its words and expressions become fixed in the brain before its spirit will fill and thrill the soul. There is no more important part of the Christian Endeavor pledge than that which requires its members to read a portion of God's Word each day. Our Saviour was made strong to resist temptation by being full of the word of God. The word of God is the sword of the Spirit, and when we are full of that word then the Spirit has something to work with. The truth of God is a lamp unto our path, and when we are full of that truth then the Spirit has something to illumine our way with. No other words are so suggestive, no other words are so penetrating, no other words are so revealing, no other words are so quickening, and no other words so satisfy the soul as the words in which the Spirit has been pleased to reveal God's will to us.

One verse of the Bible incarnate in one life develops that life more than all the schools and all the rituals of a whole generation. It is communion which develops the mind, and heart, and soul. The poet communes with great ideas in nature. The scientist communes with the rocks, and the stars, and the forces of nature. The artist communes with some great thought as it whispers to his heart in the harmony of sound until his soul is fired and thrilled with a passion which finds expression at the keys of the organ, or in the matchless powers of the human voice in song. Thus when the redeemed soul opens itself to the Word of God in meditation, and to the Christ of God in prayer, and the saved man communes with his Saviour as lover communes with lover, then higher, broader, deeper, and clearer views of truth come into the mind, and sweeter, intenser, and richer love burns in the heart, and faith stronger and stronger enters into that within the veil, and hope brighter and brighter rises above all tears and all fears, and joy like the beams of the morning makes the world a chariot of victory upon which the Christian rides into glory.

The closing exercise was the "quiet hour," conducted by Mr. C. N. Hunt, of Minneapolis, president of the Minnesota Christian Endeavor Union.

In the adult Sunday-school room Mr. George Judd presided, and directed the music, with Miss Minnie Roberts as pianist. Mr. C. N. Hunt spoke, and was followed by Dr. Smith Baker and Rev. J. G. Muir, pastor of the E Street Baptist Church, Washington. It was a very profitable "overflow" meeting.

First Baptist Church.

The young people of the First Baptist Church were the hosts of the Virginia delegation.

Rev. Chas. Stakely, pastor of the church, ascended the pulpit and opened the meeting by requesting the choir of twenty picked voices, under the leadership of Prof. N. Dushane Cloward, with Prof. John Porter Lawrence at the organ, to sing the doxology. Dr. Stakely is known all over the North and South as one of the youngest and most successful Baptist preachers; and in the invocation which he offered, some heartfelt words were delivered when he spoke of the great blessing which the delegates were receiving in being able to be present at one of the largest religious conventions of modern times, Washington City being doubly blessed in being the place of the Convention. Rev. W. F. McCauley, from the Buckeye State, read the Scripture lesson, taking the twelfth chapter of Romans, and followed it with a short prayer.

The first speaker to be introduced was Rev. Edgerton R. Young, of Toronto, Ontario.

Address of Rev. Edgerton R. Young, of Toronto, Canada.

Said Henry Martyn, the devoted missionary, " Live more with Christ, catch more of his spirit; for the spirit of Christ is the spirit of missions, and the nearer we get to him the more intensely missionary we shall become."

Said Paul, the great apostle, " I beseech you therefore, brethren, by the mercies of God, that ye present your bodies a living sacrifice, holy, acceptable unto God, which is your reasonable service."

Says Christ, our Lord and Master, "Go ye into all the world and preach the gospel to every creature. . . . And behold, I send the promise of my Father upon you; but tarry ye in the city of Jerusalem until ye be endued with power from on high."

This enduement of power is the scriptural means for "deepening the spiritual life." The Holy Spirit is life, and the origin of all life. At creation's dawn he brooded over this new world, and from him came that vitalizing energy that brought life universal to this fair world of ours. "By his Spirit he garnished the heavens." If this is true,—and we believe it is, that the Holy Spirit, the Third Person in the Blessed Trinity, is the author of physical life,— it shows us how great is the interest he takes in us, as well as God the Father and God the Son.

But it is in the great redemptive scheme that we see in the fullest light the greatness of the work assigned to the Holy Spirit. There is no deepening of spiritual life, for there is no spiritual life at all, without him. Hence, absolutely essential is the Holy Spirit. Until his vital, energizing, blessed influences are felt in human hearts, Ezekiel's vision is a sad reality.

"Can these bones live? O Lord God! thou knowest." Cheering is his answer, and glorious have been the results throughout all the ages. And it is the same to-day, for God's plan of salvation in all its fulness and blessedness is from the beginning of days.

This deepening the spiritual life is a glorious possibility, and Omnipotence has done his part for its accomplishment.

"Tarry ye in the city of Jerusalem until ye be endued with power from on high." Those disciples and the other loving ones obeyed, and there came the promise of the Father, the Holy Spirit, in a way so real and glorious that they all were very conscious of it, and so were all their friends and also their enemies.

Peter, once so cowardly but now so brave, said a great many glorious things that day; but there is only one of those blessed truths we wish to quote here, and it is this, — "For the promise is unto you, and to your children, and to all that are afar off, even as many as the Lord our God shall call." Surely this is one of the "exceeding great and precious promises." It reaches down to us who are here gathered from many States and provinces and distant lands, worshipping with the saints that are in Washington at this great Christian Endeavor Convention.

Yes, Peter, we are glad that, under divine inspiration, you uttered those words; the promises are to such as "are afar off." They reach to us here, and we accept them in their full significance; and we, with humble, lowly, contrite yet believing hearts "receive the gift of the Holy Ghost." This is the promised Comforter, "even the Spirit of truth, whom the world cannot receive, because it seeth him not, neither knoweth him; but ye know him, for he dwelleth with you, and shall be in you." Beloved, do you know him? Does he dwell in you? "Have ye received the Holy Ghost since ye believed?" If so, happy are you.

We know not who selected this very important subject for these opening addresses at this great Christian Endeavor Convention. We are not careful to know; but this we do know,—that no more important or vital subject could have been suggested. For two reasons this is evident. First, for the spiritual happiness, the soul restfulness, and the Christlikeness of every loyal Christian Endeavorer, and for every child of God everywhere.

Augustine wrote, "The soul is restless till it rests in God." Very true, indeed, is this, and millions have found it out.

"There remaineth therefore a rest for the people of God,"—a rest of soul, a sweet rest in the atoning sacrifice, a foretaste of the rest, sweet rest, where "the wicked cease from troubling, and the weary are at rest." But it does not mean spiritual indolence. Just the reverse. Time is for employment; eternity, for enjoyment. This brings us to the second reason why the Holy Spirit's work of deepening the spiritual life is so necessary and important. It is that there may be rendered to Him whose we are and whom we serve, the highest and most efficient service. We are called not only to be like him, but also called to be co-workers with him. He, the Lord of lords and King of kings, asks us — and somewhere in his plan has he the niche for us to fill — to enter into partnership with himself. Marvelous condescension, amazing love! And he says, "He that believeth on me, the works that I do shall he do also, and greater works than these shall he do, because I go unto my Father." Greater works! Surely that must be a mistake. O no! for Jesus himself uttered those words. Then what do they mean? Why, they mean that if any of us are the instruments in God's hands in the conversion of an immortal soul, we do a greater work than was the miracle of the raising of the body of Lazarus from the dead. Our work is for the regeneration of immortal, eternal spirits, whose existence shall run on and on through all eternity with that of God himself. This is the call of the Master. These are the marching orders to all his followers: "Go ye into all the world, and preach the gospel to every creature." This is the great commission. With the equipment of the Pentecostal baptism, our work is clearly marked out before us, — an ignorant world to be instructed, a polluted world to be regenerated, an enslaved world to be disenthralled, a dark world to be illumined, a sinful world to be saved, a redeemed world to be brought to his feet.

Beloved, this is our work to which we are called — we, instead of the angels. Let us get, by the Holy Spirit, illuminating power, larger, grander conceptions of the responsibility as well as the magnitude of this work, — at home, as well as abroad, all the world for Christ.

And blessed be his glorious name forever; and let the whole earth be filled with his glory. Amen, and amen.

The next speaker was from New York City, the Rev. J. L. Campbell, D.D., pastor of the Lexington Avenue Baptist Church.

Address of Rev. J. L. Campbell, D.D., New York City.

There is perhaps no single expression that is more often on the lips of all believers than this: " Pray for me, that I may be a truer, better, worthier Christian." We see the ideals presented to us in God's Word, and then we look at ourselves. Between what we are and what we feel we ought to be, what we have a right reasonably to expect ourselves to be, there is such a chasm that we often become disheartened and discouraged. The subject we are considering this evening is therefore one of living interest to every true child of God. The word translated "convert" in the common version of the Bible literally means "turn." When Bunyan's Pilgrim turned his back on the City of Destruction, and set his face steadfastly toward the Celestial Gate, that moment he was converted; but how vast and wonderful the experiences which lay before him ere he reached his journey's end! The beginning of the Christian life is not the close; its inception is not its goal. In regeneration the child is born; in sanctification it grows to "a mature man" and attains "to the measure of the stature of the fulness of Christ." (Eph. iv. 13.) Justification is our title to the skies. Sanctification is our meetness and our fitness for the inheritance of the saints in light. We need not only more Christians, but if the world is going to be saved, we need also a higher standard of piety,—Christians that can be weighed as well as numbered, Christians that will be ensamples to the flock, Christians that will stand "four-square to all the winds that blow;" Christians that are out-and-out for God. Laying aside all theories of men, and looking directly into the pages of God's Word, we come back impressed with the solemn, glorious thought that there are heights and depths and breadths and fulnesses, even in this life, that but few Christians attain. Tennyson says, "I am a part of all that I have met." We become like those with whom we associate. Look at that evening sky. See yon huge mass of clouds, dark, forbidding, cold, hanging low in the west; mountains piled beyond mountains, great Titanic forms, sullen, black, repellant. That cloud can not change itself. It might toss its vapory bosom into ten thousand anxious forms, but it would remain as gloomy and dread as ever. Now try another method. Let the cloud swing its shape round into the light of the evening sun, and let it remain there conversing with the sunbeams. Just as soon as it begins to cultivate the acquaintance of the sun it commences to change into the same image. First a deep blush passes over its face. The outer edges become golden. The color deepens and deepens as the rays continue to play among the shadows, until at last the whole mass becomes transfigured, and its cold heart becomes saturated and drenched with flame, and there it stands piled like burning ships and mountains athwart the sky, changed into the glory of the king of day. A voice comes to me out of the bosom of that cloud, saying, "All this change was brought about not by my own effort to change myself, or to throw the darkness out of my bosom; I simply supplied the conditions. I put myself in right relations. I entered the light and I tarried there, and the natural result was that I was changed." Beholding, we become changed from glory to glory. " If ye abide in me and my words abide in you, ye shall ask what ye will, and it shall be done unto you." (John xv. 7.) The new man is renewed in knowledge after the image of Him that created him. (Col. iii. 10.) "Whosoever abideth in him sinneth not; whosoever sinneth hath not seen him, neither known him." (1 John iii. 6.) He who consciously lives under " the great Taskmaster's eye " will not dare go on in sin. The principle that we are now considering is a familiar one. Students unconsciously imitate the peculiarities of their honored teachers. Writers reflect the style of their favorite authors. Husband and wife are growing more and more alike all the time, until at last you have "two minds with but a single thought, two hearts that beat as one." While alone with God in the holy mount, a glory that he wist not of shone from Moses's face. Cultivate an intimate acquaintance with Jesus, and the world will lose its charm. You can not from the heart sing one stanza of a gospel hymn; you can not read one chapter in the Bible; you can not spend a few moments in silent prayer; you can not attend one prayer meeting, one sanctuary service, without being changed more into his likeness. When at last the beatific vision bursts full upon our view, we shall be *like him*, for we shall see him as he is. Then our sanctification will be complete.

If this is the goal,— Christlikeness,— what are the steps by which we are to attain it? The programme lies fully before us in the New Testament. The first step is *crucifixion*. Jesus died, was buried, rose again. So, too, with the believer. " But God forbid that I should glory, save in the cross of our Lord Jesus Christ, by whom the world is crucified unto me and I unto the world." (Gal. vi. 14.) Again, " I am crucified with Christ; nevertheless I live, yet not I, but Christ liveth in me." (Gal. ii. 20.) And again, " Likewise reckon ye yourselves to be dead indeed unto sin, but alive unto God through Jesus Christ our Lord." (Rom. vi. 12.) And again, " For ye are dead, and your life is hid with Christ in God." (Col. iii. 3.) The world is to be dead to us, and we to it. We are to be in it, but not of it.

The second step is *coronation*. After the cross came the crown. Jesus led his disciples out as far as Bethany, and then, with hands outstretched in priestly benediction, he parted with them and rose to his throne. Paul cried, " Christ has died," but he did not stop there. He hurried on to add, " Yea rather, who is risen again, who is even at the right hand of God "— the place of power — "who also maketh intercession for us " (Rom. viii. 34). The practical questions are, first, Has Christ been crucified in our lives? Secondly, Has he been glorified in our lives, — made " King of kings and Lord of lords "? As one has well put it, Has there been a coronation day in your life when " in full and glad surrender you placed the crown upon his brow, crying, 'Crown him, crown him, crown him Lord of all '? " If the Bethany scene has taken place in your life as well as the Calvary one, then Jesus is your Lord as well as your Saviour. "Whatsoever he saith unto you, do it." It is here that the study of the Bible comes in. We want to know his will, that we may do it. " Ours not to make reply; ours not to reason why." When he speaks it is ours to listen ; when he commands it is ours to obey; when he leads it is ours to follow.

The next step is *prayer*. During those ten days they were all with one accord in the upper room in the great pre-Pentecostal prayer meeting. John McNiel tells us that the Scottish bankers have published the fact that there are $200,000,000 lying unclaimed in their deposit vaults. The owners of this money may some of them have died in the poorhouse, or some of them may now be living in garrets and cellars suffering for lack of their daily bread. They know nothing of the wealth piled up yonder at their disposal, and which they would at once get if they went and claimed it. What stores of untold, unmeasured, unsearchable riches are stored up for you to-night in the treasury of God, and which you can have for the asking! Why should heirs of glory live in spiritual want and die in spiritual poverty when all the wealth of heaven is theirs? "Ask and ye shall receive." " More things are wrought by prayer than this world dreams of."

This brings me to the last step, *the glories of Pentecost.* We have followed the steps that lead up to it in every life; namely, crucifixion, coronation, prayer, and Pentecost. We know Christ in the fellowship of his sufferings; we know him in the majesty of his power, having made absolute surrender to him as our exalted King; we know him in the intimacies of our deepest supplications, and as one who never turns us empty away; then we know him in his blessing as unfolded to us by the Holy Ghost in Pentecostal fulness. Are you prepared to pay the price? Granted that there were some features about Pentecost that were external and not to be repeated ;— it marked the public inauguration of the present dispensation; there were visible signs and wonders. But in its essential character, these scenes are yet often repeated. There are Peniels yet where, after a night of wrestling, Jacob became Israel. There are holy mounts of fellowship still whence you can come down with your faces lit up with a new radiance. There are Pentecostal scenes that yet bless our world. This is abundantly attested in the lives of men like Christmas Evans, Jonathan Edwards, George Muller, Henry Martyn, and hosts of others. May it be also yours. Pre-eminent above all other things, may you and I, my dear friends, take with us to our homes more of the Lord Jesus.

The "quiet hour" was conducted by the Rev. W. F. McCauley, of Dayton, O.

Central Presbyterian Church.

Most of those who crowded the Central Presbyterian Church were members of the Canadian delegations, whose headquarters are at that church, but scattered among the congregation were delegates from the States of the Union and residents of the city. Quite a party of New Jersey people were present.

Rev. A. W. Pitzer, D.D., pastor of the church, was announced in the programme as the presiding officer, but on account of illness in his family he was compelled to be absent from the city. His place last night was filled by Mr. Selden M. Ely, president of the Y. P. S. C. E. of the church. Before the proceedings had advanced beyond the opening hymn, Mr. G. Sargent Elliott, one of the elders of the church, spoke on behalf of Dr. Pitzer as to his regret at being compelled to be away during Convention week.

After devotional exercises and the responsive reading of Psalm ciii., prayer was offered by Rev. John McMillan of Halifax, N. S. He was followed by Rev. J. Clement French, D.D., of Newark, N. J., in a fifteen-minute address on the topic of the evening. As he stepped forward on the platform, the New Jersey contingent of the audience gave him a loyal reception, waving fans, hand flags, and handkerchiefs.

Address of Rev. J. Clement French, D.D., Newark, N. J.

We all have one common theme to-night, "Deepening the Spiritual Life." We are here not for the rivalries of learning or eloquence, but for serious, earnest work. It is the call of God, as well as of men, to set the whole anthem of this Convention to the key-note of spiritual purpose and result. My single hope is to find and define to you the paramount and practical work of Christian Endeavor, which is best and grandest because of its direct and reflexive bearings. When Dr. Lyman Beecher was asked, "Doctor, you know many things, but what do you consider the greatest thing in life?" the sturdy old hero of forty revivals replied, "It is not philosophy; it is not theology; it is not controversy; it is saving souls." I have sometimes feared that this expression,

" soul-saving," or " soul-winning," may degenerate into cant, and perhaps prejudice some man who may not clearly understand it. In its connection with our Christian Endeavor it means simply that our leading, commanding purpose should be to present the religion of Christ as not only the one safe, sensible possession of the individual, but as energizing, inspiring, making more valuable everywhere experience, possession, deportment of human life and activity, just as preciousness was given to Corinthian brass by the gold which was suffused through its entire substance. To drive souls is not to win them. The man forced at the point of a bayonet to bow and cross himself and mumble prayers before a crucifix would be only a pitiful counterfeit of a worshipper. I have small faith in those conversions which have not sprung from a clear view of the moral ugliness of sin as against a pure and holy God, and in which the heart is not won by the supreme excellence and beauty of the One who saves from its condemning power. In this light nothing could be truer than the words of Lyman Beecher. Thus to win souls is the greatest thing in the world — both for those who are saved and for those who have been instrumental in saving them. Now, Christian Endeavorers, we want it to strike into our very consciousness that our work is in the very first place rescue work. But let us not talk of converting men! That is God's work. We can sow the seed upon which he will send the quickening sun and rain. We can woo and win men into the spheres where the light of God's truth is shining. We cannot make them eat of the banquet, but we can spread the table and set a chair, and invite at least one hungry soul to occupy it. We can put out the welcoming hand, and if it is not taken we shall, at least, be acquitted of coldness and neglect. We can pray mightily for them, but we must add to our prayers the personal solicitation. This is our needed equipment for winning souls. It is important to have able preachers in our pulpits, but more important to have consecrated workers in the society and in the church. The kingdom of God will never come in all its strength and beauty until the whole rank and file of Christian Endeavorship are enlisted in a hand-to-hand fight with sin. We by no means underrate the power of a few steady, consecrated souls. We remember that many a battle has been decided, many a stronghold has been carried, by a forlorn hope. We remember the three hundred men of Gideon; the single regiment of Garibaldi; the Old Guard of Napoleon; the gallant piercing of the Austrian ranks and of his own brave breast by Arnold of Winkelreid, and we are made sure that with God on their side " one can chase a thousand, and two can put ten thousand to flight." " Yes," exclaimed John Wesley, " give me one hundred men who fear nothing but God, who hate nothing but sin, and who are determined to know nothing among men but Jesus Christ and him crucified, and I will set the world on fire."

When Dr. French had taken his seat, " Saved by Grace " was sung as a duet by Miss Mamie Cowell and Mrs. N. T. Elliott. The second speaker of the evening was Rev. Leander S. Keyser of Dayton, O., a writer and speaker well and favorably known to Endeavorers.

Address of Rev. Leander S. Keyser, Dayton, O.

No man wants to be called shallow. Perhaps the shallower a man is, the more he resents the imputation of shallowness. This is true on the self-evident principle that the shallow man is too superficial even to sound his own depths. He goes on his noisy, boastful way, proclaiming his profoundness, all unaware that other people see the shallowness of his thought and character in every word and deed. He can neither see himself as others see him nor as he really is. The turgidness of a stream may give it the appearance of great depths, even when the bottom is only a few inches below the surface.

In the realm of thought there is a great deal of superficiality. There needs to be a deepening to-day of the intellectual life.

It is never safe to be dogmatic while you are young. It is safe to hold your judgment in abeyance until you have investigated more thoroughly and looked upon all sides of a mooted question. If you are sure of the truth in your consciousness, it is right to be positive, but the supercilious dogmatist only advertises the shallowness of his mental operations.

This is an age of culture — at least, of the means of culture; and in that fact lies a world of hope for the race. But our bane may be our superficial culture. We may not drink deep of the Pierian springs. Having sipped a little from them, we may fancy that we have drained them dry, and never return to them to find that their quantity is inexhaustible and their depths unfathomable. As a means of preparation for the deepening of the current of the spiritual life, I would say, Do not be satisfied with shallow knowledge if you would be a learner and help to solve the problems of the age.

From mental flippancy it is but a step to spiritual flippancy. There are religious butterflies as well as butterflies of fashion. Their religious life is as shallow as the mountain brook in a drought. They go to church — yes, sometimes they do, anyway; but for all the good they receive they might almost as well go to the opera. Before the benediction is pronounced, their thoughts are gone wool-gathering after fashion or social conquest, and after the benediction has been said, they straightway scatter the precious fragments of down far and wide.

As a pastor, have you ever felt amazed at the slight impression your sermons produce on many of your hearers? Why is it so? Because their spiritual life is so shallow, their religious experience so meagre, their range of Biblical truth like the periphery of their tiny heads. Do you wonder that so little is done by the churches in comparison to their numbers in the tables of statistics? How can it be otherwise when we know so little of God; when our souls are so empty of his love and ministering activity; when our hearts are parched and dry, like an arid desert?

But my talk must not take on the sickly hue of complaint and criticism. I shall put in the more cheerful coloring of encouragement and positive suggestion. There is need of more spirituality in our churches to-day; of a deepening of the stream of individual and church life. That is a proposition too plain to need proof. It has always been so. If you should ask me, "What is the spiritual life?" I should reply, "It is the life of God in the soul."

Now, how shall this life be deepened? Where shall we begin? That is not easy to tell, for it is as difficult to make an order of sanctification as an order of salvation. The free spirit of God and his truth cannot well be imprisoned in our cut-and-dried systems of divinity. Still, we may venture to offer a few simple rules. An illustration will serve our purpose.

Suppose a man had a shallow stream on his farm and he wanted to deepen it. He would say to himself, "The trouble with the stream is, the bottom is too close to the surface of the water." What is one of the things he would be likely to do first? I do not say first of all, for I do not know; but at least one of the first. Well, he would probably do some dredging! By means of the proper machinery, he would let down the buckets and scoops, and hoist the mud and mire and sand and debris up to the bank, and thus deepen the channel and get down to rock bottom. Those accumulations suck up part of the water of the stream, and soil and poison the rest. Yes, he removes the debris and gives the stream an unobstructed right of way.

My friends, I despair of turning God's life into our souls in a strong, deep, healthy current until there is some dredging done. How can God and Mammon dwell together in the same life and thought and purpose? Two cannot walk together or work together or live together except they be agreed. If there is wilfully cherished sin in your life, God cannot — at least, will not — soil his own life with it. Christ had first to cast out the devils before he could put the right mind and spirit into the demoniacs. Do you ask me why the religious life of so many professed disciples of Christ is so meagre and unsatisfactory and parched? It is because of sin in the heart, sin willingly and consciously harbored. What they must do is to dredge, dredge, dredge! As Isaiah says, "Your sin separates between you and your God."

But I must be a little more specific. As long as men will cherish hatred and resentment in their hearts, or envy of another, or covetousness, or greed of worldly goods, or a spirit of faultfinding, or selfishness, or doubt; as long as they will be indifferent to the claims of God's house and God's day and God's Word, or to the claims of humanity; as long as they will resort to little tricks of trade to gain advantage; as long as they will make mere forms of worship or mere religious performances a substitute for genuine Christlike righteousness;—just so long may they expect the fountains of their spiritual life to be dried up. Here is where the work of excision must come in. Men must repent and forsake their sins, casting them, root and branch, out of their hearts. Said John the Baptist, the voice crying in the wilderness, " Repent, for the kingdom of heaven is at hand." That was also the proclamation with which Christ began his earthly ministry : " Repent, for the kingdom of heaven is at hand."

Brethren, the river of God's life and grace flows only along the channel of righteousness. It is an ethical stream. For that reason the forerunner, in proclaiming the Messiah, said in clarion tones, " Prepare ye the way of the Lord; make his paths straight."

To root sin from the heart requires heroic treatment of self, and the uttermost sincerity in scrutinizing our own motives and secret springs of life; but it is the only treatment that will effect a cure. It is a surgical operation, but it is necessary. Let us not be afraid of God's scalpel. The pure in heart shall see God; no others can see him face to face.

Let me return to my original figure. The husbandman dredges the shallow stream on his farm in order to deepen and purify the current; but he still may have a small and shallow stream — a mere rill dashing over the pebbly bottom. Is not something more necessary to secure depth and fulness and power? Yes; there must be a larger flow; more water, in fact. He must find some strong, inexhaustible fountain whose waters can be turned into the channel he has opened.

That is the secret of a deep, steady, abiding spiritual life,— contact with the perennial source of life; and that source is God. You and I must see to it that the currents of grace are turned you-ward and me-ward. We must go to the fountainhead and let the life of Christ fill our life-channels. Our own lives are too meagre and shallow; they must be deepened and freshened and enriched from the exhaustless urn of eternal fulness.

Now, our communion with God must be a real, direct, and vital one. It must not come second or third hand,— through a priest, a creed, a church, or a society. These may be helps to us, but they are not the sources or even the media of our spiritual life. Religion is a personal matter, and each one must come into direct contact with the living Head of the Church. He must know for himself whether he has the Spirit's witness, and must not take the word of a confessor or of an evangelist or a society. He must first be a member of Christ, and then a member of God's visible Church.

Direct communion with the Holy Spirit is the open sesame to the real spiritual life, for it is the Spirit that searcheth the deep things of God. Is your religious life poor and shrivelled and parched? Then seek the company of the Spirit for enrichment and refreshing.

Do you ask how this is done? It is a very simple process. You may run and read. Pray, study God's Word, do the Spirit's bidding. There is no new or copyrighted way. Christ's parable of the two houses — the one built on the sand, the other on the rock — puts the golden key into your hand. The man who hears and obeys is the man whose house stands; he who hears and fails to obey is the man whose house topples in the swirl of the gale.

The deepened spiritual life leads to practical results. It does not expend itself merely in pious meditation, as the strained efforts of the mystics did. It leads the Endeavorer to greater faithfulness in meeting the requirements of the pledge. It makes him a better worshipper, a better church-member, a more generous giver, a more tender sympathizer, a more earnest soul-winner, a more patriotic and righteous citizen, and adds every element that enriches and enlarges his Christian manhood and makes him a more effective servant of

Christ and his fellow men. And all the while this active, practical devotion reacts upon his spiritual life, deepening its channel and enlarging its current.

My brother, you can never, never measure the reflex influence upon your religious life of giving a cup of cold water to the least of your Lord's brethren in his blessed name.

After the two addresses, Rev. E. T. Root, of Baltimore, president of the Maryland Christian Endeavor Union, took charge of the " quiet hour."

Gurley Memorial Church.

The meeting was opened with an organ prelude by Miss Nellie Sacrey, and after the invocation a duet, "The Evening Prayer," arranged from Hemans, was rendered. After the reading of the 103d Psalm and the singing of a hymn, the first speaker of the evening was introduced by Rev. J. R. Verbrycke, the pastor of the church. The Rev. J. H. Garrison, D.D., of St. Louis, who was to have delivered this address, had not arrived, and Rev. James L. Hill, D.D., one of the trustees of the United Society, spoke in his place on the topic of the evening, " Deepening the Spiritual Life." He dealt first with what he called the greatest American vice,— timidity, with regard to the expression of religious life. He contrasted with the natural boldness of the American in all other matters his reticence in declaring his position concerning spiritual affairs. He used the leaves of a tree as an illustration of the expression of spiritual life, and showed that if the foliage was destroyed the tree was dealt a fatal blow, and in the same way the outward expression of a Christian's religious life was essential to its well-being.

After a solo by Miss May Edmonston, "Abide in Me," by Barter Johns, Rev. L. R. Dyott, of Newark, N. J., addressed the audience.

Address of Rev. L. R. Dyott, Newark, N. J.

Christian Endeavorers and church-members in general may be divided into three classes. First, there is a large class composed of all who are below the average. Whatever may be their peculiar expression of Christian life in its entirety, it is not so perfect in quality as the life of others.

The second class is made of the average Christians. Their life is not so variable, their excellences are not so spasmodic, the evidences of success in Christian work are not so few; they are better, perhaps, than the majority of Christians, but practical, applied Christianity everywhere is not the main issue with them.

The third class is the smallest and the greatest of the three, making up in quality what they lack in quantity. They are above the average in everything pertaining to the Christian life. They are truly good; but their goodness is winsome, and not repulsive. It is not inane, awful, pale-faced, goody-goody goodness. It is not all the time shaking hands with self. It is not self-admirative. It is characteristic of this class that they are not satisfied with present attainments, feeling that there is no state of maturity that will not admit of advancement.

Christ has declared spiritual birth to be the only condition of entrance into the kingdom of God. " Ye must be born again " is not a matter of choice; it is an arbitrary command. It is the announcement of an unalterable law. A person can no more live in the kingdom of God without being born into that kingdom than he can live in the natural world without being born into it. These premises are unchangeable. What, then, is the conclusion? Shall we make the sweeping, harsh assertion that only they are Christians who are beyond the average? No, emphatically no. They may, indeed, be Christians, but we must conclude that if they are they have spiritual life.

All created life, from a blade of grass to the highest archangel that flashes his wings in the ineffable light of the glorious throne of God, all created life everywhere, is determined by three things; viz., its nature, its environments, and its limitations. I know that a fascinating philosophy teaches that we are creatures of environment. There are elements of truth in it. You were born of Christian parents and reared under Christian influences. At the same time you were born, there came an innocent babe into a drunkard's home. He was born under a parental curse. He grew in the most wicked surroundings. He was affected by them. Environments did that. But this law is not fundamental. Nature is stronger than environment. You may plant the weed among the roses. Give it the same sunlight and air. Let the same showers refresh it. Let the same sunlight flash life about it, but it is still a weed. You may plant a rose among the weeds, and they may seek to hide it; they may, possibly, even kill it, but all the weeds in creation cannot make a weed of a rose. It is still a rose — to the day of its death it is still a rose. Among human beings the same law is dominant and pervasive.

Disease in life and abnormality in development are fearful periods. But havoc may be averted. Remove the hot rocks. Let the gentle rain and the gracious dew soften the soil. Let the mighty life go very deep. Let the sun whisper through the earth sweet messages of heaven. Lo! the earth bursts. Life breathes! All is joy. Downward, upward, inward, outward, onward, Godward. Oh, who can tell the blessed possibilities of such life!

Deeper spiritual life must be in contact with human needs. It becomes stronger through duty well done. It craves private devotion — indeed, it can not do without that, but its co-relation is in practical life. It refuses to be shut in a cloister.

Deeper spiritual life is found through duty intelligently met, cheerfully borne, faithfully done.

Mr. Harry A. Kinports, of New York, conducted a "quiet hour," and asked those in the audience to search their hearts for secret faults. This period was brought to a close with an earnest prayer, and the congregation dismissed with a benediction.

Nineteenth Street Baptist Church.

When the time for opening the meeting at the Nineteenth Street Baptist Church arrived an audience numbering some twelve hundred filled to excess the large auditorium and surrounding galleries.

The exercises were opened by the singing of Hymn No. 5, " Words of Cheer," followed by the reading by the congregation of the familiar twenty-third Psalm, beginning " The Lord is my Shepherd, I shall not want." Prayer was then offered that the meeting might be productive of much good for Christ and the Church, and that the Convention prove a source of abundant blessing, not to this city only, but to the various states, territories, and countries represented here by delegates.

The "Invocation Hymn," written by Col. John Hay, was next sung by the large choir of the church, and at its conclusion the pastor, Rev. W. H. Brooks, D.D., made the following address of welcome: —

My name appears upon this programme not to speak, but to preside, and one of the qualifications of a good presiding officer is that he shall not have much to say. I shall, therefore, make my words few this evening. Nevertheless, it becomes me as pastor of this church to extend a hearty welcome to all who are present to-night, and to beseech you, as the speakers shall come before you, to lift up your hearts in silent prayer to God that the Spirit present may be made manifest in their utterances, and that the truths spoken may be so delivered, and may so impress each one, that when these speakers shall have returned to their several homes, and when this Convention shall have finished its work, and its tents shall have been folded and borne to some other place, there shall abide with us leavening influences which shall make us nobler and happier men and women, and that as followers of the Lord Jesus Christ we may have learned to take in more of the Spirit of God. Those of you who have watched the appropriations made by Congress from year to year are aware of the fact that many thousands of dollars have been spent for the purpose of deepening and widening certain rivers, so that seafaring barks might go into certain ports. I can fancy that the great object of these twenty-odd meetings to-night is to widen and deepen the human heart, so that there shall be a greater fulness and richness of the Spirit of God in us. It is a question of our capacity. We are strong Christians. We are noble Christians. We are useful Christians. But we are these only in proportion to the amount of the Spirit of God that is in us, molding our thoughts, our sentiments, and determining our destiny. Oh that the Spirit of God may come upon us all as we mingle together as Endeavorers and Christians! If we shall go from this place to-night thanking God that we have had a feast of Pente-cost, the Lord will be praised and we shall be blessed indeed.

After the singing of a hymn, Rev. P. Thomas Stanford, D.D., of Boston, Mass., was introduced as the first speaker of the evening. He took as the basis of his remarks the sixth verse of the fifth chapter of the gospel according to St. Matthew, as follows : —

Address of Rev. P. Thomas Stanford, D.D., Boston, Mass.

It is customary in the Arabian desert for the travellers, on reaching a spring, to leave a portion of food, so that if any unfortunate traveller should happen to visit the spring he would not only find water, but food also.

A traveller, making his journey, was hindered for several days by sand-storms and many other difficulties, and when he had got a long way from the place of rest his food gave out, but, knowing the custom, he pressed on, hoping to find a spring. At last, when so weak he could scarcely walk, he spied a spring and used the last bit of strength he had left in reaching it. He looked about for food. He saw the little leather bucket in which food is usually kept. He seized it and took out what he supposed to be a bundle containing eatables, but to his grief and surprise, instead of food, the bundle contained pearls of the first water, valuing some hundreds of pounds — and his body was found clutching the bag. He died of starvation.

Humanely speaking, hunger and thirst are not blessings, but great enemies, against which the nations of the earth are battling every day. This world is a battle-field.

When we are hungry we desire food, and when we are thirsty we desire drink. Nothing but food for the hungry, nothing but water for the thirsty. Gold is despised for bread. The desire of food to the hungry creates and increases the burning fever of death. The oppressed will use every endeavor to obtain it. The great and good John Bright said, " He that withholds bread from the poor, the nation will curse him. To offer them riches is to mock at their misery."

Our Lord and Saviour was a very practical preacher. In all cases, as in this, he presented the truth and worth of the Gospel in such a way that it enforced its own conclusions. How to show more clearly what I mean, let us read the text again : " Blessed are they that hunger and thirst after righteousness, for they shall be filled;" filled with joy and peace through believing.

The good Shepherd will lead them into green pastures, and make them to lie down beside still waters; and they shall be fed with all the superabundance of the Gospel feast.

This text may serve to comfort the hearts of those who do hunger and thirst after righteousness. I doubt not that it is the grief of many that they cannot serve God better Jesus says blessed are those; though thou hast not much righteousness as thou would like, yet thou art blessed because thou hungerest after it. The old saying is that actions are louder than words, but actions may be counterfeited for compulsion. Desire is the best discovery of Christian graces. There are many forced Christians, forced fruit, very beautiful, but affected at the core. Some Christians have nothing but desires; but it is highly important that those desires be put into effect. Let it be observed that hungering and thirsting after righteousness proceeds from love. If thou didst not love Christ thou couldst not desire him.

The doubts and fears to be fought against: —

Objection: "If my hunger were of the right kind, then I could take comfort of it; but I fear it is counterfeit. Hypocrites have desires."

That I may the better settle a doubting Christian, I shall show the difference between a true and false desire, spiritual and carnal hunger.

First, the hypocrite does not desire grace on its own account, but only as a bridge to lead him over to heaven. So Balaam said, "Let me die the death of the righteous." The believer desires grace on its own account, and Christ for himself purely.

Second, the hypocrite's desire is conditional; he wants heaven and his sins; but Christ's conditions are opposed to sins.

Third, the hypocrite's desires are but desires and destitute of activity. Not so with the true Christian. Illustration: The eagle and its prey; he is hungry. True desire carries the soul swift to holy ordinance, communion, and those who take it not.

Fourth, the hypocrite's desires are transient, or like a hot fire. They are soon over. They commence under sorrow and affliction. When better all is over. True desire is constant. The Greek word is in the participle, — " Blessed are they that are hungering; though they have righteousness, yet they are hungering for more." The hypocrite's desire is like the motion of a watch; it soon runs down; but that of a believer is like that of a breathing pulse — lasts as long as life. It is like the unextinguished fire of the temple, ever burning in holy affections.

Objection: " But, my hunger after righteousness is so weak, I fear that it is not of the true kind."

The pulse beats but weakly, yet if it does beat it shows there is life. Weak desires are not to be discouraged. The believer may estimate his spiritual state by his judgment, as well as by his affections. Religion consists not in an endeavor to flee from hell, or in strenuous struggles to attain heaven, but in loving and practising goodness for its own sake, so loving holiness and right as to have perils, endure sufferings, and forego joys, if necessary, in their behalf.

Objection: "But," says the believer, "I have not the earnest hunger that I once had. Where is the blessedness?"

It is, indeed, a bad sign for a person to lose his appetite. Spiritually, it indicates a decay of grace. But it is a very good sign to bewail its loss. " Ye shall be fed." A Kaffir boy, twelve years of age, was asked, when he came to the miserable settlement of the Moravians, which did he like best, his home or the Christians'? At home he had meat and milk; here he could not get either. Said he, "I wish to become a child of God, so I do not care how I have to live." To test the sincerity of a number of poor, distressed, starving beggars, a gentleman in Scotland opened a shop in a locality where they resided and had a sign put over the door, which read as follows: "Walk in, take, eat, and live." The proprietor said to all who entered, " Well, what is your trouble? " " I am hungry." " What is this? " " Bread." " What do you know about it? " While one was debating its origin, its growth, etc., he fainted and died; the last rushed in like mad, seized the bread, ate, and lived. So with the Word of God.

The address of Dr. Stanford, which had evidently made a deep impression on all present, was in turn followed by the singing of Hymn No. 159, "True-Hearted, Whole-Hearted." Dr. Brooks then rose to say he had received a letter from Rev. J. W. Hamilton, D.D., of Cincinnati, O., in which he intimated that he might be prevented from appearing, but at this point Dr. Hamilton himself arrived, and on being introduced to the audience, said : —

Address of Rev. J. W. Hamilton, D.D., Cincinnati, O.

Mr. President, Sisters and Brothers : — I have come all the way here from Cincinnati to be with you to-night. I was afraid I might not be able to reach this place in time for this meeting. As some of you possibly know, I am the Corresponding Secretary of the Freedmen's Aid and Southern Educational Society of the Methodist Episcopal Church, which is the only denominational organization, I may say, with a bit of encouragement to you, which has a co-ordinate associate secretary who is black. We have opened the doors of our church, and one of the highest officers elected by our General Conference at Cleveland was one of your own color. Yesterday our first meeting of the Board of Managers, after the adjournment of the General Conference, which has just closed at Cleveland, met in Cincinnati. I had my train and my sleeper already engaged, so as to leave for Washington promptly, but the meeting kept on and the train came on and left me behind. I put what I had on paper, so that I might have it read to you if I failed to get here, as I am not in the habit of disappointing an audience if possible to avoid it, but when I found that another train would get me here in time, I concluded to keep the paper and bring it myself.

[We regret that Dr. Hamilton's manuscript has not reached us in time for print.]

After the addresses of Rev. P. Thomas Stanford, D.D., and Rev. J. W. Hamilton, D.D., a "quiet hour" was conducted by William T. Ellis, of Boston, one of the editors of *The Golden Rule.*

Church of the Covenant.

The Endeavorers who met at the Church of the Covenant on Wednesday evening could not wait for eight o'clock to arrive before expressing their enthusiasm. Long before the opening, Buffalo's delegation, numbering nearly seventy-five, but who seemed in strength of voice many more, started up "Hail Buffalo," air "Maryland, My Maryland," then following "At the Cross," in which all of the audience joined, with "Jesus Washed My Sins Away" and "Anywhere, My Saviour" and the Convention favorite, "Scatter Sunshine." The audience was in a most excellent condition at the opening to appreciate the addresses.

On account of an important meeting of the Board of Trustees, Dr. Hamlin was unable to welcome to his church the several delegations who made headquarters at the Church of the Covenant. The Rev. Joseph T. Kelley, pastor of the Ninth Street Presbyterian Church, in a few brief remarks stated how pleased they were to welcome so many bright faces.

Scripture was read by Rev. Dr. W. E. Webster, pastor of the Baptist

Church of Hoosic Falls, N. Y., and prayer was offered by Rev. S. W. Pratt, of New York.

The first speaker was Rev. C. A. Barbour, of Rochester, N. Y., president of the New York Christian Endeavor Union.

Address of Rev. Clarence A. Barbour, Rochester, N. Y.

For deepening the spiritual life the means are manifold. I cannot hope to touch more than a single phase of the subject — only one out of many means. This can be safely said : A spiritual life, which is lived victoriously for the Lord Jesus, will ever become more strong and deep. I love to think of the Christian religion as a military religion, one in which the elements of battle and of victory are found. The Bible is a book of peace, but also a book of war. The war-song sounds from many of its pages. Not always are its heroic men men of peace. Joshua, David, Elijah, Peter — these were not men whose lives floated on in a peaceful current. The angels at Bethlehem at the birth of the Saviour did indeed sing, " Peace on earth, good-will toward men," but that same Saviour whose birth the angels heralded said, " I came not to send peace, but a sword." In its description of the Christian life the Bible has much to say of conflict, conquest, victory. Surely it is well that this is so. There are chords in the human heart that vibrate to these words alone, and from them come the strains of inspiring martial music. The conflict in spiritual life is between " that which is born of God " and " the world." Let us mention three wrong conceptions of the meaning of this phrase, " the world;" three which the Apostle John does not mean when he says, " Love not the world." He does not mean the world of nature, with its trees, and grass, and flowers, and sunshine. I pity the man who can go from the dusty and crowded city to the green fields and quiet of the country and not have his soul thrilled with the beauty of the world in which God has placed him. The one who can look upon the mighty forests without having his whole nature respond to the voice of God is not rightly constituted. The one who can look upon the sea and not be drawn nearer to God is out of touch with the voice of God in nature. The apostle does not mean, either, our fellow men when he says, "Love not the world." The hermit life is a coward life. The Bible nowhere prohibits love toward our fellow men. True, human love is elevating, ennobling. God would not take our love from those about us. John does not mean, either, our vocation, our trade, our occupation. But it is easy to say what an expression does not mean. Now, what does it mean ? The thing or combination of things in the individual life which tends to draw the heart away from God, to usurp God's place, to set itself as the chief end of life and the chief object of worship. With such a definition, no one can deny that there is conflict between that which is born of God and the world. In this conflict victory is possible, for we are assured, " Whoever is born of God overcometh the world." At the close of our long and cruel war there marched down this magnificent avenue veterans, all powder-blackened and dusty, carrying the dear old shot-torn flags — flags which, thank God, wave to-day over a united country. The people shouted their welcome with cheer upon cheer to those who had conquered on the field of battle. Ah, what a greater review is coming when the armies of the universe shall march in great review before the Great Commander ; when standards shall be lowered to him, and on that day he shall say, " Ye are my well beloved ; ye who have overcome ! " The Scripture gives us means of victory. Faith enables us to conquer by giving us the conviction necessary to progress, by assuring us of certain triumph.

The next speaker came from Ohio, and was cordially received.

Address of Rev. C. L. Work, D.D., Cincinnati, O.

The fulness of spiritual life lies in Jesus Christ. It is from him that we get our spiritual life. Deepening the spiritual life means the clearing-away of the rubbish and a removing of all the obstacles which lie in the way of the Holy Spirit's complete possession of all our powers of body and soul, our minds, our wills, our affections. We cannot for one moment think that there is any halting or hesitancy on the part of the Holy Spirit in the matter of leading men and women except as there may be cause for it on the part of men and women themselves. In the Spirit's leadership is involved full surrender on our part. We are not our own; our bodies, our spirits, and all powers of both are the Lord's. I have no right to entertain a single thought that is not suggested by the Spirit. I must be as fully at the disposal of the Spirit as was Paul, when, on his second missionary tour, he essayed to go into Bithynia, but the Spirit sent him over into Macedonia. It is only into the surrendered life that the Spirit can put whatever he may please, as may be seen by him to be necessary for the advancement of his cause among men. It was into the surrendered life of Paul that the Spirit put that stormy voyage on the Mediterranean, with shipwreck on the Island of Malta. Into that life he put also the rod, the stoning, the Philippian jail, with its midnight song, and, finally, beheadment on the bank of the Tiber. But what man ever trod the earth that was the instrument in the hand of God in lifting the world nearer to heaven that the once suffering but now gloriously sainted Paul? Leadership of the Spirit involves his choice of life's work and conditions for the saints. The undisputed leadership of the Holy Ghost will result in a deepening of the spiritual life of God's people. We are exhorted in the Scriptures not to quench the Spirit. We are exhorted to desist from all actions, states, and conditions of soul as would hinder the Spirit from doing his work in and upon us, and through us in our religious life. We need in our churches and in our individual lives a good old-fashioned outpouring of the Holy Ghost. We need such revivals in this country as swept over Scotland in the eighteenth century and over our own land in the first part of this century. In those days men and women fell down before the preached word as if cut down in battle. The Presbyterian Church was born in a revival under the preachings of Calvin and Knox in Edinburgh; the Methodist Church grew out of a revival under the preaching of the Wesleys; the Cumberland Presbyterian Church grew out of a revival in the early part of this century in the South; the Lutheran Church grew out of a revival under the preaching of Luther; and so the world has been blessed by the state of religious fervor known as revival. We need a higher grace of spiritual life in order that we may have more power with God and man. We need it that we may have revival; we need it that we may do better work in the line of missions; we need it that we may live in the spiritual life, for without it we shall surely die.

The service was brought to a close by Rev. Ford C. Ottman, of Newark, N. J., who, under God's leadership, led all to a closer walk with Jesus Christ.

West Street Presbyterian Church.

There was a large attendance at the Christian Endeavor meeting at the West Street Presbyterian Church. The large church was filled, and the members of the Maine delegation, two hundred strong, the headquarters of which are at the church, attended the services in a body.

The church was tastefully decorated. Over the altar a large frame was hung, in which was the motto: " For Christ and the Church," and on the wall in the rear were two frames of a similar nature containing the words, " Do great things for God," and " Expect great things from God." On each side of the altar were draped like curtains two immense American flags.

In the Sunday-school room of the chapel adjoining, the decorations suggested the Pine-tree State. The chapel was used as the headquarters of the visiting delegates, and had been furnished accordingly.

Members of the church expressed the opinion that their decorations excelled in extent and splendor those of any church in the city. Thirty barrels of pine-cones shipped from Maine had been used. Green and gray are the colors of the Pine-tree State, and drapery of those hues had been lavishly used in the adornment of the chapel.

The pastor of the church, Rev. Dr. William C. Alexander, presided and introduced the speakers. The first address was delivered by Rev. W. H. Towers, of Manchester, England, a member of the National Council of Christian Endeavor of Great Britian.

Address of Rev. W. H. Towers, Manchester, England.

To-night I regret to occupy the place of another Englishman, the Rev. J. Holden Byles, who is sick, and whose physician forbids him to travel for the present. Mr. Byles is an eminent Congregational minister, and out of a larger experience of Christian work and life would have spoken to you words of greater edification and helpfulness than I can hope to accomplish. However, my hope rests upon God, and if he shall guide me, maybe I shall not speak in vain in the Lord.

First of all, sirs, I rejoice to be here as a representative from the Old Country. In England and Scotland and in gallant little Wales the Christian Endeavor movement has come to be a factor in the religious life of the people. We have now upwards of 3,000 societies of Christian Endeavor, and these are winning for themselves golden opinions everywhere.

Some six or eight months ago, when there arose a cry of alarm that the two great Anglo-Saxon races on the Eastern and Western Hemispheres might suffer a rupture in their friendly relationships, and there was wild talk of some remote possibility of these two great Christian countries coming to war, the Christian spirit — which we are sure is at all times the best promoter of peace — I say the Christian spirit prompted our British United Society of Christian Endeavor to send the first word of greeting to our American brethren, which spoke of peace and good-will in the name of the Prince of peace. We hope and pray that the day may never come when these two mighty peoples shall so far forget themselves and the principles of good-will and the Christ-King as to draw the sword upon each other. I can conceive of no greater calamity than that. My brother Americans, your race and mine belong to each other; the very warp and woof of our common history are of the same thread; our language and literature and interests are identical, and the same noble Protestant faith, the same grand old holy Bible, and the same Cross of Calvary combine, like the mighty strands in an unbreakable cable, to bind us together in the bonds of eternal brotherhood and peace. War between the great Anglo-Saxon races would be a spectacle to cause men and angels to weep, and would make a jubilee nowhere but in hell.

My conviction is we shall have no war. If, in our diplomatic relationships, we find misunderstandings arising, we have a more Christian remedy than war. We have the appeal to the Tribunal of Reason; and ever since the Right Hon. W. E. Gladstone submitted to arbitration on the "Alabama" claims, I feel pretty confident my country will never be ashamed or afraid of arbitration, and that especially with our kith and kin on this American continent. Oh, in the name of Christianity and civilization and progress, and in the name of this great International Christian Endeavor brotherhood, let us pray God to scatter the people who delight in war !

I now have to turn to the topic in hand. It is one of fitting moment for the commencement of this great Convention. God is a Spirit, and when he made man in his own image, he made him spirit, soul, and body. And when, in his infinite love, he redeemed us through the life and death of his Divine Son, Jesus Christ, he redeemed us spirit, soul, and body.

These bodies of ours are his by creative and redemptive right. The physical powers of a man ought to be to the glory of God. You have sent your Yale crew to England to compete on the river Thames for the prize of pre-eminence. I hope the Christian Endeavor movement, in America and in England and throughout the whole wide world, will ever develop the muscular powers of its membership, for the soul and spirit of a man are always helped by the good sound house they live in.

Neither must we neglect the training of the mind. It has been well said, " The mind's the standard of the man ; " and it is true. Let everything that ennobles the understanding, that gives power to the brain, and that crowns youth with the diadem of wisdom be earnestly sought after by the Endeavorer. The gymnasium and the college, the arena of athletics and literature, are open before us for the proper development of mind and body.

It now remains for me to touch upon the spiritual aspect of man's tripartite nature. Many of us remember, dear brothers and sisters, how we have been born anew. Our former life, which was lived under the domination of sin, has been changed by the wonderful power of God; old habits, old tastes, old companions, have been given up for the sake of the Lord Jesus Christ, who reigns as king in our hearts; and our grandest ideal now is to be like Jesus. Here, in this first assembly, let it be our intense and earnest prayer that we may see no man, save Jesus only; then shall we drink in of his Spirit and be baptized with power from on high. Our life should be like the aim of the great sculptor Thorwaldsen, who endeavored to chisel out of a rugged block of pure Cilician marble a statue of the Christ. He worked long and he worked hard at his task, and at last he finished the work. He then called a little child to his studio, in order to know if he had succeeded in making a masterpiece; but the child could not name a person to correspond with the statue, and Thorwaldsen found he had failed. He set to work again, however, and wrought out another statue, more delicate and more feeling and more beautiful than the first ; and when it was finished it instantly struck the little child, and with the utmost reverence she placed her little throbbing hands on the cold, white feet of the statue, and said, "This is He who said, 'Suffer little children to come.'" Fellow Endeavorers, do the children see the Christlikeness in us ? That is why we are here for the deepening of the spiritual life.

Another reason why we are here is to enable the Holy Spirit of God to shed a light upon our life. We want, very solemnly and very earnestly, to let God try us. Like the Psalmist, we cry out, " Search me, O God, and know my heart : try me, and know my thoughts : and see if there be any wicked way in me." Our Christian Endeavor pledge binds us to do all Christ would like to have us do; and if in the solemn gathering of to-night God should put his finger upon some part of our life and tell us it is sin, we shall not be loyal Endeavorers if we do not give it up. The Holy Ghost is a spirit of burning, of judgment; and if he shall hurt us, it is only that we may be healed and made more meek for Christ's most blessed service. Do you ask, my dear fellow Endeavorer, how we may have more of the Holy Spirit ? I answer, Have faith in him. Read in 1 Cor. vi. 19, — "What? know ye not that your body is the temple of the Holy Ghost which is in you, which ye have of God, and ye are not your own ? "

The second address of the evening was delivered by Rev. J. L. Withrow, D.D., LL.D., of Chicago, Ill., moderator of the Presbyterian General Assembly. His address was on the subject of the evening, "The Deepening of Spiritual Life," and was well worded, maintaining the strict attention of the audience.

The " quiet hour" service lasted only fifteen minutes, and was conducted by Rev. Joseph Brown Turner, of Dover, Del., president of the Delaware Christian Endeavor Union.

THE OPEN-AIR PATRIOTIC SONG SERVICE. — THE UNITED STATES MARINE BAND.

CALIFORNIA BOOTH IN THE CONVENTION BUSINESS HEADQUARTERS.

INTERIOR OF TENT WILLISTON DURING THE JUNIOR RALLY.

Congress Street Methodist Protestant Church.

The meeting at the Congress Street Methodist Protestant Church was well attended, considering the weather. This was the first time the church was opened to the visiting Endeavorers, and the decorations for the occasion were pretty, especially the central decorations hanging from the large centre chandelier.

Rev. W. S. Hammond, D.D., the pastor of the church, was scheduled to preside. He appeared at the meeting, though feeling quite unwell, and introduced Rev. Dr. J. L. Bates, a former pastor of the church, as the presiding officer. The first address was delivered by Rev. Franklin Hamilton, of Newtonville, Mass.

Address of Rev. Franklin Hamilton, Newtonville, Mass.

Were I to tell you the story of those whom the world deems royal, I should recite to you the history of princes, queens, and kings.·

" There's such divinity doth hedge a king " that chronicle and romance have hung their richest garlands around the memory of the warrior king.

Even in this democratic age, the king of men, as old Homer defined him, ·· The first in glory and the first in place," still is esteemed the great one of earth.

" 'T is so much to be a king," says Montaigne, "that he is only so by being so."

The Divine Carpenter, however, has brought a new revelation to bear upon this thought.

Monarchs have reared their thrones on the sweat and tears and blood of humanity, while they, themselves, all too often, live and lie reclined "on the hills, like gods together, careless of mankind."

Cæsar whispered to a friend that his four triumphs had cost nine million lives. At the outset, therefore, we see that the royal life is not necessarily the life of one who sits in "that fierce light which beats upon a throne." The ruler may wield a sceptre, though in the sight of God he may not be a king. By power he may govern, though in life he may not reign. Who, then, is the real king, the real queen? Who are they whom Jesus means when he says, " I appoint unto you a kingdom, as my Father hath appointed unto me"? Who are they to whom Paul refers when he writes, "They shall reign in life"? Is the veritable king, as Carlyle says, the *koenig*, the canning, the man who can?

Are any of these the ideal kings of Jesus? Are these they of whom the apostle says, "They shall reign in life"? Are these they who live the truly regal life? Or is the life of privilege, of conquest, of glory, to be reserved until we shall have passed the Gates of Pearl? Is it true that I can not enter upon "my kingdom" until the battle of life is ended and the last veil of eternity is lifted? Is it to be with us as it was with Pilgrim Valiant, that not until in the midst of the dark river we shall hear the silver trumpets sound for us on the farther shore; not until, like that mystic king, we shall be greeted with sounds from beyond the limit of the world, " as if some fair city were one voice around a king returning from his wars "? Is it true that not until then can we get the "victory over the blandishments of the symbolic beast," and stand among the crowned conquerors in life? No! Jesus said to his disciples, while they were yet on earth, in the midst of their daily toil, " I appoint unto you a kingdom, as my Father hath appointed unto me." And Paul, while enduring stripes, perils, and weariness, hunger, thirst, and cold, and nakedness, burst forth into a song and told of a life to be lived, so royal, so radiant, so blessed, that those who live it may be said to reign as kings.

On earth, then, this kingdom is to be found. Here in the daily walks and dull, tame commonplaces of existence, its kings and queens are to reign. But how shall we find this kingdom? What is the *right* conception of the royal life? Let me borrow an illustration: "Have you never sat on the bank of a

quiet lake, and, by that phenomenon so familiar, have you never seen the surrounding objects, hills, trees, and shore, reflected on the placid surface of the
water? And as you have looked, have you not noticed that all things are
reversed in that reflection? That which towers highest above you is reflected
as lowest in the glassy mirror before you, while that which is lowest is reflected
in the watery picture as highest. This is a perfect representation of what by
and by is to happen to so many of our earthly standards." When you and I
shall have passed from the tempestuous seas of earth, to stand on that sea of
glass before the throne, having the harps of God, we shall then have a larger
vision of life. We then shall realize that, often, what here towers highest is, in
God's sight, the lowest, and that what now on earth is abased shall there be
exalted. " Gold, here on earth, is on top! But up yonder they think so little
of it that they pave the city's streets with it." Here in our narrow cave life, as
Plato calls it, men and women are mad for political place, for social prestige
and power. Here we idolize beauty, learning, and the magic of a name; but
up yonder, in the wider, unthralled life, it is seen that all these may be joined to
a shrunken soul, and so these count but as dust in the scales of that tall archangel weighing

> " All man's dreaming, doing, saying,
> In the unimagined years."

Apply now this thought to the problem of our kingdom and the royal life,
and see what a revelation it brings. Paul tells us that they shall reign in life
which receive " abundance of grace by one Jesus." Mark you, —they which
receive " abundance of grace and of the gift of righteousness, they shall reign
in life." It matters not how poor or how mean they may be, if they will but
receive into their lives the abundance of his grace and of the gift of righteousness, absolutely no limit can be put to their spiritual development. They shall
inherit the earth. They shall be so changed from character to character that
at last they shall present to the world regal lives of radiant beauty and transcendent power. Because of their acceptance with God spheres of unutterable
sacredness are open to their footsteps. With them, as Macaulay said of the
Puritans, " If their names are not found in the registers of heralds, they are recorded in the Book of Life. If their steps are not accompanied by a splendid
train of menials, legions of ministering angels have charge over them. Their
palaces are houses not made with hands, eternal in the heavens; their diadems,
crowns of glory that shall never fade away."

Here, then, at last, is our kingdom,—a reign of the Spirit. The royal life
is the life that through the transforming power of the Holy Spirit has become a
life of privilege, of conquest, and of glory. The ideal kings and queens, they
who live the truly regal life, are those who, through the indwelling Spirit of
God, have gotten the mastery over self and the world, over the powers of darkness and hell, and, in their own souls, have entered upon that beatific vision
which comforted the great Shepherd King e'er his spirit passed away to join
the harpers harping with their harps,—" What is man that thou art mindful of
him and the son of man that thou visitest him? Thou hast made him a little
lower than the angels and has crowned him with glory and honor."

But stop! That is not all. This kingdom of the Spirit is a kingdom in
which advancement goes not by favor. Nor is it obtainable by clamorous solicitation. The way to the throne in this kingdom is the *via dolorosa* of the
Cross. The palm-bearers in its realm of glory shall be they who have passed
through great tribulation. Its princes shall be they who have drunk most
deeply of his cup of sorrow.

Explain that, you say. Listen! " Behold, a king shall reign," and as he
reigns he shall be unto others as " a hiding-place from the wind and a covert
from the tempest; as rivers of water in a dry place, as the shadow of a great
rock in a weary land." What the deep, safe haven is to the storm-tossed, faint
ing mariner; what the sky-fed mountain river with its cool refreshing waters is
to the parched and thirsty desert; what the great rocks' saving shadow is to the
caravan fleeing from the sand-storm, perishing;—all these is a king in this kingdom to be unto others. " Whosoever of you will be the chiefest shall be ser-

vant of all." " Even as the Son of man came not to be ministered unto but to minister." What a revelation! What a startling conception this is! What a flood of light it throws on the utterance of Jesus and on the thought of Paul! Under its white illumination how our human standards shrivel. Now we know that the world's estimate of success is false. The world's conception of kingship is utterly inadequate. In the realm of matter the mightiest forces are the quietest. So now we realize that, in the realm of the Spirit, the most regal lives are the humblest.

A king after the manner of Napoleon? Why, such a king is a slave! A king after the manner of genius or learning? Why, the most accomplished, the most brilliant, men and women are often the worst, the most degenerate. A king after the manner of money-bags? Why, most millionaires are like butternut-trees, — they impoverish the ground upon which they grow.

"Come. now, and let us reason together." It is a grander thing by far to be nobly remembered than to be nobly born. Professor Blackie used to say, " Money is not needful, power is not needful, liberty is not needful, even health is not the one thing needful: but royal character is that which alone can save us. If we are not saved in this sense, we certainly must be damned."

> " Howe'er it be, it seems to me
> ' T is only noble to be good.
> Kind hearts are more than coronets.
> And simple faith than Norman blood."

Do you not know that one of the most regal natures that Anglo-Saxon civilization has produced was a poor Cornish miner, Billy Bray, known the world over as the " King's son "?

There was no need of those draped flags of the Salvation Army, or the sound of those muffled drums. as they bore to the grave all that was mortal of Catharine Booth, to announce that humanity that day was losing a queen. God's wondrous benediction upon the work of her hands had told that. Sleep on, thou sweet St. Catharine of England; sleep on. thou queen!

> " There is never a sigh of passion or of pity,
> Never a wail for weakness or for wrong,
> But has its archive in the angels' city,
> And finds its echo in the endless song."

Oh. I rejoice that we are beginning to exalt ourselves to this conception of the " King's daughter," the " King's son."

The second address was delivered by Rev. R. F. Coyle, D.D., of Oakland, Cal. The address was to have been delivered by Rev. W. D. Williams, D.D., of San Francisco, but he was unavoidably prevented from attending the meeting. Dr. Coyle spoke of the character of Washington weather, and stated that when the Convention came next year to California, as he understood, perfect weather could be guaranteed.

The gist of his remarks was to the effect that by patience we are to acquire for ourselves souls. We have a flesh man and a spirit man, and according to the intention of God the spiritual man should enlarge and grow away from the corporal man. He spoke of the fact that souls are not ready-made products, and need to be enlarged by man. He stated that the first impulse of man is to do the highest aim of the soul; but, when the matter is considered over, the corporal man steps in, and selfishness sits on the bench.

The thought of the "quiet hour," which was led by one of the editors of *The Golden Rule,* Mr. Arthur W. Kelly, turned on the consecration needed as a preparation for the Convention.

Metropolitan Presbyterian Church.

Not less than 1,600 persons, it was estimated, attended the meeting at Metropolitan Presbyterian Church. Rev. Dr. George M. Luccock, pastor, presided, and Dr. F. J. Woodman was musical director, with Mrs. W. F. Nicholson as organist. The principal address was delivered by Rev. W. G. Fennell of Meriden, Conn., president of the Connecticut Christian Endeavor Union.

Address of Rev. W. G. Fennell, Meriden, Conn.

The word "spiritual" has come to be a much-abused term. It is partly on this account that so many of our young people are afraid of it. The extreme ecclesiastic has long appropriated it to designate those who withdraw themselves from the world to live a monastic life. The Pietist would apply the term to the long-faced and deep-sighing souls who see so much of sin and sorrow that they consider it wrong to smile. Swedenborg, with his visions and trances, seemed to think that spirituality was the subtle power of evaporating fact and reality into something ethereal. Last of all, and perhaps the worst of all, modern religious fads have taken it up, and would fain refuse the right to use it to other than their own select few. By Christian scientists, mental scientists, and theosophists it is applied to their mental ecstasies. But any healthful mind will acknowledge that it is not good sense to ignore a truth because some people have abused it. That is one of our faults. Many have kept silent on the subject of temperance because some people had, as they thought, taken extreme positions. An honest man would say that there is all the more need of wise men in the ranks, and I must find a place somewhere. If some men have taken an unwise position with reference to spirituality, it is our duty as honest Christians to find the mean between extremes, and set up a standard to which the Church may rally. To be spiritually minded is to have the mind of the Spirit; it is to come into living relationship with God; it is normal living, recognizing the high calling and destiny of man. Such a conception of spirituality must appeal to every person, young or old, for it means making the most of life according to God's plan. In studying the spiritual development of Paul we notice that his progress was in proportion to his conception of God. We can obtain the inspiring view of God's purposes by studying God in history, above all in the Old Testament. The Old Testament is a section of history laid open. Much that governs that history is true of all history. Study it long if you would come to have the broad view that will enable you to think God's thoughts after him. The old idea of "spiritual" was too passive. Like the monk of the middle ages, it betook itself to the mountains to meditate; it was a subjective condition instead of an active force. The true spirituality, becoming deeply impressed with God's purpose in the world, would consecrate itself to the purpose of seeing that effort realized. Above and beyond all, a deeper spiritual life must come through a more complete dependence upon the Holy Spirit.

The next speaker received a royal welcome, coming as he did as the official delegate from the British National Council of Christian Endeavor. We regret we can not give Mr. Morgan's address in full.

Address of Rev. Joseph Brown Morgan, Chester, England.

If this movement stands for anything, it stands for a whole-souled and out-and-out allegiance to Jesus Christ. The obligation to personal holiness is on every Endeavorer. Words have no meaning if the Bible does not teach that. Would that Christians would honorably, squarely, face out the idea of deepening the spiritual life. I have no royal road to point out to-night by which to accomplish this purpose, but I am quite sure that to accomplish the deepening of the spiritual life there must be a definite renunciation of the world's spirit. You are called by Christ's religion to self-denial, to self-sacrifice. But be not afraid of God's altar. Does it bid you climb the rugged steeps of Moriah? Does it nail you to the great sacrifice? Shrink not from the task. There is an angel waiting for you when you reach the top. Does it place you in the path of duty? Stand for the right. Renunciation standing stiffly by itself is insufficient. There must be aspirations as well as renunciation. What do we know about the passion for holiness? Our whole soul must be put into the thirst after righteousness. The passion for holiness finds its focal point in Jesus Christ. It is in likeness to him. It is personal loyalty to a personal Saviour. The spirit of Jesus is for the world. All true progress, all real advance, is for Jesus Christ. The most important condition of all for the deepening of the spiritual life is inspiration. It is the inbreathing of God into the soul. In that God-breath lies the deepening of our spiritual life. And it is available for you and me. When self is crucified, when the vision of God is more clearly seen, when God's people are more filled with the Spirit, then shall they fly as doves to their windows; then shall a nation be born in a day!

Epiphany Protestant Episcopal Church.

The pastor of the Epiphany Church, the Rev. Dr. H. R. McKim, presided at the meeting, and the Rev. C. M. Palmer, of Lanesboro, Mass., conducted the " quiet hour " at the close of the service. The music was rendered by a choir of boys, their singing being greatly enjoyed. The Rev. Albert E. George, of South Boston, Mass., and the Right Honorable Rev. M. S. Baldwin, D.D., Lord Bishop of Huron, Ontario, were the speakers.

Address of Rev. Albert E. George, South Boston, Mass.

There is always something encouraging when we set out to do a work that gives us a foundation to build upon. It is hard to construct without this. We are asked to deepen our spiritual life, not make it. It exists in us all, and, while it may not be fully developed, it is within and has the degrees of activity and progress. When it becomes indolent and dormant it can, through a variety of means, be awakened, cultivated, and trained. It will act at our will, and, as it acts, bring us into a larger realization of the living God, moving us and testifying of our spiritual strength. The spiritual life, in short, is a life in union with God. It is the measure of his Spirit dwelling in us. To feel its existence is as natural as any law of life. It is as natural for us to serve God in some capacity as it is natural for the bud to bloom into the flower. In some degree it is a mistake to look upon God as anything acquired or cultivated. A taste for certain kinds of foods which were at one time repulsive can be acquired. But we do not acquire the spiritual life. It is with us as a natural tendency, not anything forced. Looking at it in this light, there is no other way of regarding it. We are prepared to investigate the how and why it should be deepened. It should be deepened because it is the life of God in the soul of man. We speak about God dwelling in us. Did not God make it evident? He put his Godhead in union with manhood in the person of Jesus. Jesus is the testimony of the Divine Mind. God, from that time, has been peculiarly dwelling in man. Every man in his ideal state has the life of God in him. To deny this is to lower humanity. The more we draw upon this silent dependence upon God, the more we see our spiritual life. No better words set forth the mighty truth than " Abide in me, and I in you. As the branch cannot bear fruit of itself, except it abide in the vine, no more can ye, except ye abide in me." (John xv. 4.) Spiritual life needs to be deepened because of its vast opportunities. It endows us with the gift of discrimination. It enables us to discern all things. The very secrets of life are opened. It is the true cathode ray and helps us to tell what will advance the growth of the divine life within, and what it is necessary to guard against. It needs to be deepened because of its warmth. One zealous, sincere, spiritually minded man can warm up a community; and how many have done it! Our fires are lighted by sparks from the Holy Spirit. The Pentecost is not a stationary event; it is repeating itself in the heart of every consecrated servant. How may it be deepened? The power that made this spiritual life possible is the power to deepen it. That power is God. The spiritual life that sometimes grows indistinct and even useless in our eyes, that may be cast aside, can be recovered and restored by the One that made it plain to us. It may be deepened by putting ourselves in continual union with the objects that suggest and endear God to us; by meditation upon the Divine Word, measuring ourselves according to its precepts, guiding and shaping our way by means of it. Get it into your life. Deepen every feeling for God by it. To deepen spiritual life we must feel the power of Jesus. Nothing short of this affects the mysterious union that we maintain with him. Deepen your spiritual life by Christian conventions. In a convention like this there is a blessing coming from a hundred sources. What is the aftermath of such a convention if truly and sincerely followed? More spirituality, more consecration, and more unity. Listen to the testimony of other Christians, and what is then awakened but a deeper obligation of our duty?

Address of the Right Honorable Rev. Maurice S. Baldwin, D.D., Lord Bishop of Huron, Ontario.

We are told in Divine Scriptures that God created man in his own image; beautiful and fair he was till sin came, and then sin, writing its deep impressions upon man, obliterated the marks of that divine nature. Deeper and deeper he sinks into the abyss of sin — sinks till he does not exhibit one feature that the world could say was Godlike. I would ask you just for one moment to consider how the world was utterly unable, at the time when Christ actually came, to exhibit any one that looked as the face of God. They tell us that an eminent artist on one occasion pictured a child in lovely innocence which was considered such a masterpiece that it was hung up as a goodly ornament in a great gathering. Years rolled by; the artist was beginning to grow enfeebled. A man asked him if he would not kindly draw a companion picture to that, and it was to be Vice. The artist consented, and he went to some penitentiary and selected the darkest, most repulsive face that he could find there, some one of knitted eyebrows, some one that seemed to have graduated in crime. He selected this man as the subject of his painting. He painted this face and hung it up; and after awhile it transpired that the man he had just painted was at one time the child whose face of perfect innocence was the admiration of all. The one was the child; the other was the man — the same being. One exhibits the traces and the work of the ghastly power of sin. And so it came to pass that man having lost the Godlike image which the Father intended, God at last sent One to be his perfect image; and when the Lord Jesus Christ trod this earth men as they looked into his calm face saw the face of God. Our Lord said, "Have I been so long time with you, and yet hast thou not known me, Philip? He that hast seen me hast seen the Father, and how sayest thou then, Show us the Father?" His face might be marked more than the sons of men, but that face was the face of God. As men looked into it they saw the face of the great Father of us all; and I ask amidst the followers of Christ, Is there not something that the world stands yet in awe of? Infidelity, looking at the jagged edges of our troubled lives, our thoughts, our feelings, and our sins, criticises and sometimes ridicules, often rejects, the claim we make, and infidelity sometimes attacks the very Word of God. But, after all, there is one figure that looms up from time into eternity, that has its feet upon the earth but whose face is in heaven, and that is the form of Jesus Christ, our Lord.

They that wait upon the Lord shall be like him, and I would only point out to you that this is the Lord's way, — to take his promise, to lay it down at his feet and then urge it by the sacredness of his truthfulness, by the inviolability of his promise and the sanctity of his own oath, and as the Lord liveth and as thy soul liveth, thou shalt grasp the fulness of his promise. And I would ask you to notice what it is to be like Christ. First, it is to be like a man that was put to death and buried and raised to life again. I never saw a man that was put to death and buried and raised to life again, but the first person we see like this will be like the Lord Jesus Christ. Now when St. John saw him he said he saw a lamb as it had been slain. There were the wound-prints upon his hand, the spear-point in his side. He looked like a lamb that had been slain and had been raised to life again. And when we reach the better home and these dim eyes look upon our Lord, he will look like one who did die and was buried and raised again. Now what is it to look like that? I would ask you to notice what the great mass of Christians look like, and if there is anything common it is the appearance of many Christians. You go into ordinary Christian society and you find that men and women give way to the ordinary laws that guide the world. Here is a man who says, "This person has traduced my character." He proceeds to try to traduce his character. You speak evil of me and I speak evil of you. You run me down and I will run you down. Here is a man that sings like a cherub in the church and rehearses his creeds, but some person has offended him and he says, "I will drag him to every court in the law." Yes, and that is what the world says, too. It is the law of the jungle. It is not the law of the Lord Jesus Christ.

Now when you see a man that has been put to death and buried and raised to life again, it is a man that will bless where others curse, a man that will whisper a kind word of him that is secretly undermining his character. You may say there are not many to do that; but there are not many like Jesus Christ; and I say to you, Go into the world and get the men that give their hearts to the Lord Jesus Christ, and let them be covered with ignominy, the reproach, the taunting, the bitterness, and the acrimony of the world, and let them exhibit the life of Christ. To shine out as jewels that glitter and break and refract the beam in this dark world — oh! they are the people that teach us that there is a Christ above because they see a Christ below. Yes, and that will convince the world. "Ye are the light of the world." There is something to which the world will do homage. Does Christ live in the ordinary events or in the extraordinary events of every day's rushing, busy, tumultuous existence? O child of God, show to the world that your own nature has been put to death, been buried fathoms deep, and that you live in the power of the resurrection, that you bear the wound-prints upon your hand, and the spear-point is there upon you to show that you died with Jesus Christ and live in the power of his endless life.

This is Christ's character; and just as you exhibit this you will be a light shining in the world.

The next feature of our Lord's extraordinary life is this: the food he partook of. He did not partake of the food we take. He said, "My meat and my drink are to do the will of him that sent me." That was the food the Lord Jesus Christ lived on. He said it was his meat, it was his drink, just to do God the Father's will. He could live on that. It was his food. I would like to be in that frame of mind; and whoever do reach it will look like Christ. They will be so lost in the doing of the Lord's will that they will find it meat and find it drink; they will not go with jaded feet, not go with a groan, not go from the exigency of the occasion, but esteem it as a hungry man esteems a gracious repast, and as a thirsty man drinks fathoms deep of the draft and is refreshed. So the Lord thought the doing of his Father's will was meat and drink. Dear fellow citizens, seek this: to be lost in thy blessed Saviour's will, so that thou shalt not be beaten with a whip of scorpions to thy work, but wilt be as those that find it meat and find it drink to be lost in the doing of the Saviour's will.

Thirdly, our Lord's character is seen in the position he held the Holy Scriptures. Our Lord had a model for life, and that model and that plan were in the inspired page of God. There was truth in this: that, though he was possessed of all power, all power in heaven and all power in earth, there was one thing he could not do, and that was deflect one hair's breadth from the word of God. When the disciples said, "Master, Master, that be far from thee," he rebuked them. He said to Peter, "Get thee behind me, Satan: thou savorest not the things that be of God, but the things that be of men." And when our Lord looked at the Bible, he looked at it as you look at a map. You are about to start on a journey, an unknown road, and you sit carefully down to study a map. You see your starting-point and you see the goal that you wish to reach, and you say, " I must travel that road ; " and our Lord saw his whole path from the cradle of Bethlehem to the paths of glory depicted in that Book of God, and he followed that as no other human being ever did, and he assures us that the whole source of human knowledge lies here. See him when temptations are gathered around him, when he sweat, as it were, great drops of blood; not for one moment would he listen to the voice that said, " Turn aside." His response was always, " How, then, shall the Scriptures be fulfilled ? "

O child of God, if thou wouldst put thy feet into the footprints of thy Lord, if thou wouldst climb up that same ascent and go down that same depth, thou must take God's Word and shut your ear to human cry and hold it straight before thee; for the way the Master trod was not that of expediency, of human thought, of popular maxim, or of the world's inclination, but it was as God wrote it with his finger in the inspired volume of his Book.

To conclude, — the last feature I shall mention is as follows : that whatever our Lord did he did in the power of God, the Holy Ghost. It is a mystery, but it is what we are to teach. We are told that at his baptism the Holy Ghost came down and descended as a dove. After his baptism he was led by the Holy Spirit into the wilderness. After his temptation he came back in the power of the Holy Ghost. He talked in the synagogue of Nazareth, and he said, " The Spirit of the Lord is upon me, because the Lord hath intended me to preach." Again, in appealing to the Jews of his day, he said, " If I by the Spirit of God cast out devils, by whom do your sons cast them out ? " And, lastly, we are told by St. Paul, in his epistle to the Hebrews, that it was through the Spirit that he offered himself to God and accomplished the great work of redemption. And in concluding let me say that it was by the indwelling, the mysterious indwelling, of God the Holy Ghost that our Lord, our Master and Guide, performed the great work of redemption. So, dear child of God, thou shalt do it and grow to the likeness of that Lord. Then thy features will fade away and new features come. They will be the features of the face of the Lord that died for thee.

Go home with this blessed thought: that " I too am to be like my Lord; that the Lord will take the common, sin-stained, polluted thing of earth and by his grace will transform it until it shall burn like the glory of the Saviour himself, and I shall be like him, for he shall stamp his features on my heart." May God deepen this life in us all, for Christ's sake, Amen.

First Presbyterian Church.

The First Presbyterian Church was crowded to its doors, in anticipation of a missionary address, illustrated with lantern slides, by the Rev. Frank S. Dobbins, of Philadelphia, on " The Land of the Rising Sun." The meeting was in the interest of the foreign missions, and not only was the large audience delighted by the speaker's description of missionary work in the East, but also highly gratified by his statements of the success which is now attending such work.

Rev. D. W. Skellenger, of Washington, presided at the meeting and cordially welcomed the strangers. While the audience was gathering the young people started hymn after hymn of those most familiar and dear to Christian Endeavorers. Neatly uniformed young men seated the audience, and the church was handsomely decorated with bunting, the national and Christian Endeavor colors being prominent, as were the colors of the New Jersey delegation, orange and black, the church being that delegation's headquarters.

Mr. Skellenger explained that the address would be preceded by a service of song and prayer, conducted by Dr. Dobbins. All were asked by Dr. Dobbins to bow their heads in silent prayer, and then, as the hymns were flashed upon the large canvas screen in front of the pulpit, each hymn being accompanied by appropriate illustrations, the audience, led by the choir, sang a verse or two of each one, Dr. Dobbins interpolating sentences appropriate to their themes. The feature of this service was the rendering of the grand old hymn, "All Hail the Power of Jesus' Name." First a verse was sung by a single voice, one of the young ladies of the choir. Then the choir sang another verse, the women in the audience, only, rendered another verse, and all present joined in singing the concluding verse.

The Rev. Dr. Byron Sunderland, pastor of the church, in invoking the divine blessing, spoke of the day as being one of the grandest in Christian history, saying that the Christian Endeavorers were the elect of God, who were to take in their hands the banner of Christ.

Dr. Dobbins then told in an interesting way of the missionary work in Japan, India, China, Burmah, and Africa. He paid a high compliment to the intelligence of the Japanese and their love for the beautiful, saying that it is very gratifying and encouraging to know that the seeds sown by the missionaries are springing up among the higher classes in Japan.

Mr. Dobbins used about 110 lantern slides, all finely colored. First was shown the out-door life of Japan, the queenly mountain, the jinrikisha, and child-life in Japan. Following that came a study of the home-life of the Japanese people. The religious life was next considered, with illustrations of celebrated idols and temples, leading up to a consideration of the relations of Christianity to Japan in ancient days and in recent years.

Then hurriedly the lantern journey was continued through India, Burmah, Assam, China, and the Congo region in Africa. Groups of noted missionaries, the division of the missionary dollar (showing by an odd device just what becomes of money given for missions), missionary homes. certain great events in missionary history, and evidences, by the sun's testimony, of the value of missions and their great success, — all these were presented by carefully drawn illustrations, with full, yet concise, description.

First Congregational Church.

One of the most interesting features of the programme was the illustrated address on Armenia, delivered by Rev. George E. Lovejoy, of Stoneham, Mass., at the First Congregational Church. Notwithstanding the heavy rain-storm, the church was crowded to the doors by an audience which demonstrated its thorough accord with the sentiments of the speaker by frequent and enthusiastic applause.

Long lines of red, white, and blue streamers were festooned from various points in the balcony to the central chandelier in the ceiling. The rear wall was decorated with a large banner of real red, white, and blue, and the American colors in various designs were displayed at all other points of vantage.

Rev. S. M. Newman, D.D., pastor of the church, presided, and the music was rendered by the Christian Endeavor chorus of the church, under the leadership of Mr. E R. O'Conner.

"The Crescent Against the Cross" was the title of Mr. Lovejoy's lecture, and it dealt entirely with the persecutions and outrages perpetrated upon the Christian Armenians by the agents and emissaries of the Sultan of Turkey. Mr. Lovejoy told a graphic story of the recent massacres in Eastern Turkey, where the martyred Armenians were given the choice of "Islam or death," and were ruthlessly slaughtered by the cruel Turks because they heroically refused to renounce their religion. The details were suppressed, so far as possible, by the Turkish authorities, but enough was known, he said, to make the blood run cold.

Pictures of the Sultan, his palaces, the principal dignitaries who have figured in the Armenian troubles, Constantinople, Stambool, the bridge across the Dardanelles between them, several mosques in different parts of Turkey, groups of the Kurds and Basha Bazouks (the regular and irregular soldiers of Turkey), and many other interesting pictures were shown during the description.

The massacres have been a regular thing for the past two hundred years. The authorities deny any responsibility for them, but there is no doubt but that they have been ordered and directed from that source. After the massacres of last year, a Commission of Inquiry was ordered to investigate and report their causes, and enough evidence was produced to show that if they were not ordered directly by the Sultan, it was not very far from him; and the removal of one of the Governors of a province in Turkey where massacres had occurred was demanded. This was done, but he was shortly afterwards given a more honorable position, plainly showing that it was in the nature of a reward for the work he had done. This Commission of Inquiry demanded that reforms should be made, but the Turks are noted for their delays, and although these reforms have been promised, nothing has yet been done.

During his description of the massacres, views of different cities of Armenia, where they occurred, were thrown upon the screen. Among them were Erzerum, Sarsoun, Sevas, Harpoot, Van, Marsovan, Caesarea in Capadocia, Marash, Zartoon, etc., places of importance, at all of which many of the Armenians were butchered, their shops plundered, and their wives and daughters forced to lives worse than those of slaves. At some of the places named there were missionary stations and schools, and he gave graphic descriptions of the trials and dangers through which they passed during the massacres. Prompt and determined action on the part of the missionaries and teachers, and the fear of the United States government, alone saved their lives and property. Some of these stations have lost much property by fire, amounting to many thousands of dollars.

These massacres are still going on; in the city of Van, about two weeks since, there were many of the Armenians killed.

There is great need of funds in all parts of Armenia to alleviate the sufferings and to keep them from actual starvation. He stated that one dollar would afford bread for one man for three months, or for three hundred men for one day. The Red Cross Society, through Miss Clara Barton, is doing a good work among these people.

The United States has done a great deal in spreading the Gospel among this people, and through the power represented by it has been the means of protection to our missionaries and teachers there. The United States flag should float over every schoolhouse and every church, not only in this country, but over every mission school and Christian church in Armenia, and so throw the protection of this great Republic around Christianity.

The meeting was concluded with the singing of Heber's missionary hymn, "From Greenland's Icy Mountain," during which twelve scenes, illustrative of the words of the song, were shown.

The service closed with the benediction by Dr. Newman.

THURSDAY MORNING.

THE FIRST MEETINGS IN THE TENTS.

Tent Washington.

The great Convention began Thursday morning, with the certainty that the tents of meeting would be crowded, for there were only two. Tent Williston was level with the ground. Hours of steady drizzle, followed on Wednesday night by a pouring rain and a strong wind, were too much for the mighty spread of canvas. The night watchmen and patrols were zealous and faithful in their inspection, but the ground was softened, the great guy-ropes snapped, and the tent collapsed in a deplorable ruin. Benches were swept down by the wild rush of the canvas, the pretty decorations were thrown upon the ground, and later the workmen extricated drenched musical instruments, chairs, and tables.

This disaster was a tremendous test, but Christian Endeavor was equal to the emergency. Churches and halls were opened to take the place of Tent Williston. Tents Washington and Endeavor were made dry within, and extra precautions taken to make them abundantly safe. Everybody was good-natured, everybody was trustful and hopeful. Cried Mr. Foster, announcing the opening hymn, "Let us sing 'Praise God, from Whom All Blessings Flow,' including the blown-down tent!" Then, as was appropriate under those lowering skies, they sang, "There's Sunshine in My Soul." There was much laughter when Mr. Foster remarked, in announcing the next hymn, "We *need* the showers — of blessing."

Dr. Clark's first words were, "Rain can not drown Christian Endeavor, and wind can not blow it away," going on to read Job xxxvi. 27–29; xxxvii. 21, 22, "For he maketh small the drops of water. . . . Fair weather cometh out of the north." That was the spirit with which Christian Endeavor conquered the elements.

The gathering of the clans was, as usual, spirited and happy. What a constant surprise and marvel are these vast Christian Endeavor audiences! What an eloquence in ten thousand eager faces, in twenty thousand speaking eyes! These tremendous companies are responsive and flowing, bursting out here in a jolly State cry, there in a beautiful hymn; now springing to their feet with cheers of greeting to some honored leader, now waving flags and white handkerchiefs in time with a popular song, and in an instant hushed in silent prayer, "All one body, we;" with quick sympathies, with swift appreciations, and with one strong, common purpose.

In this year's assembling of the hosts, the presence of those charming flying bits of color, the new State flags, was delightfully noticeable. So were many new and beautiful State songs. And all the good old fervor and sparkle were there, unquenchable by the showers.

The fine invocation hymn, written for us by the Washington poet, John Hay, was read in unison by the audiences, and sung with a will.

Invocation Hymn.

TUNE, FEDERAL STREET.
Written for the Fifteenth International Christian Endeavor Convention.
BY COL. JOHN HAY.

Lord, from far-severed climes we come
To meet at last in thee, our home.
Thou who hast been our guide and guard
Be still our hope, our rich reward.

Defend us, Lord, from every ill;
Strengthen our hearts to do Thy will;
In all we plan and all we do
Still keep us to thy service true.

Oh, let us hear the inspiring word
Which they of old at Horeb heard.
Breathe to our hearts the high command:
"Go onward and possess the land!"

Thou who art Light, shine on each soul!
Thou who art Truth, each mind control!
Open our eyes and make us see
The path which leads to heaven and thee!

The devotional exercises were conducted by Rev. F. D. Power, D.D., pastor of the Vermont Avenue Christian Church of Washington.

Then Mr. W. H. H. Smith, chairman of the Committee of '96, was introduced by President Clark to give the words of welcome. Mr. Smith received a royal greeting.

Address of Mr. W. H. H. Smith, Washington, D. C.

" Not by might, nor by power, but by my Spirit, saith the Lord of hosts."

I wish it were possible for me at this moment to sink my personality out of sight and to be to you only a voice, and that the voice could adequately cry into your hearts the three great words which we desire shall be the key-words of the Fifteenth International Christian Endeavor Convention: Welcome! Worship! Work!

A royal welcome from the government of these United States of America, which, by its representatives in Congress, without a dissenting vote, enacted the law granting us the use of this beautiful and spacious public reservation, and by its executive officers, from His Excellency the President to the heads and assistants in the several departments, has helped us in every reasonable way to provide for your comfort and to greet your coming.

A hearty welcome from the honorable commissioners, officials, citizens, and press of this city, who have so readily and generously contributed in preparing for your pleasure and profit.

A sincere welcome from the clergy of all denominations, who, without a word of carping or criticism, have encouraged us in all of our plans.

A Christian welcome from the seventy-five churches which, without a single request from us, have been freely placed at your disposal for use during this Convention.

A loving welcome from the thousands of homes whose doors have been flung wide open for your entertainment.

A great welcome from the Endeavorers of the District of Columbia Union, with their labors and sacrifices in your behalf, and from the more than 3,000 workers upon the several committees who have planned and toiled for you.

A glad welcome from the Epworth Leagues and other societies who have cheered and helped us in many ways, and who join with us in swelling this great Convention chorus to more than 4,600 voices.

Welcome! a hundred times welcome! Welcome to all, of whatever nation or people or denomination, who own allegiance to our Lord Jesus Christ. Welcome to the hearts and homes, to the public buildings and parks, and to the wealth of the beautiful, interesting, and valuable which is here in such profusion to thrill and fill you in this, our great nation's capital.

> " Welcome to heart and home;
> Welcome to Washington,
> Welcome this day."

But is this all? Is it alone for the earthly fellowships, the social meetings and greetings, good and glad as they are, that we have been so long and so lovingly preparing for you with such enthusiasm and expectation? I am sure that you will agree with me that it were indeed worth the discomforts, weariness, and expense of thousands of miles of travel to clasp the right hand of such fellowship, whose left holds no dagger, to knit up friendships, which weave in heavenly tissues, and to color into your lives the rich treasures of interest and information which you can receive in this home of the nation. But we want more than this for you. Dear friends, if our highest hopes for you are to be realized, and we believe they are; if our most earnest longings for you are to be satisfied, and we are confident they shall be; if the fulness of that for which we have planned, prayed, and toiled is now come to its consummation, and we believe it has, then these tents are the tabernacles of God and you are in the audience-chamber of your King and have come to meet and to greet the Lord of heaven and earth, our Lord, our Saviour, our Brother, our one Master, even Christ. Oh, it is this, it is this we wish for you. May he appear before you in every prayer and song. May he be lifted up in every scripture and address. May he sit beside you in these seats. May he walk with you through these parks and streets. May his Spirit be in you and with you. Here may your lives be fully "hid with Christ in God." May this be a real Mount of Transfiguration, where you shall catch somewhat of the shining of his face and garments and realize more vividly than ever before the tremendous import of a work which stirs the interest of all heaven.

" While we to God appeal,
May each his Spirit feel,
May God himself reveal
To all, we pray."

Once again shall the voice cry unto you, and now with the intense cry of practical application for each life. Work! What is to be the outcome of all this expenditure of money, of time, and of life? What is to result from your audience with the King? Will it prove? Will it pay? If there is one thing more than another for which I love the Christian Endeavor movement it is for its purposefulness,— not simply to be something good, but to be good for something. And so I am sure that the right answer shall be given. You can *not* go out from this place upon the same level as you entered. God grant that it may be marvelously higher, nobler, purer, for the most intelligent, intense, and persevering service "for Christ and the Church." We may, indeed, wish that we could build our little mean huts of earthliness and selfish content, hoping to detain some heavenly visitant, upon these shining summits of privilege; but look! See down into the valleys and out beyond the shining, and behold the aching hearts and the twisted and blasted lives of men, made at the first in God's own image, but now so marred out of divine fashion, who need your working and wearying that they may be restored to self, to home, and to heaven. See the sin-stained and demon-possessed that God wants to reach and must reach through your life and your strength with his own cleansing and power. Behold a world lying in wickedness, stumbling and groping on in blindness, with the eternities just before, for whom Christ died, and into whose lives the Saviour shall come only as he comes through your life; and then, with all the wealth of all you shall gather into your life here, go out to do great service in the midst of great need, and sure of great reward.

If our devotion to your interests has established any claim to your affection, if our sacrifices for your happiness call for any return from you, if our efforts in your behalf place you under any obligation whatsoever, then by so much and to such extent as we have any right, we plead with and command you to "make it pay," by stepping out upon a higher plane and a broader view of life than ever before, into every place where the Master calls you, to do better and braver work for him whose incarnated life motto was, "not to be ministered unto, but to minister." So shall your Christlier life answer the pertinent question of this utilitarian age, and by every soul won to our Master, and every heart helped in his service, you *shall* "make it pay" over and over, "make it pay" for anything, everything, done for you and for this Convention.

"Search for the strayed and lost,
Rescue the tempest-tossed,
Save men at any cost;
To God be true."

The voice cries unto you in a great cry of passionate longing, Welcome! Worship! Work!

One of the oldest and best friends of Christian Endeavor, the Rev. Robert J. Service, D.D., of Detroit, Mich., then made a response to the words of welcome.

Address of Rev. Robert J. Service, D.D., Detroit, Mich.

Mr. President and Fellow Endeavorers: — We expected a warm welcome when we came to Washington and we certainly have not been disappointed. Knowing the gathering that assembles from year to year on Capitol Hill, we were quite confident we would receive a windy welcome, and in that we have not been disappointed.

But I am sure we all appreciate most heartily the gracious and the generous words of welcome to which we have just listened, and especially do we appreciate the act of the united houses of Congress in granting us this ground upon which to pitch our tents. As grateful guests, we propose to show our appreciation of your generous welcome by making ourselves perfectly at home. That we have already begun to do so the keepers of the hotels and boarding-houses and the generous hosts in private residences can testify, I am sure.

As loyal Americans, we feel that in a sense this capital city is our own; and I have no doubt that our Canadian brethren who are present already wish that they possessed that delightful sense of ownership. Possibly there shall go back to Canada's realms a great host of earnest annexationists, so impressed with our national hospitality that they no longer have any fear of refusal on our part to receive fair Canada into the galaxy of our States.

Coxey-like, we shall probably walk upon the grass and congregate in the national plaza. Nor do we fear that we shall be compelled to follow Father Clark or Secretary Baer to your prison gates. Were Congress in session we should doubtless invade her halls, and, impelled by the imperative necessities of the case, should perhaps begin missionary work. Possibly the fear of this has led to the early adjournment of that body.

Heartily, most heartily, do we thank you for your generous welcome; and with all due modesty, may I say we believe we deserve it?

Representatives we are of 2,600,000 of Christian Endeavorers whose sole object is to do good to their fellows, to lift the standard of human life, to make better citizens, to keep our government pure, that it may be stable and enduring.

History tells us that the life of republics is only about one hundred years. Then comes decay and death. Wise, far-seeing men in our own land already begin to discern clouds rising in our sky that threaten tempest and storm to our national and social life. Possibly their intense love of their country is the mother of their fears. Be that as it may, all agree and recognize that if that for which Christian Endeavor stands can prevail, these clouds will vanish as the mists before the morning sun.

As truly defenders of our national honor and stability are the hosts of Christian Endeavor as were the boys from Massachusetts and Connecticut who marched up Pennsylvania Avenue in the dark days of 1861. Right gladly did this city welcome those boys from the North as her defenders, as they have welcomed us to-day; and I believe that no portion of our great United Republic to-day more rejoices in the success that crowned the armies of those days than our brethren from the South. I believe that to-day no section of our country is so devotedly loyal and true to our United Republic as are they.

To check vice and sin in individual and national life, to keep before men the divine ideal, to awaken in the consciousness of mankind the sense of a Fatherhood enveloping men in his love, and the consequent sense of human brotherhood, whereby injustice between man and man, whereby class distinctions with their threatening dangers and perils, shall be done away with; whereby in homes, in factories, in business marts, in legislative halls, and at the polls men in purity and righteousness shall act as children of the one Father, and brethren together; — this is one of the objects of Christian Endeavor, and this will render any nation immortal.

What youth has done for the world we all realize in every line and department of life. We gather here with youthful enthusiasm to advance the kingdom of our Lord and our Saviour, Jesus Christ. Slowly, but surely, the Church is beginning to recognize, under the press of youthful enthusiasm, that she received her divine commission not as a hospital but as an army, and that there is a place for every one in the field. Already, under the press of the army idea, the Christian Endeavor idea, the Christ idea, cots that have abounded in the court of Israel, containing dyspeptic sons, are being folded, as they march with us in the ranks of the army of Christ.

I look upon this as a great council of war, gathered together to plan for the campaign of the Christ. May we all carry back to our different divisions, and regiments, the martial spirit, the spirit of our Divine Saviour in his tireless, persistent, conquering war with the hosts of evil; and let our response to the warmth of our generous welcome here be in the harvest of souls, be in purified life, be in more devoted, persistent, loyal service to the Captain whom we love and whom we serve.

Rev. Wayland Hoyt, D.D., of Philadelphia, then took the post of presiding officer. Said he, " The same unkind winds not only to some degree disarranged Tent Williston, but necessarily also disarranged somewhat our programme. So there must be some change in the order. I do not think you will object at all to the change necessitated just now, for the thing next in order is the presentation of his annual address by President Clark. He said to me just now, 'Introduce me.' What is the use? A man might just as well say to himself, 'Introduce me to myself,' as for a Christian Endeavor throng to need to have President Clark introduced to them."

Then the tent swelled with the cheer that went up. Again and again it died away, only to be caught up again and redoubled. For several minutes President Clark stood the centre of a whirlwind of enthusiasm. He tried several times to speak, but his voice could not be heard two feet away. He waited, patiently, until the fervor of the Endeavorers had exhausted itself; then he went on, but only to be interrupted every few moments by the applause that punctuated his words.

Address of President Francis E. Clark, D.D.

Fellow Christian Endeavorers : — This is a good year to build platforms. Several have been constructed already. From the great metropolis of the West we can almost hear the resounding blows of hammer and chisel as, in another platform, plank is fitted to plank.

Our Christian Endeavor platform was built for us at the beginning by Providence. Its strength has been revealed by our history.

My task is an easy one, for I only need write in words what I believe God has written in deeds.

If I do not state our platform correctly, I do not ask you to stand upon it.

But if I can read our history aright, these are its chief planks: —

First. Our Covenant Prayer-meeting Pledge,—the Magna Charta of Christian Endeavor.

Second. Our Consecration Meeting,— guaranteeing the spiritual character of the Society.

Third. Our Committees, — giving to each active member some specific and definite work "for Christ and the Church."

Fourth. Our Interdenominational and International Fellowship, based upon our denominational and national loyalty.

Fifth. Our Individual Independence and Self-government, free from control of United Society, State or local union, convention, or committee; all of which exist for fellowship and inspiration, not for legislation.

Sixth. Our Individual Subordination as societies to our own churches, of which we claim to be an integral, organic, inseparable part.

Seventh. Our Christian Citizenship plank,— our country for Christ. but, as a Society, no entangling political alliances. Our Missionary plank,— Christ for the world.

Eighth. Our Ultimate Purpose, — to deepen the spiritual life and raise the religious standards of young people the world over.

For fifteen years Christian Endeavor has built upon this platform. The history of the Society which has wrought out in practice these principles may be briefly summarized, so far as words and figures can summarize a movement, as follows: —

Forty-six thousand societies have been formed.

Five millions of Endeavorers have been enrolled, of whom more than two millions seven hundred thousand are to-day members.

Two millions of others, Endeavorers in all but name, have probably been enrolled in purely denominational societies.

Ten million Endeavor meetings have been held.

Five million copies of the constitution have undoubtedly been printed, in forty different languages, and at least fifteen million copies of the pledge.

Over one million of our associate members have come into the evangelical churches connected with fifty denominations, influenced in part, at least, by the Christian Endeavor Society; and it is certain that over two millions of dollars have been given in benevolence through denominational and church channels.

"The past at least is secure," we say.   But ah ! is it ?   Not unless we secure the future by learning the lessons of the past.   The future stretches before us,— ten times fifteen years of Christian Endeavor, please God, and ten times that. We stand yet at the beginnings, fellow Endeavorers.   The stream is yet near its source.   Our concern should be not to deflect it into any channels of our own choosing.   Let God choose its way and direct its course, as he has done these fifteen years, and then the future, too, is secure.   "We have but one lamp by which our feet are guided, and that is the lamp of experience."   By the past what does God teach us for the future ?

Let me try, as best I may, to draw out the lessons.   Christian Endeavor, as our platform shows, is a practical paradox, a reconciler of irreconcilables.   It has married opposites.   It has brought into an harmonious family, ideas which have been thought to be mutually exclusive.   I am tempted to consider this the most important work of Christian Endeavor, in the future as in the past.

Our platform specifies some of the banns that have been proclaimed by Christian Endeavor.

First.   It has married the ideas of denominational fidelity and fellowship between denominations, and has written on the door-posts of the home thus formed: "FIDELITY AND FELLOWSHIP, ONE AND INSEPARABLE."

These ideas have been thought by many to be inconsistent, if not hostile, one to the other.   Hence, many ecclesiastics are to-day afraid of our fellowship because they believe it will weaken our fidelity.   Christian Endeavor, sooner or later, will show them the groundlessness of their fears.

By combining these disassociated ideas, Christian Endeavor has created a new idea, which has required a new word, — a word which is found only in the very latest dictionary, — the word "interdenominational;" a denomination-alism which is not sectarianism on the one side or care-nothing-ism on the other. Mind your prefixes, Christian Endeavorers ; not "un," nor "non," but "inter."

Closely linked with this idea of Interdenominational Fellowship is that other great idea of International Fellowship.   Look at these intertwined flags !   They tell their own story.   They tell of our intense love for our own flag,— the Stars and Stripes, "Old Glory," if we live in the United States; the Union Jack, if we live in Canada or Great Britain.   Interlinked as they are, they tell of our world-wide brotherhood.   Our Society is an arbitration meeting which never adjourns, a peace-with-honor convention that is always in session.   On these banners is written: "LOYALTY AND BROTHERHOOD, ONE AND INSEPARABLE."

Second.   Again, if our platform is correct, Christian Endeavor stands for a self-governed society that is yet wholly governed by its own church.   I know of no way of developing responsibility except by bearing responsibility.   That man and that society will always be a dwarf and weakling that is ever managed by some one else.   In comparison with such a man, Mr. Caudle behind the bed-curtain will be independent and self-respecting.

Each society of Christian Endeavor is in a sense independent.   It works out its own problems.   It is responsible for its own success or failure.   It lives or dies according to its own inherent worth.   It manages its own matters.   It elects its own officers. It plans its own campaigns. But it is always subordinate to its own church, and seeks tô find out and obey the wishes of its own church and pastor.

Let me here take occasion to pledge myself to the Christian public, if I may be allowed to speak in any sense as a representative of Christian Endeavor. No United Society and no convention, no union, and no committee of evangelism, good citizenship, or missions, shall legislate for, or seek to control, any society in the wide world.

More and more strongly every year is this principle of Christian Endeavor established, which indeed has been fundamental from the beginning,—that each society owes allegiance to its own church. Some churches have taken advantage of this principle of subordination to compel their Christian Endeavor Societies to commit suicide, to go out of existence, or to label themselves with a local or sectarian name. Is this entirely fair? I appeal confidently to the Christian public of the future, to the sense of justice in the church at large, for my answer.

Nevertheless, and in spite of the advantage sometimes taken of this principle, Christian Endeavor has proclaimed the banns once more over these two apparently dissimilar ideas, — Self-government and Subordination. It has married these disassociated thoughts, each of which is incomplete without the other; each of which is puny and weak without the other; each of which is complemented and supplemented by the other. It has married them, and has written on the lintel of their door: "OBEDIENCE AND INDEPENDENCE, ONE AND INSEPARABLE."

Third. Again, our platform embraces Patriotism and Humanity. Patriotism is a name that is used to cover a multitude of sins. "It is the last resort of designing knaves," said Johnson. It has been made to stand for partisanship and to mask hideous corruption. It needs to be married to another idea, — the idea of humanity. This Christian Endeavor has attempted to do.

Our patriotic fervor was born at the same time as our missionary fervor. Good citizenship and missions have gone hand in hand. "America for Christ" had not ceased to echo before we took up the cry "Christ for the world." Good citizenship has too often meant in the lands where its slogan has been sounded, "America for the Americans," "Canada for the Canadians," "Great Britain for the British," "Japan for the Japanese." Christian citizenship means something more than this. It means our country for Christ, and Christ for the world. It means good rulers and good laws. It means the abolition of the saloon. It means prohibition wherever we can get it. It means Sabbath observance. It means inflexible opposition to all unrighteousness—not simply that America may be the greatest nation on which the sun rises, not simply that Britain's drumbeat may be heard around the world, but above all, that "His kingdom may come, and his will may be done, on earth as it is in heaven."

By Christian Endeavor, then, we marry the too-often disassociated ideas, patriotism and humanity. CHRISTIAN CITIZENSHIP AND CHRISTIAN MISSIONS, ONE AND INSEPARABLE.

Fourth. Our Christian Endeavor platform, once more, stands for Organization; it stands for Spiritual Power. These two great ideas, alas! have too often been set over against one another. They have been divorced and sundered far. Come, Christian Endeavor, thou white-robed peacemaker, and pronounce the banns which shall make organization and spiritual power forever one!

Two wings are essential to the bird that would soar toward the sun. Organization is one wing, spirituality is another. A poor, broken-winged eagle is that church or society that fails to use both wings.

Organization without spiritual power is the perfect engine standing upon the track with no fire under the boiler, no steam in the pipes. It is a dumb, dead, impotent thing.

Spirituality without organization is the fire upon the prairie, kindling a blaze, but driving no wheels, turning no turbines, energizing no whirring looms or flying shuttles. This, too, is an impotent, evanescent thing. But spirituality and organization may move the world.

We have the organization practically complete,—our covenant pledge, our consecration meeting, our committees, our unions. Our future conquest is a question of spiritual power, and that, O Christian Endeavorers, you must furnish. Spiritual power abides not in the machinery of itself, but it may be had for the asking. Listen to the promise, Christian Endeavorer: " Ask and ye shall receive; seek and ye shall find." Spiritual power is as free as the sunlight, as mighty as the tides. It is as abundant as electricity, but, like electricity, it must be generated. It is as omnipotent as God, but it must be applied.

The Christian Endeavor history of this past year is the story of this power. Its dominant note has been " Evangelism." " Saved to serve " has been its motto. The " new Endeavor " may be summarized as the evangelistic Endeavor, and wise evangelism is spiritual power applied.

O Endeavorers, this is your supreme mission. Be the conductors of this spiritual electricity. Be the willing wires, the live wires, along which may run the power of God to every part of our organization. This is the one, the only, secret of true success,—" Not by might, nor by power," not by organization nor by perfection of machinery, not by committees, not by methods, " but by my Spirit, saith the Lord," working through committees and methods and organization.

Oh that by some word of burning eloquence I might lay this thought on the heart of every Endeavorer throughout the world! This word is not mine to speak. It is not any man's to utter. Come, Holy Spirit, Heavenly Comforter, speak thou the word that makes our organization live.

But I *can*, I do, urge you to make this the Christian Endeavor watchword of the coming year. Each year of the fifteen years has been noted for some advance step. Each convention has been signalized by some great thought. " Citizenship," " Missions," " Fellowship," have been our watchwords at conventions past, and they are our watchwords still; for a step once gained we will not lose. And here is the greatest word, and best of all: SPIRITUAL POWER. " Washington '96 " — may it live in history as the Convention of God's power! 1896-7, the year of God's energizing might in Christian Endeavor!

Then, as steel and copper, hitherto unweldable metals, are welded together by the mighty, subtle power of electricity in a union so complete that no human eye can find the seam, so, by the fusing might of God's Spirit in Christian Endeavor, will be welded together *fidelity that is true and fellowship that is large-hearted, responsibility that makes strong and loyalty that makes humble and gentle, patriotism and humanity, organization and spiritual power, now and forever, one and inseparable.* AND " WHAT GOD HATH JOINED TOGETHER, LET NOT MAN PUT ASUNDER."

After the applause had subsided Dr. Hoyt said : —

Christian Endeavor is no whim or waft of sentiment. It stands for something. It has principles. You have heard these principles summarized and admirably explicated in this splendid address to which you have just been listening. Would it not be a good thing if we had something to do ourselves with the reaffirmation of these principles of Christian Endeavor which have been thus so clearly announced by President Clark? I think, if we all of us state back to him that these are the principles that we stand on as Christian Endeavorers, that these are the principles that we are bound to work by, it would be a good thing for him, and a good thing for us, and for all Christian Endeavorers associated with us. I propose that we make such response of reaffirmation, and that we do it in two ways, but at the same time, — by posture and by voice. I propose that if it shall please you we all rise and so express by posture our reaffirmation of Christian Endeavor principles, and that when I count three, and say three, you shall by voice reannounce and reaffirm them by saying all together, and just as loudly as you can, " Aye."

The entire audience arose, and with mighty shout gave their testimony. The next feature of the programme Dr. Hoyt introduced by saying : —

We who live under this flag have got to be somewhat disappointed, I imagine, but nevertheless we will congratulate our brethren who live under the British flag. In Christian Endeavor it is pretty nearly all the same. These badge banners that mean so much, that represent sacrifice and service and pioneer endeavor, will remain this year under the shadow of the flag of Great Britain instead of getting back under — I will say it — the better shining flag of the United States.

You will remember that last year the badge banner which was given for the greatest proportionate increase in the number of societies during the last year went from somewhere in the United States away up into the northwest corner of North America, over which floats the British flag, and now it is going a good way from Assiniboia. It is going across the ocean, and it is still going to remain under the British flag. The banner representing the greatest proportionate increase in the number of societies during the last twelve months is to go to Scotland. We have a very eloquent and admirable gentleman with us, who is to receive this banner. It goes to Scotland, and it is to be received by the Rev. Arnold Streuli, of Manchester, England, who has been called to a great church in Scotland. I do not know whether he is going there, but at any rate, he is Scotch for the present, and he will receive the banner.

Remarks of Rev. Arnold Streuli.

Fellow Endeavorers : — It is never a very pleasant thing to stand in any one's else shoes, and particularly in those of a Scotchman. I must confess, however, that until I came to America I often wished that I had been born a Scotchman. Just now the attractions of your great country are in the ascendant, but I must say that I feel a return of the old desire as I look upon this banner and envy the possession of this banner by Scotland. I wish also that I could worthily express the gratitude of Scotland for the honor done to her by the gift of this banner to-day.

Though I am not a Scotchman, I know a good deal about that country, and have seen much of the work Christian Endeavor has done there. We in Great Britain rejoice in nothing more than in the progress which Scotland has made during the last few years in her societies of Christian Endeavor. Under the splendid leadership of Mr. Fleming and Mr. Pollock, whom you know, I think, and others, Scotland has made wonderful progress. As you understand, she receives the banner this year for proportionate increase, — more than fifty per cent increase in both societies and membership. In 1895 she had 200 societies; for 1896 she rejoices in 315. Her membership last year was 9,500; this year it stands at 14,500.

I should like to say, especially at this Convention, what I heard a few weeks ago from a distinguished layman in Scotland. He said to me, " Our churches in Scotland are hungering for a deeper spiritual life ; " and I feel that it is very significant indeed that Scotland should receive the banner from "the deepening-of-spiritual-life Convention," if I may so call the Washington Convention of '96. On behalf of Scotland, therefore, the land of John Knox, the land of the Covenanters, the land of Thomas Chalmers, the land of Thomas Guthrie, I very gratefully accept this banner. I promise, on behalf of Scotland, that we shall take good care of it ; we hope we shall keep it for many years to come, and that you yourselves, when you come to one of our great conventions in England or Scotland, will have the pleasure of seeing this banner there at that time. I am sure that whenever we look upon this banner in Scotland we shall feel a special inspiration as we think of the marvelous work that God has wrought in this Convention at Washington in 1896. Many thanks.

As he sat down, a delegate arose in the rear of the tent and called for "three cheers for old Scotland," and they were given with a will. Dr. Hoyt then said : —

I saw a statue of Mercury the other day. It was lithe of form, and the face of it looked as though the brain of the deity was alert. It was swift of foot.

When I saw it, I somehow thought of Secretary Baer. I said, "Secretary Baer is the Christian Endeavor Mercury." There is not an ounce of superfluous flesh on him. He is just as quick of mind as Mercury ever was, and he is just as swift going about. He is everywhere. He does not need any introduction. Secretary Baer will now present his annual report.

Mr. Baer came forward, and this was the signal for another cyclonic disturbance. Cries of "Baer, Baer, Secretary Baer," rang out everywhere, and the young man was unable to proceed for some minutes. Then he went on with his address, which was received with applause and cheers as the various states and nations were mentioned.

Annual Report of Secretary John Willis Baer.

Christian Endeavor, — "*It is like a grain of mustard seed, which a man took, and cast into his garden; and it grew, and waxed a great tree; and the fowls of the air lodged in the branches of it.*" (Luke xiii. 19.)

Those few lines give a brief and most accurate account of the beginning and the progress of Christian Endeavor. Wonderful indeed has been its growth. Paul has planted, and Apollos has watered, but God has given the increase. Yea, verily, the mustard-seed cast into Dr. Clark's garden, the Williston Church, Portland, Me., fifteen years ago, has waxed a great tree.

I know very well that there is a law in the vegetable life which says that what grows most rapidly generally decays earliest, and that some "good and wise men" have for that reason likened Christian Endeavor to Jonah's gourd, "which," you know, "came up in a night and perished in a night." Let me remind those good friends, if their line is still in the earth, that the prophet says, "God prepared a worm, and smote the gourd, and it withered."

It has been said that "the least in nature is a better illustration of divine truth than the greatest object of art," and it seems to me that Christian Endeavor, with its mighty, God-given growth, is more appropriately comparable to the life in the little mustard-seed, the least of all seeds, than to the most famous creation of art that skilled man has produced. The whirligig of time has sped on these fifteen years, and Christian Endeavor *grows*, and has already waxed a great tree, and the fowls of the air lodge in its branches; and I, for one, am confident God has not prepared a worm with which to smite it in a night, or in a year, or in a decade; no, never!

Now let us count the branches on this great tree. It is a task upon which we enter with enthusiasm. Of the states and provinces that now have each over one thousand Young People's Societies of Christian Endeavor, the Keystone State of Pennsylvania still heads the list, with 3,273; New York next, 2,971; Ohio, 2,311; Ontario has now passed to fourth place, with 1,817; Illinois, 1,802; Indiana, 1,352; Iowa, 1,302.

These figures do not include the numerous other kinds of Christian Endeavor Societies that are now fast becoming sturdy branches of the mother tree, such as the Junior, the Intermediate, the Mothers'. and the Senior.

The Junior branch claims our first attention. God be praised for its growth. It is said a root of corn would grow an inch in fifteen minutes, and the Junior branch bids fair to surpass that. There are now 10,084 Junior Societies. Pennsylvania leads with 1,224, then New York not very far behind with 1,104; Illinois, 836; Ohio, 716; Indiana, 498; Iowa, 468; Massachusetts, 461; California, 442. Notwithstanding many of the States have made splendid advances in Junior Societies, Pennsylvania will for the third time secure the Junior badge banner for the *largest gain* in number of Junior Societies.

And the other banner, now in the hands of Assiniboia, must pass across two imaginary lines to our enterprising neighbors in Mexico, for her record for the *greatest proportionate increase* in number of Junior Societies is far ahead of all others.

Next in numerical strength comes the Intermediate Society. When this branch first put forth its stem, we know not; it is but a few years old, but promises richly. In many large churches there is need of banding the older Juniors together, for aggressive work, preparatory to their graduating into the Young People's Society. There are now 115 Intermediate Societies enrolled, and many more of which we have no record. Illinois leads with 17 recorded. California, Indiana, and Ohio each have 11 enrolled. Another year's growth of this branch will be watched with interest, as will that of still two other new branches, the Mothers' Society and the Senior Society. There are 50 of the former and 20 of the latter. Illinois leads in both, having 21 Mothers' and 4 Senior Societies. New Hampshire and Pennsylvania each report 3 Senior Societies, and Kansas, 11 Mothers', and Pennsylvania, 7.

These three last branches named, Intermediate, Mothers', and Senior, like the Junior and Young People's, have great promise of power, athrill with life as they are. As the Junior is for the boys and girls, the Intermediate for the lads and lassies, the Young People's for the young men and women, the Christian Endeavor succession graduates into the Mothers' and Seniors. As one pastor says, "It is not too much to hope and predict that the churches will gradually welcome the application of Christian Endeavor principles to all their activities. These principles underlie all Christian work, and by the force of their inherent reasonableness have the right of general application; and the day draws on apace when the Church will foster the Christian Endeavor 'idea' as another method, like unto the Sunday school, subordinate to itself, and will do through it its manifold work."

We have not time to investigate the branches in schools, in colleges; in public institutions of all kinds, in prisons and schools of reform, in almshouses, asylums, institutions for the blind, etc.; on board ships, men-of-war; at navy-yards; in life-stations and among life-savers; among the boys in blue in United States barracks; in large factories; among car-drivers, policemen, and patrolmen; in the Traveller's Union, etc.; but we cannot pass by the growth of the Canadian and foreign branches, for they next attract our admiration. All Canada has 3,292 societies, and in foreign and missionary lands there are now 6,399 societies enrolled. The United Kingdom has over 3,000; Australia, over 2,000; France, 66; West Indies, 63; India, 128; Mexico, 62; Turkey, 41; Africa, 38; China, 40; Germany, 18; Japan, 66; Madagascar, 93; and so on until every country in the world is represented, save three or four, making a grand total of 46,125 branches.

The badge banner, which is given for the *greatest absolute gain* in number of Young People's Societies, can again be carried back to England's shores. Pennsylvania and other States have made a splendid effort to keep it on this side of the "pond;" but it is evident that our brothers and sisters on the other side have a firm grasp upon it.

The banner for the *greatest proportionate* gain in number of societies for the first time crosses the "briny deep" to Scotland's shores. What will another year bring forth? Shall both banners float on the Queen's domains?

But time is passing, and we must cease our counting branches, twigs, and leaves, and get to gathering the fruit from this mighty paradox of God's planting, this tree with mushroom rapidity of growth and the sturdiness and solidity of the oak.

The fruits, what are some of them? Systematic Bible study; circulation of good literature; denominational loyalty intensified; pastors encouraged; Sunday schools enlarged; church services attended; pastorless churches assisted; mid-week prayer meetings sustained; cottage prayer meetings inaugurated; evangelistic services in asylums, almshouses, prisons, reformatories, in factories, in street-car stations, at homes for the aged, the feeble-minded, soldiers' homes, and other public institutions; open-air gospel meetings at wharves and coal-docks, in parks, and at street-corners; gospel wagons employed; public drinking-fountains erected; poor children and mothers given free river, ocean, and car rides; new churches built; old ones repaired; city missions revived; young men preparing for the ministry; Endeavor volunteers for home and foreign missionary fields; more money than ever before given to the cause of home and foreign missions.

And that leads me to make mention of the missionary roll of honor which will be unrolled in our meetings on Friday. Upon it are the names of over 5,869 Young People's Societies and 2,331 Junior Societies from thirty-five States, seven Territories, seven Provinces, four foreign lands. These societies have given $154.022.68 through their own denominational boards to the cause of home and foreign missions. In addition to this amount which has been given by these 8,200 societies that we have enrolled upon the roll of honor, we find that $206.150.21 has been given by these same societies for Christ and the Church in other ways, making a total of $360,172.89, the largest amounts given by any one society being $1.107.01, by the Clarendon Street Baptist Society, of Boston, and a little over $1,000.00, by the Calvary Presbyterian Society, of Buffalo, N. Y.

Let me make it plain that the $154,022.68 given direct to mission boards by the eight thousand societies, and their gifts of $206,150.21 for other benevolences, represent only the record of the societies that have *asked* to be enrolled upon the " missionary roll of honor."

But there is other good fruit, such as open hostility to Sunday baseball-playing and Sunday excursions, whether by bicycle, train, or boat, and every violation of the Sabbath Day; race-track gambling and lotteries antagonized; well-planned Christian-citizenship battles fought at the primaries; aggressive and organized voters' warfare against the saloon; increase of hatred for the entire liquor traffic and its power in the party politics of all nations. Aye, a more intelligent spirit of patriotism has been promoted everywhere. Christian Endeavor believes Bishop Berkeley knew what was needed when he said, years ago, " To be a good patriot, a man must consider his countrymen as God's creatures. and himself as accountable for his acting towards them."

Then another fruit, and a blessed one, has been the growth of our interdenominational fellowship. To have once tasted it is to turn it like a sweet morsel on the tongue. We want nothing to blight it. God has continued to smile upon it, and each year it is expressing itself in new leaf and blossom and bud, as convention after convention, local, district, state, provincial, national, and international, gathers, increases in numbers and spiritual power. Brethren, " forsake not the assembling of yourselves together."

Let us examine the interdenominational fruitage a little more definitely.

In the United States the denominational representation is as follows: The Presbyterians still lead, with 5,458 Young People's Societies and 2,599 Junior Societies; the Congregationalists have 4,109 Young People's Societies and 2,077 Junior Societies; the Disciples of Christ and Christians, 2,941 Young People's Societies and 1,087 Junior Societies; the Baptists, 2,679 Young People's Societies and 927 Junior Societies; Methodist Protestants, 975 Young People's Societies and 302 Junior Societies; Lutherans, 854 Young People's Societies and 268 Junior Societies; Cumberland Presbyterians, 805 Young People's Societies and 289 Junior Societies, and so on through a long list.

In the Dominion of Canada the Methodists of Canada lead, with 1,041 Young People's Societies and 150 Junior Societies (most of the societies known as Epworth Leagues of Christian Endeavor); Canadian Presbyterians are next, with 1,026 Young People's Societies and 134 Junior Societies; Baptists next, with 173 Young People's Societies and 34 Junior Societies; Congregationalists next, with 103 Young People's Societies and 40 Junior Societies, etc.

In the United Kingdom the Baptists lead, with over 900; Congregationalists next, with nearly as many; then the Methodists, with over 700, and the Presbyterians, Episcopalians, Moravians, and Friends, in order named.

In Australia the Wesleyan Methodists lead, and Congregationalists, Baptists, and Presbyterians follow.

Let me refer, in closing, to a prophecy made just ten years ago, by Dr. J. E. Twitchell, of New Haven, Conn: —

" I am no prophet, nor the son of a prophet, but I venture that the 50,000 now composing the Christian Endeavor Society in five years will become

500,000; and I would not be at all surprised if in ten years it should roll *up a round million.* It is Christian, on the right basis, and breathes the true, prophetic life. God has a place for it, and a work for it, and help for it, I am sure. How patriarchal our brother, Dr. Clark, the founder, will feel, ten years hence, if he shall become the foster-father of a million!" Well, Dr. Twitchell, the ten years have passed, and the "round million" has been rolled up, and more, for there is to-day, in the 46,125 societies throughout the world, a total membership of 2,750,000. And the best of it all is that from our Juniors 21,500, and from our Young People's Societies 210,400 have this year joined the churches of America. Praise God for that! *In all, 231,900 have from Christian Endeavor taken their place in the Church of the living God. What a blessed harvest for one year!*

Dr. Charles F. Deems, that sainted friend of our cause, said at the Saratoga Christian Endeavor Convention in 1887, that "things that grow have more intrinsic value than things that are made. Growth is natural; manufacture is artificial. What is manufactured is every moment going to decay. Whatever grows has in itself the seed of its own propagation. The first acorn God made is growing now, mightily multiplied, and spread through millions of its descendant oaks."

Christian Endeavor at that time was but six years old, and Dr. Deems thus early proved by natural reasons that Christian Endeavor germination would continue year after year.

It is because there has been a deepening of the spiritual life that this mustard-seed has waxed a great tree. More and more are its fertilizing evangelistic influences giving birth to new converts, new workers, new soul-savers, under God's guidance.

Yes, the Christian Endeavor tree *grows*. Its tap-root, the active members' pledge, which reaches down into the soil made rich by God's Word, is sending up, growing nearer and nearer to the heavens above, its mighty. sturdy trunk, "For Christ and the Church." And coming from all denominations, all tribes, and all nations, for the fifteenth time we gather under its spreading branches, crowned with a blessed fruitage, and with united heart and voice praise God that "it is a tree planted by the rivers of water, that bringeth forth his fruit in his season."

After Mr. Baer had finished, Dr. Hoyt arose and said : —

Let us express our thanks for the growth of Christian Endeavor as delineated in this report, especially for the winning of so many thousands to Jesus Christ through the Christian Endeavor. When I count three and when I say three, let us all say together loudly and distinctly, "We thank thee, O Lord."

The Convention here arose and said, "We thank thee, O Lord."

DR. HOYT: Some of the things that would have been done in Tent Williston must be done in Tent Washington because of the wind. We are nearly through, but one of the things is the presentation of another banner,— the badge banner for the greatest absolute increase in number of societies during the last twelve months. England had it last year and is to keep it this year. The gentleman who is to receive it is the Rev. Joseph Brown Morgan, the chairman of the British Council of Christian Endeavor.

Remarks of Rev. Joseph Brown Morgan.

My Brothers and Sisters in Christian Endeavor :— I never felt the gracious blessed brotherhood of this movement as I do at the present moment.

On the other side of the herring-pond, about two years back, there was a classic song much sung by the boys in the London streets, and more or less in our provincial cities and towns. I do not know whether you have had that song on this side of the Atlantic. It may be indeed that we got it from you. America has sent us many good things, and the best thing she ever sent us was Christian Endeavor. The sublime refrain of that song is: "He don't know where he are." There have been odd moments this morning when I have been fancying myself back in England. As I look into your faces, as I listen to your song, as I heard the eloquent addresses which have been presented from this platform, I could fancy myself in England. We have the same tongue, that you have. We have the same faith in God. We have the same loyalty to Christian Endeavor. As I stand here, on many accounts I have been fancying myself in England this morning, especially as I heard the rain pelting and pattering down upon the roof. There is a story of an American who once went to Glasgow, and he had there three days of Scotch mist. On the third day he could not stop in the hotel any longer, so he went out to a bootblack, and while he was having his shoes cleaned he said to the boy, " Does it always rain here, my boy?" The boy said, " Naw, it sometimes snaws."

I hope my friends in Pennsylvania, and in the other States, who have been striving so earnestly for this banner during the year, will forgive me this morning for taking it back again to England; but in the Old Country, — that little country which you could just take up and drop into Lake Superior and lose it, — in that Old Country we have advanced a thousand societies during the year, and we have added forty thousand members to the roll of Christian Endeavorers. I wish that we could all have the badge banner. As only one country or State can have it, I am glad we have got it for England. It was an American who wrote these words: —

> " Hugged in the clinging billow's clasp
>   From seaweed fringe to mountain heather,
> The British oak with rooted grasp
>   Her slender handful holds together.
> With cliffs of white, and bowers of green,
>   And ocean narrowing to caress her,
> And hills and threaded streams between,
>   Our little mother isle — God bless her ! "

I am sure that American Endeavorers will echo those words of one of the most genial men who ever trod God's earth, Dr. Oliver Wendell Holmes.

Endeavorers, we need this banner in the Old Country for one year more. I have seen it unfurled from the pulpit where Alexander McLaren preaches in Manchester. I have seen it hung up in the great Metropolitan Tabernacle over the platform from which the saintly Spurgeon preached God to men. It has been floating aloft in our great national assemblies. We have got inspiration and encouragement from it. There are kindly hearts in England to-day toward American, from having gazed in the old land upon that badge banner; and we feel sure, as you send it back with us for another year, that you will send it with your best greetings to England, and with your prayers that God will bless our land in the coming days.

Dr. Hoyt: In the last minute the very best thing of all this morning is coming. In all our Christian Endeavor Conventions there never has been quite such a chorus as we have in Washington, — not quite so large or so well trained, and that is saying a great deal. We are going to have a chance to listen to the chorus in a moment. Let nobody leave, out of respect to the chorus, and because they certainly want to hear its splendid music.

Mr. Foster: I should like to announce the number to be sung by the choir. It is not specially an anthem, but it is written by the secretary of our '96 Committee, and is on page forty-six of the programme. The choir will sing two stanzas, and then we will ask you to sing the third one.

The Convention thereupon adjourned after the benediction by Rev. Canon Richardson, of Canada.

Tent Endeavor.

If the wet and humid weather prevented any of the Christian Endeavorers from going to the great meetings of their Convention, the effect was not visible at Tent Endeavor. As soon as the tent-flaps were raised, shortly after eight o'clock, the Endeavorers began to gather, and those who came early entertained themselves with talking over the great movement in which they were all so deeply interested, and admiring the pretty effect of the decorations, or studying the steady stream of newcomers pouring into the inclosure. The seats were damp, and the clouds that piled up in the west bore promise of more rain. The streamers that stretched from the side flaps of the immense tent to the lofty center poles had lost their brightness in the persistent bath of humidity they had been plunged in for two days, and the atmosphere they swung in was heavy and hot.

The Convention came to order at 9.30 A. M., Rev. Howard B. Grose, of Boston, Mass., presiding, and Mr. E. O. Excell, of Chicago, acting as musical director.

MR. GROSE: We well knew that Washington would give us a warm welcome, but we did not know that they would give us a wet one as well. But we already know one thing: that even though the heavens seem to fall down upon us, you cannot dampen the ardor of a Christian Endeavor Convention.

The devotional exercises were conducted by the Rev. Dr. Jesse B. Colbert, of Washington.

MR. GROSE: The first thing I saw when I came into Washington was that magnificent monument which reminds us all of the first great General and President of our Republic, — the Washington Monument. And as I have gone about the city, I have been everywhere reminded by the statuary of the fact that here we are in the presence of the statues, if not the living persons, of generals. We have present with us this morning, however, one general we might think we could spare, but whose presence we shall have to endure, and that is general humidity. It does not matter whether we stick to him or not, he will stick to us.

I have now the honor of declaring the Fifteenth International Convention of Christian Endeavor open. The District of Columbia, in which we meet, is said to be the best-governed portion of our great country, and I suppose that with the exception of that State from which we come, that statement may be true.

We are now to receive a welcome from the District of Columbia, first from one of its honored commissioners, the Honorable John W. Ross, of Washington, who will now speak to us.

Address of Hon. John W. Ross, Washington, D. C.

The people of the District of Columbia have witnessed many distinguished gatherings within the past decade. They saw the white-plumed Knights Templar march upon the historic avenue by the thousands; the grizzled veterans of the Grand Army of the Republic paraded upon the line of march followed by the survivors of Sherman's army in 1865; then came the Knights of Pythias in grand encampment, and other noted organizations which have deemed it a duty, as well as an honor, to meet once at least in the city which bears the name of Washington. But the capital, in all its experience as a convention city, never before had as its guests thirty thousand young and enthusiastic representatives of such a cause and of such a purpose as that which has brought together these representative American citizens to-day.

I esteem it a great honor to bid you welcome in the name and by the authority of the people of the District of Columbia. It is an especial pleasure to extend a greeting to those of you who have come from other national jurisdictions. Your presence to-day shows that the boundary lines between nations are not barriers to co-operation among those who profess the same faith and who seek to attain the same great result. You are not deemed strangers in a strange land, but friends and brethren in a common cause.

You are gladly and hospitably received because the work in which you are employed has the sympathy and support of those who have faith in the progress and in the uplifting of the human race. Your teachings and your work tend to cultivate the better and the finer elements of our human nature; your purposes and methods call into exercise those forces of the soul of man which find their fittest expression in the worship of the Infinite, whose power and majesty are beyond our ken.

The principles which you profess and the work upon which you strive not only tend to the elevation of individual aims and character, but they are in the direction of good citizenship, and they are for good government. Every municipal officer welcomes such a force and such an influence in the community wherein he is a public servant.

There is another standpoint from which our people extend to you a heartfelt greeting. You are assembled in the only city in all the land to which all of you who are citizens of the United States can come with the same rights and privileges. You may visit the capital of the State of which you may be a citizen, and be inspired with all of the State pride in its greatness and dignity, which is natural and becoming to you when you reflect that in that State capital the laws are made and enforced which protect your rights of person and property; but you would not expect your fellow visitor and Endeavorer from another State to share fully in all of your local State pride. You meet to-day, not only as members of the Christian Endeavor Society, not merely as inhabitants of New York, and Virginia, and Illinois, and Kansas, but as citizens of the United States, gathered together in your own capital city. You are not merely guests and visitors — you are owners and proprietors, whose rights no man may gainsay. In common with all of the people of the United States, you own not only these national public buildings, these beautiful parks and reservations, but also all of the streets and avenues as laid out under the guidance of President George Washington in the original city which bears his name.

How much do you suppose your real-estate holdings in this District are worth in gold or silver dollars, whichever you may prefer? Of course it is difficult to state accurately the value of the land contained in the streets and avenues, but they are estimated to comprise more than one hundred and fifty-seven million square feet, and to be fairly worth two hundred and seventy-eight millions of dollars. Aside from the streets and avenues, the United States owns in the District buildings and grounds carefully estimated to be worth two hundred millions of dollars. In other words, the people of the United States own property here which is worth more than all the property owned by all the taxpayers in the District of Columbia. Very properly, the real-estate holdings of the federal government are not subject to taxation in the manner that that property is taxed which is owned by the people of the District. In 1878 Congress assumed entire control of the local government by means of municipal agents appointed by the President and confirmed by the Senate. This was done in compliance with the clause of the United States Constitution which provides that the Congress shall have power "to exercise exclusive legislation in all cases whatsoever over such district . . . as may . . . become the seat of government of the United States." Since that date no money belonging to the District, or raised by taxation from citizens of the District, can be used for any purpose not specifically authorized by act of Congress.

It was in that year formally enacted as a part of the organic law of the District that the United States should pay one-half of the annual appropriations made for the expenses of the local government, and the District revenues the other half. This was deemed just and equitable, because the United States owns more than one-half of the property, and is not taxed upon it, and because the plan of the city was so vast and extensive, with many streets and avenues one hundred and sixty feet in width, that no local revenues could possibly improve and care for them as befitted the capital of a great republic. Besides, the people of the United States are the direct beneficiaries of the annual appropriations made for the support of the District.

Many thousands of employees of the federal government reside here temporarily. Our public schools are free and open to their children, and to all who may come here to attend them, with free text-books in all of the grades below and including the grammar schools. Our police force guards not only the homes of our taxpayers, but also the property of senators and members, and the Capitol and White House. Our fire department is for the protection of all government property. The money expended to provide good sewerage and an adequate water supply throws safeguards about the health and the well-being of your public servants in the White House, at the Capitol, and in the great departments of the government. It is needless to attempt to prove that expenditures for keeping the streets and alleys clean and wholesome, and for keeping our seventy thousand shade-trees in proper condition, are not wholly for the benefit of the people who permanently reside here. Whatever tends to adorn and beautify, and fit to be a healthful residence, the capital city of the United States ought to appeal to the sense of justice and to the patriotic pride of the representative of every congressional district in the United States. It is the city lately referred to on the floor of the Senate by an eloquent senator from Missouri as "the eternal city of an eternal republic." They who are now associated with its fortunes and its management will soon pass away and be forgotten; but the Republic will survive forever, and its "eternal capital" should reflect its perennial lustre.

I have ventured to bring the cause of the District of Columbia into this presence and before this representative body of American citizens because we are without direct representation on the floors of Congress. Our representatives ought to be and are the senators and representatives who are accredited by you and by your fellow citizens from all the States of the Union. We believe that you will agree with us that, although we are voiceless in the halls of Congress, the end we seek to attain, namely, a model municipality in every phase of growth and development at the capital, is your cause as well as ours. When Washington founded this city, on the shore of the great river which winds its way to the sea by the sacred spot where his maturer years were passed and where his ashes now repose, it was his hope and his belief that the city so founded would surpass all other national capitals in beauty and in grandeur.

Surely no representative of this great people can win lasting popular renown by seeking to hinder or to mar that manifest destiny of his own national capital.

I will not delay your important deliberations by more extended remarks. We are all Endeavorers here this week. We will endeavor to show by our kindly acts and by courteous attention, rather than by our words, how cordial and sincere our greeting is intended to be. When the work of your Convention shall have ended, and you shall have journeyed to your homes, may you have with you in perpetual memory only fragrant and agreeable recollections of your great Convention of '96, and of the hospitality of the people of Washington.

Rev. S. H. Greene, D.D., pastor of Calvary Baptist Church, was next introduced to speak a word of welcome for the city pastors.

Address of Rev. S. H. Greene, D.D., Washington, D. C.

Mr. Chairman and Fellow Endeavorers: — I have been honored with the privilege of extending the Christian salutations and cordial greetings of the pastors of this city to you, now assembled in your Fifteenth International Convention. We rejoice in your coming; we bid you a glad and hearty welcome.

We welcome you to our broad avenues, beautiful streets, hospitable homes, historic buildings, venerable institutions of learning, and localities fragrant with the memory of the nation's great men, from "the Father of His Country" to the present time.

We welcome you to our churches, which are neither few nor insignificant; to the centres of thought and labor, where Christian men and women have toiled these many years with no small success; to an atmosphere of spiritual fellowship and love seldom surpassed; to a great and important field still "white for the harvest."

We welcome you to the privilege, with God's help, of contributing to the spiritual forces at the nation's capital, till from yonder Executive Mansion, halls of Congress, to the smallest department of the government's work, there shall be recognized and honored that "righteousness" which exalts a nation, and is in itself the assurance of divine watch, care, and love.

We welcome you in the glad remembrance that we are one in Christ Jesus; that here no undue emphasis will be laid on latitude, language, sect, or condition of any who bow at the feet of the Crucified, worshipping Him who "hath made of one blood all nations of men for to dwell on all the face of the earth."

Brothers of the continents beyond, and of the isles of the sea, I salute you! Welcome, thrice welcome to these western shores, this beautiful capital, these inspiring services, our hearts and homes.

This welcome is uttered in the remembrance that you are individually the active, loyal representatives of the younger portion of the Christian churches,— not a disaffected, disintegrating element, but living, loving members of that Church for which our Lord gave himself. The record of your fidelity and success is written in the marvelous history of the recent past. God breathed upon the churches, and lo! a mighty inspiration came, and an element hitherto largely overlooked in active work was wheeled into line and led forth to magnificent service. Enthusiasm, thoughtfulness, efficiency, marked its movement, till, like the perfume of flowers, it drifted beyond the garden walls and sweetened all Christian work.

It aimed to assist in saving the lost and developing the saved, and the endeavor has been signally blessed. Without the betrayal of denominational loyalty it has cultivated that spirit of fraternity among the churches which becomes the Gospel, and makes co-operation possible in advancing the kingdom of Christ among men. A most happy illustration of this is seen in the history of the movement in the District of Columbia. Its beautiful impress is to-day upon the young men and women who are the hope of the churches. No pastor can be more indebted for its sweet, inspiring helpfulness than myself.

We welcome you in the expectation that from this fraternal gathering, this communion of spirit, this interchange of experience, this search for truth, this union of prayer, there may come to us all a larger revelation to God, a clearer conception of his will concerning us, a higher consecration to his service.

May there come to us here such a broadening of the intellectual horizon, such a deepening of the spiritual life, such a strengthening of spiritual fellowship, as befits the disciples of our risen Lord. The week before us is great with spiritual possibilities, world-wide blessings. I pray you, let neither the attractions of this fair city nor the pleasures of social intercourse shut from your minds for one hour the great purpose for which we are gathered.

We welcome you, therefore, with the sincere prayer that this Convention at the national capital may be a Pentecostal scene; that here you may be "endued with power from on high;" that you may return to your homes and churches impressed with the fact that here you have been face to face with the Master himself, until you comprehended his purpose, drank in his spirit, shared in his power. Then across this great continent to those beyond, and to the isles of the sea, there will come a blessing immeasurable in the strengthening of God's people and the salvation of the lost. Then amid the labor, sacrifice, and hope there will come a broader emphasis on that petition taught by our Lord, "Thy kingdom come," and we shall rejoice in the signs of his approach, "whom having not seen we love."

MR. GROSE: Now that you have seen and heard Dr. Greene, I can say that he is one of the most honored and successful pastors of this capital city; and not only that, but through the years he has been one of the most loyal friends and truest workers in behalf of Christian Endeavor.

Now there will be a response, on behalf of the United Society, from one of its trustees, Professor W. W. Andrews, who comes to us from Sackville, N. B. He comes to us from across the border, but I don't know of any more loyal-hearted American, hence loyal-hearted Christian Endeavorer, than Professor Andrews.

Address of Prof. W. W. Andrews, Sackville, N. B.

I think myself happy, most worthy Chairman, that I am permitted this day to answer to these cordial addresses of welcome on behalf of our assembled millions from almost every clime under heaven. I am delighted to-day, seeing that I am a British-Canadian-American, to answer addresses of welcome from two great citizens of these United States, the heaven and the haven of the oppressed the world over.

I am delighted that a welcome has come to it from the District of Columbia, to me the most sacred place in the whole United States.

The sacred memories of your nation gather round Plymouth Rock. The foot of Providence struck Plymouth Rock three hundred years ago, but the feet of Providence,— in this place where the voice of the people becomes articulate in the laws and statutes according to which your law-abiding millions shall walk,— the feet of Providence walk to-day in the District of Columbia. And as I have walked around this city and gazed upon the White House, the Capitol, and the other public buildings, I have been disappointed in them, as I was disappointed in looking upon our Canadian-American Niagara for the first time.

But there is one thing in which I was not disappointed, whose presence haunts me even through the hours of the night, and that is that plain, simple, magnificent shaft pointing heavenward, whose presence overshadows us, to me the symbol of what Christian Endeavor is,— not a great organization, but a simple cause, a great movement, pointing heavenward.

I am happy to reply to the addresses of welcome in behalf of what we are now being accustomed to look upon as the most advanced group in economic organization, the most advanced group of Anglo-Saxon people on the face of the earth,— the people of Australia. I reply to-day on behalf of the teeming millions of India, where the multiplex populations are gradually being educated so that they may be ready for future self-government. I reply to-day for the great Dominion of Canada, whose length from Queen Charlotte Island to the eastern coast of Cape Breton is over 1,200 miles longer than the distance from San Francisco to New York,— a dominion great enough to take in the whole present population of the United States and plant them all upon land in which the flowers bloom early in May.

We are working out our own destinies. I reply to-day on behalf of this great group of confederated republics, the colonies of the British Empire; for let me disabuse your minds of one misconception which I find everywhere. I am not ruled by the Queen of England. I love her; I sing " God Save the Queen ; " but the Queen of England has not power to say to me, " Walk six feet, and walk back again." She can only say that to the servants in her own house. Only the people of Canada rule me !

And now the Anglo-Saxon people, wherever they are found, are marked by these great characteristics. We say we carry ourselves in such a way that all other nations think we want the earth, and Anglo-Saxon people, whether under the Union Jack or the Stars and Stripes, all have a marvelous faculty of thinking that they are right and everybody else is wrong. Anglo-Saxon people are marked by this characteristic : that we hold so tenaciously to our own language and to our own customs that we are the only group of people in the world that can not be colonized by other nationalities. And therefore, seeing we have these characteristics, it means much for the future of the world whether our hearts are one for Christ or not, and whether Christianity becomes supreme in our midst.

But as things stand to-day, it is this : wherever Anglo-Saxon government and civilization go, there good government goes ; there property becomes safe; there justice becomes a fact; there political freedom becomes a great reality, whether it be in Egypt or Hawaii; whether it be in South Africa or Alaska; whether it be in Venezuela or Cuba.

Christ said to his Church, " Go ye into all the world and preach the gospel to every creature." Through the centuries he has been saying to his people, " March! March!" Now, in these latter days, he is saying to his people, through Christian Endeavor, "Quick march! Go! Go quickly, and evangelize the world for Jesus Christ!" It used to be said that the blood of all the martyrs was the seed of the Church. Now it is the consecration of the blood of young hearts that is the hope of the Church.

And may God grant that abroad through the land this Society, this movement, teaching its millions of members to serve Christ faithfully, and to do whatever he would have them do, may spread and become triumphant everywhere !

Secretary Baer was then introduced to read his report, as he was expected to read it in Tent Washington ; when half way through it, Treasurer Shaw was introduced and finished reading the report.

Then Mr. Ira D. Sankey was invited to sing, and he did so to the manifest enjoyment of the vast audience.

Mr. W. H. Pennell, the first signer of the first Christian Endeavor pledge, was also introduced and heartily greeted. The presentation of the Junior badge banner to the State union having made the greatest absolute gain in number of societies was the next upon the programme.

MR. GROSE: Look upon this Junior banner. Professor Andrews told you that the Anglo-Saxons want the earth. They seem to be getting good deal of it. The Pennsylvanians want this Junior banner. They ought to have been satisfied with holding it twice, and some other State ought to be immensely dissatisfied that it has not taken it away this year.

Dr. McCrory, of Pennsylvania, who will now receive this banner for his State for the third time, has had to make so many acceptation speeches that if he were any other man, I do not know how he could have anything fresh to say. But he is always fresh.

Remarks of Rev. J. T. McCrory, D.D.

I simply have to say that this is getting monotonous. I do not mean the rain; I mean this taking the Junior banner back. I want to say to New York, and Illinois, and Great Britain, and all Europe that we would like to have them take this banner. It is too much like a family Christmas all to one's self, where there is only one man in the family. It seems to me we might have something a good deal more interesting. Why, it would be more interesting than this if a husband would some day, after his wife had given him a first-class meal, just hand her over a pocket-book and say to her, " Wife, you go down-town and get just the most beautiful diamond ring you can find, just such a ring as you think I would like to give to the most beautiful woman in the world." Why, it would be more interesting on Christmas morning, a great deal more interesting, if the wife had gone and bought that ring and had handed it over to her husband, and on Christmas morning he should hand it over to some other man's wife. It would be a great deal more interesting. So next year we want to hand this over to some other man's wife. But we do not propose to quit organizing Christian Endeavor Junior Societies.

Let me say just one thing in favor of the Juniors. I was at a State convention not very long ago, and the Junior rally was held, and when they were about through I was talking to them, and I said, " How many of this Convention can repeat the Christian Endeavor pledge? Stand up and repeat it." And the older Endeavorers remained silent, but the Juniors stood up in a body, and every one of them repeated the Christian Endeavor pledge.

Thank the Lord for the Juniors, and especially that they learn the pledge. Learn the pledge, and work for Junior Endeavorers, and come next year with more Junior Societies organized than Pennsylvania has, and we will be glad to give you this banner.

MR. GROSE: And here is the second of the Junior banners. This one is given for the greatest proportionate increase of Junior Societies. It was held last year by Assiniboia, as you have already heard. It goes this next year to Mexico. It goes from the far North into the South, and still across one of those imaginary lines that may form a political division, but in Christian Endeavor forms no division at all of heart and service.

Is Mr. Peter Grant present to receive this banner on behalf of Mexico? Mr. Grant does not seem to be present; therefore we will have no response this morning on behalf of Mexico; but we will see to it that Mexico gets the banner that her Christian Endeavorers have so nobly won.

Fifteen years ago there was a minister of God away up in Portland, Me., who sought for the right kind of a young people's society until he found it; and to-day the world honors him as the founder of Christian Endeavor.

Dr. Clark will now present to you his annual address. Now of course you all want to hear Dr. Clark, and he wants you to hear; but you will bear in mind that already, in another of the great tents, he has delivered this address. It is almost more of a strain than any human voice can bear to repeat such an address, and if you find at any point that his voice begins to fail him a little, and he needs a bit of rest, give him a chance to take a sip of water, and you just applaud until he has the chance.

Dr. Clark then read his report, which has already been printed. After singing " Loyal Soldiers," the meeting adjourned with the Mizpah benediction.

THURSDAY AFTERNOON.

DENOMINATIONAL RALLIES.

For the Church.

If the Convention as a whole abounded in illustrations of the inter-denominational fellowship of Christian Endeavor, the overflowing denominational rallies on Thursday afternoon gave a striking object-lesson on the twin principle of denominational loyalty. The Presbyterians took possession of Tent Endeavor. The action of the last General Assembly was the leading topic, and after the report of the committee appointed last year to confer with the Assembly's committee, the following resolution was passed : —

The delegates to the Fifteenth International Christian Endeavor Convention, assembled at our Presbyterian rally, representing the 5,458 Young People's Societies of Christian Endeavor and the 2,599 Junior Societies of our church, would recognize gratefully the action of our General Assembly at Saratoga with reference to Young People's Societies. We heartily and thoroughly indorse the statement therein made as to the relation of our societies to the Church, and of the duties and objects of these organizations.

MEN'S MEETING IN TENT WASHINGTON.

INTERIOR OF A TENT AT THE OPENING SESSION.

THE OPEN-AIR PATRIOTIC SONG SERVICE. CHORUS OF 4,600 VOICES UPON THE CAPITOL STEPS.

An elaborate programme had been prepared for the Baptists, who filled Tent Washington. Strictly limiting the time of the speakers made it possible to hear from a large number of leading pastors, who treated brightly and forcibly different phases of the Society's fitness to meet the Church's present special needs.

The Congregationalists, too, followed the plan of having many very brief addresses, in which the history and principles of the denomination were reviewed in their bearing on the solution of religious, political, and social problems.

The Disciples had a large and enthusiastic gathering, at which, besides other addresses, a summary of the reports of the denominational State superintendents was given by the national superintendent, Rev. J. Z. Tyler, D.D.

The Christians listened to interesting accounts of incidents connected with the extension of Christian Endeavor work.

The Methodist Protestants received cheering reports from the officers of their national union, and awarded Texas their banner for the greatest proportionate increase in membership. Unanimous approval was given a suggestion of a course in church history for Junior Societies.

The Methodists of the United States and Canada discussed the action to be taken in view of the relations between Methodism and Christian Endeavor, and spoke of the excellent results to be gained by the Canadian plan of Epworth Leagues of Christian Endeavor.

Christian citizenship was the topic of the African Methodist Episcopal assembly, and freedom of the soul was pointed out as the chief essential of a good citizen. The African Methodist Episcopal Zion Endeavorers bore witness to the good points of the societies among them.

A missionary flavor marked the rally of the Reformed Church in America, as work among the Indians, in Japan, and in India was reported.

Statements of the best points in their different Endeavor Societies were made by the delegates of the Reformed Church in the United States. The gifts of the societies during the year included the fulfilment of a pledge for a fund for church-building.

The work among the Free Baptists was reported by representatives of different sections, and support of the denominational paper was urged.

Greetings from the Luther League were received by the Lutherans, who heard from their secretary a report of growth during the past year. The harmony between the principles of Christian Endeavor and the denomination were set forth in addresses, which were followed by an open parliament.

The Cumberland Presbyterians in the interests of denominational loyalty adopted a resolution declaring their opposition to any change in the form of organization of the United Society.

The Canadian Presbyterians passed a vote expressing hearty thanks to their General Assembly for its generous recognition of Christian Endeavor, and affirming their continued loyalty.

The Southern Presbyterians reviewed the past of their church, especially in regard to missionary activity, and considered the work lying before them in the immediate future.

Testimony to the value of the Society was heartily given by United Presbyterians, and its power as a bond of unity was emphasized.

The Reformed Presbyterians found cheer in looking to the promise of the future, to be realized through the agency of the Society.

Open parliaments dealing with methods of meeting difficulties, together with addresses on giving and missions, formed a large part of the programme of the United Evangelical Church, who discussed the interests of the Keystone League of Christian Endeavor.

The Friends' denominational Christian Endeavor president, in his annual report, recommended increased organization, special courses of Bible study, and the appointment of a missionary to extend the Junior work.

The United Brethren had music by the Christian Endeavor choir of the church where they met, and the Junior Society conducted the last part of the meeting. Among the addresses was one on the best reading for young people.

Many of the benefits of Christian Endeavor had been discovered in its practical application among the Mennonites, as many speakers bore witness.

Those Episcopalians that had tried Christian Endeavor were loud in its praise, and were urgent for its further extension in their churches, as its two principles of work and prayer are essential to every church.

The highest ideal and the individual's mission in the church were topics brought before the Reformed Episcopalians, who closed their rally with a consecration service.

The good of organization and the need of it, especially in country places, were urged in the rally of the Church of God, and Christian Endeavor's fitness to meet the need was pointed out.

Reports as to increase in membership, missionary gifts, and evangelistic work told of the prosperity and earnestness of the Moravian Societies.

_____

Successful and enthusiastic gatherings were held by the German and Welsh Societies, at which the music was a prominent feature.

_____

THURSDAY EVENING.

Under two mammoth tents, in half a dozen churches, and within one of the great halls of the city, thousands of Christian Endeavorers gathered to raise songs of praise to God, and to listen to addresses by distinguished speakers on the duties of Christian citizenship. For the first time the skies did not even threaten rain, and the evening was cool and pleasant. For the first time the great throng of Endeavorers could give themselves to the full enjoyment of the meeting, and even on the street-cars choruses of well-trained voices would burst forth in well-known Christian Endeavor hymns.

Metropolitan M. E. Church.

The meeting which was to have been held at Tent Williston took place instead at the Metropolitan M. E. Church, which was not large enough to accommodate anything like the number of people that sought admission.

The principal feature of the evening was an address by President Booker T. Washington, of the Tuskegee Institute of Alabama. Dr. Washington is the colored man who so electrified an audience at the Atlanta Exposition last year by his eloquence, and at a bound leaped into public fame as an orator and as an exponent of the needs of his race.

The meeting was presided over by President Francis E. Clark, D.D., and after a service of song under the leadership of Mr. E. O. Excell, and the opening devotional exercises, a double quartet from Hampton Institute sang several times with telling effect.

A letter of greeting from Hon. Neal Dow was then read by Rev. Rufus W. Miller, of Reading, Pa., founder of the Brotherhood of Andrew and Philip, and a trustee of the United Society.

Letter from Hon. Neal Dow, Portland, Me.

PORTLAND, June 25, 1896.

Mr. JOHN WILLIS BAER: —

Dear Sir,—I am very sorry that my strength will not warrant me in undertaking the long journey to Washington to assist in the great work of the Endeavorers. They are now a great power in this country, and every year will increase their influence and force among those of our people who wish to increase the prosperity of the nation and the welfare and happiness of the people's homes. I earnestly desire that the Endeavorers will boldly resist everything that is inconsistent with the general welfare, boldly opposing it as opposed to the will of God, with no thought of any evil consequences to self. At the same time I wish them to stand up for the right without fear from any quarter. I say this because I fear that many well-meaning men shrink from any open help to a good cause lest they suffer from the enmity of bad men who may have power to do them an injury by boycott or otherwise. There is one matter to which I will especially call their attention, because they can aceomplish an infinite good without fear of any one when engaged in God's work.

The liquor traffic is a far greater evil to all civilized countries than any other by which the world is cursed; its suppression would be a benefit and blessing to the nations and to the people — greater than any other that is occupying public attention. I believe that the overthrow of this great sin against God, this great crime against the country, may be accomplished by the Endeavorers. To do this requires the courage which they have, their great numbers rapidly increasing, and a cordial co-operation with each other. Perhaps the Endeavorers may be startled if I say that the continuance of the liquor traffic, with all its horrors, largely depends upon them. That is what I think, but I hope and believe that it will not long continue to be so. The issue of the *Christian at Work* of the 29th of October, 1891, said: —

"The liquor traffic exists in this country to-day only by sufferance of the membership of the Christian churches. They are masters of the situation, so far as the abolition of the traffic is concerned. When they say, ' Go, and vote, go;' it will go." This whole question of the perpetual nuisance of the saloons, or their speedy overthrow, is a question of the ballot alone. Is that averment just and true, or is it a mistake? Does the liquor traffic depend for its existence upon the membership of the Church, or only upon the worst elements of society?

It is said that the Protestant church-members who are voters in this country are at least 5,000,000 in number. If that be true, it may be honestly said that the continuance of that great sin, shame, crime, and infamy depends upon the permission of the church membership, because their ballots, honestly employed, may easily destroy the grog-shops promptly.

In a sermon of the late Dr. Payson, entitled "Participation in Other Men's Sins," he says: "Members of civil communities partake of all the sins which they might, but do not, prevent. When a person has power to prevent any sin, he is left to choose whether that sin shall or shall not be committed. If he neglects to prevent it, it is evident that he chooses it should be committed, and by thus choosing he has in effect made it his own."

That that is true no intelligent person can deny. In Dr. Payson's day there was no preacher in the country who held a higher position in the pulpit. Christian Endeavorers, protest against the continuance of the liquor traffic. There is no other way in which that can possibly be done except through the ballot-box. He who knows the right, and does it not, to him it is sin.

NEAL DOW.

After the reading of Mr. Dow's letter, which was received with applause, President Clark introduced President Booker T. Washington. At the request of Dr. Washington, we do not print his address.

First Congregational Church.

The Christian citizenship meeting at the First Congregational Church was preceded by a song service, under the direction of Dr. F. J. Woodman, of Washington, and participated in by the choirs of the Central Presbyterian, Fifth Congregational, and Fifteenth Street Presbyterian Churches.

Rev. M. M. Binford, of Richmond, Ind., one of the trustees of the United Society, presided over the meeting, and after a Scripture lesson, in which the congregation joined, Rev. James E. Mason, of Rochester, N. Y., led in prayer.

Mrs. Ruth B. Baker, of Boston, Secretary of the Massachusetts Woman's Christian Temperance Union, was the first speaker introduced.

Address of Mrs. Ruth B. Baker, Boston, Mass.

Why do we believe that temperance reform has anything to do with Christian citizenship? Surely none need ask this question when we recall more than one shameful instance of the false representation of Christianity abroad, by our government appointing ministers or consuls who have been the centre of drunken brawls; when again and again our missionaries report that the heathen have compared our religion unfavorably with theirs, because they never drink and people whom they regard as Christians, because coming from Christian lands, *do*.

Can we ask what claim the temperance reform has upon Christian citizens when we remember the record of the past ten years, or more, on the Congo?— the years since the Berlin West African Conference?

If you are not familiar with the history, read " Free Rum on the Congo," by Mr. W. T. Hornaday. Canon Farrar, about the same time, spoke with no uncertain sound in England, and declared the present curse of the liquor traffic far more deadly than the old curse of the slave trade. At least you will remember how these words have been emphasized in years gone by by the pathetic appeals of the native chiefs and rulers to keep out the drink, and none of you who saw him can have forgotten Dr. John G. Paton, when only two or three years ago he was forced to leave his work in the South Sea Islands to come to plead with England's Queen and the President of this great and noble country, to use his own language, to prohibit the exportation of firearms and intoxicating liquors that threatened to destroy the fruit of all his years of labor among his beloved Islanders. I heard him plead in the name of the dear Lord Jesus that Christians would all unite to petition our government to act in this matter.

When we remember the effects in our own land of this gigantic evil, we cannot question whether there be any relation between the temperance reform and Christian citizenship.

All Christendom has been thrilled with horror on account of the Armenian atrocities. We have felt faint and sick as we have read of the horrible deeds committed, and they are too dreadful to repeat unnecessarily. But have you thought that intemperance causes just such suffering; that the worst that is pictured of Turkey is fully paralleled by the drink curse; that the atrocities are not less frightful, nor the awful aggregate less?

Our working people throw away every year $750,000,000 for liquor. It empties our churches; it fills our prisons and insane asylums; it brings sorrow and misery to the homes of rich and poor alike; it carries thousands to an untimely grave; it mocks at and frustrates all our efforts to Christianize the heathen. In the great sum total of misery and suffering and all forms of evil that go to compose the great mountain of sin, that is some day to become a plain, the liquor traffic is responsible for by far the greatest proportion.

We covet the active interest of the millions of Christian Endeavorers against this monster evil, and we call on you as Christian citizens to say what you will do to help in the battle for humanity.

Wellington said at Waterloo, "We want young soldiers!" We want you, young men, because you are strong; we want the young ladies, whose influence is no less strong, to show in no uncertain way that you are always and forever against the perpetuity of this great evil that so affects the happiness of thousands in this state and national, if not private, home of ours.

We want you to stand for temperance reform as you stand for missions.
First, for your own sakes you should become a total abstainer. I know many
young people think that they can indulge in an occasional glass of wine without
injury, and that they can let it alone if they wish; but there is something in the
power of the wine-cup that can best be defined by the word "deceit." "Whosoever
is deceived thereby is not wise." I believe the only absolute safety for any one
before me is *total abstinence*. But if you are absolutely sure in your own mind
that there is no danger for you, will you not sign the pledge because of your
brother?

Last year, I saw a beautiful object-lesson in London, at the meeting of the
World's Women's Christian Temperance Union. In the crowded Royal Albert
Hall, from an entrance at the rear of the platform, came fifty or more of the
children of the slums, dressed just as we see them in any of our large cities, the
only difference being in their cleanliness. There were tall, lank girls with
babies in their arms; there were thin, pinched, hungry-looking faces, and they
all looked, oh, so sad and sorrowful! As they came to the front of the platform
in the brightly lighted hall, and stood before the richly dressed throng, they
began to sing: —

> " There 's a shadow on the home,
>   Many hearts are sad to-day;
> It hushes e'en the laughter of the
>   Children at their play.
> At its coming, want and sorrow
>   Across the threshold creep,
> And amid their broken idols
>   The mourning mothers weep."

As these words were sung the doors at the front opened, and hundreds of
children from more favored homes, clad in white and holding aloft a broad
white ribbon, entered two by two, singing,—

> " We are coming to the rescue,'' etc.,

and as they finished the first verse they halted in front of the platform. Again
rose the sweet, pathetic voices of the children of the slums :—

> " There 's an evil in the land,
>   And the kingdom of the Lord
>   Is hindered in its coming," etc.,

and then the white-robed children in front, commencing once more the joyful
strain,

> " We are coming to the rescue,"

divided, coming up the stairs each side of the platform, and surrounded again
and again with the white ribbon the poor little waifs that stood there. Those
who saw it will never forget the sight. Will you not join that rescuing army,
and use your utmost endeavor to banish this evil and this sorrow from the
world? At least say, " I will stand upon my watch, and set me upon the tower,
and will watch to see what he will say unto me" in reference to this temperance reform and my duty and responsibility as a Christian citizen.

Miss May Levers, of Washington, sang effectively " The Holy City,"
and then the presiding officer stated that it is necessary for Christian
workers to mass their forces. " In this city not so very many years ago,"
he continued, " millions of our fellow citizens were set free by a single
stroke of the pen. We have with us this evening," next said the
presiding officer, " one of that race who has honored our conventions
heretofore by appearing on its programme and who is also a member
of the Board of Trustees of the United Society. I take great pleasure
in presenting to you Bishop Alexander Walters, D.D., of Jersey City,
N. J."

Bishop Walters was warmly received, and he announced the topic assigned to be " The Need of Christian Citizenship in Municipal, State, and National Affairs."

Address of Bishop Alexander Walters, D.D., Jersey City, N. J.

Solomon declared centuries ago that " when the righteous are in authority, the people rejoice : but when the wicked beareth rule, the people mourn." This truth is as applicable to-day in our land as it was in the land of Palestine in the days of the wise king.

Great intellectual, spiritual, moral, and material progress was made by the Israelites of old under the leadership of Moses, Joshua, Samuel, David, Solomon, Hezekiah, and others. On the other hand, Israel and Judah were wasted and blasted, suffered defeats and humiliations, and were finally carried away into captivity because of the sins of their wicked rulers. When Ahab said to Elijah, " Art thou he that troubleth Israel?" the prophet answered, " I have not troubled Israel; but thou, and thy father's house, in that ye have forsaken the commandments of the Lord."

We read in the Scriptures that Jeroboam made Israel to sin; that is, he opened wide the flood-gates of idolatry and used all his kingly influence and authority to keep them open. None of his successors was able to stem the tide of wickedness which was inaugurated during his reign. It is surprising how much evil a wicked ruler can bring about.

Rome reached her lowest point of infamy and degradation during the reign of Nero. No crime was too great, no sin too heinous, for him to commit. He encouraged all manner of debauchery, and as a result plunged his entire realm into an abyss of public disgrace. His name is a synonym for wickedness, and his reign a history of cruelty and bloodshed.

About the close of the seventeenth century the rulers of France declared for infidelity, in consequence of which she had a " Reign of Terror."

The morals of the English nation were at a low ebb during the reign of the licentious king, Henry the Eighth.

The endorsement of slavery by our rulers was the occasion of confusion and bitter strife, which finally deluged our land with blood, depleted our treasury, and desolated our homes. Indeed, the baneful effects of that accursed institution are being felt even to this day.

A wise ruler is of incalculable benefit to a nation. We have an example of this in our mother country, England. She has enjoyed marvelous progress in her commerce, institutions of learning, political influence, and ecclesiastical affairs during the reign of her wise and virtuous Queen, Victoria. Indeed, England's prosperity and achievements have been phenomenal since her accession to the throne.

When that fair-minded, liberty-loving giant, Abraham Lincoln, was elected President of these United States, the South seceded from the Union, for she believed that his election meant the overthrow of slavery. Her fears were well founded. His very soul revolted against oppression and wrong, therefore he could only act in harmony with the principles of right which governed him. The righteous cause espoused by him gained adherents so rapidly that in a few years he was enabled to emancipate the slaves.

Some of our large cities have been blessed with wise and just rulers. Such cities enjoyed great peace and prosperity during their incumbency. Wickedness was checked, and in many cases some forms of it destroyed. For instance, in New York City, where that abominable organization known as Tammany Hall held sway for many years, and whose power was so formidable that it seemed impossible to overthrow it. But when Christian men and women, stimulated by Rev. Charles H. Parkhurst and other ministers of New York, rose in their might and took as their slogan of victory, " Down with Tammany ! " Tammany went down; for they not only raised the cry, " Down with Tammany ! " but pulled off their coats, went to work, and continued to work until they overthrew that wicked organization. My only regret is that it was not utterly destroyed.

Christians are too ready to retire to their tents after a flushing victory. They forget the prophet's warning to Ahab after he had routed Ben-hadad. He said to him, " Go, strengthen thyself, and mark (watch), and see what thou doest: for at the return of the year the king of Syria will come up against thee." Be assured your enemy will return again to renew the attack; get ready for him. Eternal vigilance must be our watchword.

If Christian citizens expect to win, there must be no lagging in the ranks, no indifference on their part, no letting-up on the enemy. Our foes are ever on the alert, ever watchful; after every defeat they resolve to renew the attack.

If the question were asked, "How can we make good citizens?" I would reply, " First, by Christian homes; second, by a spiritual and patriotic Church; third, by efficient and patriotic public schools; fourth, by good-citizenship leagues; fifth, by voting as we pray."

In no place can the principles of Christian citizenship be so effectually taught as in the home. In order to have Christian citizens we must have Christian homes, where the father believes and trusts in God, and the mother is imbued with the Spirit of Christ; where the Bible is read and studied, prayer offered, and patriotism taught. The ablest and best men of the world were trained in religious homes. It was said of the mother of General Grant that her home was a fitting nursery for heroes, because religion, patriotism, industry, economy, and temperance were taught and practised there. It was patriotic home-training that made William Lloyd Garrison a courageous agitator of the rights of humanity. Methodism owes an inestimable debt of gratitude to Susannah Wesley for the splendid religious training of her two sons, the founders of Methodism ; and wherever this church exists her influence is felt.

We need more homes where patriotic songs are sung, where children are taught to love our grand institutions, to honor the Stars and Stripes, and to respect our rulers ; where the principles of temperance and good government are inculcated. Out from such homes will go forth worthy citizens. Character and intelligence are the true foundations of citizenship.

The need of the hour is more and better religious training in the home. If our children are taught to observe the rules of home, there will be no trouble about their obeying the laws of the land.

An important factor in the formation of Christian citizens is a live and patriotic church; a church all aglow with the Spirit of Christ; where not only the doctrines of salvation are taught, but where the principles of good government are proclaimed, sermons preached on state and national issues of the day, and the duties of man to man set forth. Such a church was old Plymouth, in Brooklyn, N. Y., in her palmy days under Henry Ward Beecher. It was said that no one could enter Plymouth Church and remain through a service without being impressed with the thought that it is the duty of Christians to aid the unfortunate and oppressed. The very atmosphere breathed love and the rights of humanity.

In the olden times the Church and State were one. Abraham was not only the head of the Hebrew nation, but the head of the Hebrew Church. While we do not believe in the matter in that particular form, we do believe that every department of our government should be controlled by the principles of Christianity. Christ has given to the Church the ideal standard of man's duty to his fellow man. Hear it! "Whatsoever ye would that men should do unto you, do ye even so to them."

The Church was established to ameliorate the condition of mankind. It is here we teach men and women faith in the Lord Jesus Christ and faith in each other.

It was the Church that gave to the world a Moses, a Solomon, a Paul, Luther, Calvin, Knox, Wesley, Edwards, Beecher, and other great leaders and thinkers, such as Frederick of Saxony, Gladstone, Newton, Douglass, etc.

For centuries the torch of civilization has been borne aloft by the Church, and the world has and is being benefited by the influence radiating therefrom. It is the light of the Church that is to dispel the darkness of ignorance, superstition, and doubt.

Another essential factor in the making of loyal and intelligent citizens is good public schools. If we would have intelligent voters throughout the nation we must have good schools in the rural districts as well as in the cities. In some sections of our country the public schools are open only two or three months in the year; this is notably so in nearly all the Southern States. Strenuous efforts must be made to correct this error. Each State ought to appropriate enough money to keep all the public schools open at least six months in the year, and nine months if possible. The great mass in the Black Belt is thirsting for knowledge; their cry is, "Give us more schools and longer terms." The greatest blessing that could come to the Afro-American in the South is further aid along educational and industrial lines, and a fair chance to be whatever in the providence of God he is capable of being by intelligence, diligence, and frugality.

As a race, we are accused of not being intelligent voters. If we are not, the fault is not altogether our own; as yet we have not had a fair chance. Give us a sufficient number of schools, competent instructors, and longer school terms, and there will not be much ground for complaint of our incompetency as voters.

The lamented Bishop Haygood, of Georgia, made the following statement a few years ago: "The illiterate vote of our Southern States is simply appalling, and this illiterate vote is increasing. From 1870 to 1880 there was an increase of illiterate voters in the Southern States of nearly two hundred thousand. In Georgia the illiterate white vote in 1870 was 21,899; in 1880, 28,571. The negro illiterate vote in 1870 was 100,551; in 1880, 116,517. The white illiterate vote in Kentucky, in 1870, was 43,826; in 1880, 54,966. The negro illiterate vote was, in 1870, 37,849; in 1880, 45,177. In Tennessee the white illiterate vote was, in 1870, 37,713; in 1880, 46,948. The negro illiterate vote was, in 1870, 55,958; in 1880, 58,601. In Texas, in 1870, the white illiterate vote was 17,505; in 1880, 33,085. The negro illiterate vote in 1870 was 47,235; in 1880, 59,609." The increase of illiteracy from 1880 to 1890 was nearly as great in those States.

We appeal to the President and Congress; we appeal to our Governors and State Legislatures, to all ecclesiastical bodies throughout our great Commonwealth, to our philanthropic friends outside of the Church, and to all lovers of good and intelligent citizenship, to aid us in our struggle for more and better schools, in order to eliminate the great illiteracy of our land.

Good-citizenship leagues are another medium through which to make patriotic citizens. I think the Church ought to encourage such organizations. If we win it must be through concentrated effort; in order to accomplish this we must have organization. Combination is the theme of the hour. We hear a great deal about combinations now-a-days,— a combination to fix a monetary standard; combinations to advance commerce; combinations to improve cities; combinations to boom real estate; combinations to lower prices, and combinations to raise them; combinations to defeat good legislation. The Christian Endeavor deserves great praise for combining the Christian forces of the world to abolish corruption by defeating wicked men and measures.

Last, but not least, if we would advance the cause of good citizenship we must vote as we pray. If we are praying for the destruction of the liquor traffic, we must vote for the men who are willing to overthrow it. If we are praying for the extermination of the brothels and gambling-dens, we must see to it that men are nominated and elected (regardless of favoritism or party affiliations) who will close them up. If we are praying for the preservation of our Sabbath, we must demand the nomination and election of men who will uphold its sanctity. In a word, we must act consistently with our prayers.

The next speaker was Rev. J. W. Fifield, of Chicago.

Address of Rev. J. W. Fifield, Chicago, III.

For a long time the Church has been asleep. Her eyes have been closed as tightly as those of Pharaoh's mummy. Seated on soft cushions, charmed with sweet song, she forgot her mission. The great bugle-calls that startled the Church in the past centuries and sent it an invincible host against evil; that caught up those words of heroism, "Let the Lord arise, and let his enemies be scattered," until despots were smitten from thrones and fetters broken from men, are no longer heard. The minister preaches about love and evolution while a weak and powerless church changes itself into a restaurant for serving soup and cake to pay the salaries. While the Church has been inactive Satan has come in and taken the land. As the frogs came out of the rivers of Egypt until they croaked in store and palace, so have evils crept and crawled with slimy trail across the nation. Like the vale of Siddim, America is full of slime-pits. Talk about the wild beasts of African jungles! Here are beasts a thousand-fold more ferocious. Their fangs are more bloody; their poisonous touch, more deadly. The lairs where they crouch and coil are paved with marble, walled with gold, flooded with song; yet they tear their victims limb from limb and lap with savage growl their blood. While the Church sentinel has slept the enemy has come in and fortified in strong places. Behind earthwork and equipped with arms it seems unconquerable. Now the Church is growing thoroughly awake and there is trouble. The young people are shaking the elders and deacons. The women are holding up the unsteady hands of the clergy. God is planting his batteries and an aroused Church is hearing, better than for a hundred years, the great words of new duties. I know some faint-hearted and sheeny lovers of peace are going to the rear; but with this great gathering in the lead the doubting brethren of the churches may close in behind.

America is God's charity for humanity. It is the open gate for the human race. Could you lift up the United States as Milton's angels lifted the hills of heaven, you could find no other place to put them down. They would cover all of Europe, and spread on into Asia and Africa. We are only true to facts when we say that this is the greatest stretch of arable land on the globe. These great conventions which take our young people across the continent are helping us to learn American geography. We are told that our forefathers once called fifteen miles west of Boston the western limit. They drove a stake there, that the sun might have a place to go down behind it. But civilization came this way. The emigrants' wagon broke down the stake. Then the Hudson River was the western limit. But the stream of civilization came on. It rushed through the Mississippi Valley, beat and dashed its way over the Rocky Mountains, and, like mighty billows, surged and bounded to the Golden Gate. What a great country is here! Colorado would make twenty-two Connecticuts. Our New England States would get lost were they to enter Texas or the Dakotas, and it would require an exploration party to find them again. Land here sufficient for the millions of mankind! The Swede can live in Minnesota and dream of Gustavus Adolphus. The Catholic may dwell in Maryland with more liberty than in Rome itself. The Quaker can peacefully stay in Pennsylvania and be as broad in his ideas as he is broad in his hat. The Irishman can stop anywhere and never fear snakes. Here even the negro, now, can own a home of his own; the morning-glories may blossom at his window, and his own chickens play in his yard; while his child, free and ambitious, may receive our civic wreaths and occupy honored and responsible positions in our land. What a great land is here! And yet, my friends, while we have room for all, while each may dwell here in peace, there is in America air sufficient to stir but one flag. That flag is the one that was baptized with blood yonder at Gettysburg and Antietam, and is holier and nobler now because of blood shed of both North and South. I want you to know what a great inheritance we have in America. To be sure, bigness is not greatness. A live dog may be of more service than an elephant. It depends on the elephant. Yet physical size gives room for opportunity, and opportunity occupied is always greatness. Our country is not only large, but good. What valleys are richer? When tickled with hoes they laugh into harvests. What mountains are more stored with jewels, and what nobler streams spring from snowy heights? Our country is God's great palace for man. Walled in by lakes and oceans; beautified with unsurpassed land-scape and unequalled waterfalls; blessed with varied, yet healthful, climate; where is its equal? Great States are our flour-bins, miles of anthracite with hills for coal-hods, birds flying on swift wing, cattle fattening on prairies, and fish diving in lakes and streams. To be sure, it is said that New England is a little stony, but even there you can raise beans and *brains*. In the swamps of the South they raise cotton and cane, — especially cane. Heaven's blessings rest upon our nation. The Almighty has grandly performed his part, and man's work alone is vile. Alas, that so many evils are permitted here! The trouble at the Garden of Eden was that Adam and Eve went out and Satan stayed in. Here we must stay in and put Satan out, and we will have paradise regained.

What are some of those evils which threaten to spoil the Almighty's design in America? What are some of the devils which Christian citizenship should cast out? The first fiend which should command our attention is the *saloon*. What a word that is! It staggers with delirium; it coils with madness; it weeps dry tears of blight; it trembles with life's saddest pathos. The saloon is the grindstone where the assassin whets his knife. It is the malarious sewer of ulcerous manhood and cancerous womanhood. Into its till, along with the dollars, fall the tears of suffering children and the fading joys of betrayed and broken womanhood. O God! how long this evil? For money, the poorest thing in all the riches of life, we are willing to blast and blight and damn. A saloon license is a written permit, signed by our government, for the saloon to snatch the boy from his mother's arms, and send him, a maddened wreck, into a drunkard's grave; it is an agreement to steal the working man's wages, and, pouring insanity into his brain, to call it a recompense; it is an opportunity to drug young women, and, breaking the moorings of virtue, send them adrift on life's stormiest sea, outcasts from God and man. The wild and savage lion protects its young. The buffalo, stopping before the hunter with maddened bellow and lowered horn, will fight for the weak and defenceless. Not unfrequently do we know of birds which died while fighting for the nest. Some animal of prey approached their young, and although weaponless, the bird began fierce encounter. Its piercing cry filled the air. With all the strength of its wings it dashed against the foe. The feathers torn from its breast, with broken wing and lifeless form it lies beneath the spoiled nest where once it sung to its young. What creature of wing or fin, what beasts of tropic or frigid zone, would invite danger to its offspring? Yet we do it, and for a pretence take revenue to build sidewalks and public institutions. " O judgment, thou hast fled to brutish beasts, and men have lost their reason." The Bible declares that no drunkard shall enter heaven. Saloons are drunkard factories. Their product is labelled for despair. The people make the saloon. By our permission they continue, for were the Church to unite its power the last saloon could be driven from the land. O Church of the living God, O children of heaven's right hand, why not cast out this evil? Let the Christian Endeavorer be the uncompromising foe of the liquor traffic, and by prayer and vote may we destroy this mighty evil now entrenched in our land. The Bible says that the wicked flee when no one pursues them ; but, as Dr. Parkhurst has aptly added, " They make better time when some one is after them."

A second great evil which on account of its direful effect may be called a devil is *Sabbath desecration*. In history and the Bible we read of a holy day of rest called the Sabbath. It is fast becoming a stranger to us. Into the midst of man's work and activity the Almighty placed a time of quiet and joy. It was a shaft of light falling across life's rugged pathway. Whenever the Sabbath has been forgotten the individual and nation have suffered. Now the fourth commandment is rolled up into a football and we kick it about as we please. The holy day has become a holiday. The Sabbath should be the salute of the nation to Almighty God. Now we salute picnics, beer-gardens, open theatres, and every sort of evil that can creep or crawl or squirm into it.

Destroy the Sabbath and you abolish the Church. Abolish the Church and the land is the breeding-place of anarchy and bloodshed. It will be well for us to keep close to God's holy law, and it is becoming in this great Christian host to set an example of Sabbath-keeping that will glorify God and tend to perpetuate the nation.

Another evil is found in the *power and prominence of wealth.* The large combinations of capital, unless they are wisely managed and unselfishly controlled, may prove among the greatest of the national perils. When God made the coal, why not sell it cheap enough so that the poor may get warm? Why should people go hungry here with our bountiful harvests? It may be that sometime we will learn that it is still a curse to corner the market and raise the price of food, although the money is given away in a great philanthropy. For years the Gospel has been given to the poor,— and that is about all we have given them,— but let it also be preached to the rich. Jesus said that we are to love our neighbors as ourselves. But can that mean the sumptuous and wasteful banqueting of Dives while Lazarus is hungry and barefoot at the gate? Now there are many miles between the avenue and the alley, although they are not far apart. Now in business life selfishness rules, the weak are ground and broken, and principles unfit for savages are used by Christians. Christ said that the way to glory lay by the cross, and one great present-day need is to interpret the laws of the cross for the business world. The trinity of commercial life is not the Father, Son, and Holy Ghost, but the Gold Eagle, Silver Dollar, and Copper Cent. Christian citizenship would place Christ in the store and factory, in the market where the poor try to buy, and among the men of wealth who control the commercial interests of the nation.

When Charles Sumner entered the Senate he was told that there was nothing for him to do, that the great issues were all settled. His informant did not know the power which lay in that scholarly mind from Massachusetts. The negro was a slave, and until he was free Sumner was kept busy. Let us not feel that the great questions are all settled. Upon our national sky are clouds as black and threatening as ever threw their shadows or rolled their thunders over a people. Place your ear to the ground and you will hear voices that bode no good to our country. Nothing to do with malignant evils about us? Have we no spirit of love? Can this great Christian movement continue and not solve some of our national issues? Apply its power to the saloon. Let it stand for the Sabbath. Let it apply the Gospel, and all of it, to the life of the nation. Around the cross, that symbol of self-sacrificing love, let us gather, until with it we shall conquer. On my study table I keep a penholder which I cut from the oak that grows by the grave of Wendell Phillips. He belonged to the Christian-citizenship movement of the Christian Endeavor. He said years ago, while spending himself for reform, that if we build our institutions as high as the Rocky Mountains, yet use in them unholy brick, the pulse-beat of a child will knock them down. On this grandest land of the hemispheres, a land enriched with the highest civilizations of the past, with the priceless legacy of such names as Washington, Lincoln, and Garfield, with its great and invincible army of God-fearing youth, let us build a nation that shall stand. Let it rest upon our great natural foundation, and rising above our battle-fields and the quiet graves of our sacred dead, let it tower up in the centuries to come as, free from g eat evils, the dwelling-place of a happy people, and receiving the favor of Almighty God.

Calvary Baptist Church.

Within the brilliantly lighted church which bears the name of that historic mount where the Christ was crucified there gathered a host of Christian Endeavorers which filled every nook and corner of the edifice.

The meeting was scheduled to commence at half-past seven, but long before that hour the familiar hymns of the Endeavorers were sung over and over again. The meeting adjourned a few minutes before ten.

Mr. W. H. Pennell presided, and introduced in a felicitous manner the several speakers. After a praise service, the chorus of the Christian Endeavor sang the anthem, and Rev. S. Domer, of Washington, conducted the devotional exercises.

Miss Jessie A. Ackerman, of Chicago, was introduced and delivered the first address. Miss Ackerman gave an interesting account of much that had come before her own eyes in her " round-the-world trip."

She especially scored the liquor traffic, and pressed the responsibility of its existence upon the " will of the people."

The singing of another song was followed by the address of Rev. William Rader, of San Francisco, Cal.

Address of Rev. William Rader, San Francisco, Cal.

In the fourteenth article of the Constitution of the United States, the legal citizenship is thus defined: " All persons born or naturalized in the United States, and subject to the jurisdiction thereof, are citizens of the United States, and the State wherein they reside." The possession of rights, moreover, does not constitute true citizenship, which properly assumes that a right is only efficient when rightly used, and that a man is no more a citizen because of the constitutional authority afforded him by the Constitution than he is an artist because he owns the brush of Rubens or the chisel of Angelo. What are known as American rights, such as free speech and political suffrage, are the political instruments of Christian men; they are not ends, but means to an end; they are the instruments of political righteousness, the legal opportunity of a Christian man to practically apply his Christianity to the State. Citizenship, then, is more than the political authority to cast a ballot; it is the moral ability to cast it right in the interests of the kingdom of God and according to the Christianity of Jesus Christ. Voting is a Christian function. It has come to pass in our own country that the conflict of to-morrow will not be between Republican and Democrat, but between the Christian and the unchristian citizenship.

In the wide-spread awakening now going on in the United States, the Christian estimate of the State is being recovered.

The citizen is finding his place in the kingdom of God. The time is passed when it can be said that a man is a good Christian and a poor citizen. The two are one, and it is impossible for a man to be one without being the other. Heresy is not the adoption of a theological dogma; it is not the doubt of the Mosaic authorship of the Pentateuch; but it is putting the bushel of political indifference over the candle of one's character on election day.

Taking an interest in politics does not mean that the minister of the Gospel should bring politics into the pulpit, but it does mean that he should take his pulpit into politics. It does not mean that he should bring politics into church, but it does mean, most emphatically, that the Church should be translated into political power. The call in this revival is for every citizen to be true to his civic obligation. This is applied Christianity.

We have had two revolutions. The principle of the first was political independence, and the master spirit was Washington. The principle of the second was personal liberty, and its guiding genius was Abraham Lincoln. The revolution through which we are now passing combines these two principles of political independence and personal liberty, and the genius of the movement is no one commanding personality, but every American citizen who has the moral courage of his convictions, who carries the principles of his Bible into the Australian ballot booth, and who is the coming king in American politics. It is enough to say that the politician who fails to count him in his political reckoning will make a serious mistake in his political arithmetic.

Something, from present signs, it is safe to predict,—some things which may be expected to occur. First, the passing of the "boss." The hierarchy in politics is doomed. We want leaders, but not bosses, in politics.

The overthrow of the king in politics is as sure in the future as the overthrow of the king is a fact in history. He cannot stand before the majesty of the people. The man who is in politics for boodle ought to be kicked out for righteousness' sake.

Second, the faithless officer, the man who wears the policeman's star and fails to do duty for the people, should be punished with the same severity as the deserter from the army or the traitor to his country. The enforcement of law is the weak point in the political life of our country.

Third, the saloon must go. Public sentiment has been hurled against it as bird-shot against the Chinese Wall, while the force of the cannon-ball has hardly been felt in this conflict. There is a passionate restlessness among the people upon the temperance question. It is finding expression in more independent thinking and a method of warfare of wider range than those of Father Matthew, John B. Gough, and Francis Murphy. The great fact is plain that in spite of the ferocity of the legalized tiger, roaring at will through our streets, we willingly cut his toe-nails, puncture his ears, pull his teeth or put a costly muzzle in his mouth, stand in our churches denouncing him, without reaching a conclusion that he deserves to die and that the patriotic, economic, and religious thing would be to shoot *him dead now*. For this, all Christian Endeavor and all right-minded citizens should strive.

In a day when political parties are greedily looking for material to appropriate to their own use, it is not surprising that the young people's movement has been led by the spirit in the wilderness to be tempted of the devil. Thus far it has refused to turn stone into bread, or to leap from some pinnacle to be dashed to pieces below. It has been conservative, and has succeeded with admirable good sense in keeping the organization out of the cog-wheels of partisan politics.

Should the Christian Endeavor Society go into politics? Emphatically, no. Should the Christian Endeavorers go into politics? Emphatically, yes. Christian Endeavor should come into politics not as an organization, but as an influence. It is not necessary for the cannon to follow its ball. Christian Endeavor is democracy.

In looking over the history of the young people's movement, it is clear that already it has been a powerful force in American politics. It is to-day a reinforcement to good government second to none in the United States. It may be too early to collect facts, but every State in the Union can testify to the helpful influence of this movement in the strife for civic righteousness. The young people came on the field at a critical moment.

There was a time, not long since, when good men trembled throughout our country, and this in the face of a hundred years of distinguished history. It appeared as if the sacred and secular were separated, segregated, and entirely distinct. It appeared as though Christianity had lost its civic sense, but that was the hour preceding Blucher. On the platform of the International Convention held in Montreal, Dr. Clark blew the bugle of a ruling idea, that of Christian citizenship, and immediately an army of young people stood ready to do his bidding. That note, may it be said, saved, in a very great degree, the integrity of American politics. That note was the prophecy of the new citizenship, and the Old Guard of New York City, with Tammany tiger on its banner, was the first to be repulsed and broken. Dr. Parkhurst and Theodore Roosevelt are possible, very largely, because of the reinforcement afforded by the young people's movement. Christian Endeavor rendered valuable assistance in closing the Sunday saloons in Philadelphia, Detroit, Indianapolis, and other cities throughout the country. It is one of the potent factors supporting the Prohibition law in Maine, and its power to make public opinion in all the politics of the nation has made it respected by every observing politician in the country.

How shall the young people carry their religion into life, and thus practise what they preach?

How should Christian young people behave in this great day of opportunity?

We must be intelligent. We must acquaint ourselves with political conditions by reading the newspapers, the study of the best literature, and by taking a hand in the politics of our own locality. We must not sing of the eternal streets of gold, and fail to pave the streets of our own town. The young man who knows more of Cuba than of his own village, and more of the politics of Turkey than that of his native city, ought to be ashamed of himself. Christian Endeavor must carry its enthusiasm into life.

The steam in the cylinder must turn the wheels until they quiver with speed and power.

Unapplied steam may explode.

We must learn *to be.* Intensive development is quite as important as extensive growth. Depth is as vital as extent. Current thought emphasizes the Altruistic duty, but we must never forget that the condition of collective morality is personal character. Being is more than doing. The world is saved, not by what we do, but by what we are. We are witnesses to the universal truth. We stand as witnessing sentinels of Almighty God.

The flag testifies. There is no action in that bunting, but a testimony which gathers up the history and genius of our government.

Character is the splendid sentinel of the nation. We need the witnessing power in the American pulpit, men of iron, who have the moral courage of their political convictions. We need men in office, from policemen to mayors, from mayors to presidents, who dare stand square to their political obligations.

To the Christian Endeavorer politics means an instrument of righteousness, and party but the scaffolding around the rising kingdom of God. Politics, government, parties, are not ends, but means.

We must never doubt the eternal truth that the secret of strength is the abiding Christ of God.

Before we can be great citizens we must be great Christians. The kingdom of heaven is within you; and if it is n't, it ought to be.

The secret of strength, that secret which the great souls of history have cherished, is the implicit and triumphant confidence they had in the co-operative help of God. " Not by might, nor by power, but by my spirit, saith the Lord " is the motto of heroic history and the inscription written on every banner of power. The Psalmist of old, looking toward the eternal help, found it when he shouted, " Let God arise, and let his enemies be scattered."

Cromwell and Savonarola, Garfield and our Lincoln, caught the same logic ; for when our dead lay in the unburied glory of their death, Lincoln rose up through the clouds of war and threw this truth on the black clouds like a ray of light: " Let God arise, and let his enemies be scattered."

The last speaker was the vice-president of the Illinois Christian Endeavor Union.

Address of Rev. Millard F. Troxell, D.D., Springfield, Ill.

The ultimate appeal as to what is truth lies in the life and the word of Him who said to Pilate that he was born to bear witness of the truth. He was and is the teacher of governors, kings, and presidents.

He drove out the money-changers and those making of the temple a place of merchandise for their personal gain; but that was a proper, if violent and forcible, cleansing of that temple where in a peculiar sense he had a right to rule. It stood for that spiritual kingdom which it had been his special purpose to set forward in this wicked and inconsistent, selfish world. When the proper time and occasion demanded, in a way just as sincere, and a word just as earnest as the word saying " Ye have made of this place of prayer a den of extortion and selfish robbery," he put the temporal and spiritual kingdoms in their proper places and in their right proportions. He did it at a most critical time for him and his cause. It was when the traps were set and the wires were laid to catch him. The Pharisees, the " holier-than-thou" party, and the Herodians, the " anything-for-office " party, had put him in a position where it seemed certain that he must either involve himself and the claims of the Jews for Messiah in ruin, or else prove disloyal to the Roman government of Cæsar, so hateful to the average orthodox Jew. But at that critical moment, Jesus of Nazareth, spiritual teacher and manly, loyal citizen, arose not only equal to the occasion, but also forever joins the temporal and spiritual kingdoms, the civil and the theocratic authorities, by giving each its place in the statement, "Render unto Cæsar the things which are Cæsar's ; and unto God the things that are God's."

It is God and Cæsar, not God or Cæsar. Many men think of only one or the other of these governments or sources of authority and of power. Some think of and render willing obedience to the one to the exclusion of the other— or to the other to the exclusion of the one. Is it any wonder that so many States and statesmen have been flopping along in history in a zigzag fashion, when one wing or the other has been clipped, shorn, plucked of its power ? The eagle neither of ancient Roman nor of modern American government can reach its possible height of vision and influence and strength except by the happy equipoise of duty and service towards both the human and divine standards of obligation.

There must be a rendering to Cæsar of that which properly belongs to human government. There must be loyalty to one's own flag and one's own country and institutions. Every one owes it to the government that has protected him, aided him, instructed him, and developed him as a citizen, to be loyal and true as long as he lives in the country either of his birth or his sincere adoption. So a man ought to be a French Frenchman, an English Englishman, a German German, or an American American. So he ought to respect the law and order of the land in which he lives. He ought both to keep the laws made by his representatives and his government, and he ought to do his utmost to have others keep them. Only in this way can the highest well-being of the individual, the family, and society be promoted.

All our services for God are purely voluntary, depending at last upon the human will. God requires of man really nothing against his will. What he would require is simply that a man do justly, love mercy, and walk humbly before and with him. Human governments are sustained and make progress by taxes and tariffs and compulsory revenues, by drafts upon the · energies and resources of the people. It is not so with God's government.

Yet there are certain relations to be maintained and principles to be fixed in one's life and mind which bring together in cordial union the necessary *must* of human law and government, and the imperative *ought* of the Divine Voice. In relation to the State and the duties of citizenship the choice should not be made as between God and Cæsar, but for both Cæsar and God. Reasons for this statement and position can be given: (1) every life has a relation to two kingdoms,— the earthly or social, and the heavenly or spiritual ; (2) our obligations to these two kingdoms sometimes seems to interfere with and oppose each other, but it is only in the seeming and ought not to be so in fact ; (3) this is because Jesus Christ, as Lord of all worlds, is the only being who can rightly and authoritatively define our duties and relations to both kingdoms — and he has done so ; (4) the benefits which we receive from the earthly kingdom give rise to certain duties toward it ; (5) our duties toward the earthly kingdom do not lessen or put aside those toward the heavenly, and *per contra* ; (6) while the earthly relations are for the highest well-being in this life, the heavenly are for our happiness throughout eternity ; (7) both our condition and our relations in the world to come will be different from those in the present world, but depend upon our lives, faith, and conduct here.

And now what can we as young people do and be, as those who must and ought to render to both God and Cæsar, that is, to both divine and human government, a proper allegiance? Related to both earthly and heavenly powers, how can we best influence and deal with the earthly so as to do with it just what Jesus, our one Master, would have us do?

1. In the first place, we can be intelligently informed, so as to know just where we stand, and why we stand just where we are. Let us not be deceived

by the cry of any that we are mixing Church and State. These two are not mixed, nor can they be in the light of Jesus' words and example. They are joined together in phrase, but not mixed in either fancy or fact. Each is distinct. We have duties and relations towards each. In the best sense it pays for each to cherish and protect the other; but as organizations, the Church and State are distinct and separate from each other, and ought to remain so for the purest and best progress of both. The first duty of a young Christian as a citizen and would-be patriot, as a member of the State, is to become informed upon all issues in order to be an intelligent voter.

It is true it may seem difficult to be intelligent on some questions that come up in politics. It may be hard to understand all or anything about the tariff, or free trade, the gold standard, or sixteen to one in the silver question, but it is not hard to find out whether or not a man running for office is a man of clean life and Christian principle. An intelligent view of the politics of the time causes one with open eyes and common sense to see that there are good men and selfish men in all parties.

It is not judicious for the Church of Christ, or Christian Endeavor, or any branch or body of the followers of Jesus, to become a political party; but it is the common-sense thing to do to take a stand for the principles of Christ in any and every party where a Christian may feel called upon to serve his country, in rendering unto Cæsar the things that are Cæsar's. It took a miracle on the part of the Master, at one time, to fulfil his obligation to the earthly government. To some of us it may seem like a miracle required of some of our friends to affiliate with this or that political party and yet be good, consistent Christians. But let us give them the same credit for honesty and sincerity of purpose which we think we possess, and which we ask from others for ourselves. We all need to remember, in trying to perform our civic duties in any political party, George Herbert's noble words: —

> " Next to sincerity, remember still,
> Thou must resolve upon integrity.
> God will have *all* thou hast, — thy mind, thy will,
> Thy thoughts, thy words, thy works."

2. Along with intelligence on all the public and political questions, we can, as young people, hold to an unswerving and unfaltering devotion to the peculiar principles of our Christian faith and calling. These principles may all be covered with the three terms, so far as civic relations are concerned, " purity," " honesty," and " sobriety." I mean by these a pure personal or home life, an honest administration of public affairs, and an unfalteringly clean and consistent attitude against the worst single enemy of the home, the Church, and the country, which is the saloon and the drink devil of our day.

I love the branch of special work called Christian citizenship because it stands for a pure social and home life as the fountain of personal purity for the stream of public administration.

Then it stands for honesty in the administration of public office as well. In all our cities and smaller communities the young people can have and ought to have open eyes to search out and behold, and then clarion voices to brand the bribe-takers and all who steal from the public purse. How often legislation is transformed into brokerage! How often votes are bought, sold, and intimidated! How often public offices are made the place of private pilfering instead of being administered as public trusts! The doctrine of Christian citizenship stoutly maintains that whether the office seeks the man, or the man the office, no man ought to ask or expect the votes of the people for a second term who has not honestly and cleanly administered a first term; and if such a man does ask for office, every true believer in Christian citizenship will say, " You cannot have my vote or influence." No man ought to be put forward or voted for whose record for honesty in money affairs and whose integrity of word or oath is in the least tarnished or even suspicious. We have good men in all our communities, men of sterling honesty, men of Christian character, who stand ready to fill the public offices, and who will consider an office a public trust, to be accounted for as conscientiously as any other matter of confidence and responsibility. We have it in our power to create a public sentiment favoring this view of the question concerning public office where it may yet be needed. In time past there has been so much of corruption and dishonesty and insincerity in public administration that it is wonderful how kind providence has been to our nation and communities. It has been so remarkable that the observation of the old French abbe made some while ago seems justifiable. He said, "A sort of special providence seems to brood over little children, old women, and the people of the United States." Perhaps he spake with a little tinge of sarcasm, but none of us can fail to feel that we have withstood shocks that have overthrown nations stronger than ours.

I love the branch of special work called Christian citizenship because it stands for an honest and clean administrating of public trusts. I love it because it means to place the principles of purity and honesty, of the Golden Rule, in every one of the thousands upon thousands of our offices, — from that of president, judge, and congressman, down to mayor, justice of the peace, and even city alderman. I love it because it means to make it the popular and patriotic thing to put bad men out of office, and to keep them out, and so to make it the popular and patriotic thing for good men, and good men only, to apply for office.

Lastly, I love the special branch of our work called Christian citizenship because it stands for an unfaltering opposition to the saloon and the drink devil. It means that the saloon must in the end be outlawed. It means that the drink devil will be laid low. It means that a David has come forth from the camp of Israel to meet and slay the boasting Goliath, not with the weapons of King Saul, but in the name and faith of the Lord of hosts. It means that the banner of our country's freedom is being lighted from above, that it is being carried and placed in the white search-light of the fresh Christian conscience of our robust young manhood and womanhood of to-day. All hail this day when the radiance of the Cross of Christ, made beautiful by the beams of the Sun of righteousness, is being cast all about the red, white, and blue symbol of our country's freedom. The saloon and whiskey traffic, the drink devil, all foes of our homes, of our best institutions, the Church, and the Sabbath, are to-day marked as the foes not only of God and his people, but also as a combined force plotting against Cæsar, all that stands for a just and equable government. In the saloon the worst things of our civilization are found. From it flow our most poisonous sewers, breeding disease and causing death. The saloon sewer makes men insane, criminal, debauched, licentious, domineering, selfish, brutal.

Knowing this, what can be clearer than that we young Christians, and that all Christians and all good people, should press the principles and power of our holy religion into every avenue of life, into court-house and council-chamber, into legislatures and governors' offices, into Congress and the White House, until the law of Jesus Christ, the law of love, duty, and service, to God and Cæsar, to the Church and to the State, shall be the law of every Christian and of every citizen; until this our high ideal shall be pushed on to the very ramparts of victory? From this position and this standard let us know no retreat.

Foundry Methodist Episcopal Church.

At the old and historic Foundry Methodist Episcopal Church there was a well-attended meeting, and those who came were rewarded by excellent addresses. The music was well rendered by the Endeavor choir, under the direction of Mr. J. A. Rose. The meeting was opened with a praise service and anthem, followed by devotional exercises conducted by Rev. J. T. Anderson, of Washington.

Then the presiding officer, the Rev. H. F. Shupe, of Dayton, O., introduced the first speaker of the evening, Rev. H. K. Carroll, LL.D., of New York City, editor of *The Independent.*

Address of Rev. H. K. Carroll, D.D., LL.D., New York City.

I want to take as my text on this occasion a single sentence from the last Episcopal address of the Methodist Bishops. It is this: "A man may be as much a missionary of God in the politics of America as in the forests of Africa."

This I hold to be good gospel. If the religion of Christ is anything it is everything. It is not given from above simply for delightful meditation on quiet Sundays, or exhibition in church or prayer meeting; it is not alone a balm for sorrow, or a cordial for approaching death; it is a mighty, intellectual, moral, reformatory, and spiritual force, applicable to every problem and exigency of life. It is intended to be established in the heart of man, that from the citadel of his being it may command every thought, control every impulse, suggest every word, and inspire every deed. It is meant to be, and is capable of being, the all-in-all of every life.

We must get away from the thought that religion is something which we put on, like a coat or dress, for special occasions. If it is something to be put on, it is something to be put off. Our pulpits tell us often enough that we must not be Sunday Christians merely, but every-day Christians; but we retain much of the leaven of an old and slowly passing heresy. We have not only our religious days and seasons, our religious manners and garments, but we are still in the habit of dividing our lives into several distinct parts, each with a different label. Part of our life we devote to Bible-reading, prayer, meditation, and religious work, and we are conscientious enough to make it a generous part and to reserve it religiously, not allowing other concerns to intrude and interrupt. Six days in the week we give to business, and count it a distinct part of our life. Another part is made up of recreation, pursuit of pleasure in many forms, public duties, and the like. Here are three divisions, and it is idle to deny that they are more or less separate in our thought, our plans, and our purposes. What we do for the Lord we do in a religious spirit; what we do in business we do with all our might, having the single object, success, constantly before our eyes; in our pleasures the engrossing thought is to get as much out of them as possible. It is all right to keep business out of pleasure; but religion ought never to be out of place. And yet is it not? If I were to question the average church-member I believe the answers I would get would run somewhat as follows:—

"Do you consciously serve the Lord when you are at your prayers, your Bible-reading, your place in church, your religious work?"

The answer would come quickly and confidently:

"Yes, of course I do."

"Do you consciously serve the Lord when you are pushing your business interests, trying to make money?"

The answer would come slowly and with obvious doubt:

"Well, I don't know; I am not quite sure. In business in these days you have got to do as others do, or you will fail. You cannot be over-particular as to methods. You must follow the customs of business life, or make up your mind to drop out of the race. I try to be honest; but I have to do some things which I would rather not do. Still, I keep up my church work; I give liberally for the support of religious enterprises; I bring up my family in Sunday school and church, and I always have family prayers. I guess I am a pretty good sort of Christian, after all — as good as the great majority of church-members."

And now for the third question:

"Do you serve the Lord when you are pleasure-seeking and in your public duties?"

The answer would come, after great hesitation:

"This is pretty sharp cross-questioning. You cannot be expected always to have the Bible on your lap. You cannot go to church seven days in the week. A man cannot always have his thoughts on dying and the resurrection and heaven. One who constantly studies the words on tombstones, 'Prepare to meet thy God,' will be too gloomy to enjoy life. When you are on pleasure bent you must give yourself up to the enjoyment of the hour. As to public duties, what have a political caucus and church in common? A man hunting for votes cannot be expected to proceed as an evangelist hunting for souls. Everything in its place, I say. Religion is religion, business is business, pleasure is pleasure, politics are politics. You cannot mix church and caucus, or religion and business, or piety and pleasure, any more than you can mix oil and water."

I think the average church-member would answer these questions in about the way I have indicated. You will observe that a distinction is clearly made between work for the Church and work for the family or the State. One is regarded as purely religious, the other as purely secular. And many think that religion has a sphere of its own, and that it must be confined to that sphere, as though the sun should not flood the earth, the moon, and the universe with his light! When we speak about the members of a Christian Endeavor Society becoming interested in civil affairs, it is as though we proclaimed some great heresy. "What! carry religion into politics? The next thing will be to carry politics into religion!" And the way this is said shows that those who say it believe it to be the *reductio ad absurdum*, that it would bring ruin dire upon the Church, and that to dip the Church into the dirty pool of politics would be a baptism of the devil.

The best way to answer those who are so zealous for the Church and fear that it will be contaminated if brought into close relations with all the concerns of life, is to study Christ's life and see what his method was. Of course Christ was religious, and no one questions the wisdom and righteousness of anything he did. "Wist ye not that I must be about my Father's business?" What was this business? We say that it was to preach and teach, to reveal the gracious purpose of the Father, live a perfectly holy life, and be offered in sacrifice for the sins of the world. But after that memorable conversation, Christ returned with his parents and became a carpenter. He worked at Joseph's trade. He had his living to earn, and he earned it. Before he began his public ministry was he a carpenter and a devout Jew, or was he a devout Jewish carpenter? Did he carry religion into his business, or did he try to separate the two? Was not his religion as characteristic of him as his manhood, and as indelible in the lines of his life as his Jewish lineage? I can not imagine that he was any the less engaged in his Father's business when he was handling the saw and the plane than when he went into the Temple on the Sabbath. I can not imagine that he ever held that a carpenter must suspend his religious obligations while engaged in his trade. When he began his public ministry he did not confine his religious teaching to the Sabbath, nor to the Synagogue; nor did he cease to take an interest in the business affairs of others. We do not learn that his Sermon on the Mount was a Sabbath sermon. He did not refuse to teach great spiritual lessons on working-days, and some of his most effective teachings were drawn from events in the "secular" world, as we sometimes call it. On more than one occasion he was with his disciples when they were fishing, and he did not seem to think that it would be incongruous to mix the truths of the Gospel with the fish of the nets.

A little girl who was about to leave New Jersey for a summer vacation in New England said in her prayer the night before the journey, "Good-by, God, I 'se going to Maine." That is what many men and women practically say when they propose to do anything not definitely religious. They believe that God and business, God and politics, and God and pleasure are, and must be, divorced. This is why the business operations of Christian men are so often in violation of the Decalogue; why politics appear to many to be so godless; why pleasure is so worldly and anti-spiritual. They say you must not drag business, or politics, or amusements, into religion, because they will degrade it; nor religion into these secular concerns, because it is unseemly, incongruous, out of place. At a great political convention, some years ago, a gentleman, recently a candidate for a high office, apologized to me for not introducing a man who interrupted our conversation a moment. "That man," he said, "is the notorious Blank, of Blank City. He is not the kind of person one likes to present to gentlemen; but he is very necessary and useful to the party. He does for us a peculiar kind of work which others could not and would not do." This is godless politics. This is the result of drawing a line between a man's duties to religion and his duties to the State, allowing God to rule over the one and the devil to claim the other. Some Christians are horror-struck at the idea of associating politics and religion. Politics are such a wicked business, so defiled, so degrading, that good men must have nothing to do with them. They are not always and everywhere so bad; but why are they ever bad? The answer is easy to find. Take the light out of this room and darkness becomes supreme. To banish the darkness, you have only to bring back the light.

The great need of the world is that God should be everywhere and constantly present. We want God in our business as well as in our churches: in our amusements as well as in our devotions; in our politics most of all. What are politics? In the language of President Hitchcock, politics are "the principles by which nations should be governed and regulated," and are "only a branch of ethics," or rather "a special application of the principles of morality and religion." It is a fair field for Christian Endeavor; and I believe that any Endeavorer may be as much a missionary of God in American politics as in the forests of Africa. He should go to the primary, the polls, or the political convention as regularly, as religiously, as he goes to church or to conference or to prayer meeting. Let us all be not only Christians, but citizens; not Christians in the church and citizens out of it, but always Christians, always citizens,— citizen Christians, Christian citizens; then will love to God and love to men and love to country flow pure and strong and free from the same heart.

At this point Miss Florence McNally sang a contralto solo very pleasingly. Owing to the illness of Bishop Abram Grant, D.D., of Atlanta, Ga., Bishop W. B. Derrick, of New York City, spoke in his stead.

Address of Bishop W. B. Derrick, D.D., New York City.

To-night we say we are pleased to be present as Christian citizens, not simply as good citizens. A man could be and can be a good citizen and a moral man, and yet not a Christian citizen. Christian citizenship is the most exalted of all citizenship, but no man can be a Christian citizen unless he is a good citizen. He must be a good citizen; good, not simply to receive the plaudits and praisings of men, but good because it is good to be good; and then, by being a good citizen, in all that the word "good" implies,— respectable, intelligent, and moral,— accepting the truth as in Christ Jesus. He is then transformed from being good to Christian citizenship, with a title not to earthly inheritance, but to that inheritance which is incorruptible, undefiled; that which shall never fade away. To-night, it is to that I would call your attention; but I repeat that before any professing Christian, before any church membership, before any church organization, can consistently claim to be citizens of the commonwealth of Israel, they must be completely stripped of all the nonsensical prejudices, and recognize the man, whether he is dressed in yellow or in black or in white or in red, so he can testify to the fact that he is a Christian and that he understands the workings of the Spirit of God in his heart. We say, Mr. President, as a portion of the Christian family standing here to-night, as men dressed perhaps in a different hue, we belong to that species of men in the Church of our Lord and Saviour Jesus Christ who would not dare to place manhood or womanhood simply upon race or color; but we place Christian citizenship upon Christian character. God looks not at the outward appearance, but he looks at the heart; and the man whose heart has been thoroughly cleansed, the man whose heart has been washed in the blood of the Lamb, whose heart is in harmony with the teachings of the Gospel of God, that man who can testify that God is the Creator, Christ the Redeemer, and man the brother, that man is suited to become a citizen of the commonwealth of Israel.

The good brother, in introducing me, said that we represented the Afro-

American Societies, and they were glad to hear us talk on this subject. Let me tell you to-night, as to good citizenship of America, that there is no class of people in America which is more humane in the exercise of good citizenship than the people whom I represent to-night. So we come to you to-night with implicit confidence in approaching this question of Christian citizenship, and we are proud and we are glad to know that we can stand as equals before the bar of eternal justice. In this world citizenship may be thwarted; the judges upon the Supreme Court bench may pass an adverse decision, saying that a citizen is entitled to certain rights; but regardless of all their biased and prejudicial decisions, we are marching to a bar where the Judge of all judges will declare that " none but the pure in heart shall stand before me and enjoy the happiness of my upper sanctuary."

It ought to be carrying coals to Newcastle to bring instruction concerning Christian citizenship to the capital of the nation. But if one may carry live coals to Newcastle, he may at least set a fire. Sir Philip Sidney once said to his brother, " Whenever you hear of a good war, you go to it." To hear of a good war and not go to it is something very difficult to a good man. Now a good war is not a war of bloodshed ; such a war is a weapon, an erudite weapon, of a rude people in a rude age. It will be abandoned ; it must be put away ; it is already an antiquated thing. It is both a mode and a measure of Paganism; it settles nothing and never did settle anything. In making these seemingly startling statements, I am met by the whole course of human history, and I must therefore convince you that the work of this world very largely has been a failure, that it will have to be done over again, for since the world began the classes have been set over against the masses. This has occasioned strife, embittered feeling; it has waged war. The history of the world has been only a history of battles, and there have been only three things for which the world has fought. From the very beginning it has been the rule for the stronger to prey on the weaker; second, so much like it as to be akin to it, extension of territory; and, lastly, only another name for it, balance of power. That is the history of the world. It has been a system of competition on the 'one hand ; it has been a condition of lord and master, servant and slave, on the other. But you and I live in a new era, under a revolution. The American Republic was in itself the projection of a good war, but it was a war of a very different kind and for a very different purpose. Alexander, and Cæsar, and Hannibal, and Napoleon were the soldiers of the first war; Paul, and Luther, and Wesley, and Edwards, of the second war. The American people expected every citizen to be a soldier. It could not have been otherwise. We are glad to know to-night that the history of two hundred and fifty years has been the history of a continuous war. The citizens of the new country have been a standing army, and the nation's progress has been signally a series of voluntary surrender after the battles were over. The new kingdom is one of Christianity, I say ; it is not limited in its movements by the Church ; it has gotten out of doors and is in the wide, open air. This is the first Christian century since Jesus died. There has been something of Christianity in all centuries, but this century is the century of humanity as well as the divine teachings of the Gospel. Commerce is coming to be Christian; society cannot avoid being Christian; and the State, turn and twist as it may, submits to the will of the Christian people. There is no longer distinction between personal and political relations, private and public duties. My brother was right when he said your Christianity must go into your politics. The Bishop of Cologne was heard swearing by one of his parishioners, who held up his hands in holy horror to hear a bishop swear. The Bishop apologized, however, by saying that he did not swear as a bishop, that he swore as a man. " Yes," said the parishioner, " but what will become of the Bishop when the man goes to the devil for his swearing?" There is no distinction between private and public duties in a Christian State. The Christian man must be the Christian citizen. The public policy, no less than the private character, demands it. Christianity is everywhere. It will not do for a man to serve a Christian State, therefore, who is not a Christian. Christianity is in the ground; you can not bury it. It is in the water; you can not drown it. It is in the fire; you can not burn it. It is in the air; you must breathe it. We are a Christian people. Why is it that you discuss a question in this country that has cost us more than a hundred times what we have expended for Christian missions? Why is it that you here to-night frankly discuss a question that involves the ill or weal of every home within this district, and reaches out from this capital to every corner of the nation? You might burn down this church and every other in every other city, and take the income of the liquor traffic for one single year in the business itself, and rebuild every structure that has been destroyed, and supply every pulpit and pay the salaries of all the preachers. It is a proper question for us to discuss, when the State is involved; and you cannot discuss a question to-day in a Christian State where this question is not involved. Here is a great party, of which I have been so warm an advocate, because a soldier carrying a gun, and a stalwart one. I came home with my own present feelings, which are that it has been difficult for me to ever utter a criticism of the political party to which I belonged, and yet it can adopt a platform of three hundred and twenty-one lines, and on this platform that involves more than any one platform, including the currency, the tariff, and all the other questions before the public to-day, this party can sum up its principles in such ambiguous language as to give all sides to the controversy an opportunity to follow and vote its ticket. Here we are to-night, face to face with the problem that we do not know what to do with politically. When I say to you that the taxes in the State of Ohio (from which I came) on the liquor traffic last year were $5,000,000, and that they say they dare not give up this $5,000,000 of taxes, I simply tell what every man in that State knows, — that $30,000,000 are involved in the business, with $30,000,000 more to some way or another offset the ravages of the same business. I spoke in Denver, in my own State, a few weeks ago, and before I entered that large hall where we had been invited to speak on this particular topic, I met a man at the door, and I said to him, " Sir, what would be the argument that would be urged in this town against the preservation of the liquor traffic in this town?" He said, " You forget, sir, that up on that hill we have a building here that furnishes almost all the business of the town, in which there are almost a thousand inmates." When I went inside I inquired what the building was. I found that it was an asylum for the insane, and when I went up to look into the business of that institution I found that more than 800 of the 1,000 inmates were brought there through the use of strong drink. I might traverse the country, and find that similar institutions for the feeble-minded had in a majority of cases been filled from this same source. Yet, to-day it is a difficult matter in most of our Christian churches to get an expression of political opinion concerning what we must do with this question. " License it," says one man. Would you license murder? Yet there is murder. Would you license stealing? Yet there are thieves. Yet there is scarcely a man who drinks to excess who at some time or other would not steal.

Now any system of legislation that assumes to deal with these matters after a principle that is involved in all our personal relations to the Church, any principle of political legislation that involves the Christian character of the nation, that every moment stirs one's soul concerning the questions of Christian citizenship in such a way as to even put the churches upon a doubtful issue,—I am here to say that there is for this and all other questions, where it may mean some pandering to appetite, some threatening danger to the home or to the life of the state and the nation, but one Christian way in which we can deal with all wrong; and the man, like Abou Ben Adhem, whose tribe would increase must write his name as the friend and lover of his fellow man, and to do this must involve some thought of some keeper that like a brother would care for his fellow man. We unveiled the other day in Boston a statue to a man who made his reputation on these lines. If I could fasten them in your memory, I would fasten the key not only of the relationship of brother to brother, but of Christian citizenship upon the Christian as well as the Christian legislator.

> " ' What is the real good?'
> I asked in musing mood.
> ' Order,' said the law court ;

> ' Truth,' said the wise man ;
> ' Pleasure,' said the fool ;
> ' Love,' said the maiden ;
> ' Beauty,' said the page ;
> ' Freedom,' said the dreamer ;
> ' Home,' said the sage ;
> 'Fame,' said the soldier ;
> ' Equity,' the seer ;—
>   Spake my heart, all sadly :
> ' The answer is not here.'
> Then within my bosom
>   Softly this I heard :
> ' Each heart holds the secret ;
>   Kindness is the word.' "

First Presbyterian Church.

It seemed particularly appropriate that one of the five large meetings should be assigned to the First Presbyterian Church, of which Rev. Dr. Byron Sunderland is pastor, and that the topic should be "Christian Citizenship," the one question of all others in which Dr. Sunderland is most interested, and for which he is known all over the land for his connection with it. A section of the large Convention choir was present and rendered the first number of the programme, a praise service, under the direction of Mr. Russell Barnes, of this city. Rev. William Patterson, of Toronto, one of the trustees of the United Society, presided. Preceding the principal features of the programme, Rev. W. J. Howard made the opening prayer.

The first speaker was Rev. Franklin Hamilton, of Newtonville, Mass.

Address of Rev. Franklin Hamilton, Newtonville, Mass.

When the Continental Congress laid down the proposition that all men are created free and equal and endowed with certain inalienable rights, among which are life, liberty, and the pursuit of happiness, "men, under the spell of that call, started out of their lethargy like exiles from their childhood who hear again the dimly remembered accents of their mother-tongue." Patriots in other countries had had for their object privilege or power. The American patriot fought for a new commonwealth. The weal of one is the weal of all.

In that proposition the struggling thought of ages came to utterance. In it seemed to be born again "the doctrine of the brotherhood of man once entrusted to the Jewish people." In it were concentrated all the earlier struggles of the Anglo-Saxon race. For it was, as our own poet says, "the drums of Naseby and Dunbar that gathered the minutemen on Lexington Common. It was the red dint of the axe in Charles's block that marked ONE in our era." In obedience to that call Faneuil Hall threw open its doors to an eloquent patriotism. The nation rocked to the utterances of a Patrick Henry, an Otis, a Warren, a John Hancock, a Quincy, and an Adams. In answer to that summons on Bunker Hill and Concord bridge,

> " The embattled farmers stood
> And fired the shot heard round the world."

The second great patriotic movement occurred when the slaveholder sought to divide the Union. Then was witnessed the grandest scene of history. Then it was the whole world was moved by the very pathos of American patriotism. The homes of the people were turned into arsenals of war. What was written of the Knights of St. John in their crusades could be said of the multitudes, all unknown and unheard of before, — " In the forefront of every battle was seen their burnished mail, and in the gloomy rear of every retreat was heard their voice of conscience and of courage."

Suppose the spirit of our country could stand before us on this platform to-day, and say, " Come up here and lay down for me your life ;" how many do you think would obey that summons? Yet nearly two millions of our bravest and our best did that, — gave themselves, at their country's call, to flying bullets and to flashing steel; and, to-day, they sleep where they fell, on every field of the South. Their bones are whitening on every hillside. Unknown, unmarked, they lie hard by some lonely brook, where, all unnoticed, the pacing sentinel fell; or in some forest glen where only the soughing winds know the resting-place.

That hour is past. The Grand Army of the Republic is a vanishing army; their work is done. I believe, with the poet, that some sweet bird of the South shall build her nest in every rusting cannon's mouth; that the note of the bluebird will be the only sound that shall be heard from the iron throat of these instruments of death. I believe that "never again in this land for civil strife shall there be fighting men abroad or weeping maids at home."

The arbitrament of arms shall give way to arbitration. Less and less shall the human heart respond to a patriotism of the sword, until at last a day shall dawn when

> " The battle flags are furled
> In the Parliament of man,
> The federation of the world."

And yet I stand before you this evening to emphasize the third great occasion in our national history for a patriotic war. Never has there been such need of an exalted Christian patriotism as there is to-day. There is abundance of jingoism, tawdry, and barbaric, which would stand, possibly, for country, right or wrong. There is a superabundance of the dirty partisanship which has crushed out the moral life of all party politics. But where do we find an ardent and intelligent patriotism that the lust of office does not kill, or the spoils of office cannot buy? Where is the love of the fatherland that once illumined the fair morning of our national life? Where is the consecrated devotion that inspired the free-soil patriots for whom Wendell Phillips spoke, when, on that morning never to be forgotten, he said, "Many times I have counselled peace. One of the journals announces to you that I come here this morning to retract those opinions. No! not one of them! I need them all, every word that I have spoken, every act of twenty-five years of my life, to make the welcome I give this war hearty and hot." Where do we find such patriotism to-day?

We do not find active in the heart of the great common people this spirit that once flamed through city, hamlet, and prairie cabin,— " We are coming, Father Abraham; we are coming six hundred thousand strong !"

> " He hath sounded forth the trumpet
> That shall never call retreat;
> He is sifting out the hearts of man
> Before his judgment-seat.
> Be swift, my soul, to answer him;
> Be jubilant, my feet;
> The Lord is marching on."

The great common people of America, to-day, may be divided into two classes.

The first class is that of the worthless immigrants and the detritus of our American life. Penniless and ill-fed, unwashed and unlearned, many of them degraded by ages of tyranny, they bear with them the seeds of all that is lawless and un-American. They are the vagabond children of hunger and despair. Their flag is the red flag of anarchy. Their fatherland is the country which they can most easily plunder. It has been computed that there are in America 85,768 tramps. More than one-half of them are of American parentage.

The second great class of the common people is that vast body of wage-earners whom political economists term "producers and consumers." They are the bone and sinew of the nation. This is the class which back in those sober religious days of sturdy New England Puritanism was distinguished by its non-conformist conscience. To-day it cares nothing for the heritage of the Puritans. Its heart is fixed on "a community of pelf." Its religion is the gospel of the horse-leech's daughters. Its motto is "Enrich yourselves." It bids the Son of God stand still before the giant selfishness of business. It has inaugurated an era of Epicureanism that is sweeping this whole nation into the mad, wild dance of folly around the calf of gold.

Behold the results! Politics a pandemonium where blind guides which strain at a gnat and swallow a camel compass sea and land to make one proselyte, and when he is made they make him twofold more the child of hell than themselves. The liquor traffic, freshly incorporated legally to be fattened, as, with fangs lengthened and sharpened by a new whiskey trust, it sinks its poison deeper into the body politic. The social-evil vampire licensed and protected by the guardians of public purity. Capital and labor hopelessly embroiled Capital, a soulless sweater, greedily refusing to Christianize the laborer's environment. Labor, like a mad dog, "gasping, yelping, and snapping, helpless in the swirl and suck of monopoly's maelstrom." Pauperism, with her demoniac daughter, socialism, fermenting strikers and riots that partake of civil war. The Afro-American, that "image of God carved in ebony," still heaped, in the white name of liberty, with dastardly indignities and bestial outrages. Massachusetts ostracising and South Carolina disfranchising the negro, Florida making it a penal offence to educate white and black children together, while Romanism, as if to sound the ossification of the public conscience, dares in the open streets of Boston to spit on the symbol of the national school system and to insult the American flag.

The Church stands impotent before these wrongs because for a generation she has avoided them. She has not ventured the only remedy,—self-giving. She has not dared to become a divine incarnation brought down to date. We have lived so long in the piping times of peace that we have lost our civic muscle. "We are in the condition upon which autocrats and dictators feed." If we would not as a people forfeit our divine inheritance, the hour for a new patriotic warfare has come.

This is not the call of a Continental Congress to shoulder a musket or buckle on a sword. This is not the bugle-note of an endangered fatherland for patriots to assemble and to hurl themselves in one huge embodiment of zeal and vengeance upon a traitorous foe. This is the call for the awakening of the civic conscience, the demand that truth and righteousness shall become our standards as a people.

This is the summons for every citizen of moral muscle and spiritual backbone to awake, to arise from his sleep of civic indifference, and to heed the voice, "What doest thou here?" This is the summons for every soldier of Jesus Christ "to bear the star of Bethlehem, not only in the blue ground of his flag, but also in the white sinews of his arms and in the red tissue of his heart."

They tell me that patriotism in America is dead. I do not believe it. I concede, with Robertson, that if moral evil were clothed with flesh and blood, and marshalled as an army to invade our homes and ravage the country, there would spring forth an opposing army to meet, resist, and utterly destroy the invader. But our weapons are not carnal. We war a warfare with principalities and powers, led by the Prince of the Power of the Air. And I believe, with Plutarch, that though there may be a delay in divine justice, that justice ever comes at the last, swift and sure. But we who are the defenders of our homes to-day will be faithless cowards if we court indifference or flee from the struggle, which demands our noblest aspirations, highest courage, and bravest endurance. The honors which await us will evade us and flee to our children, who will win what we ought to have won. We will transmit nothing but our inheritance, and that impaired by our neglect.

> "Others shall sing the song,
> Others shall right the wrong,"

another generation will take our crown.

Our country needs a new conception of patriotism, a comprehension of civic duty that shall summon the youth of this land to unite, "fair as the morn, clear as the sun, and terrible as an army with banners," determined that by the help of Him whose word is as a thousand swords, America shall not be given over to anarchy, to self-will and the devil. To whom shall our country look to give her these but to us, her Christian young people? We have here no continuing city. We are the patriots of a heavenly country. We are the sons of God. We are the trustees of posterity. On whom else shall she call "to wake the deep slumber of careless opinion, to startle the torpor of an immoral acquiescence, to kindle burning aspirations, to set noble examples?" And God made woman to be man's equal. With our sisters we will strike hands that this country shall cast out her devils, and, sitting at the feet of Jesus, be clothed and in her right mind. We will no longer be silence-keepers to hell, but we will live for God; we will fight for God. And when we can no longer fight we will pray for the mildew of God's wrath on "whatsoever worketh abomination," or would delay the coming of the kingdom of God. We will put an iron heel on the dram-shop. We will hound colorphobia back to its lair. We will teach anarchists and religious bigots that adherence to a red flag or a red robe shall never cloak violence or lawlessness. We will give no clean votes to dirty politicians. We will carry the Gospel into the Tibet land of American trade. We will shame religious shams. We will force respect for the Sabbath. We will cleanse the Augean stables of the press. We will quicken the dying sense of the holiness of marriage. We will defy the arrogant tyrannies of that public sentiment which builds on the love of money and the lust of spoils. We will lift up our hearts and our hands to welcome the purest patriotism that the world can know,— a patriotism that shall measure all things by a divine standard, and shall act with the sense of a divine captaincy. We have a passion for the planet,— we will exalt Jesus and humanity; we who are

> "The heirs of all the ages
> In the foremost files of time,"

we will consecrate ourselves to the one work of winning men to the standard of the Cross, until this whole nation is come to the Christ,

> "And green forever be the groves,
> And bright the flowery sod
> Where first the child's glad spirit loves
> Its country and its God."

The next speaker was Mrs. J. Ellen Foster, of Washington.

Address of Mrs. J. Ellen Foster, Washington, D.C.

We condemn the use of alcoholic stimulants. They do not build up the body; they retard the assimilation of food, they weaken the vital organs, they degenerate the muscles, they paralize the nerves, they cook the brain. The use of alcoholic stimulants has another and more subtle effect on the human organism ; this poison effects the mental and the moral nature; it causes obliquity of vision and dulness of conscience. The victim does not see, neither does he understand, and, saddest of all, he does not care. Drink is the most subtle and the mightiest enemy of man's body, brain, and character. It debauches manhood, it despoils womanhood, it slaughters childhood, it desecrates the family, it embroils communities, it pauperizes the masses, it threatens the State. Away with it ; drive the swinish thing into the sea. Let no Christian citizen, let no son or daughter of the King, touch the accursed thing.

When imagination paints the race as it will be when the accursed thing no longer defiles the earth, and faith makes the vision a reality, then I shout with America's beloved daughter, "Mine eyes have seen the glory of the coming of the Lord." No man liveth to himself and no man dieth to himself; the Christian finds himself not only in the family and in the Church, but in the State, and he must render to Cæsar the things that are Cæsar's.

When one inquires, How shall the Christian citizen stand in relation to political action? it is well first to remember that civil and political citizenship under our flag are not conditioned on moral character. "All persons born or naturalized in the United States, and subject to the jurisdiction thereof, are citizens of the United States and of the State wherein they reside." At the beginning, in some of the colonies, political citizenship was withheld from non-church-members. A study of the efforts of the Fathers to found either a Church-State or to unite the Church and the State as illustrated in Massachusetts and Connecticut is most interesting. These efforts were often illumined with the glow of heroic purpose, and sometimes shadowed with the grotesque arrogance of bigotry; but this has now passed away, and nowhere in the United States is religious belief made a test of citizenship. The Christian has no eminence under the law; he has no priority of title to civil or political preferment; in civil and political relations he is known only as a resident of the community, a tax-payer, a voter.

When Jesus said, "All ye are brethren," he uttered the prophetic truth upon which popular governments and republican institutions rest. This "brotherhood" permits no coercion in religious belief. It puts no restraints on individual conduct, except the necessary limitations whereby all may enjoy the fullest liberty in the pursuit of happiness. The law informs us what these limits are; Christian and Jew, Pagan and Agnostic, are all equally bound; none are exempt.

What a Christian voter shall do in the wide range of political action he alone can decide when the duty is imminent; we may, however, know the outline of his duties. He should vote; he should render to Cæsar the things that are Cæsar's. I have known intelligent men, leaders of thought and teachers of public morals, who for one reason and another did not perform this simple duty; I have known others who scorned to take any hand in "practical politics." It is no exaggeration to say that at every election — more especially local and State — there are hundreds and even thousands of men who do not vote, and even disparage as shallow enthusiasts those who magnify political effort and responsibility. In all aggregated responsibility there is danger that the unit will lose itself in the mass, and weakness and utter disregard of effort be the result. Does not the citizen who will not "mix up in politics" assume arrogance as well as lack of appreciation? Does he not imply that he is made of better stuff than other citizens, and therefore will not lose his identity in the mass? This sentiment may not be formulated in his own mind, but does it not lurk behind his failure? In this country the average citizen wears the crown of sovereignty; good and bad, intelligent and ignorant, meet at the ballot-box and determine what this average is. He who withholds an intelligent Christian vote by so much lowers the quality of the average vote.

" Practical politics " to the Christian citizen should mean that he will use his greatest endeavor to nominate and help elect the very best men which the local sentiment will support. This " best man " may not be an ideal Christian citizen, for ours is a representative government; but Christian citizens should support those who because of their own character and political affiliations may be reasonably expected to give their support to the highest present attainable good in civil and political life.

Political parties are a recognized agency in the administration of constitutional government. Party politics more properly deal with questions of administration in government than with moral questions not yet a part of the government. Party issues are made when differing conclusions are reached as to the wisdom or unwisdom of certain forms of administration. Protection and Free Trade, Bimetalism and Monometalism, are illustrations of legitimate party utterances. These questions are in no sense moral issues, although to the individual "silverite " or "gold bug " there exists the moral obligation to support the policy which his individual judgment approves.

The questions involving material interests, which are championed by political parties, ought not to be despised by the Christian citizen.

The last speaker was the president of the Pennsylvania Christian Endeavor Union.

Address of Rev. J. T. McCrory, D.D., Pittsburg, Pa.

The following declaration was made in the Senate Chamber yonder on the hill, a few years ago, by a representative of the Christian commonwealth of Kansas: "The purification of politics is an iridescent dream. Government is force. Politics is a battle for supremacy. Parties are the armies. The Decalogue and the Golden Rule have no place in a political campaign!" I have heard of an eccentric and zealous old Christian who was in the habit of "speaking out in meeting" and signifying his approval or disapproval of the sentiments uttered by his pastor. A strange minister occupied the pulpit one day and was detailing some dazzling heresy and was quite paralyzed to hear from the pew the unctuous and emphatic response, "Thank the Lord, that is a lie." One could wish that somewhere in the Senate Chamber or the galleries there had been such a Christian patriot to greet this sentiment of Senator Ingalls in the same way, for, thank the Lord, that is a lie. That sentiment has been characterized as both infamous and brutal. If the senator was right, then Christ has no place in national life and my theme is a misnomer. But he was not right. Ten thousand voices in this country declare that characterization of American life is false. "This is a Christian nation." That declaration came from the Supreme Bench since the other was made in the Senate Chamber. But the subject I am to discuss should have a text. We Endeavorers want to feel that we are on the " Rock " in politics as everywhere else. My text is an incident that occurred in the beginnings of the Gospel in Europe. Paul had responded to the vision from Macedonia and had come, in his journey, to Thessalonica. His enemies, the Jews, sought to drive him out. They declared he was a revolutionist; that he proclaimed another king in opposition to Caesar; that he was turning the world upside down with his doctrines; that he proposed to dethrone Augustus and put Jesus in his place. Of course that was not true as they meant it. Still it was true that Christ would, in some real sense, displace the Roman tyrant and revolutionize the Roman government, for he is a revolutionist. His purpose in coming into the world was to produce a complete, radical revolution in all the affairs connected with human life and society. In describing his own mission he declared, " I came not to bring peace, but a sword." Every prophesy that heralded his coming told the same story. It is true these prophesies are also bright with the visions of a golden age; a blessed peace that is to embrace all the earth is the thrilling hope inspired by the promises of his coming. But does not that very fact foreshadow revolution? Does not the fulfilment of these promises necessitate the turning of the world upside down?

Let me call your attention first to the fact that the aspect of the Cross is undergoing a great change in this regard. There was a time, not so long ago either, when the Cross was viewed almost exclusively in reference to the salvation of the individual. We looked at Calvary amid the shadows of the awful day and heard the sweet assurance given by the suffering Saviour to the dying thief, " This day shalt thou be with me in paradise," and were disposed to conclude that the whole meaning of that mysterious and merciful sacrifice was summed up in the rescue of the individual sinner. We have taken that picture which brings tears to every eye that looks upon it, where the shipwrecked woman clings to the cross standing there upon the rock where beat the billows of an angry sea, while the broken vessel is dashed madly upon the shore, as the full representation of the saving purposes of the Son of man. But our conception of his work and mission has been mightily enlarged. That transaction on the hill back of Jerusalem almost nineteen hundred years ago concerns not only every man but every interest and institution of humanity. It has grown upon us as some of the great events and battles of the world have grown. Marathon was more than its age thought. It was more than a battle between two peoples. It was the turning-point in the tide of civilization. There the hordes of barbarism were turned back and civilization took up its march toward the new day. Waterloo means more to us than it did to the contending forces on that desperate field. The coming of Blucher not only saved the day for Wellington, but changed the map of Europe and gave to despotism the staggering blow from which it is never to recover. Gettysburg was a glorious victory even as we understood it on that memorable Fourth of July, 1863, when the lightning flashed the glad tidings across the continent and around the world. But we were mistaken in the thought that it was only a victory for the North against the South. It was a turning-point in history for the mighty American nation both North and South. We stand with uncovered head on that immortal field to-day after the lapse of a generation and try to realize the solemnity becoming the place where the everlasting purpose that " free government " should not " die out among men " was sealed in the best blood of all sections of this great country. He who stands yonder where Pickett's dauntless thousands hurled themselves in deathless energy against Hancock's fearless and immovable battalions to speak in boastful tones of either side in that desperate fray has no soul for the courage and conviction that sent those eager thousands forward into the embrace of death or held the lines they hurled themselves upon with daring unsurpassed. Gettysburg was a battle-field that is of primary interest to all the world. So we conceive it to have been with Calvary. Those wide-stretched arms of the dying Christ were extended for the uplift of the race. But the uplift of the race means the elevation of all the institutions essential to the welfare of humanity. That means civil government. We are beginning to appreciate this fact more and more as civilization advances. As Christians we must believe that this world never can be restored to an ideal state, morally, socially, or politically, until Christ is enthroned. I can understand how unbelievers may contest this proposition; but to the Christian the only salvation for this world is found in the Cross. Now, if I understand it aright, it is one purpose of this great Endeavor movement to enthrone Christ in our national life. Be patient with me then while I present some practical suggestions for your consideration and assistance.

1. Christ is in national life in a practical, telling way when he is represented by the makers and executors of the law and the founders and fashioners of political institutions. To illustrate: (*a*) Christ got practically into our national life when the Pilgrim Fathers, in the cabin of the *Mayflower*, entered into that solemn compact setting forth that they had undertaken that perilous voyage for the purpose of planting a colony for the glory of God and the advancement of the Christian faith, and pledging themselves to frame civil institutions with that end in view. To that pledge they and their descendants were loyal for the next five generations. During that formative period many things were wrought that they had not calculated on, so that, in the end, a new order of things developed under the influence of the Gospel leaven. It will hardly be claimed by any one that the first settlers, wise and progressive as they were, intended to found the free, republican institutions which came into existence with the Declaration of Independence. But they had unconsciously provided for just this outcome when they had given Christ a place in our national life. The advanced political institutions of this great Republic are the inevitable result of the place given to the Gospel at the beginning of our civil order. (*b*) Then, again, Christ got practically into our national life by means of the Declaration of Independence. When the representatives of the thirteen colonies, appealing to the Supreme Judge of the world for the rectitude of their intentions, and with a firm reliance on Divine Providence, mutually pledging to each other their lives, their fortunes, and their sacred honor. took their stand on the side of the rights of the people, as against the Old-World doctrine of the divine right of kings, which was only another name for despotism, they put Christ into our national life. That was so because the doctrine they announced was eternal truth. It was in line with the entire teaching of the Bible. Christ in national life, as everywhere else, stands for the rights of the individual. It is his purpose that every man shall be a free man. He is in the world to paralyze every arm of oppression, break every bond of despotism, dethrone every foe of human freedom; to annihilate every sullen, selfish force and influence which the arch-despot has employed for the enslavement of the world, and let the race go free.

Christ has not wrought out his entire purpose concerning this nation yet. He has not been accorded the full place to which he is entitled and which the welfare of this country demands in our national life. It is not my wish to dishearten any one, as we turn our faces toward the future and consider the work yet to be done on behalf of righteousness in this great Republic. But I must be honest and straightforward with you. I must, therefore, say to you that this is no holiday or dress-parade business in which we are engaged,—getting Christ into our national life. It never has been and never will be. He has never come in on the tidal wave of popularity by the votes of majorities or the applause of the multitude. He comes in just as he came into Thessalonica in Paul's day, through suspicion, false accusation, mob violence, imprisonments, and martyrdoms. Mind that. It will help you some day when you are suffering for this cause. Christ gets into place and power in national life just as he got into his place and power at the right hand of the throne yonder in the heavens,— by Gethsemane, Gabbatha, and Calvary. There is a must-needs-be for the bloody sweat, the crown of thorns, and the cross on the way to the enthronement of righteousness in this world. Over yonder, in Scotland, they have just been engaged in doing honor to the memory of the martyrs of former centuries. Who were these men? They are the men who sought in their day to get Christ into national life, and they lost their heads for it. They stood, in their day, for what they called the "crown rights of King Jesus," the same thing precisely that the Christian-citizenship movement of Christian Endeavor stands for in this country to-day. Let us then make up our account to suffer for it in some way, if we propose to take any serious part in this important business. It must come to this.

2. Our enterprise will be desperately antagonized. Consider some of the forces that will oppose us. (*a*) We will be opposed in the name of religion. Extremes will meet. The narrowness of so-called Liberalism will be joined by the despotism of Roman Catholicism. This is not theorizing. This is history,— history that will, inevitably, repeat itself. Take, for illustration, the common-school question. When the assault was made some years ago on the Bible in the schools of Cincinnati these extremes were found banded in one fell purpose to secularize this characteristic American institution and so work its destruction. And they partly succeeded. The same thing was seen in Boston and other cities of the country. You are for " The Little Red Schoolhouse." But, if I understand that phrase, you do not mean simply a building with walls and shingles and plaster, to shelter the young between the ages of six and twenty-one from the summer's heat and the winter's cold. You mean a place for the training of men and women for American citizenship. You believe, as that great document, the ordinance for the government of the Northwest, declares, that, "religion, morality, and knowledge" are necessary to good government and the happiness of mankind. You believe that we should therefore cultivate the fear of God and the love of country, and that, hence, the open Bible should be always inside the schoolhouse and the old flag forever float above it. This is one of the foremost issues of this hour. Let popular education be abandoned and multitudes will grow up in ignorance, fit tools for despotism. On the other hand, educate the brain of America without the conscience and you but prepare the way for our speedier destruction. We must, in sheer self-defence, look after the education of our future citizenship or suffer the consequences. But we do not want, and will not have, any priest business in that education, nor will we submit to the immorality of atheism or unbelief of any kind. We want the Word of God to get straight at the understandings of the young by means of an open Bible. This will cost a struggle. (*b*) For another thing we must count on the opposition of base partisanship and political prejudice. I do not believe that voter fairly represented the average constituency of any existing political organization when he declared that if his party nominated the devil for office he would vote for him. I do not believe it is altogether so bad as that. Anyway, I question whether the devil would give up his general oversight of all parties for the highest office in the gift of any of them. Partisanship, nevertheless, is standing squarely across the pathway of

every reform. Take the matter of the government of our cities. You will not find a sane man anywhere but believes municipal government all over this nation is a menace and a curse. Through robbery and jobbery and bribery taxation is fivefold what it should be. What is it that stands in the way of reform? Nothing in this wide world but the partisanship of politics. The case must become desperate before the average voter will say "No" to the "boss;" And it is altogether likely that if he says "No" at this election he will endorse at the next the villany he opposed. Look at New York City. Out of sheer disgust with the vileness of Tammany, three years ago, the people rose up and seemingly shook off the clutches of the "Tiger" from their throat. But partisanship robbed them of their victory and they are soon to be back again under the old despotism. It is thus in every city that has attempted reform.

Or take the effort for the destruction of that *monstrum horrendum* of nineteenth-century civilization,— the saloon and liquor traffic. No decent man defends the saloon. The universal verdict from people of even average morality is that it ought to die. The evangelical churches represented in Christian Endeavor and standing for not less than forty millions of our population have declared again and again, with burning emphasis, that the liquor traffic is "the sum of all villanies," an offence against high heaven and a curse to the world, and that its legalization is a sin and a crime. It is pointed out, over and over again, that this traffic is the cause of nine-tenths of the poverty, degradation, crime, and general political and social corruption of the times. The cry is heard from a million of these Christian homes every year, "The saloon has got my boy," "The saloon has ruined my daughter," while a hundred thousand graves, with not a gleam of resurrection hope, hide away each year the heartache of as many wives and mothers in the person of the dead which the saloon has robbed and murdered and damned. And yet there it stands in all its hellish enormity and brazen effrontery, pointing to its justification in the license decreed it by the votes of American citizens, five millions of whom are members of our churches and Christian men; five millions of whom have said in their church resolutions that it ought to die, that its legalization is a crime and a sin. Why have they not made that declaration good at the ballot-box? The answer is, "Partisanship and political prejudice." It is said that some years ago Rev. George R. Stuart was preaching in Kentucky, and in the midst of his sermon a poor Irish woman started down the aisle, crying, "Mr. Stuart, the saloon has my boy." He stopped and asked, "How many other mothers are there here who can bear that same tragic testimony?" Hands went up all over the house; kid-gloved hands, toil-hardened hands, hands of all classes of people. Then Mr. Stuart said, "Men of Kentucky, I do not know what kind of stuff you are made of; but I am made of the kind of stuff that will stand for these mothers against the saloon and the liquor traffic," and that entire congregation rose to its feet. Why do not the five million Christian men of America rise to their feet on election day, and stand for the robbed and broken-hearted mothers against the saloon, as our church resolutions have pledged the world they will? The answer is, "Partisanship and political prejudice." That spirit can only be cast out by the fuller coming of Christ into our national life. I might refer to many other phases of opposition to the entrance of Christ into national life; but let this suffice. You see what I mean. Now the thing to be done is that we consecrate ourselves anew to the business of preparing the way for that coming. We may only be John Baptists. There may be Herods to oppose us. There may not be the dungeon or the headsman's axe in response to the appeal of the harlot, the political boss, or the drink; but there will be the crack of the political whip, the cry of "fool for throwing your vote away." There will be the propositions for compromise that "would deceive even the elect," especially if they thought there was the least chance by means of the deception of being elected. There will be that "thief of time," procrastination, "just wait till this election is over," and the good intentions with which hell is paved, which are never put into action, and a thousand other things to baffle and oppose you in your good work. But you get right with God, and consecrate yourself to the enthronement of righteousness and hold firm, and Christ will yet be supreme in our national life.

IN FRONT OF THE CAPITOL DURING THE PATRIOTIC SONG SERVICE.

IN FRONT OF THE SENATE PORTICO DURING THE PATRIOTIC SONG SERVICE.

CALVARY BAPTIST CHURCH.
ARMORY, CONVENTION BUSINESS HEADQUARTERS.

FIRST CONGREGATIONAL CHURCH.
WESLEY M. E. CHURCH.

FIRST PRESBYTERIAN CHURCH.
FOUNDRY M. E. CHURCH.

NEW YORK AVENUE PRESBYTERIAN CHURCH.
CENTRAL HALL.

Central Hall.

Central Hall, beautifully decorated, with streamers and bunting stretching to and from every part of the building, with flags and shields tastily arranged together all over the walls, held a big crowd, which did not show any lack of interest from beginning to end.

The musical director of the evening was Chas. S. Clark, chairman of the music committee of the Convention. The presiding officer was Mr. Frank E. Page, of Chicago.

Chairman Page, in his opening remarks, said that a few years ago it might have been necessary to apologize for introducing the subject, "Christian Citizenship," into a Christian Endeavor meeting, but it was now a timely topic.

Then Mr. Page introduced as the first speaker on this subject Mr. H. L. Castle, of Pittsburg, Pa., one of the reform leaders of that city.

Address of Mr. H. L. Castle, Pittsburg, Pa.

The one thing supremely needful to correct the committed evils in American politics is a wide-awake, active, unsubsidized, incorruptible Christian conscience. The affections of the average American are true; but the conscience is perverted, and the sense of absolute right in politics is dethroned, and in its place policy or party necessity reigns supreme. This condition has made of our Christian citizenship a byword and a jesting. From four to six million men in our land who should possess this acute conscience and unsuborned principle of right in the highest degree of development have slept, or but faintly protested, at unimportant times and by inefficient means, while year by year on the auction-block of greed, avarice, and ambition, all that the Church holds dearest in the affairs of government has been sold to the saloon interests of this and foreign lands. Just see how it has affected our civilization. The name of Washington naturally suggests the thought of Christian citizenship, for it brings to our mind the image of a Christian patriot who on bended knee in the Continental Congress committed this land to God. In the dark hour of his country's need he rested on the arm of Jehovah, spurned the gilded bribe of a king's crown, and in resigning his sword to Congress commended "the interests of our dearest country to the protection of Almighty God, and those who have the superintendence of them to his holy keeping." But the name of Washington City, as the political centre of our country, with its cold-tea bars, its "where-am-I-at" representatives, its mad plunge for power at any sacrifice of principle, and its godless atmosphere, has in it no more suggestiveness of Christian statesmanship than do the muddy roads over which Coxey's army tramped to this city suggest the golden streets of the new Jerusalem. This degeneracy in politics is not because the world is growing worse, for it is not, but is day by day being lifted nearer to God. It is not because there are no good men in the control of politics, for there are men whose personal life is blameless; but it is because the organized, legalized liquor traffic is in partisan politics. It formally entered on June 5, 1861, when, at a National Brewers' Congress held in Chicago, they resolved: " That we will sustain no candidate, of whatever party, in any election, who is in any way disposed toward the total abstinence cause." So complete has become their dominion that we have the humiliating spectacle presented of a high official of government leaving his seat here in Washington to go to a distant city and appear before a brewers' congress with these words upon his lips: " I am here for the purpose of learning your wants. Congress has given you an internal revenue law, milder in its provisions, less burdensome than any law affecting an equally great interest. Yes, you have begun well. Let us take no backward step. I say, Let *us*, for I am with you. Every patriotic citizen is with you. The President is with you. Every patriotic citizen is with you if you will hold to your course. If there be any regulations or anything whatever which you may deem unreasonable, I beg that you will not hesitate to express your views."

It is true that no man can be elected to any office of importance who is known to entertain feelings of active hostility to the traffic. While the liquor interests have thus been steadily following the letter of resolution, see what the Church has been doing.

Laboring under the delusion that it is the business of the government to make men rich, we have been attempting to vote ourselves financially prosperous, while we have stood watching the foulest monster that ever had legal life crawl up and down through our nation, and, as he goes, leave behind him a track of blood that can never be washed out, feeding him our money at the rate of $3,000 per minute. His foul breath has died the fire on thousands of hearthstones; in his clammy embrace has been hugged to death the dearest hope of millions of hearts; charmed by the gaze of his red eye, lawyers have tottered from their throne of greatness, statesmen have fallen from their empire of power, ministers have dropped from their pedestal of exaltation, been caught in the wide-open jaws, and, ground to a pulp, swallowed into the belly of habitual inebriety, where they join thousands from the humbler walks of life; and over the wretched termination of their human existence, the kindliest prayer that might be uttered in their behalf would be, " O Lord, that in this life or another they might never awaken ! " This is the condition begotten of saloon resolutions and waved aside year after year by the Christian citizen that we might vote ourselves rich.

Here I stand before you, the representative of the Christian youth of America, and I call upon you to " strive to do whatever He would like to have you do." This traffic ought to die. This is attested in the broken heart of every father, mother, brother, or sister that is being slowly torn to shreds, drawn as through a sieve of despair, burned over the slow fire of anxious waiting for the coming doom of a dear one; in every hearthstone now cold and damp, whose very shadows form themselves into the ghost of bygone brightness; in every brain from which has been erased the image of Godlike manhood, and upon which has been imprinted the hateful image of the Prince of darkness. The liquor traffic ought to die. This is truth. I summon the young men of America who have no strong political ties to bind them, no political foes to punish or friends to aid; whose vision of political righteousness has not been narrowed by the astigmatism of party polity or obscured by the cataract of party greed; whose political hearing has not been deadened by the din of the unmanly shout, " Don't let the other party win; " whose political tastes have not been perverted by the unwholesome food of victory at any sacrifice of principle; whose political touch has not been dulled by the handling of the gruesome pestilence of machine politics; but whose vision is so clear that they can see the Son of righteousness; who can hear the still small voice in the soul; who can taste the sweets of doing right; who can lay hold of the hand of God in the politics of our land. You, young man, with God in your soul, I call you to rise and stand at the polls of this nation this fall for the destruction of the liquor traffic as the one great, overshadowing, overmastering, all-embracing foe to this nation's credit, honor, and manhood.

Young man, I call your mind to the fact that your Master, to whom at the altar of some church you have surrendered your life, is to-day on trial; even now, in the temple, he is surrounded by his would-be murderers ; and where are you and the church that so lately made proclamation of allegiance to him by notifying the world that " no political party need expect the support of Christian men so long as it refuses to put itself on record in open hostility to the saloon," — that has even been so ready to chop off the ear of some harmless, jabbering servant? Where are they now? For the most part, warming themselves beside some silver or gold fire, while their Lord is in the death-struggle with the power of evil. Do not accuse me of overdrawing the picture. It can't be overdrawn. Within the last thirty years the consumption of liquors has increased from a trifle over four gallons *per capita* to over eighteen gallons *per capita* per year; and if this increase shall continue for another thirty years, American Christian civilization goes out in night; and if it were true that Freedom shrieked when Kosciusko fell, the very angels of heaven shall drop their pinions of light and weep, for a thousand years of Christian effort centres in the birth of the twentieth century. Shall all that effort be lost? If it is, it means incalculable loss here and in the hereafter. And the political conditions are so shaping themselves that whether you wish it or not, the call is coming to each of you to stand upon one or the other side of the question, and you must answer fairly and squarely, or skulk or cower beside some fire of pelf, compromise, or cowardice while the eyes of the dying Lord are turned in pity and amazement upon you, the very serving-maids deride you, and the cock of time proclaims another opportunity lost. There never was a time when the single, burning question, " What will you do with the liquor traffic? " was so clearly pressed into notice as now, and God has his Elijahs, standing for the most part alone, upon our Mount Carmel, while the priesthood and the crowds and the majority are against them; but still we hear the challenge, we must hear it: " How long halt ye between the god of silver and gold and the God of pure manhood?" I tell you some day our God will answer by fire,— some day, when upon the altar of sacrifice and consecration the Christ-citizen lays his loyalty to self, that will not permit an alliance with wrong for personal reward; loyalty to home, that will not consent for a day to postpone protecting it from its greatest foe by promise of immunity from questionable ills; loyalty to country, that will decline to permit the Stars and Stripes to float over and protect a liquor saloon; loyalty to God, that will subrogate everything to his honor and glory. Then will come sweeping down from his holy mountain the fire of his glory and power; their sacrifice will be accepted, and the bewildered, condemned, false prophets will be swallowed up in another Kishon, and the land will be refreshed by the rains of his grace and blessing.

The call to you, as present duty, is to array yourself with the Elijahs, even though the crown may be small. And this is a call of ownership; ye are bought with a price, precious, single standard, full weight and fineness in the circulating medium of heaven, even the blood of Jesus Christ, and this purchase includes your citizenship, for Paul says, "Our citizenship is in heaven." Imagine the citizenship of some of us in heaven!—its material manufactured in 240,000 saloons, held together by tariff and silver, lined with broken hearts, bound with blood money, padded with lost spirits, and worn in the name of party fealty, and, thus clad, made to parade Jerusalem Avenue in the New Paradise under the inspecting eyes of Abraham, Isaac. Paul, Silas, Stephen, John, and the thousands of those who have washed their robes and made them white in the blood of the Lamb.

Endeavorers, I have not improved this opportunity if I have not brought your conscience face to face with a duty as great as lay before Moses when he stood by the burning bush, as weighty as rested upon Joshua on the banks of the Jordan, as real as fell upon David when the king's crown pressed his brow, as solemn as burdened the cross-ladened Christ as he toiled unsupported up Calvary's hill. It is a duty of standing in the political market-place of this nation in the ides of next November for the destruction of the liquor traffic. It is as great as was Moses's duty, for it means the freeing of a great people; as weighty as was Joshua's duty, for it means the conquest of a great power; as real as was David's duty, for it means a kingship of righteousness; and as solemn as was Christ's duty, for it is a part of the plan to usher in his kingdom.

Now, dear friends, a word of warning in conclusion. It may be that something which has been or will be said here to-night has filled you with new desires and aspirations after political righteousness, but you rise and go out in the world, and presently the devil, or one of his emissaries, will catch you up and bear you to a high mountain of excitement. He will show you all the kingdoms of preferment and power; judgeships, senatorships, even presidencies, will pass in review before you. A land stacked with gold and silver, where money is as plenty as water, will be made to appear before you. A country so protected that you can't see over the walls, and all within them are dwelling in palaces, is reviewed before your vision, and the devil will tell you, " All these things will I give you," if next November you will bow at the nation's altar and, with ballot in hand, worship me. Don't believe him; he always was a liar, and he never will be anything else. There are no honors for you that will compensate for dishonor before God. There is no plenty for this country while we continue to worse than waste $1,200,000,000 every year; and there can be no universal family happiness while it is true that a million besotted wretches are staggering out into the blackest night at the rate of 120,000 per year, and that the recruiting-stations of death are laying hands on one bright boy from each fifth home every year to keep this army of the lost full. You must not allow a drum-beat to answer for the voice of conscience, nor crowd to carry you with them to do evil; but, as did thy Master, turn thou upon the political devils, who are all about thee, seeking thy life, and to all their fair promises make answer, " Thou shalt worship the Lord thy God, in all thy ways; and him only, and at all times, shalt thou serve."

After Mr. Castle's address, the Rev. F. M. Lamb sang a solo, which appealed mightily to the hearts of all.

The second speaker introduced by Mr. Page was Rev. Alexander Alison, D.D., New York City.

Address of Rev. Alexander Alison, D.D., New York City.

What saith the Scripture? " The powers that be are ordained of God." If this be so then human government is a divine appointment. As such we must give it honor — not only theoretically, but practically. In this fair land of ours citizenship means more than anywhere else on earth. We have here the best result, defective as we may sometimes think it, of the republican idea; that is, a government " of the people, by the people, for the people."

While I do not believe that a "form" of government is the all-essential in matters of State craft, any more than I believe that Presbyterianism or any other form of church polity is essential to the existence of the " body of Christ," — the Church,— yet I do hold that our form of government, the "republican," is the one which most nearly conserves the rights of the individual as well as the high interest of the masses. But a government of this kind can only attain its highest operation through the diffusion of general knowledge among the people as to its *modus operandi*. If manhood suffrage shall exercise the franchise, then we must see to it that no stone is left unturned that twenty-one years of age shall find the individual citizen duly qualified to put in practice his sovereign rights. What is such a doctrine as this? It is nothing more nor less than the carrying into the State the instruction of the children in patriotic and governmental principles. This is a fundamental idea. Under such a régime we begin the building of the house at the cellar.

I, for one, do not believe that the country is in the hands of the Philistines numerically. For instance, I do not accept the proposition that Romanism is so strong in this country that it dominates our rulers. As a matter of fact, it has a good deal of influence. Why is this the case? Is it because the papacy is in the ascendency here? Not at all; the Romish communion is not occupying any such position. But the politicians have the idea that the Catholic population votes all one way. While this is not altogether true, it is very largely true. But politicians are not as well informed as they ought to be on this subject. The priesthood is politic in endeavoring to keep up the impression of Rome's influence.

But I am quite certain the Catholic vote, so called, is not so large as many politicians believe. The priest cannot always deliver the goods. They know this themselves. What is the real strength of the Roman Catholic Church in the United States? There are not quite ten thousand priests in the whole country. How many Protestant ministers are there? Over one hundred thousand, in all the evangelical denominations. Suppose these should stand together for good-citizenship training and for our country's governmental interests; where would the power of the one-tenth represented by the priesthood be? Shall the nine-tenths be governed by the one-tenth? Does the priest have more influence over his communicant than the average Protestant pastor? I deny it. History has not shown it. Evangelical Christianity must ever be defensive. It must not fight unless it has to; but when it does stretch forth its arm, its cry must ever be, " Death rather than surrender."

We want in this land to train our children to understand that no religion is worthy of the name that does not unselfishly stand for good government and patriotism. We have dangers in this land of ours that will have to be met in the future by stalwart men and women. Those who will be required for service will be those only who have but one sentiment emblazoned on the banner under which they shall march,—" For God and native land."

We have evils among us that must be overcome. The American saloon will have to go to the wall. American journalism must be elevated in its tone. The atmosphere of the editorial sanctum has become vitiated by reason of the Sunday-newspaper filth. There has been a letting-down all along the line. Where are the Horace Greeleys of to-day? Is the American tribune in this land of ours really what it ought to be, the palladium of our liberties? If not, it should be.

It rests with the coming generations to make it so. I have great hope born in my soul as I contemplate the magnitude of result for good that may accrue from the movement among the young people of the Christian Church which is the chief characteristic of the evening of this, the grandest of the centuries, and which may toll the death-knell of partisan politics and political demagoguery and all the evils that have retarded not only our progress as a nation, but have been tremendous stumbling-blocks in the way of the Gospel chariot.

Young people, arise and proclaim yourselves! Let not the Philistines capture the camp of Israel! Do not forget your strength, your power. Remember, if you please, that nothing is here to stay which God disapproves. The works of darkness, both in Church and State, must come to naught.

The Old Testament history is full of illustrations that " it is not by might, nor by power, but by the Spirit of the Lord, that victory comes." The minority always won in the wars of Israel when God was a partner in the struggle. I believe that the hosts of law and order are greater in our country than the converse. I believe we are in the majority. But it matters not. Abraham Lincoln never spoke more truly than when he said, " He who is in a minority with God is in the majority." Let this be our conviction as we go forth with the one cry, " Our country for Christ and the Church."

The last speaker was Mr. Thomas E. Murphy, the well-known leader of reform fights in New York City, and a temperance lecturer of world-wide renown. Mr. Murphy is a great favorite with Endeavorers and has spoken before at International Conventions. We regret that Mr. Murphy did not supply manuscript.

New York Avenue Presbyterian Church.

The meeting at the New York Avenue Presbyterian Church was a great success, and three admirable addresses were made in advocacy of Christian citizenship. A large choir, under the direction of Mr. Page Zimmerman, rendered the musical part of the exercises in a very spirited and pleasant manner. The Rev. Gilby C. Kelly, D.D., of Birmingham, Ala., one of the trustees of the United Society, presided, and after the choir had participated in a service of song he introduced the Rev. G. O. Little, of Washington, who conducted the devotional exercises, during which Mr. Melville D. Hensey rendered in excellent style, " One Sweetly Solemn Thought."

Dr. Kelly then introduced the first speaker of the evening.

Address of Rev. D. F. McGill, D.D., Allegheny City, Pa.

I am to speak to you to-night upon the subject, "A Christian Citizenship Platform." Such a platform seems to be needed. For the same reason that a society has its constitution, a church its creed, and a political party its platform, the Christian citizen needs a concise statement of the principle and policy upon which his work for Christ and Church and State is to be done.

A Christian citizen is a man who enjoys his rights and privileges and performs his duty as a citizen in such a way as to manifest the Spirit of Christ and of his teachings. And yet, without a more definite statement than that afforded by the definition, one's duty might seem to be just a little vague, as when over-anxious and solicitous parents are wont to enjoin impressively upon their children some dozen times a day that they shall "be good," whatever that may mean. Our observation has been that it means anything, or little, or nothing, according to the more or less confused or vacant condition of the mind of the child. And as we have heard men talking fluently of this new movement among the Christian Endeavor hosts, this thing that we call "Christian citizenship," we have wondered whether most men have a much more definite idea of its significance than this, — that it just means being good, or, perhaps, being goody-goody. What does it mean? If Christian citizenship is of the Lord, then its platform ought to be found in the Bible. I am persuaded that it is to be found there. Peter and John had been speaking boldly in the name of the Lord Jesus, and working miracles. The priests and sadducees, being displeased, commanded them that they should speak no more in his name. The answer of the apostles was, "Whether it be right in the sight of God to hearken unto you more than unto God, judge ye." That was the spirit of Christian citizenship cropping out. These men were beginning to feel that they were apostles first and citizens afterward; so they went back to their work. They wrought signs and wonders. Multitudes were healed and multitudes were saved. The apostles were arrested and cast into prison. The angel of the Lord opened the prison doors and said, "Go forth and preach." Again they are arrested and brought before the council. Again they are threatened and examined by the angry council. Their answer is, "We must obey God rather than men." Noble words! That was the bugle-blast for a conflict that has never ceased and that will continue until every citizen shall be a Christian citizen and every nation a Christian nation. A Christian citizenship platform in seven words! In seven thousand words it could not have been improved upon. If it is not a gold platform, it is a platform of pure gold. If it is not a silver platform, it contains that the merchandise of which is better than silver. If it is not a broad-gauge platform, it is a broad platform. We must obey God rather than men. Christian Endeavorers, I submit to you that one who, as a Christian, marches under the banner of King Jesus, and who takes for his motto, "Whose I am and whom I serve," ought to be most willing and happy to stand as a citizen upon such a platform as this.

The adoption of a platform supposes a conflict. The two great political parties of our country have just put forth their declaration of principles, and the conflict is on. The apostles declared their position in seven emphatic words, and the conflict was on. With them it was a question of principle or policy, of duty or expediency, of singularity or popularity; and as the same conflict goes on to-day, the same alternatives are presented to every one of us. Principle or policy, duty or expediency, singularity or popularity,— which shall it be? Our platform will decide every question for us. We must obey God rather than men.

All Christians claim to be Christian citizens. There is not a single voice from the Church against Christian citizenship. But let a man examine himself. Am I standing squarely upon the platform of the apostles? Do I refer every question to the will of God? Do I live and act and speak and vote as would the Son of God himself, if he were in my place, a citizen of this free country?

Political parties press their claims upon us. They point to their records, and remind us of the principles for which they have stood and of the services which they have rendered the individual and the nation. They give us their promise for the future and declare their policy, and ask us for our support. And this is right. We are not here to dispute the claim made by any party, or to cast reproach upon any party. We only want to find a platform and a straightforward, consistent policy for every Christian citizen. Let it be supposed that every point in every platform of a political party is well taken and that every statement made is true. God also has his claims upon us ; and these are immeasurably greater. There are those who have a lively appreciation of the blessings of a protective tariff. The Christian citizen will be willing to admit, however, that these are not to be compared to the blessings of a protective Providence. Political parties are wont to hold themselves responsible for our blessings of civil and religious liberty. Even these, however, are not to be compared to the glorious liberty of the children of God, for which we are indebted only to the King of kings and Lord of lords. It may be freely admitted that political parties, by the wisdom of their principles and policies, have done much to promote the welfare and increase the wealth of our country ;— not so much, though, as God has done by his free grants of rain and dew and sunlight and heat, to the value of untold billions of dollars. And when to these we add the spiritual blessings whose value can be estimated only by the price that was paid for them, surely we are ready to admit that we are under obligation to obey God rather than men.

But what will our Christian citizenship platform require of us ? What effect will it have upon the life and conduct of the men who stand upon it ? The work of reforming the world has been committed by the Lord Jesus Christ to his people, to be carried forward in his name and according to his will. It follows, therefore, that the Christian citizen must be a reformer. It is just at this point that many who claim to be Christian citizens become discouraged. To be a reformer—what does that mean? It means hard work. It means fighting against the current. It means to be called a crank, it may be ; a Puritan, a fanatic, a friend of the Blue Laws. But it means, also, loyalty to Christ, who was himself a reformer, and who would be one if he were here to-day. Bad bills become laws in our State legislatures by the energy, patience, and persistence of bad men. Thus are our laws of marriage frequently assailed, the Sabbath destroyed, the school system undermined, the saloon enthroned and relieved of restraint, and government, municipal and state, converted into a vast machine for collecting revenues and disbursing them in the interests of the powerful and unscrupulous.   How shall these evils be remedied, if not by the energy, patience, persistence, and self-denial of good men, who stand upon the platform of the apostles ? We must obey God rather than men. Influential Christian legislators must be chosen by Christian citizens. All legislative matter must be thoroughly and rigidly inspected by men who are capable of judging of its moral effect. Moral legislation must be secured, if at all, through the efforts of good men, Christian citizens, who believe that not evil, but Christ, has come to stay. If you are not willing to be a reformer for Christ's sake, do not call yourself a Christian citizen.

A political party that gets on the wrong side of any moral question forfeits its claim to the support of a Christian citizen. Jesus Christ, whose we are and whom we serve, asks that we shall be found on the right side of every moral question, and that by our lives, our voices, our influence, and our votes we shall serve always and only one Master. More than one master we can not serve; and when the question is one of obedience to God or man, our Christian citizenship platform would seem to make our course very clear indeed. The Christian citizen must declare eternal warfare against every foe of God and man. He who belongs to God must not, can not, belong to any party. He must not, can not, vote with any party for that of which his one Master disapproves. This is what Christian citizenship means. It means having *one* Master, belonging to God, voting for Christ. In Paul's letter to the Philippians, there is a sentence in the margin of the Revised Version which reads, " Behave as a citizen, worthily of the Gospel of Christ." Christian citizenship again! Government is instituted by God himself. He has ordained the end for which it is instituted and the purpose which it is to serve. He has declared the character of the men who ought to be chosen to carry out his ideas of government. How, then, shall one behave as a citizen worthily of the Gospel of Christ? By using his citizenship so as to serve the purpose which God has in government. Speaking only a few days ago to a State senator on the subject of some proposed anti-Sabbath legislation, he said in his effort to defend himself, "Even the Lord Jesus Christ could not please everybody. How can I be expected to do so?" It was not difficult to answer, "It is quite true that the Lord Jesus Christ did not please everybody, but he did always please his Father in heaven; and the public official who always tries to do that will never have occasion to be ashamed or afraid of his record." To this we may add in this presence that the Christian voter, who casts his ballot for Christ rather than for any party, will not need to be ashamed or afraid of his record in the day when the fire shall try every man's worth and every party's platform, of what sort it is.

We must obey God rather than men. Then what shall be our attitude toward the saloon and the liquor traffic? Attitude is the position appropriate to the expression of some feeling. It indicates opinion or purpose regarding anything. What position have we Christian citizens assumed that gives expression to our feeling and purpose regarding this institution that has done evil and only evil all the days of its life? You have never been in a saloon in your life! That is a magnificent record, but it is not an attitude. You are a total abstainer. So far, your attitude is only one of indifference. You are leaving the saloon alone with the expectation that it will leave you alone. You may discover some day that you have been terribly deceived. I know a Christian mother who never had anything to do with a saloon except to hate it; but it took hold of her only son and made him at times a demon and finally a sot, until in her agony she cried out, "Why did God not take him from my arms when he was an innocent babe?" I know a father who never did anything for or against the saloon; but it degraded his son and debauched his daughter and ruined his home. There are hundreds of thousands who have left the saloon alone only to discover that the saloon would not leave them alone. I think this has been the great mistake of the Christian world. It has left the saloon too severely alone. It has not come up to the help of the Lord against the mighty. Jesus Christ did not leave evil alone. We can not and be true to him. We must obey God rather than men. All that evil asks is to be let alone. The devils made that prayer of Jesus Christ, but he did not grant them their request.

What shall be our attitude towards the saloon and the liquor traffic? I pray God that it may be one of open and uncompromising hostility. Nay, that is God's prayer to us. We have been heedless and indifferent too long, while this great enemy of God and man has entrenched itself in the political and commercial life of the nation, until many are ready to affirm that the saloon has come to stay. If that were true, it would not relieve us of our obligation to wage unceasing warfare against it. Disease has come to stay, and we fight against that. Poverty has come to stay, and we fight against that. But it is not true of intemperance, or of Sabbath desecration, or of impurity, or of any other evil, that it has come to stay. The Holy Spirit has come to stay; Jesus Christ has come to stay; the kingdom of God has come to stay; and, thank God, we believe that Christian citizenship has come to stay until every one who bears the name of Christ shall stand upon the platform of the apostles, and shall practise in his life that which he professes with his lips,— that we ought to obey God rather than men.

After the choir had rendered in a spirited manner the hymn, "Onward, Christian Soldiers," the chairman said that as a Southern man it gave him special pleasure to introduce a young man of a race for whom the Southern people entertain only the kindest feelings ; in whom they believe, and in whom they repose great confidence. He then introduced Mr. W. L. Board, of Wilberforce, O., a young colored man who has attained quite a prominent position as an orator.

Address of Mr. W. L. Board, Wilberforce, O.

What to do and how to do it are questions that puzzle temperance reformers. I am glad that we meet to-night not as Prohibitionists, not as local optionists, not as high-license men, not as government regulationists, but as Christian Endeavorers, seeking a better tone of Christian citizenship, and countenancing nothing that bars the road to such an end. To whatever faction of temperance workers we belong, we oppose the rum traffic. Let us then lay aside our prejudices, forego our preferences, and stand together for principle, and not method. The temperance workers have been mistaking too long method for principle. We have already wasted too much time hurling missiles at each other, instead of joining in one mighty band and concentrating our fire upon the enemy. Let us surrender our preferences and take hold of the method that promises most unity and efficiency. I offer no apology when I present for your consideration the method pursued by the Anti-Saloon League. It is a temperance method about which I know most, having been associated with the Ohio Anti-Saloon League. It is interdenominational and omnipartisan. Its methods are so arranged that all good Republicans, good Democrats, good Prohibitionists, good Populists,— good citizens all may join issue against a common foe, without giving up their party affiliations. How can we help the cause of good citizenship? By being practical citizens. By rallying to the primaries and seeing to it that dishonest boodlers are not nominated and elected to administer law in the interests of saloon-keepers.

I am not advocating that every minister of the Gospel, and every good citizen, should become a politician, but I do advocate that it is the duty of every good man and woman to go into politics. There is as much difference between going into politics and becoming a politician as between a patriot and a politician. The one wishes to do all he can for his country; the other wants the country to do all it can for him. I have endeavored to impress upon you something of the dignity and grandeur of American citizenship; I have pointed out to you its greatest living foe, intemperance; I have dared to suggest to you a method to assuage this evil. If you remember nothing more, do not forget that the success of the temperance cause lies in unity of action and purpose. Let differences be compromised for principle. Let all the temperance squads unite and form a company, the companies a battalion, the battalions a regiment, the regiments a brigade, and finally uniting in one grand army of Christian citizens, let us go forth to battle, as one has said, " not to enslave, but to free; not to destroy, but to save; not for conquest, but for conscience; not for ourselves, only, but for every land and every race."

Then will the Church awaken to the awful chorus of an army of 500,000 hopeless drunkards in America crying to her eternal shame; then will politics, journalism, society, and religion see themselves as cringing slaves before the crime-besmeared banner of King Alcohol; then will that sense of right and duty inherent in the American people take its proper place in the affairs of state, and demand of legislation the enactment of just, practical, and effective temperance measures.

Another hymn was sung by the choir, and then the chairman introduced Mr. S. E. Nicholson, of Kokomo, Ind. Mr. Nicholson is a member of the Indiana legislature, and "father" of the famous "Nicholson Bill," and has done much effective work in the promotion of Christian citizenship.

Address of Hon. S. E. Nicholson, Kokomo, Ind.

In the discussion of this theme to-night I shall try to avoid technical definitions and minute and unimportant distinctions, that only tickle the fancy of the fastidious critic, but I shall endeavor, rather, to utilize the enthusiasm of this occasion as an overpowering agency in the busy humdrum work of the days to come.

Were we to follow the close framing of the pessimistic reformer and see only the dark side of American politics to-day, we might be sure that there is a glaring paradox in the statement of my subject, and it must be admitted that there is some evidence to warrant this belief; but when our eyes are lifted, and we behold the bright dawning of the present civic revival, and see a new type of citizenship, directed by a Christian conscience and energized by the new life-blood of young, consecrated, Christian hearts, we may dare hope for the future, that through the untiring devotion of patriotic Christian Endeavorers, Christian citizenship will soon be the dominant force in the politics of the nation.

Civil liberty and governmental prosperity are based in a special sense upon religious liberty and the development of righteous ideas.

It is not enough to say that Christianity is an important factor in human development, but in all justice it must be claimed that human government, whether in the Church, society, family, or the State, is a failure except it be measured by the infallible standard of absolute right as found in the Word of God. It was undoubtedly a part of the original divine plan that the people of earth, whose interests were largely common, should be associated together in separate individual nations, governed by rules and regulations peculiar to their needs and conditions, and that these nations should just as truly obey the laws of God as the individual members of these nations themselves.

Infidelity may attack Christianity with all the subtle arguments that the natural mind can command; scoffers may pour out their venom of wrath upon it; men may try to freeze it out in the atmosphere of a cold intellectuality; yet still the religion of Jesus Christ flows onward in a mighty, consuming stream that purifies the heart, directs the destinies of its willing votaries, and reveals to mankind a conception of the ideal standard of truth, found in the Gospel preached two thousand years ago. In all authority and legislation there must be a certain vitalizing force that gives energy and strength to the creation. For centuries men tried to find this in a system of caste that gave regulation to society; then in an aristocracy that sought obeisance from the overburdened masses; later on, in an absolute monarchy that would rule by the innate power of command; and finally, in a universal suffrage and freedom of conscience that placed men on an equality in government, church, and society. Governments are slow to learn the truth that a system laid in unrighteousness is doomed from the beginning. Ever since the law came thundering upon Mount Sinai, and the Decalogue proclaimed the human duty to God and to fellow man, there has existed a spirit and a force that ought to become the centralized idea of every organization. And any nation that either in the beginning or in any subsequent combination of elements fails to recognize the potency of Christian citizenship, measured in terms of the law of absolute right, may know that, as surely as there is a God in heaven, sooner or later it must fall, by the very imperfection of its building and the decay of its central doctrines.

We have reached a critical period in American history. The question of supreme importance is, Shall our government be maintained in its original purity and for its original purposes? In short, it is the question whether government shall be prostituted to serve the selfish ends of the depraved and the ignorant and the vicious of our country. To-day there have entered into our national and social life a great many ideas that are altogether foreign to the original purposes of the American government.

Anarchism and socialism are not nearly so threatening as that the patriotic feeling of the native citizen may be stifled. With all due sympathy for the reformer to-day, I ask, What need is there to waste centuries of energy in revolutionizing sentiment and laws, if every vestige of the original nationality is to be obliterated? What hope is there in demanding any reform, when there are so many people — apparently good citizens — ready to join the immoral or the law-defying elements, either for the sake of party domination, or under the guise of allowing personal liberty? In our own citizen life we need a revival of patriotic sentiment. We need to be lifted out of the cesspool of wrangling where demagogues hold sway. We need to call a halt upon the introduction of alien parasites, and place such restrictions that the United States will no longer be the dumping-ground for the offscourings of the world. We need to check the legislators as they play upon the ignorance of the new-made citizens to perpetuate themselves in political ascendency.

The saving grace of our own Republic, and the beacon light, to guide the world, lies in the complete recognition of Christianity as the central fact of authority. Citizenship must be measured by this absolute standard of truth, or be relegated to the rear for incompetency and unavailability.

I am not unmindful of the difficulties that menace the civic and social reformer of to-day. It is easier to suggest the remedy than to apply it. But the task is not an impossible one. Christian energy and wisdom applied to the machinery of government is the panacea for every national ill.

Happily the day is past, or at least is passing very rapidly, when a still and a deadened conscience is the price of party loyalty. And I declare to you the fact to-night that they are the best party men who stand for the right and who stand for the best interests of the people. And as a partisan myself, I dare to assert that no party in this country is worthy of success which must achieve it at the cost of degraded manhood and by pandering to the low and the vicious elements of our citizenship. I declare here to-night that whenever the Christian voters of this century come to the point of decision, when they are known to be eternally and forever against any man or class of men who favor the non-enforcement of law or the perpetuation of the liquor traffic, and are willing to register their protests at the point of greatest effect, — the ballot-box, — as do the liberal elements, then will we not only see conditions changed, but the day will be hastened when Christian citizenship enthroned by the franchises of a free people will be sought after as the only potent agency in American politics. It will only be when Christian men, whose thought has been quickened by the divine life and energized by the Holy Spirit, are elevated to places of trust and honor, and lauded as heroes by the patriotic sentiment of the Republic, that Christian citizenship will have reached the acme of its claims, and the government will become in fact as well as in name a Christian government. Christian Endeavorers, the key to the situation is with you and your Christian co-workers. By your honest battle for a better citizenship Christian conscience now passes current at the political exchange, and honest effort is redeemed at face value in the majority of political conventions throughout the country. In every State and city and village and hamlet the people are organizing for civic righteousness.

Catholicism may threaten religious toleration, and infidelity may mock at the shrine of holiness, but let us hope that the spirit that revolted against European superstition and made a new land the birthplace of freedom will in time again cause complete national recognition of the Supreme authority, and that the fellowship of saints will make Christian thought the basis of a pure government.

Tent Washington.

Tent Washington was one of the popular resorts for Christian Endeavorers on Thursday evening. By half-past seven o'clock the space covered by the canvas was filled, and the sides of the tent were lifted so that the throng that had gathered but could not be seated might join in the services from their standing-places outside. The delegates did not wait for the leader to start the singing. A band of Marylanders started " My Maryland," and then one after another of the popular hymns of the Society were started and joined in by the vast assemblage.

The exercises were opened by a service of song under the direction

of Mr. P. P. Bilhorn, of Chicago. Devotional exercises were then conducted by Rev. J. J. Muir, D.D., of Washington.

Ex-Postmaster-General John Wanamaker, of Philadelphia, was the
presiding officer of the evening.

Address of Hon. John Wanamaker, Philadelphia, Pa.

Christian Endeavor Comrades: — Our meeting at Washington, the greatest of
American cities, and upon the grounds of the nation, is in the blessed hope of
another meeting on the broader common grounds of faith by the grace of God
in the only city that is greater than any earthly city.

This country has never had but one Lincoln and one Grant and one Clark.
In the order of Providence, each came at the time of a particular need to fulfil
a sacred trust. General Clark heads and commands the largest organized army
the world has ever known. It bears no sectional banners, yet it constitutes the
majority of the truest citizenship of the land. It is the young undergrowth of
the best manhood that the world has ever seen, the hope of the nation in this
strange, but not hopeless, time.

I saw a fortnight ago in Boston, cut in letters of marble high up under the
outside cornice of the stately and matchless Public Library, these words:
"This Commonwealth regards the education of the people as the safeguard of
liberty and order." Neither the magnificent bay, nor the great avenues of splendid houses and churches, not even Boston Common, left such an impression
upon me as that noble legend of our Pilgrim Fathers.

Well may the nation to-day, and not for the first time, follow again the lead
of Massachusetts, adopting a national creed to read: This nation, throughout
its forty-six commonwealths, insists on the education of the people as the best
safeguard of liberty and order.

In the brightening dawn of the twentieth century, with the light of the
world's long struggle shining clear and steady upon us, the lamps of science
and philosophy and experience reveal the distinct fact that the elevation and
happiness of the people necessitate more than the development of the intellect. The largest temple in the world to-day is not the Parthenon of Athens,
once dedicated to philosophy, but a church for the worship of Jesus Christ,
named after Peter, the apostle, who one day denied the Lord, who was without
an open friend on all the earth. That Christ, who never carried anything in
his hands but nails, is conquering the world — not by any sword or force, but with
his appeal to the heart as well as the head. And I submit to you that this is
the proper time and place for the two millions of Endeavorers of the United
States to send out from the capital of the nation a declaration: We believe
solemnly and affirm that the safety and advancement of the people requires not
only the training of the mind but the education of the heart in knowledge of
the Word of God, which is the only rule of life for the permanent happiness of
the human race.

I think the enthusiastic two per cent of our membership in convention
assembled will vote aye on such a deliverance at this time, and I think I hear
from all over the land the rising of a voice louder than the voice of many waters,
like the thunder of the summer sky, sending up the shout of approval from the
hearts of the ninety-eight per cent of loyal members not here who desire to
stand together with us for the kingdom of Christ on earth.

Beloved brethren, it remains for us to combine the intelligence, influence, and
wisdom of the young manhood of the time to work out the destination of the
nation. It will require patriotism before partisanship.

The wars of conflicting ideas sometimes work as much suffering and loss to
a country as military battles on sea and land. It behooves us to patiently master the principles of finance and government and take our part in the strife by
voice and vote, not in the interest of party names, but of Christian citizenship.

Each man must judge for himself where and how he can do his best; but let
him do it. Christian Endeavor is not simply saying over texts and pledges and

holding consecration meetings. It is doing something. If I could, when once a year occasion required it, adjourn a consecration meeting to the town meeting or to watch over and take a proper part in a primary election, I would count it both practical politics and practical religion to do so.

The political world, as I believe, is thus far only highly amused at the talkative grumble and do-nothingness of churchmen, young and old, in public affairs.

I was once in Geneva, Switzerland, one summer Sunday afternoon, with perhaps a dozen friends, sitting under the trees in the grounds of the Rev. Leonard Woolsey Bacon, then the American minister at Geneva. We were studying the Sunday-school lesson leaf. The Hon. Henry P. Haven, of Connecticut, was in the chair. We were all startled by the sound of a gun close by, and its shot came rattling down from leaf to leaf, falling on the gravel walk. Mr. Haven said, "Well, this is the Lord's Day, and this is the Lord's Book we have in our hands. We are in the Lord's hands and are safe from harm." Mr. Bacon instantly rose, put on his hat and started off, saying, "Well, I think the Lord wants me to help him find that man with the gun and warn him off."

My friends, the noise in the air around us suggests that the Lord wants his people to help him, and we must rise up straightway.

In the hope of a kingdom of heaven, patriotism, I salute you this day and bid you Godspeed.

The first speaker introduced was Rev. Howard H. Russell, LL.D., of Columbus, O. Dr. Russell has done heroic work at the head of the Anti-Saloon League in Ohio.

Address of Rev. Howard H. Russell, LL.D., Columbus, O.

When that gallant and effective saloon-fighter, the late Hon. John B. Finch, was yet a boy, he saw a drunken man stagger from a saloon door and fall senseless upon the street. His mother pressed her boy's hand closer and said, "Promise me that you will never touch nor taste that which makes men drunk." "I never will," said the boy; "and when I am a man I will shut these places where they sell it." The dauntless young people of America have beheld with amazement and patriotic shame the multiplied horrors of poverty, disease, and crime resulting from the curse of drink, and they have registered, with John Finch, the holy vow that they will close these places where they sell it. And they will keep that covenant, because to high Christian faith and heroic Christian Endeavor nothing is impossible.

Wherever Christian Endeavor has attacked the saloon it has found the spoils-politicians entrenched behind the screens. The anti-saloon campaign is, therefore, a war in which organized good citizenship moves victoriously upon the fortifications of bad citizenship. I am hopeful this present generation of young people here represented will in time abolish the liquor traffic, because of the conspicuous and honorable part which you have borne in the recent revival of civic patriotism. The Young People's Societies were in the van during the World's Fair Sunday campaign, in the temperance revivals in Illinois, Indiana, Ohio, Massachusetts, and other States, and especially in the hot municipal conflicts in the great cities. These experiences have been of untold value in exposing to our view, as never before, the bad character of many of our civil officers and the rottenness of municipal management, and have aroused a deep determination to enter upon and co-operate in systematic, permanent, and effective reform. Christian young Americans have reached the condition of mind of the long-suffering Quaker who had been assaulted and grievously maltreated. Looking up from where he lay he said, "Thee has broken my nose and kicked me down stairs and broken two or three of my ribs, and upon my word, if this goes on much longer I propose to take some notice of it." Allied young Christianity, organized to promote applied religion for the individual and community, has learned that the public offices, instead of being public trusts, sacredly executed for the public weal, are too often controlled and farmed out by rings, combines, and bosses; and we will take some notice of it. Bad citizenship wins to-day in many of our States and municipalities because it is more ready than good citizenship to pay the price of success. Bad citizenship is organized, alert, and diligent to do the necessary things to secure the induction into civil office of the men under its control. Good citizenship, on the other hand, will permanently win when it regularly brings to the primary elections and the polls more members of the dominant parties, acting in unison, than are brought to the same primaries and poles by bad citizenship. As Josh Billings remarked, "We shall never have an honest horse-race until we have an honest human race;" and it is equally true we shall never have honest politics until honest people become the politicians and control political affairs. The boss must be supplanted by the patriotic good-citizenship chairman, who is in the work, as his compatriots are, not for boodle nor for spoils, but for the sake of good social order.

Good citizenship begins its practical work in choosing civil officers, as bad citizenship universally does, before the primary election is held. I do not mean that the work in the political arena is to supersede educational work and public sentiment building; and the organized work must also be interpartisan or omnipartisan. I now come more particularly to the liquor traffic. The Christian Endeavor Societies here find a common foe to federate against. All the great denominations are with us. You will be interested to know that in the great Methodist denomination the presiding elders have recently united in an address to be read by the pastors in all their churches, which address has been signed by every presiding elder in Ohio; and this address appeals to the people to support everywhere the Anti-Saloon League and Haskell Bill. This unity of the Methodists characterizes all the other Protestant denominations. You will also be interested to know that the great Roman Catholic Church has wheeled in side by side with the Protestant Church in battle array.

The laws are enforced as they never have been before in the history of the reform. The number of saloons has been greatly reduced. For five years before the league was formed the saloons increased over 400 per year. In the last two years the number has been reduced over 400. We are assured we are now upon the right track, and our success is due to the unification of the people who are opposed to the saloon. We need in this campaign, now spreading into the other States, the cohesion of welded and hammered iron, which shall give us tension enough for a "long pull, a strong pull, and a pull all together." My heart was touched to know that a poor woman was giving one dollar per month — twelve dollars for the year — toward the support of our league, and the money was earned by washing. She was one of the many who daily pray for the enactment of the County Option Bill, that her husband may be delivered from the man-trap of an open saloon. I am sure everything is summarized and wrapped up in this. We shall get healthful political activity, and the forces of God will be marshalled to the pre-primary, the primary, and the polls when we reach blood-earnestness. We shall come together in fraternal union, and our personal pride and sensitiveness and dogmatism as to methods will all be put away for the sake of unification, and our work will not be spasmodic but permanent. We shall have iron cohesion and endurance, and we shall be ready for all downright personal blood sacrifice when we get terribly in earnest about this most important practical work, next to the conversion of men, that the children of God have on hand. Oh for a flash of heaven-sent inspiration that will set our souls aflame with zeal, and then while we muse the fire will burn! I believe if this company of young people could be brought face to face with the horrors I have seen, caused directly by the saloon, you would go forth with me into the thick of the fight.

If there were no other calls upon you for earnestness in this battle, the helpless children, orphaned by death and worse than orphaned by divorce, assaulted and maltreated by the cruel greed and outlawry of bad citizenship, should be enough to call you into action. Look about you! Is not this hell-sent curse at work in every place where the saloon is found?

I stand to-night as the attorney for blighted childhood, martyred woman-hood, and dethroned mankind, and demand that you make earnest business of this civic revolution. Young people of America, organize everywhere for the destruction of the saloon! Forward, to reinforce the wavering battle-line and turn defeat to glorious victory! Assert your God-sent citizenship; strike with your votes at primaries and polls! In the name of Mount Moriah's Christ, braid with Australian ballots a whip of small cords to lash the money-changers of hell out of the rum-ruled temple of American politics!

> " O children of bravest fathers, will ye falter
>   With all they left ye periled and at stake?
> Ho! Once again on freedom's holy altar
>   The fire awake.

> " Prayer-strengthened for the conflict, come together;
>   Gird on the armor for this mortal fight;
> And, with the blessing of your Heavenly Father,
>   Maintain the right."

After the singing of a hymn, Secretary Baer was introduced to make the following announcement: —

MR. BAER: For three or four years the California delegation has come to each successive convention expecting to take back the convention of the next year following.

I am very glad indeed to announce to you to-night that the trustees of the United Society have decided to hold the Convention of 1897 in San Francisco. (Great applause.) (Cries of " Hurrah!") And I want to introduce to you for just a moment one of the workers, who has for four years waited patiently to give you a hearty invitation to California,— Mr. E. E. Kelly, M.D., of San Francisco.

DR. KELLY: I dare say there are some in this audience who, about four years ago, were coming down the St. Lawrence River on an excursion, and expecting to shoot the rapids; and for some reason, which I can not tell, not being there, the trip had to be postponed. And perhaps you will remember that some of you became very impatient because you could not complete the trip at that time; and some pretty warm words were being expressed, when some one in the company began this song: " Wait, Meekly Wait, and Murmur Not."

We have been waiting for four years for the privilege of standing before you in the capacity in which I stand before you to-night, to announce that the convention is definitely coming to San Francisco, without any " if's."

There was an old German on the train coming over with me from San Francisco. He had gone to San Francisco forty-two years ago, and he had gone from the East by the way of Cape Horn, and had no idea whatever of the vastness of our territory. And after looking at the territory, and admiring the magnificent farms of Nebraska and Iowa and Illinois, he was filled with wonder; and as I was talking to him, he said to me one day, " My, oh my, vat a beeg country ve got! I never thought so mooch aboud it before in my life!"

So it is with all of you. You will have a liberal education as to the vastness of the empire which we have inherited.

And we have an empire upon the Pacific Coast which we will take great delight in showing you. We have become accustomed upon the Pacific Coast to think in a large way. We have the largest valleys of any State in the Union, because we have the largest State. If we could lay California down upon the Atlantic Coast, it would reach from Maine to South Carolina. And we have a thousand miles of seacoast, and a mountain range which contains the highest mountain in the United States. We have the Yosemite Valley; and we have the hundreds and thousands of other great things that I can not mention now. And one of the greatest things, and one of the things that we prize the most in the State of California, is a State Christian Endeavor Union with over 40,000 members. And we think that is the greatest of all.

What will you give us? I would like to have you remember that California was settled by the Argonauts, and, after the days of '49, by those adventurous characters who came from every corner of the globe in the search for gold. And they were not very religious; and we are not very religious to-day. There is no premium on religion in California. No man is religious because it is popular to be religious, nor because it pays to be religious, but he is religious from principle. And now, if you come to us, what will be the reflex benefit of an army like this in the State of California, showing that there are men of business, that there are educated young people, that there are thousands of college presidents and school-teachers, and thousands of the most intelligent young people of the land who are not afraid to acknowledge Jesus Christ as King?

Ah, what the influence of that will be, I can tell you. It will be to enhance moral ideas upon the Pacific Coast a great deal. And in that way you will help us to win California for Christ, as is the motto of the Christian Endeavor Societies of that State.

Now I am not going to take any more of your time to ask you to come. I know you want to come; but I wish to say this much: that if you will come we will give you the far-famed California welcome; and there will be no wine in it either. (Laughter.) And I am very glad to announce to you that we can give you all the drinks you want, but they are guaranteed to be strictly temperance drinks from our thousands of natural springs, than which not even Germany herself can boast of more or better.

Therefore I invite you to come to California in '97, the land of gold, the land of sunshine, fruit, and flowers. (Great applause.)

Mr. Wanamaker then introduced Dr. MacArthur, who held the vast audience for nearly an hour by a masterly address.

Address of Rev. R. S. MacArthur, D.D., New York City.

It is altogether fitting that the duty of patriotism should be emphasized by a convention of Christian young men and women. One element in the thought and work of all true Christian Endeavor Societies is duty to country as a part of our duty to God. It is quite true that all Christians are citizens of another country, even an heavenly; but it is not less, but all the more, their duty to be loyal citizens of the earthly country. The better the Christian the better the citizen. We must strive to make this world as speedily and as nearly as possible the kingdom of Jesus Christ. We can have but little patience with Christians who claim that they are too pious to have any relation to patriotic politics, who say that they are so interested in the other world that they cannot do their duty in this world. I think that kind of men will never see another world as good as this world.

I hear men say that the pool of politics is very dirty, and so they must keep away from it. I admit that the pool is not remarkably clean; but I deny the inference which they draw from that fact. Just because the pool is dirty, Christian men ought to go near it; and, with the instinct of American patriotism and Christian loyalty, strive to cleanse it.

I believe that patriotism and piety are twin flowers, growing on one stem, whose root is obedience to and love of God and man. We can not separate the two. "What God hath joined together" let no American citizen attempt to put asunder. I sympathize with the idea of the old Hebrew who joined his piety and his patriotism in most tender fellowship. He said, "Let my tongue cleave to the roof of my mouth if I forget thee, O Jerusalem! Let my right hand forget its cunning." So say I, if my right hand is lifted against the country that I have sworn to support, or if my right hand is used in depositing a false ballot against Christian citizenship.

I am sure that we all sympathize with the words of Dr. Johnson in his "Journey to the Western Islands," when he says, "That man is little to be envied whose patriotism would not gain force on the plain of Marathon, or whose piety would not grow warmer among the ruins of Iona." That sentiment we heartily endorse.

I am only an adopted American citizen. I was born under a corner of the British flag. I was never disloyal to that flag. As a boy, I rose in my place and uncovered my head and sang, " God save our gracious Queen." As a man, I transferred my allegiance from that flag to the Stars and Stripes; and I now sing, " My country, 't is of thee, sweet land of liberty, of thee I sing."

It was not a pure accident that both songs were to the same tune. Many of my good British friends have said that Americans stole that tune from Great Britain. The fact is that we both stole it from Germany. And perhaps Germany stole it from Italy. And whence Italy stole it this deponent saith not. And no one can tell.

I think it is not accidental. I think it is providential that we should sing the same song out of hearts glowing with similar fervid patriotism.

And now, in the interests of true American citizenship, I think that the Christian Endeavor Society ought to use all its influence in preserving peace within our own borders and in our relations with all of the nations of the earth. We agree with Milton, when he said : —

> " Peace hath her victories,
> No less renowned than war."

There is an American patriotism that is noisy ; it is bellicose ; it is boisterous ; it is practically worthless patriotism ; it is lingual ; it is labial loyalty; it is pulmonary patriotism ; it is not cordial ; it does not reach the heart ; it struts and stares and defies and threatens war.

Well, now, there is another patriotism that is quiet, that is gentle, but that is true ; that does its duty in lowly places ; that is loyal to God and country in the home, in the office, in the shop, and, especially, at the ballot-box. That patriotism I am here to-night to endorse. Believe me, the time is coming when all international disputes will be settled by international arbitration, when the partisan feeling of the time has gone. I tell you that General Grant will appear, in the days to come, as brave as a statesman as he was soldierly as a soldier. We know well that some of the grandest pages of American history were written by the sword of Grant and by the pen of Lincoln. But in the days to come, Grant will be known because of his connection with the settlement of international disputes in connection with international arbitration. The time was when all personal disputes were settled by personal encounters. That day has gone by, never to return. We now settle personal disputes by resort to courts. The day is coming when all international disputes will be settled by reference to an international court of arbitration, whose word shall be final in all the civilized nations of the globe.

I believe that Christian Endeavor has a great part to perform in bringing about that result. During the last one hundred years eighty cases of arbitration among the nations have settled eighty cases of disputes among the nations. I know that the school-books do not tell much about that, because the histories would rather tell the story of an unjust war than narrate the facts of a peaceful solution of national and international difficulties.

Another reason is that so many of our school-books are unfair in their treatment of historical questions as between Great Britain and these United States.

Those school-books often represent Great Britain as a tyrant; represent Great Britain of to-day as the Great Britain of the days of George III. Great Britain has learned lessons as to the treatment of her colonies since the days of George III.

I am free to say to you that I would regard a war with Great Britain as a war of fratricide. Such a war would put back the hands of progress in civilization, in literature, in science, and in missionary effort round the globe ; would put back the hands of progress at least a century on the dial of humanity.

I would regard such a war as being a dishonor to our civilization ; as being an indignity (if it is not a war necessary to vindicate our honor; that is another matter). A needless war would be an indignity upon our common humanity and a reproach upon the civilization of the closing days of the nineteenth century.

I tell you that these two great English-speaking and Protestant nations are marching, side by side, to the music of Christ's name for the conquest of this world. . I want to see this American flag the noblest flag beneath God's stars to-night. This flag, that is the hope and the inspiration of humanity from sea to sea and pole to pole, I want to see blended in inseparable union with that other flag; and over both, thus united, I want to see the banner of Emmanuel float,— that banner which is the symbol of God's sublimest revelation to man, and of man's divinest aspiration toward God.

I believe, Christian Endeavorers, and largely through your influence, that the time is coming when the words of the laureate — now the sainted laureate, Tennyson — shall have their complete fulfilment : —

> " When the war-drum throbs no longer,
>   And the battle flags are furled,
> In the parliament of man,
>   The federation of the world."

Well, now, Christian Endeavorers must take note of some of the dangers to which this Republic is now exposed.

One danger is that of indifferentism on the part of the so-called " best " American citizens, with reference to their duty to their country and to their God. I have sometimes been out of patience with these so-called " best citizens." We know that there is a class of men in all our cities who will vote early, and who would, and who, in New York, *used* to, vote often, as well as early. But, by the grace of God, we are limiting their voting to the *early*, and not to the *often;* for we have overthrown the gigantic power on Manhattan Island that dominated the politics of the city, the politics of the state, and, to some degree, the politics of the nation. And God help us to *keep the tiger down!*

Now we must stimulate our best people; we must show them that it is a duty which they owe to themselves, to their country, and to their God to do their duty at the polls.

Another one of the great dangers to which we are exposed I can name in a single word,—foreignism.

Now I have already intimated to you that I was a little bit of a foreigner myself ; and I have always observed that when a fellow gets here, he isn't so very particular as to whether the other fellow shall get here or not. It depends, however, I think, a little upon the fellow, in both instances.

Reference was made by the preceding speaker to the question as to whether or not the women should have the ballot. I tell you, if all the women in these United States were like the Christian Endeavor women, I would give them the ballot. I wish all the men who have it were like the Christian Endeavor men. It is not, after all, a question of women or of men, but it is a question of intelligence and capacity and of loyalty to the country and loyalty to duty.

Now we had an idea once that all foreigners who came to us were De Kalbs or Lafayettes. Well, I have watched a great many incoming steamers of many nationalities ; and for the life of me, I can t pick out the De Kalbs or the Lafayettes. Perhaps they were there ; but they were very greatly obscured, if they were.

This country, I insist upon it, deserves the best of every country in the world for American citizenship. There are two classes at least that we shall not allow to come here. If steamship companies bring us their paupers, many towns (curtesy forbids my naming countries) paying the fare of these paupers to get rid of them — I say, if the steamship companies bring them, we will make those steamship companies take them back! We will make them take them back and dump them in the countries whence they came! We shan't permit the American shore to be longer the dumping-ground for the worst populations of Southern Europe. And we shan't allow the anarchists to come to this country. No, we shan't. When a man comes here with a red flag of anarchy in one hand and a dynamite bomb in the other, by every instinct of patriotism, and by every element of divine grace, we 'll quarantine that man for the rest of his natural life !

Now I want to suggest some immediate duties that press upon us as Christian Endeavorers and as patriotic American citizens. And first, we must see to the preservation of the purity of the ballot-box. In countries where kings reign, if a man slays a king he is guilty of regicide. If he kills another man he is guilty of homicide. Well, now, in our country, where the people reign, when a man smites the ballot-box he smites the sovereignty of the American people. The ballot-box is the ark of the covenant of this American Republic. I tell you that I could wish that the hand that deposits a false vote might be paralyzed, and that the tongue that makes the report should cleave to the roof of the mouth of its owner. It is a terrible thing in this country to give us false returns, or to deposit false ballots.

Now another duty that I must insist upon is the entire separation of Church and State throughout this land. Our fathers came to this country with many erroneous ideas of the relation between Church and State. We, fortunately, have outgrown most of their errors. But we did see, until lately, almost all the denominations in America putting their hands into the public treasury at Washington, to take out money for Indian education. I tell you that every dollar of that money taken out of the public treasury for that purpose, for sectarian education, was against the spirit, if not the letter, of the American Constitution.

Some denominations had their hand in up to the wrist; others to the elbow. But the principle was the same. All honor to the American Congress in its last session for the position it took on that point.

Let the whole country send up to-night a *Te Deum*, because we are advancing to the only consistent position for the American Republic in that regard. We shall keep on advancing. There shall be no backward steps in this land of progress. The same principle will lead us to give all intelligence to our voters to fit them for their work, and there will come in the public schools. And we shall say, so that our voice shall be heard from the mighty Atlantic to the mightier Pacific, "No politician of whatever party, no ecclesiastic of whatever church, shall touch the public schools of America!"

Now let me relieve your patience in a word. I believe, as you see, in the dominance of moral forces, and so I make my appeal to Christian Endeavorers. I tell you that one of the saddest sights in the world was in 1855, in the Crimean War, when out of fifty-five thousand British soldiers eighteen thousand were in hospitals. Never were brave Britons so badly managed. They marched in snow with boots without soles; and they lay down at night to sleep on ice or in pools of water. Generalship was helpless. Statesmanship was speechless. Dr. Russell wrote a letter to the *London Times* that stirred all England. What could be done? Who should go?

Then uprose a queenly English woman, Florence Nightingale; and she went!

She was born in the same year as Queen Victoria; and she is a queen — Queen Florence — worthy to be placed alongside of Queen Victoria!

What have we seen lately? We have seen the trembling tyrant sitting on his tottering throne on the banks of the Bosphorus, and Armenia lying dying, bleeding at every pore, and all the nations helpless. Because of national delusions and because of political precedents they could do nothing.

What then? All honor to American womanhood! Then uprose Clara Barton, and at the touch of that American woman's finger every door into Armenia opened wide, and she went as the angel of God to the suffering and the dying.

I tell you, men and women, there are forces silent as the dew but mighty as the storm. There are forces trackless as gravitation, but resistless as the fiat of Almighty God. To these moral forces I to-night make my appeal. I was in Lucknow, in India, a few months ago. I, as a boy, read to my father and mother the story of the battles of the Sepoy Rebellion in 1857, for, in Sir Colin Campbell's regiment of Scotch Highlanders both my father and mother had relatives who died for country and queen on that Indian soil. And many a time as I read my voice trembled, and their eyes were moistened with tears. I saw the place where the brave Scotch woman, Jessie, lay on the ground waiting for the deliverers to come to Lucknow. None others heard it; but in her excited state of mind she caught the notes of the music, and she said, "It is the pibroch! Dinna ye hear it? 'T is the slogan of the MacGregors, the bravest o' them a'!"

To-night, Mr. Chairman, ladies and gentlemen, the first time I have ever had the honor of addressing a Christian Endeavor Convention excepting when you met in Saratoga, when I spoke with the lamented and honored and beloved and sainted Dr. Deems — to-night I before you lay my ear upon the ground. I hear the coming hosts of Christian Endeavor shouting their songs for truth, for country, for purity, for Christ! I hear the music of the twentieth century. Oh, it is sweet, sweet music! Listen to it! It comes echoing down through the intervening years. It is music that tells of a purer faith, a sweeter love, a more ardent zeal, and an intenser loyalty for Christ and for humanity.

Amid all its notes I hear the song sung only once to human ears by an angelic choir, sung over the plains of Bethlehem the night the Christ was born, —" And on earth peace, good-will toward men!"

The benediction was pronounced by Rev. J. L. Withrow, D.D., LL.D., of Chicago.

Tent Endeavor.

Hundreds stood around the circumference of the Tent Endeavor, the flaps of which were thrown up in order to allow the air to circulate, and all were deeply interested in what was being done under the canvas. The gathering was a picturesque one, under the glow of the numerous electric arc-lights. Looking from the choir platform, it was a mass of color, the bright dresses of the ladies heightened by the gleaming badges which decorated their bosoms, and made the red, white, and blue streamers and the parti-colored flags that swung above the audience seem dull by comparison. The chorus, from the audience seats, was equally as pleasing in its optical effect, and its largely augmented ranks rendered the familiar hymns of Christian Endeavor with a vim and energy that was enjoyable in the extreme. The singing was commenced immediately after the crowd began to gather, under the leadership of Mr. Percy S. Foster, and was continued without intermission until the meeting was regularly opened. Postmaster-General William L. Wilson was the presiding officer of the evening.

Rev. Sterling N. Brown, of Washington, conducted the devotional exercises.

Remarks by Hon. W. L. Wilson.

It is not necessary for me to announce that the subject to be considered is "Christian Citizenship," and I need hardly add that no more worthy theme could be given a place on a programme of exercises participated in by men and women from every section of the country. With such a country and inheriting such institutions, the duty of a citizen is ever present and strenuous. What constitutes good citizenship must always be the serious theme of consideration on the part of every man. This consideration was never more timely than now, when the country is on the eve of a great election, at which a President of the United States is to be chosen and the policy of our government is to be decided for years to come. The world never saw a grander or more inspiring sight than 70,000,000 free and enlightened people going up to the ballot-box, choosing their rulers, and declaring the way in which their laws shall be shaped. How shall we at such a time perform the task so as to assure happiness to ourselves and our countrymen and prosperity to our country, unless we ponder well the foundations upon which American citizenship must ever rest? It needs no long reach to ascertain what these are. The declaration was made long ago, and is still familiar, that "religion, knowledge, and morality are essential to good government and good citizenship."

For the Christian citizen, the honest exercise of his franchise is not only a civic duty, but a divine command.

We have been told to render unto Cæsar the things that are Cæsar's, and unto God the things that are God's. That means not that we must be careless and corrupt in our civil duties, but careful and honest, and, if need be, self-sacrificing in the exercise of them.

The next speaker was the President of Colorado College.

Address of President William F. Slocum, Colorado Springs, Col.

We mean by Christian citizenship that which is Christlike; that which finds its rule of action in those principles which governed his life. We are told by the so-called "practical politician" that high ideals like those,—that it is better to suffer than to do wrong ; that the Golden Rule should be the working principle of every man's action — are mere theories, and have really no place in our political life, and also that the day has gone when the public has any right to expect any such ideas to obtain in our great political movements. They do not, we are told, bring success as working theories; and as success must be secured at any price, they must be set aside again and again in our practical politics.

There is no necessity of our examining the various theories of government like the paternal,—the one that the government is simply an evolution from the idea of defence, or that it is a theocracy ; but I wish to call your attention to a certain false theory that is playing a very dangerous part in our nation to-day, and which is essentially unchristian. As you all know, at the time our nation was born politically French ideas had great influence among many of our leading thinkers upon political matters. One theory which had great influence at that time, and played a serious part in the French Revolution, was that all government should be based upon a social contract. That is, the thing upon which a government rests, in the last appeal, is the agreements or contracts that the people make with each other; that the government of a city like Baltimore, for example, rests upon the agreements or contracts that the people of that metropolis make with each other. Now this is a half-truth, but, like all half-truths, when left to themselves they are very dangerous. Let me remind you how that theory worked itself out in the French Revolution. A certain philosopher in England said, " The basis of society, religion, and government is found in experience." That is, he meant that if people would come together and compare their experiences they would find that the truth they discovered in their common opinions would furnish the truth on which all human institutions could be built. This seemed to just suit the French political movements that preceded the revolution. The leaders of the people said, " Yes, this is the true basis of all institutions. Our opinion is we do not want a king. Off with his head ! The old codes of laws are good or bad just as we think them good or bad. We think we do not want them. Let us make laws for each day as it comes. The home is built on the law of marriages, but the communistic notion suits us better. We think the home is unnecessary and there is something better, therefore the marriage contract must go. Religion depends upon the idea of God. We are of the opinion that there is a God, and so there must be one. Therefore religion, the Church, and the absolute code of morals stand. But we have concluded that there is no God, and, therefore, there is no God. The social contract settles it, and religion and the Church are gone." Then the commune swept through the streets of Paris, and after that the cannon of Napoleon belched grape and canister into the faces of the mob, teaching them there was authority deeper and stronger than their fickle opinions.

This is the theory that has crept slowly and surely into our American political life. It has appeared in a different way, but it is here and always has been here. The basis of government is a social contract, we are told. Let us study it a little in our American life to see what our Christian duty is. If I speak seriously, it is simply because my heart inspires this seriousness and because I believe there is a duty and an opportunity before you Christian young people, the like of which has never been surpassed in the world's history. A great religious impulse has come to you that perhaps has never been equalled. It must all lead to a duty, and I believe that duty in large measure is the preservation of our nation from dangers that threaten it. This rescue must be achieved by the application of the principles of our Saviour to the problems of our political and social life. This is why I wanted to come from my home by the great mountains and give you the message that has been in my heart these many days.

As one turns back to the birthday of our nation and asks, What was it that was the corner-stone of our great declaration and constitution? does he find that it was simply the agreements of certain people one with another over there in Philadelphia, who said, "If we do not hang together we shall hang separately"? Were these ideas of liberty and the rights of the individual founded on the opinions of those brave men who stood ready to give their heart's blood for their declarations, the basis of all that grew out of this deed? Where did those ideas come from which they enunciated? Did they create them? Did they change them one iota? Did their opinions have anything to do with their truthfulness, or did they simply discourse the truth that had always been, and build stronger than they knew, because their opinions could not modify eternal principle? Those were the same ideas that made the Magna Charta, that were victories at Marston Moor and at Naseby; those same ideas launched the *Mayflower* and brought the Cavalier to Virginia and the Pilgrims to Plymouth; but no man made them, no man's opinion affects them one iota. They come from out the centuries; they come from the eternities; they are from God. Do you think for a moment that any man's opinion, or the agreements of any number of people, can modify in the least the eternal truth of God? I have no quarrel with the contracts which men make one with another, but when they place their contracts or agreements at the basis of government and society, I must ask first of all, not whether a certain number of people agreed to this or that, but, Are these agreements right — right as God and his Christ pronounce them right?

The Christian citizen asks, before all else, Have we discovered in this or that movement the thing that is true? Is this the trend in our American political life? I am not denying that there is much that is true; that there are men in our public affairs who would stand for what was right, no matter what was arrayed against them; but behind all this there still remains the serious and undeniable fact that our so-called practical politician asks, first of all, What will succeed in getting votes?

This is the thing to which we must agree, and, having made our contract, we must call that the truth. This, I say, is the working theory in very much of our public life.

The next step is the one that makes the end of political movements to agree to that which will create a majority, as if the one thing of all others was to be in the majority, no matter what the means by which the majority is secured, for we are told it is the majority which always controls. Here is another dangerous half-truth. Is it the majority that always controls? I love to think of that brave apostle standing in the old pagan city when the mob was hooting him, and crying in their foolish madness about the greatness of their goddess. Who has ruled, the majority of that day, or the man who stood alone against the great majority? A few years ago men were digging in the débris of that same city, and discovering a ruin, they measured it and found it was the foundation of that great temple at Ephesus. Somehow the temple, the goddess, and the crowd have lost their power, and the minority of that day rules in ten thousand hearts. The history of the centuries shows that it is the men who have stood alone for what was right, and stood because their position was right, that have guided the destinies of the world. When will we learn that "one with God is a majority"?

Was there a grander moment in the life of our Lord than when, the world having turned its back upon him, he stood with the glory of a triumphant

Christ in his face and said, "Ye shall leave me alone, and yet I am not alone. Be of good cheer."

One of the first marks of a Christian citizen is power and willingness to stand alone for a principle.

There is another test of Christian citizenship that is very simple, and yet it is one of the most far-reaching principles in all political science. It was the ideal of the ablest philosopher of the century. Let me illustrate it in a very simple manner. If I had a blackboard here, I should place a dot upon it and ask you to let it represent an individual, a citizen. Then I should draw round that a circle and let it stand for that institution which comes nearest the individual, the home. No one ever becomes a perfect human being unless he stands in some real relation to the home, unless in some way he gives himself to it, gives of his thought, his time, his strength. So it is that there wakes in him that noble passion, love of home, one of the deepest and most beautiful things in the human soul. Now I want to draw a second circle round this first and call it society. I use this word in its larger sense. I mean infinitely more than that for which people dress extravagantly, in which they tell lies to each other and worse ones behind their backs. Society is the coming of people together for any purpose, either good or bad. There is society in the slum and on the avenue; there is society in the factory and the coal-mine; in the bank and at the university. Just as the individual gives himself in some real way to society, to his fellows, to humanity, does he find himself, his own deeper nature that is born of love for his neighbor.

Let us draw another circle around these two, and call it government. There is abroad in the land the false theory that a government exists simply to take care of the citizen. It must take care of the pauper and the feeble-minded; but one's government, which in a peculiar way stands for one's native land, one's country, exists to be cared for, supported, and upheld. To give one's self to one's country is the true idea of loyalty, and this it is that rouses another splendid passion in the human heart, love of country. So it is that man continues to find himself. Woe to us as a nation if this passion passes away from the people, and the citizen simply asks, What will the government give me? rather than, What can I give of devotion, thought, service, to my country?

But we must draw one other circle round these others, for it embraces them all, and call it God. Just as the individual gives himself, directly and also in and through all these other things, to God does he find his deepest, his truest, his real self. So it is that he realizes himself, discovers his own soul. This is the philosophy of all true citizenship in the kingdom of God. "He that would find his life must lose it" is the profoundest of all philosophic principles. It is also the simplest and sweetest law of daily life.

But is some one saying, This all sounds well, but after all, what am I to do? What am I to do when the majority is against me, and it seems as if I were in a hopeless minority? What if I find myself alone? Life is short, and it is not so easy to stand against dishonesty and selfishness. I want my life to amount to something, and I do not want to be forever on the losing side.

A few summers ago, I sailed through the great lakes, and talking with the pilot of the steamer of the great winter storms that sweep over those inland seas, I asked him, "What do you do in those fiercest gales?" "We keep her head on," was his reply. "Well, what do you then?" "We keep her head on." "But what do you do after that," I continued. "We keep her head on. Last winter we met one of those southeasters just where we are now, and for hours, with every pound of steam we could carry, we kept her nose up into the gale; but at last the storm abated, and we made our harbor." That is my advice to you. *Keep her head on.* Keep your faces up into the storm. You are never alone. Our land needs brave and earnest men and women, who shall save our country from the false theories and base deeds that threaten her. I do not ask you to seek office. Let the office seek you, and, if it does, take up the burden with just as high an ideal as that which led to the consecration of those young lives at the haystack in Williamstown, years ago; but above all, in word, in deed, let no low ideal of the duties you owe to your country take possession of your mind and heart, and let no man persuade you, either by false argument or base sneer, that the teachings of Jesus, our Master, do not and can not obtain in all our political affairs.

Treasurer Shaw then presented Mr. Rolla V. Watt, of San Francisco, chairman of the Endeavor Convention committee of 1897, saying that next year the Endeavorers would go to California and help win the Pacific Coast for Christ. Mr. Watt told what Californians were going to do to entertain the Endeavorers. The California committee had already collected all the necessary funds for entertaining the Convention. He believed the trip across the continent would be an education to every Endeavorer. He wanted all to come, and promised a warm and hearty welcome.

" Not only will the Golden Gate be opened to welcome you, but the gates of our hearts and our homes," he said, earnestly, in conclusion.

Mr. Foster called for everybody to sing " that favorite song of Californians, ' Sunshine in the Soul.' " It was sung with a splendid swing.

The closing address of the evening was delivered by the Rev. Dr. P. S. Henson, of Chicago, and was probably as strong an arraignment of the saloon evil as has ever been delivered on a public rostrum. In vigorous and graphic strokes he pictured the saloon as the greatest danger that threatens the safety of the United States. He held his hearers spellbound until points were reached when they could restrain their enthusiastic approval no longer, and the applause at times was as much by the voices as by the hands of his auditors.

We regret the stenographic report was mislaid. Below we give a part of the address.

Address of Rev. P. S. Henson, D.D., Chicago, Ill.

[From a Washington paper.]

I believe in the pulpit, and I believe in the polls. I believe in the prayer meeting, and I believe in the primary, and I believe it to be my duty to be at one as much as it is to be at the other.

It is the habit of preachers to perish in the platitudes. They aim at nothing all around an imaginary circumference and hit it every time, but I propose to aim at something and fire. If my language smells of brimstone, no one must mind it, because my subject is very close to the mouth of hell. When Joshua crossed the Jordan he was at the head of an army of the most remarkable cranks the world had ever seen. They were armed with rams' horns, and they marched around the walls and blew, not on horns of silver, but on rams' horns. And the high and mighty muck-a-mucks of Jericho looked down on the crowd with derisive laughter. They continued to tramp and blow until one day there was a great shout, and the walls of Jericho tumbled down. That was the great object-lesson for God's army to be unmindful of the obstacles that confronted it, faithful in the assurance that in the end they would be overcome.

The Gibraltar of the devil, the strongest fortress he has on earth, and whose guns are the longest, is the saloon. I do not propose to speak of the wine of communion, fermented or unfermented, or of the medical uses of alcohol, or of the subject of dietetics, where a man has beer and beef on his own table. I want to invoke the thoughtful consideration of the saloon as a menace to our civilization.

Both great parties, all great parties,—and there seem to be a number of them in this year of bolts and thunderbolts,—seem to believe in protection to a greater or a less degree. The protection they talk of, however, is of sheep, pig-iron, salt, and such things; but it is for the Christians to defend protection of homes and hearts and human souls. I hear a good deal of talk also about the currency, about honest money and debased money. Jeroboam once set up in his kingdom a couple of calves, one at Dan and one at Bethel. I don't know what metal those calves were made of, but I reckon one was silver and the other gold. I reckon we can call the gold one Dan, because a golden calf was molded out there, and now Chicago is Bethel, for a silver calf is being molded there, and 70,000,000 people are dancing in idiotic ecstasy around them both. I want to know if there is nothing nobler for the American people to consider than these political makeshifts. Is not debased manhood something? They talk about the circulation. How about pumping millions and millions of damnation into the body politic every year? There's circulation for you! One of the great parties, I'll not say which, is afraid of the Irish; another one, which I will not name, is afraid of the Germans, but neither of them is afraid of the Lord Almighty, as they ought to be.

The saloon question is the serpent in the path of the public man, like the serpent that the Lord placed in the path of Moses, which only needed to be taken up to become a sceptre of regal power. The saloon is the breeding-place of the anarchist. I am not afraid of anarchy if you will close up the saloons. It is not the red flag in the anarchist's hands, but the red light of the saloon on the corner that threatens the stability of American institutions. The real anarchist is not the shock-head fellow who carries a piece of lead pipe under his coat, but the saloon-keeper. The bogus anarchist we hang; the real anarchist we make an alderman out of. I do not believe in the pessimist who predicted catastrophe to the country, for I feel sure that when God placed the American people in the Western world he intended that its future should be great and glorious.

The audience was dismissed with a benediction by Rev. Dr. Seymour, of Philadelphia.

FRIDAY MORNING.

Tent Endeavor.

The praise service with which the regular meeting began was under the direction of Mr. Percy S. Foster.

The devotional exercises, consisting of responsive Scripture reading and prayer, were led by Rev. Hugh T. Stevenson, of Anacostia, and at their conclusion Rev. John T. Beckley, D.D., of New York, who presided over the meeting, introduced Mrs. Francis E. Clark, the wife of the founder of Christian Endeavor, and she was given the Chautauqua salute and an enthusiastic greeting. Mrs. Clark then read her paper on " The Mothers' Society of Christian Endeavor."

Address of Mrs. Francis E. Clark.

The whole object and purpose of the Mothers' Society of Christian Endeavor is really included in the first sentence of their pledge: " Trusting in the Lord Jesus Christ for strength, I promise him that I will strive to do whatever he would have me do, especially that I will endeavor to bring the children to Christ and to train them for him." Surely Christian mothers everywhere desire above all things to draw nearer Christ themselves, and to bring their children to him and train them for his service. Is there any better way to do this than by banding themselves together for this very purpose? There are now a few societies in our own and other lands which have taken this name of " The Mothers' Endeavor Society," and are regularly organized and pledged to do this work.

There ought to be in every church, by whatever name it may be called, some organization that will be in very truth a Mothers' Endeavor Society, an organization whose definite purpose should be not only prayer, but prayer *and work* for the children. There are already in many of our churches Maternal Associations and ladies' prayer meetings, having for their object, in part at least, to pray for the children. Why could not these organizations pledge themselves definitely to do this work in co-operation with the Junior Endeavor Societies, even if they do not care to change their own name or have a more formal organization? Why should there not be in every ladies' prayer meeting or Maternal Association a Junior committee whose work should be to consult with the Junior Superintendent and report to the meeting any plans for helping the children. The Junior superintendent might be invited to come once a quarter to the mothers' meeting to give a five-minute talk about her work, its encouragements and perplexities and needs. It would be her opportunity to appeal to the mothers for their help and counsel and prayer.

Could it not be planned that occasionally the little Junior secretary or president should attend the mothers' meeting and give a report of the work? Perhaps the members of the sunshine committee or some other committee might sometimes go together to the mothers' meeting and tell how they are trying to do their part of the work, and ask for the prayers of the mothers. Perhaps, too, it might be possible to plan as often as once a year to have a union meeting of the mothers and the Juniors, when both societies could learn more of each other's work and be drawn into closer sympathy.

The meetings of the Maternal Association in many churches are held every month, and many heartfelt prayers are offered for the children ; and yet the children themselves know little or nothing about it, and there is nothing done in the way of following up these prayers, and so the definite results are not what they might be.

It sometimes happens, too, that in the course of time these mothers' meetings come to be largely grandmothers' meetings, because the younger mothers do not attend.

It would be very helpful not only to the Junior Societies, but to these mothers' meetings, too, if they could in these ways or in other ways be more closely connected and work and plan together. By consulting together, new ways of working would be always opening up to both societies. The mothers would find many ways of helping the children, and the children would take great pleasure in the discovery that they, too, could help the mothers in many little ways.

Suppose the mothers should decide that it would be well to send printed or written invitations to some of the younger mothers who do not attend their meetings. Surely the sunshine committee would be glad to divide the work among themselves, and run on these errands. Do all the mothers of Juniors in the church attend the ladies' prayer meeting? If not, then it might be well to have some daintily printed cards of invitation to give out in the Junior meeting, that each boy or girl may take one to the mother at home.

It would be well that quite often the mothers should send representatives from their meeting, not more than one or two at any one time, to visit the Junior meeting, and often the Junior superintendent would be glad to ask one of the mothers for a five-minute talk upon the topic of the day from a mother's standpoint.

Let the Mothers' Society occasionally give a social to the Juniors, and let it be the pleasantest social of all in the year. Let the mothers occasionally give the children a pleasant surprise, in the shape of a new banner, or some new pledge-cards, or any other little things the Juniors may be needing, and a new link between them would be forged.

If some such plans were put into practice, should we not see not only more children coming into the church, and growing up to be earnest workers there, but also more mothers who were living really consecrated lives, and who were themselves walking more carefully in the way they would see their children walk?

Many existing Maternal Associations would have more real life and earnestness if they were better organized for definite work, with perhaps a lookout committee to bring in new members, and a prayer-meeting committee to select topics and arrange leaders for the meetings, and a social committee to arrange for an occasional sociable to which not only the mothers, but sometimes the babies, should be invited, with a committee of Juniors to entertain them. Something of this sort would put new life into many a dead-and-alive ladies' prayer meeting; and if the mothers were thus working with and for the children, it would be a real Mothers' Endeavor Society, by whatever name it might be called.

May God's blessing rest upon all the mothers who are trying in any way to bring the children to Christ, and may this be a year when many children shall hear the voice of their Saviour saying to them, " Come unto me." God grant that very many of them may, indeed, come to him, and may begin in a simple, childlike way to be about their Father's business.

The next speaker was Rev. C. L. Work, D.D., of Cincinnati, O., who gave his address, " The School of Prayer."

Address of Rev. C. L. Work, D.D., Cincinnati, O.

Luke ii. 1 : " Lord, teach us to pray."

I am to speak to you to-day on some phases of prayer as seen in the Bible. God's people are as weak in the matter of prayer as elsewhere, and so need to be taught here as elsewhere.

1. There is a school of prayer for God's people. If God's people do not know how to pray acceptably, they may learn to do so. I do not believe that we have prayed as effectively as it is our privilege to pray. There is here a magazine of powder to which many of us are entire strangers. Prayer is a matter in which to make progress as followers of Christ.

There are several things which indicate the existence of this school: (*a*) Christ's conduct when he was asked by his disciples to teach them to pray. He immediately taught them the Lord's Prayer. He thinks as much of a disciple now as then, and prayer is as important now as then. If it were important that the disciple know how to pray then, it is equally as important now ; just as much depends on prayer now as then. (*b*) Again, the work of the Spirit in connection with the matter of prayer leads us to believe that not all that God intends to do for his people in this matter has been done, and that nothing now remains to be done. We are directly taught that "the Spirit helpeth our infirmities." Here is the present tense of the word " help," leading us to understand that the work is a continuous one. It is interesting here to study the make-up of the Greek word translated "helpeth." The word is " sunantilambanetai ; " it is a word made up of three others,—" sun," with ; " anti," opposite, and " lambane-tai," to take hold of, or to seize. The idea is that the Spirit takes hold of our burdens and crosses and duties as a helper opposite us, as if to look us in the face and lift the same burden with us. It is the same word used by Martha when she asked the Lord to bid Mary to come and help her with her household duties. You have only to look into the eighth chapter of Romans to see that this help here mentioned is in reference to prayer, and you will also see that the "infirmities " here mentioned are infirmities in connection with prayer. The time never was when God's people did not have infirmities or weaknesses in the matter of prayer. Hence the work of the Spirit in this matter must be a continuous one. He will show us our sins, and thus lead us to confession ; he will show us our wants, and thus lead us to the matter of petition ; he will show us the blessings of God, and thus help us in the matter of thanksgiving ; he will show us the dangers of the lost, and thus help us in the matter of intercession, and in many other ways will he help us in the matter of prayer. We are led by the statements of the eighth chapter of Romans to believe that there is a peculiar part of expression in the matter of prayer that only the Spirit can perform. His helpfulness comes in groanings that can not be uttered. To excite these in the one who prays is the peculiar work of the Spirit. They seem to be essential to the right spirit of prayer in us, and hence we must be constant. Thus the work of the school of prayer goes on. There is a school of prayer for God's people. We must matriculate in this school. This is the formula of matriculation : " Lord, teach us to pray." Let each child of God place his name to this matriculation formula in the school of prayer.

2.   Under certain conditions we may be sure of prevailing in prayer. This is the plain teaching of the Word of God. If this be not the correct position to occupy in this matter, then I fail to see why certain records are found in the Word of God.

Prevailing prayer is not something into which we can plunge, as a rule, immediately, as a bird rising on the wing from the ground. There is precedent thought, such thought and realization of facts and the relation of these to our present and future condition as will awaken us to an unusual realization of our state before God. It is a condition of soul or state of mind in which everything but our eternal interests is most insignificant. Our surroundings are intended to agonize us. In the light of the teaching of God's Word, how sad the condition of the unsaved! The awful Turk is throwing Armenian babies in the air and catching them on his bayonet as they fall. Many mothers almost faint when they think of it. But think of a child damned in hell forever. This is not an unbiblical thought, as Paul says to the Galatians, " My little children, of whom I travail in birth again until Christ be formed in you." (Gal. iv. 19.) The Psalmist says, " Horror hath taken hold upon me because of the wicked that forsake thy law." (Ps. cxix. 53.) Again he says, " Rivers of waters run down mine eyes because they keep not thy law." (Ps. cxix. 136.) Isaiah saw the coming doom of the unrepentant, and hear his words : " I will weep bitterly, labor not to comfort me, because of the spoiling of the daughter of my people." (Isa. xxii. 4.) Hear Jeremiah: " Oh that my head were waters, and mine eyes a fountain of tears, that I might weep day and night for the slain of the daughter of my people." (Jer. ix. 1.) It is our duty to be solemnly moved in this way. McCheyne used to visit his dying people on Saturday, that he might be more moved in his pulpit on the Sabbath. Whitfield used to cry out before his vast audiences, " Oh, the wrath to come, the wrath to come !" and then sit down overcome with emotion. It is the agony of Peter in the hour of penitence and bitter tears; it is the agony of David weeping over Absalom ; it is the agony of the Saviour, as on the last day of his ministry he sat on the Mount of Olives and cried in indescribable agony, " O Jerusalem, Jerusalem, thou that killest the prophets, and stonest them which are sent unto thee, how often would I have gathered thy children together, even as a hen gathereth her chickens under her wings, and ye would not." (Matt. xxiii. 37.) Would to God that his people were thus agonized all over the land ! Only when this agony of prayer seizes God's people will we have a wide-spread revival.

3.   Another Bible idea concerning prayer is that we are warranted in expecting answer to specific petition more frequently than we sometimes think. I do not think that the explanation is universal and final when we say that if we do not get what we ask for we will get something better. That is a lazy Christian's way of putting it. Why do we not get just what we ask for? Our theory is that the Holy Ghost indicts our petitions, he suggests our prayers; but do we not stultify ourselves when we pretend to pray a prayer suggested by the Spirit, and then explain away the failure to get an answer by saying that if we do not get what we ask for we will be sure to get something better? My humble opinion is that under such circumstances we will get nothing. Our explanation does not explain. It is in some sense an insult to the Holy Spirit. It is the equivalent of saying that he does not indict the petitions of his people, or that he made a mistake and indicted the wrong petition. The only proper way to do is to say that we have prayed a petition that the Holy Ghost did not suggest, and therefore we will get no answer to our petition. Now, let us suppose a case.

We pray for the conversion of a friend and our petition is not answered. Now bring in the stock explanation: "If we don't get what we ask for we will get something better." What would it be? What could it be? The only explanation allowable under the circumstances is that while the specific petition for the conversion of a person is in accordance with the will of the Holy Ghost, yet he did not indict such a petition in the given case on account of some fault in the one who prayed. God can not answer prayer without due regard for the character of the one who prays. Just here let me say that there is great need that we so live that the Holy Ghost can be able to indict for us any petition that may suit his purpose. We must not overlook the fact, in our discussion of the subject, that prayer under God's own conditions is an essential link in the chain of causes. Alas! how often is the chain broken at the prayer link. Jacob got just what he asked for at Jabbok; Hezekiah got just what he asked for when he prayed God to spare his life; Moses got what he asked for when he asked the Lord to spare the children of Israel; John Knox got what he asked for when he asked for Scotland; Jesus Christ got what he asked for when in the garden he asked that the bitter cup might pass from him. He did not there pray against the cross, but against the bitterness of that specific hour of suffering in the garden. In answer to his prayer it passed away, for he came to his disciples finally with words of victory on his lips. "Sleep on now, and take your rest: it is enough." (Mark xiv.41.) What we all need most is to so pray under the direct and specific direction of the Holy Ghost that we will ask for the right thing and get it. I am not saved to serve until I am so saved that I can prevail with God in prayer. Let us go to our Jabboks and Gethsemanes of prayer, and never give God rest till he answer all our Holy Ghost indicted petitions. "Ye that make mention of the Lord, keep not silence, and give him no rest, till he establish, and till he make Jerusalem a praise in the earth." (Isa. lxii. 6,7.) The drunkard may pray specifically for deliverance from his cups, and be contented with nothing less for an answer to his petition. The debauchee may pray for purity and get it. The liar must pray for truthfulness and get it. The parent ought to pray for the conversion of his child, and not be contented until he gets exactly what he asks for. It is our privilege to besiege the Throne of Grace and get what we ask by the teaching and help of the Holy Ghost.

4. I ask you, in the next place, to notice the importance of the matter of prayer in connection with revival, as seen in the Word of God. The pentecostal revival was preceded by a ten-days' prayer meeting. It was through prayer that Elijah reached the reformation of the people in his day. This has always been the rule of revival. I wish I had time to follow this part of my subject to a good length. In a little book entitled "Great Revival of 1800," you will find this description of a scene down in old Kentucky, at Cane Ridge: —

"We arrived upon the ground, and here a scene presented itself to my mind not only novel and unaccountable, but awful beyond description. A vast crowd, supposed by some to have amounted to 25,000, was collected together. The noise was like the roar of Niagara. The vast sea of human beings seemed to be agitated by a storm. I counted seven preachers all preaching at one time, some on stumps, others on wagons, etc.," and this is but a fair sample of the way the Spirit wrought among men in those days. All through that little book to which I have referred you will find constant reference to the way the people prayed. These great revivals were born of fervent, prevailing prayer. The Presbyterian Church of Western Pennsylvania was born of the prayers of Joseph Patterson, a layman in Vance's Fort, in the winter of 1778. (*Supra.*) If I have stated the relation between prayer and revival correctly, are we not responsible, before God, if we do not down to our knees and pray all Christendom into a white heat of revival? It can be done; it must be done; it will be done, before the coming of the Blessed Master. If you follow the history of revivals you will find that they have always been the times of earnest, fervent, and continued prayer. Revivals are begotten in prayer, born in prayer, and remain with us only when nurtured by prayer. If we would have our conventions promotive of revival, we must not forget to make them places of prayer. It is all well enough to gather in great numbers, wave our flags, make speeches and shake the hands of antipodal delegates, and send messages of greeting to the distant corners of the earth; but unless prayer be the alpha and omega of it all, it will be useless.

All great soul-winners have been men of power in prayer. It is said of Richard Baxter that he stained the very walls of his study with the breath of prayer. Here I can best express myself in the language of another: " When the disciples prayed, Pentecost appeared; when John Wesley and his companions prayed, England was refreshed; when the Sabbath-school teachers at Tanneybreake prayed, 11,000 were added to the Church in one year; 'when John Knox prayed, Scotland was revived; when Luther prayed, the papacy was shaken; when Baxter prayed, Kidderminster was awakened; and in the lives of Whitfield, Payson, Edwards, Tennent, whole nights of prayer were succeeded by whole days of soul-winning." (" Outpourings of the Spirit," page 136.)

Let us down to our knees, and may Washington City, under the influence of prevailing prayer, become a volume of flame like the burning bush at the feet of Moses; and then may it be given to the members of this great Convention to carry back " crosses of fire " to the utmost bounds of the earth.

Dr. Beckley then introduced Mr. Ira D. Sankey, who sang the hymn " The Ninety and Nine," after which he offered prayer.

The next subject was " The Joy of Soul-Winning."

Address of Rev. W. F. Wilson, Toronto, Ont.

It is not necessary, in the discussion of our subject, that we define the soul. We accept the statement in the Bible concerning it, " as being satisfying and sufficient."

As the sword is not the soldier, as the pen is not the poet, as the chisel is not the sculptor, the house is not the tenant, neither is the body the man; but soul and body, dust and deity, combined is man.

More thought, time, and money is invested in the study of man than in all other subjects in the world together. The great sages and seers of history have established schools and written unnumbered books on the dignity, fall, and redemption of man. Sin has weakened man's body and dethroned his soul; consequently man's soul is one of God's wandering stars, tarnished jewels, faded flowers, and lost sheep; and to win back this treasure is difficult in the extreme. You can easily win a man's money, secure his vote, gain his friendship, or have his applause, but not his soul; yet, marvelous thought, God is expecting from man service in winning the imperishable souls of men.

Question: Which is worse, a Christless man or a manless Christ? — the vine with no branches to bear the flowers and fruits that cluster in the character divine. God has faith in Christ, for " God so loved the world that he gave his only begotten Son, that whosoever believeth in him should not perish, but have everlasting life." Christ has faith in himself, — " And if I be lifted up from the earth, I will draw all men unto me."

Yes, and Christ has faith in man, for he commissions him to win souls. Not to buy them, for they are already bought with the precious blood; not to force them, for the diadem of freedom rests on every brow; not to convict them, this is the Spirit's work; but to persuade and win is ours. To do this we must get rid of our pride and fear; these paralyze and destroy. Remember God's your Master. Remember how he helped David with his sling, and Paul in Nero's prison; and he is still able to save and sustain to the uttermost.

All have not the same opportunities to work, nor the same gifts and graces for work. There are those with two talents and those with ten.

God gives one man great eyes to see. He thus blest Dickens and said, " Charles, write me a book against England's school and social wrongs," and he did. To another he gives great courage; he thus endowed Washington, and said, " George, strike for liberty," and the thirteen jewel States were freed. He gave Spurgeon a great voice; he gave Livingstone great faith, and George Peabody great wealth. But before them all he gave our own Clark great plans, and said, " Francis, organize for me," and he did; and here gathered in the capital of the greatest Republic beneath the stars is this world-famed Convention, because Francis E. Clark found unspeakable joy in winning souls. Daniel Webster once said, "The day will come when the proudest boast of man will be 'I am an American.'" No, Daniel, there is something even better than that; it's this: "I am a Christian,"—a working Christian, a joyful Christian, winning precious souls to shine in the diadem that spans the brow of Christ. Oh the joy of soul-winning!

First, there is the joy of knowing you helped to bring light, life, liberty, and love to the sin-enslaved of our world.

Men have done much to win liberty for their fellow men. To this Cromwell, Garibaldi, and Wellington gave their splendid powers; but before them all is the imperishable Lincoln, whose name shall live linked with liberty long as thought and heart shall live.

Intellectual freedom has had its champions. The names of Huss, Luther, Ridley, and Bunyan are stars that shall never dim nor die. But to impart spiritual liberty surpasses all the service ever rendered by the ransomed powers of man.

You remember the story of England sending General Napier and an army of 10,000 men to Magdala in Abyssinia to liberate a single prisoner — spending $25,000,000? What for? To show the world the English flag guarantees life and liberty to all who claim its protection. But, soul-winner, your object is the soul, and all God has is in it. He breathed it into man. He gave Jesus Christ to ransom it. His Holy Spirit comforts it. His angels minister to it. His heaven is prepared for it. Oh, think of your work!

I do not undervalue the great blessings and benefits conferred upon the human race by the noble spirits of the ages. John Howard brought hope to the imprisoned; Florence Nightingale brought joy to the suffering; at this hour Clara Barton in the wilds of Armenia is battling with pestilence, disease, and hunger. Yet, Christlike as all these services are, they are eclipsed by the joy of winning man's deathless nature to the life and service of Christ.

Then, fellow Endeavorers, remember you are pledged workers, inspired workers Christ is your model, and "The world for Christ" is your motto. Make your service joyful, ever remembering "They who turn many to righteousness shall shine as the stars forever."

Second, there is the joy in soul-winning of knowing that the world's purity, charity, and service for Christ is increased; in other words, you multiply goodness. Ananias, who helped Paul to Christ, was multiplied a thousand times in the unquenchable zeal of the great apostle to the Gentiles. Andrew, who led his brother Peter to the Messiah, was multiplied ten thousand times in the unparalleled service rendered the cause of righteousness by the preacher of Pentecost, under whose ministry three thousand were added to the Church in a single day.

Oh the joy of multiplying goodness! Who started John Knox Christward? What voice called John Bunyan from the slums of sin? What worker first quickened the spiritual energies of John Wesley, General Booth, and our own Francis Clark?

Pardon a personal illustration. Some years ago, in a small Canadian town, there was a devoted cripple girl who took six boys, and never ceased to pray with and work for them until she saw every one of them in the ministry of the Church of Christ. Her pulseless form sleeps in the village graveyard. No sculptured stone bears the record of her name, and yet, methinks, not until the last sermon has been preached and the last prayer has been offered will it be known how much good, under God, she mothered.

Oh this joy, when the sunset hours of life have come, when we shall look back and thank God we increased the spiritual service of man for Christ!

Third, there is the joy of knowing you are engaged in a work that will always give intense satisfaction. This is what we all want. We live for it; we toil for it; and work for Christ alone will give it. A person might discover a continent, as did Columbus, and yet die in misery, as did he; or compose an immortal song, as did Mozart, and yet die in poverty, as did he; or create an empire, like Napoleon, and yet die in exile, as did he. But in soul-winning it is different; this service gives joy and satisfaction the passing years shall never dim.

Surely, if material service could satisfy, the matchless Gladstone, of all men, would be most happy; but what are the facts? During the past few months he has dedicated his splendid powers to the writing of a book for the glory of God and the spiritual enrichment of his fellow men.

It seems to me Christ's greatest joy was in winning souls. He was misunderstood by his nation, persecuted by his Church, betrayed by his disciples, forsaken by his friends, and crucified by his enemies. His burden was very heavy, and his life was very sad. But he received satisfaction, not from the number of blind and diseased ones that he had cured, but that he had helped many precious souls to see His light and know his love. So with us; our soul-winning is our capital beyond the stars.

Lastly, there is the joy of expectant reward; the glorious home-coming, bringing our sheaves with us. There is the reward of seeing Jesus; there is the reward of meeting the good of all the ages; there is the reward of meeting old companions and near and dear friends; but greatest of all, there is the reward of seeing those whom we have helped to save, and of being introduced by them to Christ before an assembled world. And now, as every soldier steps forward in obedience to the command of his officer, so may the representatives of all the churches in this great Convention step forward in obedience to the command of our Lord, to speedily take the kingdoms of this world for our God and his Christ.

After a moment of silent prayer, the congregation joined in singing "Throw Out the Life-Life."

Rev. John W. Beckett, of Baltimore, then sang "Jesus, Saviour, Pilot Me."

Next was the unrolling of the missionary roll of honor by the Rev. Chas. S. Lane, of Mount Vernon, N. Y. The roll of honor was produced, and Rev. Mr. Lane spoke as follows:—

Remarks of Rev. C. S. Lane, Mount Vernon, N. Y.

If Mr. Moody at Boston could count it one of the opportunities of his life to address that gathering, I may well count it a double honor and privilege to be thus placed upon the programme to speak even for five minutes upon the great cause of missions; for this is not only a grand Convention, but the theme is the grandest that can claim our thoughts. Whether we regard the actual triumph of missions in the changed lines of individuals and communities, in the glorious possibilities, the dawn of which has brightened the amazing record of missions, its lofty motives, its record of personal heroism and saintly character, or whether we think of it as the simple, straightforward obedience to the King's command, in every aspect it is the grandest work that can claim the intelligence, the interest, the enthusiasm, and the energy of consecrated hearts and lives.

The five minutes allotted to this service is not our estimate of its importance, but only that it is the spirit of Christian Endeavor not so much to dwell upon what it has done as to look forward to what there is still to do. So we give longer time to addresses of instruction and inspiration than to recounting our past achievements; but it is my privilege to unroll this missionary roll of honor. It contains the names of those societies which have contributed to the home and foreign missions abroad for their own church during the past year. In Boston, the honorary roll was made up of those who had given a certain small amount. There were certain objections to that money limit, and it was a very small one; but it was one that if you were going to give anything you would give as much as $10, and it was felt that the naming of a sum perhaps made some think that that was all they needed to give, and so there was nothing said about an amount this year, and all that have given to the missions for their own

TENT ENDEAVOR.   TENT WASHINGTON.   TENT WILLISTON.

THE WHITE LOT FROM THE STATE, WAR, AND NAVY BUILDING.

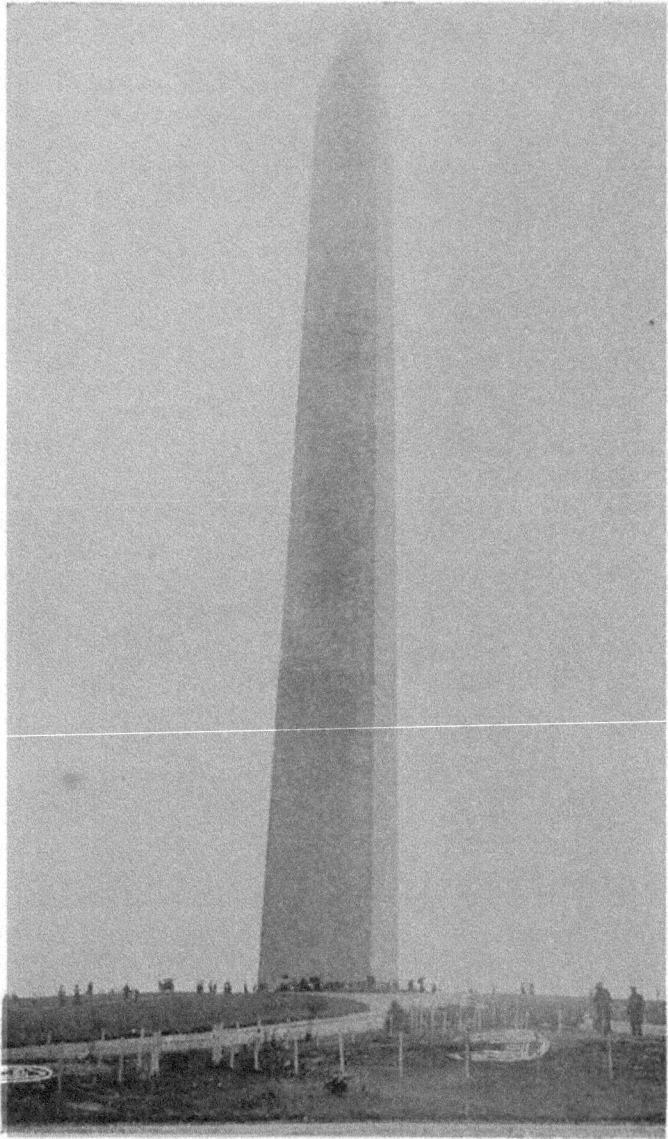

THE WASHINGTON MONUMENT, SHOWING FLORAL DESIGNS AT THE BASE.

church recognize their obligations, and in that way are on the roll of honor. And there are, as Mr. Baer told us yesterday, 5,869 of these societies, besides 2,331 Junior Societies of honor of the boys and girls that are beginning to bear the burdens of the Church. There are 8,200 societies, as against 5,500 last year. The thing is growing. The tide is rising, and they come from all over this country. Is your society on the list? Well, it ought to be next year if it is not this. We ought to have them all on the roll.

We only unroll it in the figure of speech. I would like to give one end of it into somebody's hand to be carried out to the end of the tent, but you would have to carry it out there and back and back, I do not know how many times, for there is no room here to unroll it. It is 600 feet long.

Before I tell you more, as magnificent as this roll of honor appears in its physical form, it is far greater in what it stands for. For one thing, this roll of honor is the answer to those who have any question as to the loyalty of our Endeavor Societies to their own denominations. There have always been those who have feared — and there may be a few left — that the young people may be drawn away from allegiance to their own church, and that they may lose something that binds them to the church of their fathers. But one of our principles of Christian Endeavor is loyalty to one's own church. If there is anything Dr. Clark insists upon with greater fidelity or with more burning eloquence than he does anything else, this roll of honor is one witness to it. It is the record not of money given to them for miscellaneous causes, good enough in their way; not of money given for missions in general; but of money given to the mission boards of our respective churches,— the official channels through which we are to give. This roll of honor is one record of our loyalty to our own churches, and then, too, this roll of honor stands as an answer to those who think that Christian Endeavor has a kind of sentimental gush, and is a sort of annual religious jubilee. Those of us who are in it know that Christian Endeavor means Christian work, week in and week out, the whole year round; and this roll of honor stands for not merely an enthusiasm of words and songs, but the kind of enthusiasm that is transmuted into downright service and hard dollars and cents. It used to be said that the prayer meeting was the thermometer of the Church. There is a profound truth in that, of course, and yet is it not a practical truth to-day that the test of a church's piety or an individual's piety is in their foreign missionary collection? How clearly and how fully do we recognize our obligations to God? And this roll stands for the loyalty we have to our own church; it stands for our loyalty to God's work, the expression of our purpose that we will do what we can, that we will use what God has given us for his service and his glory. May I not urge also as a thought to lie under all these and to lead us to larger giving, that Christianity is essentially a missionary religion? That is a great deal more than saying that missions are important. Christianity is essentially in its very nature a missionary religion. Missions are a part of Christianity,— so much a part of it that it is not the real Christianity without missions.

The church in whose pastorate I have the honor to serve, fifty years ago wrote its platform of principles in this matter: "The Presbyterian Church is a missionary society whose purpose is the conversion of the world, and every member of the church is a member of that society, bound to do all he can in the prosecution of that work." And about the same time the church used these words also: "The time has now come" (and remember that was fifty years ago; how much more must it be true now!) "that no church and hardly any individual can refrain from giving something systematically to missions without grave dishonor and sin." We cannot be indifferent. The work of missions rests upon our hearts, and I plead with the Christian Endeavor members of this host to plead with God for the cause; be honest in our faith, and let us lift the burdens of the heathen of the world not lightly with our finger-tips, but let us pray God with strong crying and tears for mercy not only upon our Christless brethren across the sea, but upon the Christlessness of our own souls, upon our shallow sympathies, our hollow self-denials, our callousness to the evils of the world, that we take up this work for which God pledged his Son and to which that Son gave his life.

The Hampton Octette then rendered the song, " Let the Heavenly Light Shine on Me."

DR. BECKLEY: There is a motto that hangs in our homes, "The Lord will provide," and the Lord arranges our programmes for us often after we have made our own arrangements and printed the programme, and sometimes the very best programmes are those that have been arranged after the meeting begins. We will not be able to hear from the last speaker on the programme to-day, but the Lord has sent Bishop Baldwin, of Canada, and I know you all will rejoice in the privilege of hearing him now.

Address of the Rt. Rev. Morris S. Baldwin, D.D., London, Ont.

My friends, I only speak because I feel that I have been called upon to do so, and I recognize a higher power than the chairman. I therefore would say but a few words on the subject of Christian power, and I would begin by af-firming that the Gospel of Jesus Christ is the power of God in the highest and most unrestricted sense. God has given us what power is in the Gospel of his Son, and I would therefore point your attention this morning to the evidence of that power in the kingdom of Christ.

Now, to begin with, we find that the Church of God is not a granite build-ing, not some huge, immobile structure, but a tree, living, growing, and expand-ing, whose leaves are for the healing of the nations. The simile of the church is not stone. It is not that which is fastened and secured and absolutely with-out motion, but something whose progress is commensurate with the great mis-sion of our Lord; and therefore a church without power is like Samson without his locks. It is an anomaly. And wherever we see pulpits without power, wherever we see communities that are rich and where perhaps the Gos-pel is preached, yet where there is an absence of power, we see something that is in direct contravention to the whole economy of God. Now when we look at God's power we see this manifested in the work of God the Holy Ghost, and God the Holy Ghost is that mighty power by which God communicates life, refreshes the weary, strengthens the weak, and brings back millions to the fold of the Son of God. Now let me ask you to notice that there are four rivers mentioned in the Word of God, and it is to these four rivers that I would draw your attention this morning. They are rivers that bring us to that work of God the Holy Ghost to which I have referred.

The first river is that of the Garden of Eden, where we see one great river flowing through the garden and dividing itself into four great streams, showing that for the garden there was blessed refreshment and power, a power that went forth over the great nations of the earth.

Secondly, we see another river,— and it is mentioned in the Psalms,— that river the streams whereof make glad the city of our God. It is the same river, but it is here in the city. It makes glad, and the Psalmist, in speaking about the tumultuous life around him, says, " Therefore will we not fear, though the earth be removed, and though the mountains be carried into the midst of the sea." There is a river which is the broad, deep, glorious river that flows to make glad the city of our God.

Now, dear friends, the city here is the Church of God, and that river is the same stream. It is the Holy Spirit that is to make glad the Church of God— not the wealthy millionaire, not the rank nor the power of the people, but what is to make glad the Church of God is the presence, the power, and the manifes-tation of God the Holy Ghost. It takes the sorrow out of our hearts and fills our dim eyes with joy.

The third river is that just mentioned in the book of the prophet Heze-kiah. It is the river that comes out of the temple, and it flows from that tem-ple in an ever-increasing stream. First, it is only ankle-deep; then it is to the knees; then it is to the waist; and at last it is the great river that one cannot possibly wade, and that river is the same mighty and Holy Spirit that is going forth from the temple of God. It is the Church Christ has purchased, and if the Church is to do its work, that river must flow out again, broadening, deepening, expanding, the river of God's Most Holy Spirit, for the deepening of his work and the gathering-in of souls against the coming of our Lord.

And, lastly, there is a river, and it is the same river that in the fourth instance is close up to the throne of God. The first was the river of the garden ; the second, the river of the city ; the third is the river of the temple ; and the fourth is the river of the throne, and it issues from the throne of God, showing us where that Holy Spirit comes from — not from the councils of men, not from human cause, but fresh from the throne of God, flowing forever and forever out upon this vast world, for strength, for healing, and for power. And what does this Holy Spirit teach ? With this I conclude. Just as the magnet of the compass points only to the north, though storm and sunshine come upon it it is always to the north, so God the Holy Ghost, through ages upon ages keeps pointing to the Lamb of God that taketh away the sin of the world. And I say to you, dear young men and Endeavorers of this vast conference, you will receive abundantly that river of joy into your own hearts. Tell it to the old, ere they sink into eternity ; tell it to the young in the freshness and vigor of life ; tell it to the men of business, absorbed with the rush and turmoil of their work : that there stands before them that great Redeemer whose blood can cleanse them from their sins, and who waits to be gracious. You have no exhausted brook to draw from, but a river broad and deep, that makes glad the city of our God. Drink of it, bathe in it, and go forth in the power of the Holy Ghost ; and let your life be a laying-down of your homage at the Saviour's feet to gather in souls against that great day when Jesus Christ shall come again in the glory of his Father to take his waiting bride and place her forever in the joy of heaven.

Central Hall.

Owing to the fall of Tent Williston, the big meeting which was to have been held there took place at Central Hall.

President Clark was present at Central Hall and presided over the meeting. A large section of the chorus was on hand, and the first half-hour was devoted to a musical service, under the leadership of Mr. P. P. Bilhorn, of Chicago.

When Dr. Clark advanced to the stand to formally open the exercises he was greeted with enthusiastic applause, as he is every time he comes before an Endeavor audience.

The devotional exercises were conducted by Rev. Adam Keoch, of Washington.

The first topic was "The Intermediate Society of Christian Endeavor."

Address of Rev. Chas. A. Dickinson, D.D., Boston, Mass.

The Intermediate Society is to the Christian Endeavor movement as a whole what the trunk is to the tree. It is, or should be, that part of the organism which connects the roots and branches. It conserves and regulates the flow and counterflow of those influences which are to determine the character and quantity of the blossoms and fruit. It covers that nexus of critical years which joins infancy to young manhood and womanhood.

The discussion of the question at this time is but a natural result of that wonderful evolution which has characterized the Endeavor movement from the beginning.

Each succeeding year has presented to the common sense of the Christian Endeavor hosts its special questions, and most of these questions have been followed by practical and helpful solutions. Thus the work has grown from the tiny beginning to the world-spreading tree.

In speaking of the trunk of the tree, it goes without saying that it requires as much care as the root and branches.

Trunk-shielding and trunk-straightening and trunk-pruning are some of the most important parts of arboriculture. I have seen a row of maples every one of which was scorched and shriveled on the southern side the first year after they were transplanted. Their trunks were not protected from the burning sun, and, as a result, they will always have a mass of dead wood at the core. The woods and fields are full of crooked trees which might have been straight had withes and stakes been applied to them when they were young.

The adolescent age, comprising the early "teens," is in a special sense the trunk-training age. Everything depends upon the protecting, straightening, and pruning which are given during this period. It is here that the tendencies of infancy are strengthened or perverted; here that the man or the woman is shaped; here that the tremendous dynamos of passion and ambition and aspiration are changed for life's weal or woe.

It is here that the Intermediate Society does its gracious and beneficial work.

In my judgment, the Christian Endeavor movement owes its phenomenal success and great prosperity to the fact that it started as an Intermediate Society, and adapted itself from the very outset to the peculiar needs and perils of the adolescent period. The first society was composed very largely of boys and girls.

It was this class which most troubled the ministers twenty years ago. "What shall we do with them?" said fathers and mothers and clergymen. "Where will they be safe? They are too big for the cradle and too small for the church." "Take them under the wing of the church and organize them into a working society," said Dr. Clark. Take them while they are plastic and train them in Christian service. Give them five or six years of continuous practice in Christian thought and prayer and expression and activity, and when they are eighteen they will be shapely young men and women.

This was the God-appointed mission of the Society of Christian Endeavor. It was here that it did a work which no other organization had done, and it is only by adhering closely to its original charter that it can hope to continue its beneficent influence.

The years in their merciless revolution push us forever on. Youth comes but once in a lifetime. The boys and girls of the first society are now the young men and women of the community. The happy tendency is to forget the flight of years, however, and to imagine we are still the original Endeavorers. And it is just possible that, with this sense of our own perennial youth increasing, even under our gray hairs, we may forget the real boys and girls who are just now jumping out of their cradles into the shoes we wore fifteen or twenty years ago, and so pulling the Endeavor Society along with us into middle life, leave no adequate provision for the young folks who come after us.

This tendency has been noted in some of our churches. There is a disposition on the part of those who were boys and girls fifteen years ago to separate themselves from those who are fifteen years old to-day, and to monopolize the privileges of the Society. They do this almost unconsciously. And herein is the danger which threatens the permanency of the Society, and which, unless arrested, will tend to make the Endeavor movement the convenience of a single generation, instead of what we believe that it is designed to be, the blessing of the ages.

The Intermediate Society is adapted to avert this danger and solve the many difficulties connected with it.

The formation of Junior Societies was an important step toward establishing that law of circularity by which organizations and institutions become permanent through the infusion from year to year of the fresh young life of the community, but there is a long distance between the Juniors and adult societies. The graduate from the Junior Society is in no sense fitted to become an active member in the older society, as it exists to-day in most of our churches. He does not feel at home there. He is overshadowed and silenced. I am not sure but that this fact will become so apparent as the evolution of the Society goes on that some such provision as the intermediate department will seem to be a necessity in every church. Indeed, I am inclined to think that the Intermediate Society in future years will be considered as the essential part of the Christian Endeavor movement.

For some years to come, however, this need will not be so much felt as it will be when the present societies have practically become the rank and file of the churches and have assumed the work and responsibilities of the older generation. In the larger churches the need is felt to-day. The societies in these churches are, as a rule, too large for the conscientious fulfilment of the pledge and the most efficient service.

They are made up of many adults who, because of their larger experience, are expected to assume the official duties and do most of the planning and talking.

Several years ago it was thought advisable in a number of these large churches to break up these societies into division bands, in order to secure a more general participation in the duties and privileges of the meetings, and the formation of the intermediate branch is one of the results of that movement.

In my own church we organized some two years ago a second, or intermediate, division, which comprises to-day some sixty of the brightest boys and girls of the parish, whose average age is about fourteen or fifteen years. They are full of life and fire. They are sometimes mischievous. They once in a while laugh out in meeting and do things which the good old saints consider very frivolous ; but on the whole they are ideal Endeavorers, full of the spirit of ministration, genuinely devout, earnestly desirous to serve the Lord and obey his commands.

One of the pastors of the church is always present at their meetings. Advice and direction are given when needed. They are always amenable to loving guidance, and under it they give promise of becoming a strong right arm of the church. They are learning what few adult Christians learn in their youth; namely, that Christian life means service. A little five-year-old nephew of mine said to his father the other day as he was waiting for the after-dinner dessert, " Papa, do you know what custard pie is ? " " What is it ? " asked his father. " Why," replied Robert, with a bright twinkle in his eye, " it is all swallow and no chew." A pretty good definition, I should say, of some of the old-time religion, which came very near turning our churches into intellectual restaurants for feeding lazy Christians with soft custards. Against this whole idea of an easy-going faith the Endeavor movement has set itself from the beginning.

And, under God, it has been wonderfully blessed in raising up a vast host of active workers.

The best worker of to-day is the young man or woman who came ten or fifteen years ago as a boy or girl into the Endeavor ranks. The workers of the next generation will be the Endeavor boys and girls of this. So long as Endeavor shall hold the boys and girls God will use it to bring on his millennium.

The next speaker's topic was " Every Talent for Christ."

Address of Rev. John Neil, Toronto, Ont.

The central thought in this address is that God will accept and use every power we possess if we consecrate all to his service, and that the Christian has scope for the exercise of all his talents in the service of God. This has been denied. There are those who have said that Christianity narrows a man ; that it has impoverished art and is inimical to true culture. Such is not the case. Culture has been defined as having a high ideal and training heart and brain and hand and eye to reach that ideal. Now Christianity sets before us the highest ideal, and it trains heart and brain and hand and eye to attain to that ideal. John Stuart Blackie has truly said that man's chief end is to develop every power of mind and body and soul to the fullest extent. If he does that he will glorify God and enjoy him forever.

Christ invites us to come to him with all we have, and the two talents will be made four, and the five, ten. In endeavoring to prove this, let us first consider that God has given man every power which he possesses and has made provision for the exercise of all. When man was created he was endowed with all the faculties he possesses. His love of the beautiful and his power to produce the beautiful all came from God. In this respect he was created in the image of God himself, who loves the beautiful and has made everything beautiful in its season. He also commanded him to cultivate all the powers he gave him, for when he told him he was to cultivate the earth he did not mean the external world around him merely, but his own nature as well, with all the powers it possesses.

When he was creating a world in which man was to dwell he did not merely make provision for man's necessities, but he also created a world filled with forms of beauty, and which minister to every part of our being. No part of our nature, no talent, is left unprovided for. The same was true when he was providing a revelation for man. He did not content himself with declaring his will in a few brief, comprehensive statements, but he gave a revelation which appealed to every part of man's being. The Word of God has come to us through history, parable, simile, poetry in all its forms, so that every part of man's being is touched. His intellect, his emotions, his æsthetic nature,—all are used as channels through which His truth reaches heart and conscience. If God had no place in his kingdom for all man's varied talents, it is not likely that in all these varied ways he would have ministered to them all.

We find that God has in the founding and developing of his Church used all the powers man possesses.

When founding his Church he did so. In the construction of the Tabernacle and the Temple, in which God was to dwell in the midst of his people, the mechanical skill and genius not only of Israelites, but those of other nations, were placed under contribution. In making provision for the Temple service, the greatest poets and the sweetest musicians were employed by God. In the revelation which he was giving to man, he placed under contribution the learning and the genius and all the varied talents of men who had given themselves to him, — the learning of Moses, the wisdom of Solomon, the poetical genius of Isaiah, Jeremiah, and Ezekiel. When that revelation was to be completed, when Christ came, we find him training his disciples and using their individuality and their varied experiences in the declaration of his truth,— the learning of Luke and Paul, the methodical training of Matthew; also the sanguine temperament of Peter, making him the apostle of hope; the fervent nature of John, making him the apostle of love; and the ethical instincts of James, making him the apostle of the ethical side of Christianity; so that all the varied gifts and talents and experiences of those men were utilized by God in the founding of his Church. The same was true when he was bringing his Church back to a knowledge of the truth. She had become corrupt, and a false philosophy had concealed or distorted the truth. When the time came to bring men back to the light we find all men's varied talents employed. What varied gifts were exercised in the Reformation! Luther was not only a great preacher, but he was a sweet singer, and he produced the battle-songs of the Reformation. Holbein was a great artist, and from the canvas he taught the same truths which were preached and sung by Luther. Calvin was the greatest logician of his age; Erasmus, the greatest scholar. All were used; not a talent was rejected.

The same was true when God's Church was to be revived. We find God laying his hand on men of varied talents. Whitfield, the marvelous orator, who could for hours hold thousands spellbound; John Wesley, not only a great preacher, but the great organizer; Charles Wesley, the poet, who wrote some of the sweetest hymns which have enriched our books of praise; — all these were used.

We find the same is true now, when we are disseminating the truth. This is the age of missions. It seems as if each age of the Church had its own special work to do, — at one time to defend the truth, at another to disseminate the truth. This is the age of missions. The Church has her ears open to hear the command of her Lord: "Go ye into all the world and preach the gospel to every creature." And now as never before since the first centuries she is seeking to obey that command. And what do we find? God is using and blessing every invention, every advance in science and art in this great work. Men and women find that every talent they possess can be used in telling the story of Christ's love to a lost world. Medical missions are opening doors for the entrance of the Gospel. Scientific knowledge in other places is being employed. The Gospel sung is reaching hearts which were closed against the Gospel preached; and we find that God is calling on all and using every power he has given to man in furthering this great work, so that all through the past and in the present, in the founding and developing of his Church, God has, and is recognizing, all man's work or gifts.

We find also that when men consecrate their powers to God's service they are developed in a way they would not otherwise be. Moses was a learned man and possessed great natural talent, but would he ever have possessed the power he did had he consented to be called the son of Pharaoh's daughter and refused the call of God? The disciples of our Lord would never intellectually have been the men they became had they not yielded themselves to him. Bunyan had a vivid imagination and possessed native humor, but he would never intellectually have been able to write the "Pilgrim's Progress" had he not dedicated these gifts to God.

And so it has ever been. If we have any talent, we find that talent is increased and developed by giving it to God. We yield it to him; he gives it back enriched. It is reasonable that such should be the case. The story is told of a great musician who was also a mechanical genius. He was not satisfied with any of the musical instruments at his disposal, and constructed an organ for himself. Others could produce sweet music on that organ, but no one could call forth its powers as he who had made it. So with us: God has made us; every power we possess has come from him, and it is only when we yield our lives to him and allow him to use us that the full music of which our lives are capable is evoked. Now when we consider all this, when we think that God has created all the powers we possess; that in the world he has created and in the revelation he has given, he has made provision for them all; when we think that in the founding and development of his Church he has used all the varied talents men possess, and when we consider that it is only when men have yielded themselves fully to him that they have produced all of which they are capable, can we have any doubt that God will accept and will use all we bring to him? Do not fear that if you become a Christian it will narrow you. On the contrary, it will enrich your life and give it a beauty it does not now possess. Do not let us be satisfied with merely coming to Christ that our sins may be pardoned, but let us bring every gift to him and use all for him. If there is any one here who is not a Christian, I would say, Why remain away from Christ? You may have much in your life that is sweet and beautiful, but you are like the wayside flower; it is beautiful and fragrant, but it is exposed to the chilling winds and is in danger of being trodden down by the feet of those who are passing by. Let that flower be transplanted by the gardner and he will watch over it, shelter it from the storm, and it will put on a richer beauty and have a sweeter fragrance. So with you. Come to Christ with all you possess and he will not only guard and defend your life, but he will beautify and enrich it, and it will go on developing through the ages of eternity.

After the singing of a hymn by the chorus, Rev. Cortland Myers, of Brooklyn, N. Y., was introduced to speak upon the subject, "The King's Business."

Address of Rev. Cortland Myers, Brooklyn, N. Y.

There were twelve millions of men who laid down their lives to satisfy the ambitions of a Cæsar. There were four millions of men who laid down their lives in the war-path cut by Napoleon Bonaparte through Europe, and whose bones lay bleaching upon the shore of a foreign world. There have been millions throughout the history of the world who have simply followed obediently the standards of an earthly king. There are in the world to-day millions of men who would rise at the first sound of the word " Go " from the king's or the queen's lips. The Czar of Russia commands his thousands, the Emperor of Germany his thousands, and the Queen of England her thousands. They are ready at the first instant to move to any part of the world at the command of their sovereign.

If those who obtain only a small part of this world to call their kingdom, and a single house or two which they call their palace, have such implicit obedience as history testifies to, what shall we say this morning as to our relation to our King,— the King of kings and the Lord of lords. Not only a small part of this world is his, but the whole planet. All the flowers and all the conservatories and fields of the world are in his conservatory in one palace. All the grass and all the meadows of the world comprise his lawns. All the mountain-sides with their trees and their verdure comprise his parks. The oceans themselves are the baths, and the rivers and lakes are the fountains for that palace. All the sunrises of the morning and sunsets of the evening are the pictures upon that palace wall. All the stars in the heaven are his thousands of candle chandeliers.

If that is the contrast between your King and Napoleon Bonaparte, what ought to be your duty this morning to that sceptre that swings above the head of every Christian man and Christian woman? Just one attitude of implicit and immediate obedience. We have a theology of justice emphasized and a theology of love exercised, a new theology and an old theology; but I declare this morning that it seems to me about time in the kingdom of God that we had a theology of obedience.

The last word of your Divine King was one monosyllabic word, but a word stupendous in its size, after all,—that one single round " o " encircling the world and the crooked "g" the chain which binds that world fast to the throne of God. "Go, go," was your Master's command, and not stop until the last square foot upon the planet had been touched by a drop of blood from his veins. That command covers preacher and hearer. It covers every man and woman and child beneath the sceptre of the Son of God.

In the world's bright field of battle, alas! it is too often true in the bivouac of life you will find the Christian soul represented by his wife. And the men of this kingdom of our Lord have not yet learned the lesson which I speak this morning as well as the women have learned it. They have not learned it in the home field and they have not learned it in the foreign field,— the implicit obedience demanded of them by their King.

We must follow implicitly the standard of the Christ, no matter where it takes us, in any part of this home-land or the foreign land, before this planet shall be ever given to its rightful owner. We must learn more deeply than we have ever learned it yet, the necessity, the demand, that runs through the entire kingdom of our Lord Jesus Christ to be obedient to our King. If we had one-tenth part of the obedience which is given to the kings of this world in their kingdoms how long do you think it would be before this world would be given to Christ entirely, bound with golden chains to the feet of God? How long, think you? Before the close of this nineteenth century, and you would not need to plan a Christian Endeavor Convention in England. Wherever you would go you would find your Convention before the throne of God.

If we would simply move up to the standard of Christ in obedience to our Master's voice, ah, quickly, quickly, would the world be given to him. Tennyson, in his " Light Brigade " says:—

> " Theirs not to reason why,
> Theirs but to do and die..

Into the valley of death
Rode the six hundred.
Cannon to right of them,
Cannon to left of them,
Cannon in front of them,
Vollied and thundered.
Into the jaws of death,
Into the mouth of hell,
Rode the six hundred.''

If that was our attitude towards the commands of our Divine Master,—never to reason why, but to do and die,—what mighty progress there would be in the kingdom of our Lord upon earth!

What is our message, and what is our business as Christian men and women? We are here in this Christian Endeavor Convention, and we say our mission upon earth is to fulfil the mission of Jesus Christ and to save men; but next week we will be back in our business places and our homes, and our business, if we are truthful, is not that; it is more often to get more of this world's goods in our hands, or to climb to a higher summit; or some other object than the one supreme object. We are hearing a great deal to-day about gold and silver. One part of this land is falling down before a golden calf, and another part of this land is falling down before a silver calf, and nearly the whole land is waltzing and dancing around those two calves in its excitement and its insanity. Almighty God is sending the message from his throne: "What doth it profit a man," if he owns all the silver-mines of a Bland, or a Boies, or a St. John, or all the gold of the gold-bugs of Wall Street, if he loses his immortal soul? What value is it if we have all the wealth of this world in our hands if the soul is lost? What value is it to your fellow man if his soul is lost? The most valuable thing upon earth and in heaven is the soul of man. It is your business and mine to save that soul through the grace of God. We have been hearing much recently, and rightly so, about Armenia and the persecutions of the Turk. I have had my own blood boil, and I am prepared this morning to pause right here and pray to God Almighty to send our white squadron yet up the Dardanelles and shatter that old Turkish throne into atoms and send the pig-headed monarch where he belongs. I have prayed it. I prayed it before three thousand people and have been preaching it to them almost every Sunday for the last month. I am prepared to pray that that old Turkish rug, crimsoned with blood-stains, shall be rolled up off this world's floor and be given to the rag-pickers of perdition, or hung out upon the lines of the world, and the winds of justice be made to sweep through it, and the moths to be taken out of it.

There is more for Christian people and more for the kingdom of God to work for upon earth even than that. It is the sublimest of all occupations, and that which is coveted by the angels, next to the throne of God, to seek and to save that which was lost. And it shall be done. This magnificent mission shall be accomplished only by the divine method. It can not be done by any amount of machinery. It can not be done by any process of war. It can not be done by any other means than the Peter method, and the Andrew method, and the Nathaniel method, and the Philip method, and the Christ method. It must be done by soul touching soul and imparting the divine love.

Christianity is love. There has been too much emphasis laid in these latter days in the Church of Christ upon education and upon benevolence and upon other things which are to help and elevate human kind. We have been placing too much emphasis upon brain in the pulpit; even Christianity is not primarily that. It is love. It is not intellect. It is passion. It is not an idea, not a philosophy, not a science, not anything else than a passion for the souls of men. Why? Because Christianity was born in love. It had its inception in the heart of God. It was love which produced a Gethsemane and a Calvary and a Sepulchre to save human kind; and it is precisely that element which must go out from your heart in order to acomplish this sublime mission of which I speak to you to-day,— the King's business upon earth.

We are so afraid of a little enthusiasm and a little sweat and a little of anything except formality and coldness! My heart is just bleeding and aching when I recall this morning that down in the battle-field from which I come a million people in my city never crossed the threshold of a Christian church on the Sabbath Day; and more than a million over across the river in New York live in the same depths of heathenism. The churches of our Divine Master almost without exception are empty. I know only one church in the whole City of Churches that has to turn people away from its doors. I believe this morning it is not due to the sin which is binding this world as much as it is due to the coldness which is shackling our Christian hearts.

I have declared to you this morning that the immortal souls of men amount to infinitely more than that. This kingdom of our Master will never be laid at his feet until we realize that our mission is the highest mission upon earth, and it shall be accomplished by only one method. You can have all the machinery you wish and you can have all the equipments you wish, but it seems to me it is a sad, pitiable thing to hear, pathetic to hear, for any church of Christ to say, " We are in a poor location; we can't be anything where we are." The church at Pergamos was in a poor location. The church of Ephesus was in a poor location, and all the rest of them were in a poor location. They say, " Because we are down-town, we can't do anything." " You can't do anything in down-town New York." " You can't do anything in down-town Brooklyn." I know one poor, weak specimen — the whole church, the board of deacons, trustees, and everything — who said, " You can't do a thing. The greatest preachers in the land have preached in this beautiful church for years, and they have preached to as many as seven people on Sunday night. You can't do anything down here,"— and that was in the centre of a quarter of a million people. They were not able to do a thing to save any one.

If the Church of our Master will rise right up to its level, to its possibility of divine enthusiasm to save the souls of men, you can fill any building on earth and you can save anybody on earth.

Oh, what splendid opportunities are given to those in the Christian Endeavor Societies to-day, and in every part of this kingdom of our Lord, to save men! There never were opportunities like those, in every part of our world, that there are in this day,—opportunities in the literary world, opportunities in the scientific world, opportunities in the commercial world, opportunities in the professional world, opportunities in the inventive world, opportunities everywhere. We think we have done wonders in these last days, and we have; but I believe in the next twenty-five years we are going to see more wonderful things by far than were ever seen in these last twenty-five years. You will simply laugh about some of the electrical apparatus and steam apparatus and apparatus of other kinds and machinery of these latter days. I should not be surprised if we were to make a journey to the moon within the next twenty-five years. I do not know about it. I haven't bought my ticket for it yet. I do not know that I would go in the first train; but it will not be surprising if we do go. There are growing up in these days more opportunities for young men and women to make a magnificent success in every department of life. Don't you believe it when they tell you you are being crowded out. There is plenty of room at the top, and there will be more. Don't put any confidence in that expression at all. There are opportunities in the moral world, in every part of the world, to elevate human society. You were pleaded with last night, some of you, I suppose, to make better citizens, better government, for a purified political life; and it was declared that that was the arena of most splendid success for young men and women in these days.

I care not this morning whether you heard that or not. I do declare that it is not true. The best, grandest, greatest arena for the success of young men and young women to-day is to be soul-savers. You could purify the politics of hell, perhaps, and yet that would not be the saving of the lost. The most important work on earth, I have said, is to save men. The most magnificent work given to human kind is to save your fellow men.

Our churches to-day are not realizing just this message of this morning, to my mind, to one single part of the degree that it has been realized in the days past. With all the splendid equipments we have, with every emolument to advance the interests of our kingdom, with every possibility ahead of us, we ought to accomplish ten thousand times more than we do.

Ought we to be satisfied with just a few conversions in our society a year, just a few in our churches a year, simply to keep up the record? No, we ought not to be satisfied with anything less than a Pentecost. If they had a Pentecost, with the men they had it with, with the money they had it with, in the environment they had it with, what ought we to have to-day? They·had three thousand saved in one city in a day. Forty thousand would not be a comparison with a Pentecost; and the same Spirit of God moves and reigns upon earth, and the same Spirit is given to his Church upon earth.

What does it require? It requires simply a consecrated heart, not brains. Not that does God always use. Not ability along indefinite lines, perhaps Not that does God always use. Our Heavenly Father has seen fit to use our. poor efforts. What would some of us do this morning if his mercy had not left it that way? He uses the weakest instruments upon earth, if they are only consecrated to his service, to save the souls of our fellow men.

There are pulpits to-day which are being used as the instruments of blasphemy,— a morocco case, the leaves unrolled, the struggle is simply this: to bring all of Webster's dictionary into a single man's vocabulary, and to place it in grammatical, rhetorical sentences. I have known a man to spend an entire week doing the same thing that they do in order to learn to ride a bicycle,— spending an entire week constructing a grammatical sentence and riding it down the asphalt pavement of some rich church. I would rather utter every sentence ungrammatically, have only twelve words in my vocabulary, if those words could come from a burning heart, all aglow with fire. Twelve words would be enough,— "The blood of Jesus Christ his Son cleanseth us from all sins."

I don't care whether I can express myself very well or not. That does not amount to much as long as the purpose is plain and the destination is reached. I stand at the foot of my Master's throne and he places the crown of royalty on my poor brow and the sacred lips give the message: "Well done, good and faithful servant, enter thou into the joy of thy Lord." He will touch my lips and make me never to stutter again. As sure as his throne stands, that will inevitably be the result. It was that same determination that sent Henry Martyn to Arabia, Carey to India, Morrison to China, Atchison to Africa, Patterson to the Islands of the Sea, and every man and woman into every part of God's kingdom, which has shaken this world and brought us nearer to his throne. When this is done, oh, what a glorious morning will pleasantly dawn! I am waiting for it. There is not a pessimistic drop of blood in my veins — not one, because I believe in God the Father, in Jesus Christ the Son, my King, in the Holy Ghost, my helper; and this world is bound to be his.

I am pleading with you simply to have a share in it, not because it will not be done. It will be done; but you will be sorry some day that you did not use every one of those talents to the saving of your fellow men. I am pleading with you for that purpose, because it is bound to come; but with this great army of Christian Endeavor, and the millions of the Church of our Master, I can hear the tread of the oncoming host this morning, and the battle is soon to be won.

The next exercise was unrolling the missionary roll of honor.

Remarks of Rev. J. W. Weddell, Philadelphia, Pa.

In imagination you have before you the roll which records 8,200 societies of Christian Endeavor who have given within the last year to missions, $150,000 and more. Besides this, $200,000 and more have been given to other benevolences, making a round sum of $360,000 given by the Christian Endeavor Societies of the country to general missions and benevolence,— a noble record indeed.

Of this company, the Clarendon Street Baptist Church has a Christian Endeavor Society that has given $1,107 and has the honor of being first. The Calvary Presbyterian Society of Buffalo gives $1,000, and stands second. I am very glad, dear friends, that we have such a record as this, and that we have the promise of good things to come in the year which is before us. The only feet that are called beautiful in the Bible are the feet that are moving. "How beautiful upon the mountains are the feet of him that bringeth good tidings, that publisheth peace."

I thought, as they were singing here to-day, of the watchmen that shall lift up their voices together when He shall bring again Zion; how he is bringing Zion by means of his ransomed host. So when we are doing a mission work, giving to Christian missions, we are living the most beautiful and most graceful Christian life. I believe also that we are strongest in our Christian life when we are giving in this Christian fashion. There is a text of Scripture that says, "If the salt hath lost its savor, wherewith shall it be salted?" The salt of this whole world is the Church, and the salt of the Church is missions. If the Church shall lose its missionary interest, its enthusiasm for missions, it is like the salt that are lost its saltness, to be trodden under the foot of man; and it is so trodden wherever churches of Jesus Christ lose the missionary spirit. The strength of our Christian living is in our Christian giving, as the beauty of our Christian living is in our Christian giving.

The word that our brother accented was "go." Some one has put along with it another word, "lo." I should say the two balance each other. In God's Word, at the last of Matthew, it is: "Go ye" and "lo, I am with you." God himself comes into the midst of the people. We go in answer to his cry, following out the Master's direction; and as we go he is with us and we enjoy his presence.

As we take the roll of the missionary agents of this Society we are laying hold upon the world of Jesus Christ, and we can say, "Gideon is mine." When you and I go forth under the Master's direction and pattern we have entered upon the conquest of the whole world, and the strength and might is with us.

There in my old city of Chicago a colored man stood up one day, and when questioned as to how he was getting along in the Christian career, he said, "I am having a good time. Oh," said he, "I am having so good a time as I go along as a Christian that when I goes up to the gates of heaven, if they shuts me out, I will say, 'Anyhow, I had a good time getting here.'"

Fellow Christian Endeavorers, we are having a good time on the way, and it is not to be wondered at, for as Jacob went on his way the angels of God met him. He was going on God's way, and how could it be otherwise than that he should meet God's messengers? Christian Endeavorers, go God's way as Christ set the fashion,—"Go ye into all the world and preach the gospel to every creature. Lo, I am with you alway, even unto the end of the world."

Tent Washington.

By nine o'clock there were about fifteen hundred people in Tent Washington, and the stream of incomers was steadily growing larger. Those who had come early sat quietly and without displaying any of those signs of great enthusiasm that marked Thursday morning, until at about ten minutes after nine the Tennessee delegates, sitting near the front, began to sing the "Nashville, '98" song, a medley of "Dixie" and "Yankee Doodle." It breathed a good spirit of welcome and broke the damp silence and served to warm up the delegates. There was a hearty round of hand-clapping, and the Southerners began their other song, "Tennessee," to the tune of "America." When there was quiet again some man in the crowd, inspired by a thought of the moisture of the past few days, called out, "How's the weather down there?" An enthusiastic Nashville delegate shouted back, "It's dryer than it is here."

Then ensued a remarkable rivalry. The Philadelphians, sitting in the north end of the tent, opened up with their song of invitation and welcome, "Come to Philadelphia in 1898," sung to the tune of "John Brown's Body." It was bright and catchy, and soon many others than the Quaker city folks were sounding forth the strains of the famous old march. They put it through all the verses about four times, and then the Nashville people, growing a bit jealous of the attention the Endeavorers from the City of Brotherly Love were attracting, started up their medley again without waiting for their rivals to cease. The two songs did not harmonize very well, but that mattered not, for there was a touch of friendly rivalry in the effort, and the delegates who were not rivals for the convention two years hence enjoyed the efforts of the two delegations keenly. For a few moments there was a running fire of mingled cadences and chords, and then a crowd of folks in another part of the tent started up a hymn that smothered out the other songs. Finally there came other aspirants for convention honors, — the Endeavor crowd from Louisville,— and their song was probably the prettiest of all, the refrain of "Louisville in 1898" fitting in very nicely with the rhythm of "The Red, White, and Blue."

It was half-past nine o'clock; Right Rev. Samuel Fallows, D.D., of Chicago, stepped forward on the rostrum and called for order. He then asked Mr. Excell, of Chicago, to lead in the song service. Mr. Excell took the platform and called for "All Hail the Power of Jesus' Name." There were about six thousand voices in the great choir that swelled out the notes of the grand old hymn to defy the pouring rain that was falling by gallons on the canvas walls.

Rev. N. C. Naylor, of Washington, conducted the devotional exercises.

The first speaker was Miss Haus, of St. Louis, Mo., whose topic was "The Junior Society of Christian Endeavor."

Address of Miss Kate H. Haus, St. Louis, Mo.

The membership of the Junior Christian Endeavor Society should consist of children of all ages, up to twelve and fourteen years — babies in arms, if they can be brought; anyway, have a baby roll attached to your Junior list; you can pray for them and their parents, and by so doing keep the brothers, sisters, and members interested in the younger ones, and often win indifferent parents to a lively co-operation and sympathy in the Junior work. The babies can not become acquainted too early with what ought to be their future home.

In this primary department of Christian Endeavor and Church work is taught the spiritual alphabet and the simple fundamental principles of Christian mathematics.

Here they get not only the key-notes that unlock all Bible teachings in words, but they get the heavenly geometrical truth, which, if followed, helps solve all problems of life; namely, that a straight, pure life is the shortest distance between earth and heaven.

No church or mission field is complete without this class for Christian training, any more than a district or grammar school would be complete without its primary department.

The Junior Christian Endeavor is not to take the place of the home training of the parents, or of the Sabbath school or Church, but to supplement, emphasize, enlarge, and help make complete the spiritual life and training of Christ's little ones.

We have had commentaries, lesson helps, papers, religious magazines, and what-not, to the exclusion of the Bible. The Juniors should be taught to know their Bible as their main object — not the poll-parrot repetition of verses, without thought, but an intelligent, prayerful study of the Bible, that will bear fruit in purity of thought, word, and deed.

The outcome of such training in mature life should be a clean soul, a pure heart, in a sound body, and all under the control and guidance of the Holy Spirit.

To have this result means a Junior superintendent wholly consecrated to the work, continually active, and having the help of parents, pastor, church, and seniors, through prayer, sympathy, counsel, and advice.

There must be no summer vacations for Satan to pull down the spiritual life faster than all combined can rebuild. Continue the meetings all summer, if only one child comes.

Have the grit, Junior superintendents, of the old Scotch woman who was left alone on the membership roll of her church. When the presbytery came to disband this useless church of one member (as they thought) they were met by her, and she said, " Ye canna disband this church, for I winna be disbanded," and not gaining her consent, they were forced to continue the faithful church of one member that became, through her prayers and work, a powerful influence for good in that community. Take no vacation unless Satan does or the Bible teaches it.

Teach the Juniors what God says about idlers in his vineyard and about Sabbath-breakers, and train them to practise the teachings, and we will need no future laws for Sabbath observance, and there will be no more closing of churches and Sabbath schools in the summer.

How simple and easy would it be to train the Juniors to observe the Sabbath if the Christian men and women would help by their example ! But the Sunday newspapers and elaborate dinner are found in the Christian's home. ·The ice-cream, milk, baker, and butcher wagons stop at the Christian's door on the Sabbath. The mail, telegraph, and telephones carry the messages of the Christian on the Sabbath. The cars and bicycles hold Christian riders on the Sabbath, and the riders are not always bound for religious meetings.

" Remember the Sabbath Day to keep it holy " seems to be a useless law, broken into numberless pieces, but, Christian Sabbath-breaker, each broken piece cries out to God in judgment against you, as did every drop of Abel's blood shed by Cain cry out for vengeance. God is speaking to this nation in financial disasters, tornadoes, and judgments of various kinds to return to the sacredness of the Sabbath Day and help preserve it for the little ones whom Jesus loves.

Christians, will you help the Juniors in this vital matter and help keep many little feet from straying ? The Juniors should be taught to memorize chapters as well as single verses of the Bible ; taught where to go for help from the Bible — in times of trouble and temptation, in joy or sorrow, sickness or death, study, work, or play.

Take up in simpler forms all the various kinds of church and committee work that the children can easily be trained to perform well.

Have the regular officers and business meetings. Train them to systematic giving, as well as to every other work. Train them to loyalty to their own church services. Don't have them mix their interdenominational fellowship with interchurch fellowship so that they become well acquainted with every other church and pastor but the one to which they belong. Train them, so that loyalty to their own church stays by them and is a part of their life as long as they live.

Use the simpler form of the Junior pledge and teach the Juniors it means just what it says, and when once taken, is taken for life, and though often broken through forgetfulness or ignorance, it should never be wilfully or deliberately broken.

Oh that we would guard more carefully our lives, and live up to the solemn obligations of even the simplest Christian Endeavor pledge! How much better, nobler, and more effective Christians we would become!

The lack of a Junior Christian Endeavor Society in any church or mission field shows a careless or sleepy condition of affairs, or something wanting, on the part of those who are supposed to have the spiritual interests of that field at heart.

How can we hope to see retained among all ages of our Church the child-like faith, character, and love Christ commended and insisted upon his follow-ers having, if the lasting foundation is not laid in early childhood, and we do not do our part toward helping keep the children ever near the great, loving heart of the Saviour, so they may never have the opportunity or inclination to become aught else than humble followers of Jesus Christ?

Let us pray God to teach us to realize the awful issues of eternal life or everlasting death that lie dormant in every little soul born into this world, as thoroughly as Satan knows it.

The next speaker was Dr. Williams. His subject was " Saved to Serve."

Address of Rev. Hugh Spencer Williams, Memphis, Tenn.

The general theme which commands the thoughtful attention of this great Convention to-day is " Saved to Serve."

Christ stamped "service" with his own image and superscription when he declared that the Son of man came " not to be ministered unto, but to minister," and laid down as a principle in the economics of his kingdom that we are saved in order that we may serve. Service is thus made the most Christlike and divine aspect of our mission as his redeemed. Our purest joys, as well as our highest honors, are experienced and enjoyed as the result of our becoming the "servant" of all. The incentives to such a life of service are truly glorious.

First, service is self-ennobling. It always brings out the divinest and best in our nature and character. God has made it impossible for us to become true benefactors by any real service rendered in any capacity without also becoming beneficiaries. We truly receive more than we give always. The true giver, the real helper of others, the humble and self-forgetful servant, constantly experi-ences the truth of the Master's maxim, "It is more blessed to give than to receive." This is so; because he becomes rich faster in real assets of ennobled Christian manhood and character by giving, helping, and serving than it is pos-sible by any process of direct bestowments upon him.

Second, the great moral motor which moves us as a mighty incentive to this blessed service is, as expressed by the apostle, " The love of Christ con-straineth us."

1. The conception of this infinite love of Christ, which carried him from the throne to the cross and emptied his blessed heart of its divine blood in order to redeem and save me, draws me as a captive and willing slave to his feet, crying, "Lord, what wilt thou have me to do?" The sense of loving gratitude for saving me from the jaws of eternal death overwhelms me, and I bind myself with the cords of my most sacred vows to his holy altar, as a living sacrifice, holy and acceptable in his sight, wanting to be used as he may choose ; not as my own, but his, " bought with a price, even the precious blood of Christ."

2. The conception of the scope of this love, that " he died for all." The love of Christ outlasts the ages and reaches the remotest edges of the human race. Hence, the redeemed — those who are saved — enter into the Christ spirit at once, because they thus judge that if one died for all then were all dead. Then that the purpose of his death was that they that live should live not henceforth unto themselves, but unto him which died for them and rose again. This was the mighty secret spring that moved Paul to Macedonia as a missionary of the cross; made him enter Ephesus, Corinth, Athens, and Rome, and made his missionary journeys co-extensive with the then known world. Christ had died for a world dead in trespasses and sin, and they that live must

not live for self, but obey the divine mandate of the Master," Go ye into all the world and preach the gospel to every creature." This same spirit made John Knox cry aloud, " Give me Scotland or I die," and Wesley to exclaim, " The world is my parish," and moved Dr. Carey to leave all for India. In short, this almighty incentive, " the love of Christ," is the *esprit de corps* that is massing and moving the Church of God in a solid phalanx upon the heathen world, to take and capture it for Christ; and this is what moved Dr. Clark fifteen years ago to ask the question how to interest and use the young men and maidens of Christendom for Christ and the Church.

The third great incentive to serve is the infinite value and greatness of the soul and the eternal interests involved in its salvation. He who understood man as no other being in the universe could understand him asked, " What shall it profit a man, if he shall gain the whole world, and lose his own soul? Or what shall a man give in exchange for his soul? "

The greatness, the majesty and infinite value of the human soul, when in any measure properly conceived of by the saved, as an object to be rescued from peril, sweeps like a tempest over the mighty deep of the soul until every power is aroused and the passion for lost souls becomes intense and they cry out, " Oh that my head were waters, and mine eyes a fountain of tears, that I might weep day and night for the slain of the daughter of my people," and with Paul say, " I could wish that myself were accursed from Christ for my brethren, my kinsmen according to the flesh," and like Christ the Master, who wept over Jerusalem, saying, " How oft," etc., " How can we have any conception of this mysterious being, such as will thus stir our souls with a passion for his salvation? " Consider his majestic intellect in the light of his masterly achievements. Man's mind has acquired a knowledge of the structure of the earth on which he lives, familiarity with almost every square mile of its surface, its products, and climates; he has fathomed the depth of the sea, of atmosphere surrounding it. Then he has time to spare to scan the heavens, count, measure, and weigh the stars that are in sight. Then he invents the telescope that he may sweep the more distant heavens in search of systems which lie beyond the reach of the naked eyes. He still has time and powers unexhausted, and begins to soliloquize thus : Who made all these? Who is he? Where is he? Whence came he? And it is truly marvelous what deductions his majestic mind is capable of concerning the infinite first cause; and he reasons from cause to effect in his great laboratory of facts as he finds them. But the greatest and most wonderful feature of his mental greatness is his power to think upon his mysterious thinking self. He asks, What am I? Whence came I, and whither am I going? Not at all strange that the Psalmist should have declared, " I am fearfully and wonderfully made." This marvelous mind is, however, but one feature or department of this living, thinking, sentient, and active being. In the realm of sensibilities we find the moral powers, consciousness, conscience, love, hate, hope, fear, and all other sentient aspects of our complex being. These are the faculties through the medium of which we come in touch with the infinite. Herein is spiritual hunger and thirst experienced. Intellect finds out that he is but the heart alone, by reaching out the finger of faith can touch the hem of his garment, and the soul is thrilled with the consciousness of his presence and wraps himself in his mantle, like Elijah on Mount Horeb. It is the function of conscience to hear the still small voice of God and recognize it, and of faith to see him, and that of love to lean on his bosom. All this and infinitely more is to be found in the *sanctum sanctorum* of these emotions or sensibilities of the soul.

From here we pass to the power which makes man responsible for his acts and his destiny. This mysterious power we call will. This can accept or reject any proposition the eternal Jehovah may make to man. " Choose ye this day whom ye shall serve." This in brief is the soul akin to God in its nature, the offspring of the eternal, destined to live with God and enjoy him forever, or to be banished from his presence into outer darkness, lost forever. Is the possibility of saving such a pearl not an incentive to even superhuman efforts? The thought of such a magnificent being as this to be in jeopardy, on board a sinking ship in a refuge of lies destined to be swept away, leaving him exposed to the fury of outraged justice, must sweep across the heart-strings of the saved and call them to serve in rescuing this great and precious pearl from peril.

This conception of the majesty and greatness of the soul must excite every one of God's redeemed to shout, "Throw out the life-line, some one is sinking to-day." Nothing short of some adequate view of the value of immortal souls and the pending peril can arouse the Church to earnest service; but when this great truth dawns upon the minds and hearts of pastors and people they will never fail to be on fire with a passion for saving and serving men.

The fourth incentive that we shall name is the certainty of the outcome of the service. (*a*). "The whole earth shall be filled with the knowledge of the Lord, as the waters cover the sea." "They all shall know him, from the least to the greatest of them." So that there is absolute certainty that our labors shall not be in vain. Success is the eternal decree of Jehovah. (*b*). Not only are we sure of success in our labors to enlighten the nations of heathendom by the spreading of the Gospel of Christ among them all, but the reign of righteousness is to be brought in Christ's coming to reign on earth a thousand years, and then is to be a new earth wherein righteousness shall reign, truth shall triumph, virtue shall be crowned as victorious forever and forever. "Holiness unto the Lord" shall be inscribed upon the horse's bridles; every blade of grass shall become an Æolian harp, as it waves in the breezes of the morning, making music to the coming of the King. The branches of the trees shall clap their hands together in the hallelujah chorus of the universe. Mountain-top shall echo to mountain-top, "Heaven and earth are full of his glory," and Gabriel shall take up the shout that the kingdoms of this world have become the kingdoms of the Lord and his Christ. It is only a matter of time. Heaven and earth shall blend their alleluia in one eternal chorus of praises to their conquering King. This unalterable assurance of ultimate success fires the souls of his servants and becomes an all-powerful incentive to diligence and faithfulness until the Master comes.

Looking at the world this late in the evening of the nineteenth century, with more than two-thirds of its inhabitants who have never heard of Christ, and at Christendom, with its millions of sceptics and scoffers, and many more millions of dead formalists and hypocrites, it would appear as if the number of the finally saved would indeed be small. But upon a closer examination of facts, even within our narrow limitations, we find the reverse of this to be the unquestionable truth touching this interesting and important matter. We arrive at this conclusion: (1). From Scriptural intimations, that there are multitudes who are his "sheep," though not of this or that denominational fold. Like Joseph of Arimathea, and Nicodemus, they are disciples in secret. They are his, nevertheless, and will be revealed as such at his coming, when he shall make up his jewels. (2). From the hope which the Word of God warrants that many shall come from the East and from the West, from the North and from the South, who shall sit with him in his kingdom, who never heard the sweet name of Jesus while here on earth. Listen to the declarations of God's infallible Word. "For when the Gentiles, which have not the (written or revealed) law, do by nature the things contained in the law, these, having not the law, are a law unto themselves: which show the work of the law written in their hearts, their conscience also bearing witness, and their thoughts the meanwhile accusing or else excusing one another." (Rom. ii. 14, 15.) We are thus led to hope and believe that millions of heathen through the long line of past ages have been saved, through the atonement of Jesus Christ, although ignorant of him. We cannot believe that these countless generations of heathen have been born to be damned. "God so loved the world." "Christ tasted death for every man." "The true light lighteth every man that cometh into the world." So we dare believe and hope that the great God has been gathering golden sheaves from the vast field of heathendom to fill the heavenly garner. (3). We are confirmed in this intelligent conviction that the throng of the finally-saved will overwhelmingly outnumber the lost by the fact that more than one-third of the inhabitants born into this world die before reaching the age of five years, and one-half die under twelve years of age. The blessed Christ has settled the question of their salvation when he said, "Suffer the little children to come unto me, and forbid them not, for of such is the kingdom of God." Thus we find that possibly one-half the human race is thus saved before reaching the line of personal responsibility. This we know according to this blessed declaration: that every child dying before reaching the line of moral accountability to God goes straight to heaven, whether they be infants born in darkest Africa or India, China or the Islands of the Sea,— Christ claims them as his own. Never went an infant to hell from any spot on the face of the earth. No! no! no! Every one of such is borne from its mother's arms on cherubic wings into the bosom of the Shepherd, who "bears the lambs in his bosom." Alleluia, the mediatorial administration of our King is a triumphant success! The hosts of his redeemed outnumber the stars and discount the sands on the seashore. Brother, such a prospective salvation is worthy our noblest service. Such a glorious hope must fire with holy ambition. For such prospective triumph it is glorious to live or die.

Unrolling the roll of honor came next. Mr. W. L. Amerman, president of the New York City Christian Endeavor Union, was in charge.

Remarks of Mr. W. L. Amerman, New York City.

Not every speaker has the manuscript for his remarks in this convenient form. I have five hundred and sixty feet of it here, and am prepared to go on all day. But, prudently, the committee have limited me to five minutes, so I must unroll it at the rate of something over one hundred feet per minute. And rather than attempt that, I will just, in a word, call your attention to the significance, not of what is on this roll, but of what is not on it.

We have here gifts recorded from some 8,200 societies. That does not mean that the other 38,000 gave nothing to the home and foreign missionary boards of their own denominations, but it simply means that they did not ask to be enrolled.

We know very well that they gave large sums, doubtless a larger sum than the $152,000 which is inscribed upon this roll.

And we should note also that this $152,000 does not represent the total of the gifts of the members of these societies to Christian work, nor, indeed, to home and to foreign missions.

Whoever heard, for instance, of a Sunday-school teacher who only gave to God's work what she gave in the collection in the Sunday school? And yet the great mass of our Endeavorers are Sunday-school teachers. We know very well that their gifts in other ways outnumber their gifts through Christian Endeavor sources ten to one; but we are speaking of what they have given as societies of Christian Endeavor — not the total of their gifts as societies of Christian Endeavor to God's work, but the total of their gifts to the home and foreign missionary boards of their own denominations.

We know very well that their gifts to their local churches, their own churches, have been far larger than their gifts to home and to foreign missions, in many and many a case. We know that they have given liberally to other objects. We need to realize that this roll of honor is restricted to the gifts of these societies, as societies, to the home and to the foreign missionary boards of their own denominations.

Those who are familiar with the missionary statistics of the Church, and who know of the thousands of churches in all the prominent denominations that give not one dollar, never give one dollar, to home or foreign missions through the denominational channels, will realize what this record means.

There are societies here who have found it a struggle to get upon this roll of honor; there are societies here that have never tried to be enrolled, and have never reported their gifts; there are societies here, I believe, and many who are not here, who are struggling to pay their expenses, to discharge their duty towards their own church, and who have not been able to give the amount that would entitle them to a place upon this roll of honor. And in spite of all these things, in spite of the limited number of societies which this represents, and the immense amount of money which has been given by those societies in other ways, this roll of honor, thank God, is growing larger every year!

Then followed the address of Dr. Whitman.

Address of President B. L. Whitman, D.D., Washington, D. C.

The two Testaments have a common key-word, "Emmanuel." Its interpretation is "God with us." Its significance is the will of God to dwell in the midst of men, that men may be transformed by the indwelling. The theme appeals to us in three phases :—

I. *A method of revelation.* Man has never been left in ignorance of God. Successive disclosures have been made of the divine character and will. As men were able to receive it, the divine purpose has been spelled out. Slowly but steadily progress has been made in the conception of truth. Instruments have been many, but their use has been one. Many forms have been followed, but the central idea has remained the same. Moses looked to Jehovah as Redeemer. The latest saint finds his faith satisfied by the same thought; only in the fulness and clearness of the thought has there been change. The time came when the message could be delivered in completer form. "God, who at sundry times and in divers manners spake in time past by the prophets, hath in these last days spoken unto us by his Son, whom he hath appointed heir of all things, by whom also he made the worlds; who being the express image of his person, and upholding all things by the word of his power, when he had himself purged our sins, sat down on the right hand of the Majesty on high; being so much better than the angels as he hath obtained a more excellent name than they." (Heb. i. 1-4.) In this manifestation the issue of all revelation was made clear. Then "Emmanuel" was written in the beginning of the Gospel in token that the fellowship which God had offered, and to which he called men, was at last accomplished. Christ was but the culmination of revelation. In him God made of himself a personal offering so that men knew that he had accepted the lot of their life to the end that he might win them to his life, and so abide with them forever. This is the theme of Sacred Writ from Genesis to the Gospels.

II. *A principle of life.* We have to consider :—

1. The meeting-point of the divine and the human life. The simplest outline of psychology will make this clear. Man is partly physical and partly spiritual. The spiritual part is essentially the man. In the spiritual part we find a fourfold function,— intellect, sensibility, desire, and volition. In this fourfold function we have not four different things at work, but one thing working in four different ways. Intellect is the soul knowing; sensibility is the soul feeling; desire is the soul craving; volition is the soul willing. The four functions are closely related. Knowledge awakens response in feeling of satisfaction or dissatisfaction. Feeling passes into desire or aversion. On the basis of desire or aversion will is determined for attainment or avoidance. The step in the process of importance to us just now is that by which we pass from desire to will. Will never acts without desire in the form of motive. Motive is desire accepted as controlling. Unmotived volition is a contradiction of terms. Of course, the choice of motive is not without reason. It is no mere clamor of impulses with ear given to the noisiest. It may be that the impulse weakest at the outset is found to have sanctions which authorize it to take precedence of all others. Once accepted as controlling, the desire or impulse becomes the motive, and will acts according to it.

2. A new impulse imparted by the touch of God. One has only to regard man in his usual condition to see what is needed. His life is dominated by wrong motives. The inheritance into which man is born is sinful, at least in tendency. Theology easily mistakes an inheritance of consequence for an inheritance of penalty. But the simple awful fact that faces every life is that, whether as consequence or as penalty, its impulses are largely evil. It is beau-

tiful to talk about developing the soul into the kingdom, but first we have to reckon with the stubborn fact that until the soul comes under the domination of a new impulse it has no place in the kingdom.

3.   The new impulse become regnant, the source of new life.   We understand now the importance of the law by which an impulse may become a principle.   Choice may be so often repeated that a habit is formed.   On the basis of habit what we call second nature grows up.   Second nature is simply the self that is developed by choice, that has become habitual.   Whether it is good or evil depends upon the character of the choice.   Under the touch of God a right impulse is imparted which is accepted as dominant, and which presently shapes the life.   Not without struggle.   Impulse is not exempt from struggle because regnant.   Only at cost of continual struggle does it maintain mastery.   Appetites and appetencies of an ungodly sort assail it constantly.   One has only to read Romans to find the outline of the struggle in his own life.   Fleshly impulses impel downward.   Spiritual impulses impel upward.   God or the devil — which shall the soul have?   The man who makes his choice of God finds that the earthward impulses have lost dominion over him.   With any kind of faithfulness the upward impulse grows in power.   More and more of life is brought under it.   Presently every thought and feeling is made subject to the divine will and the divine nature becomes second nature.   Henceforth the way of life lies along the heights.

What has been said may be taken as in brief the natural history of regeneration.   It emphasizes a point we are forever missing,— regeneration, while supernatural in its effect, is natural in its method.   There are two methods of self-examination about equally defective.   One takes the form of excessive analysis.   It treats the soul as one would treat a botanical specimen — and with the same results.   It takes it to pieces, labels all its parts, and leaves it a thing of shreds and filaments, with no life and with no use.   The other takes the form of incantation.   It treats the soul in bulk, regards it as a meeting-place of mysteries, and waits to see what will come of it.   The divine way with the soul is very different from these.   It compels recognition of the truth, gives peace in believing, awakens desire after better things, and impels the will to worthy choice.   There is no man but needs it.   In the most spiritual Augustine's cry finds echo: " O God, thou hast made us for thyself, and our souls are restless until they find rest in thee."   There is no man but may be moved by it.   Take the veriest savage, with just soul enough to keep him from going on all fours. He hears the truth.   Impulse is awakened.   His course is set toward heaven. Somehow, an instinct for better things seems to be everywhere waiting for the voice of God.   Christianity is the embodiment of that voice.   It is a moral dynamic quickening the entire life.   Its literature is stamped with the same purpose.   The Bible is not a dictionary, or grammar, or book of etiquette.   Its mission is an impulse, illuminating the intellect, transforming the affection, cultivating the taste.   The manifold work of Christ is but the perfected form of that impulse.   As prophet he opens and interprets the world of truth.   As priest he satisfies the conscience.   As king he takes possession of the will.

III.   *A pledge of attainment.*   The motto of the redeemed life is, " Saved to serve."   A man has a very meagre notion of salvation — if, indeed, he is saved at all — if he regards his life as an end in itself.   Far better is the conception that the saved life is part of the great order in which righteousness is working itself out in the universe.   The man who has found his life renewed stands for the first time in right relation to the order of things.   We need to keep in mind : —

1.   The universe as law.   We have not dropped into a world of chance. Events do not happen.   Two and two do not make four to-day and something else to-morrow.   An axiom is an axiom as long as the order lasts of which it is a part.   Counteracting of effect is not subversion of law.   A table may be interposed or a counter-attraction applied, but none the less the stone tends toward the earth in obedience to the law of gravitation.   As fast and as far as it is left undisturbed the stone will follow the force that tugs it centreward.   It is not heavy one day and light the next.   The universe is order.   It is what it is be-

cause God is what he is. Its guarantees of stability are furnished by the unchangeableness of his nature. Because we believe in him we accept truth with perfect confidence in the result. Two lines started from given points in given directions will move on and on and never meet. They may encircle the universe and return upon themselves, but they will be as far apart as when they started. You can not follow the parallels around the universe; but you know they will never meet, for the power that fixed the relation of those lines is the power that wrote the law of your thought, and the necessity of your law of thought is the guarantee that the facts are as the law declares them. Two other lines will meet a million miles away in space. You have never been there to see it, but you do not doubt it, for God fixed the relation of the lines and the law by which your mind accepts the result.

2. Obedience as adjustment to fundamental relations. The immediate form of life under the domination of the new impulse is obedience to the will of God. Its ultimate form is free development under a central and symmetrical impulse. Accretion may be from without. Development is from within. The tree does not need a chart of its upward progress, but a vital germ. The soul does not need a book of rules, but a principle of life. You do not find the Bible discussing styles of dress and codes of manners. Its message is, Do the will of God. There is much involved in that, no doubt. " Do thy duty and thou shalt know what it is that is within thee," says Goethe, chosing the words of Jesus. " If any man willeth to do his will he shall know of the doctrine." The whole sum of life is simple : Do the will of God. Life is a circle. We know only a small segment, but it is enough to the show curve. Knowing the formula for the segment, we know the formula for the circle: Do the will of God. This helps us understand how Jesus could speak so confidently concerning man. "Jesus saw not the primeval savage living in caves, fighting with stick or stone. He saw not the half-civilized man of early ages, struggling in constant and fierce rivalry with others in the sharp competition of existence. He saw not merely the hero of Grecian mold or of Roman fortitude. He saw not merely the modern philanthropist perking about a little, beginning to live for others, building hospitals and asylums, and talking about altruism or universal benevolence. He saw the ultimate man, the complete man, the true Son of man who came down from heaven." (Rev. E. B. Mason.) He saw man in right relation to God.

One of the banks of London had a very unique and ingenious arrangement to watch its watchman. Each square in the marble floor of the bank rested upon a steel point, and that steel point connected with an electric wire, and each square in the bank was numbered, and each wire numbered. Those wires ran away through the building to the private office of the bank officials.

The watchman was told to keep awake, and to keep moving. He said the place was safe. So he took a newspaper or a novel, and sat down on a chair by the light. There he would sit and read, when he should have been looking about. One day they sent word to him that his services were unsatisfactory. He went in great indignation to see why he was discharged. They told him that he had been reading or asleep in his chair. He said that it was not so. He knew there was no person who could see him, and there was no person allowed in the building; he knew he had the keys, and the time-lock was on that safe; so he felt sure no one could have seen him. In indignation he threatened the president of the bank for accusing him of telling a lie when he denied that he had sat down at all in that chair. Then they called him into the office. They took out a piece of paper which represented all the squares on the floor, and then, taking the time-lock checks, put them beside it. " Now, my man, at three minutes of eight you stepped on that square, and then on that one, and then on that ; then you immediately turned around, and went back and stepped on this one, and you did not step from this one for two hours. Here it is. Every time you stepped on a square, it telegraphed that you were on it."

The world is God's. Obedience to God is adjustment to the laws by which the world moves. This is the secret of success in lives that, consciously or unconsciously, have got into line with God. The blossoming of power we call genius is but perfect obedience to law. Success is more than the product of work. To succeed, work must be according to law. The seeker after gold may wear himself out digging on the seashore. To get gold one must dig where gold is. One may blunder on the start, and that is well. One may study gold and the geologic strata in which gold occurs and so come upon it intelligently, and that is better. In either case, when gold is found it is found because the seeker worked in accordance with the law of gold. In absence of such accord there may be much motion, but there will be no progress. When such accord is assured every stroke counts. When a man gets into line with God's law he stands for God. The great workers have always wrought in this representative capacity. Results which stagger belief are simply the product of harmony with the power which rules the universe and which speaks through law.

3. Life as realization of divine order and application of divine power. How great the marvel is after all the dynamic conception of the universe proves to be the truth, that atoms are centres of activity, that the formula of the molecule is a formula of motion. Oh the joy of the thought that the living, personal God is working through all! Atom calls to atom, and planet to planet, across immensity; and atom answers atom, and planet, planet, because they are akin by right of birth. Man is no stranger in the world in which he walks. He has only to open his eyes to find God. Let him travel where he will, though it be to the remotest star, he will still be at home with God. The atom is God's handiwork, and so is man. But man's relation to God is unique. God was not lonesome or lacking before man was created. But the glory of the creation is the life which God begat in his own image that henceforth there might be in the universe some to work in God's way. Through them in special sense God works his will. We have only begun to realize the possibilities of our life. But better things are coming. The dawning of the day of triumph already reddens the sky. With better sense of ourselves as instruments of the divine purpose we shall find the day hastened. The vessel for God's filling; the instrument for God's using; the messenger for God's sending; the redeemed for God's witness;—this is our glory and joy.

If we have not thought amiss while doing our duty at every turn, we shall be braced for greater faithfulness in two lines:—

First, we shall be willing to let God provide for part of his work through others. A noble thing is told of Mr. Charles H. Haseltine, whose building stood next the building of the Baptist Publication Society and was burned with it. Mr. Haseltine was teaching his class in Sunday school when some one rushed up to him with the news that his building was in flames. Mr. Haseltine turned again to the lesson. "But what are you going to do?" excitedly asked his informant. "I am going to teach this lesson," was the quiet reply. "I am not a fireman and can do nothing to help put the fire out."

Second, we shall be content to accept God's plans for us as best.

> "Sometime, when all life's lessons have been learned,
>   And suns and stars forevermore have set,
> The things which our weak judgment here have spurned,
>   The things o'er which we grieved with lashes wet,
> Will flash before us out of life's dark night,
>   As stars shine most in deeper tints of blue,
> And we shall see how all God's plans were right,
>   And how what seemed reproof was love most true.
>
> "And you shall shortly know that lengthened breath
>   Is not the sweetest gift God sends his friend,
> And that sometimes the sable pall of death
>   Conceals the fairest boon his love can send.
> If we could push ajar the gates of life,
>   And stand within and all God's workings see,
> We could interpret all this doubt and strife,
>   And for each mystery could find a key.
>
> "But not to-day. Then be content, poor heart;
>   God's plans, like lilies pure and white, unfold.
> We must not tear the close-shut leaves apart;
>   Time will reveal the calyxes of gold.
> And if thro' patient toil we reach the land
>   Where tired feet with sandals loose may rest,
> When we shall clearly know and understand,
>   I think that we will say, 'God knew the best.'"

The last speaker was Dr. Chapman.

Address of Rev. J. Wilbur Chapman, D.D., Philadelphia, Pa.

This morning I want to speak very briefly to all of you on the subject of one baptism with the Holy Ghost for all believers. Many in-fillings with the same Holy Ghost are possible, and sometimes necessary. The last point, — special anointings of the third person of the Trinity are to be sought for for every special service upon which we enter.

It will be necessary for you to say with me a few verses of Scripture — not in every case a whole verse, sometimes just a clause; but will you allow me to say the verse first, and then ask you to repeat it with me?

This is the first: Acts i. 5: " John truly baptized with water, but ye shall be baptized with the Holy Ghost, and with fire, not many days hence." Say it with me: "John truly baptized with water, but ye shall be baptized with the Holy Ghost, and with fire, not many days hence." Second clause: Acts ii. 4: "And they were all filled with the Holy Ghost." Say it: "And they were all filled with the Holy Ghost." The last verse: Luke iv. 18: " The spirit of the Lord is upon me, because he hath anointed me to preach the gospel to the poor." Say it: " The spirit of the Lord is upon me, because he hath anointed me to preach the gospel to the poor."

I dare to assert this morning, with the Word of God for my authority, that every single Christian Endeavorer in this tent, in all these tents, in the city of Washington, in the United States, in America, in the world, may have, if he will, the baptism with the Holy Ghost. It is only necessary that we should be willing to pay the price, for God is no respecter of persons. Some of you here to-day stand for culture. That is no barrier. As an illustration, let me present the woman who is to speak to us in this conference, Mrs. E. M. Whitmore. I believe that she is one of the most remarkable women of this day,— a woman of high social position, and yet a woman so filled with the Holy Ghost that to stand in her presence, even if she opens not her lips to speak, is to feel the mighty presence of God. Some of you do not stand for culture, and possibly you might lay claim to ignorance. Do any of you know who it was that Dr. John Hall said he counted the most influential man in Christian work in the great city of New York, in all his acquaintance with it? Do you know his name? He did not preach on Fifth Avenue. He did not stand as the leader of a congregation of millionaires in the city. Dr. John Hall said that the man that seemed to him to be the mightiest illustration of the power of God in all the city was the poor old river thief in days gone by, Jerry McAuley. And I say that if to-day you are pleading ignorance, ignorance is no barrier. The promise is for you. Some people say the baptism with the Holy Ghost is every Christian's privilege. It is not Scriptural to state it. The baptism with the Holy Ghost is every single Christian's birthright. It is his birthright, and it is yours for the claiming. Some of you may say to-day, " Well, I don't stand for ignorance. I stand for quite the opposite." Then I hold before you that man who has been an inspiration to me in evangelistic work, that man the very sound of whose name, when I was a student, was an inspiration and an uplifting power,— Charles G. Finney. He was filled — nay, he had been baptized — with the Holy Ghost; and so I state here to-day that this blessing is for you; and I thank God this blessing is for me.

I think I ought to give you another verse of Scripture. Listen to it, for if we can not find Scripture to fortify us in this position, our opinions will profit us nothing. The second chapter of the Acts of the Apostles, and the 32d verse: " Repent and be baptized, every one of you, for the remission of sins, and ye shall receive the gift of the Holy Ghost." But, friends, while it is not inconsistent with the plan of God to give to every one of his children, the moment they enter into saving relations with him, the full baptism with the Spirit, how many people do you know that entered into the full blessing at the moment of conversion? How many? Well, I know a good many of the Christian workers; I know almost all of the evangelists; I know many of the men and women whom God has blessed. I do not know one single soul, man or

woman, that entered into the full reception of the Holy Ghost at the time of
conversion. Every single Christian has the Holy Ghost for life, and, therefore,
if we want the enlarging blessing, we need not pray for his coming. He is
here. He abides in me. It is his work to abide in me. If I want to be filled
with the Spirit,—nay, if I would be baptized with the Spirit,—I need only to take
away the hindrance, take away the hindrance. This morning I talk to you
along that line. Now, then, a great many people talk about getting hold of the
Holy Ghost, and getting more of the Holy Ghost. Why, bless your souls,
friends, you have had more of the Holy Ghost since your conversion than you have
used. That is not the need; that is not the need. I remember going through
one of the World's Fair Buildings and seeing, away at the end of the building,
what I thought was a man. He had his hand on the crank of a certain kind of
a pump, and he was turning it round and round. I stayed in the building an
hour, and the man never stopped work for an instant. I said to myself, "He
is not constructed on the same plan that I am or he would have grown weary."
But when I came nearer to the spot where he stood, I found that it was not a
man. It was just the figure of a man, the form of a man, and I found that he
was n't turning the crank at all, but that the crank was turning him. Well, friends,
that is the secret. I do not want the Holy Ghost that I may mark out a channel in which he may run for me and my glory; but, before God to-day, I crave
for myself and for every Christian Endeavorer that the Holy Ghost might come
upon me and upon you and send us whithersoever God will. That is the
secret of power.

Now, I have an idea. Possibly some of these ministers who know far more
about the truth than I would not agree with me. Nevertheless, I think it is a
good illustration. I think that when Jesus said, "John truly baptized with
water, but ye shall be baptized with the Holy Ghost not many days hence," he
was using the figure of baptism as an illustration that the baptism of water
stood as an illustration for what the baptism with the Holy Ghost might be.
Now, then, if that is true, I have three points to make quickly : —

1. Baptism is always a definite experience. How many of you know just
when you were converted? How many of you? Well, lift up your hands if
you know the day and the hour. Up with your hands. (Part of the audience
raised their hands). Now, listen to this. How many of you do not know the
day you were converted, and yet to-day you say, "I know I have passed from
death to life"? Up goes my hand first. (Others of the audience raise their
hands.) Ah, friends, I believe a man may be a Christian and not know just
the time he crossed the line into the kingdom. But I do believe that no man
in all this world can be a Christian, filled with all the power of God, without he
has a definite experience touching the Holy Ghost — a definite experience
touching the Holy Ghost.

If you do not know the day of your surrender to him, make it to-day. If
you can not put your finger upon the hour, make it this hour. If you can not put
it upon the minute, let this be the minute. Baptism with the Holy Ghost is
definite.

2. Baptism signifies complete surrender — complete surrender. Well, now,
take the figure immersion, though I could take the other just as well. When a
man presents himself for baptism, what does he do? Well, he does n't say to
the administrator, "I want to be baptized forward." or "sideways," or "backwards;" what does he do? He simply puts himself without question into the
hands of the administrator. Well, my friends, I believe that, whatever your
intellectual equipment may be, no man in all the world can receive the
baptism with the Holy Spirit without he surrenders absolutely to God every
single thing; give up every single thing, put upon the altar, and then, hands off
forever — forever!

3. Baptism as a formal rite is the death of self — the death of self. No man
can ever claim this blessing so long as he allows the flesh to come up. The
Rev. F. B. Myer says, "If you want a good definition of flesh, drop the letter
'h' and spell it backwards,— s-e-l-f." I heard of a man, one of our own ministers, who delivered an address over in London the other day lasting twenty

minutes, and in the twenty minutes he used the personal pronoun one hundred and twenty times. Well, friends, the Spirit of God does not lead us to do that. The death of self! Have you a definite experience? Will you take it to-day by faith? God help you to do it!

Now, then, I think the manifestation depends upon the individual. Some persons think if they were baptized with the Holy Ghost they would be preachers, and they would stand up in the presenc of this congregatiou, and they would sway men's hearts and minds, and sweep them by the thousand into the kingdom. "Ah," you say, "I know that; that is the reason I want it." Why, friends, there is flesh in that—flesh in that. Hear me when I say that Simon Peter was filled with the Holy Ghost and swung 3,000 people into the kingdom, I know. But hear me again. Stephen was filled with the same Spirit, and was stoned to death. I think the time has come when the influence of Jesus Christ might be further advanced if men should take such a stand for the truth that they would be actually stoned to death upon the streets.

The next thing,—if we are baptized with the Holy Ghost, what shall we be? Witnesses. Where do we begin to witness? Well, a great many people want to begin at the wrong end, at the uttermost parts of the earth. "Well if I could just go out there to China!" God never sends a man to a higher position until he has filled to overflowing the lower position —never! What does the Scripture say? "Ye shall be witnesses unto me in Jerusalem first, then Judea, then Samaria, then unto the uttermost parts of the earth."

If you are filled with the Holy Ghost at the Fifteenth Annual Convention of Christian Endeavor, the first thing you will do will be to go back home and let your wife know that you have gotten something that you have never had before, and you won't have to tell her that you have it. A man is responsible for the atmosphere that is around him. I have a great many persons that I call friends who make me mad when I come within ten feet of them — well, when I come within a hundred feet. I have other friends if I come within a thousand feet of whom my heart begins to burn, and I say, "This is a foretaste of heaven."

Well, I can not say anything about the filling of the Holy Ghost — I make a distinction between the baptism and the filling — except this: if I have had the definite experience,— and I thank God I have, October 16, 1892,— it is written on the book at half-past three in the afternoon. Not perfection; not sinlessness; not boasting myself that I am better than other men, for God knows and I know that that would be untrue; but if I have had the definite experience, then if I am going to keep in touch with the Spirit of God, I must every single day be filled.

I walked along the streets of Northfield, Mr. Moody's home, with the Rev. F. B. Myer, on one of the most beautiful mornings that I think God could make; and I said to him, "Mr. Myer, I have had a definite experience. But something is wrong with me. What is it?" And the great teacher, whom I delight to honor, took my hand in his, and said, "Your difficulty is the same as mine." He says, "Stop a minute. You never breathe out physically without first of all breathing in." Well, now, let's just stop a second and see if that is n't true; you begin to breathe now. See how you do it? Breathe in first and out second. And the Rev. F. B. Myer said, and I should have gone around the world to have him say it to me, "I need, my brother, and so do you, to keep all the time breathing in, and breathing in spiritually." That is keeping filled with the Holy Ghost.

The last point,— special anointings for special service. I think a minister ought never to preach his sermon without waiting before God for an anointing of the Holy Ghost. And I believe, brethren in the ministry, that it be a good thing sometimes if our people would go into our churches and find the pulpits empty while you and I wait for the anointing of the Holy Ghost. I think that no man should ever sing a hymn without asking for the anointing of the Spirit. I believe that no Sunday-school teacher should meet her class without asking for the anointing of the Holy Spirit.

Harry Morehouse, the great evangelist of years gone by, who came across to this country and preached in Mr. Moody's church seven nights, on John iii. 16, came back the second time to Chicago; and they had billed the whole city, that " Harry Morehouse, the great evangelist," was to speak in Farwell Hall. The hour came, and the historic room was filled. Harry Morehouse came out on the platform; to the right of him sat Mr. Moody; to the left of him, Mr. Jacobs; back of him, William Reynolds, and I don't know but Mr. Sankey. All about him were the leading Christian workers of that great western city. And Harry Morehouse stood up and announced his text, and then stopped. He read it a second time and stopped again. He read it the third time, and then deliberately closed his Bible, and Mr. Moody said he left the platform and went into the little anteroom. They waited fully five minutes, and he did not come, and then Mr. Jacobs went down. " Why," said he, " Morehouse, what does it mean? Here we have billed the whole city, and Farwell Hall is filled to suffocation. There will be great disappointment." " Ah," said the man that knew his God so well, and was so filled with the Spirit, "that is the trouble; that is the trouble. It has been all ' Harry Morehouse', and it has been nothing of the Lord. And I can not preach."

And Mr. Jacobs fell on his knees beside him, and Mr. Moody bound his arms about him. And Mr. Reynolds prayed, as the tears rolled down his cheeks; and they waited for twenty minutes, and the people sat in silence in the other room. And then Harry Morehouse, with his face shining like an angel's, with his heart burning with that fire that comes down only from on high, stood before the crowd of people and, filled with the Holy Ghost, he swayed them with the power that comes from above until it seemed as if a hundred people and more had pressed their way into the kingdom.

O brethren in the ministry, that is what we need; that is what we need! To-day I dare to stand and say, with this old Book in my hand, and resting upon it as my authority, that there is not a Christian Endeavorer here but what might go back to his home with his life transformed, if he were only to surrender to the Spirit of God.

Are you ready to do it, friends? I don't know but that I am going beyond my bounds; but I will take the liberty. Are you ready to do it? We have come to Kadesh-Barnea; Canaan is just beyond us. The fruit of the Spirit is ours for the choosing. Will you enter to-day and put it down, July the 10th, 1896, at 12 o'clock and 8 minutes, " I surrender to God"? Will you say it, friends? If you will, I would like to pray with you. Will you say it? Every Christian Endeavorer in the house that would just like to say to-day, " I want to enter into the land that flows with milk and honey," stand to your feet.

The audience rose, as requested, and was led in prayer by the speaker. Mr. Sankey sang and led the Convention in prayer, and then the audience was dismissed.

Wesley M. E. Church.

Junior Workers' Meeting.

One of the most interesting and profitable meetings was the meeting of the Junior workers, held in Wesley M. E. Church. Long before the hour for the exercises to begin the beautiful little edifice was filled, and the delegates sang one after another of the Christian Endeavor hymns, until the musical leader, Mr. Chas. S. Clark, of Washington, took charge of the singing. Secretary John Willis Baer presided, and after a short service of praise, introduced Rev. M. Ross Fishburn, of Washington, who conducted the devotional exercises.

Miss Grace E. Hyde, of Winchendon, spoke first of " A Model Junior Society."

Address of Miss Grace E. Hyde, Winchendon, Mass.

At a flower exhibition in London there was one plant far more beautiful than all the rest. Beside this plant stood its owner, a little girl in a patched calico dress. When the man in charge told her that her geranium had won the first prize, he asked her how it happened that among so many beautiful plants hers was the most luxuriant. The little girl told him how she had cared for it. She lived in a large tenement-house, but on the fifth floor, where the air was pure and the sun shone all day. Each morning she had put the plant in the east window, where it would catch the first rays of the sun ; in the afternoon she had changed it to the west window, turning it around so that the other side would receive the warmth until the sun went down. Under the influence of pure air and warm sunlight the plant grew in symmetry and beauty.

In a similar way the model Junior Society expands the lives of the children into beauty and usefulness. Flooded with the warm sunshine of God's love, growing into his likeness by contact on all sides with Christian influences, the children develop into the most beautiful blossoms in Christ's kingdom.

In the catalogue of the Harvard College Summer School is an announcement of two courses in physical training ; one is a course in theory, the other in practice. Each is valuable in itself ; one supplements the other ; but to one who is striving for the perfect development of his muscles, of what worth is the theory without the practice ? In our spiritual training the Sunday school gives the theory of Christian living ; the societies of Christian Endeavor, the practice. In the Sunday school children are taught to know Christ and to love him ; in the Junior Society they are taught to work for him. "Love is idle that knows no service." In a model Junior Society then, the boys and girls are trained *to serve*. A Junior Society makes service intensely practical. In one of our model societies in Massachusetts, the Juniors were interested in collecting orange-peel for a poor old lady who dried it and sold it for making extract. In another they brought eggs, which were carried to poor sick people or to the hospital.

At the entrance of a beautiful garden this sign is said to have been placed : "Joy and cheerfulness found in this garden by all who bring them." In a model Junior Society Christ is found by all who bring to its meetings a spirit of willingness to learn about him and to speak for him, a spirit of helpfulness and of unselfish kindness toward one another.

In a model society the superintendent (who should be a permanent officer) is wise, tactful, loving ; she understands children and guides them trustingly into God's kingdom. The superintendent and her assistants are present at every meeting. The Juniors are attentive, responsive. They play the piano, sing, lead their own meetings. They hold regular business meetings and give committee reports. They have frequent socials. They give systematically for missions. They each have some definite work to do. The boys and girls are taught to show Christ in their lives. A strong testimony in favor of our work is one given by the public-school teachers in a town where it was thought that the Junior Society would be disbanded on account of the sickness of the superintendent. These teachers said, "The Junior Society must not be given up. You have no idea how wonderfully it has improved the deportment in our schools. We can not spare it."

An old Scotch woman once thanked her pastor for the helpful sermon he had preached the previous Sunday. He asked her what particular thought had helped her,—if it was the text. No, she did not remember the text. Was it any one sentence? No, she could not recall any special sentence. "Well," said her pastor, "you said my sermon helped you ; yet you do not remember anything in it. I do not understand you." "It is true," replied the woman, "that I do not remember the text, or any one sentence ; but I see the effect in my life. I am a better Christian for having heard that sermon."

The boys and girls in our Junior Societies may not be able to tell why they love Christ and serve him, or to explain fully the meaning of their pledge ; but if they are so trained that they live Christ every day, then your society is a *model Junior Society*.

The next speaker was Miss Jennie T. Masson, of Indianapolis, Ind., whose topic was " A Model Junior Superintendent."

Address of Miss Jennie T. Masson, Indianapolis, Ind.

The work of the Junior superintendent is to be done on earth, hence the word "model" does not mean perfect or angelic. It means, the best to be had. Model Junior superintendents are not born, but made.

Any society can cultivate one, provided there be, to start with, a good-tempered Endeavorer in love with the boys and girls. No society lacks such a member. Indeed, once in a while in a society can be found a sweet-tempered, children-loving Endeavorer who can sing and play, give chalk talks, tell fascinating Bible stories; who has the power to control; who is as alert as the sunrise, as placid as the first lily that bloomed in the Garden of Eden, as definite as a railroad track, as spiritual as the thoughts of an angel, as full-grown as a California welcome. Such, however, is a shining exception. God evidently is not Christianizing the world by means of prodigies.

Still, the model Junior superintendent has all these qualities. She does not always, however, combine them in her own person. Happy is she if she can herself teach the ready lips to pour out the music of Junior songs. But just as happy may she be to inspire interest and attention and order while some singer from the Junior committee of the senior society performs the pleasant duty. She can talk up such a pleased anticipation of a blackboard exercise that even before the artist comes his chalk-talk will have begun to bear fruit. She can love the children so much that she will not be jealous if others share with her the adoration of the child-hearts. Oh, she can with God's help and the support of the senior workers become an acceptable Junior superintendent. That is the chief motive of this paper, — to inspire some one to try to be cultivated into a model Junior superintendent.

This is the report that came the other day from a State superintendent of Junior work, — twelve Junior Societies disbanded because of no one to superintend; and all, very probably, because those who might have done the work were afraid. Afraid of yourself; afraid of making a mistake! Probably you will make a mistake, but it could not possibly be so great as the mistake of disbanding.

We carry for our motto, " The world for Christ," and yet every disbanded Junior Society, every failure to organize, delays the consummation of that motto. Shall that delay occur because we will not learn the above given meaning of a model Junior superintendent, — take the best you have and do the best you can?

Right here is about as good a place as any to remark that the feminine pronoun seems to be the one generally used to stand for a model Junior superintendent. It is not necessarily true that the superintendent be of this sex, but in this day of the church membership where the women outnumber the men 16 to 1, it is very probable the Junior superintendent will be a young woman. It is to be hoped that she can secure much help from the young men, for manly influence is most needful to a successful Junior Christian Endeavor Society.

In the cultivation of a model superintendent, communication with the State Junior superintendent should be kept up constantly. Christian Endeavor conventions, with their inspiration, new ideas and methods of work, greatly assist. A prayerful study of these methods helps the superintendent to decide what can be used in her especial Junior Society. The aid of the senior society is indispensable. The church services are always chief assistants, the superintendens advising the boys and girls not only to go to church, but to sit in the church pews with their parents; and this suggests that great bugbear roaming some parts of the world in the shape of the opinion that children should not be allowed to join the Church. I feel toward that opinion as the baby boy did toward the big dog of the house where he was on a visit. Having a dreadful fear of the dog, they talked to him until the coming manly pride was aroused in him, and this was the result. One day while alone in a room the child was startled by the dog coming in. Watching the child from the next room, they say him start for a chair, remarking aloud to himself, "I'm not afraid of him. I wish he wasn't there," meantime hastily climbing upon the chair. "I'm not afraid of him. I'm not afraid of him. I wish he was dead, for Jesus' sake."

We need not be afraid of that opinion, for it cannot keep the children out of the Church. We're not afraid of it, but we wish it was dead! The model Junior superintendent need not teach the destruction of this idea. Her intelligent, well-trained little Christian Juniors are living arguments in favor of its annihilation.

So add to the helps mentioned, belief in Junior church membership, conferences with the pastor, possession of every scrap of literature regarding Junior work, correspondence with workers in other societies regarding Junior work, correspondence with workers in other States, an abiding interest in the organization of Mothers' Societies, good cookery, knowledge of games, a carefully-cared-for body, constant communion with Christ. These helps are the scaffolding which God provides for us in building that beautiful character, a model Junior superintendent.

A discussion of these papers then took place and many present offered suggestions for making the work successful.

Mr. C. J. Atkinson, of Toronto, Ont., then addressed the meeting on "Some Things To Avoid."

Address of Mr. C. J. Atkinson, Toronto, Ont.

Avoid doing all the work yourself. The Juniors will learn to do by doing. You plan, they will carry out; you touch the button, they will do the rest. Juniors are working interrogation points, and only require responsive superintendents to suggest the what and the how. Give them something to do or they will soon lose interest. Maintain good order and discipline by occupying surplus time and energy; remember that it is the idle hands that the father of mischief finds work for; it is the business of Junior Christian Endeavor to preempt this field. Teach the Juniors early the valuable life lesson that it is better to try to do something and fail than not to try and beautifully succeed.

Avoid making your Junior Society your society. Don't selfishly monopolize all the pleasure of superintending. Have several assistants, say one to look after each committee in the society, and place responsibilities upon them. You will thus educate superintendents for other societies and insure the future of your own. If a Junior Society disbands it will be found, in nine cases out of ten — if that number can be found — that it is due to lack of a competent superintendent. In training superintendents you are not working a question in addition; it is one in multiplication.

Avoid increasing members at the expense of thoroughness. Strive for quality, not quantity. Hand-picked fruit keeps much better than windfalls. Make pledge-taking a serious business and the consecration meeting a solemn hour. Deal personally and privately with every applicant for active membership. If possible have them visit you at your home, and with open Bible and bended knee and the Spirit's guidance, draw the lambs gently into the fold. The blessing will be mutual, and the superintendent and Junior will be intimate, confiding friends ever after. Those little conferences will become the greatest joy of your life, the memory of which will dispel the little irritations and add to your zeal in the work.

Avoid ruts. Variety is required not only to make the weekly meetings attractive, but to maintain interest in the work of the committees. If superintendent and assistants lack original ideas here is a receipt for making a good substitute: get all the text-books, periodicals, and helps on Junior work that are within reach; have your note-book at every convention where Junior work is discussed; go with it yourself, if possible; swap plans with every Junior worker you meet. Squeeze the best out of all these, sweeten to the local taste, and serve in small quantities. Jam always takes well with Juniors.

Avoid sentimental gush, a long-faced demeanor, and the calling of Juniors "dear little children." Teach a real, matter-of-fact religion that Juniors can practise in the school-room, running messages, riding a bicycle, or playing baseball. If we must have long faces, let them be long crossways. Treat your Juniors not as prudes and prims, but as healthy, fun-loving girls and boys. Boys? Yes, boys; and you can have boys from twelve to sixteen years of age in your society in as great numbers as the girls, if you recognize that they must have exercise sometimes or something will break, and that they must have fun sometimes or something will burst, and that they aspire above everything to be considered manly while in their teens.

In conclusion, don't use as many don'ts as I have this morning in the next six months, but substitute instead the verb active, "do." This subject was not of my choosing.

Miss Nettie E. Harrington, of Janesville, Wis., read a paper on " The Relation of the Juniors to the Older Society." We regret Miss Harrington's manuscript was not preserved.

Miss Kate H. Haus, of St. Louis, Mo., took charge of the open parliament, and conducted a discussion on " How To Keep the Juniors Interested." The parliament proved to be a lively and instructive feature of the programme.

Miss Lottie E. Wiggins, of Toronto, Ont., interested her auditors by an address on " The Relation Between the Parents and the Juniors."

Address of Miss Lottie E. Wiggins, Toronto, Ont.

We have talked much about the relation of children to parents, but very little about the relation of parents to children. How strange that we have overlooked the divine command to "become as little children," and have always been holding up adults as the examples for children to follow! Which of us consider the conventionalized, warped, distorted, indirect, half-fair, untrusting mode of thinking of the adult a good substitute for the spontaneous, genuine, direct, just, and trusting mode peculiar and essential to childhood?

Junior workers are not competing with parents in training the Juniors, but co-operating. We also believe that the best work for the Juniors can not be done without home co-operation. Our Juniors are leading their parents deeper spirituality, and thus the Junior Society is fulfilling the predictions of our Lord regarding the foremost age of all history,—"A little child shall lead them." We, therefore, organize a Parents' Society of Christian Endeavor, not enlisting the mothers alone, but the fathers also. Too long the entire management of the home has been left to the mothers, while the fathers have guarded our larger home, the nation. Both governments have signally failed, and now we learn the lesson that neither home nor nation is well governed unless there are "two heads in council." Parents best realize their responsibility to the Juniors when they live the principles they desire to see the children live.

How often we find parents lax in their own practices in honesty, and boasting before the children of some sharp trick by which they gained advantage in a business transaction! If they but realized that it is the little leaks that sink the ship, they would be more careful to be true under all circumstances. Parents should be so true that when the Juniors weigh their actions in the balance they shall not be " found wanting."

" Child-nature " should be studied. The gardener studies his plants and knows how to treat each. The farmer studies his fields and knows what best will grow in every field. But parents think all children alike, recognize no differences in character, and do not adapt plans to develop different natures.

Parents should possess the utmost confidence of the Juniors, sympathize with them in their aims, study their tastes, encourage their development; should have great faith in the children, that, though mistakes are made, they desire to do the right ; should not make promises unless certain of being able to fulfil them; should not bribe children to be good by promises of reward and payment for every service.

Parents should think more about the physical development of the Juniors,— see that they take proper exercise, proper food, and go to bed early. Some persons' digestion has a good deal to do with their religion. Children's tempers are often caused by too much pastry and sitting up till midnight. Make allowances for failures. Let the children down as easily as older people. Five-year-old Flossie said to her mother on being reproved, " When it 's me, you say ' cross ; ' when it 's you, you say ' nervous.' "

Mothers and fathers who expect their children to be angels must have forgotten their ancestry. As far as possible parents should co-operate with the superintendents in carrying out the plans of the Junior Society. The Juniors are encouraged by the interest of their parents, as well as the parents benefited by the Juniors' work. The Parents' Society should meet at least once a month and talk over the work, hear the Junior superintendent's monthly report, pray for blessing on the Juniors. In an informal way parents and workers may talk over the work with mutual benefit; discuss difficulties, but also state the blessings and benefits of Junior work. At home the Juniors may be more easily encouraged to read the Bible and pray every day. Parents may note whether Christian principles are lived in home life, in school life, and in the playground. Parents should not only pray for the Juniors, but with the Juniors. Many a difficulty between parent and child will be sweetly reconciled as, together, hearts are lifted to the Father on high. By this mutual sympathy and help the spiritual life of the threefold nature, which is one in the unity of the spirit and the bonds of peace — husband, wife, and child — shall be exalted, our family altars will mean more, and over the homes of our country shall be written, " Holiness to the Lord."

Mr. Thomas Wainwright, of Chicago, conducted the question box, and gave his opinion of various ways for getting along with the boys and girls of the societies.

The next speaker's topic was " The Pastor and the Juniors."

Address of Rev. Peter Ainslie, Baltimore, Md.

Some time ago I stood by a naval constructor as he directed the laying of the keel of a great vessel. He watched it daily, and, after many months, it was successfully launched, with the Stars and Stripes floating over its newly christened prow. In these days when childhood is largely, and in some cases entirely, given over to the Church for religious instruction, it seems to me that the pastor has a magnificent opportunity of aiding more than ever before in the building of the child-thought and the child-life. Without discussing the hold that the home is losing upon childhood, certainly this condition has thrust upon the pastor a new and large responsibility. It compels him to be more than ever before the servant of the child. The Junior Society meets the want of forming the children into an organization to bring the pastor in closer touch with them, that he may study their individual lives and press to their hearts as near as possible the divine mold. In fact, this is his business. He is pre-eminently in the world to make men and women better; but since it is easier to plant a truth in a child's life than to uproot evil or disfigured truth in a mature life, his opportunity and responsibility are measureless. It is his as never before to directly influence manhood and womanhood and make a safe passage, as far as in him lies, in the launching of human barks upon the rough and pathless sea of life.

Somebody has said that the child is the best copy of Adam before he tasted the fruit. At any rate, it is the flower bursting the calyx that holds the child-blossom, and the pastor's prayers, words, and life should combine to keep fragrant the opening flower. He should pray for them individually. It is easier to prevent a leakage than, after twenty-five or thirty years, to attempt to chink a weather-bitten craft. He should know the children by name. " How do you do?' and "Good morning," may suit men and women, but "How do you do, Jim?" and "Good morning, Mary," is the only salutation that will suit boys and girls. He should play with the children. You can not touch men unless you get on equality with them; neither can you reach young children unless you become identified with them in their toys, games, books, and sports. The pastor then must be a child, or, if you choose, "an overgrown boy," as somebody once called Henry Ward Beecher. After all, this is just where Jesus wanted every one of us to make our starting-point,— at childhood.

The crowd in attendance on the service was so great, and so many could not be accommodated with seats in the church, that an overflow meeting was arranged and held in the lecture-room, speakers from the main meeting going to the overflow meeting and repeating their addresses, Rev. Geo. B. Stewart, D.D., Harrisburg, Pa., presiding.

During the service Rev. Mr. Lamb, of Maine, sang solos and captivated his hearers.

Mrs. Francis E. Clark was present at the meeting, and, although not engaged to take a part in the service, was called upon and was given a warm reception by the audience. Mrs. Clark spoke of methods for interesting young people in the Junior Society, and believed there was no rule that could be adopted as applying to all societies.

The meeting was closed with prayer by the presiding officer, Secretary Baer.

FRIDAY AFTERNOON.

"Committee" Conferences and Advance Lines of Work.

"To the work," said the score of practical conferences along special lines of Christian Endeavor work, held Friday afternoon. The earnestness of the delegates and the definiteness of the discussions gave these meetings a character that will be impressed on thousands of societies in months to come. "Advance, Endeavor," was the key-word. "There remaineth yet very much land to be possessed," was the prevailing sentiment, and in the conferences on old topics, and in those that considered the later enlargements, the desire for greater things was clearly manifest. Especially cheering was the good attendance and great interest at the meetings where were considered the Intermediate, Senior, Mothers', and Parents' Societies, the work for life-savers, the Travellers' Union, the Floating Society, and the information committee.

Corresponding Secretaries' Conference.

This conference was held in the upper room of the Church of the Reformation, Lutheran, corner of Pennsylvania Avenue and Second Street, S. E. There was a large number of corresponding secretaries present, a majority of whom took part. Mr. J. M. Lucas, of Des Moines, Io., presided. The object of the conference and the discussion of the work were well defined and outlined by the chairman. The chairman also spoke in a general way of the subject, defining the duties and work of the secretaries, and then extended an invitation to the officers present to take an active part in debating the many points of interest as they were successfully brought out. This request was most liberally responded to.

It was the evidence of nearly all present that the reason we failed to receive prompt and accurate reports and responses from thousands of our secretaries was the fact that the records of our recording secretaries and church clerks are so poorly kept that it seemed almost impossible to secure the information desired. At this conference it was fully decided that it was a most important duty of all corresponding secretaries to help to inaugurate a glorious reform in their respective societies and churches in seeing that the records of the same are more systematically kept. Many plans and methods of work were freely discussed. This was a very enthusiastic, interesting, and successful conference. One very important fact was brought out in the meeting; namely, corresponding secretaries should be prompt in answering all communications sent to them from proper sources, and be very active in placing in the waste-basket all forms of advertising matter being unduly imposed upon our Endeavor Societies which should not be recognized by them. It was proven to be a fact that many unscrupulous advertisers are trying to place their wares, etc., in the hands of many of the Endeavorers by using this means of advertising same.

Junior Superintendents' Conference.

One of the most interesting conferences of the Convention was the meeting of the superintendents of the Junior Societies, held at the Wesley M. E. Church. Miss Cordelia Jamison, of Beltzhoover, Pa., the State superintendent of that State, presided, and the meeting was one of the largest of the afternoon, the church being crowded by the Junior superintendents and many others interested in that important branch of Christian Endeavor work. A praise meeting of ten minutes preceded the business meeting, Mr. Harry G. Kimball, of Washington, conducting it. Miss Lottie E. Wiggins, of Toronto, Ont., read an interesting paper on "Junior Business Meetings," Miss Kate Haus, of St. Louis, following with a valuable paper on "Aids to Superintendents." Mr. Henry Small, of York, Pa., gave many interesting suggestions in an address on "Personal Work."

A feature of the meeting was a short talk by Miss Elizabeth W. Olney, of Providence, R. I., her subject being "Bands of Mercy."

Mr. J. A. Shannon, of Kansas City, Mo., illustrated the right way and the wrong way of teaching the Bible in a very interesting story, and for several minutes Mr. Thomas Wainwright, of Chicago, conducted a question box, answering many inquiries as to the best way of conducting Junior work. The exercises were closed by the audience repeating the Christian Endeavor pledge.

Conference of Missionary Superintendents.

This was the first attempt at holding a conference of missionary superintendents, and though the attendance was not large, the deep interest manifested proved the idea a good one. The leader, Rev. Willis S. Hinman, of Columbia, Pa., opened the conference with prayer, after the singing of two or three missionary songs. In a few earnest words he reminded those present that in many societies the missionary work depended largely on the guiding influence of the superintendents. Then he called for an interchange of thought in answer to the twofold question: *What have you been doing; what do you propose to do?*

Miss Frances B. Patterson, superintendent of the State of Illinois, reported the State thoroughly organized. Courses of missionary extension lectures had been held in nearly all the important towns and cities, often under difficulties, especially in the country districts, where speakers were sometimes obliged to drive long distances. The cost had been entirely met by the fees. She had sent out a great deal of literature. The two-cents-a-week plan is in satisfactory operation in many societies.

The superintendent of one of the districts in Chicago gave an interesting account of the methods used in his district to keep up the interest of the missionary committees. District meetings are held, for which careful programmes are prepared and at which bright, pointed talks on methods are given by the best speakers obtainable.

Another State superintendent told of work done at the State convention. A room was secured and an elaborate display was made of missionary literature, pictures, books, maps, and curios. Several student volunteers were in attendance constantly, who made it their business to talk missions to every visitor, explaining maps, showing curios, and distributing literature.

Mr. Hinman reported nearly every county in Pennsylvania organized, and all parts of the State kept in close touch with the State superintendent through an efficient corps of district and county superintendents. Missionary extension lecture courses were held in about forty towns and cities, with gratifying results.

Then followed a half-hour of informal conversation concerning the work, during which there was a lively exchange of questions and answers, helpful suggestions, and bright bits of experience.

A series of prayers for God's blessing on the work of missionary superintendents, in which many of those present participated, brought the conference to a close, every one feeling that the hour and a half had been spent profitably.

Local Union Officers' Conference.

The centre of attraction Friday noon for the officers of local Christian Endeavor Unions was St. Paul's English Lutheran Church. A conference of local union officers was held there, with Mr. William L. Turner, Jr., of Philadelphia, Pa., as chairman, and with union officers from every section of the country, from Maine to Texas, and from Washington to Florida, in attendance.

A song service followed by prayer opened the meeting, and then the presiding officer announced that the general subject to be discussed was, "How Can We Best Further the Interests of Our Local Unions?" After several had talked on that topic, opinions were given on how best to conduct the union of societies, and an explanation of the idea of city unions was made.

The union of widely separated country societies occupied attention for some little time, and later it was agreed that a large attendance at quarterly union meetings might be secured by the liberal use of printer's ink, by following good programmes, and by uniformity as to time. Among others, the presiding officer asked the question, "What do you expect of your lookout committees?" and many interesting and instructive answers were made by the delegates.

"Where did you get your form of organization?" was another question put to the meeting. The foregoing is a sample of what was done at the gathering, which was in session for an hour and a half. There is no doubt that when they returned home their respective societies profited to a very great extent from the exchange of views between the officers of the local unions at Washington, '96.

District Secretaries' Conference.

Secretaries are always industrious persons, no matter what organization they belong to, but the duties of district secretaries of Christian Endeavor Unions are manifold and seemingly endless. A small but interesting conference of these officials was held at the First Baptist Church, with Miss Martha E. Race, secretary of the Florida Endeavor Union, presiding. The first topic brought up for discussion was that of "The District Secretary." This and each succeeding topic was subdivided, any person present volunteering his or her views on the subject. Some of these opinions showed much serious study, but all concurred in thinking that at least three requisites were indispensable in a district secretary; namely, that he should be "business-like," "energetic," and "open-hearted."

District secretaries have, of course, multifarious correspondence, and similar heavy work, but the local secretaries are nearly as busy, and have in addition many duties that the others have not. Under this head a world of work, much of it not named in the category of ordinary secretaries, was brought up by those present. One delegate expressed in a nutshell a quality that is wanted in everybody as well as secretaries,— more "grit," less "quit."

Sentiments such as these about filled up the afternoon, though time was found near the close to develop old methods and discuss new methods of work.

State and Provincial Officers' Conference.

The conference of the State and Provincial officers, which was held at the Sixth Presbyterian Church, Sixth and D Streets, S. W., was one of the most important meetings conducted. Judge L. J. Kirkpatrick, of Kokomo, Ind., president of the Indiana State Union, presided. After a short welcome address by the chairman, prayer was offered by Rev. O. W. Stewart, president of the Illinois Union. Music was furnished by the choir, under the direction of Mr. Sweet, of Colorado.

The first subject offered by the chairman for discussion was " The Grouping of State Conventions for the Purpose of Enabling Speakers To Attend Conventions of Different States with Less Expense to the State." The subject was freely discussed. It was considered feasible to group adjacent States, and a committee was appointed for the purpose of considering such matter more fully, with power to consult with the State officers and make such groupings as might be mutually agreed upon. The next topic discussed was, " The Payment of Expenses of State Conventions." It was unanimously agreed that each State committee should see that all expenses of the convention are promptly paid. Especial emphasis was placed upon the duty of such committee to see that all the incidental expenses of speakers are paid, as well as car-fare, that the amount tendered should fully reimburse the speaker for all expenses incurred. It was also urged that the same plan of payment be followed by the district secretaries of the several States in holding district conventions. " The Uses and Abuses of State Papers " was next considered. This topic called forth much discussion. The majority present thought it well for each State to have such paper, provided it be kept under the management of the State committee and made self-sustaining. It was considered unwise to allow a private individual to conduct such paper as an individual enterprise without giving the State committee the power to direct its policy and to know at all times the character of the articles published. The enterprise in many States has proved a financial failure, and great care was urged in providing for its support by advertisements and circulation. " How To Raise Money for State Work " was the last topic presented by the chairman. The plan which has proved most successful in many States is for the treasurer to send his call for pledges to each society prior to the convention, requesting the society to send in the pledge by the time the convention convenes; also, to have subscription blanks and envelopes distributed through the convention hall, so subscriptions may be made during the convention. Mr. M. M. Shand, of Washington, acted as secretary of the conference.

Lookout Committee Conference.

The Lookout Committee Conference was held in the McKendree Methodist Church, with quite a large attendance of Endeavorers from almost every State in the Union. The lookout committee is an important committee of the Society, as its duty consists chiefly in bringing in new members and keeping a sharp lookout on the old members to see that they do not neglect their duties.

Mr. Guy W. Campbell, of San Jose, Cal., was chairman of the conference. In opening he spoke quite earnestly of the importance of the work of the committee, which he declared to be quite as essential a part of the Society as any other committee. Some members, he said, were inclined to be neglectful of their duties as Christian Endeavorers. and it thus became necessary for some one to remind them of their backwardness and impress upon them the necessity for more earnest consecration to the cause. This it was the lookout committee's function to perform, and the spiritual success of the Society depends largely upon the efficient and conscientious manner in which their duties were performed.

In the open parliament following Chairman Campbell's remarks quite a number of practical suggestions were made as to the best manner in which this work may be performed. Above all things else, the members were most earnestly urged always to observe the tenets of the pledge, and not to substitute in its stead any of their ideas as to the best policy for the members of their society to pursue in cases in which special legislation seemed to be necessary.

Mr. Campbell suggested the following outline: —

LOOKOUT COMMITTEE.

DUTIES.

Bring in new members.
- Who to secure.
- How to get them.
- What is to be required of them?
- How can we insure faithfulness and guard against careless, indifferent, and inefficient members?

Introduction of new members to work.
- Method of receiving new members by the *committee.*
- How introduced to the society.
- How interested and enlisted in the *work.*

Affectionately look after and reclaim any that are indifferent to duties as outlined in pledge.
- What methods are employed to determine who are negligent?
- What course pursued with negligent members?
- Shall we expel?
- What is being done to maintain the spiritual life of society and membership?

Sundry duties.
- Committee duties { Meetings. Reports — Blank reports of United Society.
- Duties to pastor.
- Duties to church.
- Duties to society — Society in general — Loyalty — Defence.
- Special duties toward associate members.

Prayer-Meeting Committee Conference.

One of the most largely attended of the committee conferences was that of the prayer-meeting committees at the North Presbyterian Church. This is one of the most important committees of the Society, and the conference brought together many of the best workers in Christian Endeavor in the United States.

Mr. H. H. Grotthouse, of Dallas, Tex., was the leader of the conference. He kept things moving right merrily, allowing no time to be lost, and gave all a chance to tell about the methods that had been successfully adopted in their particular societies.

First, there was a song service, followed by a series of sentence prayers for the work of the prayer-meeting committees.

The first question discussed was, "What is the ideal prayer meeting?" These were some of the definitions of an ideal prayer meeting in the opinions of the various Endeavorers: "A place where we get the blessing of God;" "A meeting led by anybody, taken part in by everybody, monopolized by nobody, and in which everybody is somebody;" "A place where Christians are made joyful;" "Not the battle-ground, but just the place where the canteens are filled;" "The place where we bring heaven to earth and we get God into our hearts;" "A place in which we wait on the Lord for a blessing."

The leader called attention to the valuable help he had received from "Prayer-Meeting Methods," by Amos R. Wells. He said that if any one bought a copy and found it an unprofitable investment, to send him the bill and he would send checks on his bank-account in heaven.

A lengthy discussion on topics connected with making a prayer meeting a success followed. The best music to be used, which a majority of the Endeavorers present thought was the old gospel hymns; the most profitable manner in which to conduct the prayer meeting; the most desirable manner in which to select leaders; — these and kindred subjects of interest to the members of the prayer-meeting committees were thoroughly discussed by the Endeavorers and many practical ideas brought out, which the delegates eagerly jotted down in their note-books to carry back to their home societies for the benefit of their fellow workers who were unable to attend the Convention and hear the talks themselves.

In regard to the most profitable manner in which to conduct the prayer meeting, the majority of sentiment was in favor of allowing the appointed leaders to carry it on in their own way, but it was suggested that it was not well to have too much prayer, too much talking, or too much singing. It was said these features can be used to better advantage if there is a proportionate quantity of each.

The best method of selecting leaders for the meetings was said to be to so arrange matters that each member would have the opportunity of conducting a meeting as often as possible.

The conference closed with a number of brief prayers for the blessing of God to rest upon the labors of the prayer-meeting committees.

Social Committee Conference.

One of the best of the committee conferences was that of the social committee, at the Church of the Covenant. The programme was much changed, quite informal, and altogether delightful. Mr. Raymond R. Frazier, of Madison, Wis., ably conducted the meeting.

The first speaker was Rev. William Patterson, of Toronto, who thoroughly captivated his hearers by an informal talk, which was both witty and full of good common sense. Mr. Patterson stated that some men can be reached through their intellectual side, some from their physical side, some from their social side. " I hear ministers preaching sometimes on the topic, ' Will We Know Each Other in Heaven ? ' " said Mr. Patterson. " Now it seems to me the best way to be sure of that is to get acquainted on earth first. Christ never refused an invitation to a social gathering. His first miracle was at a wedding feast. I think the social committee's work is the most important of all, because theirs is the duty of bringing in new people." In concluding, Mr. Patterson remarked, " Some folks say I talk like a Methodist, others say I look like a priest, and I am a Presbyterian. I came from Scotland some 200 years ago, but more recently from Ireland ; I live across the line, but while I 'm here I am trying to be an American. I hope this rambling talk may help to break the ice." And it did.

Following this there was a general discussion, in which many original ideas were brought out, and which must have proved helpful to all.

Rev. Henry Faville, of Lacrosse, Wis., then spoke on the need of getting young men in the cities without any social opportunities into the societies. " I was announced to speak on money-raising by social committees. I shall not. I am not in the money business — I am in the young man business," the speaker concluded.

After another general discussion, the meeting closed.

Information and Press Committee Conference.

The information and press committees met at Concordia Church, where under the leadership of Mr. Wm. T. Ellis, of Boston, Mass., questions on the best methods for disseminating Christian Endeavor news were discussed. Mr. Ellis advised the societies to divide up a city into sections, and to have some one attend to supplying the secular and religious papers with news concerning the work of the organization which it would be beneficial to the work to have spread abroad. He advised the committeemen to avoid furnishing the papers with trifling matters, and thought it would be well to have Endeavorers everywhere look for and urge the newspapers to furnish the news of their societies on which they wished to be informed.

Sunday=School Committee Conference.

The Calvary Baptist model Sunday-school building — one of the best and most thoroughly equipped in the world — was the scene of a practical and intensely spirited conference. Of the many Endeavorers present were numerous pastors, Sunday-school and primary superintendents, and teachers. Mr. J. L. Dixon, of Springfield, Mass., was chairman.

Inasmuch as not all of our young people are found at the Sunday-school conventions, and inasmuch as Endeavorers are always anxious for the best in whatever they attempt, the chairman presented at the outset the following chart, in which was emphasized the normal and home departments: —

THE SUNDAY SCHOOL AS AN EDUCATIONAL INSTITUTION.

No. 1.

ORGANIZATION OF THE SUNDAY SCHOOL.

DEPARTMENTS.

Age 2—8 Primary	Age 8—12 Junior	Age 12—16 Intermediate	Age 16—19 Senior	Age 19 Adult	Normal	Home	Libr.
Advanced	GRADES 1 2 3 4	GRADES 1 2 3 4	Junior	Young Women's	Junior	Scattered	General Sec.
Primary			Middle	Young Men's	Senior	Neighborhood	Teachers' Sec.
Kindergarten			Senior	Men's Bible	Reserve Class	Correspondence	
				Women's Bible	Tea. Meeting.		
				Congregational			

SUPPLEMENTAL INSTRUCTION.

PRIMARY	JUNIOR	INTERMEDIATE	SENIOR	ADULT	NORMAL	HOME
Lord's Prayer	1 Books of the Bible	1–2 O. T. Biography Catechism	1 Church History	Old and New Testament Introduction and Analysis	Reading Courses	Library Church Papers
Beatitudes	2 O. T. Hist. & Geog.	3–4 N. T. Biography Catechism	2 Christ. Evidences			
Commandments (Shortened)	3 N. T. Hist. & Geog.		3 Doctrines			
Psalm 23	4 Commandments (In full) Church Hymns Selected Verses Selected Chapters					

PROMOTION.

DAY.—Annual, near the beginning of the year.
EXAMINATIONS.—From Primary, oral; from other departments, written.
TEACHERS.—Advance with classes through their department.
NORMAL GRADUATES.—Join the Reserve Class or teach.

The question was then asked, " What can Christian Endeavor do in helping to bring about this ideal, so much desired in principle at least, in all of our churches?" Rev. Chas. Roads, of Philadelphia, ex-president of the Pennsylvania Union, and a member of the Pennsylvania State Executive Sunday-school committee, made answer in the following:—

THE SABBATH SCHOOL AND CHRISTIAN ENDEAVOR.

MUTUALLY HELPFUL.

TO BECOME ONE AND INSEPARABLE.

THE SABBATH SCHOOL STANDS FOR		CHRISTIAN ENDEAVOR STANDS FOR
1. Systematic Bible study. 2. Denominational Christian truth. 3. World - wide organization for lessons and missions. 4. Training to teach the Gospel. 5. Soul-winning.		1. Pledged all-comprehensive Christlike work. 2. Interdenominational fellowship. 3. Spiritual power. 4. Training in service. 5. Enthusiasm.

Let them clasp hands.

CHRISTIAN ENDEAVOR IN DETAILED SUNDAY-SCHOOL WORK

Secures New Scholars.	Does Home Dept. Work.	Fills Normal Classes.	Is loyal To Supt. And Pastor.	Creates C. E. Atmosphere In the Sunday school.

It was designed that the conference proper should divide its time in the consideration of two phases of the Sunday-school committee work: what can Christian Endeavor, and thus the Sunday-school committee, do in helping the Sunday school, first, in what might be termed the more untried ways, — under which were classed the normal and home department work; and, second, in the somewhat well-beaten paths, — as visitation, issuing invitations, and welcoming strangers to the Sunday school? Owing, however, to the discussion aroused over the first topic, which at times was not a little vigorous, and revealed the fact that the Christian Endeavor Sunday-school committee requires wise tact and the thoroughly Christlike spirit in order to make *to-day* any helpful effort possible, the principal thought of the conference centred about the normal department.

Mr. Percy H. Bristow, the salaried superintendent of the Calvary Sunday school, opened the discussion by the presentation of the "Bible club" as in operation in his Sunday school. If any one desires to know how to conduct a successful teachers' meeting under the broader name "Bible club," he will obtain no little information by writing Mr. Bristow.

Among the many open doors for usefulness for the Sunday-school committee, as briefly indicated under the second division of the topic, were mentioned, securing new scholars, visitation under the direction of the Sunday-school superintendent, organizing Sunday schools in the outlying districts, conducting Bible study in the jails, old ladies' homes, almshouses, etc.

Temperance Committee Conference.

A small but earnest company of workers gathered at the Temperance Conference at the appointed time and place. Mr. Geo. W. Coleman, advertising manager of *The Golden Rule*, Boston, presided. In the devotional service, prominence was given to the sentiments of brotherly union as found in 1 Peter iii. 8–17, "Be ye all of one mind, having compassion one of another, love as brethren, be pitiful, be courteous: not rendering evil for evil, or railing for railing: but contrariwise blessing." In the same passage is found also an injunction to fearlessness:— "But and if ye suffer for righteousness' sake, happy are ye: and be not afraid of their terror, neither be troubled." With the thought, therefore, of brotherly union and fearlessness against a common enemy, and after a season of hearty and spontaneous prayer, the company settled down to a serious consideration of ways and means.

Every one present had some direct connection or special interest in some form of temperance work, and for two hours the discussion of methods went on without any lagging of the interest and without any loss of time. Frequently several men were on their feet at once seeking recognition from the chair.

In this brief report it will be impossible to even mention any of the very many excellent plans and devices that were suggested for the assistance of workers in every department. A good twenty minutes was taken up in telling how the temperance committee in the local society does its work among the members of the society and in the church and congregation. The most effective methods of using temperance literature was discussed with animation, together with pledge-signing in all its various forms. How to conduct public meetings in the interest of gospel temperance or no license brought out a great variety of suggestions. "Gospel Temperance in the Slums" was a topic not at all unfamiliar to this company of young people, and their discussion of it manifested a practical, personal acquaintance with the work. And so on to the end of the list, one department after another of the work was taken up, and the discussion almost without exception was directly to the point and very helpful.

It is not often that so many divisions of the great temperance army are represented in one meeting as were gathered together at this conference. There were on the one hand the very beginners in the work and on the other the well-known Edward Carson, connected with one of the national temperance societies, a man who has given the best of his life to temperance work, and who, he said, saw a greater promise for the future of the cause in the children and young people than in any other direction.

In one aisle of the church sat a man who had been rescued from the drunkard's grave by the kind word of a child; in another sat Vice-Chairman Taylor of the Committee of '96, who brought in his testimony as a police judge charging the great majority of crimes to the evil of strong drink. There were present and took active part leaders in the W. C. T. U. Nearly every political party was represented and numerous workers in special fields. Notwithstanding all the difference of opinions in such a company, on such a topic, there prevailed from opening to close a beautiful spirit of brotherly union in which there was abundant room for the many fearless utterances that frequently found expression in the course of the conference. The company adjourned acknowledging with one accord that it had been good to be there and that much help had been given and received.

Good-Literature Committee Conference.

The conference of good-literature committees was held at the Nineteenth Street Baptist Church, on Friday afternoon. The appointed leader was Rev. W. P. Landers, of Middleton, Mass.

Mr. Landers conducted the conference upon the plan of an open parliament, throwing into the discussion these topics : "What Is Good Literature ?" "The Importance of it ; " " The Relation of Christian Endeavor to Good Literature ; " "Its Publication ; " "Christian Endeavor Ink ; " "The Circulation of Good Literature ; " "Sources of Information Regarding the Work of This Committee."

A large number participated in the animated debate which followed the presentation of each topic. Experiences and successes were related. Many suggestions were offered, among them the distribution of religious tracts through what is known as "silent evangelism ; " the opening of reading-rooms in churches and elsewhere ; the distribution of suitable literature in jails, railway stations, and in car-stables; and the use of the local press in the regular and continued appearance of a Christian Endeavor department.

The discussion upon what constitutes good literature, and the relation of the Christian Endeavorers to it, was especially helpful. It seemed to be the opinion of those present that "that which emphasized and distributed the good in literature" can be called good literature. The relation of the Endeavor Societies to it is one with that of Christianity.

Christian Citizenship Committee Conference.

About 150 or 200 delegates gathered at the E Street Baptist Church. Mr. Frank E. Page, of Chicago, presided. Earnestness and enthusiasm marked each moment of the meeting, and made up for the meagreness of the attendance. Talks of three or five minutes opened the discussion, and were given by Revs. M. R. Lyon and C. S. Bullock, of Chicago, Hon. Mr. Nicholson, of Indiana, Hon. H. L. Castle, of Pittsburgh, Pa., and several others. These speakers not only aroused the enthusiasm of the conference, but spoke of actual good work done, of work planned, and of practical methods. Little time was given to bewailing the condition of affairs. Each speech had the true ring that promises so much for the success of this vigorous forward movement. A delightful solo was sung by a local Endeavorer, and then the discussion became general. Delegates from all parts of the country reported excellent work. Some told of failures, some of perplexities and difficulties; some asked for advice and help, which were readily given. The most inspiring feature of the meeting was that all work done or planned was manifestly in the name and for the sake of Christ. It was a great regret that Mr. E. D. Wheelock, the assigned leader of the conference, was unable to be present.

The Brotherhood Committee Conference.

The brotherhood committee met at the Western Presbyterian Church. Rev. Rufus W. Miller, the founder and president of the Brotherhood of Andrew and Philip, presided, and in opening gave a brief history of the organization with which he is so prominently connected, and compared its work with the work done by the Christian Endeavorers.

Rev. John H. Elliot, rector of the Church of the Ascension, in bringing the greetings of the Brotherhood of St. Andrew to the sister association, gave a thoughtful and entertaining address on the idea of conducting brotherhood organizations.

The meeting was thrown into the form of a conference upon brotherhood methods in Christian Endeavor work, and reports were received from various chapters.

An address was delivered by Rev. John Conkling on work being done in Springfield, Mass.

Rev. J. Wilbur Chapman, D.D., testified to the benefit of the brotherhood at his home in Philadelphia, where he is pastor of Bethany Church.

Rev. Howard Wilbur Ennis spoke in reference to the brotherhood work in this city, and the meeting was brought to a close by a devotional exercise conducted by Rev. Ford C. Ottmann, of Newark, N. J.

Missionary Committee Conference.

The Missionary Committee Conference was held at the New York Avenue Presbyterian Church, Rev. Ira Landrith, managing editor of *The Cumberland Presbyterian*, Nashville, Tenn., presiding. The main body of the auditorium was well filled with chairmen and members of missionary committees, returned missionaries, secretaries of mission boards, and volunteer missionaries. The conference was designedly wholly informal and seemed to be all the better on that account. There were no long speeches. In the two hours there were more speeches than minutes. The conference was grouped about what the leader called three good "Endeavor G's" — *Growing, Giving, Going.* The first section of the conference was devoted to answering the question, "What is your society doing by way of growing in missionary information?" The second section answered the question, "What is your society giving, and how?" and the third, "What is your society doing by way of going to the regions beyond?" Miss Rice served as secretary of the conference, and recorded the fact, among many others, that there were no less than eleven board secretaries present, perhaps a score of volunteers, and quite as many who, during the conference, announced their willingness to become missionaries. Among the plans suggested for missionary information were reading-circles, written examinations on missionary subjects, talks by missionaries, missionary libraries, magazines, etc. Under the subject of giving, the haphazard method was emphatically denounced, systematic and proportionate giving being in high favor. The entertainment for revenue only appeared to have but one friend in the conference. A Chicago lady said that in her society the members who thought they could not give two cents a week were told that they should write a letter to the Lord each week, putting a two-cent stamp on the envelope, and thereby tell him they were too poor.

The singing was led by a young lady and was in all respects admirable. From beginning to end there was not an instant of intermission, every moment of time being taken up by song or speech or prayer.

Mothers' Societies' Conference.

The Mothers' Societies of Christian Endeavor held their conference in the Wesley Chapel. The interest of this meeting was largely added to by the kindness of two of the Washington Endeavorers, who, by song and recitation, gave pleasure to the audience. Miss Knight sang a solo very delightfully, and Master Ralph Quinter made a plea for the Juniors. Greetings were received from Mrs. A. B. Fellows, of Chicago, also the assurance from Mrs. Cleveland's secretary that matters pertaining to the right training of little ones was of great interest to her, and that were she in Washington she would extend her earnest wish for the far-reaching good of our conference. From Miss Willard, who is in Ryegate, England, were words of love and encouragement to the mothers in all lands.

It is very much to be regretted that all of the words of the speakers can not be scattered broadcast through all homes, for the help of mothers not privileged to listen to them. Miss LeBaron, Junior superintendent of the Chicago Union, very forcibly impressed her hearers of the absolute need of the mothers' co-operation to make the Junior Society the kind aimed at. The Mothers' Society of Christian Endeavor is indispensable to the leader and the little ones. Mr. Rader, of San Francisco, made all feel that out in California they knew how to conduct model societies, and that the mothers must not be selfish, but generous, and open the ranks and admit the fathers to the privileges enjoyed by their calling the new branch the Parents' Society of Christian Endeavor. Glad will be the day, indeed, when in perfect atonement father and mother shall seek the highest and best for the children "lent them of the Lord," both delighting themselves in the Lord, and he fulfilling his promise to give them the desire of their hearts, the salvation of these dear ones.

Dr. Robinson, of Englewood, knew whereof he spoke when he told from a pastor's standpoint the wide range of usefulness that the Mothers' Society of Christian Endeavor has. He cited personal instances in his own pastorate, and showed that the influence was possible to permeate all the interests of the Church. After Dr. Robinson had invoked God's especial blessing on absent mothers, and on all interested in the welfare and training of the young, the Mizpah benediction was pronounced, and the audience quietly dispersed.

Intermediate and Senior Societies' Conference.

The conference of Senior and Intermediate Societies held in the Kendall Baptist Church was probably one of the most interesting meetings held in connection with the Christian Endeavor Convention.

Rev. Charles A. Dickinson, of Boston, Mass., was the first speaker, his subject being "The Chip-Basket." During his talk he said, "The Intermediate Society arose from the systems of divisions in large societies. Their age should be from eleven or twelve to seventeen years, and is very important. These original young people are now old enough to hold office and carry on the work they do. Are we drifting into an adult society or are we to keep to the original purpose," he asked, "that of saving the boys and girls for the Church of Christ? From the age of seventeen to twenty-five or thirty years the Endeavorers are ready for absorption into larger church life and should enter the next society."

He then suggested five classes that are ready for this older society, as follows: (1) the young people who find it impossible to go to the Y. P. S. C. E. meetings any longer; (2) those who are so absorbed in other church work as to have no energy for Y. P. S. C. E. work; (3) those who are affiliated members; (4) those who go to the midweek prayer meeting and do not take part, and those who forget to go to the prayer meetings; (5) our honorary members.

Rev. W. F. McCauley, of Toledo, O., had for his subject "The Membership," about which he talked entertainingly for a quarter of an hour or more.

Miss Kate Haus, a well-known Junior worker, spoke of "The Intermediate Society's Place in the Church."

In addition to taking charge of the question box, Prof. Amos R. Wells, of Boston, Mass., spoke on "Organized Systematic Work."

The meeting was in charge of Mr. Geo. B. Graff, subscription manager of *The Golden Rule*, of Boston. The music was made especially interesting by the presence of Mr. Percy S. Foster.

Floating Societies of Christian Endeavor Conference.

An earnest company of workers and sailors gathered in Peck Memorial Church, which was effectively decorated. Unique blue and white shields bearing the names of Floating Societies and committees were suspended overhead, and a big anchor from the navy-yard, with flags everywhere, gave a nautical welcome.

Here came a naval chaplain, an ex-marine just home from a cruiser, a big gunner's mate from a battleship, and deep-water sailors; a sailor-boy's mother, a sister who said, " Floating Christian Endeavor was the means of my brother's conversion," and workers from organized work in Portland, Me., Vineyard Haven, Mass., Brooklyn, N. Y., New York, N. Y., Philadelphia, Pa., and Norfolk, Va.

A brief praise service was led by one deep-water sailor, and the opening prayer was offered by another.

In opening the conference, the leader, Miss A. P. Jones, of Falmouth, Mass., said in part : —

Floating Christian Endeavor workers must never lack two essential qualities,—*thorough consecration to Christ* with a *special burden for souls*, which is of far greater importance than knowledge of sea life and sailors ; and *thorough knowledge* of, and loyalty to, *Christian Endeavor principles.*

Forty-seven Floating Societies of Christian Endeavor, nineteen on shore, twenty-eight on ships, and eighteen Floating Christian Endeavor committees of five to thirty consecrated young men and women, have been earnestly serving the past year, while work has been broadened and strengthened, with many special blessings to report, far more encouraging than figures would indicate.

To organize a Floating Christian Endeavor committee, *first find your chairman.* Choose one who is deeply in earnest for the souls of men, especially *sea*men. True success never follows *forced appointment.*

Appoint a *live leader*, abounding in faith and resource, *for chairman*, and one who has made a success in other lines of Christian Endeavor. This chairman by a tour of the local societies will obtain a picked committee of evangelistic Endeavorers.

Avoid haste in organizing either a ship or shore society, unless you have many strong Christians for members, but *be led of the Spirit* in all work.

In no way do we interfere with established seamen's work, but there is ample room in so great a harvest. In districting a city for Floating Christian Endeavor work, the one which includes established seamen's work may have less assistance, and it should be extended as desired.

Best results follow work organized *first in seaports.* If a *State superintendent* is first appointed he can not so well urge the work on seacoast societies as for local workers to feel the special call to service.

Carefully admit members. Quality before numbers. Observe courtesy to a society on a ship when a member of a ship's crew desires to sign the pledge. Systematically solicit comfort-bags, by circular letter, and enclosing the little story "Dan's Comfort-Bag," with description. Examine contents carefully and mark Testaments.

Even inland societies can have a Floating Christian Endeavor committee to help seacoast work. Fly a blue flag with white C. E. monogram or the C. E. with anchor interlaced, for ship or shore services or for the launch.

Bits of news come daily from sea and land,—a temptation overcome, workers encouraged, a great need met, another life consecrated fully to God's service, and all showing how God owns and blesses Floating Christian Endeavor.

One member already on the mission field in China as a gospel minister.

Services held on ships rich in blessing.

Five Floating Societies of Christian Endeavor report 22 sailors uniting with the church during the year.

A bluejacket gives $25 to Red Cross for Armenians.

The Christian Endeavor home for Seamen, in Nagasaki, Japan, founded by the U. S. S. Charleston Floating Society of Christian Endeavor, bought and opened.

Pray much, plan carefully, work quickly, for time with the sailor is short, remembering the prophesy in Isa. xlii. 10 can be fulfilled to-day, and that "All — seamen — are brethren."

Greetings were sent from workers and sailors in distant ports, and from lands across the sea.

Mr. Lewis W. Destler, of Philadelphia, Pa., gave a clear, enthusiastic description of his Floating Christian Endeavor committee and their work, which is so planned and executed that already ten miles of their city water-front is each week covered by Christian Endeavor visitation and services, resulting beneficially to sailor and worker, and to non-Christians who desire to assist.

Another Philadelphia worker told of visitation and services.

An open conference followed. One query, if Floating Christian Endeavor did not lead a sailor away from church or Bethel, *to a society*, brought forth the earnest assurance that Floating Christian Endeavor serves faithfully under the Christian Endeavor motto, "For Christ *and the Church*."

Mr. Deans, of Norfolk, reported their Floating Christian Endeavor committee work among the men in the navy-yard, and services held on naval ships.

Portland, Me., work was well represented.

Mrs. Jane Cassera, New York, a veteran sailors' missionary, now of the new Christian Endeavor Bethel, told of her work among ocean-steamship men, the trials and bravery of sailor Christians, and testified to the helpfulness of the Floating Christian Endeavor Society.

Mrs. J. P. Kelton cordially extended the greetings of Woman's Army and Navy League, of Washington, which has so kindly and practically co-operated with Floating Christian Endeavor in furnishing organs and singing-books to naval ships, and for use of workers among naval men.

With more earnest consecration for soul-winning and service the coming year, "God Be With You" was sung, and "Mizpah" closed the conference.

Work Among The Life-Savers.

The announcement of an illustrated lecture, "Christian Endeavor Among the Life-Savers" as the subject, attracted an audience to the Fourth Presbyterian Church that jammed the large auditorium even beyond the doors. It was an immense gathering, and in spite of the heat earnest attention was paid to every word spoken.

Rev. J. Lester Wells, of Jersey City, N. J., was the lecturer, and he called upon Rev. S. Edward Young, chairman of the international committee on sea-work of the Christian Endeavor, to preside. After a few words by Rev. Mr. Young, the fourth annual report of the committee was read by Rev. Mr. Wells.

Full statistics have not yet been gathered on the work for life-savers, but from the United States, Dominion of Canada, the British Islands, and Germany the government reports have been received. The grand total for these four countries alone is 7,339. Nearly all the stations in the United States have been communicated with by the secretary, and up to date about half have reported. These reports reveal the fact that on the average there are five persons to each family. In the life-saving stations there are eight families represented in a crew, eleven in the light-ship, and one family in the lighthouse; thus 21,320 souls are connected with the life-saving stations, 6,215 in the light-ships, and 34,025 with lighthouses, making a total of 61,560 persons. And we can truthfully report over 100,000 souls who may or are coming in touch with the influence of Christian Endeavorers in the four countries mentioned.

Wherever feasible, Christian Endeavor Societies have visited the stations and held thousands of appropriate services for the surfmen. In many locations revivals are reported, and especially along the New Jersey coast, where the work for life-savers first commenced, many from the crews have been converted. The work of these heroes is well known. The name of Maebelle Mason, only fifteen years old, will be associated with Grace Darling in deeds of heroism as a life-saver. Her father was keeper of the Mamajuda lighthouse, Michigan, and while he was at church one Sabbath Day a signal for help came from a passing steamer to that station. Maebelle quickly sprang into the life-boat, and, with great fortitude, pulled the oars two miles to a drowning man. She drew him into her boat half dead, and brought him safely to the island. Well did she merit the gold medal (a Maltese cross) presented by the lake masters of Cleveland, O., and a silver medal presented by the government. But these are only samples of noble characters among our sisters who are charged with responsibility in the lighthouses.

The world-round representatives of the work in life-saving stations, lighthouses and light-ships can clasp hands and band the globe. The spirit of the Master, like an electric current, has gone from hand to hand and heart to heart in the progress of the work.

As the international committee enters upon the fifth year of our work, we would turn our ears to the future and strive to hear the voices as they come floating over the sea from life-saving stations, lighthouses, and life-ships of the world: voices that call, saying, "Come over and help us." "Come to our stations and conduct religious services." "Come and cheer us in our lonely and often dangerous tasks." We then turn to hear what Christian Endeavor has to say in answer, and the response is: "Here am I. Send me." Christian Endeavor has found the words of Jesus true: "Inasmuch as ye have done it unto one of the least of these, my brethren, ye have done it unto me."

Next followed the address of Mr. Wells, which was illustrated by stereopticon views in colors, giving a graphic description of the life and work of the brave men who man the life-saving stations, lighthouses and light-ships of the world, and what Christian Endeavor can do and is doing for their intellectual and spiritual good. Portrayed upon a large canvas screen in pleasing succession were views of dangerous coasts, collisions at sea, storms upon the ocean, ill-fated ships, throwing out life-lines, the rescue of passengers, and other heroic deeds. In connection with the views, Rev. Mr. Wells made a running explanatory and descriptive talk, which added greatly to the pleasure of the meeting. A large number of persons who had been uninformed in regard to this important branch of Christian Endeavor work undoubtedly profited to a great extent by the lecture.

Travellers' Union Conference.

Evangelist Ralph Gillam, of Malden, Mass., was leader of the Travellers' Union Conference, at the Fifteenth Street Presbyterian Church. While the attendance was small, there were several travelling-men present, and the meeting, which was a very impressive one, resulted beneficially. A service of song opened the meeting, the choir of female voices leading in the singing of " I Am Trusting in Thee, Lord Jesus."

Miss Carrie Burrill, president of the society of the Fifteenth Street Church, welcomed the visiting Endeavorers.

After Scriptural reading and prayer by Mr. George W. Brown and Mr. Henry Lee, and a solo by Miss Amelia Tillman, the Rev. Gillam opened the conference by telling his hearers that nine years ago he was a travelling-salesman, and therefore he knew something of the life of these men. The question now is how to reach them. He spoke of the many great temptations to which these men are subjected, and said that this organization is endeavoring to put them in a position to have them resist these temptations and save their souls.

Mr. H. W. Johnson, a travelling-salesman for a Philadelphia firm, who was present, gave his experience, and suggested a means of helping his fellow travellers. There are 380,000 drummers, most of them between twenty-five and thirty years old. "They are the flower of the men," he said, "sharp and intelligent, and if they constituted a drilled army they would be invincible in battle. But," he added, "I am sorry to say there are but few of them who have knowledge of their God," and he said he was glad to know that this organization is making a noble effort to save them. He told of a plan to send invitations to travelling-men at the different hotels for them to attend service on Sunday, and he remembered that on one occasion when this plan was practised, more hotel people attended church than had ever done so before.

Mr. George W. Brown said he thought this was one of the best movements he had ever heard of. He told his hearers that Christians who do not go out in the byways and hedges, and to the hotels, are selfish. "Keep your Endeavor pledge," he said, "and you will seek to save every one, including the travelling-men, and when the end shall come it will be well with your soul."

Brief addresses were made, and the meeting closed with a service of song and benediction by the leader.

FRIDAY EVENING.

Tent Williston.

For the first time during the Convention, Tent Williston was used Friday evening for a meeting-place. It was no small task to put up the big stretch of canvas that went down in the storm of Wednesday, but a big force of workmen was put at it, and before sunset the finishing touches were completed, and all was ready at last. As if to celebrate the occasion, an immense congregation gathered, and the exercises were marked by the greatest fervor and enthusiasm. In opening the exercises Secretary Baer paid a high tribute to the energy of the Committee of '96 in so quickly raising the tent.

Mr. Ira D. Sankey was to have led the meeting, but he was compelled to leave town in the afternoon, and in his absence Secretary Baer conducted the service, which, like those in the other tents, was on the topic "Saved to Serve." The opening prayer was made by Capt. H. B. Shaw, the superintendent of the seventh district of the United States life-saving service, coast of Florida. He is an active member of the Christian Endeavor Society. Mr. P. P. Bilhorn, by special request, gave as a solo "Sweet Peace."

The first speaker of the evening was Rev. S. Edward Young, of Newark, N. J., who is in charge of the work among the life-savers. Mr. Young is a young man of pleasing personality and address, and his talk presented an eloquent word-picture of the conditions and needs of the brave men who risk their lives to save others.

After Mr. Young's address the big chorus and the audience sang the stirring hymn, " Throw Out the Life-Line." " Sing it as you never did before," said Mr. Bilhorn. And they did. Mr. Young's address had worked his hearers up to a high pitch of enthusiasm, and such an appropriate hymn as this gave them an excellent opportunity to express their feelings. " Throw out the life-line,"—it was an earnest prayer in song to bring assistance to those unfortunates who are sinking in a sea of temptation.

"Christian Endeavor and Missions" was the theme of an eloquent address by Rev. J. E. Pounds, D.D., pastor of the Central Christian Church, of Indianapolis, Ind.

Address of Rev. J. E. Pounds, D.D., Indianapolis, Ind.

Let me give some reasons for affirming that the Endeavor Society is essentially missionary in its nature ; that missionary work is not something it may do, but something it must do ; and I suggest that this is true because the Endeavorer makes daily study of the great missionary book of the world, for no one who reads the Word constantly enough to get its real meaning can fail to have the missionary spirit. The Word of God is quick and quickening. I pray for more faith in it,— a faith like that of Jesus. Perhaps there have not arisen in Israel prophets of greater faith in the truth than Luther and Carey and Raikes unto this day. But what was their faith compared with that of the Man of Nazareth,— he who, living between the sectarianism and superstition of the Jew on the one hand and the idolatry and sin of the Gentile on the other, gathered twelve unlearned men about him and taught them apart of the truth? And when eleven of them partially understood what they heard and feebly accepted it, he confidently declared that the problem of the world's salvation was solved, its redemption from sin begun. The " It is finished " of the Cross is to me the sublimest word of history, sacred or profane ; and to doubt that he who reads God's Word every day will be active in missionary work, which is taught on every page of it, is to doubt the power of truth itself.

Some have been afraid that the Endeavorers would not be loyal to the teaching of their respective denominations. But if humbly reading the Bible every day will not make the young people of any church loyal to its teaching, then I tremble for that denomination; and if every young man and woman in the world could be induced to make that pledge and keep it, then we might stand on the hill-top and shout home to God, " The victory is won, for the earth is full of the knowledge of the Lord, as the waters cover the sea."

Again, the Endeavor Society is essentially missionary because of its definition of Christianity,—that it is a service. " Trusting for strength" suggests the performing of labor rather than the forming of dogmas; and " striving to do what He would like to have me do " implies action rather than sentiment, and there is more religion in motion than emotion or commotion. Various definitions of Christianity prevail, with as various results. Many think it a sort of life insurance company, and so seek it as a good place in which to die ; this seems passing strange when we consider how very dead they are already. Some believe it to be a resting-place, and thus they seek in it what they call a "church home ;" and they seem to think of a "church home" much as a dog views his kennel,—a good place to sleep and growl in. Others consider church membership to be a ticket on a through express train to heaven, with no stops, sure to arrive on time in the grand station; and all such want to ride on a *free pass* and in the *sleeping*-car. The kingdom of heaven is thought by many to be meat upon which they may feed their ambition for personal renown, and so grow great. Others look upon it as drink to satisfy the thirst for social position. " The four hundred " must greatly change their opinions before they will be ravished by the thought of a heaven which contains "ten thousand times ten thousand," among whom Lazarus has the place of honor, the bosom of Abraham. The Church has been thought to mean ecclesiastical power, a synonym of which is "pope." The Endeavorer believes that Christianity is service of the Saviour, the result of which will be the conversion of the world to the Christ.

Another reason for saying the Endeavor Society is missionary is because of its spirit of obedience. "Striving to do whatever He would like to have me do" is so much like " Lord, what wilt thou have me to do?" that the Endeavorer will be like Paul, zealous for the conversion of the whole world. I once overheard a man say to another, concerning a young clergyman, " Yes, he has studied theology, but he has not taken orders yet;" and using the word in a different sense, it may serve as a definition of a Christian Endeavorer,— one who has taken "orders;" one who, believing in the divine right of the King of heaven and earth to give orders, has taken them to execute, not to argue about. " Theirs not to reason why, theirs but to do and die." It is high treason to argue concerning a command; and treason, being a capital crime, is punishable with spiritual death. There have been plenty in the Church willing to give orders, but too few to take them. But Endeavorers are learning obedience, both in letter and in spirit, and so they are going into all the world, and will go more and more.

And since the Endeavor Society must do missionary work, if true to itself, we should consider how it can best do it. As a rule, the best way to work is through the regular missionary boards of the Church. Let individual societies do all the special work they will, or can be persuaded to do, but let it *be special* work. By all means let us have some particular work for our societies to unite in doing, but let it be selected, or at least managed, by the general boards. I have several reasons for saying this. One is that it is in harmony with the fundamental idea of Christian Endeavor that it is a society in and for and through the Church; this principle is cardinal,— it is vital. The reason why the Society exists at all is the reason why it exists as it is. To train young converts for more spiritual living and efficient service in and for the Church is its mission. There can be no higher calling; and to do this well is surely a sufficient work for any one organization. But some who do not understand what the real work of the Society is, or else do not appreciate the importance of such work, think that if it does no special work it is really doing nothing. They view it as a Niagara of power, beautiful to look at, but entirely wasted; and being "practical," as they call it, they hasten to dig power tunnels and set this "wasted force" to doing the work *they* want done. President Clark says, "We have come to the 'grind-my-axe' period of the Christian Endeavor." He is surely right, for it seems that every man with an axe — and every hobbyist has at least one — wants it ground at the Endeavor grindstone. I attribute this rush of business to the scarcity of good grindstones, for it is surprising how few organizations are capable of really helping a cause; and when a man invents a new reform or a novel plan for "saving the masses," he looks around for some means of advancing it to success. If the Endeavor Society will accept it, the thing is done. The glory of this young Society is its strength. This strength is all expended in doing the work to which God has called it; but the Philistines of glittering theories and petty reforms want amusement; and, can they but blind this Samson to his real mission, they will set him to breaking sticks and carrying loads for them, and he will himself perish in the ruin that must surely follow. But, thank God, the leaders of the movement understand this, so there is no real danger, for the principle of working in and for and through the local church will be maintained. And then the regular church boards are already the missionary boards of the Endeavor Society, for the Endeavorers are represented in every regular church offering. The amount reported by the secretaries as coming from the Christian Endeavor Societies is only a tithe of what they have given to missions. They give with the Church, first of all, and this is the best way for them to give; it trains them to regular and systematic giving, which is more to be desired than much fine gold. And because the regular boards are our boards they are managing our special work, or we manage it through them. Thus the work does not fall a prey to designing men.

But hear another reason,— the most important I have to offer. Endeavorers must work through the regular missionary boards, that they may learn to do so. Suppose they did nothing but special work for the next ten years. By that time the number of those who are supporting the Church missionary work will be largely diminished, and then what is to become of the general work? For if our Endeavorers be not trained to work for and through the missionary societies for the next ten years, they will not be in as vital sympathy with them as we could wish, for where our treasure is there will all our hearts be also. After a century of effort to get the older people into sympathy with co-operative work let us not make the fatal mistake of alienating the young people by giving them work to do in some other way. He who does so will be no true friend to either Christian Endeavor or missions.

It might also be said that having our Endeavor work in common with all the Church is more in harmony with the Christian union spirit of the Society. On the night of Gethsemane, the eve of Calvary, Jesus prayed the Father that his people might be one. God will answer this, the most earnest prayer of his only Son, as soon as we, his people, are willing. I speak it reverently. Christian Endeavor is the John the Baptist of to-day, standing in the wilderness of sectarianism and crying, "Prepare ye the way of the Lord, make his paths straight, for the kingdom of heaven is at hand."

And the last reason I would suggest for doing our work through the regular church channels is that it **is in** harmony with the humble spirit of Christian Endeavor. It was of humble beginning, and of humble purpose; it was born to service; it serves the Sunday school; it serves the prayer meeting; it serves the Church in every way,— by attending all the services; by financial support; by winning thousands to the Church and preserving tens of thousands who are already Christians. If it be true of organizations, as of individuals, that the greatest is the servant of all, then Christian Endeavor is the greatest of all societies; and if it ever falls, which God forfend, it will be by ambition; for when it shall seek to rule instead of serve, its candlestick will be removed out of its place. The Society is of humble birth; the pastor of the Williston Church was of humble spirit; and when the Lord shall come, bringing his reward with him, and shall crown William Carey, the apostle to the heathen, and Robert Raikes, the apostle to the children, he may have a coronet of no less brightness for Francis E. Clark, the apostle to young Christians. And the noble thing about all of these is that no one of them tried to form a great organization, or do a heroic deed; but when the Pharisees of the Church were bringing their showy gifts of theological arguments and elaborate schemes for "saving the masses," Carey and Raikes and Clark came and cast in their two mites of consecration and service,— their all. Their coming was unobserved by all who were in the temple, except only the Man of Nazareth. By blessing the work so largely he has said, "These have given more than they all." I rejoice to serve a Master who sees such gifts.

We might also consider, in the third place, the spirit in which the missionary work of Christian Endeavor should be done. In a spirit of joy — joy is characteristic of Christian Endeavor, as of mission work. Endeavor work is winsome; it is pleasant. I like Christian Endeavor because I like it. I don't like everything that I like, because some things that I enjoy are not wholesome in their effects; but when I do like a thing, I like it all the better because I like it; and in missionary work is found the deepest of even the Christian joys. It is the experience of the great truth, "It is more blessed to give than to receive." The missionary has fellowship with the Christ in the joy of the cross: "Who for the joy set before him"— the joy of seeing the world redeemed more and more — "endured the cross, despising the shame;" the joy the missionary felt when he declared that he could not understand how heaven could be heaven without some heathen to save.

Again, the work must be done in the spirit of faith, or "trusting in the Lord," as the pledge has it. "Business in Christianity" is becoming quite a motto. It is a good one; but the work of missions cannot be carried on successfully on strictly business principles. We need principles as accurate and careful as those of business, but as large as those of faith. Business principles do not make enough account of the "silent partner," the "Lo, I am with you alway." The business eye does not see the invisible gold and silver that are in the treasury of the Church. Had Carey waited for business principles he would never have gone to India, or Judson to Burmah. By faith we are saved, and by faith we save. The armies of God, when they marched by faith, have never lacked supplies. Christ is present to multiply the loaves and fishes. All we have to do to feed men is to help them to get hungry; for "Blessed are they which do hunger and thirst after righteousness; for they shall be filled." The missionary boards will have no bother to pay their bills if they only make them big enough. There will be no trouble to fill our mission churches to overflowing if we only build them large enough; for if we will but prove the Lord, he will open the windows of heaven and pour out such a blessing as there shall not be room to receive.

And then the work must be done in a spirit of self-sacrifice,—and genuine sacrifice, too,—not the giving-up of a few unwholesome luxuries, but the giving of some of the capital of our money, some of the necessaries of life. A business man remarked to me recently, "Religion is a very expensive luxury." I intimated that I considered it one of the necessities of life, rather than a luxury. "But," said he, "you know a man must live." "No," I replied, "I did n't know that." John the Baptist did not know it; the martyrs were not aware of it; Peter and John, before the Sanhedrin, did not declare it; but they did say, "We cannot but — we must — speak the things we have seen and heard;" their Master did not teach it when he said, "It is expedient for you that I go away." The cross of Christ forever contradicts it. We *must* preach the Gospel, and then if we have enough left to buy a loaf of bread, we may eat it and be innocent of the blood of all men.

But what can we sacrifice, money? Yes, we understand that, for except we leave houses and lands we can not be his disciples. Something of self also. I like the old expression, "To spend and to be spent." One who saw Christ die on Calvary spake a truth which, had he understood the meaning of his own words and spoken them in earnest, would have made him immortal: "He saved others, himself he cannot save." The same may be said of his disciple. But what of self can we give up? Something of intellect, perhaps; not that we should become intellectually weak, but intellectually indifferent, not caring whether we be considered great preachers or not; willing to become fools for Christ's sake; willing to be considered crazy, even if our madness be not attributed to much learning, as was that of Paul; willing to speak the language of the slums where that is best understood; yea, even learn to live and think in that language and forget the other, as Judson forgot his English. One of the greatest errors of Christians is that they insist upon doing their own thinking concerning matters of which God has spoken. When the Christ says, "Go into all the world," some have dared to express opinions concerning the wisdom of such a course. There is a neglected command in the New Testament. I have never heard it even quoted, except for the sake of the other parts of the verse: "Thou shalt love the Lord thy God with all thy . . . . *mind*." We will never take the world for the Master until we love him enough with our minds to trust his wisdom above our own.

We must sacrifice something of the will, too. Paul subscribed his letters in a peculiar way; not "yours truly," nor "yours etc.," but "Paul, a servant (literally, bond slave) of Jesus Christ." A bond slave had no desires, no will, no choice, no method, no motive, no end of his own; but when his owner said Go, he went. We might sacrifice something of natural love also. Give up home, friends, family, the graves of our fathers, to live in a strange land,—there to die, and to be buried there.

And then we may have to sacrifice something of spiritual culture. When the Master went apart for an hour's spiritual refreshment and communion with the Father, if the multitude followed after, he turned and taught them instead;

and some of us may have to fill positions in life and business and society not the most conducive to spiritual growth. We must do it for Christ's sake, and only satisfy our impatient hearts with the thought that we shall be like him when we see him face to face.

And then we must deny ourselves our self-denial, and give what we give cheerfully. Quit boasting to ourselves and others of our sacrifices; for when we have done all, we have only done that which it was our duty to do. We should wash our faces that we may not appear unto men to fast; we must take our martyrdom to the stake; give up giving up: sacrifice our sacrifice; be not only too proud to be proud, but too humble to be humble; counting it joy that we are permitted to suffer for His name's sake.

Does sacrifice seem hard to you? Does it seem like a hard saying, that "he that loveth father, mother, son and daughter more than me is not worthy of me"? I am sure it will not seem so when you consider the last words, "not worthy of me." Then, O Lord, those who forsake these things are in some sense worthy of thee. Worthy of him! O my soul, who is! O our Saviour, may we be! God forgive us if the thought shall unduly exalt us! Shall we not count all things but refuse that we may win Christ, and at last be found worthy to be with him, where he is?

Following Dr. Pounds's address came another appropriate incident, the presentation of a handsome silk banner, suitably inscribed, to the local union which contains the largest number of members who have given not less than one-tenth of their incomes to the Lord. The presentation was made by Rev. S. B. Meeser, of Worcester, Mass. Mr. Meeser's presentation remarks were of a very high order and aroused enthusiasm. For two years past the banner has gone to Cleveland, but this year the New York Local Union reported eight hundred and fifty-eight such members, and the banner went to it. When the announcement was made a hymn was started by the New York delegation. The feeling was intense. As a sort of relief some of the New York delegates set up a cheer : —

> "Rah! Rah! Rah!
> Who are we?
> N. Y. Y. P. S. C. E."

The banner was received by Mr. W. L. Amerman, president of the New York Local Union, who made a few brief remarks, expressing the intention of the union to do even better next year, while an enthusiastic New Yorker mounted the platform and waved the big blue and white flag of the union. Then came some singing by the octette from Hampton Institute, and chorus and audience sang "Marching to Zion."

Rev. J. Wilbur Chapman, D.D., the pastor of Bethany Presbyterian Church, of Philadelphia, was then introduced to deliver the closing address of the evening, on the subject "Christian Endeavor an Evangelistic Force."

Address of Rev. J. Wilbur Chapman, D.D., Philadelphia, Pa.

It is the opinion of thoughtful people in all branches of society that we are coming on to some sort of a great crisis. Some believe that this is the coming of our Lord; others, that it is to be a great uprising of the working forces; while others simply stand in wonder and amazement and look for they know not what.

I believe that we are at the beginning of what may be called a great evangelistic era, and yet this is to be a work not such as has been conducted in the past, but a work peculiarly identified with the pastors of the churches, the members of the churches, and the societies of the churches. In saying this, I put no mark of disrespect upon God's credited evangelists, for I believe that the office of divine appointment; but in the natural order of things, with the changing of other systems and methods, this new evangelistic era is to be under the control of the Church of Jesus Christ and her specially appointed leaders. In this work the Christian Endeavor Society is to play no small part. I know of at least five cities of importance in our land already planning to enter upon such a campaign with the beginning of the Church life in the fall; and I am profound in the conviction that the season of 1896 and 1897 shall witness such an outpouring of God's Spirit, and such an ingathering of such as shall be saved, as we have not seen for many a year.

But what can the Christian Endeavor Society do? In the first place, if the pastor is to be instrumental in this work he will need to have done for him what the people did for Moses; namely, to have his hands uplifted. This may be accomplished by means of prayer. No man in the pulpit can be strong in the best use of that word if he is without this atmosphere; and no man in the pulpit would be weak if a faithful band of people should lift him up to God for a special manifestation of his Spirit. This is the first move for the Christian Endeavor Society,— pray for your pastor.

Second, organize praying bands for the lost, and then be definite about your petitions; ask God for certain individuals, and ask him for them at a certain time. Believe that what you ask you will receive, and set it down as a rule that when one begins to pray for the unsaved he naturally turns to make an effort to help God to answer that prayer; and if the Christian Endeavor Society of the world could be pledged to pray for the unsaved men and women of the world, this year would witness not one Pentecost, but a hundred, and that would mean three hundred thousand souls for Christ.

Third, as a preliminary to a special series of meetings in a community, let the Christian Endeavor Societies carry the Gospel to the people who will not go to church to receive it. Every city and town in this country ought to have during the summer months, also September and October, numerous outdoor services, where direct appeals can be made to the unsaved who seem to be indifferent, but who actually are longing to know the peace of God. This was the way the Saviour worked; and if on a certain day the whole Christian Endeavor Society would turn out from the Church to preach upon the streets, its highways and its byways, in one day there would be thousands of souls brought to Christ, and tens of thousands more deeply interested.

Fourth, at the first favorable opportunity make an effort to unite the churches of your cities or your towns in a straight-out campaign in behalf of the lost. The counsel of the pastors will be needed in this; and in behalf of these men of God I am prepared to say that hundreds and thousands of them over the country wait to-day for the first word of encouragement which would lead them to spring into the very thickest of the fight, and there is hardly a minister of the Gospel in the land to-day but what I believe would be willing to enter heart and soul in this service if he were sure simply of the support of his own people. Behold, I say unto you, Lift up your eyes and look on the fields, for they are white already to harvest; and I summon the great Christian Endeavor Society to follow the Master more closely than ever in these days that are before us, so that this year upon which we now enter may be the very best of our lives in point of victory.

Calvary Church.

Another great meeting was held at Calvary Baptist Church. Anticipating a crowd, Endeavorers and their friends began to arrive before seven o'clock; and when Rev. Ralph W. Brokaw, of Springfield, the presiding officer, opened the evening's exercises, there was scarcely a vacant seat in the entire church. The first twenty minutes were devoted to a praise service, and then Rev. Dr. Greene, pastor of Calvary Church, conducted the devotional exercises.

The first topic, "Frank Talks with Our Associate Members," was divided into two parts. The first address was "Who Should Do It?"

Address of Rev. J. L. Campbell, D.D., New York City.

Associate members occupy a peculiar and interesting relation to our societies. If there are many of them, it indicates that the meetings are attractive, reaching those who are outside and bringing them in. Their number, or lack of number, is a sort of thermometer which shows a growing or a declining organization; then, too, they constitute in themselves a most important class. While they do not make any profession of religion, they are so far favorably disposed to it that they come out and attend the weekly gatherings. The society of Christians, the singing, the speaking, and all that goes to make up a meeting has sufficient attraction to cause them to leave other company and be found there. Many of them are like the young ruler,—lacking only one thing. They will not remain in this position; either they will before long come out on the Lord's side, or they will soon grow weary and drift away and become lost to us. Of all persons anywhere they should be the object of our deepest solicitude, and most fervent prayers. They are of good character; they are young; they are interested; they are yet unsaved.

1. Who should speak to them? The pastor. He stands at the head and his example will be contagious. The strong wish of every true pastor is to get into thorough touch with all the young people of his congregation; he will make any possible sacrifice to bring this about. My friend Uncle Boston Smith visited a Minnesota village where the young people were living in total disregard of the churches and the Sabbath. He went in among them, played baseball with them, helped them win a match game, got hold of their sympathies, and then they came to church and large numbers of them were converted to God. Being crafty, he caught them with guile. Other ministers resort to other means, social or intellectual, so as to get near their young people. Once their confidence is won, the steps after that become comparatively easy. No one ought to know how to deal with souls as a pastor can; it is the work to which his life is consecrated; no matter how eloquently he may preach, it is the man who does the hand-to-hand personal work who is pre-eminently successful as a soul-winner.

2. Who should do it? The members of the Church. The Christian Endeavor Society stands for Christ and the Church. The Church should also stand for Christian Endeavor. One of the dangers of organizations of this kind is that the young people may constitute one group, and the rest of the Church another group, and that both may gather themselves in opposite camps. With wonderful wisdom, the leaders of the Christian Endeavor movement have sought in every way to prevent any such line of cleavage. One of the most vital and cardinal principles emphasized in every way is the duty of unqualified, unswerving loyalty to the Church. There is a corresponding duty, too, on the other hand. The members of our churches must not stand aloof from the young people; there must be the completest reciprocity; action and reaction should be equal; every chasm should be filled up, and none ever suffered to exist. The future pastors, and deacons, and trustees, and editors, and teachers are to-day in our Christian Endeavor Societies. Our interest in them is simply our interest in the future of the cause of Christ in the world.

3. Who should do it? The active members. They have as their peculiar work the spiritual interests of the associate members; they belong to their own years, and come into direct contact with them. In every step and act of life we are molding character and shaping the destiny of those by whom we are surrounded,—savors of life unto life, or savors of death unto death. A blithe and merry bricklayer one gloomy day was working upon a scaffold, building the wall of a house, and all the while he wrought he was singing and whistling as

bright as a lark.   Little dreamed he up yonder at his daily task that the melan-
choly eye of Thomas Carlyle was sadly watching him from a dark chamber, and
that his unconscious, cheerful example led him to re-write and then complete
his great work on the French Revolution.   Harriet Beecher Stowe, who has
just died, and her brother Henry both received their bias toward the colored
race through the modest, unconscious influence of a black man named Charles
Smith, who was a servant in the farm-parsonage of their distinguished father.
How vast the influence of that humble man in the destiny of this nation !   Had
the impression made by his life been the opposite of what it was, the history of
our country might have been different to-day.   The humblest Christian Endeavorer before me in his or her most unsuspecting moments may be touching springs
that will shape the future of the nation and change the history of the world.
Solemn, stupendous thought !   Not simply what I say, but what I do; not
simply what I do, but what I am,— this is the measure of my responsibility.
We are not going to heaven or to hell alone.   Every conversation that you have
with an associate member, every contact of life with life, of character with
character, of magnet with steel, will endure

> " When the sun grows cold and the stars are old,
> And the leaves of the judgment book unfold."

It is yours, therefore, to so live before them that everything you do and say
will tell the unconverted about you " more about Jesus."

4.   Who should do it ?   Those Christians among you who are personal friends
of the unsaved.   Andrew found Simon Peter, and brought him to Jesus; Philip
found Nathaniel; Martha found Mary.   There is some one over whom you have
more influence than all the rest of the Church put together.   Use that influence
for God ; tell your own experience,— how God first spoke peace to your soul.
This was what Paul did.   When they brought him before courts and kings, he
rehearsed the way that Jesus met him at noonday near the gate of Damascus,
and how he was saved.   This was an argument they could never answer.   Do
it with your unconverted friend, and a blessing will rest upon your own soul,
and God will use you in bringing others to his feet.

The next division of the topic was " When Should It Be Done ? "

Address of Rev. W. H. Robinson, D.D., Englewood, Ill.

I am to speak to you to-night on " When Should It Be Done ? "   I have
three points that will enable you to know how fast I am using up the time.
The first one is that we should decide the question by our own condition,— that is
to say, we should have a frank talk with an associate member when we have
been impressed by some great truth of emotion ourselves.   It don't do to talk
to an associate member, or any other young person,— and the younger the person you are talking to the truer it is,— on religious subjects, unless you feel it
yourself.

Once there was a very worldly mother who had trouble to make her child
mind, and a good, unworldly mother spoke to that worldly mother and told her
to use moral suasion with her boy and she could manage him.   She said, as
some people say, " Go to; now I will be religious."   She said to her own self,
" Go to; now I will use that kind of a machine.   I will use moral suasion on
that boy of mine."   So she thought up all the good things she could.   She got
that little boy on her lap and talked machine-talk to him.   When she got
through, her closing appeal was, " Now, Walter, you will do better, won't you?"
" Why, ma, all the time you were talking your upper jaw did n't move at all,
and your under jaw kept a-going all the time."   He was an observant boy.   He
knew that she was talking for the sake of talking, and he watched how that
kind of machinery worked.

So then, when you are going to talk to an associate member, be sure that you
have within you something that fills and thrills your own soul.   Then is when
to do it.   When you have a sense of worth of your own soul and the associate
member's soul, when you see that neither silver nor gold, nor the election of

Bryan nor the election of McKinley, when you see that nothing else is of any consequence at all, compared to your own soul, then is the time to talk to an associate member about his soul. And when you feel eternity near you, and it becomes real to you that that other world is so near that the sweet closing of an eye may bring you there, then is the time to talk to your associate member about eternity.

Point number two is that the question is also to be decided by the condition of the associate member.

" There is a tide in the affairs of men which, taken at the flood, leads on to fortune." And there is a tide in the affairs of the associate members, in his soul, which, taken at the flood, leads on to everlasting life with God and Jesus Christ. Neglected it may never, never again come. There is such a thing as opportunity. Take the associate member when he is in a susceptible mood. Jesus talked with people once about rejoicing, and when did he do it? Did he take them at a time when they were not enabled to be joyful? Oh, no. They had been through the villages of Galilee, the seventy, and they returned with joy. They had had some good fortune that they did not expect. They said, " Why, Lord, even the demons are subject to us! We tried, tremblingly, thy name upon them, and we were able to cast them out." He entered into their joy for a minute,— what tact! — and he said, " While you were passing out the little devils, the demons, I saw as in a vision the prince of devils, Satan himself, as lightning fall from heaven." It is glorious work we are in, but notwithstanding, in this rejoice not especially that the demons are subject unto you, but rather rejoice in your individual salvation, if you have it, that your names are written in the book of heaven.

Don't you know when any one is in great grief that is the time to say, " Your brother shall rise again," as He said to Martha? And he led her on and on until he said to her, " I am the resurrection and the life." So take the time when the associate member is susceptible. There are such times. They have their sorrows and their joys, and if you have a sympathetic heart kindled by a companionship with Him who had such strangely insertive sympathies with the sorrows of mankind, at a time when an associate member feels grief, just then tell him in that susceptible hour of the Man of sorrow, acquainted with grief. In their hour of gladness, when you see they are full of gladness, tell them of Him who was anointed with the oil of gladness above his fellows.

Take the associate member when he is alone. Some man has been writing a chapter in a book lately to the effect that Christianity now works with individuals, whereas heretofore people have been taken in masses. Not at all. God always began with one. He commenced with one man in the Garden of Eden, and it was not until later on that he even had the man's other self, the woman, there. He took one man, Abraham, and out of Abraham's seed he took Isaac, and from Isaac's children he took Jacob, and so on ; and through his one Son, Jesus Christ, he brought in redemption to the world.

Remember this: that Jesus did not hold an immense convention in a tent. Such things are good, but beware that you who attend these immense meetings from year to year do not think that big tent meetings or big church meetings are the chosen means of bringing the kingdom of God into the world. They are not. That is indicated when you see him taking Nicodemus alone by night, and the woman of Samaria alone by the well, and when Philip findeth Nathanael and bringeth him, one man, alone to the Christ. Get the associate member alone after meeting. I wish I might tell you of a tree,—I need no picture to see it,—one tree and one piece of sidewalk, seen dimly in the gloom, when my only sister said to me at a time of revival, which was not having more effect upon me than medicine upon a stone statue, " Willie, don't you care anything about these things? " That was the beginning.

Thirdly, let me say that you are to talk to the associate member whenever the Spirit moves you. I know that is used for a slang phrase, but you know that as that phrase came in its original meaning it is a very sacred one. Was it not when Philip was going down toward the south country, and the eunuch, a great authority in the court of the Queen of Ethiopia, had been to Jerusalem to worship and was returning? He sat in his chariot reading the Word of God and the Spirit of God said to Philip, " Draw nigh to this chariot," and so on. Does the Spirit of God ever say anything to you or to me? I think it does. I think the Holy Spirit is here now. I think that just as surely as the trade-winds blow across the sea, so surely does that Spirit which Jesus said was like the wind move in its great carrying tide over the ocean of human life. What we need to-day is to hoist the sails. I believe the light is forever shining upon you and me, only we do not put up the shutters. That is all we need. I believe that the river of God is forever about us, only it is so magnificent that we do not realize it.

There were some sailors once that had used up all the water of the ship. They saw another ship coming. They hailed the other ship with the signal of distress. The answer was, "What do you want?" "Water, water; we are choked for the want of water." " You are in the mouth of the Amazon; dip it up." I know that is an old story, but it applies most perfectly to this thing. The Spirit of God is ready to be given to you when you ask the Father for it.

I have done with these three points, and am ready to stop. All three of them sometimes come together. Sometimes the associate member is in a susceptible condition, and sometimes you have a great truth in your heart, and then also you are conscious and he is conscious of the movement of the unseen power which we call the Holy Ghost. Those are the great days when souls are born again.

And so, in answering this question, I should say, "Speak to the associate member; have a frank talk with him every day. Sunday is a good day. You know events make the calendar and the red days on it, and the calendar does not make the events. There was a Monday that is like our day Monday,—a sacred day in Jerusalem,—a common day. Men went about their business. There was no religion. It was not a worship day. It was a Monday. It was the first day of the week. Sacred day was over. The Sabbath was past, and just then Jesus rose from the dead. Search your Bible through, and find where Jesus says to transfer the Sabbath from the seventh day to the first day. You can not do it. What did it? What put those red letters on the calendar that mean Sabbaths? A mighty event. And so you can make any day — Monday, Tuesday, Wednesday, Thursday, Friday, Saturday — the holiest day in the week for any associate member by making it the day when Christ rose from the dead within their souls and unto new life, and transformed them into his likeness."

Do not keep after the same associate member all the time. I do not mean that when I say speak to him every day. Don't you be guilty of that machine-work of nagging at one soul all the time and saying, " James, don't you want to be a Christian?" and then the next day, " James, don't you want to be saved?" and so on and on. I used to hate those fellows that came after me that way. They never had any effect on me. Don't do that. That is not divine husbandry. John Sterling's father gave him some seeds, and John planted them, and the next morning he dug them up to see how they were getting along. Then he put them down again, and the next day he took them up to see how they were getting along again. Poor John Sterling! He could not wait.

When the soul of the associate member is in the right condition, and you are in the right condition, and the Holy Spirit moves you, speak to that soul, plant the seed in it, watch over it tenderly, carefully, lovingly, and let it rest until the rain of God shall come down on it,—the early and the later rain, perhaps,—and then after a while go and cultivate it a little. You do not hoe corn—or we did not when I was a boy, if I remember — more than once or twice before the crop comes.

When you have sown that seed go and try another soul, and another and another, and by the time you have got a certain distance it will be time to go back and cultivate again.

Mr. Fred S. Ball, of Montgomery, Ala., then conducted an interesting discussion concerning Endeavor work. He paid particular attention to the bringing into the fold of active membership the associate members of the different societies. He wanted to find out, for the benefit of himself and all Endeavorers, the different plans of the several societies for bringing about this much-desired end, and he called upon members and delegates present to explain how they did it. This invitation brought delegates from every part of the United States to their feet, who gave interesting data concerning the number of associate members in their respective societies, and their plans of transforming them into active members.

The meeting closed with an address by the Rev. Dr. Rufus W. Hufford, pastor of St. Matthew's Lutheran Church, of Reading, Pa. His subject was "Individual Responsibility for Soul-Winning."

Address of Rev. Rufus W. Hufford, D.D., Reading, Pa.

The subject before us is "Individual Responsibility for Soul-Saving." That is a most interesting subject when you come to think of it — a most important subject. It is oppressive in its earnestness,— individual responsibility for soul-saving. There was a time centuries ago when men were discussing the question as to whether people had souls or not. Some of the Jewish rabbis discussed the question as to whether women had souls or not. A Scotch writer has lately called attention to this : that it is the Lord Jesus who has enabled us to save, who has brought into this world the thought that the soul is worth something, and that it is always worth something, that we are ever to make an effort to save it. Jesus has brought that into the world. He illustrates it in this way : for a long time it was not known that there were any diamonds down at a certain place in Africa ; but once there was a bright stone discovered there. Some one kicked it, picked it up and looked at it, and found out that he had a diamond. He found out that those pebbles there were valuable.

A short time ago in our own land a man picked up a stone and threw it at a cow. He was driving his cow home and the cow was a little inclined to wander off to the bushes. He picked up a stone to throw at her to make her get back into the road. The stone seemed very heavy. He began to examine it. The weight of it startled him. He did not throw it at the cow. He took it home with him and had it examined and found it was very rich in gold. That man who was poor before that was very soon worth $100,000. He had found something that was very valuable right there in the road.

We have valuable souls all about us. We are living with them. They are growing up in our households. They are in our Sunday schools and Young People's Societies. They are in the Church and outside of it. They are on every street and highway. Wherever there is a human being there is one who has an immortal soul, that which is infinitely valuable ; and because it is infinitely valuable, the question comes to us as to our individual responsibility for saving souls.

In hastening on, I wish to call attention to just this. In the first place, recognizing the value of the soul, we ourselves are to feel that we are to put forth individual efforts to save it. When we talk about a soul being valuable, and working to save it, I think the first impression that is made upon the average person is, I wish I could get a chance to approach those people. The first impression is, If we could just collect around us those persons and begin to say what we have to say about their welfare ! That is the disposition ; that is the temptation ; but it is not the wise thing to do at all. We are talking about individual responsibility, and that presents two things. It is the individual who is responsible ; and in order to do his best work he must work upon the individual. It is a very great mistake to suppose that the best work is done, as has been said to-night, by getting people in the mass and talking to them there.

I think there has been an immense amount of time wasted by young men who have thought that they were suddenly called, without any particular amount of preparation, to become Moodys, and preach to the people. I think there has been a good deal of effort wasted just in that way. I do not under-rate, I trust, the efforts that are made in all of our societies. I believe any-body who has the opportunity and ability to talk a minute ought to talk a minute as it is given to him, or two minutes, or even five minutes. He ought not to kill the meeting by talking ten minutes, as a rule.

But there is something a great deal better than that. It is set forth in just these words, that we are to reach the individual,—the individual is to reach the individual. As has been said to-night, that was the Lord's own method. He who knew the value of the soul reached the soul as a rule in that way. He went to the woman at the well and talked with her. The disciples were sur-prised that he should do such a thing. They did not consider her soul as of any great value. They did not think it was to his credit or theirs that he should be seen talking to her. Yet he did talk with her, and his talk resulted in the salvation of her soul. There was a woman of lower repute even than she, and it was the Lord's teaching that saved her. Mary Magdalene, out of whom he cast devils, was the one who bore the intelligence first that Christ had risen from the dead.

He gives us this example of reaching the individual soul,— just hunting up some one and talking to that one. It is not a difficult thing to do. Every one can do something for them. We find them everywhere. It may be difficult to get a congregation together, but it is not difficult to find just one. I remember a young man, in a church over in Pennsylvania, who made up his mind that he would like to teach a Sunday-school class. He had never been a faithful Sun-day-school scholar at all; he had never had patience enough with his own teacher to attend regularly, and did not care enough for the teachings of the Bible to be a good scholar, but he wanted to teach a class. There are a good many such persons fond of having some degree of prominence in some way.

He wanted to teach a class. He asked permission to get up a class for him-self, as none was offered in the Sunday school. He thought he would hunt up those who would come in. Permission was given to him at once. He was told, "You can have your class; get it up and teach it." He spoke to a number of boys, and then on the following Sunday morning he came there and looked in. The boys had given him something of an evasive answer, I presume, a half-promise that meant nothing. When he came there in the morning and looked in, hoping to see his boys, he found the pew where they were to be just as his particular part of it had been when his teacher came to teach him. The boys were not there. He went back disappointed with his idea of teaching. He wanted to teach. He wanted that degree of prominence. There is something of that probably in the most of us. We like prominence; we like popularity. We like to have persons around us who will recognize us as a little higher and wiser than they are.

There is nothing of this kind needed in what we have before us here to-night. As we think of the individual responsibility of soul-saving it brings to our minds just this: as we have opportunity let each one win one. There is a "win-one" society in this country somewhere. I don't know just where the chapters of it are, but there is such a society, and the very inspiration of it is that one so I shall try to win another. That is a good thing to do. It would be an excellent thing to make the effort right in one's own household.

You would be surprised if you were to know how in many professed Chris-tian families there are unconverted young people, who do not go to Church and who are getting farther and farther away from the Church, caring less about the Church. Yet the fathers and mothers in those families may be very devoted to their church; they may go quite regularly themselves; they may take part in various meetings of the church; but somehow they are not able to reach those right in their own family. What is the matter? They have not gone about it in the right way; they have not felt as deeply as they ought to feel, in all human probability, that it is their duty to win those who are right there at home.

Make it your business in the various relations of this life to pick out one here and one there and follow him up with prayer and talk to him as you have the opportunity, and show kindness to him, so that he will know you feel an interest in him.

You will remember that in the Old Testament Scriptures there is a prophecy of a grand time when the influence of the Spirit of God shall be felt, and it is said that one of the signs of that time shall be that the hearts of the fathers shall turn to the children, and the hearts of the children shall turn to the fathers. That would be a most excellent result,— for fathers and mothers to feel such an interest in their own children that they could go to them and confess mistakes that they had made in their bringing-up; that they should acknowledge the fact that they have permitted their children to go away from them.

I remember a meeting that I attended not long ago where an old man stood up and said something like this: " Mothers can have an influence over their children. Sunday-school teachers can have an influence over their children. Pastors can have an influence over the different families of the congregation; but it seems to me a very difficult thing for the father to talk to his own sons and daughters about religion." He said, " There seems to be such a chasm between them that you can hardly pass over it." I replied to him in a few words afterwards that there was a time when that was not so, and in every family there is a time when that is not so. There is a time when the father, if he is religious, can talk to his son or daughter about religion without any trouble. He can talk with them about God, about the Lord Jesus who died for them; about what they owe him, and about this life that is passing; about how much he cares for them, and about when this life is over he will meet them in another and better world.

One of the finest things in all literature is the letter written by Horace Bushnell to his own daughter. He was in Europe and seemed not to know whether he would return again. He said to her, " I expect to see you again; but we know not what a day may bring forth. I hope to meet you in that better world, and in order that this may be so we must both be followers of Christ. You must choose him for your Saviour, as I have chosen him for mine." It is always possible in every household for a father or a mother to talk to their children. Don't let the chasm form at all. Keep close to your children and to your Sunday-school classes. Sometimes we see classes grow up and the teachers keep right along with them. The class goes right into the church. In other classes the scholars seem to go away from the teacher. The teacher's influence does not seem to reach them. Somehow the teacher has not gotten hold of the mind and learned to control it. When they are little boys and girls then you can talk to them; then you can reach them and bring influence to bear upon them; and if that is kept up wisely and persisted in prayerfully it will at last succeed.

This individual responsibility for soul-saving — we ought to feel it. That is the first and most important thing; let it be in our hearts that it must be done —that something must be accomplished. It is said concerning John Knox, that he said, " Give me Scotland or I die." He must have that nation saved to the Lord. We can take a far smaller contract. We can say, " Give me one soul; let me follow it up; let me save it for the Lord Jesus Christ." We ought to feel this individual responsibility. We ought to follow up those with whom we come in contact. We ought not to feel that it is ours to gather them together, but we should reach them individually, as the Lord Jesus Christ reached them.

The Scripture tells us that " he that winneth souls is wise, and they that be wise shall shine as the brightness of the firmament." It does take true wisdom to win a soul to Christ. You can win a soul to yourself. You can bring a little circle around you and make them love you and follow you, and yet that may not mean that any one of them has been won to the Lord. That may not mean that any one of them has left the sin of this world and entered into the service of Christ. You can win people to the Church, and still you may not have won them to Christ. You can have a great mass collected, and hold them for years, and then they may melt away like snow under the sun. You may win them to your Christian Endeavor, and hold them there for a while. You may feel that it is very interesting to keep them there and have them join in your singing ; and yet they may go away, not one of them having been won to Christ.

"He that winneth souls must be wise." He must put himself out of sight. He must behold Christ as the Saviour of the soul, and he must make the soul feel that in order to have a hope of life everlasting it must be by a complete self-surrender to Jesus as Saviour, and as Lord and as Master. Then, when they have been won, when they have been gathered in, we treasure them up. We think about them. We pray for them. We feel as the Apostle Paul did when he said that these were the trophies of his work ; that he felt that these were the very crown of his rejoicing,— those who had been saved through his preaching and teaching, and brought to the Lord.

First Presbyterian Church.

The presiding officer at the First Presbyterian Church was Rev. Dr. M. F. Troxell, of Springfield, Ill., who is the vice-president of the Illinois Union. The evening began with a song service, after which Rev. Edward Warren, of Washington, led the devotional exercises.

The general topic for the evening was "Our Work." The first speaker's topic was "Duties To Be Done."

Address of Mr. J. Edgar Knipp, Baltimore, Md.

The common, every-day duties of life must be performed. Such duties are incumbent upon us all, whether we are officers, chairmen of committees, or individual active members of a Christian Endeavor Society. As a river is composed of drops of water, a dollar of pennies, and an hour of minutes, so life consists of *little* duties, characters are formed by *daily* actions. The student who would become a scholar does not pass by one mighty bound from the bottom of the ladder to the top, but attains the desired goal by performing heartily the *daily* tasks assigned by his instructors. The beautiful rose which is admired by all does not develop in one day ; first a bunch of very small leaves appears at the end of the stem ; a few days later the tip of a tiny bud is seen ; this gradually grows larger and larger, and as the weeks go by it changes into a beautiful rose. Its development was slow. Daily there were supplied to it moisture from the ground, light and heat from the rays of the sun, material from the earth, and carbonic acid gas from the atmosphere. From such common, ordinary materials the lovely rose was formed.

In the same way the faithful performance of our daily tasks transforms our characters into Christlikeness.

Of these common daily duties which we must fulfil a very important one is morning secret prayer. As Endeavorers we have promised Christ to make it the rule of our lives to pray every day. We all need to talk over with our Heavenly Father in the morning the work of the coming day ; for the Christian who waits until he is about to retire before he communes with God is like the engineer who starts to make a trip with a small supply of water in the boiler, and expects to fill it up at the end of the trip. He is very apt to need, before he reaches his destination, more steam than the water he has will supply, and a long delay and great inconvenience will result.

We ought to tell our Father in heaven the details of our work and the difficulties which will beset us ; we need to ask him for guidance and help in overcoming the temptations and difficulties that will come upon us.

By thus telling God the details of our work, and by asking his help in performing it, our strength will be renewed and we shall realize more fully and more constantly the presence of Christ with us during the day.

Many of the failures in our daily living are due to the lack of morning communion with God. As Christian workers we do much sowing, but often we reap small harvests. The cause is found in the fact that we have not been a sufficient time alone with God. The busier Christ was, the more time he spent in prayer. He passed the whole night in communing with his Father previous to the choice of the twelve apostles and the preaching of the Sermon on the Mount. At another time, when he was busy preaching the Gospel in Capernaum, and he was engaged in healing the throngs of sick persons which pressed about him, it is recorded of him that he "arose a great while before day and went apart into a solitary place and there prayed."

Sometimes when we have a very busy day's work before us, we are apt to hurry through our morning prayer. But it is in just such times as this that we ought to draw very near to our Father, for if we do not, the tendency will be to forget him during the day, when we are actively engaged in our business, or household duties, or even in Christian work.

Martin Luther, upon being asked one time by a friend what his plans were for the following day, replied, "Work, work from early until late. In fact, I have so much to do that I shall spend the first three hours in prayer."

He did not maintain the heavenly life in his soul without continually separating himself from man and communing with his Father. If he needed such secret prayer in the midst of his work, how much more do we! As he did, we ought also to spend much time in secret prayer. Perhaps many of us have heard of J. Hudson Taylor's method. As he is kept busy at work continually during the day, and since there is always some one wishing to confer with him about the work, his habit is to rise between three and four o'clock in the morning in order to spend two or three hours alone with God. Is it any wonder that his life is so fruitful?

In addition to daily, intimate, morning, secret prayer, we must commune with God by reading his Word. He who enters upon a day's work after praying but without reading God's Word has omitted the more valuable part of his private devotions. It is more important that God speak to us than that we speak to him. This is what he does when we *earnestly* and *reverently* search the Scriptures. Like Samuel, we then say, "Speak, Lord, for thy servant heareth." We must come for a personal message as though the Bible had been written for no one but ourselves.

In what spirit do you inquire at the post-office at your church headquarters for mail in the morning? Don't you ask hoping to get a letter for yourself? It may be that you inquire also for the mail of several friends; but how pleased you are if you receive a personal message for yourself! As you stand at the counter, you see a young lady come up who is for the first time taking a long trip from home. As you watch her, you see how anxious she is to get a letter from father or mother, or perhaps from her most intimate friend. If she receives a letter how glad she seems to be! Her face is wreathed in smiles. In the same spirit the Bible should be read by us. To it we should come desiring, hoping for, and expecting a personal message from our Heavenly Father. Although we may receive some lessons for our Sunday-school scholars, if we are teachers, or helpful thoughts for others to be mentioned in the Christian Endeavor meetings, yet we ought always to be sure to secure God's personal message to ourselves. In order to do this we must read with the prayer of David on our lips: "Open thou *mine* eyes that *I* may behold wondrous things out of thy law." With our natural eyes we can not see the bones of our hands; but the X-rays can readily disclose them. So the Holy Spirit can reveal to us a personal message when of ourselves we would not see it. The Spirit must unfold to us the Scriptures. He alone can make known to us God's message.

As we pray and read the Bible daily, new duties and responsibilities will be revealed to us. To these we must yield a whole-hearted obedience. What we learn we must put into practice. Like clay in the hands of the potter we must be in the hands of God. As it is shaped and molded according to the potter's wishes, so we should submit ourselves entirely to God, to be molded into vessels fit for the Master's use. It is not sufficient that at one particular time we make a complete consecration of ourselves to God. We must always be on the altar, ready to do God's will as it is revealed to us.

Our daily prayer and Bible reading will help us realize constantly that we are not our own, but that we have been bought with a price. We shall be brought to recognize God's ownership of ourselves, so that we shall not ask the question, "How little can I do and yet remain a follower of Christ?" or "Can I do this and still be a Christian?" but rather we shall want to know: "Lord, what wilt thou have me to do?" And as he makes it known to us in his Word and by his Spirit through prayer, we shall willingly and gladly yield ourselves to God and shall be ready to do whatsoever our Lord the King shall appoint.

It will not be long before we learn that confession of Christ with the mouth is one of our duties. It is not enough for us to lead upright Christian lives. The secret of our lives must be interpreted to others with the mouth. Jesus himself did this. "He did not trust to the silent influence of his life; he wanted men distinctly to understand what the root and aim of his life was."

"In his teaching not only did he reveal the will of his Father and show what the Father is, but he also continually spoke of his own personal relation to the Father. Time after time he told men that he came as a Son sent from the Father, that he depended upon and owed everything to him, that he only sought the Father's glory, and that all his happiness was to please the Father." As Christ acknowledged to men his dependence upon the Father, so we must confess our dependence upon Christ.

May our experience be not like that of a professor in a leading college. He says, "When I was a young man, I thought other young men would resent any appeal I might make to them in regard to their personal relations to Christ."

How many of us, when we draw a glass of water from the spigots in our homes, think of the source of the water in the mountain springs, and of the pipes hidden under the ground which convey it to our homes? Or when we light the gas in our rooms, do we think of the coal which has been dug from the depths of the earth, and from which the gas is made by means of fire? In the same way our unconverted friends may see that streams of influence for good flow from us, for Christ said, "He that believeth on me, as the scripture hath said, out of his belly shall flow rivers of living water." From us also there may shine forth a light, for it is written "Ye are the light of the world." The source of our light is God's Word. We dig from the mines of God's truth precious ores, and bring them to the surface, where they are transformed into light by the fire of the Holy Spirit. This light which shines through our lives and the streams of good influence which flow forth from us are seen by our unsaved friends, but they do not think of their source.

My wife's cousin, a young fellow not yet of age, lived in our house for six months. My dread of meddling was such that I never asked him to be present at family worship, or spoke to him on the subject of religion. He fell into the company of a wild set, and was rapidly going to the bad. When I reasoned with him I spoke of Christ.

"Do you call yourself a Christian?" he asked, assuming an astonished look.

"I hope so," I replied.

"But you are not. If you were, He must be your best friend. Yet I have lived in your house for six months and you have never once mentioned his name to me. No, he is nothing to you."

May we never receive such a rebuke as this, but let us rather speak out for Jesus, and tell our friends the blessedness of Christ's friendship.

To the every-day duties of prayer, Bible reading, submission to God's will, and open confession of Christ, every Christian must add that of support of his own church. Comment upon this duty of church support is hardly necessary, for every one already realizes its importance. If any one is not a loyal church member after taking the pledge, he is not a true Christian Endeavorer.

These five duties I have mentioned must be performed. We may talk of them, consider and meditate upon them, but we must not stop there. They must be done. Let us remember them in a somewhat different order by the letters Y. P. S. C. E., beginning Scripture quotations:—

Yield yourselves unto God,
Praying always.
Search the Scriptures.
Confess with your mouth the Lord Jesus.
Enter into his gates with thanksgiving and into his courts with praise.

Probably by many present these duties are already considered privileges: but still, to all of us, they are duties to be done. However, if we enter upon them heartily, it will not be long before they will become pleasures as well as duties. According to a fable related by Dr. J. R. Miller, birds were first made without any wings. Then God made the wings, and put them down before the wingless birds, and said to them, " Come, take up these burdens and bear them." The birds had lovely plumage and sweet voices; they could sing, and their feathers gleamed in the sunshine, but they could not soar in the air. At first they hesitated when bidden to take up the burdens that lay at their feet, but soon they obeyed, and taking up the wings on their beaks, laid them on their shoulders to carry them. For a little while the load seemed heavy and hard to bear; but presently, as they went on carrying the burdens, folding them over their hearts. the wings grew fast to their little bodies, and soon they discovered how to use them, and were lifted by them up into the air. The weights became wings.

This is a parable. We are the wingless birds, and the common tasks and duties of support of our own church, confession of Christ. submission to his will, Bible reading, and prayer are the pinions by which God will lift us up and carry us heavenward. If they are still burdens and weights, let us lift them cheerfully: let us bear them with love in our hearts. and they will become a source of blessing and help to us. On them we will rise and soar towards God.

After the close of Mr. Knipp's address, the choir sang the well-known hymn, " Banner of the Cross," and then Rev. A. F. Richardson, of Grafton, W. Va., was introduced to speak on " Dangers To Be Encountered."

Address of Rev. A. F. Richardson, Grafton, W. Va.

Endeavorers and Friends:— We must not imagine for a moment that the most ardent and consecrated adherents and supporters of the Christian Endeavor movement have ever unwisely assumed that such a mighty agency for good would go unchallenged and be exempt from bitter opposition and grave dangers. Such at least has been the experience of all grand movements looking to the exaltation of society, the salvation of men, and the glory of God: and in proportion as the movement has been nurtured by the good, and blessed of God, have the agencies of evil combined to check its influence and minimize its power.

I can but glance at the dangers this evening, leaving to the Society to weigh their importance, and to a consecrated Christian Endeavor conscience to supply the remedy.

1. *The danger of unlawful personal ambition.* Paul says. " If a man strive for masteries, yet is he not crowned, except he strive lawfully." There are summits to be reached, but the paths leading thereto are ofttimes narrow and demand " grit and grace," and the Endeavorer needs to be met at the very base of this ascent by that safeguard of our Lord's Prayer, " Blessed are the poor in spirit, for theirs is the kingdom of God."

Remember that to be a Christian Endeavorer does not secure to you an indemnity on sin; does not secure to you absolute control over those passions of the human soul that are seeking continually the ascendency, and which, if unchecked, will dwarf into insignificance the lawful ambition and holy enthusiasm which marked the beginning of your service. We must not forget that association with the blessed Master himself was not sufficient to banish selfishness from the minds and hearts of the disciples, who were unduly concerned about the place of honor in his kingdom. History, sacred and profane, teems with instances where principles, grand and glorious in their conception, have been sacrificed upon the altar of unholy ambition and inordinate desire. Remember we are "saved to serve;" and he serves Christian Endeavor best who serves Christ the best: and truest service to Jesus Christ often means the lowest place in his kingdom; and, thank God, the lowest place in the earthly kingdom may mean the highest place in the kingdom of glory. " I am among you as he that serveth ; " and he washed their feet.

2. *The danger of relaxation.* We can not believe, as some one has ungraciously expressed it, that "the Christian Endeavor movement will prove a boomerang to the Church of Jesus Christ." Christian Endeavor has already proven her mission divine. Nor do we believe that there can be any rebound sufficient to cause even a serious wavering in the ranks of this mighty army battling for Christ and his Church against the hosts of sin; but there may be an unhealthy stagnation of the tributaries, the loosening of the tension, the unbending of the energies, a relaxation of effort, a shrinking of that fervid, soul-inspiring, and life-giving power which has made Christian Endeavor an almost irresistible force in the Church and in the world since its inception. God's law of growth and development must be applied zealously here as in the other departments of Church work ; the activities of yesterday will not suffice for the needs of to-day; past achievements and past successes, while helpful and inspiring for the conflict yet fiercely waging, are not a safe passport to victory to-day or to-morrow ; and not until " the kingdoms of this world become the kingdoms of our Lord and of his Christ," dare the soldiers in this army of God relax their vigilance, allow their ardor to cool or courage to wane, or lay down their weapons of spiritual warfare.

3. *The danger of sacrificing world-wide endeavor to the narrow limit of sectarian bigotry.* There is a tendency, mainly individual, to sever the relation borne by the denomination to the Christian Endeavor movement as a whole ; having received a baptism of Christian Endeavor grace, to withdraw and live in seclusion on the gracious fruits of that baptism ; a feeling of unrest and alarm lest the distinctive denominationalism be swallowed up of the broader interdenominational fellowship. Well, if it be a swallowing like that of the whale with Jonah, why not ? Jonah became a tenfold better man by the operation, and it served, doubtless, to increase the dimensions of the whale ; and as long as it works that way I am inclined to believe that God's children everywhere have great reason to rejoice. But we hope that those received and nourished in the bosom of this splendid fellowship will appreciate the necessity of perfect digestion and assimilate all that is true and good and Christlike, and not serve simply as an emetic, as in the case of Jonah.

The past phenomenal success as well as the future progress and glory of Christian Endeavor rests upon its fidelity to this interdenominational fellowship idea ; and it is this idea brought so prominently before the eyes of the unsaved masses that has done more perhaps than all other methods combined to commend this movement to the thoughtful and earnest consideration of those who have hitherto looked with at least suspicion upon the Church of Jesus Christ, *apparently* hopelessly divided, and ofttimes bitterly at war over creeds and dogmas, necessary perhaps, but not essential to the salvation of a single human soul. The creed of Christian Endeavor may be expressed in one short sentence, " Christ and him crucified."

4. *The danger of entangling alliances.* As true as the needle to the pole must Christian Endeavor be to its prime object and mission: go its divinely appointed way, using its divinely appointed means. Christian Endeavor to be true to her mission must have no affiliation with party organization; as such she cannot afford to risk her future upon the uncertain wave of human aspirations and human passions, to be borne helplessly along upon its crest of fierce fanaticism, but girded in the strength of God, guided in the wisdom of God, her watchword is, " Forward," in the truth and freedom of God. And we place our hearty seal of approval upon the attitude of President Clark and the officers of the United Society in the recent attempts to draw the Christian Endeavor host into the whirl of politics. To suffer this is to rob this movement of its distinctively Christian character, create confusion in its ranks, and place it at the mercy of designing and unscrupulous politicians ; not that those who seek such alliance may not be thoroughly honest and conscientiously zealous in their desire of such union, but they are unfortunately misguided in their judgment of Christian Endeavor methods and principles.

Christian Endeavor stands for Christian citizenship, for the abolition of the saloon, for reform in every department of our civic life, for the rescue of the Sabbath and the salvation of all that is good and pure and noble in man; but she must arm for the conflict and enter the arena untrammelled by party feeling, party whim, and party lash, the slave only of a consecrated Christian Endeavor conscience, and casting "for God and home and native land" a consecrated Christian Endeavor ballot.

Let the consciousness that there are dangers to be encountered in this stupendous but heaven-guarded task of winning the world for Christ not dismay, nor frighten, but serve to nerve and strengthen for the combat, so that when the final struggle may come, whether we live to share its triumph or not, we may go in the sweet consciousness that we have never lowered the standard of Christian Endeavor. And it may be that some of us, who may never live to share the blessing of another convention, like Moses of old, God will lead in spirit upon the mountain-top and allow our consecrated vision to sweep this land, saved. purified, and glorified through the faith, sacrifice, and service of Christian Endeavor.

The last topic was " Encouragements To Be Given."

Address of Rev. William Justin Harsha, D.D., New York City.

I. *Encouragements to be drawn from the work already done.* It is proper for us to look at the past, to take heart for grace out of it, as well as to avoid its dangers. In one sense, truly, we are to " forget the things that are behind," but in another sense we may very properly remember them. If we grow more humble in our opinion of ourselves, and more confident in our conception of Christ. by looking at the way over which he hath led us, then it is our bounden duty, as it is our blessed privilege, to consider the past. When we come to consider the Christian Endeavor movement we are amazed and overwhelmed by the amount of good that has already been done. It is a good of a distinctive and uniform kind, as I have already remarked ; but it is wide in its charity, and many-branched in its blessings. Take any number of *The Golden Rule,* or look at any denominational paper in these days, and you will be astonished to observe in how many practical directions the work has already spread and is ever extending.

A movement which lays hold upon so many diverse things as mothers' meetings, reading-rooms for sailors, selling Bibles, helping shirt-makers, paving streets. and putting the Bible into public schools has surely shown that it has a right to be, and in its past has manifested undeniable encouragements for its future.

In addition to all this we would need to see how the latent power of the Church has been brought out, how cordiality has been increased, how denominations have been united in spirit if not in letter, and how in tens of thousands of churches, at home and abroad, the mystic initials "C. E." have come — as one pastor has expressed it — " to stand for the five points of modern doctrine, as follows : (1) Christ exalted; (2) Church educated; (3) Christians elevated; (4) Continents evangelized ; (5) Christendom everywhere." When in Rome I did as few Romans do. I went out on the Appian Way to the side of the Appii-Forum and the Three Taverns, of which we read in the twenty-eighth chapter in the book of Acts. I pictured to myself what occurred there on that memorable day when St. Paul, having landed at Puteoli and having taken all the weary journey from that seaport, was met here by some of the earnest Christians of Rome. The brethren had heard of the worn traveller's approach, and they went as far as the Forum and the Three Taverns to welcome him. They put their arms around him and gave him such whispered encouragement as the warm Christian heart knows how to utter. They told of the faithful work and witnessing that had been done in Rome, and he in his turn told them of what had been accomplished in Cesarea and Jerusalem and upon the Steppes of Asia Minor. Then the record is that Paul "thanked God and took courage."

Tidings of what had been done lifted up his heart in the hope that much more might be done. So it may be with us. Far be it from me to seem merely to glory in the past of the Christian Endeavor movement; but the sunshine of God's favor on the phenomenal landscape we have left may cheer us for a further progress.

II. *Encouragements to be drawn from the results anticipated.* In some lines it is dangerous to anticipate results. "The best laid schemes o' mice and men gang aft a-gley." This is when God is not taken into account; but when God is on our side and God's promises have been pledged in our support, we are safe to anticipate results and draw encouragement from our anticipations. What are the prospects? I will answer you as that splendid old missionary, Adoniram Judson, did, when asked the same question. He had been toiling in darkest heathendom for many years, and apparently there had been few results. "Prospects?" he repeated, "They are bright as the promises of God." This I would say to you. Expectancy is the proper thing in prayer; why should it not be equally proper in Christian service? The first verse of the eleventh chapter of Hebrews tells us that faith is the actual "substance of things hoped for." Hence by faith we may lay hold upon the real substance of the triumphs yet to be. Joab's addresses to his men on the field of battle are even more thrilling than Napoleon's. Take, for instance, 2 Sam. x. 11, 12. The Syrians and Ammonites had massed themselves against him and his army, but Joab was not afraid. He went down the line and cried out to his soldiers, "Be of good courage and let us play the men." He counted upon God's help, and his heart was lifted up in sureness of victory. Christian Endeavor has passed out of an experiment into a certainty. The General Assembly of the Presbyterian Church at its last session simply voiced the overwhelming victory which the young people by their simplicity and faith have obtained in the councils of the elders. The General Synod of the Church which I represent entertains like sentiments, and I fancy that even the General Conference of the M. E. Church has a lurking love for the movement and will yet come around. What results may we expect? Along the line of Christian citizenship, a platform in which Christ's name and Christ's spirit are honored. Along the line of purification of the cities, a thousand Parkhursts and enough assistants to place one, at least, in every centre of population. Along the line of temperance, including the deadly cigarette, the utter discouragement and destruction of both tasting and traffic. Along the line of Sabbath observance, including the use of the beguiling bicycle on that day, a holier reverence for the day and a truer rest in God. Along the line of foreign missions, the Gospel to be preached as a witness to all nations early in the coming century. Along the lines of home missions, Christian Endeavor churches to be built by Christian Endeavor offerings in all denominations, as they are being built in the one I represent. Is this anticipation too rosy? I am certain it is not, if, relying upon the grace of God, the Christian Endeavorers unite in their multitude and in their might to do the work which the Master has put into their hands.

III. *Encouragements to be drawn from the personal presence of the Trinity in us.* One of the notable things in the epistle to the Galatians is that it reveals each person of the Trinity as residing and operating "*in me.*" "They glorified God in me" (Gal. i. 24); "To reveal his Son in me" (Gal. i. 16); "The same Spirit was mighty in me" (Gal. ii. 8). As with Paul, so with each one of us. The humblest Christian may have this sweetest and highest of all blessings, "the Trinity in me."

1. The Father in us. What an encouragement it is that we may count upon the inflow of the Divine Life, constant, peaceful, and strengthening, in all the ways and perplexities of service! There are some beautiful incidents of Scripture which illustrate and enforce this truth. In the twentieth chapter of Judges, for example, we have an account of the distressing conflict between the people of Israel and the children of Benjamin, and at the twenty-second verse we read that the former "encouraged themselves *in the Lord;*" that is to say, by prayer and fasting they opened their hearts to receive the inflow of strength and peace from God the Father of all. We read of a dark time in Daniel's life

when the people gathered themselves into angry knots and scowled upon him and spake of stoning him. (1 Sam. xxx. 6.) Then David did what it is our privilege to do,— turned his back upon his enemies and his face unto his God. " David encouraged himself in the Lord his God." He pulled himself together; he toughened his inner confidence and composure by receiving the power of the Divine indwelling. Referring to these experiences of his, David wrote two of his most striking Psalms. In one of them he said, "Wait on the Lord: be of good courage, and he shall strengthen thine heart: wait, I say, on the Lord." (Ps. xxvii. 14.) This was written in the wilderness, when he was fleeing from Absalom, and was exiled from God's house; yet in those trying circumstances he had but to look up and breathe into his heart the Father's strength in order to be encouraged. In the other Psalm he says, "Be of good courage, and he shall strengthen your heart, all ye that hope in the Lord." (Ps. xxxi. 24.) This was written in a time of great anguish and danger, when he had crossed the Jordan and battle was imminent. Oh, may we thus also realize that the Father is within! Let us wait upon him there.

2. The Son in us. Paul, as we have seen, gloried in the fact that God's Son was revealed in him. This rejoicing was based upon the promise which Jesus had made. " If a man love me, he will keep my words: and my Father will love him, and we will come unto him, and make our abode with him." (John xiv. 23.) This is a blessed promise, but there is a more blessed one still. It is implied in what Paul says, "Most gladly therefore will I rather glory in my infirmities, that the power of Christ may rest upon me." (2 Cor. xii. 9.)

The Word here really means that the power of Christ "tabernacles upon" the working Christian, folds a tent of hallowed protection and sure blessing over all his way and work. If this is *more* blessed, we may go on to the *most* blessed of all. " My little children, of whom I travail in birth again until Christ be formed *in* you." (Gal. iv. 19.) The thought here is so holy and sacred that one hesitates to speak upon it. It is just this: as Christ by the overshadowing of his Spirit was formed in the womb of the Virgin Mary, so is the Christ-life formed in our hearts by the same Spirit of God. And it rests with us whether the little babe shall be dwarfed or shall grow to his full strength; shall be crippled or shall be able to exert his full power. What a strange ability we have to interfere with the growth of the Christ-life within us! No mother, how-ever vile or impatient she may be, is able to will, or would desire to will, that her child be born crippled, or deformed, or lacking in some sense, or limb. But we *can* will that Christ shall be deformed and crippled within us. By our frivolity or our impatience or by our thoughtlessness we may so impede his growth that he shall not be able to do for us and be in us what he desires. But what an encouragement, what an uplift, what a heartening, to have Christ fully formed in us!

3. The Spirit in us. Webster gives as synonyms of the word" encourage," " inspirit," " comfort," and " strengthen." We will see at once how all these apply to the Holy Spirit, who is the " paraclete," or " strengthener,"— translated "comforter" in the authorized version,— who abides ever in our hearts. I need hardly say to you that living as we do in the dispensation of the Holy Spirit, it is our privilege to be so filled with the Spirit that we shall be in constant strength and encouragement.

Have you ever read attentively the little sermon which Rahab preached to the spies? You will find it in Joshua ii. 9–13,— a sermon of only five verses, but full of spiritual truth. The point I would take from her discourse, to-night, is the fact she mentions that her countrymen, when they heard of the approach of the people of Israel, had " no spirit left in them," consequently no " courage" remained. That is the trouble too often with us. No spirit, no Holy Spirit, abides in us "to will and to do;" consequently we find ourselves in desperation and dismay. We have grieved him away because of our inattentions and sins; consequently we have no power.

I note a very significant scene described in Ezra x. 1–4. The people were in despondency; their power was gone, their courage departed, the work of refor-mation in worship in the temple delayed, and all was perplexity and wrangle.

In that juncture Ezra calls them together, and after praying with them and for them, charges that something is wrong with their lives. This boldness on the part of the preacher wins a satisfactory result, for they confess their sins, not in general, but their sin in particular. Then courageously they put that sin away, and power and cheerfulness instantly return to them; and Ezra, with enthusiasm breaking over his face, cries out, "Arise, be of good courage and do!" And I note another scene described in 2 Chron. xv. 3–8. For a long season the Israelites had been without a knowledge of the true God and without a teacher or priest and without law. Troubles fall upon them, and then they feel out after God, if haply they may find him. Asa is their king, and with wonderful faithfulness he put away the idols, and then the hearts of the people were strengthened. In the eighth verse it is said: " He took courage, and put away the abominable idols." Oh, it takes courage with us to dethrone the idols which so often have robbed us of power and of peace! May the Holy Spirit show us where the lurking sin is that prevents him fully entering in, to give us the best of all encouragements. I think usually the trouble is that we have not surrendered our wills.

First Congregational Church.

" Scatter Sunshine " was the opening number of the praise service at the First Congregational Church. Dr. F. J. Woodman, of Washington, was the musical director, and under his inspiring leadership a hearty enthusiasm was noticeable about the singing. The choir of Mount Vernon Place M. E. Church was in attendance.

After the second hymn Mrs. Hattie Meads Smith sang a solo, accompanied on the organ by Dr. J. W. Bischoff, of Washington. The number was warmly received, and proved one of the features of the evening.

Rev. J. M. Lowden, of Olneyville, R. I., presided over the meeting, and introduced Rev. S. M. Hartsock, of Washington, who conducted brief devotional exercises.

The singing of "There's a Royal Banner Ready to Display for the Loyal Soldiers of the King" was followed by the introduction of the first speaker of the evening, Rev. Kerr Boyce Tupper, D.D., pastor of the First Baptist Church, Philadelphia, Pa.

Address of Rev. Kerr Boyce Tupper, D.D., Philadelphia, Pa.

The influence of a choice book in the formation and development of a choice character none have overestimated. "Next to personal religious conviction," writes a gifted author, "the best safeguard for us is a taste for good reading." "Whoever," wrote wise Richard de Bury, 500 years ago, "whoever acknowledges himself to be an earnest follower of truth, happiness, wisdom, and even faith, must make himself a lover of books." Alexander the Great, revealing valor and patriotic fervor, slept with the Iliad. The life of this same Alexander made Charles the twelfth of Sweden a man. Cotton Mather's essay on doing good shaped Benjamin Franklin's life. Abraham Lincoln attributed much of his elevation during his political career to Plutarch's "Lives."

Never in the history of the world has there been such a demand as at present for choice literature with which to counteract and destroy the impure books and degrading pamphlets which yearly curse our land. The elder Pliny said 1,800 years ago, "No book is so bad but that some part may be read with profit." This was not so then; it is far less true to-day. There are books as barren of example of noble manhood and womanhood as the African desert is barren of roses and peonies. From New York City alone no fewer than 200,000 books, either trashy or impure, are annually sent out. The influence of these must be recognized and heroically and manfully destroyed.

And most desirable is it that in our day of choice literature, much of which is not essentially Christian, we emphasize the books that tell specially on spiritual growth; books that lead the young of our churches to love what God loves, and to yield their lives in affectionate self-surrender to Jesus Christ. It is well enough for them to read widely in history, Carlyle, Freeman, Froude, Guizot, Hallam, Prescott, Rawlinson. It is well that they get considerable acquaintance with the world's poets, as Homer, Horace, Dante, Shakespeare, Milton, Browning, Burns, and Tennyson. It is well enough that they read with care the choice works of romance, as George Eliot, Scott, Bulwer, Thackeray, MacDonald, Miss Muloch, and Howells. It is well enough that they read extensively our most gifted essayists, Bacon, Macaulay, Addison, Foster, and Emerson; but necessary to the spiritual culture of these young men and women is the perusal of books that deal with a higher relation of the soul.

Let me, therefore, give you a list of 150 of the choicest books, as far as I know, that dwell upon the aspects of spiritual life.

1. Books that develop the devotional life.
2. Books that mark out practical methods of Church work.
3. Books that impart missionary intelligence.
4. Books that confirm Christian faith. (At this point Dr. Tupper distributed several thousand copies of 150 books on the subjects of choice literature as suggested.)

Each of the books I have here recommended is worthy of high place in our hearts, libraries, and homes; but best of all is the Word of God, which stands above all other books, its author God, its subject man, its object salvation, its aim the development of the immortal nature. Take this book ever as the article of faith, the manual of devotion, the charter of liberty. It is full of the richest strains of poetry, the most memorable of history, the most inexhaustible source of philosophy; but above all these, it meets the spiritual needs of our race, relieving the conscience, elevating the intellect, illuminating the spirit, and transforming the life. Young men, young women, read it, study it, meditate upon it, translate its heavenly thought into your earthly life. Let nothing in our proud world cause you to lose faith in it; but believe in it, and rest on it with a faith which no philosophy can destroy, no sophistry disturb, no scepticism touch.

Rev. Dr. Tupper's address was enthusiastically applauded, and next the choir sang "The Cross of Victory," after which Mr. W. O. Atwood, of Baltimore, Md., conducted an open parliament on the pledge. In opening, Mr. Atwood made it plain that he expected those in the congregation to participate actively in the parliament. He asserted his belief in the Christian Endeavor pledge. "No society," he said, "can exist for any length of time if organized without it; one might just as well endeavor to construct a house of bricks without mortar. With the pledge," he added, "it is possible to go out armed and equipped to strike for Jesus."

For some little time thereafter Endeavorers in all parts of the church arose and briefly stated their views the pledge. Questions were asked and answered, and, altogether, this portion of the meeting was unique, interesting, instructive, and enjoyable.

Then followed two addresses on the subject "Our Duty to the Sunday Evening Service," by two brothers, pastors in Wisconsin.

Address of Rev. Henry Faville, La Crosse, Wis.

First, friends, we have to meet certain facts concerning this Sunday evening service. I have a theory that our Sunday evening service ought to be an evangelistic service,— fifty-two in the year, if possible. But here is the fact: most of us are not evangelists. I am not sure but some of us could be if, in the first place, they would relieve us of all pastoral work and other services in the church, and then entertain us at a hotel, and then appoint committees for the work, and then all of the churches in a town or a city would go in together.

I am inclined to think that then we might be evangelists, more of us than are. But the fact is, the average minister, at least in my church,— it is the Congregational Church,— is not an evangelist; and we have to meet that fact, that we cannot hold fifty-two strictly evangelistic services during the year.

We have to meet another fact. The average adult church-member is not greatly in need of an evening service for himself. He ought to be at the morning service; he ought to be in the Sunday school as a teacher or learner. He goes to the Young Men's Christian Association; and then he needs an evening with his family, ofttimes — at least, he could better spend the moments there than elsewhere, if he is an active, adult member in the church, I say. I do not preach this, you understand, at home; but it is a fact, all the same.

I urge no one to stay at home. But they have duties at home that must be and should be attended to, ofttimes, if they have been faithful to their duties during the day.

But now, another feature: the average community and city does need the evening service — whether in this city, whether in New York, or whether upon the banks of the Mississippi, where I come from. I found this in my own city. I believe in my own city; I love its people. We have a growing city. Five years ago it had 25,000 people. It has somewhat more now. But, by a rather careful estimate and inquiry upon the attendance in all the churches — some twenty-six in that city — I found that the average attendance upon the evening service in Catholic and Lutheran and all other Protestant churches was 2,050 out of 25,000 people. That means that we are largely not a church-going people — certainly not in the evening.

I think perhaps we are exceptional in the number that attended the evening services there five years ago. But the fact is that there are at least 10,000 people in that city who would be far better off in the evening services of our church than in any other place in the city. Granting that there are 15,000 who are children, or who have not the physical ability to go to church,— and let that include some of the parents, too,— it is a wide margin to say that 15,000 might be at home. We ought to have 10,000, I realize, rather than 2,000, in our churches.

Now, the question was how to meet these facts. I set myself to work upon them somewhat personally about five years ago, for I wanted to do something for the city, and I came to this conclusion for my own church; and you will allow me to speak somewhat personally from this time on.

I felt that we have something to give to the city; that we must, as a church, throughout evening service, try to do something for at the least 8,000 people who might be in church, who ought to be in church, who would be blessed by an evening service.

I have this feeling: that many of us, as churches, have got to fulfil this great thought of Christ's, and lose our life as a church in the community, to a certain extent, in order to find it in some larger life. And so I said that we as a church are not to think of our deacons, of our Sunday-school teachers, of our young people, indeed, only, but to think of the eight thousand outside who might be blessed if they would come into church on Sunday evening.

And so I said this: "We must go upon the principle of giving, as far as possible. In the next place, we must give our best, if we are to do aught as Christians." You know how it is, you pastors at least, if you have any such conditions as we have; the pastors, if they have a specially good sermon, preach it in the morning, while the choir always has better music in the morning than in the evening; and I said, "This is wrong if we are to do the work of Christians, and give. We ought to give the very best that we can to this evening service." And on that principle we went out.

There is another thing to consider, also. I am not enough of a preacher to draw men to my church by personal power, at least in such a city as La Crosse,

But I said, "They ought to be helped, and I am here to help them. And now we will add a little something to this." This was the addition: —

First, additional music in the service.

Second, a programme in which all were to take some part,— a printed programme, with hymns and responsive readings.

Now about this music that we added. Tell it not in Gath, sir; I am not sure, but sometimes, in our first vocal — perhaps not in the vocal, but certainly in the instrumental — quartets, the garments of some smelt not of myrrh and aloes, but of the saloon. I am not sure but we had some musicians who knew more about the saloon than about worship. We did not really mean to have that kind. We certainly wanted respectable congregations, and men and women of character in our additional musical service. But at first we did not have all such as we would like. But you may publish it in Eschalon that in the city of La Crosse the most popular music-teacher, teaching vocal music to perhaps twenty in my own church, and teaching instrumental music also, is one who, through this service, by being invited to assist in a Sunday evening service, was taken from the saloon, and to-day is a new man through that instrumentality. So I am not as fearful as I was at first to introduce occasionally one who is not in sympathy with our work, and who knows but very little about it,— especially in a German and Scandinavian city like our own,— who is but very little acquainted with our methods of evening service.

We have helped them, and they have helped us. It is true there was some criticism of putting in additional music, such as a stringed quartet. Not among my own people,— for, let me say, I have the best people in the earth outside of your own church, of course,— I want to say that among them there was no criticism, but only a ready co-operation in adding to this service. There were some who were like the old gentleman who was very deaf and yet very argumentative; and he would always get in an argument, if possible, and then would say, "I don't understand a word that you say, but I beg leave to differ with you."

There were a good many that did not understand our motives, our plans, our purposes, at all; but they begged leave to differ with us. But it has been a success, a great success, in reaching out after some whom we needed and who needed us.

Let me say that at first we organized a little helping band which was known as the Pastor's Auxiliary. But I wanted that more perfect touch with the church; and so, a little later, the only addition as far as machinery was concerned in connection with the evening service was this:—

I said that we ought to have more associate members than we have. Possibly some would come in touch with our society if we should say to them, "We have a little work for you to do in the church; we want you to help usher in the evening service." And so we have as an addition to the Christian Endeavor Society to-day a committee that is called the Young Men's Auxiliary, with the one purpose of assisting in the evening service, so far as any assistance is needed. It means but very little,— some do not usher for more than one or two months, perhaps,— and yet it sometimes brings a young man in touch with the Christian Endeavor Society. We say to the young man, "Young fellow, we have a place for you, some service that you can do if you are willing to do it; won't you usher for us for one month or two months in our evening service?" Many a time they are glad to do it, and many a time it has been the first step into active membership.

Don't leave what we call out West the wheel-horses off from the evening service, though you may introduce these associate members of the Society as workers. I mean this: keep upon the committees, keep upon the staff of ushers, some of those who are to be depended on through thick and thin, through storm and cold, through hot and dry.

Christian Endeavorers, don't turn aside entirely from the old deacons or Sunday-school superintendents or trustees or church workers. Remember that they can serve the evening service with you, and without them, even though you should follow our plan, you shall, after all, have not the most of stability in your evening service. The deacon and the pastor, however, will get interested, if you make the right kind of a race for the evening service.

Then Rev. John Faville, of Appleton, Wis., took the platform.

Address of Rev. John Faville, Appleton, Wis.

Our Young Men's Sunday Evening Club has solved for us the problem of the evening service. Believing it has some features that will help others, I am to speak of it. Our city of Appleton has fifteen thousand people, seventy saloons, twelve churches, one synagogue, and a Christian college. In six of the churches services are conducted in German; in none of them are there large evening audiences. The chief industry of the city is the manufacture of paper.

Four years ago last February I invited twenty-four men to lunch with me at the hotel. (Generalship!) One-third of these men were church-members, one-third attendants, one-third non-attendants. They were business and professional men, ranging from twenty-five to forty-five years of age. They were not doing anything by way of church work except to make a subscription to the current expenses, and not all even that. I unfolded to them my ideas, which I got largely from my brother, as to the possibility of helping the evening service. Almost without exception they entered heartily into the plan, and February 7, 1892, the club was organized with twenty members, and February 21, we began our first service with its assistance.

Two general ideas were prominent in our efforts : —

First, to make a *better* service. Not to attempt something entirely new; not to depend on innovations nor sensations, but to put more time and money and enthusiasm and consecration into the parts of the service we had. My brother has perhaps sufficiently emphasized that fact, but it is important to keep it in mind. As many a church financial system is good enough if worked at its best, so we believed the evening service in its general design and method was good if *worked*. Aside from using musical instruments other than the organ, we have had nothing in our service that could be considered an innovation, unless it was the numbers,— simply a better, a more varied and vigorous use of what is considered the standard for this Sunday evening hour in the church.

Second, general idea. To take the men of the community into partnership, as far as possible, in regard to this service,— the men not identified with other churches, and also the men not now burdened with church duties. To make some one beside the pastor and choir and organist and a few stragglers and still fewer faithful church-goers in part responsible for this service. To make it a democracy (not political, here) rather than a monarchy or aristocracy, as a service.

If we made the better service we felt we wanted more people to profit by it. So in order to improve the service and to enlist others, the Young Men's Sunday Evening Club was organized. It is a simple association with a single aim, expressed in its constitution,— " To increase the interest and effectiveness of the Sunday evening service."

The conditions of membership in this order we made neither creed nor character, but — a dollar. It was not stated whether it should be a silver or gold or paper dollar, for we organized four and a half years ago, but simply a plain, ordinary dollar. Was it wise to make that one condition for a club that was to identify itself with the Church? Remember what we were after,— simply a better Sunday evening service. One essential was more people. Any man, then, who had any desire to help to this end we wanted. The duty of the members was such that it was no compromise to join the club, even if not up to a standard of life that must be required of a church-member. We were not after the church-members, but those away from the Church so far that they were not even attendants. So we asked a man, not simply to come to church, but to join our club that was aiming to improve this service. The invitation to come only would have accomplished much; but to join the club, to invest a dollar, and then be asked to do a little work, to assume a limited responsibility, that was taking hold of a new side of a man. To ask a person to do something instead of stand around and see some one else do it is a far surer way of winning him.

With these two dominant ideas we began our work as a club. We have succeeded far beyond our anticipation. We have made a better evening service. It has been a prompt, varied, business-like, religious, people's service. The motto of the Pleasant Sunday Afternoon Association of England, " Brief, Bright, Brotherly," would not be inappropriate for us. Printed programmes with responsive readings, hymns, and order of service are handed each person at the door. We do not confine ourselves to the same musicians for the special music, but try to enlist all who are available. The sermon is usually by the pastor, and has been written in full and read. The remark of the judge who, when asked what the length of a sermon should be, said, " Fifteen minutes, with a leaning to the side of mercy " has been heeded. As a recorder of facts, I must state that one of the popular features has been the sermon, i. e., the shortness of it. (Here again, generalship.) Seriously, this is an item. It is better to work a day on a fifteen-minute sermon than a half-day on a thirty-minute. It is better to talk fifteen minutes to seven hundred people than thirty minutes to one hundred, especially if you get practically the same thought in the former address. We have made a better service. It has cost more in time and money, but it has been worth more than it has cost.

It is, I repeat, a distinctly religious service, but varied in this : it attempts to touch the community on many sides ; e. g., we have one-half dozen times a year special nights, and ask some class or association to be our guests, such as a " clerks'," a " teachers', " a " temperance," a " benevolent society," a " citizens', " or a " children's home " night, — City Council and officers. And in such a service there is not only a response on the part of those invited, but a new bond between them and the Church.

But after all, it was the club itself with us that made the greatest change. We began with twenty members. There are now on our membership roll six hundred and eleven names. Of this number six hundred are living, and over five hundred are now in our city, and but with rare exceptions they can be relied on to assist in helping to make this service a success. They are all but one men under eighteen years of age. They include at least fifty vocations. These men are appointed on committees, which are changed monthly so that none may be burdened with the duties or the honors. The officers, who hold for three months, are an executive committee to make the monthly appointments. We bring the men on in alphabetical order, and the monthly committees are published on the programme. We know by this who are responsible for special work that month. The success of the service that month rests upon these committees largely,— as far as attending to the detail work is concerned. The attendance on these services has been from the first night uniformly good. The club has held one hundred and eighty-five services. From one hundred and twenty-five to fifty was the average evening audience before it was started. Six hundred and fifty has been the average since, and often a thousand — except during a few weeks of summer. We as much expect an audience that will fill the church and often require chairs in the aisle as we expect a fair morning audience. Helpful factors, however, are these : —

The church itself. From the first the club met with a hearty reception from the church. The trustees gave the evening collection to the club to help defray expenses for printed programmes and special music, and the club has never lacked sufficient funds for its work. Our church has in it no cliques and classes that are obtrusive, no " wings" that are trying to take it in different ways. It has an exceptionally large and vigorous Sunday school, and it is an attentive, eager crowd. There are many in it who five years ago did not attend church at all, and there are many young men in the club who without it would be on the streets, or in worse places, Sunday evenings.

So the results have been far greater than we dared hope along the line for which we were organized,— the improvement of the evening service. This is all the club has contracted to do, but it has done much more than that. It has assisted by its committees in the morning service, increased the size of the parish, developed a better social life, helped in the finances of the church, carried on for three years a successful, high-grade lecture-course, identified itself with the local charities of the city, and in other ways has helped to make the church a " house of life."

As I try to gather up the elements that enter into this movement, or analyze the forces that have helped to so completely transform our service, and that have helped turn many non-attendants toward the church ; as I try to suggest to others that they can go and do likewise, I find it difficult to express my convictions clearly.

We have a good church-building, well located, and are in spirit and make-up somewhat of a people's church. As another factor, I had been a pastor at Appleton six years before attempting it. I knew the field. I had done considerable special pastoral work among the men. I had learned from personal contact that most men have a warm place in their hearts, if you can reach it, for the Church as an institution ; they do not want it to go down. I learned that many a man needs sympathy and encouragement more than he needs condemnation. I learned that the thing to do to help him is to go where he is, and begin with him there, instead of insisting he must first come where you are. I learned that it was safe to ask a good act of any one, and put the responsibility of refusal on him. I learned that the fear of compromising something,— or somebody,— if you make a new departure in order to win men, is born too much of cowardice and prejudice. I remembered that Christ did not ask Peter to preach the sermon on Pentecost the first time he met him. He, instead, went fishing with him. Call a man a gentleman and he will generally straighten up and try for the moment to be one. Assume he is a rascal and you have lost your grip on him.

Again, the club's success is in its not attempting to do everything. Some write me, asking if the club has many conversions, and how many church-members from it, etc. My answer is that the direct religious results have been more than I anticipated, but the club was not born to do everything. Other agents and forces of the Church are to supplement its work. If it helps the evening service its mission is accomplished. It has done much more than it promised, but it has been successful in the fact that it has not attempted to do everything. But beyond this the success has been in asking so many to do something. " A little from many, instead of much from a few," is our church motto. This utilizing just as far as possible as many as possible is one secret of success. My brother has emphasized giving something in this evening service to the community. That is good ; that is the unselfish spirit. But there is another side ; viz., each member of the club or community giving something to this service. Give all you can in this service, but get all you can to give of themselves to it, is our thought. So there has been work done by the club. The service has not continued a steady success for four and a half years because it had a club or varied music or short sermons or some favoring conditions. Wide-awake men, accustomed to succeed, have put constant work in it. The membership committees have gone after men ; the music committees have given time to their duties ; the ushers have been prompt and cordial ; the officers, interested in their duties.

It has been clear from the first that this service would not run itself. These six hundred men have all been placed on committees. Some of these committees some months have nothing to do as a committee, but all are supposed to be interested in the general work, and to turn the tide in favor of church attendance. I have never met more faithful workers for any church enterprise than many of these club-members, who before its organization were doing nothing, and the progress of many shows the principle they are putting into this work is most gratifying.

But underneath all, I hold, has been as the most important factor, faith in men,—a faith that has dared ask them into this organization on the simple basis of a membership fee ; a faith that dares take them into partnership just as far as they would go. To say to men outside of the Church, " This evening service needs you ; you can help it if you will," touches and inspires the best in them. So we have tried to make a sweet, Catholic-spirited, positive, Christian service. We have tried to magnify our likenesses and minify our differences. We have tried to turn the current of the community toward the Church, knowing that under its influences and out of its messages will come better things to the lives of men. And this has been true. One example, to be multiplied by a score: an ex-saloon-keeper is president of our club to-night. It is no mean honor now to be at the head of our association,—a current saying among us being that it is as great an honor as to be mayor of a city,—and yet this man is now worthy of this honor, and he owes this worthiness more to the men's club than to any other one organization or agency.

So I believe in our Young Men's Sunday Evening Club. The evening service offers a splendid field for experiments, as has been said. The average morning congregation shows a lively indifference, a masterly inactivity in regard to it. And yet there are conditions that ought to make this service a power. There are plenty of people. Here is a closing hour of the Sabbath, a day that we have devoted to sacred service. Here is an open field, and here are vast unutilized forces in the men in every community as related to the Church. To multiply agencies, to increase machinery, seems dangerous, but not when, as in the case of our young people organized in the Christian Endeavor Society, you can find unutilized power. Now if the men by any simple association or movement can be enlisted in the evening service, there is no danger of the machinery becoming too much for the power.

This is my suggestion as a possible duty to the service: a rally of the men to make it a centre of influence; a platform for the best things of God, a Christian force. The Young Men's Club is simply an attempt to utilize the unutilized, to find something to do for every one who is willing, be it ever so little. It says, " Come and help us" instead of, " Come and hear us." It says to all men, " We want you to make the Sunday evening hour one that you will not be ashamed to think about on Monday." And I have thought if out of these past failures as pastors to make this service what we wanted or felt it ought to be, we have learned it is not the business of the preacher alone to build it, that it is not the duty of the members who are now doing their share, that it must not be laid upon the women who are doing more than their part, that it is not the Christian Endeavorers' mission, though they can help, but that it is the duty of the men, the men who are now outside, and absorbed in other things, to take hold of this work, not alone for their own sake but for the public good; if we, out of the decline of the evening service, learn, as pastors, that we must trust men more, co-operate with them better, then we shall all be benefited by past failures, the Church will in the end be the stronger, and the kingdom of God will be the sooner triumphant in this world.

Foundry Methodist Episcopal Church.

The pastor of the Foundry Methodist Episcopal Church, Rev. Oliver A. Brown, D.D., presided over the meeting. The musical programme was in the hands of Mr. Russell Barnes, and was a success. After devotional exercises by Rev. Chas. B. Ramsdell, D.D., of Washington, the topic of the evening, " Three Elements of the Pledge," was taken up; and the first speaker was from England and was royally received.

Address of Rev. W. H. Towers, Manchester, England.

My Dear Brethren, Christian Friends and Fellow Endeavorers:— I rejoice to stand before you to-night as a representative of the Old Country, and to bring you the greetings of our ever-growing Christian Endeavor host from Great Britain. We rejoice for this Christian Endeavor movement. We rejoice in all America, England, Scotland, Wales, and Ireland. In this church where we meet to-night they have a chapter of the Epworth League. We rejoice for this movement also. I trust that these two branches of Christian work may be married very soon. Indeed, I want to claim the privilege of John Bull, and publish the banns here this very night. I hope the next time I come to America we shall find that there has been accomplished this union, and that the churches of Christ are realizing through their young people the great prayer of our great Master when he said, " That they all may be one." The one flag that we all should follow should be the standard of Jesus Christ. I pray the unity of Christendom may be so advanced in this nineteenth century that the twentieth shall find the Anglo-Saxon race banding together, speaking the same tongue, and following the same Saviour in the same battles; that the world may be one for Christ.

Our topic to-night is the Christian Endeavor pledge,— the three elements of the pledge. We have but to square our lives according to that pledge, and we shall find that there grows within us an increasing reverence for God; that there grows within us an increasing knowledge of God's blessed Word; that there grows within us an intense desire to speak to God.

To-night, in speaking to you of the private devotion of the Christian Endeavorer — oh, I would that my God should put words into my mouth, words that should live in all our memories for all the years which are to come !— let us ever remember that God made us in his own image ; let us ever remember that God loves us with an unspeakable love ; let us ever remember that God redeemed us at an unspeakable cost,—" For God so loved the world that he gave his only begotten Son, that whosoever believeth should not perish but have everlasting life." Oh, the love of God ! That men would say, " Our Father loves us and provides for us and desires to have us to himself !" Oh, I think that is one of the great mysteries revealed to us in the Word of God that we have been slow to comprehend. God wants us, you and me, for himself. Love ever wants to talk to the object upon which its affection is fixed, and God comes to us to-night, and tells us that if we will come apart from the world we shall have close communion and blessed fellowship with the Father himself.

Fellow Endeavorers, fellow Christians, in the midst of the worldly excitement of the politics of the day, in the midst of the distractions of business, in the midst of literary society and of recreation, God says to every one of us that we need to come into our chamber and shut the door upon the world and pray to him in secret ; and He who prayed in secret will reward us openly.

Will you allow me this evening to tell you, very affectionately, in the name of our Master, for the sake of him who loved us ; will you permit me to urge upon you the claims of the Almighty in asking us to come apart from the world, and give him our time, and give him our best thoughts, and give him an opportunity to speak to us ? Surely, I may speak to you on this subject.

Now, first of all, God wants us to give time with him for meditation. We do not want to be superficial Christians. We do not want to be carried away merely by a wave of enthusiasm, good as it is ; but we want that the fire of enthusiasm shall be aided with the oil of meditation, that God may say to us what was said by the Psalmist in the fourth Psalm, " Commune with your own heart, and be still."

We want to revere God, and put him first in our hearts and in our lives. We should read his Holy Word. This we promise to do in our pledge. The best time to read the Bible is in the quiet of the early morning, when we can peacefully commune with God through his Word.

Look at Martin Luther and the Reformation; at Oliver Cromwell and the Commonwealth. Think you that we should have had Puritanism if the Puritans had not loved the Word of God? Look at John Milton, the great poet. They were all men who loved the Bible and who honored God ; and God says, " They that honor me I will honor."

O fellow Endeavorer, do not begrudge the time you give to God in private prayer, in private meditation, in reading the Word of God. These things will all repay you.

And then as a part, and as a helpful part, of our private devotion, we come to God, lifting up our souls in prayer; and as we pray to him we find that our voices are never raised in vain. The men who have accomplished the most, the men who have been raised to the highest pinnacle of fame in the realm of the

Church, have been those who could wrestle with God in prayer. Oh, if we only knew the power God has given to us in prayer! So it was with Carey, who opened the doors to India, a field to which the Christian Endeavorers are succeeding. So it is with the Armenians of the present day. God grant that the unspeakable Turk may be wiped out of existence.

Brethren and sisters, I have not said what I wanted to say to you to-night on this first line of our platform, the Christian Endeavorers' private devotion; but, oh, if I failed in delivering to you the message to-night, I pray God that he will take a few crumbs and make them to be a feast indeed!

When this great Washington Convention is over, and we have returned to our quiet homes once more to pursue the even tenor of our ways, then shall we say to God, early in the morning, before we start the engagements of the day, " My God, I have come before thee this morning with all the refreshment of the night's rest. I have come to thee this morning that thou mightest renew my faith and renew within me thy spirit in this quiet hour, and that thou mightest speak to me thy will." And when he speaks to you be obedient. When he speaks do his will. Remember it was the great burden of Christ's life to do the will of his Father; and we shall walk in his footsteps when we follow him in the path of obedience and fulfil in the hours of the working-day the commands that were given to us at our private devotion.

The next sub-topic was " Support of Church Services," and the speaker was the President of the Ohio Christian Endeavor Union.

Address of Rev. J. H. Bomberger, Columbiana, O.

I coined a beatitude sometime ago, " Blessed is the pastor who expects much of his young people." I sincerely believe that it will stand the severest practical test; that the young people in almost any congregation are ready to respond heartily to any pastor who will approach them with tact and sympathy, with a challenge to engage in church work. Ye ask and have not, because ye ask amiss. I have little to say in defence of those Endeavorers who forsake the assembling of themselves together in the regular services of their own church home. But on the other hand, I believe that ordinarily the pastor is also at fault when this is the case. Let any pastor enter into the interests and thinking of his young people with cordial sympathy, and judiciously, and I doubt if he will ever know a time when they will not loyally rally to him and be ready to manifest their loyalty by regular attendance at the services of the Church. Let him once convince them individually and collectively that they are near to his heart, and he will generally find them near to his pulpit. This end will not be reached all at once, but will be the result of patient *training*. Whether pastors and congregations improve the opportunity or not, it is a fact that the Christian Endeavor Society offers them an inestimably important opportunity for developing, controlling, and determining the character of their participation in the activities of the Church. There are few congregations in which, under the inspiration of the young people's movement, a number of the young men and women have not stood ready to offer themselves to the pastor as subjects for this training. Many pastors, wise in their generation, have taken advantage of this God-sent opportunity. As a result, probably 5,000,000 of our young people are undergoing the training which will give the character to the church activity of the next generation. Additional importance is given to this when it is remembered that whether this special training is given or not, it has come to be generally admitted that one of the special characteristics of the Church of the next century will be a largely increased *lay activity*.

The conception of the relation existing between pastor and people is undergoing a clearly defined change. He is no longer merely their spiritual entertainer and comforter. He is their leader, the one who inspires them for zealous effort and unflagging endeavor. They do not need so much specific information with regard to Gospel truth, as to have those truths, which have oftentimes lost their edge through familiarity with them, made real, brought home by a sort of spiritual shock to their consciences, and all this leading up to noble and Christlike deeds. It has been said of art, " It is its province not to present specific details, but to impart a feeling." He is the truly successful pastor who, through his sermons and his mingling with his people, can communicate spiritual impulses which will manifest their presence by producing increased activity in all lines of work in the Master's vineyard. "Support of church services" means, first of all, an *attendance* upon them so regular that it can be counted on.

Many a pastor has been kept in a state of chronic disheartenment by his uncertainty as to whether his next Sunday evening congregation would be a churchful or a handful. When the impulse seized them, his people were there in force. Inspired by the memory of a large attendance, he had been led to hope that it would be a permanent thing. In this hope he has prepared with special care for the next Sunday evening, only to find that Rev. Mr. Catch-the-crowd across the way was billed to preach on " How To Be Happy Though Married," and that his sheep have all gone a-grazing in his neighbor's pasture. Now the Christian Endeavor Society has not banished all this, but it has done two things. In scores of cases, and almost wherever the pastor has cordially identified himself with it, it has inspired him with the comforting certainty that he has a loyal band who would be proof against all such enticements to church-wandering, and on whose loyalty to their church and its services their pastor and fellow members could depend at all hazards. And in the next place, it is constantly instilling the idea of unflinching loyalty to the local church and its interests, and faithful attendance upon all its services, into the hearts of hundreds of thousands of those who will make up the church membership of the next generation.

But this "support of church services" means more than your mere presence there; it includes the *enlistment of your social talents* on the side of Christ and his Church. Professor Wells has recently written an admirable little book, with a still more admirable title: " Social to Save." That is a Christian Endeavor idea in large part,—that social pursuits should be made a means of grace, should be utilized for soul-winning. Not social merely for "fun," but social "to save." And the important bearing of this upon my subject will be seen at once, when you remember that the social atmosphere of a congregation often does more to win or repel souls than the pastor's best sermons.

There are some churches whose social atmosphere is so Arctic that it is difficult to tell whether they remind you more of a cold-storage warehouse or an ice-factory. I have read of a poor fellow who was drowning. One standing near-by ran to his rescue, and picking up a plank, as the first thing available, he pushed it out over the ice through which the drowning man had broken, and called to him to lay hold of it. He tried to, but the end toward him was coated with ice, and his grasp slipped, until in desperation he cried, " In God's name give me the end of the plank that has no ice on it." And how many a one has reiterated that cry in our churches when repelled by our cold and formal greeting, if they even got that! You have heard of that commercial traveller who dropped into a church of his own denomination in a distant city one Sunday morning. He felt a little touch of homesickness, and longed for the cordial greeting of fraternal fellowship from some Christian who, though he might be a stranger in the flesh, could be recognized as a joint heir of the kingdom. No one responded to the wish of his heart, either before or after the service. He determined to make the advance himself, so, standing at the end of his pew, as the congregation filed out, taking no notice of him, he accosted a pleasant-faced old gentleman, saying, "Are you a member of this congregation?" The man answered, "Yes, sir, I am a deacon; but you have the advantage of me, I do not remember ever having met you," and passed on out.

And in this way the members of our churches often lose opportunities for social effort for Christ, and in support of the services of their church. It is the aim of our Endeavor Societies first of all to help the young to cultivate the social graces, and to teach them to look upon them as talents held in trust for the Master.

No pastor can have a more important ally in his efforts to develop and improve church attendance, and to make the services more inspiring and helpful, than is right at hand in his Young People's Society, if he is able and willing to utilize it for these purposes.

The last speaker was Rev. W. H. York, of Ithaca, N. Y., a longtime friend of Christian Endeavor, and a pastor of a Methodist Church. His topic was " Public Confession."

Address of Rev. W. H. York, Ithaca, N. Y.

There are two vital elements in public confession. One is the manner of its expression and the other is its constituent composition.

Some have tried to quiet their consciences with the idea that their duty was done if they lived in such a way as to exemplify the teachings of the Master. They forget that there are about them a multitude of those whose lives may be blameless, who are totally opposed to Christianity, So great has been the power of the Gospel in our land that multitudes have been unconsciously influenced by it, and they are shining like the moon by a borrowed light, but, alas! like the moon, are destitute of life. They forget that a witness who refuses to testify may be a positive hurt to the case when it goes to the jury. Christian Endeavor defines public confession as taking some part aside from singing,— a verbal testimony given personally ; or, in case of necessary absence, a written testimony may be given.

It does not for a moment admit that the full duty is done when a song has been sung or a number called out for the rest to sing.

Much care should be given to the composition of a testimony, for such is the carelessness of some in this respect that it would have been better sometimes that no testimony had been attempted. We are to avoid the public confession of private sins. Ofttimes the influence of a meeting is seriously injured by the indiscreet publications of private matters. The account of a long line of failures in one's attempt to serve the Master may do serious harm to the cause, while a long. inopportune exhortation to others about their failures may fail to help the interest of the meeting or the cause.

A public testimony should be, first, a clear statement of personal faith in Jesus Christ, and then a firm testimony of an experimental knowledge of the saving power of this faith.

The apostle said, " I am not ashamed of the Gospel of Christ, for it is the power of God unto salvation." We are also to confess our great love for Christ. The need of a public confession may be seen in our own lives, for the very beginning of a Christian life involves a confession of Christ. You can not have fire without heat; no more can you have a true Christian fire in your soul without some warmth being felt by others. Public confession is essential for the perpetuity of this experience. It is but a step from silent discipleship to indifference and doubt, then open denial. Public confession of the help Christ gives us helps to continue humility and to remind us from whence cometh our strength. But more than all else, our hope of heaven is closely allied to a confession of Christ. The Master says, " Whosoever shall confess me before men, him will I also confess before my Father which is in heaven; but whosoever shall deny me before men, him will I also deny before my Father which is in heaven."

Our personal influence will be measured by our public confession of Christ. There is a vast difference between a guide-board standing by the roadside, with its mute utterance, and an intelligent, communicative guide that can answer our questions. Justice to our Master demands that we give testimony for him. Of the ten lepers that were healed, only one returned to acknowledge the power of the Master. How sad must have been his heart as he witnessed their ingratitude when he said, " Where are the nine ? "

It is sometimes given as an excuse that diffidence is so great that the testimony will be unworthy so kind a friend; but the Scriptures teach us that out of the abundance of the heart the mouth speaketh. If the heart is filled to overflowing it will find that testifying for the Master is a delight and a privilege.

Some falter because they realize that their life is not what it should be; the remedy is easy,— correct the life. It may be that this faltering comes from a false humility and we are mistaken about ourselves. Genuine humility does not hinder service, but adds to its value.

But the most common hindrance to public testimony is the habit of silence. One has come to feel they have no duty to do, and so think nothing about it and almost feel it an intrusion if the matter is brought to their attention. The recurrence of neglected opportunities soon stifles conviction of duty and they drift on heedlessly. The revelation of the value of a human soul and their responsibility for keeping silent ought to stir the most sluggish. If we would only realize that our testimony is an effort to throw out the life-line, and that if we fail to do this we are in a measure responsible, it may help us to overcome the hindrances that cause us to falter.

New York Avenue Presbyterian Church.

The attractions elsewhere had little or no effect upon the attendance at the meeting at the New York Avenue Presbyterian Church, for the church was crowded to the doors, and the large audience enjoyed two admirable addresses on the topic of the day, " Saved to Serve," excellent singing, and a very interesting discussion of how best to serve the pastor.

Major Charles A. Bird, U. S. A., presided over the meeting, and the chorus of some seventy voices was led by Director J. A. Rose, rendering in a splendid manner many beautiful selections during the twenty minutes' praise meeting which preceded the devotional exercises conducted by the Rev. J. B. North, of Anacostia. As the first speaker of the evening, the chairman introduced the Rev. Asher Anderson, of Meriden, Conn., who addressed himself to the subject of " How May the Society Help the Pastor? "

Address of Rev. Asher Anderson, Meriden, Conn.

A correct answer to the question will bring us to the very root of things in Endeavor life. Indeed, if we do not mistake the purpose of the organization in its inception, it was almost assuredly the object our beloved president had in view when he gathered the young people of his parish in his parlor in Portland, that in training them for Christian work they might become the most useful possible in the church of which he was the pastor. Like all true pastors, he not only saw the great need of developing the lives of young Christians in the work of the Gospel of Jesus Christ, but he also realized most profoundly how necessary trained workers were if he himself would accomplish any permanent results in the larger field of his Church.

It will be a revelation to some, I know, if I say that the pastor needs the help of his young people. To a large extent does it obtain with churches, that it is the individual member who needs the pastor; although he does not consider the very important fact that the pastor needs him just so much. There ought to come a time when the Christian who has been educated in the doctrine of the kingdom of Jesus Christ, and made strong in the spiritual truths of the religious life, and to whom has been discovered the wonderful opportunities for splendid service, should, instead of making such large demands upon the pastor's resources, himself provide for the pastor, that the strength of his ministry might be greatly increased.

We do not expect in the home that children will remain babies, never growing beyond the solicitous attention of wearied mothers. We do not expect that a young man entering upon a business career will never get away from the particular instruction of his employer. Yet what appears to us so unnatural in every other sphere seems to be the natural thing in the life and work of the Church. Babies are all right, interesting, and full of promise; but babies grow. Some babies presently get large enough to cast aside swaddling-clothes and the nursery bottle, large enough to be profoundly ashamed of baby talk; but how many spiritual babies there are in our churches, who, if they were in their right places, would be in the promising department of the Sunday school. Think for a moment of the years through which they have listened to good, plain, helpful preaching; think how long they have been in the Sunday school studying the Bible; and they are still without religious doctrine that is definite, or spiritual faculty that is resourceful for service. I was told only the other day of a man who had been identified with the Church from his childhood, and was a principal of one of the public schools of his city, who asked his pastor in all seriousness how old Jesus was when he preached his Sermon on the Mount, remarking that he must have been about twelve years of age. And the various agencies which are employed under the auspices of the Church are certainly sufficient to create a good deal more intelligence on the part of the members than the average member illustrates.

The most inconsistent thing in the Lord's universe is an endowed soul ceasing to grow in the knowledge of the Lord Jesus Christ. The most discouraging element in Church life is the spirit which sets aside the importance of coming up to " the measure of the fulness of Christ." And on the other hand, there is no element that is at once so inspiring and so helpful to an ambitious pastor as the spirit which, like the noble Bereans, gives itself to study to know whether these things are so or not.

Those are the workers in the Church and the great helpers to the pastor who know the most about their Bibles. Like all Gaul, a church may be divided into three parts: one seeks for reasons to oppose the pastor; another is indifferent, and a third part works in the cause. The Christian Endeavor stands to develop intelligent Bible workers. It makes the pastor's work very hard if doctrine goes without being inculcated, if nourishment is given without becoming assimilated, or if direction is given without response in service. It is in the help given to a pastor that the Society really justifies its existence. To be conspicuous solely as an Endeavor Society, to have no reference to the larger work of the Church life, is totally contrary to both the genius and end of the Endeavor movement. I am not telling any tales out of school when I say that not a few pastors have found a preference bestowed upon the Endeavor meeting and not upon the services of the church. Wherever that is known the Endeavor Society fails of its purpose and had better disband. Nothing is so natural to life as activity. The absence of force is proof that vitality has ceased. and from these the society that is not doing anything gives proof that it does not really exist. The constitution may be carefully formulated; the pledge may hang like a beautiful painting on the wall; a number of names may be on the roll ; but if that great work wished for and planned by a wise, judicious pastor is not accomplished it is not a genuine Endeavor Society and does not deserve to be called by that name.

A soul for hearty service in this cause must be dominated by the Divine Spirit, willing to serve, ambitious to fill some place ; and only under the blessing of that Spirit will any Endeavor member make what is oftentimes too much a form. Nor can we come to the place where our consecration will be helpful, except we have received that blessing. Let us compare the careers of Wolsey and St. Paul, the sad lament of the politician who lost all for temporal glory, with that of the Christian servant whose joyful acclaim was, " I have fought the good fight." For Paul's end, if we could conceive the basis of it, we must go back to the time when, flooded with the vision which fell upon him, he cried out, " Lord, what wilt thou have me to do ? "

Mr. Anderson's remarks were followed by a duet, "Saved by Grace," finely sung by the Rev. B. F. Lamb and Miss Ella Knight. Then Mr. J. H. Banton, of Waco, Tex., was introduced to conduct an open parliament on the line of Mr. Anderson's subject. Remarks were limited to a minute, and many interesting suggestions were made during the ten or twelve minutes allowed. One stated that her pastor was helped by the Christian Endeavorers making a special point of coming to church when the weather was so bad that few other people would go. Another explained that he came to Washington at personal inconvenience to represent his pastor. One pastor was helped by excursion socials held to raise funds to pay his way to Washington. Then another was helped by one of his congregation seeing to it that strangers were brought to the church and made welcome, and so on the suggestions ran.

The Rev. Mr. Lamb sang a solo in a very pleasing manner, and the last speaker of the evening was introduced, the pastor of the First Presbyterian Church, Boston, whose topic was "How May the Pastor Help the Society?"

Address of Rev. Scott F. Hershey, Ph. D., Boston, Mass.

In this magnificent sunset hour of the nineteenth century we are rejoicing in the fulfilment of the prophecy of the prophet Joel. Young men and women are weaving into the meshes of every-day life, spiritual and immortal dreams. If the spread of the Gospel in the classic countries of Eastern Europe in the first century was of God; if the patriotic and moral, the intellectual and religious, new birth of Central and Western Europe in the sixteenth century was from God; if the great missionary age inaugurated in the first part of the nineteenth century came down out of heaven from God, then is the movement of Christian Endeavor, rising so strangely and growing so rapidly at the end of this century, an unseen but not unfelt ocean wave of divine truth, inspiration, and power, which had its rise at the foot of the Cross.

The Lord moves swiftly sometimes on his operative providences, and works on a large scale; as when he led a nation out of Egypt, or gave to his church at Jerusalem its first Pentecost.

The Christian Endeavor movement is a new Pentecost, which has fallen from God upon the young people of our churches. Identified with this organized effort in Christian life and work are a great majority of the most pious and consecrated of our young people. They constitute the volunteer arm of the Christian activity of the Church, and the recruiting is unremittingly going on. Full of life, consecrated in purpose, ready for duty, these raw recruits stand with the experienced Christians, and are just as ready to be instructed, trained, drilled for the service of the Master and for usefulness in their day and generation. What can the pastor do for these willing and waiting young men and maidens to bring and keep their life and action in harmony with the spirit and mission of the Church and the will of God? They want to be loyal to the Church, true to duty, and faithful in Christian life. What can the pastor do to help them?

He must win them to himself, as the proper leader in Christian life and work. Sympathies, most cordial in character and strong in confidence, must speedily be established. Personal attachments must be formed, so strong that they may rightfully be characterized by the word "friendship" — aye, even by the word "love."

Personal devotion for, personal interest in, and personal remembrance of their followers show the secret spring of the personal power of the great leaders of the world. Socrates mingled socially with his pupils in the Athenian gardens; Jesus bathed with the cool water the tired feet of his disciples; Paul identified with himself in the work his followers; and in the last chapter of Romans he makes kindly mention, as he holds in loving remembrance, thirty-two of them.

If the pastor has so won his Christian Endeavor Society his young people are ready as his pupils to receive his teaching. If he has reached their hearts they are prepared to sit under his words. And here, commensurate with his opportunity to teach the values, the sublimities, and the hopes of the Gospel, is his responsibility to teach that Gospel as it flows from the well-springs of truth and undefiled by human theorizing.

The sole effective remedy for the ills of life and the evils of the country is the redemptive truth of the Lord. The pastor must have ideals of conscience, of duty, and of life. The heroes of patience, endurance, perseverance, and suffering, from Joseph to Paul, and from ancient martyr to modern missionary, must be examples of those ideals each of which is being duplicated in Christian life about us. He must have hanging in the picture gallery of his mind, and cherish in his heart, the high ideals of the Madonnas of art, the Beatrices of literature, and the Jeanne d'Arcs of devotion; and the Jenny Linds and Florence Nightingales and Clara Bartons of charity and service.

If they are given the truth as it is in Christ, unadulterated and undiluted, both as touching the degrading forces of sin and the elevating forces of righteousness, there will be an accentuated Christian life, in which men and women will stand for both righteousness and right with increased emphasis.

Leading young life into sweeter and holier ways of affection, into richer experiences with grace and truth, into higher ranges of meditation, into loftier aspirations, into greater attachment for and clearer understanding of the Word of life, into more sun-lighted walks of trust, into more force and strength of Christian character, into happier and more joyful and more hopeful natures, and as a crown over all, into a larger and more blessed service for God among men,— if this be not the greatest and happiest field for the exercise of leadership, then, indeed, are the aspirations of a pastor carnal and not pious.

The call now is for more intelligent loyalty to the Church to which we belong. It may sound strange, but it is nevertheless true, that in no denomination is denominational loyalty so lightly regarded as in Presbyterianism. Though considered doctrinally narrow and somewhat creed-bound, the passage into other communions is easier than is found in other denominations, or from other denominations into ours. People of wealth and liberality among Presbyterians make large and frequent gifts to interdenominational institutions and to other denominations; we put no questions about a subscription to a creed to those seeking admission into our communion. There will be no disloyalty if pastors rightly teach the history, explain the triumph, and point out the glory of Presbyterianism. In contributing both to the spirit and form of civil and religious liberty, representative government and equalities of law in the new empire of the western continent, Presbyterianism has won remarkable testimony from jurists, statesmen, and *literati*, from Burke and Macaulay to Carlyle and Bancroft.

There is another side of Christian Endeavor duty where the pastor's leadership must neither be mistaken nor misunderstood. Next to love of God is love of country. Stalwart religion and true patriotism go about over the world, and have come down through the past hand in hand. No one will look to the pulpit to take the lead in the controversy over the tariff or currency or mere administrative economy; but the very logic of consistency requires that in every great struggle over a moral cause, in which is involved the complete circle of those moral interests which most affect the welfare of the people, the maintenance of free institutions, the preservation of the sovereign rights of the individual conscience, and in all that is closely related to the salvation of souls, the pulpit must go in advance in creating sentiment and leading in action. Here no minister dare abdicate his leadership without humiliating himself before the throne of his own manhood and becoming an imbecile in the judgment of all right-hearted and right-minded people.

The young people of Christian Endeavor, in all the denominations, will thank me for saying to-night that they are ready to proclaim that there must be no more war between Christian nations, but instead, a high sovereign court of the nations, permanently sitting for the peaceful settlement of all international frictions; that the saloon must be driven from the strongholds of political domination at the ballot-box, in the Legislature, and in the courts of justice ; that demagogues in financial and civil circles shall be held up with increasing disapproval before the scorn of righteous judgment, and that all interference with organic forms of law, and all attempted subversions of free institutions and general intelligence, whether arising from Mammonism, Mormonism, or Romanism, must cease absolutely, so that the nation may fear God, keep his statutes, and enter upon the twentieth century the safeguard of liberties of the world and the guaranty of the peace of the earth.

Central Hall.

The meeting was presided over by Prof. J. L. Howe, of Lexington, Va. After the praise service, led by Mr. Charles S. Clark, and Rev. H. R. Naylor, D.D., had read the devotional service, Prof. Howe introduced Bishop J. W. Hott, D.D., of Cedar Rapids, Io., who spoke on "The Individual Responsibility of Soul-Winning."

Address of Bishop J. W. Hott, D.D., Cedar Rapids, Io.

What is it to win a soul ? It is to put in the soul a motive and an inspiration, and about the soul an influence and power, which, combined, will cause it to follow these enticements.

To win a soul to Christ is to bring into and about that soul so much of Christ as will draw it away from sin and attach it permanently to Christ. The soul left to itself will never come to God.

The purpose and plan of all grace shown in the Christian system is to so touch the soul by all influences that the strongest motives and solicitations to accept Jesus as the one and all-sufficient Saviour may be brought to bear effectively in human salvation.

What is the great inspiration to be stirred in the human soul ? What is the supreme power to be brought to bear upon the heart of our fellow man to lead him to Christ ?

There are many things that may be done and ought to be done. One thing *must* be done. Jesus Christ must be so represented to the soul as to attract and draw it to himself. We exhort too soon and present Christ too imperfectly. This revelation of Christ will show the soul its own need of him. He is not only the soul's supply, but he creates the demand. This shows a saving Christ,— a soul-cleansing, soul-renewing, soul-inspiring Christ.

The perfect attestations of Christ before the bar of the human conscience by his chosen agencies and representatives will do all that God can do in winning a soul from sin and death. He is the face of beauty, the heart of love, the smile of heaven, the welcome of God, that can alone call the soul out of itself into God. Jesus said, " If I be lifted up, I will draw all men unto me."

To make this presentation is, under the superintendence of the Holy Spirit, the supreme business of every true believer in Jesus Christ. It is the great work of the Church on earth. To it every member of the Church is personally bound with indissoluble bonds. Men are not saved by herds but by individuals. These are not employed in saving others in other ways than as individuals.

I. *The basis of this personal responsibility for soul-saving.*

1. It is not in organization. Organization and organized Christian society are only the aggregation or synthesis of individualism and individual responsibility. It is to be feared that sometimes we enter organization with the delusive idea that we shall lose or perhaps pool our personal responsibilities.

But we can not make even the most splendid organization reach further than the stretch of individuality combined in an aggregation of power. The basis of all responsibility is in the individual, and so is purely personal.

May the importance of this theme be emphasized as it is brought before us in this Christian Endeavor Convention. There is a growing sense of responsibility in the use of money,— Christian stewardship,— and it is well. There is a sincere interest in the work of education in all departments, and the cause of good citizenship enlists our hearts, while we have a profound sympathy for the heathen world. All this is intensely well. But while men feel that they must do greater things in these fields, we must emphasize the fact that the *greatest of all work is soul-saving.* We can not do this by paying money alone, or by proxy. To this work we are held personally responsible. God does not take substitutes for us in the great work of winning souls.

2. It lies in our adaptation to the work. There is a utilitarian argument we can not but reckon with. What ought to be done at all ought to be done in the best way and by the means best adapted to its doing. Primary obligation rests there. The use of human methods by the Lord is an old subject for theology. For us, as the organization of the young of all Christendom, the question is a practical one.

You all know this work is largely with the young. It is the young we hope to reach in our homes, in our churches, in the country, in the hamlets, and in the great cities. It is so in most of the foreign mission fields I have visited. This is the age of the young.

The use of the young, with their power and methods, shows God's plan. He takes the practical and simple and natural and emphasizes its power and makes its ministry divine and mighty. In the Christian Endeavor movement, this is no longer a theory but an attested fact. Thousands of pastors in all parts of the world testify to the power of the young people's organization in leading souls to Christ. They are the very hand-touch of Christ. I once looked a long time at a painting in one of the galleries of Berlin, Germany, representing the raising of the daughter of Jairus, by Jesus. The picture is a beautiful one. The calm Christ is the central figure. Beside him are the father and mother, whose faces of inexpressible sorrow, agony, and anxiety one can never forget. Near-by are the three disciples. The half-grown maiden is just waking from the sleep of death, as the hand of Jesus is reached out to help her. Somehow, as poor a critic of art as I am, I could not help but feel a weakness in the picture. I recalled a work of one of the master's, I think Kranach, which I had seen in the Crocker Art Gallery in Sacramento, Cal. It presents the same scene in almost all the details, only in it Jesus has taken hold of the maiden, and she is alive. It is true to Christ. And he "took her by the hand, and the damsel arose." That touch has warmth and life in it. The young people's organizations are the warm hand-grasp of Jesus and the Church. Without that touch the picture is weak and defective. What personal responsibility if your hand fails in the grasping of some soul nearest you!

The direct command of God no Christian can disregard without disloyalty to him. The Bible plainly shows us that we are our brother's keeper. "Go ye into all the world," as it fell from the lips of Jesus upon the ears of the disciples on the unknown mountain of Galilee, falls still on our ears upon these ends of the world have come, with a no less power. After over 1,800 years we are just beginning to see and feel what Christ really is to this old world, and what his commission really means. He is still and now more alive than ever before. In our parlance we have put it, "Go, or send;" the facts are we must do both. You know the command; why should I dwell upon it at length? What have we to do but to obey?

II. *What are some of the fruits of a sense of this personal responsibility of soul-saving?*

1. Deep humility before God. Who can do this work? It must be done under God's directions, by his methods, and all to his glory. We are nothing. All our success will be due to God, and all power and honor his. A proud, boastful, self-sufficient spirit or self-praising spirit is shameful in the professed

Christian. The prince who came into the death-chamber of his father the king wearing his crown, to see how it would fit, was asked to wait till the king was dead before putting on the crown. As long as God lives it becomes us to go humbly about our work. Let Jesus wear the crown.

2. It should lead us to the largest possible preparation for this greatest of all works. He who has a note in bank to meet will strive to meet it promptly. He who feels this responsibility will gird himself for the task.

3. Personal acquaintance and familiarity with the Christ we are to represent to others. Intelligent and reasonable men will not readily follow mere philosophies in matters of religion, and especially that which pertains to giving up of sin and to faith unto salvation. Speculation in spiritual things does not reach men's hearts. Paul was a great soul-winner. Though he was a mighty reasoner, he would now belong to the realistic type, and not the idealistic. He would often exclaim, "We know." He put this down in the most trying conditions and places and rested all upon his vision of Jesus. In this "we know" he was like his Master, however different may have been their methods of knowing or sources of knowledge. This personal knowledge includes the Word of God so constantly emphasized in these great gatherings.

4. It means that we are to be filled with the Spirit of Jesus by constant communion with him. I once climbed down into the cell of awful gloom in which Lord Byron had himself incarcerated all night, before he would write his soulful description of Venice, the Prison, and the Bridge of Sighs. If he would thus be shut in with the gloom of death that his soul might be chastened with horror of horrors, how much rather should we, conscious of our personal responsibility for the saving of souls, be shut in with Christ, and filled with him and his Spirit, when all our success will depend upon the faithfulness with which we should represent him to our fellow men !

5. Personal responsibility means personal work in soul-winning. It is this delusive idea of soul-saving in masses that opens the way for the neglect and loss of the individual. Jesus preached his first sermon to one man, Nicodemus, one of the Sanhedrin. His next great recorded sermon is to a lone woman of the Samaritans at the well of Jacob. We may learn some good lessons from him. Often the great sermon of nowadays is lost because it is not followed by personal conversation with the unsaved. In the greatest and most permanent revival I ever labored, in which over 300 persons were converted, nearly every one of these hundreds was brought to Christ by direct personal effort. When a church thus has personal interest in converts they are not so soon let go. If you rescue a man from wreck, and carry him to the hospital, you naturally have a lasting interest in him. It is none the less so in winning souls to Christ.

6. It will lead us to do that which is nearest at hand. I believe in a call to the foreign field, but somehow can not help questioning the call of a man or woman to that field who has not heart or hand for the work at home. It is doing what is at hand that gives proof to a call to a wider field. The representatives of the Young Men's Christian Association, who have had such good success in India and other distant lands, had great success in our own land. How can we expect to be of use in the most difficult foreign field when we have been of no use in the comparatively easy field at home? "Return to thy house," was the command to one whom Jesus saved in Gadara, and "declare how great things God hath done for thee." So he would say to us now. Begin with the one at your elbow. There your responsibilities are first and greatest. If you can win souls here you may do so in the foreign fields.

7. It should lead us to the use of the best and most effective means, and the employment of all our powers, in winning souls to Christ. The presentation of the vast resources and means in soul-winning is beyond this address. One thing it does suggest. Personal responsibility means that we are to use ourselves. Large-hearted sympathy and love are essential. A cold-hearted, dry soul will accomplish but little. Love for the message, love for those to whom we bear it, is essential. The one element of Jesus which surpasses the world and all that went before him and all who have come after him is his love, his

great soul. After the accumulating light of eighteen centuries we are just beginning to read that love in some measure of its fulness. That is the Christ power to-day. His spirit of justice, tenderness, and love is our weapon of all mightiness.

8. It must prompt unwearying patience. Souls are not always won in a day. "Love hopeth all things" in soul-winning. We can not consecrate ourselves entirely to soul-winning unless we consecrate ourselves eternally to this sweet task.

9. This sense of personal responsibility must prompt us to self-forgetfulness and to the most thorough work possible to our present state. It will not allow the care for ourselves or for our own ease to let us stop short of our best in the most thorough work. For a soul to be deluded by a false hope, based on a wrong conception of God and our relation to him, or on a false life and character, is an awful thing. Our anxiety to do much work may lead us to do defective and superficial work.

A few months ago, in the home of a Christian gentleman in Beatrice. Neb., while at dinner I mentioned an incident in connection with a burning of a home in Dayton, Wash., a few years ago. The gentleman, with a saddened voice said, "We lost our all in our dear old home near Ottumwa, Io. in a fire which burned it when I was young." "What," said I, "did you lose?" He replied, "We lost all we had in that fire that night. I lost three brothers." I asked how they were sleeping, and why they were not gotten out, since he was saved. Said he, "One was sleeping in the bed with me, and two were in another room." How I wished I had the inquiry back! — but in my anxiety I asked, "Could not you have awakened your brother?" I shall never forget the unutterable sadness of that face as he said, "I thought I had him awake when I fought my way through the smoke and flame." How sad for you, and you, and for me, if in our appeal to those sleeping in sin we only partially awaken them and have to say at the last, "I thought I had him awake;" "I thought I had her heart won to Jesus." May the Holy Spirit fall on us as upon those in the beginning, and use us in winning souls to Jesus, who now places these interests of eternity in our feeble hands!

Mrs. Nellie Wilson Shir-Cliffe sang "My Soul Cries Out." An open parliament was then held, presided over by Judge John D. Ellis, of Newport, Ky., when practical evangelistic methods were discussed.

The beautiful white banner, with the inscription "Christian Endeavor Fellowship, Presented by the United Society of Christian Endeavor," was then presented to Chicago for having the largest net increase of Christian Endeavor Societies during the past year.

Philadelphia has held this banner for the past two years. It was presented by Mr. William L. Turner, president of the Philadelphia Union, and accepted for the Chicago Union by Mr. Frank E. Page, an ex-president.

Then Rev. F. C. Ottman, of Newark, N. J., delivered the following address on "The Sword of the Spirit."

Address of Rev. Ford C. Ottman, Newark, N. J.

In the Epistle to the Ephesians, the Apostle Paul conceives of the Christian as engaged in a conflict. This conflict is not with flesh and blood, but with principalities, and powers, and rulers of the darkness of this world, and wicked spirits in heavenly places.

In order to compete successfully with these forces, Paul urges the Christian to be clothed with the armor of God, which has been provided for this purpose. The loins are to be girt about with truth. The heart is to be covered with a breastplate of righteousness. The feet are to be shod with the preparation of the Gospel of Peace. The shield of faith is to be worn, and the head is to be covered with the helmet of salvation.

The only offensive weapon of which the apostle speaks is called " the sword of the Spirit, which is the Word of God."

We have seen that the Holy Spirit has come into the world on a mission, both to the unsaved and to the believer, and the instrument for the accomplishment of this mission is here given us. It is called "The Word of God."

The Spirit of God is a person, and has come into the world upon a distinct mission. The Word of God is the expression of God's mind and purpose concerning us, and this Word is the instrument which is used by the Holy Spirit in the accomplishment of his mission. The Word is here called " the sword of the Spirit," and this is by no means an unusual symbol for the Word of God. When the Apostle John had a vision of the Son of man standing in the midst of the seven candlesticks, he saw issue from his mouth a sharp, two-edged sword.

It would be impossible to make any mistake as to the meaning of this symbol, when we read the statement of Jesus concerning the judgment: " He that rejecteth me, and receiveth not my words, hath one that judgeth him: the word that I have spoken, the same shall judge him in the last day." (John xii. 48.)

We read of the sword for the first time in the book of Genesis: " So he drove out the man; and he placed at the east of the garden of Eden Cherubims, and a flaming sword which turned every way, to keep the way of the tree of life." (Gen. iii. 24.) Evidently the sword here is also a symbol of the Word of God. God had commanded the man not to eat of the tree of the knowledge of good and evil, under the penalty of death; and when man violated this command, God placed the flaming sword before the Tree of Life, lest man should eat of the fruit of that tree, and live forever, and so violate the integrity of his Word.

In addition to these references, showing that this symbol is not uncommon, we have the familiar passage in the book of Hebrews: " For the word of God is quick, and powerful, and sharper than any two-edged sword, piercing even to the dividing asunder of soul and spirit, and of the joints and marrow, and is a discerner of the thoughts and intents of the heart." (Heb. iv. 12.)

The mission of the Spirit is to convict the world of sin, and of righteousness, and of judgment, and the weapon by which this conviction is wrought is " the sword of the Spirit, which is the Word of God." We need to remember that this Word of God is the sword of the Spirit, and not of man.

There is a practical side to this subject that needs to be considered in conclusion. The Apostle Paul declares that in meeting the temptations of life we need to be armed with this sword of the Spirit; by no other weapon will it be possible to achieve the victory. Just after his baptism Jesus was driven by the Spirit into the wilderness, where for forty days he was tempted of Satan. The final assault was made upon him after the forty days were ended. Jesus was human, and he was hungry. The devil said to him, " If thou be the Son of God, command this stone that it be made bread." This was a real temptation, for Jesus was really hungry; but he won the victory over Satan by the use of the sword of the Spirit. " It is written," he said, "that man shall not live by bread alone, but by every word of God." These words he had found in the eighth chapter of Deuteronomy. The sword of the Spirit, which is the Word of God, served him in the hour of need.

A second time he was assaulted by Satan — taken to a high mountain and shown the kingdoms of the world. " The devil said unto him, All this power will I give thee, and the glory of them; if thou therefore wilt worship me, all shall be thine." Jesus, again drawing the sword of the Spirit, said unto him, "Get thee behind me, Satan: for it is written, Thou shalt worship the Lord thy God, and him only shalt thou serve." These words he found in the sixth chapter of Deuteronomy; and in this second assault he won the victory by means of " the sword of the Spirit, which is the Word of God."

The third time he was tempted, when the devil brought him to the pinnacle of the temple and said unto him, " If thou be the Son of God, cast thyself down from hence." And the devil, himself drawing the sword, but destitute of the Spirit, adds still further, " For it is written, He shall give his angels charge over thee, to keep thee: and in their hands they shall bear thee up, lest at any time thou dash thy foot against a stone. "

Jesus, answering, said unto him, " It is said, Thou shalt not tempt the Lord thy God." These words he found also written in the sixth chapter of Deuteronomy. And for the third time the victory was won by means of the sword of the Spirit, which is the Word of God. On a single page of the Holy Scripture Jesus found a sufficient foil to this threefold assault of Satan, and with the wreath of victory fresh upon his brow, went down the mountain-side.

This is a practical and valuable truth for us to learn : if we are to conquer in life's temptations, we must be armed with the weapon by which alone the victory can be won. This is a spiritual conflict; it is not with flesh and blood; it is against the principalities and powers of evil, and God has given us an armor which affords protection. He has also been pleased to place in our hands this aggressive weapon, " the sword of the Spirit, which is the Word of God."

Tent Endeavor.

The services were presided over by Rev. Dr. Wayland Hoyt, of Philadelphia, who made a most genial chairman. He made a playful allusion to the hats of the ladies that caused a great many feminine fingers to search for hat-pins preparatory to filling their laps with the achieved dreams of milliners. The praise service was conducted by Mr. E. O. Excell. The devotional exercises, consisting of responsive Scripture reading and an eloquent prayer, were conducted by Rev. L. B. Wilson, of Washington.

Dr. Hoyt, in explaining the absence of Mr. Giles Kellogg, of San Diego, Cal., who was to have told the story of the Floating Society of Christian Endeavor, said that it would be unnecessary to say that Mr. Kellogg could not possibly be present, as it was perfectly well known that an Endeavorer never failed to be present when he had a duty to perform, if he possibly could. The Floating Society, said Dr. Hoyt, showed the adjustability of Christian Endeavor. It was fitted for churches widely differing in their theology, and was at home and useful in every place and among all classes. In lieu of Mr. Kellogg's address, he read interesting and copious extracts from the report of Miss Antoinette P. Jones, superintendent of the Floating Societies.

The audience and chorus sang " Throw Out the Life-Line " with fine effect, and then was heard a voice from the other side of the world. Dr. Hoyt introduced Miss Margaret W. Leitch, of Jaffna, Ceylon, who made an address on the pressing needs of foreign missions, in which work she has been engaged for seventeen years.

Address of Miss Margaret W. Leitch, Jaffna, Ceylon.

The evangelization of the world should be the great work of the Church and not merely a small part of the Church's work. If the evangelization of the world should be the great work of the Church, then it ought to be the great work of every member in the Church, and it ought to be *your* great work and *mine.*

Jesus said, " Seek ye first the kingdom of God." First does not mean second. Are the Christians of America making the evangelization of the world their first, their great, work? Are they consecrating to it their highest talent, their most devoted service? Or are they simply making it a byplay, a May holiday ?

Nearly all of the great missionary boards are burdened with debt, and as a result reductions have been ordered in many mission fields. Let us try to make vivid to our minds what these reductions mean to the work. As a result of the reductions ordered many mission village schools will this year be closed and some thousands of children turned out, who will eagerly be welcomed into the heathen opposition schools. In these schools they will be taught from heathen books which will be put into their hands; they will be taught to ridicule and make a mock of the birth, life, and death on the cross of Jesus Christ. Young men from the higher mission schools will this year be turned out, men who are being trained for the teachers, colporteurs, and evangelists of the future. The printing and circulation of Christian literature will this year be curtailed. Many trained catechists and evangelists will this year be dismissed, and that through no fault of theirs, and their work abandoned. The hearts of all Christian workers and of all members of the Christian community, where these reductions are enforced, be appalled, and the hearts of the opposers of Christianity will be elated and jubilant. Hinduism, Mohammedanism, and other false religions will, in this way, receive such an impetus as they have never had before. The faith of whole communities in the stability, permanency, and final success of Christianity and of Christian mission work will receive a staggering blow, and mission work, in not a few fields, will be put back many years. The heathen and Mohammedans will say, "Christianity has begun to die out in America. The Christians of America are reducing their work this year; next year they will reduce still more, and in a few years the missionaries and their work will be cleared out and Christianity will have proved a failure." And thus the name of our Lord Jesus Christ, that name which is above every name, and which ought to be dearer to us than life itself, will be ridiculed and dishonored by multitudes of people.

The Hindu and Mohammedan preachers will proclaim the news of this reduction far and wide. Their papers will be full of it. It will be the one great subject of conversation in the villages. How can your missionaries face it? How can they explain it? Will they say that the Church of Christ is too poor to carry on the work which it has begun? Or will they *tell the truth*, and say that professing Christians love their luxuries more than they love their Lord?

Will these reductions mean nothing to you? They will mean something to the heart of your Christ. They will mean something to those, your most noble missionaries, who are cheerfully giving up their lives to this work. These reductions will break the hearts of some of them. Your missionaries are brave men and women; they can look death in the face without quailing; but they will not be able to look these reductions in the face without quailing.

Are the Christians of America too poor to carry on, unimpaired, the work which their fathers and mothers began with so much prayer, sacrifice, and consecration? I could imagine in this country such distress and wide-spread disaster that, looking up into the face of Christ, the Christians of America might be able to say, "Dear Lord, thou knowest that we can not carry on our foreign mission work." But does any such state of affairs exist? This country in eight months exported to other countries merchandise which it did not require at home, to the value of $600,000,000. Is this a poverty-stricken country? Of all the changes which have taken place in this country during the past seventeen years, since I went as a missionary to Ceylon, the change which strikes me with the greatest astonishment is the increase in luxuries. Look at the way in which the majority of Christians are living. Are not their homes comfortable and even luxurious? Are not their tables loaded with dainties? Do they not "fare sumptuously every day"? Are they not "clothed in purple and fine linen"? Do they not have magnificent churches in which they may worship, with one, or perhaps two, highly-paid choirs?

The Christians of this country expended last year only about $5,000,000 for foreign missions; but last year the people of this country expended $22,000,000 for chewing-gum; $50,000,000 for bicycles; $400,000,000 for amusements; $600,000,000 for jewelry.

Have the Christians of America forgotten that there are in the world to-day a thousand millions of heathen and Mohammedans, half of whom have never heard that the world's Redeemer has come?

The great work of world-wide evangelization will never be accomplished until Christians deliberately turn away from the pursuit of honor, wealth, and pleasure, and choose instead a life of daily self-denial, in order that they may be able to carry out the great commission, entrusted to them by Jesus Christ, of preaching the Gospel to every creature.

This vast work can never be accomplished in any easier way. Jesus says, "If any man will come after me, let him deny himself and take up his cross daily and follow me."

Not only must there be more self-sacrifice on the part of Christians; there must also be in future a *closer and more personal* tie between the home and foreign workers, and a clearer realization of *personal responsibility.*

It is a striking fact that while nearly all of the great denominational boards are in debt, the women's boards, as far as I have been able to learn, are not in debt, and reductions have not been ordered in connection with their work.

What is the secret of this? The women's work is pledged work. The women's boards present each year to the Women's Missionary Societies of the Church a statement of the sums needed for the support of the missionaries on the field, and their work, and the support of the new work which it is proposed to inaugurate. The women's auxiliaries and State branches become responsible for the support of certain definite missionaries, who thus become their personal representatives in the foreign field, and take shares in some definite part of the work, which thus becomes their own work.

These Women's Missionary Societies in the churches have, as a rule, a monthly missionary meeting, for prayer and for the study of mission fields. They write to their missionary and hear from her in return,— some ideal societies sending a weekly letter, and some ideal missionaries returning a weekly reply. They pray for their missionary every day and at their monthly meetings.

When the missionary magazine comes to hand they open it eagerly to see if there is anything from their missionary or about her field or work. Their interest and their gifts grow with their growing love for their missionary and growing knowledge of her work. Is it any wonder that when hard times come these ladies in your churches have cheerfully sacrificed comforts and luxuries rather than sacrifice their *pledged work* or leave *their missionary* and her native helpers to suffer?

This is how the women of the churches conduct their work. But how do the men of the churches conduct their work? Many pastors and churches think they have discharged their responsibility for missions with an annual contribution gathered on one Sunday and sent to the missionary society. If the Sunday is hot, or cold, or wet, so much the worse for the missionary cause.

In the majority of churches there is no monthly concert of missions. *No responsibility* is felt for the support of any one missionary, or station, or any one department of the foreign work. No one missionary is remembered by name at the family altar. When hard times come the first collection to suffer is the missionary collection.

A well-known writer has said : —

"The missionary of Christ with his great commission is treated like a beggar, to be discharged with an alms, and not as a yokefellow in the Gospel, to be supported by daily co-operation. As a consequence, missionary contributions do not grow with the growth of the churches, and missionary interest does not increase with the increase of communicants. Missions to the heathen are not made the first, the great, work of the churches. The churches at present turn over their responsibility to boards, boards relegate it to executive committees, executive committees to secretaries; and thus the work of extending the cause of Christ, which belongs essentially to every disciple, is devolved upon some twenty or thirty overburdened men.

"This state of things must come to an end. Let every church become a foreign missionary society, having its own field or station and its own representatives, for whose support, through the channels of its denominational board, it is directly responsible.

" Let the local churches co-operate in the work of missions, without funding their responsibility in a common treasury. Let the burden of support of missionaries and mission stations rest directly on the local churches. Let the trials and discouragements of the foreign field be made an immediate and sole concern of these churches, and what a new and wonderful stimulus to prayer it would furnish !

" '*Responsibility is the mother of activity*.' Only as Christians are sensible of their obligations will they be moved to active consecration.

" Let a church have its own missionaries, who will starve unless it supports them, and there will be a possibility that some at home will go hungry in order to feed a far-off workman.

" The most pressing demand of our day is more responsibility for missions in order to greater importunity for missions.

" Never can the resources of the Christian Church be laid under contribution until in some way the missionary enterprise is understood to be the principal business of the Church, a business which can not by any possibility be entrusted to any ecclesiastical commission-house.

" ' Churches to the front !' must be our watchword, and a policy of missions which will multiply a thousand-fold the eyes that watch for their success, the hands that work for their prosperity, and the prayers that plead for their blessing."

I know a church in New Jersey which is not stronger nor richer than thousands in this favored land, but it is supporting, through its own denominational board, two home and three foreign missionaries and nineteen native helpers.

It raises more for its benevolences than it does for home expenses. Once a quarter, on review Sundays, the whole Sunday school is resolved into a missionary society, and this Sunday school provides the support for one home and one foreign missionary.

The women of the church hold a monthly missionary meeting and support a home and foreign missionary.

A few years ago the pastor discovered that the men and boys of the church were not having a proportionate share in the missionary work. In order to inform them and enlist their co-operation, the Friday prayer meeting, once a month, was converted into a monthly concert of missions. As a result the men and boys of the church are now supporting not merely their own missionary, but their own mission station in China, providing for the support of their missionary and nineteen native helpers.

As a further result of this blessed missionary work this church is enjoying an uninterrupted revival, and fifty members were added last year to this church home. "Give and it shall be given you." "There is that giveth but yet increaseth."

An address on " Christian Endeavor an Evangelistic Force " was delivered by Bishop Arnett, of Wilberforce, O. Bishop Arnett, one of the trustees of the United Society, was introduced by Dr. Hoyt as one who externally is a colored man, but who has as white a soul as it is possible to find. "Thank God," said Dr. Hoyt, "Christianity knows no color line."

Address of Bishop B. W. Arnett, D.D., of Wilberforce, O.

We have met here as Christian citizens, members of the body politic, having the interest of our country and fellow men at heart. We have not come to usurp the prerogatives and authorities of the President of the United States, nor to supersede the National Congress, nor exercise the functions of the law-making power. We are not after the gowns of the Supreme Court, for from their decision there is no appeal. I admit that a few months ago, when the

Supreme Court gave its anti-Christian, its anti-American, anti-human decision, affirming the heresy that the States had the right to discriminate against a human being because his God made him black instead of white, I felt like calling a Christian Endeavor Convention to elect Christian Endeavor judges who would recognize the fatherhood of God and the brotherhood of man, for I believe that no man ought to wear those gowns except those who believe in the Ten Commandments, the Declaration of Independence, and the Golden Rule. We have come here to marshal the moral and religious forces under one banner, and that is the banner of the Cross, and to contend against a common foe. But as I look over this vast audience, the question occurs: What has brought these people here? There can be but one answer, and that is, Love to God and love to man. It was the love of Christ that constrained us to leave our homes and business and make this pilgrimage to the nation's capital. Our love for God and man has enabled us to do our duty to our fellow men, and hath given us power to break down the denominational walls and join in a united effort to put down the foe to humanity. We must declare war against ignorance and sin in high and low places, unfurl the banner of the Cross, draw the sword of the Spirit, and march our united forces against the saloon, the greatest foe of our home and native land. Ignorance and the saloon are the common enemies of all men, all families, all races, and all nations. Therefore all Christians, all denominations, and all religions should form an alliance offensive and defensive against them. We are to find a common ground to stand on. We can all meet at the Cross of the Crucified One. We can all obey the command of the carpenter's Son; we can all serve the Son of Mary; and by being supremely loyal to Jesus Christ, the Son of the living God, we can conquer the world, the flesh, and the devil. The Christian Endeavor Society is an educational force. It is the fond hope of the Society to see the little red schoolhouse multiplied until one shall stand at every crossroad from the Atlantic to the Pacific, and on every teacher's desk the Bible, and from every gable shall float the Stars and Stripes. The educational forces of our country ought to be considered and brought under the controlling influences of Christianity; and one of the missions of the Christian Endeavor Society shall be to make Christianity popular in our homes, social circles, and institutions of learning. Two of the largest denominations of the negro race are organizing the Christian Endeavor Society among the young people; and soon the pledge, prayer, and song of the Christian Endeavorer will be familiar to our sons and daughters from Huron's lordly flood to the Everglades of Florida. The Christian Endeavor Society is an evangelistic army of men, women, and children, all endeavoring to work out their own soul's salvation. Each individual member is an evangelist, one who believes the history, doctrines, precepts, actions, life, and death of our blessed Saviour, Jesus Christ; authorized preachers, but without congregations, commissioned to instruct in the Gospel, — to preach the Gospel to the poor, to convert the unconverted to the belief of the Gospel, and bring sons and daughters from afar. Our organization is endeavoring to hasten the reign of righteousness throughout the world by practising denominational reciprocity, by recognizing the co-relations of the religious forces, and by inaugurating the era of peace and good-will between men; and we resolve, in the name of the heroic dead that sleep in yonder cemetery, that in the future we will do all that lies in our power to have in fact what we have in theory,— a government of all the people, and by all the people, and for all the people.

" The Call to Missionary Service" was the topic of the last speaker, Rev. Arthur J. Brown, D.D., of New York City, secretary of the Board of Foreign Missions of the Presbyterian Church.

Address of Rev. Arthur J. Brown, D.D., New York City.

I am asked to close the session of this inspiring meeting to-day by emphasizing the thought that the service for which we are saved, while it begins with the man on our right hand, belts the globe to the man on our left hand. At our nation's capital, and on ground which teems with patriotic associations, we can not forget that this is our country's providential task. We want to win this land for Christ. God has raised up America for the purpose. Its unique history, its extraordinary opportunity, its unparalleled resources, combine to make that purpose clear. God would make us a new Israel, through whom spiritual blessing shall come to the right. In the words of another, God considers that we should be satisfied with nothing short of coming out squarely upon the track of God's own word and providence.

As much as home missions may mean to us in our national capacity, we have not got to the bottom of home missions until we have grown to feel that to the all-seeing eye of God it is all home, centred on one cross as its one universal axis. How plainly our national history indicates this thought of God! Think what purposes had this fertile continent alone, undiscovered for thousands of years. God has intended us to be a missionary nation. When we let our visions span the oceans we understand why God has charged us with such a providential mission. We see millions suffering for the want of that which Christianity has brought to us. I might speak of the blessings of Christian civilization, of schools and books, of justice and social order, of the asylums for the blind and the hospitals for the sick, of all the comforts and conveniences of the Church, unknown beyond the pale of the true religion. Were the benefits of Christianity confined to this life, foreign missions would yet have a duty. So numerous and mighty are the humanitarian influences of the Gospel of Jesus Christ! God's grace is not to find the visible missions. We have no authority to go beyond his Word, and that Word, from Genesis to Revelations, in prose and poetry, in prophetic warning, and apostolic preaching. Aye, in the words of the Lord, Jesus himself declared that man is sinful, and that the consequences of his sin are something terrific, but God has supplied us a way of salvation, and we know it, and in knowing it we are debtor to those who know it not, and are bound by the most solemn obligations of philanthropy to carry the Gospel to all nations, as we can no longer come to these people in the spirit of condescension. Recent events have helped us to a truer understanding of the worth and dignity of man as man; to an understanding that back of almond eyes and under the olive skin are all the faculties and possibilities of a man. We have learned to respect and admire the intelligence of the Japanese and the industry of the Chinese. And if we are to speak of the negro race, I would not only speak of Frederick Douglass and of him who has spoken to-night, but I would think of those blacks who tenderly prepared the body of Livingstone, laying his heart in Africa's bosom, and who then carried that body on their shoulders through forests and swamps, over mountains and plains, amid the warring of elements, with persistence inflexible and courage superb. These are brother men, men like ourselves in the image of God, for whom, as well as for you and me, Christ died. Ruskin reminds us that mud is composed of clay, sand, soot, and water; that clay may be molded into the noblest work of the sculptors; that the sand may develop into the fairest opal; that the soot may be crystallized into the diamond; and that the water may develop into a star of snow. So with the vilest men; they may be fitted by the Son of God to live forever with God and to stand upon the feet of Christian humanity. If anybody tells you that the heathen can be converted you can say to him, "My dear sir, the heathen are being converted." Since this Convention met one year ago in the city of Boston, how many souls do you think have been brought out of the darkness of heathenism into the light and liberty through the Gospel of Jesus Christ in the foreign field? One hundred thousand. I am told that there are about forty thousand Christian Endeavorers in the city of Washington to-day. What a great multitude! And yet if you could get into this great Convention all those who have been converted from heathenism this last year, then the magnificent hospitality of the city of Washington would be taxed, for that Convention would be two and one-half times as great as the Convention which now meets here. I fancy sometimes I see them coming, 300 a day, 2,000 a week,

8,500 a month, 100,000 a year, a mighty but motley host, redeemed out of every nation under heaven, red, black, and yellow, speaking various languages.

I want to speak a word of sympathetic admiration for the missionaries who are in the forefront in this battle. In addition to the heat, dust, and fevers, fleas, bugs, snakes, and all the discomforts of a typical Oriental country, the missionaries are frequently called upon to endure great physical danger. This last year many missionaries have been brought into contact with the scourge of cholera; others have lived for months surrounded by smallpox; others have been endangered by mob violence. In the Turkish Empire our property has been destroyed, their work interfered with, their freedom restricted, and their very lives menaced. How many of you know that on Wednesday, March 25, the Sultan of Turkey promulgated a decree ordering every American missionary to leave the empire? And if it had not been for the providential discovery of that decree by the British Ambassador, and his prompt peremptory interference, great calamity would have resulted. In the meantime a strange thing is happening at home. Not only many newspapers, but some men in high official positions, one in the Senate of the United States, declared that if our people leave their country to go to a far distant country, semi-civilized, bitterly opposed to their movement, we can not follow them there to protect them; they ought to come home. And for once I was ashamed of my country. Is the missionary's business less legitimate than the trader's? Is a man entitled to the protection of his country when he goes to an Oriental country, and does he forfeit that protection when he goes there to preach the Gospel of protection and peace? In that same Senate-chamber, Senator Frye reminded the people that about twenty years ago England sent an army of 15,000 men down the coast, across 700 miles of barren sand, to batter down iron gates and stone walls, and reach down into an Abyssinian dungeon, and to help out of it one British subject, who had been unlawfully imprisoned. It cost England $25,000,000 to do it, but it made a highway over this planet for every common son of Briton; and the words, " I am an English citizen " are more potent than the sceptre of a king. And it was because of that reputation, that when Sir Philip Currie, the British Ambassador at Constantinople, drove up to the door of the Turkish minister of foreign affairs, and demanded the cancellation of that order expelling American missionaries within twenty-four hours, the Turk cringed and obeyed.

Mr. Chairman, shall America allow herself to be ridiculed by the Turks? Shall we vociferously curse England one day, and the next day depend upon her representatives to help us out when our missionaries are in danger? This is not a question of jingoism, whatever that may be. It is not a question of abusing the Sultan; it is not even a question of missions or religion; it is a question of treaty, a question of national honor, a question of self-respect. We do not ask any special privileges for the missionary. We simply ask that he be counted a citizen and a man, and that he be protected in those rights granted by treaty to the meanest American, and that it be counted a shameful thing to subject him to the criticism of a pack of men who put expediency before principle, and up whose backs run cotton strings instead of spinal columns. But of one thing you can be sure. The missionary will not run. Several months ago, when we foresaw the trouble, I wrote to our missionaries in Turkey, assuring them that we would stand by them, and giving them freedom of action, and saying that they had full authority to leave their posts, if they deemed it their duty to do so; and not one man or woman of them swerved. Why? For the same reason that the Spartans did not run away at Thermopylæ; that your revolutionary sires did not run away at Lexington and Bunker Hill; that the railroad engineer did not jump, when he knew that he was facing death; that the mother did not forsake her boy, when she saw him stricken with diphtheria. The missionary is a soldier. His station is a post of duty, and that missionary stands there. In battle, it is not so hard to be brave. There is there the inspiration of bugle and drum, and the sense of comradeship, the relief of action. But the missionary has none of these outward supports. He stands purely alone, far from succor, and entirely unarmed, forbidden to fight, prepared to look death squarely in the face. To endure such circumstances requires heroism surpassing that of any battle-field. Yet there they stand to-day in the great Turkish Empire, like that man of whom Victor Hugo wrote in "The Toilers of the Sea," on the point of solitude and danger, exposed to the fury of the elements, the bitterest glare of the sun, the fiercest side of the ocean, and yet standing with patience indomitable, with courage magnificent, battling for the truth and for God. O young men and young women, will you not go back to your churches, sending to these missionaries the inspiration of your sympathy and prayers and greetings, and divide with them a part of the sentiment for the work which the Holy Ghost has laid upon the Church, and the men and women whom the Holy Ghost has sent forth to do it? So the march of events gives new emphasis to the glory of God. Criticisms there are, but I am not here to-night to reply to them. With so much warrant for missionary service, I am not standing here on the defensive. I am not standing here to make apologies; I refuse to cheapen this great cause by begging for money.

General Sherman said that the commanders of the Army of the Potomac failed because they failed to get into action more than three-fourths of their army, and that the commanders of the western armies succeeded because they got into action nine-tenths, and in some instances all of their soldiers. How can the Church of God expect to conquer the world when only one-fourth, to say nothing of three-fourths, is thoroughly alive to the great work of foreign missions? At a critical moment in the Battle of Waterloo, when victory and defeat rested in the balance, the Duke of Wellington sent out the command, "Advance all along the line," and because that order was promptly obeyed victory was won. And we want you to go back to your churches, and put forth all of your best efforts, until the Church of the living God shall advance as one man into this great conflict. This is the duty of the hour, and it is a sublime opportunity. The call is clarion; it is God's orders; it is Jesus Christ who leads; it is the Holy Ghost who prompts.

Dr. Hoyt promised to show the assemblage a truly great and good man, one referred to by Bishop Arnett as a true friend of the colored race, and he introduced Justice Harlan, of the Supreme Court, who bowed his acknowledgment of the great applause which greeted him, but declined to make a speech.

Tent Washington.

Tent Washington was crowded at an early hour. The services were presided over by President Francis E. Clark, D.D., the musical director of the evening being Mr. P. S. Foster. The devotional exercises were conducted by Rev. E. B. Bagby. Dr. Clark introduced Mr. Amos R. Wells, of Boston, who has made so wide a reputation as managing editor of *The Golden Rule*. The popularity of the writer was evidenced by the warm reception he was given. His topic was "The Senior Society of Christian Endeavor."

Address of Prof. Amos R. Wells, Boston, Mass.

Ten years ago there were in the world 50,000 Christian Endeavorers. Where have they gone? Eight years ago the number had risen to 300,000. What has become of these myriads? Seven years ago there were nearly half a million Christian Endeavorers. Where are those half-million young people now?

Well, some of them are married. I hope all of them are, and married to Christian Endeavorers, too. Some of them are in active business, — I hope all of them are,— and about their Father's business, too. Most of them — nay, all of them, I verily believe — are in the Church, that dear Church to which, with

Christ, they promised their faithful allegiance ten, eight, seven years ago. But as regards the Christian Endeavor Society where are they — these half-million young people that joined our ranks a week of years ago ?

I am really afraid that thousands and thousands of them are in the Young People's Society still. Why should n't they be there? Because there is n't room for them. Because during these seven years the Junior hosts have gathered and are pouring their fresh young cohorts into the older army. Because during these seven years 2,000,000 young people have flocked to our standard. Because societies that once could rattle around in their meeting-rooms like the filbert in its shell are now holding overflow meetings or splitting up into sections, and hours that once had room for a yard of talk from each member now have n't room for an inch. Why should n't they be there? Because they are in the way. Because the younger Endeavorers look to them too much. Because they are taking work right out of the younger Endeavorers' hands — work those hands need to do in order to grow strong. Why should n't they be there? Because they need to be somewhere else. Because they have become too familiar with the work of the Young People's Society, and it has become too easy for them. Because they need new work, and harder work, and a different kind of work. Why should n't they be there? Because they are needed somewhere else. Because the Church needs their full time and undivided energies. Because when they enlisted under the banner, " For Christ and the Church," it was understood that they were in training for the Church, and a good training-school is known by its good graduates. Because graduation is one of the Christian Endeavor principles — graduation from the Junior into the Young People's Society, and graduation from the Young People's Society into — into what ?

Not into the Church, for they are in that already. Shall it be graduation into less strict fulfilment of duty? No! That would be to graduate backwards, like a crab. Shall it be graduation away from the idea of covenants? No! Graduation from daily Bible-reading and daily prayer? No, no! Graduation from systematic work for Christ and the Church? No! Graduation from regular testimony in a prayer meeting? No! Graduation into what, then? Why, into what shall it be but a Senior Society of Christian Endeavor !

The Christian Endeavor pledge is helpful to a young man of twenty-five. Will it not be equally helpful to the same young man ten years later? Systematic committee work gives business-like efficiency to your Christian service now. Will it not do the same a decade hence? Your consecration is fanned to a fresher flame by the breath of each consecration meeting. Will there ever come a time on earth when your consecration will not need periodical revivals?

Does any one object that our young men and women, leaving the Young People's Society, should, without any Senior Society or pledge, go right on and do for the older church just what they have been trained to do in their Endeavor Society? The objector has forgotten the stimulus that comes from organization, and the energizing force of definite obligations. One at a time our Endeavorers drop out of the Young People's Society, out of its strenuous atmosphere of strict requirement and the close shoulder-to-shoulder of its working fellowship. They *do* go into the full activities of the older church. They *do* take part in its prayer meetings and do their full share, usually more than their full share, of its work. But any one that knows human nature will know how much more they could do if, on graduation from the Young People's Society, they were received into another eager, compact body of Endeavorers, trained like themselves, using the same methods, seeking the same goals.

But does any one object that this Senior Society would mean another meeting? It would not. The prayer meeting of the Senior Society is the regular church prayer meeting. To this it transfers its full Christian Endeavor pledge. And how much such a phalanx of trained workers might do for our church prayer meetings ! With Christian Endeavor zeal, they would fly to the weakest point. Are prayers lacking? They would pour them in,— ten, fifteen, twenty, at a time. Does the singing drag? They would focus their fresh young voices into clarion leadership. Are the speeches too long? The Senior Endeavorers would drive in the hot shot of testimony with cannon-ball brevity. Do awful pauses yawn through the meeting? The Seniors would systematically fill them. The Senior Society meeting is the church prayer meeting. Do not forget that.

And does any one further object that this will mean more church machinery? It will not. If your pastor will serve as president, install him in that office for life. You will have no records, and will need no secretary. You will have no money, and will need no treasurer. The simplest of constitutions — send to the United Society for a suggestion of one — and the pledge — that is all you need. No business meetings? Once a month, after the church prayer meeting, the Senior Endeavorers should gather under the pastor's leadership and spend a few minutes in prayerful search for new work. " How can we better the church prayer meeting?" they will ask at these monthly meetings. "How does the Young People's Society need our help?" "What needed work, unattempted by others, can we take up?" What pastor would not rejoice in such a meeting of trained workers? Save this brief monthly conference, there is nothing visible about the Senior Society. Its mission work is the Church's, its social work the Church's, its temperance work the Church's, its finances the Church's. The Senior Society would not Endeavorize the Church — though that wouldn't be such a terrible thing — but would simply churchify Christian Endeavor.

Do you want to make the experiment, pastors? because if *you* do not want it, no one wants it made; but if you do want to experiment, it is very easy. Begin with a few. Don't remove all the older workers from the Young People's Society at once. Let them withdraw gradually, in the meantime working to make themselves unnecessary, training their successors as Elijah trained Elisha. The best way to start is for these older Endeavorers to belong, for a time, to both Young People's and Senior Societies, gradually weaning themselves from the younger organization. Begin with a few. Single out the young men with mustaches, and the young women with diamond rings on the third finger of the left hand. Add a choice selection from the honorary members and all the past members of the Society you can lay your hands on, and you have the nucleus of a Senior Society.

Try it, Endeavorers, try it! Your pastors co-operating, try it! To strengthen the Young People's Societies, to conserve for the Church their full vigor and enthusiasm, try it! In many parts of Australia and in a few American churches the experiment has been made, and in not a single case has it failed of glorious success. Since the Junior movement, no phase of Christian Endeavor has compared in importance with this. Do not wait for others to move, but be a pioneer yourself! Connecticut, that State of bright ideas, has a Veterans' Christian Endeavor Association, made up of its old State officers. Everywhere, everywhere, Christian Endeavor has trained its veterans. Now let them band together, and forward, march! for new victories. I hear the tramp, tramp, tramp, of the regulars. They are cadets no longer. Trained, they have found out that they were trained for something. Their manual of arms is not for the parade-ground, but the battle-field. Forward, Senior Endeavor, for Christ and the Church!

President Clark then introduced Rev. J. L. Withrow, D.D., LL.D., moderator of the Presbyterian General Assembly. His topic was "Meetness for the Master's Use."

Address of Rev. J. L. Withrow, D.D., LL.D., Chicago, Ill.

Yesterday, at the Presbyterian Rally, I said I was pastor of six Christian Endeavor Societies. As soon as the service was over, one of my young people came to me with both hands up and said, " Why didn't you say eight societies instead of six? We have eight societies in our church."

Now I really begin to think, since I heard that old gentleman a minute ago, that we will have to have a Senior Endeavor, a ninth society. I wondered what on earth he was going to make out of " Senior Endeavor Society." Now I see it and I approve of it. Whether I can get all my friends to see and approve of it remains to be seen; but I am to have a subject with you to-night, and that is " Meetness for the Master's Use ; " under the general topic of the day, " Saved to Serve," a most suggestive topic.

What fits us for the Master's service — meetness for the Master's use ? Well, a pleasant recollection comes to my mind of a colored boy. It came to my mind as these boys walked up here and sang to you; a colored boy in my college days. He was the aid or the assistant to the professor of physics ; a very illustrious and world-wide known man was the professor. Now Buck, as we called him, thought he was nearly as important as the professor. All he had to do was simply to care for the apparatus in the laboratory, to prepare for experiments, and then to prepare such instruments as might be used by the distinguished professor. But, oh, how important that young man felt himself to be ! His learning was scant ; all he had in this world was little, except his consciousness that he was the servant of the great professor. He looked down upon us boys sitting in the forms, with a sort of pitiful air to think how little we were compared to him,— we sitting there only receiving, and he serving the great gentleman who was behind the stand.

Well, I have thought a good many times of that in the course of my life. How it lifts up a man if you are only serving a great deal greater one, and how it lifts up Christians to realize who our Master is !

That is a dignified view of Christianity. That ought to make a man go up toward the Son as he takes hold of the thought.

But now I am to take the time allotted to me to speak of what fits us for his service ; and in order to be as brief and condensed as possible I propose to say first that there are some things he does not require. He does not require great endowments, nor the promise of great accomplishments. First of all, God assures us through Christ as our Master that he does not require for his service that we shall be greatly endowed. Now, do not suppose, do not let any one think, that I have an undervaluation of the importance of endowments, powers of nature, powers of education, or anything of the kind. I have not; far from it. There is not anything in any of our powers equal to the work that God can call us to do. That is a place for the greatest of brains and biggest of hearts in his field of work. The leaders of the world have been the Lord's men, and the leaders of the world to-day are the Lord's men. When he wanted to have a law given us he chose a man whose fame as a law-giver should last while time lasted. He found him in Moses; and when Moses began to give laws all the jurisprudents of the world took pens and stood ready to copy. There has been no improvement on the laws of Moses, and the greatest jurists of the world have in the greatest respect looked to that teacher who was taught in the desert by God as his teacher.

God wants big men. He can use big men. When he took up that little boy into his own private care and kept him through childhood and until he was thirty years of age, secreted him so no person could mislead his education, and then brought him out on the banks of the Jordan, crying " Prepare ye the way of the Lord, make his paths straight," God had a man there big enough to awake a world that had been asleep for centuries. He uses big men. Men of the world who have been leading characters have been God's men.

When he started in for a great reformation in his own Church he had a man who was vast enough in all the possibilities of his nature to rise above every objection and every position and persecution, and the name of Martin Luther can not be blotted out of human history. I could go on and multiply instances indefinitely of great men God has chosen to do his work.

But while God has chosen these big men for his uses, thanks be to his holy name, we who can not claim any such extraordinary powers he does not require to possess any great endowments.

I spoke about Moses. Now Moses had a mother. Her name was Jocabed. I venture to say that some of you hardly know where she was born, who her fathers were. I do not suppose Jocabed was ever president of a woman's club. I do not suppose she ever read a paper before a lotus club. I do not suppose she ever gave an afternoon tea in her life ; but as the mother of Moses she was immense.

Pharaoh on his throne, proud and tyrannical potentate that he was, had a daughter, and while his miserable bones have mouldered for centuries without respect to his memory, all the world rejoices that his daughter was there to take up the little baby out of the bulrushes. If she had not been there we would not have had the big man.

It is possible for the Lord to use such a very small thing! He does not need to use a big man ; he can use the other as well — he can use the commonplace for his purpose.

I rejoice that Paul, that man whose name stands first, next to Jesus Christ — as big a man as he declared that not many are great among the Lord's men. God chooses the weak things of the world. That is his way. He does not need great endowments. If we have them, he takes them. If we do not have them, he does not need them. Moreover, he does not need absolutely that we shall have great promise of accomplishments in order to get us to accomplish a great deal. I was trying to get a young man a place in Chicago not long ago, and the first question that the proprietor of the establishment to which I applied asked me was, " Where has the young man been ; what has he done ; has he been a success ? " I said, " Well, I am sorry to say the poor fellow has not gotten up very high so far as worldly success goes." The gentleman replied, " Then I do not want him. He could be of little use to me. My business is a big one. I do not want any man around me who has not already given good promise of success. That is a rule in my business." Continuing, the man said, " I am out of patience with these failures in life, and unless a man has proven a success you need not bring him to me."

That is the way the business man of the world looks at it. Another great business man who hires thousands of men said to me when I was trying to get a young man a place in his factory, " In our factory a man's stool is worth so much to us in his expense account. He has got to know before he goes there how to fill that stool and give good promise that he will succeed. Otherwise, he can not have the stool."

Now, blessed be the Lord, he does not ask me whether I am to be a great success or not be a great success. You have probably heard people say that often when there are three or four boys in a family, and one boy has not as much brains as the other boys, they decide to make him a minister. If a man does not know anything more than to pray, and sing, and preach, they put him in the pulpit ; but the brainy boys they make business men out of.

Now I am inclined to think there is a little correction needed on this line. I was talking to one of my fellows about that, and he was speaking of ministers being of the other world rather than of this world ; and I said, " Look here, my dear boy, are you not a little wrong about this ? The largest educational institutions that this country has ever produced have been founded by ministers and controlled by ministers. They were the boys that had no brains, you say, and therefore were made ministers. You are mistaken in that, I am sure ; " and I gave that fellow several other illustrations, and I might have added this : " Do you know in the great thought of God it occurred that there had better be a Christian Endeavor movement in the world; and he did not take a business man to think it out. "

All the wonderful wisdom manifested in the management of this unparalleled successful movement has been in the hands of those who, perhaps, when they were boys, were thought by mama and papa to be rather the weaklings; who could not stand the rough work of the world, and so they let them go into the ministry, — praise the Lord!

Where would we be to-night if they had not? The Lord does not need accomplishments to begin with. What does he need? I think God requires of us, first, a self-effacing affection for his personality; unhesitating obedience to his word, and abounding confidence in his power to conquer and his assurance of reward. I think those are his positive conditions of fitness. First of all, a self-effacing affection for Jesus Christ, our Master, as a person. Who were the mighty Christians of history? Who are the strongest of them now? Those who believe in a form of religion; who are very much interested in the ceremonials of religion, or creeds of religion. I believe in the creeds of religion. I believe in the ceremonies of religion, but I maintain that is not the beginning of power. I believe the first thing is self-effacing affection for Christ. The trouble is that we get our personality between him and us,—our personality. I think of what Bishop Phillips Brooks said in his course of lectures, when he talked of the man behind the sermon, the Christian behind the Christian profession,—the personality. How big is that? Is it so big that you and I are everything, and Christ a small affair? Occasionally I think we regard Christ as a sort of nonentity that the Church has got to talking about, and we have lost the mighty power of a personal view of him. There is something sublime in those old words in the Hebrews, "Seeing him who is invisible." I believe firmly with those who profess that Jesus Christ is the One who was invisible. You recollect that they did seem to have a view within the veil that many of us know nothing about. You take the strong Christians whose names stand out in history: Thomas à Kempis and William Law, that man whose books ought not to be out of circulation as they are. There is a nearness of view that such men had that made them irresistibly mighty in their Master's service. Dear Dr. Gordon, of Boston, that man whom I love as I hardly love any other minister, has written a song that seems to me to surpass anything else he ever wrote,— "My Jesus, if I ever need love thee, my Jesus, it is Now." It was the close approach of his soul to Christ that empowered him, made him fit for service. Nothing else does. When Diogenes asked the monarch Alexander what he could do to serve him, Alexander said to the old sinner, "Stand out of my light." I think we are inclined to get between our Master and the thing we do; instead of having him everything, we are the big factor.

Talking to Dr. Clark last night, I was delighted to hear him say what he has said many times before, publicly and privately. When I was expressing my admiration for our Christian Endeavor work, referring to the fact that it is not organized to death, that there is some freedom and liberty, he said, " Oh, it is my constant desire to keep the hand off the ark." Let our personality not come in the way of Christ. Let us first have a self-effacing affection for him. That is the first condition of service. Another thing; that is, we must keep out our professionalism. What an expression that is of Paul, when he says of those in Corinth that one says, "I go for Paul;" another, "I go for Apollos;" another, "I for Cephas;" and then some poor little disciple peeped up and said, "I go for Christ." Christ had to come in last, after three others. And so some of you say you are a Baptist, or you are a Congregationalist, or you are a Presbyterian; and another, "I go for the Lutherans," and another, " I believe in the Methodists." Now, is it not quite possible that the Church is ofttimes bigger than our Lord, and that it is often " I am a Presbyterian or a Calvinist" rather than a disciple of the Lord Jesus Christ? I fear it is. How is it with you in your Church? Do you hear more people say, " I am for Christ " than " I am for Cephas," and " I am for the pastor," or " for the last pastor,— I am for the new pastor"? Principally for the last pastor.

Obedience is better than sacrifice. Obedience that is based on a promissory note never gets paid. What he wants is obedience to the letter; obedience that is paid on demand. That is the kind of obedience my Master wants of me. Not that I am going to take this, or do this, next week, but do it now. Procrastination taught me when I was a child that it was the thief of time, and I have learned that it is the forty thieves in one. So I say if we can only get the idea of what it means, be actually ready at any minute, that means everything.

Friends, it is really good to get one of the great figures of history before you. I like to look at Abraham. He was a man the size of whom you don't see grown nowadays. I want to know if anybody here can tell how black his hair was; how his features looked, and can re-produce them as if a photograph had been taken of his face? How was the strength of that face mostly shown? It was never shown at all until God called that man to stand out alone from the world. Every other man on the earth was an idolater, and God called him to stand out; and when Abraham heard the voice of God when he said, "Leave your own land and your father's house," he did not tell him where he was to go, he did not promise him a foot of ground, but said, "Go forward." That was all Abraham knew, and he did not hesitate. And when you see him a little later, starting with that only child, on whom his heart was set as never yours has been set on your children, as much as you love them — when we see that man following an unseen God, listening to a voice that was not addressed to his ear, but his heart, and going up one day, the second day, the third day, to the top of the mountain, and lifting up that knife to strike his son,— that is obedience.

When you and I have the Spirit like that the Lord will make ten men out of one of us. That simple spirit of obedience, the spirit that we are following God, makes us irresistible. That is what we want,— obedience.

It is told — and I have no doubt it is true — in regard to the first time Mr. Stanley went to Africa, that he was in Paris when Mr. Gordon Bennett saw him and said to him that he wanted him to go to Africa as his representative — I have never seen this contradicted. He went to his hotel, and knocking on his outside door was admitted, and he told Mr. Stanley what he wanted, and Stanley consented to go; to go into the interior of Africa where but one white man had ever trod, and no one knew whether or not he was alive. "When are you ready to go?" said Mr. Bennett.

"To-morrow morning," answered Stanley.

That is the kind of obedience I am sure pleases God,— not that I will do it by and by, some other day, some other convenient season, but now.

There may be somebody here who is not a Christian. If so, he has probably promised himself to become one at some future day. He wants you to do it now,— now. Obedience unhesitating right now! That is the way every parent likes his children to act. I do not like this thing of "Just wait a minute and I will do it." I have heard of a boy who was asked by his mother to bring a pail of water. He said, "By and by." Every few minutes she would say to him, "Have you brought that water?" and he would answer, "No, but I will bring it in a minute or two." And the day wore on, and at night his mother called him and said, "Have you brought that water?" and he replied, "I declare I have forgotten that pail of water."

And so it is every day with the children of God,— we are putting off from day to day what we ought to do now. Instantaneous, absolute obedience — that is what we want to be better Christians.

There is another thing necessary. It is abounding confidence in our Leader, that he has power to conquer. I tell you it is the Christian who believes that this world is to be for Christ that will work for that end. Just as soon as we can get our hearts full of the thought that this world is to be for Christ, the kingdom of God will come. With that thought in our hearts we will become mighty compared with what we were.

When Wellington was at his best, had never lost a battle, he came on the field one day where defeat stared him in the face. But there went up the cry, "Here come 30,000 men." The soldiers were filled with new courage and confidence; the victory was won.

We are all familiar with the victory of General Sheridan in the Valley of Virginia, how he turned defeat into victory by coming on the field, because his men had confidence in him as a leader.

A man who has no faith in the success of missionaries does not contribute to the cause. It is only when we feel that this world is to be for Christ that we are ready to go to work. Christ said to his disciples the first thing, "Go you and stay by this until you receive power from on high, and you shall receive power when the Holy Ghost has come upon you," a full conviction that will result in the incoming of grace that will make us clarified, new men and women. That is an essential of successful service.

Never since I began to preach has the relation between Master and man been more strained than it is at the present time. In all the country there is anxiety as to what may next come. This anxiety is largely because they that are paid for service are being paid so poorly that the wage question is likely to be a wedge question to split us if we do not have it arranged better than this. When we think of a woman who has to work all day and get but seventy-five cents for making a dozen shirts, a woman finishing off a fine cloak for four cents, working twelve hours in the day, and getting one dollar at the end of the week for her service, it is sad! Think of it. Oh, it is sad we have this way of rewarding work in this world. Our blessed Lord did not look upon this as right.

When Thomas Hood wrote,

> " With fingers weary and worn,
> With eyelids heavy and red,
> A woman sat in unwomanly rags,
> Plying her needle and thread.

> " Work, work, work!
> Her labor never flags.
> And what are its wages,— a bed of straw,
> A crust of bread, and rags,
> That shattered roof and this naked floor,
> A table, a broken chair,
> And the wall so blank
> My shadow I thank
> For sometimes falling there,"

he did not write from his imagination. It was a real scene that Hood described. This day my eyes fell upon some lines written by a privileged friend of the merry poet, Dr. Holmes, who always sung on his pages as if he were full of blithesome gladness, and nothing else. This privileged friend told me that while in conversation with Dr. Holmes he heard him say, " Oh, I laugh outside, but I never laugh inside ; I cannot, it is impossible, the world is so sad. Oh, the poor women ! " he says, " it breaks my heart to think of what the poor women endure. "

Now let us look at the Lord's side. There came a poor woman with a little box of ointment, and poured it on his head, and the odor of it fills the world to-day. There came another poor woman into his house. She had but a farthing, but she loved God so truly and personally that she put her one farthing into his treasury, and Jesus looking said , " Wherever this gospel shall be preached, it shall be told of her that she has done that. " That is his way of rewarding ; and to you who have not even a penny — not a penny — he carefully put it down that if you will give but one cup of cold water to thirsty lips because you love him, and for his sake, you will not miss your reward. Do not let us lose heart to think that we are not going to get anything. Let us bear in mind that our life here is brief, but in the world to come we are to have life everlasting.

Christians, let us get ready, recognizing the conditions, and then we will all meet together in a day of rejoicing, to sing of the reward.

The last speaker introduced was Rev. Frederick J. Stanley, D.D. Mr. Stanley, while now residing in New York, spent many years of his life in Japan.

Address of Rev. Frederick J. Stanley, D.D., Newburgh, N. Y.

Touch the Christian Endeavor button, as electric current, and the thrill is felt at the four corners of the globe.

This world for Christ ! Most certainly. The decree declared, per Psalm ii., verses 7 and 8: " I have declared the decree. . . . Thou art my Son. . . . Ask of me and I shall give thee the heathen for thine inheritance and the uttermost parts of the earth for thy possession."

The four grand lines along which the Christian Endeavorers now labor, as four cardinal points of the compass, " The World for Christ," the north, or magnet, to which the needle ever points, guiding the unified body. " Evangelistic Endeavor," " Christian Citizenship," and " Rescue of the Sabbath " are the other three cardinal points.

Four great movements in this last century — as the century of centuries. These by young people, as a rule, and for the young.

Modern Sabbath school (Robert Raikes, little over forty), in 1781, for the young; modern mission movement, in 1794, by young William Carey, and in 1806 by young students in Williams College, of America; Y. M. C. A., in 1844, by young George Williams, in London; the climax of all, the young pastor in Portland, Me., in 1881 (only fifteen years ago), giving to the Church the Christian Endeavor organization, for and by the young of the world. This is the culmination of all the previous great movements of this marvelous century of centuries.

Nearly one and a half millions of communicants sit down to the Lord's table in heathen lands to-day. A hundred years ago scarcely a hundred, says one, and but five missionary societies, whereas, to-day, there are 139, besides their many hundreds of auxiliaries.

What means this? The time has come for the Christian Endeavor army to march in and largely be God's instrument to take this world for Christ.

What hath God wrought already in this century?

The Bible translated into 386 languages and dialects, so that nine-tenths of all the race can read (not do, but may read) the Word of God in their own tongue; whereas, one hundred years ago, but forty-four languages all told, as the result of eighteen centuries' translation previous to this nineteenth century. Only "make Jesus King," a voice from the distant lands to the Church of Europe and America, accentuated by the fact that every nation echoes the plea around the globe to-night.

Were our ancestors of seventy-five and a hundred years ago to return for twenty-four hours to this mundane sphere, they would stand aghast at the wonderful achievements, as they look at this world moved mightily by gas, steam, and electricity!

But gas, steam, and electricity have been latent powers in and around this earth for thousands and millions of years. Only within the past seventy-five years have these latent powers been developed to produce such marvelous results.

Twenty-five years hence some will stand on the platform and marvel that for centuries the Church allowed the powers and talents of the young to remain latent, and only within the past half-century — it will then have been in 1920, A. D. — shall these powers of religious activity have been developed to bless the Church and mankind in bringing this world to the Cross, to crown Him King of kings and Lord of lords.

Dr. Stanley wanted a new interpretation of the letters Y. P. S. C. E., so that it might read "You Preach Salvation, Christ Everywhere." The Christian Endeavorer should be world-wide. Gladstone had said that the great question before the world was Christianity as the thing wanted for uplifting the people; and the great Chinese diplomat, Li of China, had pleaded with a Baptist missionary to send more Christian missionaries to China to lift up the people of his country. If the Christian Endeavorers did not go into the whole world with their Society some other organization would be raised up to take its place.

SATURDAY MORNING.

Tent Williston.

The Junior rally took second place to no other meeting of the Convention. Its size was not even limited by the confines of Tent Williston, but stretched out onto the White Lot, where thousands gathered to see and hear. The enthusiasm was unsurpassed. Again and again and again did the audience rise up and cheer and applaud and wave handkerchiefs, fans, hats, and umbrellas. No one who did not see the thrilling sight can appreciate the beauty and inspiration of the great Junior rally.

The Juniors themselves, all except the seven hundred on the platform, occupied the seats in the front of the tent to the number of more than a thousand. They bore their banners and badges, and were an impressive spectacle. A large band of Juniors from the orphan asylum were among the last to arrive. On the platform was a scene lovelier than any of the city's floral displays. The Juniors were massed together with beautiful effect. A hundred girls all in white, bearing American flags, and wearing red, white, and blue sashes, occupied the front rows. Behind them were a large company of Juniors in various foreign costumes, each carrying the flag of the nation he represented. Still further back, and to the sides, were the Juniors of the chorus.

Several songs by this chorus, under Mr. Percy S. Foster's leadership, opened the exercises. How they did sing! And how they were applauded!

Rev. Joseph Brown Morgan, of Chester, England, led the devotional exercises, in which the Twenty-third Psalm was repeated responsively. A welcome in verse was manfully delivered by a Washington Junior, Raymond Miles.

Address of Raymond Miles, Washington, D. C.

Juniors from North and West and South,
  All over our broad land,
The boys and girls of Washington
  Together with you stand.
We want to bid you welcome here,
  But find no word to say
How earnestly and joyfully
  We greet you all to day.
It 's " Welcome home " we say to you—
  This is your city, too,
Dear to each boy and girl beneath
  Our own Red, White, and Blue.

To you, dear friends from other lands,
  Who 've journeyed far to come,
We give an earnest welcome now
  From every heart and home.
You can not feel like strangers here—
  Such thing could never be.
" One is our Master, even Christ,
  And brethren all are we."
And tho' we work in different lands,
  Our work is still the same,—
To do what boys and girls can do,
  In Jesus' blessed name.

And as friends speak this afternoon
  Strong words of help and cheer,
Hark! From Juniors everywhere
  A mighty chorus hear!
From Juniors who, with their own flags,
  Christ's banner lift unfurled,
And who, with glad, unfaltering step,
  Are marching round the world.
Then let us pass the greeting on,
  And so—in our small way—
Help make the world the happier place
  Because we met to-day.

The presiding officer, Rev. George B. Stewart, D.D., of Harrisburg, Pa., responded.

Address of Rev. Geo. B. Stewart, D.D., Harrisburg, Pa.

Oh that I were a poet! I never wanted to be able to compose poetry so much in my life as I do now, for nothing but poetry of the most rhapsodic character could give expression to our feelings of delight in responding to this most cordial and happily expressed welcome. It has fallen to my lot to make answer to this address of welcome, and unfortunately, you have to listen to nothing but prosaic prose of the most prosaic character.

It may have seemed to some of you a few moments ago that I used language of extravagance when I asked the question whether heaven could be very much better than this. It at least seems to me that we have to-day a very large section of heaven here. Our Lord has given us abundant assurance that children are to be there, and are to be there in force. The Word of God said that the streets of that New Jerusalem were to be filled with boys and girls. It would not be heaven, it seems to me, if there were no children there. What is home without children in this land? Would God that every home had children! Oh, that the condemnation of society might rest upon those homes that scorn children! We here to-day not simply give our endorsement to Junior Endeavorers and our efforts to save the children, and make them of value in their young years unto the State, but we here give our most solemn pledge to the land that the Christian Endeavor Society the world over proposes to put its seal of approval upon childhood. I rejoice that it has given me the privilege to-day to preside over this rally.

What are boys good for? Lots of things. They make men of them, and that is one of the best things. And the girls? Why, they make women of girls, and that is a great deal better. You never heard of a man selecting a man for a wife. Why, we would not have one. A boy said to his father, "Papa, when I get to be big I am going to do just as you do. I am going to have a soft snap and make Ma run around and wait on you and do everything you want her to do." Oh, that to me — I do not mean it in its servile character, there is altogether too much of that — but that to me in its essence is the proud distinction of woman. She serves the home; she serves the country; she serves her God. Girls, be such a woman! Boys, never get in late! Always be in the front row! Be assured that your best days are coming, and they are many. Somebody has said, "Oh, for the glad days of youth and its careless abandon and its freedom from care, thought, and anxiety!" I tell you what it is, boys. If I know anything about life the best of your life is yet to come. There is no joy, there is no happiness, there is no blessing like the blessing that comes to men in the pursuit of the higher callings of manhood. When you go out into the activities of life, when you go out into the full power of your vigorous and mature years, then indeed have you come into the blessings of life. I heard Sir George Williams — a name that is known around the world and always honored wherever known — I heard Sir George Williams say a few months ago, in Exeter Hall, "There are some who think that youth is the happiest period of manhood. I want to say to you young men that the very happiest period of a man's life are the years between seventy and eighty. You will never know what happiness is until you come to those mature years of seventy and eighty. I know what I am talking about," said he. But some one spoke up out of the audience and said, "Yes; but you must live as boys and young men as Sir George Williams lived to be able to say that." And that is true, too. Start right and you will go right. Success is at the top. You must begin right at the bottom if you wish to get there.

I respond with all my heart for myself, for this large representation from America on both sides of the Lake and below, and in the neighborhood of the Gulf, for the countries beyond the sea that is called Pacific, and beyond that sea which is anything but pacific, to bid you a cordial welcome. It is a great joy to us to be in this Junior rally, to be present with you in this promised heavenly Jerusalem, the capital of the universe of God.

After song by the chorus, Dr. Stewart said : —

We will now attend to the Junior exercise, which has been arranged by Mrs. James L. Hill, of Salem, Mass., entitled, " The Juniors' Love of Country," and it will be rendered by the Washington Juniors.

The exercise, " The Juniors' Love of Country," was prepared to give special emphasis to good citizenship. The love of home is felt in every land, and good citizenship is as appropriate to one clime as to another, and flourishes in every soil, and so boys and girls representing the loyal Juniors of different nations spoke the praises of the various countries in which Junior Endeavor Societies exist. At the beginning of the exercise a young lady personating Christian Endeavor, and called Saint Christian Endeavor, came upon the platform leading a procession of forty-eight girls, dressed in white, with red, white, and blue sashes, each bearing two flags and representing the states and territories of our own land. After some very pretty movements the marchers halted in a double semicircle about Saint Christian Endeavor, and made a thrilling effect by lifting their ninety-six flags and singing " The Star Spangled Banner." The marchers then withdrew and Juniors gave brief recitations on patriotism.

At the end of the second section of the march, which contained different figures and evolutions from the preceding one, the girls halted in a column four by twelve upon one side of the platform, and the Juniors representing the different nations, with their various banners, came in upon the other side. In this position all the boys and girls of the Queen's countries having Junior Societies (England, Ireland, Scotland, Wales, Canada, Australia, and India) sang responsively, with the girls of the flag march, "God Save the Queen" and "My Country, 'T is of Thee," each company in turn holding aloft its flags while singing its national air. The marchers then withdrew, passing under the English and American flags crossed above them, and left upon the platform all the foreign Juniors, who gave brief recitations expressive of their individual love of country.

The third section of the march contained the most complex evolutions of all, and the coiling and uncoiling of the two lines of marchers seemed like a brilliant dissolving view. The marchers having halted in the form of a semicircle, Saint Christian Endeavor, with the missionary and temperance committees (important factors in good citizenship), came into the semicircle space. As the scenes at the close of the two previous marches gave emphasis to the patriotic idea,— the first march terminating with " The Star Spangled Banner " and the second making conspicuous the banners of different nations,— so this section of the exercise gave special prominence to the religious element, and with Christian Endeavor flags held aloft, all sang " The Banner of the Cross." Missionary and temperance recitations and songs followed, and then came the fourth and final march. In this the marchers came

up in twos, in fours, in eights, and in sixteens, and halted in solid phalanx sixteen abreast. All the Juniors of all nations and committees
who had taken part in the exercises quickly grouped themselves
around the marchers, and together with the whole Junior chorus, who
had risen in their places, chanted with great impressiveness, " Trusting
in the Lord Jesus Christ for strength, I promise him that I will strive
to do whatever he would like to have me do," the Junior Christian
Endeavor pledge set to music by Mrs. Hill. All the Juniors remained
standing, and the audience rose, and the orchestra lending its aid, all
joined in singing as a final full chorus,

> "Christ for the world we sing,
> The world to Christ we bring."

President Bagby, of the Washington Junior Union, was introduced,
and spoke of the fact that the day was Mrs. Hill's birthday, and that
the Juniors wished to remember it. She was then presented with a
large bunch of roses by a tiny girl. Mrs. Hill, who had been received
with much enthusiasm, made an appropriate response.

Dr. Stewart then introduced President Clark, and he was given a
hearty greeting by the boys and girls.

Address of President Francis E. Clark.

Dear Juniors, Boys and Girls :—I am put down on the programme for a greeting; but I do not bring greetings. I want you to send the greetings. I want to
take the impression of this great audience and this beautiful sight with me all
the coming year. One week from next Thursday, on the 23d of July, Mrs. Clark
and I sail for the other side of the sea. We shall see many Juniors in many
lands, and I want to take with me your greetings, and I want you to send them.
I think you are all ready to send them, and when we get to these lands and
look into the faces of strange Juniors with different complexions from yours,
and in different costumes, we shall think of this beautiful sight and the greetings that you send. Now I am going to ask you to send them by standing
and waving your flags or your handkerchiefs, or if you have not any handkerchiefs, by clapping your hands, and then I will take them with me. Over there
they do not like whistling, but they like every other kind of demonstration ; just
as much noise as you can make, except whistling.

Now in the first place, we are going to Germany, and we shall see some
German Juniors. Do you want to send your greetings to them? If so, let me
know it. (Great cheering and waving of flags and handkerchiefs by the chorus.)
There is a cheer from the Juniors, and now I want to take the same greetings
of the audience here as well as the audience there. (Cheering by the audience.)
Then we shall go to Scandinavia, to Sweden, to Norway, and Denmark. Do
you want to send your greeting to those countries? If so, say so. (Great cheering and waving of flags and handkerchiefs by the chorus and the audience.)
And I shall go to France probably for two or three weeks, and see something
of the Juniors in sunny France. What will you say to them? (Great cheering
and waving of flags and handkerchiefs by the chorus and audience.) And then
to Old England, dear Old England, Mother England, as we all love to call her
just as much as Mr. Morgan or Mr. Towers or any of the English friends who
are here. I shall go to Great Britain before the end of the year probably, and
what message will you send to the Juniors of dear Old England, Scotland, and
Ireland? (Great cheering and waving of flags and handkerchiefs by the chorus
and the audience.) That is the best of all. And then before the year is over I
expect to go to India and see a great many of the dusky Juniors. Do you send
a cheer for them, too? (Cheering and waving of flags and handkerchiefs by the

chorus and audience.) And one more country I expect to visit, and that is South Africa,— Cape Town, and Port Natal, and those countries,—have you a cheer for them? (Great cheering and waving of flags and handkerchiefs by the chorus and audience.) I thank all of you Juniors. I go loaded down with all these messages and blessed greetings. I am glad to take them. Just a minute longer. There are two or three here who are going to speak about fifty words each, and I know you will all be glad to hear them. They are from far-off lands. They are especially connected with Junior work, every one of them; and first I will present the Rev. Fred. C. Kline, formerly of Japan, the first Methodist Protestant missionary of the world and the founder of the first Junior Society in Japan.

MR. KLINE: Having assisted my wife to organize the first Junior Society among the Japanese, about five years ago, I bring you most heartily their cordial greetings. They hail you in Christ's name, and they wish for you every earthly good. They pray the Master to abide in your hearts unto the enrichment of you in all spiritual forces and agencies, that you may become mighty in the Word of God, successful in leading others to Christ, and to exalt his name supreme among the nations. Christian Endeavor, live forever!

PRESIDENT CLARK: And another, Miss Anna F. Webb, of Spain, who formed the Junior Society three years ago in San Sebastian, Spain.

A letter from Miss Webb was read: —

Dear friends, as one of our number is going to the great Convention we had thought to send you this letter, and we are so glad to do so. We are very happy because we can be members of the Junior Endeavor Society, and now we wish that not only was there one Junior Society, but many, and we ask God that he will establish and create a great many more, both of Young People's and Junior Societies. Our Society now bids to you good-bye, and sends you all our love and the praise of a hymn that we all know in England: —

> "Jesus loves me; this I know,
> For the Bible tells me so;
> The little ones to him belong;
> They are weak, but he is strong."

PRESIDENT CLARK : Just one more; and any one who goes out will miss something, I assure you, for the last one who brings greetings is from far-off China, from Shanghai,—Miss Mary Posey, from the Southgate Presbyterian mission in Shanghai, where are some of the noblest Juniors in all the world.

MISS POSEY : With a heart full of love and gratitude to God, and prompted by loyalty and devotion to you, our dear Doctor and Mrs. Clark, for coming into our midst a few years ago, when God sent you to us, we, the superintendents and teachers and members of our Junior band in Southgate, Shanghai, China, extend to you most cordial greetings, and may God bless you and the noble work of the Y. P. S. C. E. We want this banner (presenting beautiful silk banner) to speak a message of love to our Juniors and to those interested in Juniors, in Junior work, especially to those who have been so much to us in help and prayer. We want it to speak a message of joy, and tell you how it is for us who are engaged in the blessed service of bringing the Gospel to those who know it not in heathen lands. We want it to be a mute appeal to you to do more and diffuse the blessed Gospel among races in other parts of the earth. Many of our dear Juniors a few years ago had no light of the world to guide them. Now they rejoice in the same Saviour that you and I do to-day. I want to call your attention to this little Chinese girl (referring to a representation of a Chinese girl on the banner) with large feet, with natural feet, the kind that God made for her in the first place. She is pointing there to her flag. You see the cross of Christ has obliterated the dragon. Now these dear children here to-day should welcome this glorious thing, for the dawn of this light is just breaking in this far-off land.

PRESIDENT CLARK: I am very glad, indeed, to accept this beautiful banner, so beautifully presented by Miss Posey. I can assure her and the Juniors of Shanghai that we will prize it among our dearest treasures, and that we shall keep it not only as individuals, but as representatives, if we may, of you, and we will keep it safely for you; but the Junior member of my family is Mrs. Clark, and I want to hand it over to her, to give it in her safe-keeping, and then I will know that it is all right.

Mrs. Clark, in response to calls for a speech, said : —

I remember three or four years ago in Shanghai taking a wheelbarrow ride with the lady who has just brought this banner, and as my education in wheel-barrow riding had been somewhat neglected, and as the Chinese wheelbarrow is often more complicated than an American one, I distinguished myself by falling off; but when we arrived at our destination, and I saw those little Chinese boys who sent this banner, my heart was touched, and I am sure if you could see those boys you would all want to send not only your greetings, but your prayers and your sympathies to the boys and girls in China. I thank you for my share in this.

DR. STEWART: And now we are about to close this meeting. I am sure that the missionary to Iceland who described heaven as a very warm place was right. For it is very warm here and it is very heavenly; but before we close and have the benediction we will listen to a song which was sung in the early part of the service, and for which numerous requests have come from the audience.

The chorus repeated the hymn, " Who Will Follow Jesus ? "
After benediction, at 11.30, the meeting adjourned.

Tent Washington.

No gospel gathering is so thrilling as one that brings together large bodies of *men* grandly in earnest for Christ. Is that because of the sad rareness of the sight? At any rate, the masculine regiments that thronged into Tent Washington for the evangelistic meeting for men only, the splendid men's choir under the leadership of Mr. P. P. Bil-horn, that gave its ringing Gospel invitations, the cries of " Amen ! " and " Praise God ! " and " Hallelujah ! " from the throats of enthusiastic men, the magnificent singing of those thousands of men, the strong appeals of the manly evangelists,— men every inch of them,— all this was glorious.

The songs were mainly patriotic, and great enthusiasm was manifested for " America " and " God Save the Queen." Mr. Bilhorn's sweet songs, too, were very popular; but one of the features of the morning was Consul Booth-Tucker's little Prussian violinist, with his broken phrases and his singing instrument. Secretary Baer presided, and introduced the general secretary of the Young Men's Christian Association of Washington, Mr. W. N. Multer, to lead the opening devotional exercises.

Mr. Multer called on the men to sing again the second verse of " America," and then to give the Gospel hymn, " Come, Thou Almighty King," to the same tune. This was done with fervor, and after an alternate reading of selections of the Psalms, Mr. Multer led in prayer.

" Throw Out the Life-Line " was next sung, under the leadership of Mr. Bilhorn, who tried his favorite plan of raising the key half a note at each succeeding verse. This kept the voices going higher and higher, until they rang forth with a power that was unsuspected at first.

Secretary Baer then introduced the first speaker of the morning, Mr. C. N. Hunt, of Minneapolis, president of the Minnesota Christian Endeavor Union, a lawyer who has abandoned his profession to work for Christ.

Address of Mr. C. N. Hunt, of Minneapolis, Minn.

Heb. ii. 3, "How shall we escape if we neglect so great a salvation?" and there is no answer to the question. If there had been God would have put it in his Book. It is asking the question, "What shall it profit a man if he gain the whole world and lose his own soul?" There is no profit. It is only loss, loss, eternal loss. I want to bring to your attention two or three verses of the Book, —for I am going to stick pretty close to the Book, that is all I have,—one of which is in John xii. 32, "And I, if I be lifted up from the earth, will draw all men unto me."

I am glad to say to-day what you already know: that what we most want to think about here, in a meeting of men, is that Jesus Christ was a man. I am also glad to say that Jesus Christ was a young man. Jesus Christ died for men. Jesus Christ lives for men. Jesus Christ lives in men. Jesus Christ to-day works through men. The invisible Christ in the world to-day is in men, dwelling and abiding there by the Holy Spirit.

Now turn again to the third chapter of John, and I read these words: "Except a man be born again he can not see the kingdom of God." . . . "Verily, verily, I say unto thee, except a man be born of the Spirit he can not enter the kingdom of God. That which is born of the flesh is of flesh; and that which is born of the Spirit is Spirit."

Here is the entrance into this Christ life. Men have long been seeking to live a true life, an abundant life, but it is only found in Jesus Christ, who said, "I am the door: by me if any man enter in, he shall be saved, and shall go in and out, and find pasture. . . . I am the way, the truth, and the life." Jesus Christ came not to take away from men honor or reputation, ability or power. He came to give men honor, reputation, ability, and power. I may be mistaken; I have been in political life, I have been in legal life, ten years; I have met men along the plane which men of business and professional men walk—I say I may be mistaken, but if I can see aright the future I believe to-day that the shortest cut to any place of position and power in this government, nation, or state is by upholding boldly, manfully, everywhere the principles of Jesus Christ.

I heard a woman say from this platform the other day just what I wanted to say, and I am glad to say it, taking it from a woman's lips. She said, speaking geometrically, that "the shortest cut between earth and heaven is a religious life." But I believe something that has not gotten into the hearts of men: that the shortest cut between the lowliest place on God's green earth or under his blue sky, not only between earth and heaven, but between such lowly place and the White House on the hill yonder, is a righteous life.

The kingdoms of this world are not only to become, but they are becoming now, and will continue to become, the kingdoms of the Lord and Christ. And so I am glad to-day to uphold to you this great salvation. I can not tell you what it has done for me. I can not tell you where it has lifted me from, or to what point it has lifted me. I can tell you this: that when God's Word entered my heart — there it is (holding up the Bible) — then it was my blinded eyes were opened; then it was I had a vision, not only of heaven above, but of heaven here below. I believe what John saw on the hill of Patmos is not very far away: "And I John saw the holy city, new Jerusalem, coming down from God out of heaven, prepared as a bride adorned for her husband. And I heard a great voice out of heaven saying, Behold, the tabernacle of God is with men." Is with man — not with angels, but with man. I am glad to say it, because I find everywhere, as I go about over the land preaching this blessed Gospel of Jesus Christ, men say, "You are visionary; you are up in the sky." Down our way preachers are often spoken of among some people as "sky pilots."

Now there are a great many places in this earth not very far from where we are standing, in this beautiful white city of America, that are very, very black. If there are any great lights in this Convention, in the Christian Endeavor Convention anywhere, oh, I tell you there are plenty of places for them this side of heaven ! I do not much believe they will get into heaven hereafter unless they get into heaven right here now.

That is why I think it is a great salvation. It is a great salvation because it saves a man. Now I am going to say what some of you may not agree with, but I have found it to be true, and so I am going to say it. It saves man from himself. If I were to spell devil I would spell it with four letters, s-e-l-f. I do not know how you may be. I heard a brother who was being examined the other day say he did not believe in a personal devil. I do, and I don't know anything about theology either, and I don't know very much about heaven, and I don't know and don't want to know very much about hell. But I do know if I could get rid of self and of selfishness that heaven would become very much a part of me and my home, of my daily life, of my mingling with my fellows, of my social and of my municipal life, and of my life as connected with this great government.

And so we are saved from ourselves. I am not going to speak very much of the greatness of this salvation as it pertains to heaven, because I would not speak of that of which I do not know ; but all I say as I go about among men and see men who are giving all their time and talent to the things that fade and perish, is " Oh, to get a vision of Jesus Christ, and his righteousness, and his power, and kingliness, and his manliness, then these lesser things will fade away ! "

Jesus Christ is here now in this place as the Saviour of men. How may a young man cleanse his ways ? The great Psalmist said, " By taking heed thereto." We have gotten too far away from the Word of God. This greatness of salvation in Jesus Christ is going to take us right back to the simplicity of the Word of God. I tell you we need it everywhere. You tell me that the principles of this book are not practical in politics ? I tell you that they are, and the politicians, not only of this fair city, or that congregate here, but of all the fair cities of this fair earth, are, within the next ten years, —and I am not a prophet, or a son of a prophet,— going to recognize the fact. But that salvation must come in you, and through you. Jesus Christ saves cities, he saves nations, he saves states, he saves societies, he saves homes, only as he saves the individuals. You can never get away from that.

There is only one way I can read logically or legally in this book, whereby Jesus Christ can save men; it is by saving man. That is how. And you, and you, and every brother on this earth can only be saved in that way, for we are all brothers in Jesus Christ, thank God. Paupers may be fit for princes, and princes may be fit for something less, —they very often are, are n't they ?—but Jesus Christ knew not only what was in men, but what man might become as the love of Jesus Christ entered his soul ; and so, I say, Jesus Christ saved men as the seed of this book commenced to find a lodging-place in their hearts. I do not think it necessary to know anything about theology to be truly religious. I know nothing about theology. Men become very prosperous farmers without knowing anything about agriculture, in a technical way ; men become lovers of flowers, and cultivate them, without knowing much about the science of botany ; men become successful politicians without knowing anything about political economy. And so I believe that the religion of the Lord Jesus Christ, from the Word of God itself, must find a lodgment in your souls, and that it is something to save you. It is not going to be a process immediate. I am not going to live for selfishness and sin here, and then, when I die, because I have sung songs, be transported to heaven; nor will I, because I have neglected some theological doctrine, or plan, be sent to the lowest hell. But if I refuse Jesus Christ, the great light of the world, if I refuse to let him into my life, seeing his wonderful light among men ; if I refuse to let that power have control over me, what then ? Have I not, deliberately, chosen the darkness, and has not God made me a free moral agent, to choose the light or not to choose it ? Jesus

Christ did not come to condemn; he came to save the world. And you have the proud position of being one of his lieutenants, one of his captains, in this great salvation work,—every man here, and every man you may come in contact with. I think we all want to be saviours of men. I am thankful to do anything for this great salvation.

In '32, it is said, one wandered by the shores of Galilee. He looked at the footprints of the Christ on those shores. He saw what he had done, what he was doing, and then it was that he said, rising out of his darkness and unbelief, these wonderful words that may bring light into many a soul to-day: "If Jesus Christ be a man and only a man, I say of all mankind I will cleave to him, to him will I cleave alway. If Jesus Christ be a God and the only God, I swear I will follow him through heaven and hell and earth and sea and air." And so will I; and any man who will may not only be saved, but better than that—according to the motto of yesterday, starting from the place where he lives, he may be a saviour of men. That is the greatest business God ever called any man to, for he gave it to his only begotten Son, Jesus Christ.

MR. BAER: First and last there are many amusing things that come to a convention. President Clark received a letter, I think since his arrival in Washington, urging this great Christian Endeavor Convention to take steps at once to kill the two Salvation Armies in this country, the American Volunteers and the Salvation Army. The writer said that the mission of the Christian Endeavor was to kill them. Well, I am very sorry indeed that the writer takes a different platform and view from what I think you do. I regret that Mr. Ballington Booth was unable to accept the invitation to be present with us here in Washington, but I am glad to say to you that the commander of the American forces of this great world-wide Salvation Army is with us. The Salvation Army, like Christian Endeavor, has gone around this wide world saving souls for Jesus Christ. In America it is America for Jesus Christ. I am glad to introduce the new commander, who recently came to us from India, Commander Booth-Tucker.

Address of Commander F. De L. Booth-Tucker, New York City.

Mr. Baer and Friends : — I am sure the warmth and heartiness and spontaneousness of your reception will do what Mr. Baer stated some one has suggested — it will kill me. I think if Mr. Ballington Booth had been here it would have killed him also, and then you could have put us both in a grave together. And I am sure there is enough fire and fervor in this meeting, and enough faith in it, to have had a resurrection. That would have been the best of all.

I accepted this invitation with great hesitancy because I felt that at the present time I have come to America very much in the position of a learner. However, I am an American citizen, and am proud to be one. My ancestors have been American citizens, so I am only following in their footsteps. Yet, I feel that I come on this occasion as a learner, because I have spent twenty of the best years of my life as a missionary in India. I feel I have all my experience to gain, and I come in the position of a baby American citizen. But somehow or other the baby is always an interesting member of the family. I belong to the family, and I shall realize after this meeting more than ever that I am a real member of the family, and have been accepted as such. Even if the baby coos it is interesting; if the baby caterwauls, it is almost as interesting. Somebody must run for the bottle, and if the bottle is not at hand they must get the comforter, and there must be something done. I feel proud of this opportunity, but, as I say, I feel unequal to it. I suppose, however, even in the position of a learner, the pupil-teacher going on with his learning may at the same time say a few words.

I feel there are classes of Christian Endeavorers for whom it is not necessary for me to say a word here to-day, but perhaps there are some others who may be somewhat in the same position that I am; that whereas they may have been American citizens a long time, perhaps they have not been followers of Jesus Christ for a long time, and perhaps their Christian endeavors have been of a limited character and were not commenced a very long time ago. Well, I would like to stand before you to-day and say there is encouragement for every one of us. As I came here to-day I thought, Supposing I were to go around and ask all the Christian Endeavorers here in Washington what they would like me to speak about from my own little bit of personal experience of Salvation warfare — what they would like me to mention. It came to my mind that the problem was, Who are we to Christian Endeavor in the way in which the one life we possess shall be used most for the glory of God and the salvation of souls? How are we to do it? How are we to Christian Endeavor? I feel very much afraid to go on and give any ideas of my own, because you have had this laid down to you so often and so much more clearly than probably I would be able to make it — so clearly that you can hardly have further light thrown upon the matter. Yet, as a representative of an organization which has made a special study of the art of saving souls, which has made that its special object, which has been created for that purpose, I feel that I may say something.

We now have on an average some 250,000 kneeling at the penitent form year by year, seeking salvation there. Out of those 250,000, from the lowest calculation some 25,000 are drunkards. I think that may encourage me a little, not for my own sake, but because I am the representative of that Christian Endeavor work which is carried on by the Salvation Army throughout the world; a work that has its representatives, no doubt, in this city, and that has its representatives, no doubt, by many thousands, in this country, that has a representative on this very platform, who was formerly a Prussian Cavalry officer, and who was reduced to the lowest depths of degradation by drink, until he entered one of our American Salvation Army meetings on the Bowery of New York as an ordinary bum, dressed in rags and tatters. He was sleeping at the time in a lumber-yard, and came and knelt at the penitent form, and sought salvation, and found it. He went back to the lumber-yard every night and slept for fourteen nights until he got his first job. Now you see him on the platform, and he is a beautiful sight to look at. I would like you to have a look at him.

Dr. Nyce came forward at Mr. Baer's invitation, and said : —

My precious friends, this is one of the greatest honors which God has ever bestowed upon me, that he has called me before you to give my testimony for his glory and his honor. From the position I was in the blood of Jesus alone can save. I know that his blood can cleanse and save even a drunkard like I was once. From rags and tatters I came to Christ, and I cried out, "Jesus, save me, or I perish," and the Lord spoke to me; and my rags fell off and new clothes were put upon me, and he gave me a new heart; and to-day I am proud that I am a follower of Christ Jesus, my blessed Master.

COMMANDER BOOTH-TUCKER: Now, I tell you, I have come to the country with fear and trembling. I thought, as I stepped on American soil, Now I am going to tread the soil trod by the saintly Charles G. Finney, who has had more influence upon my life, so far as religion is concerned, than anybody outside the Salvation Army. I say, I came to this country of great religious leaders with fear and trembling; but I turn with a measure of comfort and satisfaction to that organization which has been made up of little people, and I think that is perhaps why Mr. Baer picked me out,— when I was the wrong person for him to pick out,— why he invited me to come and speak on behalf of the little ones; speak a word to the little ones; and I might say to you who are not Talmages, and Cuylers, and Finneys, and who are not the great leaders we have had in this country, that there is a chance for all of us; that God Almighty has a need for you and me, and I will rise up and try to do my best.

There is no telling what we can do until we rise up and try to do it. I was myself one of the most bashful young men that ever walked the face of the earth; one of the most timid; one of those who possess by nature very little natural courage. Some seem to have courage born in them. I had not. What courage I have has come by the grace of the Lord Jesus Christ and through his precious blood. I was one of his cowardly ones, and I look back and see how he has raised me up; and so I say there is not an old man nor a young man here whom he can not take hold of and whom he can not use.

I was looking at those wonderful verses the other day in the good Book where a description is given of Moses and the burning bush; how he stood in the desert and looked on that marvelous sight,— the bush that was burning, yet was not consumed. While he was looking at it he received that wonderful call of his to go forth to the salvation of Israel. He was at the time a common shepherd; he was in hiding somewhere — in concealment, in such circumstances that when the call came to him it came to him as a surprise and seemed to him an impossibility. I think I can see him pleading with the Lord. "The fact of the matter is, I have a family and a business here demanding my presence." I can see him arguing the matter out with the Lord, and saying that he would have to take care of those poor sheep. It seems ridiculous that under such circumstances he should stop to argue that it was important for him to give his attention to a few paltry sheep, but yet that is probably what he did; and he probably said when he came along there that the other shepherds had gotten the start of him, and that after he had begun to have some business he ought not to be called away; that he was a man eighty years old, and that there were others who could be called. Finally, he probably said, "I am a stammerer; I am not an eloquent man. Though I passed my examinations in Egypt with credit, and graduated yonder and passed one thing and another, yet still, as a speaker, I was a stammerer, and therefore there is no use for me to go. In the debating societies in Egypt they used to make fun of me. I never could make a speech. So there is no use of my going. There are others better qualified than I am."

So I wonder how many there are here saying in the same way, "Send whom thou wilt, but send not me." But you know the Lord put his foot on every objection; and Moses with his family, and Moses with his business to be left behind him, and Moses the old man of eighty, and Moses the stammerer without ability, without courage, was selected by God to do that great work that he did. Moses was the one chosen by God.

I look around me now and I am convinced of the fact that there are plenty of Moseses. And there are burning bushes for you to look at. The Christian Endeavor is a big bush blazing with the power of God, and though it blazes away it is never consumed. The Salvation Army is a big burning bush which is burning away and yet is never consumed. And God speaks to us through these burning bushes and says, "I want to send you out for the deliverance of nations, or for the deliverance of drunkards, for the deliverance of backsliders, and I want you to rise up and put aside your excuses. I want you to do what Moses did, to settle the question on the spot and rise up and say, 'Here am I, send me.'" Realizing your weakness and realizing your unworthiness for the position, yet with all the difficulties to overleap you will surmount those difficulties by the grace of God, and say, "I will go at once, and I will seek to save that which is lost." And mark my words; the weakest of you will become the strongest, and the most narrow the most wise, because the mere fact of your weakness will cast you more utterly on God Almighty for the help and assistance which he is ready to give.

Now I want you to make this meeting a settling-point in which you shall go forth anticipating some difficulties to meet you. I want you to make up your minds that this shall be a meeting from which you shall go forth to accomplish in the name of Jesus something great. Persist until you get it; seek until you find it; knock until the door of opportunity is open.

I remember reading about the great General Garibaldi —that on one of his campaigns he camped one night, and as the soldiers were sitting in their tents a woman came to the opening of the General's tent crying, and he had her brought in to him. The General had a great heart, and he asked her what was the matter. Was she in need of money? If so, she should have it; he would help her. She said no, that it was not money that she wanted, but that she had lost a little lamb; that the lamb had been the pet of the household, and that she could not bear the thought of not seeing it again; that she had searched everywhere without success, and she was despairing of finding her pet. Garibaldi turned around to his staff-officers, his generals, and majors, and others, and he said, " Gentlemen, let us go and find the lamb for the poor woman." The officers looked a little curiously at one another as they started off with their sabers dangling and clashing at their heels. They went out, and after a time had elapsed, one after another came back to the camp without the lamb, and darkness set in. But Garibaldi did not put in his appearance; he did not return till the other officers had gone to sleep for the night. When the sentinel in the morning came to wake up the General he found him sleeping soundly, a little extra tired, and he had to shake him to awaken him. "General, it is time to be marching ; " and as the sentinel shook him he noticed that there was something a little big in the General's overcoat, and upon examining, there was the little lost lamb. He had searched until he had found ; and not until he had found that lamb did he return to the camp and seek his rest that night.

When the angel of death comes, when the sentinel of the skies comes and lays his hand on you and tells you it is time to take the last march to the land beyond, shall he find the lamb in your bosom? Shall he find you have sought until you have found? In the slums, in the saloons, in the highways and hedges,— you will find your lamb if you will but search.

The example of the Salvation Army stands before you as a testimony that God will use the weak thing, and I tell you — and with this I will sit down — I once made up a little jingle, and it has been a great comfort to me : " The joy of joys is the joy that joys in the joy of others." There is no joy like that joy, — the joy of being the saviour of souls.

When I was in India there was an officer engaged in our work who was a High Caste Brahmin. He had been very delicately brought up as a boy in the city, and he was sent out to do work where the food was poor and the surroundings bad, and he had many difficulties to contend with. He went forth to his work. The leader over him was a delicate young girl, a solicitor's daughter, who had left a home of luxury to go out and labor for the Lord. She was very anxious about this dear officer. She wrote him a letter and said, " I know it is very hard for you, and I know the food you have to eat is bad, and the people you come in contact with hard to get along with but do it for Jesus' sake." And he replied, " Do not be anxious for me ; the Master's blood is always before my eyes, and nothing appears difficult."

I would write those words upon your hearts. I would give you that as the talisman of victory,— " The Master's blood is always before my eyes, and nothing appears difficult."

Secretary Baer then introduced Rev. J. Wilbur Chapman, D.D., of Philadelphia, Pa.

Address of Rev. J. Wilbur Chapman, D.D., Philadelphia, Pa.

I have a verse of Scripture with which I should like to start my few remarks, in which every man among us to-day believes. I remember making this same statement at the beginning of an address in a Western city, and a man sprang to his feet and said, " That is untrue, for I do not receive a single word of the Scriptures." Nevertheless, if there should be a man in such an unfortunate position as that here, I say again, I have a verse of Scripture with which to start my remarks in which every man believes, even though he turns from the Book.

I remember at another meeting, some time ago, when I made this statement, a man came to me after the meeting, and said, " That is not true, for I do not believe in the existence of God." If there should be a man in such darkness as that here this morning, still I repeat that statement. My verse is one in which we can all unite and agree. Hebrews ix. 27, " And as it is appointed unto men once to die." We believe that, don't we? You all believe that. But the part of the verse I want to emphasize is what follows: " But after this ; " " But after this; " "But after this, the judgment." "The judgment!" I am not concerned about it myself, for I believe in Jesus Christ as a personal Saviour. I have his own word for it that I shall not come into condemnation. I am not concerned about it myself, for I have the words of the great Apostle Paul when he said, "There is, therefore, now no condemnation to them which are in Christ Jesus." But my heart goes out to the man in bondage, to the man who is a slave to his appetite and his passion; and I say to you since sitting in this meeting this morning and listening to the powerful appeals of the brothers that have preceded me, I never in all my life have had such a longing as I have this moment to go out to endeavor to turn men away from the wrong lives they are leading. God send us out after the lost, that they may flee from the wrath to come !

I will tell you why I wanted to speak on this subject. First of all, it is a very personal thing. I suppose you can say this morning, as I can say, that you have friends in this world that would die for you. I know I have them. I believe I know people in this world for whom I would count it a great honor and privilege to die. I believe you know them. But, my friends, while you have people who would die for you, there is not a man in all the world that is human that could ever stand for you at the judgment. Personal! Personal!

I was on my way from New York City the other day, and picking up one of the great metropolitan papers I read the story of an old Irish woman who had been doing everything in her power to save her boy from drink. She had washed for the money to send him to the Keeley Institute, and that had failed. The conduct of the boy grew from bad to worse. Finally she said, " I think I will go to the court and I will ask his honor, the judge, to commit you, and if you are free from it for thirty days, possibly I can help you." And she took him to the court and told the story to the presiding judge, and finally the time came for the commitment. He was standing before the judge, and he was half through with the commitment when the old Irish mother started back, staggering down the aisle, reaching out her arms, and when she reached the judge's desk she said, with tears rolling down her cheeks, " O your honor, I can 't do it. He is my only boy, and my heart will break if he goes. I can not, I can not." And she fell at the feet of her boy ; and when the officers picked her up and carried her out for medical attention, the physician said it was too late, she had died of a broken heart.

My mother has been twenty-five years in the skies, but if she had lived until to-day — and God bless her, she would have died for me — yet she never could stand for me at the judgment. Personal! Personal!

I will give you another reason. I have found that when men are insensible to the plea that is found in the Word of God sometimes they are made to stop at the cry of this word. Hear it! Hear it! Judgment! Judgment! Sometimes a man hears it in the ticking of a clock at midnight as he lies in his bed. Sometimes he hears it above the great din and bustle and roar of the city. Judgment! Judgment! And you know, men, I believe that the very sound of the word causes many a man to stop and think who, without it, who, but for that stopping to think, would have gone down to hell. And so this morning I sound it out.

One of my friends was conducting a series of meetings in the Southern cities. There was an old sheriff who was well-nigh persuaded to become a Christian. He attended the meetings from day to day, and as I say, he was almost persuaded; but he did not make up his mind, and the meeting closed without the sheriff becoming a Christian. My friend returned to that town a year later and he met a man who said, " The old sheriff is just about ready to die, and he is still unsaved." My friend went into the room and sat down by his bed. He held his thin white hand in his, looked into his dim eyes, and then said, " Mr. Sheriff, the doctor says your end has almost come, that you are about to die." When he said "die" the old sheriff's hand began to tremble and twitch and his eyes to flash. "Yes," said he, " I am going to die, and I tell you, sir, I am not afraid." They say the old sheriff was one of the bravest soldiers in the South during the war, a man who had faced death a hundred times, who had marched in obedience to his master's command again and again up to the cannon's mouth. "I am not afraid," said he. My friend said he waited for a second and then said, "Well, Mr. Sheriff, it may be you are not afraid, but how about the judgment; are you ready for that?" And the old sheriff drew away his hand, closed his eyes, and great tears began to trickle down his thin cheeks as he replied, "The judgment, the judgment! God pity me, I am not ready, I am not ready."

To-day I stand with this old Book back of me and say that every man who dies unforgiven must stand face to face with the God against whom he has sinned, and I sound out the note of *judgment* that you may stop and think.

But that is not all. I believe that the very thought of the word and the day makes men honest and true. The fact is most men out of Christ are not honest about spiritual things. You know that as well as I do. For example, a man says he can not be a Christian until he has the feeling. That is dishonest. No man ever had the feeling of a lawyer until he practised law; no man ever had the feeling of a merchant until he bought and sold goods; and no man can have the feeling of a Christian until he takes a stand for God. But many men declare that they can not be Christians because there are hypocrites in the Church. Of course I believe that; I know that there are hypocrites in the Church. I have been a minister of the Gospel for fourteen years. I have had four churches in that time, and I have had hypocrites in every one of them. I believe that. I never shall forget one church that I had, but I never tell where it was any more. I once made a mistake and gave the name of the city and had to make so many explanations and apologies on account of that mistake that now I simply say that I was the pastor of a church in a certain city. There was a man who had a seat four rows from the front — I would not call him a gentleman, but a man. When I announced my text he always began to read the hymn-book; and when he got tired of that he would read his church paper while the sermon was going on; and when that failed to interest him, he would bow his head as if he were asleep. That was his Sunday life. We had prayer meeting Friday evenings, and this same man would stand up and pray. I wish you could have heard him. He had the most sanctimonious way of shutting his eyes and kind of rolling them upwards. With a most pious voice he would pray. Indeed, he looked so pious that one might almost imagine wings to be sprouting, and think that that man would soon depart and leave us; and I might say that many times in the depth of my heart I wished he might. That was his Friday life. Hypocrite! Hypocrite! Why, I dare to say that I believe that man was one of the chiefest of all hypocrites, and his name, I am sorry to say, was on the roll of my church. Ah, but men, five seats back of him there sat the sweetest Christian woman I ever knew. I never knew her to utter an unkind word in her life; I never knew her to do an inconsistent thing. I can put my hands over my eyes now and hear her voice as it rose above the singing of the great congregation. I turn my eyes backward and I think of a dear woman years ago in the State of Indiana, who was the sweetest Christian mother that ever God gave to a boy. And I say the Church may be filled with hypocrites and yet there was enough sweetness and consistency in the life of my mother to offset it all. The man who dares to say that he is out of the Church because of the hypocrites in it is untrue.

Infidels are as a rule untrue — not always. I count it an honor to know some who are honest infidels and honest men. Such a man says, "I can not believe what you believe, but you go on according to your own way of thinking and I will not disturb you." On the other hand, I have no sort of confidence in the man who sticks his thumbs in the corners of his vest, and, not believing himself, tries to sneer me out of my hope for eternity.

Then again we meet the man who is not in the Church because he says it is an old-fashioned religion — that he has grown away from it. Has Gladstone, the greatest mind, possibly, that thinks in the world to-day — has he grown away from it?

My friend the Hon. Wallace Bruce told me that he sat one day under the influence of the splendid oratory of Ingersoll. He heard Ingersoll say, "When

I think of the Christians and their Bible and their God I am thankful I am not a Christian." " And then," said Bruce, " he gave one of those word-pictures that fairly set people wild with enthusiasm." " I would rather," said Ingersoll, " be the humblest German peasant that ever lived, sitting in his vine-clad cottage over which the grapes hang, made purple by the kiss of the setting sun as it sinks in the west, at peace with his friends and surrounded by those he loves, shod with wooden shoes, clad with homespun, without thought of God — I would rather be such a German peasant living as he did than to be the mightiest Christian in the land." " And I tell the truth," said Ingersoll. And when he said it, men sprang to their feet and shouted with enthusiasm.

Why, men, that is a play of the orator on words. I do not profess to be an orator, but I will change the word so that you can share in the picture. When I think of all that infidelity has done, nay, of all that it has failed to do, I am glad that I am not an unbeliever. When I think that it would take from me the hope of one day looking into the face of my mother I am glad that I am not an infidel. When I think it would reach down into the depths of my heart and take from me the thought that one day I shall see my child, bone of my bone, flesh of my flesh, I thank the God in whom I believe that I am not an infidel. I would rather be the humblest German peasant that ever lived, shod with wooden shoes, clad with homespun, sitting in my vine-clad cottage, over which the grapes hang, made purple by the kiss of the sun as the day dies out from the skies, at peace with the world, at peace with my God, my family about me, my open Bible on my knee, and singing with those whose voices would join my own that wonderful song of the great Martin Luther, " A Mighty Fortress Is My God,"— I would rather be the humblest German that ever lived than be the mightiest infidel that ever trod the world— yes I would, a thousand, thousand times. Men, what do you say ? (Shouts of " Amen ".)

" It is appointed unto men once to die, after this the judgment." You say it (indicating). You say it (indicating).

The congregation here repeated the verse.

" It is appointed unto men once to die, and after this the judgment." God save us all from it ! (Cries of " Amen ".)

I have just a word to say as I go on to the end. It is a place where a man is going to meet his conscience. As Sam Jones has said, " Where he is going to meet his record." The colored people in the South have a song they sing which I like. It is, " He sees all we do, he hears all we say, my God is writing all the time." It is a place where a man is going to meet his sin. God save him from it !

I have come to the end of my message. I beseech every one of you here this morning to lay hold of Jesus Christ. Ah, men, you are going to need him. You will need him when trouble comes, when death is upon you, when temptation rises before you high as a mountain. But you will need him most of all at the judgment.

Twenty-five years ago, when I was a boy in Indiana, one morning early the nurse, who had been in the household for years, knocked at the door of us children. She called out, " Boys, boys, if you would see your mother alive, come quickly." Although it is twenty-five years ago, it seems like yesterday. I was the oldest boy. I jumped up from bed and hurried the others into their clothing. Hurry though we did, when we reached the door of the room that had been like heaven to us for a long time,— for our mother had been suffering there for months,— hurry though we did, the same nurse met us at the door and said, " Children, she has gone home." If ever there is a time in a boy's life or a man's life either, for that matter, when he feels as if his sun had been blotted from the heavens, it is when he hears those words, " She has gone home." My father was there, and we crossed the threshold and knelt down where he was already kneeling by the bedside. When he heard us there he lifted up his face and turned to us and said, " She has gone ; but thanks be unto God, her Saviour is still here." And we got down on our knees, and he put his arms about every child that he had brought into the world, and he commended us there to the Saviour. We took her to the cemetery there in Indiana and laid her to rest and I went across the State the other day just to stand at her grave. If I could have opened the casket and have seen what was left, I think I should have said, " Is this all?" Listen! I think the angels would have said, " This mortal has put on immortality, this corruptible has put on that which is incorruptible." And I think I could shout until the angels would hear me, "Thanks be unto God who giveth me the victory through the Lord Jesus Christ."

And men, you will need him, oh, you will need him! What is the word?

THE CONGREGATION: The judgment!

DR. CHAPMAN: What is it again?

THE CONGREGATION: The judgment!

DR. CHAPMAN: "It is appointed unto men once to die, and after this the judgment." How many of you men here in this men's service this morning before God and under the touch of the Holy Ghost will dedicate your lives from this morning to do something for men? Who will promise before God that from to-day you will make an honest effort to live a clean life? Think of it, men. Who will so do? (Cries of " I will.")

Tent Endeavor.

The canvas of Tent Endeavor, Saturday morning, framed a composite photograph of American womanhood. Within its vast embrace there were gathered several thousand representatives of the "gentle sex," and the few men present in the shape of ushers and reporters only served to accentuate the preponderance of femininity.

Shortly after the exercises began half of the seats in the tent were occupied. Long before the addresses commenced there were few vacant places, and besides a fringe of just as attentive listeners were all around the big inclosure. The choir, composed of hundreds of women's voices, sang well. In the great semicircle of the chorus platform there was scarcely a place unoccupied.

The regular exercises were commenced with the singing of " Tell the Glad Story Again," by the audience and the choir, which had by this time assembled, under the direction of Mrs. Frank Byram, of Washington. This was followed by " Anywhere, My Saviour," and several other hymns.

Mrs. John Willis Baer, wife of the secretary of the United Society, presided. Mrs. Francis E. Clark conducted the devotional services.

Remarks of Mrs. John Willis Baer, Boston, Mass.

Dear friends, we are not only saved by Christ, but we are saved for something — we are saved to serve Christ. Let us in our meeting this morning realize that God is showering blessings upon this Convention. Let us use these blessings to elevate our spiritual life, to elevate our hearts and minds, so that when we go from this meeting back to our homes, we may lead more consistent lives, and live nearer to Christ. For that reason this meeting was called; let it be evangelistic in spirit. Let us all feel that there is something for each one of us to do. Let us forget for the time this great crowd of people, and let us close our eyes to this throng and try to feel that we are in a small room together, sisters in Christ; that we are expected to do something for him. Let us open our hearts to receive the blessing which he is so ready to bestow.

All the speakers this morning are ladies who have been wonderfully blessed of God in their special lines of work. These lines of work they will not present in full this morning in any way, as that was not the idea of this meeting. It is purely an evangelistic meeting, and they will bring in their lines of work only as they best illustrate their efforts for Christ.

The first speaker of the morning — it seems specially fitting to me—is a Washington woman. She is a woman who has been called to a grand work, the work of the Florence Crittenton Missions of this country. We all know of the great work which that mission has accomplished. Thirteen years ago it entered into the heart of a very noble man to found a mission in New York City in memory of a beloved daughter whom he lost at that time. Would that there were more man who were like minded! This man, not satisfied with founding only one mission, has followed it up; until now, after thirteen years of existence, there are thirty-four organized missions with the Florence Crittenton name.

The lady who is with us this morning has been very much blessed in her work in this special line. As superintendent of the national organization of the Florence Crittenton Mission Mrs. Kate Waller Barrett, of Washington, will now speak to you.

Address of Mrs. Kate Waller Barrett, Washington, D. C.

We, as an American people, are proud to be able to say that the blot of slavery has been wiped from our escutcheon. It is not true. There is a slavery in our midst to-day that knows no North or South, no Mason and Dixon line. These slaves are not of an alien race; they are our own Anglo-Saxon daughters. Knowing as a Southern woman may know the evils of slavery, I unhesitatingly say that in any aspect the slavery of which I speak is far worse than the slavery of the negro was. Immorality was one of the worst effects of the slavery of the negro. Here are a race of slaves kept for immoral purposes alone. The negro slave was a chattel, it is true, but he was a valuable chattel. His preservation and well-being meant added income to his master; but the white slave, the "slave of civilization," has no such monetary value in her master's eyes. Experience and proficiency do not add to her value; she soon becomes an incumbrance, and the insatiable desire for variety which led to her acquirement pleads that she be gotten rid of as quickly as possible, so that her master may be left free to enslave fresh subjects. The swiftly succeeding steps of the brothel, the jail, the hospital, and the potter's field she is quickly hurried through.

The negro slave had but few rights in the eyes of the law, but he had some. The white slave has none. The State of Missouri has declared by a decision of its Supreme Court that the general character for unchastity in a woman impeaches her character for veracity as a witness. It further goes on to state that "such character in a man does not in like manner affect his character for veracity." So far as I know, this is the first State to legally declare such an attitude, but one familiar with the police court annals has had ample opportunity to discover that there is an unwritten law to this effect everywhere. Not only is her character for veracity impeached, but the belief seems to have gained undisputed ground that because a woman has lost her chastity, or her virtue, as the common expression goes she has lost every virtue.

Often the slave has been bought and paid for by her master. If not, sne is owned body and soul by the keeper in whose house she lives. A great mountain of debt has been piled up against her, her trunk has been "nailed to the floor," as they express it, to show the impossibility of moving it. If she dares to leave under these circumstances she is arrested for stealing, for even the clothes she wears do not belong to her. Knowing as they do the slim chance for justice which they will have when once the hand of the law is laid upon them, they dread arrest more than they long for safety. Intimidated by the iron will and marble heart which is a characteristic of the keepers,— for as low as a woman sinks when she lives from the earnings of her person, she who lives upon her sister's earnings sinks still lower,— knowing no law, friendless and hopeless, is it any wonder that when once brought, snared, or coaxed into this slavery, she should not have the nerve to make the effort to free herself? You say, Why does n't she run away? Perhaps she has starved as a virtuous woman and she does not think that the world will be any kinder to her because she has lost her virtue. Everybody that comes in contact with her is in a conspiracy to keep her where she is, for personal reasons.

There is a very prevalent opinion that women are harder on their sinning sisters than men are. Even Dr. Lyman Abbott takes that view in his eloquent sermon on the social evil. I do not agree to this. Women are not responsible for the views they often express. They are like the chameleon; they take their color from any object to which they cling. Most of them cling to some man, and so it is his sentiments and not hers that she often voices when she condemns our compassionate, our unfortunate, sister. I have not yet seen a woman cast a stone at one of her fallen sisters that the stone was not slipped into her hand by a man.

The illogical ideas and methods which have been put into effect from time to time in dealing with this class are enough to excite the wonder of any reasoning person. Segregation, compulsory examination, attempting to elevate it into an institution,—almost every one of them has had as its object to surround this evil with as many safeguards as possible, to make it safe and pleasant for the male sinner; to put upon the weaker shoulders all the burden and disgrace. But the talk of robbing prostitution of its material evils; the offering up upon the altar of a false hygiene the bodies of hundreds of women with like possibilities as ourselves of happy life and glorious immortality! The thought is appalling, even if it were proven to do all for the human body that its friends claim for it. What gross materialism that which would save the body and do nothing whatever for the soul. The worst thing about prostitution is prostitution; the physical diseases which inevitably accompany it are as nothing compared to the moral disease which necessarily follows it. It is not the diseased body we deplore; it is the diseased mind, the prostituted soul. This body of ours, care for it as we may, will soon lie in the dust, with no worshippers but worms, but the prostituted soul lives on through eternity.

When I contrast the just and equitable laws that govern the relationship of the sexes among animals with the social laws of human beings; when I recall the thousands of girl-mothers in the Florence Crittenton homes, going through the trials of motherhood without any strong arm to protect or comfort them; when I think of the selfishness, and cruelty, and suffering that my own sex has to endure in the unjust relationship of the sexes; — if I thought that this was God's doings I would be an infidel. You who believe that it is so, get down upon your knees and pray to the terrible God that you worship that he will turn back the wheels of progress and make us once more as the beasts of the field. But we know that it is not so. He who is "the same yesterday, to-day, and forever" said to her taken in the sin, "Neither do I condemn thee. Go, and sin no more." He declared God's attitude to be hatred for the sin, but love of the sinner.

Secondly, I want to show how God has blessed our work among this class, in spite of the difficulties which lie in its way. There are many movements on foot to carry the Gospel to these poor outcasts. I stand here as a representative of one of the largest of these movements, the National Florence Crittenton Mission, that has as its object the regeneration of these wandering children of God. We have thirty-four rescue homes, where any unfortunate who comes to us will be gladly welcomed, and everything done to help her back into the paths of rectitude. Our beloved president, Mr. Charles N. Crittenton, has put himself into God's hands to carry on this work, and every year a princely fortune is spent by him for its maintenance.

Our being able to present our work here before this splendid gathering is in direct answer to prayer. For many years it has been our earnest prayer that this magnificent gathering of consecrated young womanhood — the future wives and mothers of the nation — should open their ears to the truth upon this most important subject. I have attended many of these inspiring gatherings, and my heart has gone up in deepest thanks to God for the founders and officers of this Christian Endeavor movement. I have listened, as one after the other has brought in the report of the sheaves gathered; but I have felt that the circle would not be complete until this neglected corner of the vineyard had been tilled. Ah! my dear friends, you who have put on the whole armor of God and gone forth in this warfare against sin, can you find a more necessary, or a more promising, or more Christlike campaign than this?

Many of these for whom I plead are guiltless of any thought of wrong. Their tender years, their innocency, their gentle disposition, will convince you of this. True, many of them are weak; but Isaiah tells us we must "strengthen the weak hands," and again we are told that "God hath chosen the weak things of the world to confound the things that are mighty." Many of them are great sinners, but He came not "to call the righteous, but sinners, to repentance." Our faith reaches out to claim the promises of God, that "though your sins be as scarlet, they shall be as white as snow." We believe it is as easy for him to save a Magdalene as it was to save the beloved disciple, and that when she is saved she is just as thoroughly saved. He who knows the secrets of all hearts knew that a redeemed woman could be trusted, and he sent Mary Magdalene forth to his disciples to testify to the great fact of the resurrection. To the power of this fact we owe it that we to-day have our Mary Magdalenes in every department of life, and in every city almost, testifying to a risen Saviour, who is able to save and to keep.

The time is short to do this great work in. The average life of an abandoned woman, according to the statistics in Europe, where they are registered, is only five years. We must be up and doing. "Work while it is called to-day, for the night cometh when no man can work."

The next speaker introduced was very early called to Christian service in the Young Women's Christian Temperance Union.

Address of Miss Belle Kearney, Flora, Miss.

Never in the history of the world has the influence of women been felt so strongly as now upon all great questions that affect the human race. She has attained for herself a position that shall not be taken away from her, in law, in society, in religion, in politics. Above all, as a leader of philanthropic movements she stands pre-eminent.

A presiding elder of the Louisiana Methodist Conference in a letter written for his church paper sometime since took occasion to say, "These W. C. T. U. women want the earth, the smaller stars, and the nebulæ." As the boys say, we do not deny the allegation, nor do we defy the alligator. Our brother was exactly right. We do want the earth for Christ, and all the smaller stars, if they are inhabited by sin-sick souls, such as those in this world; and we would like to brighten the nebulæ, if the haze is as cloudy as some people's perception and as dense as their prejudices.

This has been essentially a woman's century. Thank God, the next century will be humanity's.

As is well known, the civilization of all lands depends upon the position that women occupy. Look at China, where superfluity of girl babies are put to death and where woman is regarded as very little better than the lower animals. Look at India, where children are wedded almost at their birth, and if the husband dies the child wife has to go perpetually unmarried and wear the sables of mourning and disgrace. Look at Turkey, where women are shut up in harems and live only to serve their lords and masters, going through life veiled and dishonored. Look at Corea, where women are regarded as of such little importance that they are not allowed to look out of a window without the consent of their husbands, and when their children are caressed by one of the opposite sex, they are regarded as forever contaminated, and the only expiation they can make to their parents is to commit suicide, which they do continually.

In comparison to the women of the East, look at the English-speaking nations of the Western Hemisphere, — at Great Britain, for instance, where women are given the highest education, and where they are allowed to exercise the elective franchise for all offices, except Parliament; where they go into political campaigns like men, mount the rostrum, and occupy pulpits. Look at

Canada, where almost exactly the same conditions prevail. Look at the United States, where women are admitted to every position of honor to which they aspire, from managing a farm or a silver-mine to pleading a case before the Supreme Court or performing a difficult surgical operation. My observation has been that, favored as women in many countries are, it is in the United States that they have come nearest to entering into their full possessions, although Great Britain is ahead of us along the line of women's political emancipation. In many other respects, it is very far behind.

I visited the San Sebastian catacombs with a party of friends who were with me at Rome. In the shaft that leads to the vaults beneath we were met by a bare-footed friar, dressed in a gray gown with a rope around his waist, who presented each of us with a little wax taper and led us to the altar, where they were lighted by the fire that burns there continually. Then one by one, in a long procession, we moved toward the catacombs. An iron gate slammed behind us with a thunderous sound, shutting out the world. We found ourselves in a long, dark, narrow passage with vaults on either side, many of which were open, revealing their horrible contents. The way led down forever, it seemed, into miles of subterranean passages, each step more and more slippery and uncertain, and the darkness deepening; but our hearts did not fail us, for each had a light in her hand, whose flame was started at that altar. Ahead of us was our guide, who knew every step of the way, every defect in the defile, and almost every skull in the open graves.

Those of us who have selected the narrow way, especially the leaders of reform movements, are set apart in isolation from the multitude. The way is dark and the atmosphere dank and cold. We pass daily by open sepulchres where lie the ashes of dead hopes; but our hearts do not fail us; we do not shudder nor turn back, for each has a lamp in her hand whose flame was started at the altar of consecration, the brightness of which will lighten the way for our own feet, and, thank God, for the feet also of those who shall come after us.

Ahead is Christ, our guide, who has been along these same sad paths and knows every step of the way. The lamp in his hand is the light that shall bring all men to the knowledge of our Lord and to the glory of that unending day when his will shall be done on earth as it is in heaven.

I don't know what you think about it, but I think the women who lead philanthropic and religious enterprises are the bravest women on earth. God only can ever be able to know the crucifixion they have endured in carrying the blessed tidings of this latter dispensation to the souls of the starving and the heavy-laden. From the beginning they have been laughed at and reviled and scorned; but they have gone on their way undaunted, knowing that they were fulfilling a divine commission and were backed by the power of God.

> " They did not hope to be mowers
>   And gather the ripe golden ears,
> Until they had first been sowers,
>   And watered the furrows with tears."

None but God can ever know the crucifixion of having to go into homes where there is an utter lack of sympathy, where in each smile there lurks a sneer. None but God can know the hardness of pushing the work in places where people do not care to receive it; the constant strife with the liquor traffic and the political power back of it; standing for principles that the world regards as useless or insulting; the battle of radicalism, which means Christ brought down to dull earth, against conservatism, which means selfishness. No one but God can know the loneliness of spirit, the bodily fatigue, the constant strain on brain and heart and nerve, that fills the days of these workers; but we are willing to undergo it all if by our sufferings one soul has been brightened or one community brought into touch with God.

The women of these philanthropic and religious movements are life-saving women. They walk up and down the rock-bound coast of the world waving the danger-signal to the souls that pass by on the great deep of temptation.

They too have worn steep paths into the stony ground; they too have felt the icy winds and tasted the brine of the salt spray; they too have slipped upon the rocks and been swept into the sea of eternity; but their places are supplied. The watch is kept up; the signals are given. Storm-tossed craft sail by into the harbor of peaceful lives under the shadow of the Most High. But out on the ocean there is now a floating spar too far away to catch the gleam of the danger-signal. In this sad world there is many a face that tells the tale of a heartache, and many a life that bears the history of a wreckage.

In this world daily there is a conflict being waged between the home and the saloon. The liquor traffic, an indomitable host of blood and iron, is bearing down upon us. Our homes are being wrecked; our hearts are being broken; mothers are crying out in woe unspeakable, " O saloons, give me back my sons."

Oh, the heartache of the world! Oh, the pain of life! Oh, the mystery of it! My friends, I ask you to-day in the name of God to help ease the burden, to cool the fever, to still the throbbing, aching pulse in the heart of humanity.

MRS. BAER: I am sorry to tell you that the next speaker on our programme is not with us this morning. We are very sorry not to have Mrs. Whittemore with us this morning, and doubly sorry for the reason which prevents her being here. I have a letter which I will read to you, explaining that her daughter Emma, seventeen years of age, is suddenly and hopelessly ill. I know you will all unite together in raising a prayer that this dear girl may be restored.

At these annual gatherings we all delight to call ourselves a Christian Endeavor army. We have with us a representative of another branch of God's army which has done an equally good work with us in another way. I take pleasure this morning in introducing to you a representative of the Salvation Army. We had hoped that you would have the privilege of hearing the daughter of General Booth this morning, Consul Mrs. F. De L. Booth-Tucker; we had also hoped that Mrs. Ballington Booth of the American Volunteers might be here; but Mrs. Booth-Tucker has met with a painful injury, and Mrs. Ballington Booth was unable to accept the invitation of the committee. I take great pleasure, however, in presenting Major Swift, of the Salvation Army.

Address of Major Susie Swift, New York City.

Mrs. Chairman and Dear Friends :—I regret with you the enforced and unexpected absence of my dear leader, Mrs. Booth-Tucker, but I feel so deeply the value of the moments which you lend me in her name that I dare not waste them even in expressions of regret.

I trust that I may be able to make you hear me; and yet if my voice is not as strong as I could wish, will you bear with me when I tell you that for weeks it has been keyed to the low pitch of sick-room and death-chamber, and that I have learned to hush it, as we do instinctively hush our voices when we stand in the outer court while a soul is passing to the presence of the King.

I have taken it for granted that, leaving out of sight all questions of specific religious creed, I speak to women who desire to better the world; to women with aspirations, with plans, with purposes; and I rejoice to know that I need waste no moments in speaking to you of those generalities which are sometimes styled "the elevation of the masses," but that I may confine myself to the practical knowledge which I have gained during the twelve years in which God has privileged me to work among a people who, their enemies themselves being judges, have had exceptional success in the single point of making bad people good people.

My own call, when I rose from my knees, after the fifteen minutes' face-to-face communion with the Lord Jesus Christ which changed all life for me, was to the poorest and to the lowest and to the weakest and to the worst. When I came face to face with Jesus of Nazareth, and recognized him as a living spiritual presence, and felt as never before that Jesus of Nazareth, who fared coarsely, and dressed roughly, and who went to the stupid people and to the ignorant people and to the bad people, was not only my Saviour but my personal Friend, I wanted to follow him ; and I believe that that is the universal experience of the truly converted soul.

But you say, Are we all to become missionaries and all to be workers? Yes, in that Christian Endeavor means, if we believe the Word of God, Christian success. Yes, in that the bettering of the worst and most miserable must be our chiefest aim.

My own conceptions of human need have somewhat altered. My views perhaps have widened. I stand before you to-day more cognizant of the miseries of the rich, more appreciative of the fact that soul starvation may exist in those whose bodies have never hungered, than on that day twelve years ago when I vowed myself to the service of God's weakest, and worst, and furthest-strayed children; and yet I believe that the soul-starved rich are best helped by us Christians keeping before us that original conception of going first and foremost, of going in the greatest numbers, of going with the most persistent intensity, where the need is greatest.

I feel so strongly the limitations and perversions to which the human intellect is subject, and I realize so strongly the almost infinite capacity for confusion and misunderstanding and interpretation existing in our human vocabulary, that I hesitate to make my estimate of the soul status of any man or woman, for this world or the next, existent upon their religious belief. At the same time I am forced to the conviction, after these years of experience, that direct belief in a few fundamental points is absolutely essential to us if we want to help up to God the people who are farthest away from him. Our own articles of war, our own profession of faith in the Salvation Army, only brings out such points as we consider to have the most definite effect on a man's own character, and therefore on his power of helping others. First and foremost as Christian workers, you and I, if we are to go to those who are sunk in sin with a method which is to be of the slightest avail to them. must believe in a regenerative religion.

Mrs. Barrett was speaking about the girls whom she gives her life to help. My mind went back to my own first tentative effort at rescue work, long before I realized that the power of God on the human soul could change all life and all purpose, long before I realized the full force that is bound up in that word "regeneration."

My mother had sent me, in one of my vacations from Vassar College, down to New York to bring her back a servant. In a way that I need not stop to tell you of, a girl whose eyes blazed fire had planted herself in my way and said, in spite of the superintendent of the Intelligence Office, who tried to prevent her from even speaking to me, with her soul in those black eyes, " Oh, take me. I heard you say you wanted a girl to go up into the country. I want to be good. I know," she said in her brusque way, "I have raised the devil for six years, but I want to be good; and if you will only take me and give me a chance, I will promise to serve you faithfully."

In my girlish ignorance and inexperience I only faintly appreciated the past that lay behind that other girl ; but something in my heart was reached and I said, " By the grace of God, she shall have a chance to be good." I took her up with me. I told my Christian mother just as little of what I understood of her story as I could. I took her up into the fresh, green country, and put her under the charge of a Christian housekeeper, who regarded it as her God-given mission to try to help the servants under her to be good. Mary wanted to be good, and I thought her Christian surroundings would help her ; but I had nothing in my heart to put into her heart, and after about six weeks of the country life and of the hygiene, and my own careful study of her, and all I could do for her, my girl came to me again, and again her eyes blazed fire. She said, " I am going back now. I have tried to be good, but I can't do it. Your religion is not strong enough for me ; " and looking into my own heart and my own life, I realized that had I been born where that girl was born, had I been bred as she was bred, had my playground as a child been in the streets and in the city slums, had my only pleasures in my growing girlhood been pleasures with poison at their heart, the semblance of religion I had would not have been strong enough for me, either.

But the day when I rose from my knees at the penitent form of the Salvation Army, after I had laid my hopes, my aspirations, and my all at the feet of the God who took my body and soul, one of my first memories was of the black eyes of that girl far away in New York City; and I said, "Thank God, I have got a religion now that is strong enough for Mary."

After these twelve years I feel that I have a religion in my own soul strong enough for all the lost girls like my Mary, and that the regenerative religion of Jesus Christ is the one for the lost, and the fallen, and the outcast. Then, too, we must have a belief in God's will and God's power to do all that is necessary to make people good. People say sometimes, "Do you really believe that God will take the desire for drink from a drunkard? That is as much as to say that he will make a new coat for a drunkard's stomach." Thank God, we of the Salvation Army believe that if it is essential to make a new coat for a drunkard's stomach to make a sober man of him, that God who fashioned all that delicate, sensitive tissue that we call the mucous membrane is able to re-make it as well. In every land our annals tell of men and women who testify that the very desire for evil of all sorts has been taken from them.

I wish to God I had time to tell you how God can alter the whole brain habit of the sceptical, and make believers out of those whom we call born infi-dels. We must believe that God will give us a definite consciousness of the forgiveness of sin. "Heaven itself can not make my past as if it had never been," said a fallen girl of New England to me one day, a girl who had been ruined before she was twelve years old by her own father. "No," I answered, "heaven itself can not make a past like yours as if it had never been, but the love of Jesus Christ can, and the love of Jesus Christ can enable you to save other girls like yourself and help them up to him."

Finally, I want to speak for a moment on a qualification which has not the slightest possible connection with any doctrinal views, and yet which is the foremost essential for us as Christian Endeavorers, as Christians who are putting forth real efforts for the salvation of other souls. That is, personal holiness of heart and life; we must not only be given up to God's service, but possessed of him. A full soul, a soul that is cleansed from all sin, is the kind that looks attractive to the sinner. On beyond the change of heart and life and will that is involved in conversion, there is something more, something further,—the cleansing of our hearts by the inspiration of God's Holy Spirit, that we may by his grace perfectly love him and worthily magnify his holy name in our lives.

I do not say that no one can work for God without this, but I do say that until we have that perfect cleansing and that full possession we are checked and hindered and hampered and thwarted at every turn. The pure in heart see God in this world as well as in the next. I have hinted already that my own communion was interrupted by sceptical doubts and seasons of darkness, but once I surrendered my all to God, brain and mind, as well as body and soul, he made me understand how it was that the peace of a Christian could indeed flow as a river. The path of the Christian brightens more and more steadily unto the perfect day, as we are promised in the Bible it will do.

Do you really believe that it is possible for you, dear sisters, to have the mind that is in Christ, to be kept from wrong feeling and wrong desires, as well as from wrong words and wrong actions? If you do not, let me ask you to study your Bible, to ask all living witnesses, to fully inform and establish your own mind as to what God's will and purpose for you is. But if you believe this morning that this is attainable for us, then let me beg you to surrender your all to God, going out into the dark with him alone. God's path for me did indeed involve going out from my country, out from my church, out from my home, out from my friends, to poverty and to exile and to strangerhood; but in going out into the dark with God, one finds himself in the light with him, and hidden in his presence the surrender seems absolutely nothing.

One of our slum workers, who was a cultured teacher in a Brooklyn seminary, said, after she had been at her work in the slums, her work of attending the sick and caring for little children and speaking always to the poor and ignorant for a few months, that she used to lie on the floor in prayer at night and say, " O my God, I am brain hungry." The weeks went on; her work went on, and her knowledge of God grew. I came face to face with her one day and said, " Well, dear, are you brain hungry still ? " She said, " Ah, Major, I have not stopped to think for weeks whether I was brain hungry, because I am so soul satisfied."

After the cleansing must come the indwelling, and then the love of God and the grace of God and the peace of God rippling out of us naturally and spontaneously will make our Christian work so effortless that even the glorious blessed name of your Society will seem to you at times almost a misnomer, because the Endeavor will have no conscious effort, the burden being laid on the indwelling Christ.

SATURDAY AFTERNOON.

Capitol Hill.

What a spectacle ! The wide space enclosed by the east and west wings of the national Capitol was one sea of human beings, a flowing sea, with currents and tides, with streams of humanity pouring into it from all avenues, with great bays stretching out along East Capitol Street and Delaware and Maryland Avenues, and with three mighty waves breaking upon and covering the flights of Capitol steps.

Fifty thousand souls, to judge from the more than five thousand in the choir,— that great choir which, ranged upon and around the centre steps, was only the shining nucleus of the throng. A dazzling sight indeed was that fair bank of human flowers, those thousands of young girls in their fresh gowns of pink and white and dainty blue. And a manly sight were the regiments of tenors and basses. In front was seated on a platform " Uncle Sam's " white-uniformed Marine Band.

And to the right and left, as far as could be seen, reached a mass of heads. In the shadow of the beautiful dome the mass was light with straw hats; in the bright sunshine it was dark with umbrellas. As the shadow spread, the crowd brightened. Sparkles of gay color everywhere,— umbrellas of every brilliant hue, and in hundreds of places there rose above the assembly the red, white, and blue banner of the Convention, Ohio's garnet flag, New Jersey's orange and black, Pennsylvania's blue and red, and many another State ensign.

An unequalled setting for such a glorious scene were the lovely Capitol grounds, shining in the afternoon sun; the new national library,— a superb piece of architecture; and that building of buildings, that epic in stone, our national Capitol. And the Capitol windows were crowded, and the crowd overflowed on to the library grounds, and surged up on the pedestals of statues and the bases of fountains; and pushed hard on the full areas allotted to carriages. Yet it was, *of course*, a joyous and an orderly crowd, and the police had nothing to do but enjoy it all.

And the white figure of George Washington rose serene from the midst of it all. Was the spirit of the great patriot there, rejoicing over this, the mightiest gathering of young patriots ever seen in the country he loved, or in this wide world?

Never before has our government permitted the area around the Capitol, the very heart of the nation, to be used for other than governmental purposes. And indeed a governmental purpose was that, since the 50,000 represent nearly 3,000,000 young people whose force of character will make them the country's governors before many a moon has passed. That grand exhibition of young manhood and womanhood is the clearest omen yet seen of the coming time when Christ, whose right it is to reign, shall be supreme on Capitol Hill.

The trustees of the United Society filled one stone outpost. Justice Harlan's strong face and giant form was conspicuous in the fair setting of the topmost rows of the chorus. The speakers' stand was filled with Dr. Clark, Secretary Baer, Chairman Smith, Director Foster, Dr. McCrory, of Pennsylvania, and Dr. J. Z. Tyler, of Ohio.

"Holy, holy, holy,"— fit opening chorus, that! And how the over 4,000 young voices bore that glorious hymn to heaven! Dr. McCrory offered prayer, and then Dr. Clark made a brief address.

Remarks of President Francis E. Clark, D.D.

This is not to be a speech-making occasion. I regret to say that Hon. John Wanamaker, who was announced to speak from this platform, has been obliged to return home. His name was put on the programme when he was upon the water, returning from Europe. We could not wait until he got here for his acceptance, but we thought he would be able to be with us. He found he could not, and has been obliged to go home.

This will be essentially a Christian citizenship praise meeting. We have speeches often. It is not often that we can have a chorus of 4,700 voices. I am sure that we want to hear them sing, and to join with them in their songs.

Just a word before I present the banner to the local union that has reported the best work in promoting Christian citizenship.

What a glorious spectacle is this,—these tens of thousands! I think this scene will be photographed upon our minds as long as we live. We shall never forget the sight at the capital of the nation.

It means that Christian Endeavor stands for Christian citizenship. That is the significance of this meeting. It does not mean that we are partisans, that as a society we belong to any one political party. It does mean that because we are Christians, we are Christian citizens. It means that we stand for temperance, for purity, in a word, for righteousness; and I am glad to say that one city union has obtained, by its specially good work in Christian citizenship, the banner. Many cities have done excellently, but Cleveland excelleth them all.

Last year Syracuse had the banner. She deserved it, and she held it nobly. She has done good work this year. Other cities have also done nobly, notably Chicago; Hamilton, in Ontario, across the line,— Christian citizenship means just the same thing in Canada that it does in the United States,— Hamilton, Ont., should have honorable mention ; also Newark, N. J., and Jamesville, Wis., and others.

But there is one city that especially deserves and will receive the banner. In the estimation of the committee, the city union of Cleveland has reported the best work.

In the name of the United Society, I present this banner to the representative of Cleveland, the Rev. J. Z. Tyler, D.D., who will accept it in the name of the fair city by the lake.

Take it, Cleveland.   Take it, and keep it as long as you can.

Remarks of Rev. J. Z. Tyler, D.D., Cleveland, O.

Fellow Citizens (applause), *Fellow Endeavorers* (Cries of " That's better "):— From the salt marshes of Syracuse to the forest by the unsalted sea, the banner moves westward.   It stands not simply for Christian Endeavor.   It stands for citizenship exalted.   No clearer demonstration of the divine touch upon the heart of him who has led us in this movement can be found anywhere than in the suggestion that Christian Endeavor shall give special attention to Christian citizenship.

I believe that the Christian Endeavor movement has done more to contribute to the new patriotism than any other one thing, for it must be recognized that there is coming a civic revival throughout the Republic.   This does not mean that Christian Endeavor is in any sense to ally itself to any one party, whatever may be its purpose, its principles, or its record, but that every Endeavorer stands for himself, and will do his duty as a Christian citizen.

I shall carry this banner with pride — a just pride, I hope,— back to that city which had the honor and the pleasure of entertaining the convention in 1894 ; and we shall hold it until some other city shall be able to take it from us.

After these stirring exercises came the praise service.   Of course the Marine Band made matchless music.   Of course the fifty regiments of Endeavorers zealously applauded each patriotic piece, gayly swinging flags and hats and umbrellas to the more sprightly tunes, such as " Yankee Doodle."   And of course Mr. Foster's tremendous chorus took hold on the very heavens.   The international hymn, " America," " There's a Royal Banner," Dr. S. F. Smith's " The Cross and Victory," and Mr. Foster's own " Loyal Soldiers;"— those were the songs they sung.

Finally came the march down historic Pennsylvania Avenue.   The Marine Band led the way with inspiring strains.   There followed the trustees of the United Society.   Dr. Tyler bore his Christian citizenship banner.   In the centre were the officers of the United Society.   Very appropriately there followed the noble Committee of '96, and then came the mighty army of Endeavorers, pouring down Capitol Hill in an endless stream.

The route of a mile and a third was lined all the way with a dense crowd of spectators.   All windows were filled.   The Endeavorers sang as they marched, the favorite song being, of course, " Onward, Christian Soldiers."   As they passed the gayly decorated State headquarters they saluted, and similar honor was rendered to prominent Endeavor leaders of whom the procession caught sight.

The procession was dispersed at the Treasury Building.

SATURDAY EVENING.

Meeting of Citizens of Washington in Tents Washington and Endeavor.

It had been a matter for regret at earlier conventions that those living in the city so generously opening wide its doors have been in so large measure barred out from the meetings. At Washington special provisions were made for the citizens. Meetings especially for them were held in Tents Washington and Endeavor on Saturday evening. These were intended to set forth the aims and possibilities of Christian Endeavor, and the speakers were all trustees.

In Tent Washington Rev. J. Z. Tyler, D.D., told some of the objects that Christian Endeavor does not aim at. It does not seek to carry out any one's pet schemes of social reform. It does not strive for size, but for strength. It aims at the enthronement of Christ. It aims to promote religious activity by working outward from within. It aims to exalt in Christian life the idea of a covenant.

Bishop Alexander Walters, D.D., spoke powerfully of the inspiration that had come from the scenes of the afternoon at the Capitol, and felt that the city had not been praised by the committee as highly as it deserved. His race had been set free by a declaration issued from a spot not far from that tent, and Christian Endeavor is engaged in freeing souls from slavery to sin.

In his effective way Dr. Wayland Hoyt described Christian Endeavor's efforts to win the young. When William the Conqueror sailed to take England, a golden boy was the figurehead of his vessel, pointing to the goal. Christian Endeavor seeks to secure the devotion of the golden youth to Christ, thus pointing the way to a noble future. It does this by making Christ supreme, and by training them for service.

After the speaking the audience listened with delight to several selections by the Hampton singers.

The "ebonized trustee," as Dr. Hill styled Bishop Arnett, gave the first address in Tent Endeavor. He said that the Society aims to make a good man out of a bad man, and then to make every man feel his duty. If a man has true religion, the devil will know it, as well as God. The best way to test a man's religion is to ask his wife about him. The Society aims to make patriotic citizens, and the scenes witnessed this week are greater than any of the historic scenes of the time of Lincoln and Grant.

Rev. William Patterson said that we are told a woman's history can be written in a few words : She was born, she lived, she chewed gum, she died. So the history of many a man could be written in a few words : He lived, he dressed himself nicely, he chewed tobacco, he swung a cane, and after a while he died. Christian Endeavor gives a purpose to life. It means practical work, too, and not mere theory. A man might write a whole book on the theory of the bicycle, on how to get on, and how to start, and all that, but you put him on a bicycle, and say, " Off you go," and off he does go — to the ground.

Dr. Beckley stated the work of Christian Endeavor as teaching the young to do something. God help a man that can do anything. You do not want him ; you want a man that can do something. It is fostering the true Christian fellowship. He would not waste his breath in talking about Christian fellowship as a sentiment ; we need it as a power.

The fellowship of Christian Endeavor, it was pertinently suggested by Dr. Hill, who presided, was illustrated by the fact that the speakers were a Methodist, a Baptist, a Congregationalist, and a Presbyterian.

State Rallies and Receptions.

Washington hospitality was so hearty that all the visitors would have been glad to stay longer. Illinois found this out when trying on Saturday night to plan in regard to a special train for the return trip. Votes were taken for one day after another with so little result that finally those that had decided at all on the day of their return were asked to rise, and very few responded. With such feelings between hosts and guests the State receptions, the delightful social feature of the week, could not fail to be a great success. The common thought took a pleasant form of expression in the case of Iowa, which had a double reception at the church assigned as its headquarters. The society entertaining the State held a reception in the lecture-room, and then all adjourned to the church, where the compliment was returned. Pennsylvania had to have two rallies in different audience-rooms of the church, because the attendance was so large. Enthusiasm ran high in all the gatherings, even those where but few delegates could be expected, as at the rally of New Mexico and the Floating Societies, while Chatauqua salutes and applause were as frequent as in the largest meetings of the Convention.

At almost all the receptions the exercises included addresses of welcome by representatives of the local church and Endeavor Society, with a response by some State officer. In addition to this some of the States had arranged more or less elaborate programmes with a number of speakers. The president and secretary of the United Society were in demand and spoke at several places. Rev. B. Fay Mills spoke at the New York rally, and Dr. Crafts, who also addressed the Endeavorers from the Keystone State. Ex-Governor Ordway and a Nebraska Indian delegate addressed Dakota's rally. Rev. Stanley Matthews, D.D., of England, was at Ohio's reception; Rev. Thomas Marshall, D.D., of the Presbyterian Board of Foreign Missions, was welcomed by Illinois; and Maine claimed once more Dr. Clark, and Mr. William H. Pennell, whose home is now in Washington. Wisconsin and Indiana were entertained by graphic accounts of their journey.

Music, of course, played a part in the programme. The Canadians sung their national hymns, and Massachusetts kept "Boston, '95," in mind, not only by the many "white and crimson banners," but by singing by three hundred of the Boston choir. State songs or songs and hymns written for the occasion were heard at the receptions of Massachusetts, Maine, Illinois, Kentucky, Ohio, and New Jersey.

The thought of future conventions gave color to some of the gatherings. Tennessee was tired out with celebrating the promise of "Nashville, '98," but not too tired to celebrate some more. Kentucky consoled herself with the thought that for many the road to Nashville must lead through Louisville. Pennsylvania with flags and songs roused enthusiasm for the State convention at Scranton in the autumn. There was entertainment of lighter sort. Light refreshments were served. Alabama and Louisiana had an exhibition of the phonograph. Introductions in many of the rallies were accomplished by means of cards furnished each delegate and bearing his name. In some cases these were used later for collecting autographs or for playing a game. Those furnished Rhode Island were pleasant souvenirs bearing the picture of the new church building soon to be erected by their hosts, the Mount Pleasant Congregational Church. Oklahoma and Mississippi were given photographs of the Eastern Presbyterian Church, their headquarters.

Indiana returned the compliment of the souvenirs and kindness that they received by presenting their hosts with a silk flag. Massachusetts expressed its feelings in a similar way, and there was not a State that would not have been glad to join Kentucky in passing a vote of thanks by rising. The evening had strengthened greatly the ties between entertainers and entertained, as well as those between delegates from the same State.

SUNDAY MORNING.

Church Services.

The clause of the pledge relating to daily reading of the Bible was the topic for Sunday morning's early meetings. When the hour for the Sunday school arrived, the Endeavorers in great numbers came with it. They were interested to see the model arrangement in some of the larger schools, and they were not less interested to join in study of the Word.

By the time for the church services to begin the churches were overflowing. A Washington paper remarked that the visitors had been in all respects teachers by object-lessons, and that Sunday's lesson showed how practical Christians observe the Sabbath, the unusual feature of the text being, " Do as I do, and not merely as I say."

It was not because the capital is at all lacking in strong preachers whom the visitors would have enjoyed hearing, but it was according to custom, that the pulpits were chiefly filled by leading ministers in attendance on the Convention, and naturally most of them were influenced in their choice of themes by the thought of the special character of their audiences. Many of the delegates went to their church headquarters, but they also scattered much.

The Christian Endeavor meetings in the evening were characteristic, testimony, prayer, and song filling the minutes to the utmost ; and no one was heard to complain that the young people did not remain to the second service. In the majority of cases this second meeting was a preaching service, but several pastors improved the opportunity to arrange " platform meetings," with many brief addresses from different visitors.

SUNDAY AFTERNOON.

Denominational Missionary Meetings.

One of the valuable new features of the Convention was the holding of denominational missionary rallies separate from the denominational rallies, that have already become so familiar and popular. In twenty-two different churches were gathered the young people of twenty-two different denominations to listen to their missionary leaders and the most prominent pastors in their churches while they stirred them with the thrilling pictures of missionary heroism, or moved them to greater zeal and consecration by strong representations of the present missionary crisis,— the debts of the boards, the many open doors, the appalling need of money and of men.

Whenever the denomination had a church in Washington, the rally was held in that church. Several of these rallies, compelled to meet in churches of another faith, had much to say about establishing churches of their own in the capital city.

It would be impossible in our limited space to give full accounts of these twenty-two crowded sessions. Only a few glimpses are possible.

The three denominations most prominent in Christian Endeavor — Baptist, Presbyterian, and Congregationalist — occupied the three great tents.

Large space in the meetings was given, of course, to the missionaries now in this country. The main feature of the Methodist rally was the stirring address by that heroic missionary to the far North, Rev. Egerton R. Young, of Canada. The eloquent Miss Margaret W. Leitch, of Ceylon, spoke to the Congregationalists, together with the home missionary, Rev. Warren Goff, Rev. Rufus Clark, of Japan, and Dr. Todd, of Turkey. "Uncle" Boston Smith, that original home missionary of the Baptists, famous for his chapel-car ministrations, addressed their great rally, and also Rev. W. H. Sloan, of Mexico, and Rev. W. M. Thomas, Burmah, who has translated the Christian Endeavor pledge into two languages, and said that, if God gave him more tongues, he would translate it for still other peoples. Rev. George P. Goll, the Lutheran missionary, who has established thirteen Lutheran Christian Endeavor Societies in Liberia, spoke at the Lutheran rally, which was especially notable for its size and enthusiasm. The Friends listened to a missionary returned from Palestine, who sung them an Arabic hymn. The rally of the Reformed Church in America was addressed by Rev. Henry Stout, D.D., returned from their field in Japan. From the United Brethren mission in Western Africa came Rev. L. O. Burtner, to carry Africa's appeal to the young people of his church. Three Mennonite home missionaries told their rally about their work among the Indian tribes in the West.

These gatherings were conspicuous also for the presence of missionary secretaries, who wisely made use of this splendid opportunity for reaching their young people. Among these were the Congregationalists, Dr. C. C. Creegan and Rev. A. F. McGregor, of Canada; the Lutheran, Dr. Hartman; the Baptists, Dr. Mabie, Dr. Seymour, and Dr. Morehouse; Miss M. Catharine Jones, of the Presbyterians; the Disciples, Rev. B. L. Smith and Rev. F. M. Raines; and Dr. Fullerton and Rev. J. W. Laughlin, of the Cumberland Presbyterians.

Among the prominent speakers were: Southern Presbyterians, Professor James Lewis Howe, a trustee of the United Society; Dr. James L. Hill and Bishop Arnett, two trustees, who addressed the African Methodist Episcopal rally; Canon Richardson, another trustee, who addressed the Episcopalian rally; Rev. B. Fay Mills and Dr. Wallace Radcliffe, who spoke to the Presbyterians; Dr. J. Z. Tyler, a trustee, Dr. F. D. Power, Dean Willett, of the Disciples' Divinity House of Chicago University, and Miss Jessie H. Brown, editor of *The Lookout*, all of whom spoke to the Disciples; Bishop Walters, who addressed the African Methodist Episcopal Zion rally; Dr. H. S. Williams and Rev. Ira Landrith, editor of *The Cumberland Presbyterian*, who spoke before their own young people, the latter also addressing the Welsh rally, which brought together many Welsh Endeavorers, a large part of whose exercises were in their native tongue. There were besides, of the Lutherans, Miss Laura Wade Rice, editor of *The Children's Missionary*, and Rev. W. S. Hinman, so prominent in young people's work; of the United Brethren, the musician, Rev. E. S. Lorenz; President T. H. Lewis and Rev. R. B. Whitehead, of the Methodist Protestants, who also held a very enthusiastic meeting of the National Christian Endeavor Union of their denomination. Then there was Rev. W. E. Barton, D.D., the Congregationalist; Dr. Clarence Barbour, the Baptist; and Rev. P. A. Canada, Dr. Barrett, and Rev. G. A. Conibear, of the Christians.

Dr. Bell, United Brethren missionary secretary, illustrated his address with charts, and many of the speakers used similar aids. The United Evangelical rally took earnest and practical steps to help that young denomination start out in missionary work. The Free Baptists listened to some of their most active home and foreign missionaries. The Church of God Endeavorers held an interesting rally, addressed by Dr. Allen and Rev. C. I. Brown. The Moravians filled the church at their rally, which, as befits this denomination so prominent in missionary activity, was one of the greatest enthusiasm.

Altogether, these meetings, though held at a time when the heat was almost intolerable, were strikingly vigorous, and are sure to result in greatly increased study of denominational missions and rapidly growing contributions to denominational treasuries.

Central Hall.

Mr. Shaw, in the absence of Rev. Dr. Cuyler, who led the Sabbath observance meeting in Central Hall, said that the presence of more than 2,000 Endeavorers there that sultry afternoon was proof that the attendants on these great conventions came for spiritual purposes, and not merely for a junket. The meeting opened with the repeating, by all the company, of the fourth commandment. Mr. Foster had charge of the singing. Rev. J. E. Gilbert, of Washington, conducted the opening devotional exercises.

Mrs. McEwen, wife of Dr. H. T. McEwen, the chairman of the committee that cared for the great New York Convention, was forcible and truly eloquent. Rev. J. B. Davison, of Milwaukee, spoke nobly of the harm Sabbath desecration was doing to the laboring man, and how the Sabbath is "God's bridge over the chasm between Christ and Christian wage-earners." Dr. Alexander Alison, of New York, poured out for half an hour a fusillade of fact and argument, right to the point, on Sunday desecration in all its forms, by newspapers, saloons, bicycle-riders, railroads, and the like.

The audience, in spite of the great heat, were enthusiastic and eager listeners. The meeting ran far beyond its time to hear that eminent reformer, Dr. Wilbur F. Crafts, president of the Reform League. With sparkling anecdotes and strong truths and cogent logic, he pleaded for God's day.

Remarks of Treasurer Shaw.

There are some people who try to give us the impression that Christian Endeavorers come up to their conventions simply to have a kind of excursion, a good time, a picnic, as they call it. I wish they could look in upon the great congregations that are gathered this afternoon. They would then understand that we mean business when we come to a convention. If we did not we should not be here at this hour, and under the pressure of this atmosphere. We are not here for fun. We are here for business. I consider this one of the most important meetings that will be held during this great convention. I greatly regret that our honored friend and leader, Dr. Cuyler, is prevented from being here on account of a sudden attack of illness. His heart, I am sure, is with us. His prayers are for us. We know that though he is absent in body, he is present in spirit. We shall pray for him that many years of earnest faithful service, such as he has rendered in the past, may be yet in store for him, and that his voice may still be lifted for every cause of righteousness and of truth.

Dr. Clark received a letter yesterday from a good friend who was very much disturbed about some reports in the papers. I have also been interviewed by several good friends about some reports in the papers. I understand that one of the leading New York papers has advertised a special Christian Endeavor Sunday edition, with contributions by the officers of the United Society of Christian Endeavor. Well, for ways that are dark and tricks that are vain, the Chinese are not the only people that stand in the front ranks. There are some managers of newspapers who stand there. We have good friends on the press. They have done magnificent work for Christian Endeavor and for the cause of Christ during these passing days. On the wings of their papers they have sent out messages of truth and of righteousness; but Dr. Francis E. Clark is not contributing to Sunday newspapers, if he knows what he is doing. General Secretary Baer is not contributing to Sunday newspapers, if he knows what he is doing. Sometimes editors of newspapers may secure a contribution weeks in advance, and hold it and use it in a Sunday edition without the consent of the writer. That has been done in more cases than one. So don't be disturbed, friends, even if a contribution by Dr. Clark should appear in the Sunday edition. Don't be disturbed about Dr. Clark's orthodoxy on the question of Sunday observance. I pledge you my word, and I have his statement for it, that he is not now contributing, and he will not contribute, to Sunday newspapers; and where he stands the other officers of the United Society of Christian Endeavor stand.

Furthermore, another good friend writes that he has seen in the public press that a delegation of Christian Endeavorers from New England left home last Sunday to come to this Convention, and that another delegation from the West arrived here and spent last Sunday in excursions to some of your places of interest. I want to say that the tickets held by these Christian Endeavorers are excursion tickets from the New England States, and that they were not good for passage until last Monday. They could not be used on Sunday. I want to say that the excursion tickets from the West were not good in the territory of the Trunk Line Association until last Monday morning; and I do not believe that any of our Christian Endeavorers paid double fare from their homes in order to take a little horse-car excursion in the city of Washington.

It is not necessary for you to believe even everything that is published in the newspapers in Washington. So don't get worried about these things. Don't think the whole Christian Endeavor movement has gone over to the enemy because some newspaper may happen to make a mistake; don't think, either, that every man or woman wearing a Christian Endeavor badge on the streets of Washington is a Christian Endeavorer. Some of them may have been able to get badges. I want some other card of membership, or certificate of membership, than the mere fact that these people are wearing Christian Endeavor badges. Everybody in Washington is so proud of Christian Endeavor that they would all like to wear a badge, whether they deserve it or not. If you see anybody disgracing the cause of Christian Endeavor, and they happen to wear the badge, don't say they are Christian Endeavorers. Rather give us the benefit of the doubt, if there is one, and don't go off and sit down under the juniper-tree and mourn for the depravity of the young people in these days.

There are no stronger, more enthusiastic observers of the Sabbath Day, and none that stand with a stiffer backbone for God's holy day, than our Christian Endeavor members.

Address of Mrs. Henry T. Mc Ewen, New York City.

It is as significant as it is important that God no sooner founded the home than he instituted the Sabbath. The intimate relation between the home and the Sabbath is woman's justification for being the Sabbath's defender.

The evening of the sixth day witnessed the completion of God's creative work. The home was its consummation. The morning of the seventh day dawned not for toil, but for rest. God, who instituted the Sabbath, himself observed it. What a perfect day—the earth without sin, the curse unknown! It was the foregleam of that " rest which remaineth for the people of God."

That man would fall, and that he would have to earn his bread in the sweat of his brow, did not surprise God. The Creator knew man's possibilities and limitations. Six days of the continuous toil in the arduous struggle for bread was all that the human frame could endure. In the battle of life, the needs of the body would stifle the cry of the soul. The physical would be provided for at the expense of the spiritual. For these reasons God ordained that the Sabbath should be observed by man. The body needed it for rest ; the soul, for worship.

God penned the fourth commandment ·for the whole man, for all races, for all times. During the centuries since creation man's nature has not changed. We have the same weak bodies and tempted souls which were the portion of Adam and Eve. Our physical and our spiritual natures must be renewed to live. The observance of this commandment conditioned man's existence at the beginning, and will condition it to the end. " Remember " is employed to recall the past, guard the present, and secure the future. Sabbath desecration means individual and national desolation. It was not vengeance but mercy which dealt sternly with the gatherer of sticks on the Sabbath. " Better that one should die, than that the whole nation should perish." Of all the peoples of that time, the Hebrews are the only ones who have survived the shock of centuries. Sabbath observance has to do with national perpetuity as well as with individual purity. Benedictions followed the keeping of this covenant as surely as curses its violation.

Christ came not to destroy the law but to fulfil it. To fulfil means to fill full, or to fill completely. Did Christ fill full this law? We find that his custom was to be in the synagogue on the Sabbath Day, engaged in worship. He also fills up the law with acts of mercy. He wrought seven miracles on the Sabbath. Three of these were performed in the synagogues. Two were to heal women. Acts of necessity were justified by the Master. He had no censure but rather approval for the disciples who, as they walked through the fields on the Sabbath, plucked the heads of grain, rubbing them out in their hands. It was he who said, "The Sabbath was made for man, and not man for the Sabbath." Falling from his lips these words meant for all men, as opposed to any class or portion of men, and they meant for the whole, or entire man, as opposed to any portion thereof. Underneath each jacket two natures struggle in mighty combat. Subordination or supremacy, rather than co-ordination and co-operation, seem to be the watchwords of these combatants. Even Paul found that when he would do good evil was present with him. Man's soul is as surely related to God as his body to the earth. Outdoor sports with siren voice are luring him to mountain and sea; science, art, literature, stimulate his intellect; "But what shall it profit a man, if he should gain the whole world, and lose his own soul? Or what shall a man give in exchange for his soul?" Trained body and disciplined mind must be crowned by sanctified soul, if you are to have the complete man. Starving the spiritual, in order that you may surfeit the carnal, is demon's, not divine, work. He would be a generous master who gave six-sevenths to his servants and retained one-seventh for himself. What shall we say to this Master who not only gives us six-sevenths as our own, but would give us back, fuller in measure and richer in kind; even this one-seventh, when we hallow it to him. God did not make the Sabbath for God, but for man, the highest, noblest, truest, completest man.

Sabbath desecration is not merely robbing God of his glory; it is even more surely robbing man of his perfection. Esau, selling his birthright for a mess of pottage, was a far-seeing and wise man in comparison with those who for pleasures of body barter the wealth of the soul.

Alarmed at the prevalent and growing Sabbath desecration, and knowing that it imperilled the home, as well as the Church and the nation, a number of women of several Christian denominations met in the Calvary Baptist Church, New York City, Dec. 10, 1894.

Several phases of Sabbath observance were discussed, and a committee was appointed to consider a plan by which women might unite to secure a better observance of the Lord's Day. After deliberation the Women's National Sabbath Alliance was organized, a constitution adopted, and officers chosen. Our honored president, Mrs. Darwin R. James, has the confidence and affection of all Christian women. There are eleven vice-presidents, representing as many denominations. Christian Union and co-operation are thus realized.

All who become members of the Alliance subscribe to the following pledge : —

We, women of America, recognizing the American Christian Sabbath as our rightful inheritance, bequeathed to us by our forefathers, as the foundation of our national prosperity, as the safeguard of our social, civil, and religious blessings, as the conservator of the rights of the wage-earner, do hereby pledge ourselves to resist, by precept and example, whatever tends to undermine Sunday as a day of rest and worship; such as the Sunday secular newspaper, Sunday social entertainments, and Sunday driving or travelling for gain or pleasure; and we further pledge ourselves to use our influence to create a right sentiment on all aspects of the Sunday question, especially in reference to traffic of every kind on that day.

Pioneer work is never easy. Crowns succeed, they never precede, triumph. We have, however, been encouraged by the cordial response we have received from Christian women in different States throughout the Union. Our aim is to form auxiliaries in every city and town, that our personal, united effort may be felt by those who profane the Sabbath. In order that all Christian people may be alert to the peril and opportunity of the Sabbath, we desire every minister to preach on this theme. We realize that every woman in America is an uncrowned queen. Her subjects are numerous and loyal. To render her reign beneficent is our desire. Said a gentleman not long since, "Your pledge is almost as strict as the traditions of the Pharisees. I take the Sermon on the Mount as my rule of life, and in it I do not find any Sabbath-keeping enjoined. I think the Sabbath was made for man."

How can he read, "Blessed are the pure in heart, for they shall see God," and forget the Sabbath, instituted by God to bring him near to God? Do we find either God or purity in the Sunday newspapers? Are we made purer by the Sunday concert, baseball game, or so-called popular amusements? Do we go there to meet or catch a vision of God? How can he read, "Blessed are the merciful, for they shall obtain mercy," whilst he demands that his Sunday dinner-table shall be supplied with oysters on the half shell, or that the confectioner shall deliver his desserts on the Sabbath? By what right, human or divine, does he deprive others of the rest of the Sabbath that his creature comforts may be supplied? How can he read, "Blessed are they which do hunger and thirst after righteousness, for they shall be filled," when selfishness is his controlling motive? Is it necessary, or merciful, that the post-office be open on the Sabbath, or that letters be delivered?

Christian women wield an influence which can not be weighed or measured. Not only can this influence be felt in our homes, but in business and social circles American women possess a power not felt in other lands. What Drummond says is pre-eminently true of America: "Christianity is not all carried on by committees, and the kingdom of God has other ways of coming than through municipal reforms. Most of the stones for the building of the city of God, and all the best of them, are made by mothers." But true as this is and ever must be, it is not less true that the number of business, professional, and laboring women outside of the homes is increasing with every year. *The Union Signal* is responsible for the following very significant statements: "In this country 2,500 women are practising medicine, 275 are preaching the Gospel, more than 6,000 are managing post-offices, and over 3,000,000 are earning independent incomes. Since 1880 the patent office has granted over 2,500 patents to women, and in New York City 27,000 women support their husbands."

Women of vast wealth have a responsibility entrusted to them. Said a clergyman not long since, "Mrs.—— owns a controlling interest in the stock of the mines in which my people work. I can not get suitable elders for my church, because the mines are operated on Sunday, and my men must either work or leave. Mrs.—— is a Christian woman, and I can not believe that she knows of or comprehends this." How can Christian women oblige others to do unnecessary work on the Sabbath, or themselves set the fashion by entertaining, or attending, dinners, teas, and receptions on the Sabbath?

Of the one hundred thousand who, according to the *New York Herald*, were out on their wheels, in Greater New York, Sunday, June 21, do you suppose that all were Hebrews, or that they all belong to the so-called working classes?

A recent number of the *L. A. W. Bulletin* says, "Those who are disposed to decry Sunday wheeling should remember that the first Christian Sabbath was the occasion of a Sunday outing and a discourse on the way by the founder of Christianity. No one would now venture to doubt but that, if Cleopas and his companion had possessed bicycles they would have ridden them that spring day on their journey of threescore furlongs to Emmaus." Why did not the writer tell the whole truth, instead of a half of the truth, which is often the worst type of a lie? Did he not know that the apostles and disciples so strictly observed the Sabbath that not even one of them went to the tomb in which their Master's body lay that sacred day? As the women hurried along that memorable morning of the resurrection they do not even seem to have known that Pilate had placed a Roman guard and fixed the seal. Cleopas and his companion were not desecrating the Sabbath by walking to Emmaus. Not till the Sabbath was past did their Master rise from the dead. It was to complete a hasty and imperfect burial that the women hurried to the tomb that early morning. Not even their devotion to Christ could lead them to break the Sabbath which they and their fathers had hitherto kept. If you are a Hebrew, and devoutly keep the Jewish Sabbath, we shall not question your Sabbath observance; or if you are a Christian and keep the first day of the week, we shall be satisfied; but that to which we object is that you are a Gentile on Saturday, and a Hebrew on Sunday, thus violating both letter and spirit of the Sabbath. The day is thus turned into one of revel, instead of rest; it is made to minister to selfishness, instead of holiness. If we should read in to-morrow's papers of thousands of men, women, and children fainting at their work for lack of food, a cry of horror and anguish would be heard. Purses would open, hands and hearts would be busy supplying the need. Yet to-morrow thousands of men, women, and children will fall under the strain and stress of temptation because their souls have not been fed. Shame on a people's conscience where to starve is more awful than sin!

> " Keep your conscience pure, untainted,
> Be existence short or long;
> Hold aloft the golden watchword,
> Love of right and scorn of wrong."

It is a siege, not a skirmish, which we have undertaken. To the women we appeal against the Continental, in behalf of the Christian, Sabbath. " Who knoweth but that thou art come to the kingdom for such a time as this? " was the challenge with which Mordecai aroused Queen Esther. Her sacrifice and heroism saved a nation. If we rescue the Sabbath, we shall have saved a nation.

Address of Rev. J. B. Davison, Milwaukee, Wis.

Everybody knows that a broad chasm separates a large portion of the wage-earners from Christianity. It may not be deeper than in former years, but it is there. I ask you to consider two propositions in reference to this chasm.

1. The Sabbath has been made one occasion of this terrible chasm.

2. The Sabbath is a bridge over this chasm by which these wage-earners may be led to find and know Christ.

The Sabbath is the most prominent outward representative of Christianity. Satan has so bewildered his servants' eyes that the Sabbath has seemed to them a hobgoblin, full of gloom and evil forebodings. Looking through this distorted vision of the Sabbath at the Church, the Christian religion, and even heaven itself, they have all seemed to many sombre and forbidding. A refined lady said to me, " I used to think if heaven was an eternal Sabbath I never wished to go there."

Some of us have often looked or talked as though the Sabbath were a dull, gloomy burden. The joy of the Lord has not so filled our souls as to shine out of our faces and ring out of our speech. So we have led men to think Sabbath-keeping is probably a duty essential to salvation; but it is awfully dull. So, while they hope to keep their last Sabbath holy, and would not wish to go fishing that day, they prefer to put off such evil days, and with them they put off Christianity.

Again, some Christians have gone to church while their employees in the factory or kitchen were bound to incessant, needless toil, and so were taught to hate the Sabbath and the Church. Many who would not do this individually have been partners in the same iniquity as members of a corporation. Others, by riding on Sunday trains, going to the post-office Sunday, taking Sunday papers, asking that their freight be carried on Sunday, or in other similar ways have helped to hold in bondage to greedy employers and a thoughtless public millions whose bodies, brains, and souls cry out for release from this Sunday slavery.

Some Christians have said, " I keep my employees at work Sunday to prevent them from doing something worse." Others refuse to help release men from Sunday slavery lest they may not use their freedom rightly. Dare a Christian thus excuse his own disobedience to God and his cruelty to his neighbor?

Again, many Christian communities have allowed saloons, theatres, etc., to run wide open Sunday, inviting multitudes to ruin. In these and other ways has this memorial of the resurrection been perverted into a means of opening and widening the terrible chasm between the sons of toil and their loving Heavenly Father. One of God's chief blessings is thus turned into a curse.

It must be restored to its original beauty and glory. Then will it be a bridge over the foul chasm of unbelief, upon which thousands of wage-earners shall be led up from the dark morass of discontent into the sunlight, hope, and joy of God's love. There will they learn to know the tender heart of the Carpenter of Galilee, and be awakened to a full consciousness of their own manhood, their dignity as sons and daughters of God, co-workers with Jesus, and heirs of heaven.

The consciousness of the need of rest, and the yearning for something higher, nobler, are clearing away the mists by which Satan has hid God's true Sabbath from these toilers, wearied, well-nigh crushed under the daily grind of machinery and trade. And, lo! they see in it one of their best friends. In their own bodies, nerves, brains, homes, yea, their whole social and moral nature, they are reading this unchanging law: Rest thou one day in seven, or suffer — suffer in shattered health, nerve, and brain, shortened life, shadowed home, and weakened moral power. They see that on this law, as positive and irrevocable as the law of gravitation, as its solid foundations, rests the lower end of this bridge of divinely appointed Sunday rest. On this bridge that leads up over this chasm toward the Church of the living God, yea, toward God himself, thousands of the wage-earners are seeking to plant their feet.

Six years ago the barbers in Cleveland commenced to demand Sunday rest, and persevered till, by special State law, it was made such to all barbers in Ohio. Later, the barbers of Chicago have struggled vigorously for the same blessing. Recently the grain shovelers of Buffalo struck, demanding Sunday rest and payment of wages somewhere else than in the saloon. The whole country knows how the retail clerks of Chicago have pleaded and worked for Sunday rest. These are only samples of the way God's Spirit is awakening wage-earners all over the land.

In my Milwaukee home the retail clerks are in the midst of a similar struggle. For twenty years all Sunday laws had been a dead letter in the city, with no attempt at enforcement. Fifteen hundred saloons were wide open. More than nine-tenths of all classes of retail stores were open a large part of every Sabbath. More than ten thousand men were engaged in Sunday work. Lady clerks, as well as gentlemen, after standing behind the counters eighty hours in six days, were compelled to stand there several more hours on Sunday. They found it was killing them. They organized, they discussed, they agitated, they pleaded with their employers, till more than ninety per cent agreed to close. A few refusing seemed almost to compel all. Their only hope of safety was in appeal to the law to compel the few. They found that, as Horace Greeley said, "The law of rest for all is essential to the liberty of rest for any." The week after the "world's week of prayer for the Lord's Day," which President Clark invited all Christians to observe, a merchant was found guilty by the jury of violating Sunday law. That same week our Governor ordered that the State militia should cease their long-time habit of going to and from camp on Sunday. Now the liquor power is seeking to thrust their clerks back into bondage; but, mark this fact, the Federated Labor Union of our city proposed to help these clerks. It was referred to all the unions of the different trades, discussed in each, and then the Federated Labor Union voted $50 to help these clerks win their case in court. Remember, most of the members of these unions are Germans. Are not our working men climbing out of their darkness onto this bridge of Sunday rest?

This is especially true of the railroad men. To the World's Congress in Chicago came Hon. L. S. Coffin, sent by one hundred thousand railway employees, to plead in their behalf for the abolition of Sunday traffic. Thirty thousand of the Brotherhood of Trainmen said, "We believe the Sabbath a God-given blessing to the laboring man, and when its hours are encroached upon by the greed of capital we would be less than free men if we did not enter our earnest protest; and we do trust a thoughtful and Christian public, and the corporations we are connected with, will accord to us this rest day as our imperative need and our most sacred right."

Twenty-two thousand railroad conductors said, "We believe when this day is secured and used as the best good of each demands, it becomes the impassable barrier to the encroachments of capital upon the rights of labor."

The locomotive engineers said to Vanderbilt: "This great strain of mental and physical faculties constantly employed impairs the requisites necessary to make a good engineer. Troubled in mind, jaded and worn out in body, the engineer can not give his duties the attention they should have. Give us the Sabbath for rest after one week of laborious duties and we pledge you that, with a system invigorated by a season of repose, with a brain eased and cleared by hours of relaxation, we can go to work with more energy, more mental and physical force, and can do more and better work in six days than we now do in seven."

The leading organ of the Knights of Labor is demanding not merely talk, but united action to secure rest on the Sabbath for the laboring classes.

The editor of *The Outlook* finds the women in the tenement-house districts of New York, generally, crying, "God bless the men who try to close the saloons Sunday." One said, "I tell you, we are living a new life here. Children who have never seen their fathers sober on Sunday see them at home sober every Sunday now. Women who have never before since their marriage seen their husbands sober on Sunday pray to God on their knees, 'Bless the men who shut up those places that made hells of our homes.'"

Truly, the wage-earners are crowding the lower end of this bridge. But we must not let them stop there. They need God's soul-rest still more than rest of body. They need a day to get acquainted with wife and children. They need still more a day to get acquainted with God, and learn the joy of talking with him. So, then, the bridge must reach clear across the chasm, and have a solid abutment on this side.

That abutment must be God's law of holy rest shining through the lives of his people, making them radiant with joy in God and love to their fellow men. It is our business, fellow Endeavorers, to furnish this abutment, and to lead these masses clear over the bridge into the liberty of sons and daughters of the Almighty.

1. We must do this by our example. When God's truth is translated into and shines through human life, it becomes a living power. We can not win men over the bridge unless they see the Sabbath law dominating our lives and making the day to us intensely holy and happy. While we have any fellowship with such unfruitful works of darkness as Sunday papers, trade, or trains, we can not help the slaves of Sunday toil to see the beauty of rest in God.

2. When *our* hearts love, and *our* lives honor, the Sabbath, we can begin to educate the masses, American and foreign — especially foreign. Ignorance and prejudice are the chief causes of opposition to a true Sabbath and to Sabbath laws. The light of truth will scatter these, and that only. The majority of non-church-goers have even yet no clear idea on these matters.

Great care should be taken to enlighten all the people as to the close relation of the Sabbath to the foundation, growth, and safety of our Republic, and as to the reasons why Sabbath laws are needed. Thousands suppose they are merely to upbuild the Church and to promote religion. All good laws promote religion, but that is not the purpose of Sunday laws any more than of other laws. Their purpose is to protect liberty, health, home, and character, and thus promote national prosperity. Sunday laws require nothing religious. They protect one's right to rest, and give him a chance to worship God, if he wishes, or to refrain from all worship, if he so prefers.

3. Again, if we would lead these toiling masses over the chasm, we must get very near them. We must know their heart-throbs. Through our sympathy they must feel the sympathy of Christ.

4. We must help them secure justice and fair play. Especially must we

help them secure universal half-holidays every week,— one-half day for home, nature, and physical recreation; one whole day for God, home, and soul-growth. In every practicable way help them secure a chance for Sunday rest. Stand by every business man who closes store or factory Sunday. Patronize him as far as possible. Bring all possible pressure to bear on any who refuse to close. Make clear the mischief of Sunday amusements to man and the State.

Elect true men to office, and stand by them when elected. Awaken the public to demand of every officer the fulfilment of his sworn obligation to be true to God and man.

Finally I call upon you all gathered in our nation's capital, Hear the cry of the millions in the mail and railway service, and awaken the people all over the land to persistently demand that our government cease to defy God by compelling its citizens to trample on the law of God and the State by rushing Sunday mail-trains all over the nation and opening a post-office in almost every city and town. This is the main root of our nation's Sunday lawlessness, watered, it is true, by the saloon and some of the foreign immigration. But for this main root we, the people, are directly responsible. The Sunday post-office led to the Sunday store, and the Sunday mail to the Sunday trains and papers, all which threaten the destruction of Church and nation.

Gen. A. S. Diven, thirty years manager on the Erie Railroad, said, " The refrigerator-car removed the last excuse for a Sunday train." Vanderbilt said, " Though one great road can not stop alone, all roads can stop together with no damage." No train, unless it be a short early milk-train, can have any reasonable excuse. Sterilized milk is likely soon to do away with all necessity for that.

Shall we sit still and let our nation go on crushing the life out of these millions? Let us speak in behalf of the bill to stop Sunday mail and interstate commerce with a voice that shall be heard through the whole nation. Let us go home and arouse every philanthropist to cry out, " Let these millions go free and enjoy God's rest. Give them a chance to rise up to the highest manhood." Such a law would free nearly as many from slavery as the Emancipation Proclamation, and be as great a blessing to the nation. Shall we here and now swear eternal warfare against this and every other form of Sunday slavery?

Address of Rev. Alexander Alison, D.D., New York City.

The Sabbath Day, day of rest, cease day, or day of cessation from earthly toil, is a very old institution. It is older than our country, older than Christianity, older than Judaism. It is older than the Ten Commandments, for there it is said, " Remember the Sabbath Day to keep it holy." That word " remember" is significant. The implication clearly is that that which is here enjoined was before the enactment concerning it which was written by the finger of God upon the tables of stone. The fact is that the Sabbath is older than human sin. It was given to man prior to the fall. It has, therefore, survived the tragedy of Eden. In Gen. ii. 2,3, we read, " And on the seventh day God ended his work which he had made; and he rested on the seventh day from all his work which he had made. And God blessed the seventh day, and sanctified it, because that in it he had rested from all his work which God had created and made."

There is a craze in these days for the old, the ancient, the antique. Talk about the antique! We surely have it here. The oldest institutions we have are the family relation and the day of rest. But some one says it was the " seventh day which God sanctified and blest, not the first day of the week." Look closely at the passage, " God rested on the seventh day of his own work." On what day were Adam and Eve created? Was it not on the sixth day of the creation period? What was the first day of Adam and Eve's earthly existence? Was it not the day following the sixth day of the creation? What day was this? Was it not the Sabbath Day? What, then, was the first day of the human week? Was it not the Sabbath Day? Adam was appointed to work, was he not? Read the verse, Gen. ii. 15, "And the Lord God took the man, and put him into the Garden of Eden to dress it and to keep it." Adam, in a perfect state, was not to be an idler; but he is not to begin his week of work in the garden until he has first enjoyed a Sabbath Day. The first day, therefore, of the human week is the day of sanctified rest.

After that, six days of honest toil. Then the first day of the second week is a Sabbath, and so on. Is not this a sweet suggestion of the time to come, when the first day of the week would be formally, technically, and officially recognized by the resurrection of our blessed Lord as the first day of the beginning of the work of a redemption applied to man's salvation? The Sabbath Day, then, is a day to be revered. It is the one day that is dignified as the crown of creation. It precedes man's toil as it succeeds the work of God. Again, it is not only the crown of the creation, but it is the crown of the re-creation. It follows the divine work of re-creation, as it follows the divine work of creation. If it could be said, when God finished the natural creation, "Behold, it was very good," it could be so said when he completed the work of re-creation or redemption.

If we really appreciated the force of the fourth commandment, we would be able to decipher the full meaning of the Saviour's words when he said, "The Sabbath was made for man, not man for the Sabbath." The day of rest is essential to man's highest welfare. It is essential to his life physically, mentally, and morally, or spiritually. The Sabbath Day he can not get along without. One-seventh of the time he needs. France tried one-tenth. What was the result? In answer, the epidemic in man and beast, and the revolution, or reign of terror.

Voltaire, the brilliant French infidel, spoke like a philosopher when he said, "If Christianity shall ever perish from the earth, you must first destroy the Christian Sabbath." Another Frenchman, many years ago, said to an American tourist, "If France shall continue her existence as a nation, she must adopt your American Sabbath."

The American Sabbath! I like that expression. It has the right ring to it. There is an American Sabbath! And it is the Bible Sabbath, too. Our fathers of immortal memory brought it with them across the sea. The family relation, the Bible, the Lord's Day, — these three were brought here by our godly ancestors. They believed in this blessed trinity, those sturdy pioneers. And they believed in it so thoroughly that they were prepared, if need be, to die rather than surrender it to the advocates of a false philosophy and a false religious system.

But there is not only a religious side to the subject of Sabbath observance. There is also a secular one. We have a right to make and to enforce human statutes that shall call for the observance of the laws of God. As a matter of fact, we have in every State in the Union but one what might be called fairly good Sabbath laws. One State has repealed its laws on the Sabbath. We hope, ere long, to have this changed. We are glad the showing is so good as it is. Let us see to it that laws now in existence are enforced. Public sentiment is always potential. Christian sentiment, if crystallized, can control public sentiment anywhere. A great city daily recently said in an editorial, "If the Christian people of this city would unite as touching the suppression of any evil in our midst, the evil could be crushed in a month." This means that a united Christian sentiment will surely constrain the newspapers to be its allies. They know the power of united Christian sentiment. The trouble is with Christians, that they differ so much in regard to methods and details.

It is only by indifference of Christian people, a sentiment below par on the part of our Christian people, that it can ever be possible for the American Sabbath to be in danger.

The Anglo-Saxon race owes everything to the Sabbath. What is the great race in civilization? Is it not the Anglo-Saxon? Let us remember that no country has retrograded where the commandment "Remember the Sabbath Day to keep it holy" has been sacredly obeyed. This is true in Great Britain, New England, New York, Pennsylvania, and all the grand old States of the

American Union. What has made the East and South will make the North and West.

There are portions of our country where the Sabbath Day is the worst day in the week; we can reverse this if we are willing. The home mission problem in all the denominations will be largely solved so soon as Sabbath laws are enforced. The Sabbath question is fundamental. It underlies everything. If the Sabbath goes, so does the Church, the Bible, and the family. Who will care to go to church or read the Bible if the Sabbath becomes a dead letter?

Let us remember that man is more than animal. He is made in the image of God. The beast is to rest one day in seven. The fourth commandment enjoins this. Man, as an animal, is to rest also. But he can do what the beast can not. He can enter into fellowship with his Creator. This he is to do on the Sabbath Day. He is not only to rest from labor, from the gathering of his daily food, the manna, on the Sabbath Day, but he is to worship God.

A healthy arousing on the part of all who profess to be followers of the meek and lowly Jesus will in the next decade restore our fair Republic to its old-time devotion to Sabbath-keeping. Then shall we develop a true and abiding prosperity. Sabbath observance is more at the root of national prosperity than any questions of tariff or finance. Politicians reason out along their own lines the way to good times. May we never forget that God only is the true statesman. He holds the destinies of nations in his hand. His sceptre is the sceptre of universal dominion. Hear him, as he says, " Them that honor me I will honor; but them that despise me I will lightly esteem."

Members of the Y. P. S. C. E., let us never forget that he who fights for God, for truth, and freedom, shall never fight in vain.

Address of Rev. Wilbur F. Crafts, Ph.D., Washington, D. C.

The centre of peril and of hope to-day is the Sabbath, the citadel of Christian morality. One of our chief perils is in the breaches made in that citadel by the Sunday papers, the Sunday cycle, and the Sunday trolley. One of our chief hopes is in the re-enforcements that citadel is receiving from the oncoming hosts of Christian Endeavor.

The most plausible argument against the strict observance of the Sabbath is the specious claim that " the complicated civilization of the nineteenth century" requires that Sabbath observance and Sabbath laws should be relaxed. Nay, this is a new reason why they should be maintained and strengthened. Did Adam, to whom the Sabbath law of work and rest was given before the fall,—did he, who knew nothing of "cut-throat competition," and "soulless corporations," and "hard masters," and wearying "tricks of trade," need a Sabbath law more than we do to-day, when sin has put its curse into the Edenic blessing of labor? At Sinai, where the Sabbath law was reproclaimed, did those Hebrew herders, moving on at three miles an hour, need a law to protect them against the overstrain more than the engineers of to-day, who drive their iron dragons a mile a minute with hand on the throttle, eye on the track, every power alert? Did those dozen farmers from whose social plowing-bee Elisha was called to be a prophet,— I have seen in that region a modern plowing-bee of eighteen,— did those farmers, gossiping together as they kept step with their slow oxen, need a Sabbath law more than the motor-man who harnesses the lightning to his electric car, and drives through crowded city streets, where a moment's inattention may cause the loss of a pedestrian's life and his own position?

Turning to the more recent times, when the foundations of this Republic were laid on the Bible, the Sabbath being assigned a prominent place among American institutions, did our fathers, when they lived half a mile apart, curtained at night with the soft velvet of silence, need a day of protected quiet more than their sons in the tenements of to-day, where going to bed at night is often like the "charge of the light brigade,"—noises in the flat above, noises in the flat at the right, noises in the flat at the left, noises in the flat below; the high fiddle-diddle of a midnight dance on the floor overhead; the crash of a family jar just beyond the wall on the right; a piano through the wall at the left making love on that side and hate on this side at midnight; while the flat below does its share in the torture by an early start on a fishing-excursion to murder sleep in the morning?

When nearly all the work was in the open air, in forest and field, was there more need to protect the toilers' right to one day's release from labor, than now, when many thousands work at night and in the mine, and thousands more in stifling shops? Is there more excuse for keeping thousands toiling on the Sunday mail now, when a letter is carried from New York to San Francisco in five days, than in our fathers' day, when such a journey took five months? Was there less excuse for our fathers to issue Sunday papers when news crossed the Atlantic in two months, than there is for us, when the news of Europe reaches us by telegraph the day before it happens? More than ever before, we should see to it that neither ourselves nor others cause any Sunday work except of necessity or mercy.

Canada leads the world with its recent votes for prohibition and non-sectarian schools and rest for street-car men. A few weeks ago I started for Chicago, and told my wife to go to Halifax. She likes to go there. Halifax is the *upper* end in that contrast of cities. Canadian cities are nearer heaven than any other cities. Toronto, with no Sunday papers, no Sunday mails, no Sunday street-cars, no police gazettes, and 10,000 majority for prohibition, is more than half way from Old Rome to the Holy City.

But it would tax to the utmost the talents of the professional optimist, who makes himself the special attorney for the defence of the present, to prove that our country has progressed morally in this last third of the century; that is, since the war. During that time unimpeachable statistics show that the consumption of liquors, and, partly as an outgrowth of that, divorces and murders also, have increased three times as fast as the population; that, as additional outgrowths of the liquor increase, lynchings, labor riots, and municipal corruption have outrun, in our land and time, all other records. A recent gathering of physicians from all parts of the country sadly agreed that impurity, another branch of that same trunk, is also increasing apace in all our States. Most serious of all, the assault upon the Sabbath is also increasingly effective just when its walls should be strongest for the defence and rescue of imperilled morality.

The trouble is that while Sabbath observance *as a personal duty* is more or less urged by the churches, the Sabbath *as a social institution*, which manifestly can not be defended by one church or one denomination, but only by united, organized action in town and state and nation, is not recognized as a part of the work of associated churches. All the Sabbath associations in the country have fewer men and less money for their work than the churches of a single city of 10,000 population. There are but nine men in the United States giving their time to the defence of the Sabbath. Temperance makes a somewhat better showing, though not more deserving; but the whole force engaged in Christian reforms is but a squad of raiders, whose function is only a reconnaissance in force, preparatory to the onward march to ultimate reform triumph which must be made by the whole grand army of the Church of God. Upon Endeavorers, as the Church of the twentieth century, I wish to urge earnest consideration of the question whether the hour has not come, in the closing years of this century, for moral reform, the child of Christianity, which is treated as a distant and poor relation, to be taken into the family; that is, whether moral reform should not be made as much a part of church work as missions, of which it is indeed a home branch.

The Methodist Episcopal Church and the Presbyterian Church have both established temperance committees, and recommended the churches to take collections to enable them to promote this reform. The United Presbyterians have taken like action as to national reform. What is only a committee now, its support only enough to make the Church's neglect the more visible, will, in the twentieth century, in every church, be a "*Board* of Christian Reforms." The churches should do more or less. They should cease to recognize, by resolutions, that the crusades against intemperance, Sabbath-breaking, impurity, and gambling are a concern of the Church, or else attack these evils with something more than resolutions. They should shoot something besides paper balls, unless the paper consists of greenbacks.

As the best work of a law and order league is not to do the work of public officers in enforcing law, except enough to show that it can be done, but rather to make the officers do their duty, so the best work of a Sabbath association is not to do the work, except temporarily, which in this case belongs pre-eminently to the united churches, but rather to arouse the churches to their manifest duty in this matter.

Meantime, let each Endeavor Society prepare the way of the Lord by adding to its plan a Sabbath observance committee, and let that committee, for one thing, follow the example of the Endeavorers of Mount Vernon, New York, by securing the Sabbath closing of the post-office by a local petition to our noble Postmaster-General Wilson, who has deliberately adopted the local option plan originated by Honorable John Wanamaker.

Toronto, a city as large as Washington, which has grown faster than any American city except Chicago, shows that no Sunday work whatever need be done in the post-offices. Telegrams Saturday night and Monday morning provide for all emergencies. But if, in our large cities, it be deemed impracticable to ask for complete suspension of Sunday work at first, a reduction or re-arrangement may often be secured. For instance, here in Washington, let Endeavorers lead a movement asking that, first of all, the four carrier deliveries at hotels and newspaper offices, the only outside deliveries by carriers in our country anywhere, which have been put on without the authority of law, be discontinued; also, here and everwhere, the unauthorized collections from street boxes. As on the Sabbath men must go to the office if they wish to get mail, by analogy they should go there if they wish to send it. Let us also ask everywhere for the discontinuance of the wholly unauthorized and utterly unnecessary Sunday sale of stamps, called for mostly by shiftless loafers. And as a fourth petition in large cities, let us ask that in the inside Sunday work of the office rights of conscience and the right to rest shall at least receive larger consideration.

The movement against Sunday work in your local post-office may well include petitions to Congress for a law against Sunday work in the national capital, and in the mails, and wherever else the control of Congress extends. All this can be covered by the adoption in churches, labor unions, and other societies, of this resolution:—

Resolved, That our president and secretary are hereby authorized to petition the Honorable Postmaster-General, in our behalf, for the discontinuance of Sunday work in our local post-office, and also to petition both houses of Congress for Sabbath laws that will suppress unnecessary Sunday work in the nation's capital, in its mail service, also, and wherever Congress has jurisdiction in this matter.

For another thing, let that Sabbath committee urge that Christians by their patronage encourage those daily papers that have no Sunday editions, among which are some that have no superiors in influence; for example, among morning papers, *The Philadelphia Ledger*, *The Baltimore Sun*, *The Pittsburg Commercial Gazette*, and *The Chicago Record.*

Do not be stayed one moment in your course by that musty chestnut, " It is the Monday paper that makes the most Sunday work." The newspaper men who say that assume that there is no work required in *distributing* Sunday papers far and wide, with roaring trains and huckstering cries. As Mr. Moody said recently in Boston, the worst thing about the Sunday paper is that it employs in sinful Sunday work two hundred thousand newsboys. At the very hour when they should be learning Christian morality in church and Sabbath school they are sent into the devil's Sunday school of Sabbath-breaking and law-breaking. Those who take a Monday paper make no Sunday work necessary, for Horace Greeley, except two years of war time, made the best of Monday papers without Sunday work, and called the Sunday paper "a social demon."

Happy is the man who comes to this meeting untarnished by its tricks, who has not bought a Sunday paper even in a set of Endeavor reports, when he has the opportunity of another full set in a paper that keeps the Sabbath.

Do you excuse yourself for buying a Sunday paper, when, as to-day, it has some good reading? Or do you with equal shallowness of sophistry defend taking a Sunday train to go to a religious service? Both cases are exactly parallel with the excuse of the highwayman who "robs the rich to help the poor." We have no more right to steal *time* from God and man than to steal money, whatever we do with the stealings in either case. God did not write the fourth commandment longest for us to treat it as least.

Another thing the Sabbath observance committee of each local Endeavor Society might do is to circulate a pledge against using the cycle for pleasure on the Sabbath. Of course, there is no more objection to riding to church afoot than to walking afoot, and every church should provide a cycle stall. But *all* Sunday *pleasure*-riding comes under the ban of Isaiah's profound injunction to turn away from selfish "pleasure" and so make the Sabbath a higher "delight."

Most of all should the Endeavor Sabbath committee scatter Sabbath reform literature from door to door, as the Endeavorers of St. Paul did through all that city, and so contributed to its deliverance from a despicable "ring." Some of this literature should be in foreign tongues, such as Rev. J. B. Davison, of Milwaukee, has used effectively in that State. But American church-members need light hardly less. The firm that is breaking down the Sabbath is the firm of Thoughtlessness and Selfishness, and while Selfishness may fairly be called the foreign partner, Thoughtlessness, the American and Christian partner, is also the senior partner. Less than a quarter of a million are to-day at work behind the screens of the saloons. Ten times as many, mostly Americans, and many of them professing Christians, more or less regularly do unmerciful and unnecessary work on the Sabbath in connection with Sunday trains, Sunday mails, and Sunday papers, for which Americans are chiefly responsible, and which the churches might stop if they would.

It is amazing to what extent not only church-members, but even ministers, break the Sabbath, many of them having done it so long that they now do it unconsciously, and need what Miss Willard, in large charity, calls "the arrest of thought." Nine-tenths of the Sabbath-breakers need no other 'arrest." Their excuse is the child's "I didn't think." But that is the very thing heads were made for, not merely for hat-racks.

A month ago a temperance lecturer, whom I love for his fearless eloquence, while scoring the churches, and justly, for neglect of the liquor problem, in an illustration told us he was going that Saturday night to take a train which we knew would be a Sunday train before he left it. He would break a specific commandment of God in order to upbraid another distant audience for neglecting an implied command. A few days afterward a bishop, whom I also love, told me, without apology, that he was to take a train that Sabbath Day to reach a missionary committee in New York the next day. A Sabbath later I called on a preacher and was told by his son that he had preached elsewhere that morning, but would be home on the Sunday afternoon train. A few minutes later I called on another preacher and found a huge Sunday paper scattered over his porch. In Baltimore, one Sabbath evening, a preacher in introducing me to speak on Sabbath reform, told his people he had come eighty miles since the morning service to hear my address.

Even more than the arrest of Sunday liquor-sellers, the "arrest of thought" is needed by the Church. Let the Endeavor committee "serve the papers" from door to door in well-chosen literature.

Never before were such varied arguments available, for we have the utterances of labor unions as well as of churches, of science as well as of Scripture. Professor Hodge, of Clark University, Worcester, with Voit, and Pollikofer, and Haegler, of Germany, have shown, in an argument which, as expressed by the latter, received a hygienic medal at the Paris World's Fair, that the night's rest does not balance the day's work, and that the corpuscles of the blood and the nerve cells need frequent additional periods of rest of thirty hours or more for their restoration. Thus the latest science, as often before, confirms the earliest Scripture. Let us not forget, as we gather in the nation's capital, that the Lord's Day is not only the Rest Day also, and the Home Day, but also especially the WEEKLY INDEPENDENCE DAY.

Popular government is more secure under the British flag and ours than in the French and Spanish republics, largely because the Sabbath gives our working men what theirs lack, — intelligence, conscientiousness, and the spirit of equality, three necessities of life in a self-governing people. A king, about to demolish a historic building, as old as his capital, to put something more modern and ornate in its place, saw, when a stone or two had been removed, this uncovered inscription: "These gates, with their country, stand or fall." So in our midst stands the Sabbath citadel of liberty and morality, built of linarite granite, and of Plymouth Rock. Let not the Church, let not the State, mar that citadel; let not vandal hands, native or foreign, especially our own, tear out a single stone; for it is the testimony of Continental and South American history, in contrast to that of the British Empire and the American Republic: WITH THESE GATES OF THE SABBATH OUR COUNTRY AND OUR CHRISTIANITY STAND OR FALL.

Tent Washington.

The Evangelistic Meeting.

It was a big meeting. It was more. It was a great meeting. The limits of Tent Washington could not contain the thousands who thronged to the popular evangelistic meeting on Sunday afternoon. But more important yet, the immense congregation was pervaded by a deep, quiet spirit of resolution, that found magnificent expression before the meeting closed.

Rev. B. Fay Mills was the sole speaker. His text was Rev. v. 6, and the general theme, "In the midst, a Lamb as it had been slain." It was a wonderful sermon, of unexpected character, but the more powerful for that. It was primarily an address to Christians, pleading for the Christ-life of sacrifice.

"Self-interest, we have been told," said Mr. Mills, "is the first law of life. It is not. It is the first law of hell. Everything that is to live must have the slain Lamb in the midst. There is no law that ever has been enacted, or that will be enacted, that has in it the principle of selfishness, that can endure.

"The call of the Lord to us is that we should lead sacrificial lives. Think of it; the Church of God has been in this world 1,800 years and more, and still the world is unsaved! I would not lessen the force of the call, 'Come to Jesus,' but the message I bring to-day is, 'Come with Jesus.'"

With many more words of eloquence did the preacher hold up the Lamb that was slain, pleading that Christians would follow him in sacrifice. Then he solemnly put the question to the Christians in the audience, whether they were willing, beginning that afternoon, to undertake the life of sacrifice; to make life and love one; to count not their own lives dear unto them, for the sake of their brethren and companions, and for the sake of their Lord, the slain Lamb. Just as reverently, hundreds and thousand of the Christians present upraised their hands in an " I will."

And then Mr. Mills called upon those who were not Christians, who desired this same Christ-life of sacrifice, to rise and affirm it. One, two, three, a dozen, a score, a hundred — but it is the work of the angels, and not men, to count the number of those who turn to Christ. Each heart was moved deeply; to thousands the occasion was a very Hermon, where they beheld Christ transfigured.

MONDAY MORNING.

Tent Washington.

One of the most powerfully affecting meetings ever held was that in behalf of our suffering fellow Christians that have suffered and are suffering such inhuman cruelties at the hands of the fiendish Turk. The great throng that crowded Tent Washington was at many points moved to tears, and at others aroused to the highest point of excited indignation. Best of all, the addresses sought not only to stir the emotions, but to excite practical action; and in this they will undoubtedly prove richly successful.

Rev. F. D. Greene, a missionary from Van, Armenia, author of "The Armenian Crisis," had set sail for Turkey six years before that very day, and had now returned, a missionary to Christendom. Shame that such a missionary should be needed! He was not there to make a plea for the Armenians. He was there to say that God's thunderbolts are hot, and that they may fall on London, on Washington, or on St. Petersburg, even before they fall on the Sultan of Turkey. "Here we are, singing 'Let a little sunshine in;' but how about those terrible darkened lives in Asiatic Turkey?" There are two and a half millions of Armenians. There are the same number of Christian Endeavorers. Fifty thousand stood in that grand demonstration before the Capitol; fifty thousand Armenian martyrs stand now before God's throne, having given heroic testimony on earth; and these are all men, the breadwinners, and not women and children, as were many gathered there. Whole villages are running out to our relief-agents, crying pitifully, "We are hungry." Their children dig up the grass and eat the roots. Every glass of soda-water you save, every car-ride, saves the life of an Armenian for a week. American citizens have suffered wounds, torments, the loss of all their goods, the loss in one place of $100,000 worth of property, and not a cent of indemnity has been paid, or a single apology rendered, or a single criminal punished. The passport of an American citizen in Turkey is not as much protection as the old clothes of any Englishman. You talk about balance of power; is there no balance of justice?

" I wish my voice had not gone somewhere," said hoarse Dr. Hoyt, introducing Miss Krikorian. " I feel as if it were under Turkish rule."

Miss Rebecca Krikorian, of Aintab, Turkey, was an Armenian lady, dressed in the beautiful native costume. Her sweet face was unutterably sad, and only to look at her brought tears irresistibly to the eyes. Her voice was full of a fearful pathos, and had an indescribable undertone of horror, as, in faultless English, spoken with a quaint foreign accent, she painted some of the scenes that might be revealed of that hell upon earth into which the Turk has transformed fair Armenia,—men buried alive under heaps of festering corpses; women compelled to eat their babes that have been roasted before them; tongues cut out that refused to profess Mohammedanism; their hands and feet cut off one by one, and eyes dug out; and such common horrors only the things that can be told, while worse, far worse, are things which no man, even, would dare whisper to another man.

Said that eloquent missionary, Miss Margaret W. Leitch, of Ceylon, at the close of her address: "Miss Krikorian's aged father, a Christian minister, has just been released from a loathsome Turkish dungeon. Her two brothers still are there. Yet no word of hatred for the Turks passes her lips, but only the prayer for their conversion. This is the kind of Christian the missionaries to Turkey have been making. She is a Christian Endeavorer as well as you. Shall we desert her? No! I take this emblem of liberty and safety, and throw it over her (flinging about the Armenian an American flag), and say to her, 'The people of America will not desert you.'"

This scene, so thrilling and effective, seemed to bring the meeting to the highest possible pitch, but it was reserved for Rev. B. Fay Mills to reach the climax. A clear statement of terrible history prepared the audience for a fearful arraignment of the English and American governments, which, being abundantly able to end these outrages, had perfidiously on the one hand, and cowardly on the other, refused to interfere. The Canadians and Englishmen on the platform sadly assented to the truth of the terrible charges of broken faith brought against English statesmen, especially since Mr. Mills fairly acknowledged that English protection alone maintained in Turkey our missionaries and the noble Clara Barton. The vast audience of Americans, of all parties, assented, in a passion of shame and rage, to the charges brought against our own government at home and its representatives abroad. The vast audience sprang to its feet in its excitement, shouting, waving their hands, and manifesting in every way their condemnation of the weak, inhuman, cowardly, selfish, unchristian way in which our government, with more reason to interfere than any government, has joined all other Christian lands in their inhuman indifference.

Tent Williston and Tent Endeavor.

The World's Union Meetings.

Monday morning was a glad and significant day, not only for Christian Endeavor but for the whole cause of Christ as well. It witnessed the wonderful scene of a great multitude of Christ's disciples assembled from all parts of the earth solely in behalf of universal fellowship. The North gave up and the South kept not back. East and West sent their messengers. All spoke of the glad day that surely is coming when they all shall be one.

This first meeting of the World's Christian Endeavor Union will be a marked event in the history of Christian Endeavor. It was seemly that the programme proper should begin by the responsive reading of the Saviour's prayer for unity.

The various national flags that decorated Tent Williston were not as numerous as the living foreign representatives who were seated upon the platform. The first speaker was Rev. J. G. Hildner, the pioneer of Christian Endeavor among German-speaking churches. He told graphically the story of the beginnings of the movement among the Germans of this land and the fatherland, and as he concluded was given a vigorous Chautauqua salute by the congregation. Persia, with its 3,000 years of history, had a message for this youngest of all the great religious organizations, that it sent by Rev. Jesse M. Yonan, who claimed for Persia the first Christian Endeavor Society, the three wise men who banded themselves together to seek the new-born Saviour.

A surprise was given the audience after Mr. Yonan's address, in the presentation of the Committee of '96. It is needless to say that the most royal ovation that Endeavorers know how to offer was accorded to these noble servants of Christian Endeavor. As the members of the committee were introduced one by one, each was greeted with a hearty cheer. When all had retired from the platform, save Chairman Smith, he stood silent for a moment, and then, slowly and reverently, repeated this Scripture, adding no words of his own : "Not unto us, not unto us, but unto thy great name, O Lord, be all the glory!" Before the committee was allowed to leave the tent, Dr. Clark presented to the District of Columbia Union, through Mr. Miles M. Shand, on behalf of the United Society, a beautiful silk banner, as a souvenir of the Convention.

The Hampton Octette, which early in the Convention won the hearts of the delegates by its sweet melodies, sang several songs, and was received worthily. Great Britain then gave its greeting — and a splendid greeting it was, telling of wonderful work done by Christian Endeavor, and of the delightful prospects for still greater things — through Rev. Joseph Brown Morgan, the president of the British National Christian Endeavor Council. Mr. Morgan closed his thrilling address by an urgent invitation to all the Christian Endeavor world to visit London in 1900. Naturally, the Endeavorers answered this with unbounded applause.

Many countries that could not have personal representatives present sent fraternal greetings by cable or by post. These were next read. All of them bore the same glad tidings of the cause that is speeding onward gloriously. "The time is coming," said India's spokesman, Mr. S. C. K. Rutnam, " when we shall have an International Convention in India." Africa, too, put in a claim for an International Convention, through Rev. George P. Goll, who told some thrilling incidents of the Christian Endeavor spirit in Africa.

The introduction of visiting missionaries, a unique and impressive feature of the programme, was then announced by Dr. Clark. A Jamaica pastor brought a message of cheer from his sunny land. Nellore, India, was represented by three missionaries. India was again heard from in the person of Commander Booth-Tucker, who left the shores of India last February. His speech thrilled all hearts with its note of hope and courage. Persia again spoke through two missionaries, and Sierra Leone, Africa, delivered a hopeful message through two representatives. Dr. Cyrus Clark, of Japan, spoke briefly, and he was followed by missionaries from India, Chile, the great West, and the Holy Land. New Mexico, with its burden of Romanism, sent a plea through one of its workers, and still other missionaries from Africa, Chile, and China briefly addressed the Convention. Tarsus, which is "no mean city," pathetically said through its representative that Turkey could not invite a Christian Endeavor Convention to meet within its borders, because the sword and persecution are the only welcome that await Christians in that dark land, once lighted by the presence of the great missionary apostle.

A meeting of the charter members of the World's Union on the platform of Tent Williston was held at the close of this service.

In Tent Endeavor, where Treasurer Shaw presided, another great session of like character was held. Mr. Shaw is a breezy presiding officer, and since the meeting was one that was worthy of all the enthusiasm that could be manifested, he set the audience to applauding, "just to find out how." After they had proved themselves masters of the art, he introduced Rev. Arnold Streuli, of England, whose address was one of which his fellow British Endeavorers could be proud. The presentation of the Committee of '96, and an address by Rev. W. H. Towers, followed.

Armenia's woful message was next brought to the Convention by Rev. H. S. Jenanyan, who moved the audience greatly. He was followed by natives of Persia and India. Then came the most impressive incident of the service. Mr. Shaw called on all the delegates who were missionary volunteers to ascend to the platform. There they were grouped in a semicircle, thirty-nine of them. While thus they stood, all clasped hands, and a sentence prayer was offered by each. A few words were spoken to the audience, pointing out the need of Christian gifts to send these missionaries abroad. Every one in the great tent bowed in prayer, while supplication was made that Christians at home might be consecrated to the work of giving to the cause abroad. All who were willing to make this new consecration to a life of giving for the sake of the Gospel were called upon to rise, and almost the entire audience stood on its feet. Thus was brought to a close this splendid fellowship meeting.

Greetings by cable and letter were read from many Endeavorers in distant lands. A large number of national flags were received from foreign lands and were displayed. There were flags from England, Japan, France, Spain, Switzerland, Ireland, Germany, Mexico, Norway, Liberia, India, and China.

MONDAY AFTERNOON.

Central Hall.

The United Society officers and trustees gave an informal reception to the State officers in Central Hall. The building was filled with a joyous company,— the picked young men and women of a continent. In all parts of the hall was eager conversation, as the workers from all over the land interchanged greetings. Dr. Clark made an address which was received with every demonstration of esteem and affection. Ice-cream was most appropriate on that hot day, and cooled everything but the fervor of this cheery intercourse. Such blessed gatherings are coming to be especially characteristic of the great conventions, and of themselves would amply justify the existence of those conventions.

MONDAY EVENING.

Perhaps Paul, who saw unutterable things, or John, to whom the heavens opened, could portray in truth all of a consecration meeting at an International Christian Endeavor Convention. Certainly no one else can. The superlative of expression has been exhausted on other meetings; how, then, shall the indescribable climax of the Convention be described. It will not be attempted. The visions of that sacred hour, the resolutions then kindled, the vows registered, will be treasured by thousands and thousands. To those who were not there but a bare, expressionless outline of the proceedings can be given.

There were eight consecration services, four in churches, one in a great hall, and three in the Convention tents. Not all of these places were as well filled as the tents, but each meeting was a blessing. In the churches Rev. J. Wilbur Chapman, of Philadelphia, Rev. John Faville, of Appleton, Wis., Rev. John Neil, and Rev. W. F. Wilson, of Toronto, Ont., preached consecration sermons, and Rev. Ford C. Ottman, Mr. Charles N. Hunt, Rev. Ralph Gillam, and Dr. Chapman conducted the closing consecration services. Rev. B. Fay Mills both preached the sermon and led the consecration exercises in the enthusiastic meeting in Central Hall. Neither speakers nor audiences will forget these powerful sessions.

We greatly regret we did not secure the manuscript of Messrs. Faville, Neil, and Wilson. And only extracts of Dr. Chapman's and Mr. Mills's sermons were secured.

Extract from Sermon of Rev. J. Wilbur Chapman, D.D., Philadelphia, Pa.

TEXT:— And we came to Kadesh-Barnea. —*Deut. i. 19.*

The children of Israel furnish a perfect type of the Christian with an average Christian experience. Egypt stands for the world; Canaan stands for the life of surrender; and all the wanderings between Egypt and Canaan represent the experiences which come to us simply because, like Israel of old, we are not willing to trust God. The Pillar of Cloud going before them was like the Spirit of God convicting us of sin; the Red Sea stands for our conversion. The manna sent from heaven is a good illustration of the Word of God, upon which our souls feed. The water bursting from the rock is the type of the Holy Ghost, which every Christian has, whether he is in Canaan or out of it.

But there is more to the Christian experience than this, just as Canaan was before the children of Israel. When they reached Kadesh-Barnea they had come to a crisis. God intended that they should enter in Canaan at once. Before them was rest, fruit, communion with God; back of them was the wilderness, and there were just two things they could do: the first was to go back to the wilderness—that meant fighting and failure, lusting and idolatry and murmuring; the second was to cross over the line and forever be at rest.

God has brought us to a crisis in this conference. Many of us have been living the average Christian experience, but now we are at Kadesh-Barnea, and we may go over into Canaan if we will. To fail to go over means to lead the carnal Christian life, with its envyings, its strifes, and its divisions. To cross over means to enjoy all the fruit of the Spirit, uninterrupted communion with God, and the fulness of the Holy Ghost. This may be God's last call to you to enjoy the life of privilege. When the children of Israel failed at Kadesh-Barnea they never again had the opportunity of going in. Their failure to go in also kept out Kaleb and Joshua and the others who wanted to pass over. Your failure may keep out some one over whom you have an influence, and before God you will be responsible. One step alone settles it; if you are willing to submit your will and to believe God, you may enter to-day into a perfect communion with God, which is the life of privilege, and is therefore every Christian's birthright.

At the close Dr. Chapman asked all those of his auditors who wished to go over into Canaan, to enter this life of perfect surrender, and those who would pray that God would make them willing to be made willing to make the surrender, to stand. A large number all over the house arose. He then asked them to come out into the aisle and kneel down by the altar. They bowed for a few moments in silent prayer and sang softly a prayer hymn. Dr. Chapman asked if there were not some in all parts of the audience, Christians and others, who desired an interest in the prayers about to be offered. A great many hands were uplifted in response to this invitation. Prayers were offered by himself and others that all might be able to make this surrender and go over into the Canaan of a new life. The kneeling Endeavorers resumed their seats and all joined in singing, very appropriately, "I'll Live for Thee."

Extract from Sermon of Rev. B. Fay Mills.

I would ask your most prayerful attention to the thoughts that are suggested in the prayer we have prayed so frequently, as recorded in the sixth chapter of Matthew, tenth verse: "May thy kingdom come . . . on earth as it is in heaven." We have all said it hundreds of times; and of all the millions that have ever prayed it how many have ever really expected the answer? How many people have applied to it the principle that Jesus taught when he said,

"Whatsoever things ye desire when ye pray, believe that ye have received them, and ye shall have them." The things we pray for are that God's kingdom may come, and that his will may be done on earth as it is in heaven. Now we know what the popular idea of heaven has been in the past. I doubt whether there is any popular idea of heaven now prevalent among the people. I scarcely know two people who have the same thoughts concerning heaven. We used to have an idea of heaven as a city,— a material sort of city, with battlements and gates and streets and mansions.

I think most of us have come to be moved away from some material ideas of heaven, until at last probably all of us here would agree to define heaven as a perfect society of perfect individuals. No man can be in heaven alone, no matter how happy he be in his individual consciousness. No man can form a heaven alone.

Our conception of heaven must include individuals in a perfect society. We are told in the Bible that in heaven there will be no hunger and no thirst, no oppressive heat, no pain, no disease, no death, and no sorrow, no impurity and no selfishness. Now I do not want to destroy anybody's hope in anything that is worth hoping for. I would not want to say that we shall not be translated to some place of perfect felicity; but I do want to say with tremendous emphasis that any such conception of the work of Christ is but a partial comprehension of his mission, and is not a description of the great purpose of Christ, which did not primarily concern some far-off heaven.

God sent not his Son into the world to condemn the world, but that the world, through him, might be saved. And there is a certain sense in which no man living on the earth can be fully saved until all those who live about him are also fully saved. No man can be perfect alone. No man can be saved alone, and there never will be heaven anywhere except there is an association of men that are living in absolute unselfishness; and wherever that exists the kingdom will have come as it has already in heaven. I believe it is a place where our activities shall be devoted in a larger and more effective form to the transformation of this world.

I do not believe that we will change our prayer, but that we will labor that God's kingdom may come on the earth "as it is in heaven." We have these words put on our lips as the direct language of the Master, and the devil never executed such a triumph of his art as when he turned the attention of the disciples of Christ away from the transformation of this world. To be a Christian is to be a laborer together with him who was, as Christ, reconciling the world unto himself.

The very first words that Jesus uttered in his mission were these: "The kingdom of heaven; repent, for the kingdom of heaven is at hand." The conception of the Jews that it was to be a terrestrial kingdom was a correct one. I do not know of but one place in all the Gospel where Jesus refers to heaven in any sense that might be rightly interpreted in the ordinary idea. His call was a call to man to come and help him in the establishment of peace upon the earth.

I do not believe that the Church, for the most part in the first century, had any other idea than that the disciples were called to work for the triumphs of Jesus in this world. I even believe that Paul, up to a certain period of his life, expected to see the earth transformed and the kingdom of God fully established before he should be taken away. The eyes of the apocalyptic seer saw the New Jerusalem, the city of God, descending out of heaven to abide upon the earth, and he gave to the people the great vision almost at the close of his wonderful book. He tells us that he heard the voices crying out in heaven and singing, "The kingdoms of this world are to become the kingdoms of our Lord, and of his Christ, and he will reign forever and ever."

I am not mourning because some old doctrines are losing their grip over the hearts of men. I can occasionally weep a little on account of tender-heartedness, but I never weep on my own account, as I see the faith of men being strengthened, and their conceptions being enlarged. And while our great conventions are passing their resolutions, the Presbyterians, the Congregationalists, the Unitarians, and all the rest, defining what they mean by the Christian religion, the day of our Lord is coming as a thief in the night, and the hearts and minds of the people are being changed into the conception of Jesus Christ in such a fashion that we will have to be one under the power of the Lord.

Do you not see that when the old overmastering passion of the ministry and the Church shall not simply be to defend its dogmas, but to establish the kingdom of love, before we know it we will all be so heartily engaged in work for the same thing that we will be practically one? Even now, when we are engaged in this limited fashion in a practical effort for the uplifting of men, here come men of twelve different denominations — all Christians — and join their hands. For what? Not that we may lift up any of our peculiar standards of doctrine, but that we may have a practical aim in trying to do something in a practical fashion.

And I can conceive that as the Spirit of God goes on diffusing this great thought among men, we will have to be bound together. I can see a united Protestant Church, clothed with power and inspired in such fashion that men shall not think of what they think, but rather of what they do; and I can see the Protestant Church look into the face of her mother, and see the old Roman Church, purified by this inspiration, with all of its history of noble achievements as well as its history of shame and sorrow, united with the child for this and this alone,—that God's kingdom may come, and his will be on earth as it is in heaven.

Further than that, even to the mother of Rome, I can see that old Greek Church, called out of its slovenly inactivity by the great thought of establishing the kingdom of peace — one united Church of Jesus Christ.

Back further than that: turning to that one that was the mother of us all, crying to God's ancient people that they may come and see the Messiah visible in what he does for men, until there shall be a mighty union of all the so-called Christians with all the Israelites; and I am willing that they shall lead us if they will as we call the heathen world into this glorious fellowship, until in the darkest corners of the earth the kingdom of peace shall be established. Come and let us make a heaven below, into which the heaven above shall flow until they both shall be one, bound together in the manifest spirit of Christ, the Son of God.

And I come to say more than that; that I believe that not only is this the inspiration that is availing now and that will avail until the final triumph comes for the purifying, unifying, and empowering of the Church, but for the regeneration of society through the instrumentality of the Church. May it not be that just such a company as are gathered here this evening, who shall give themselves to the answering of the prayer that you have heard thousands of times, and let that kingdom come in you as it has come in heaven, and in the trade and intercourse of our fellows and in our politics,—may it not be that this company might make of this capital city of our country and of the communities of our homes, cities of God; and all cities throughout the nation might catch the inspiration, and one nation with the spirit of Pentecost might lead every other nation of the world into a holy fellowship of serving Christ?

Tent Williston.

Treasurer Shaw presided in Tent Williston. Here, as in the other two tents, a special song service, perhaps the best of the Convention, was given by the choir. Mr. Foster's singing of "Just as I Am" was notably affecting. The antiphonal singing by the choir of "Bringing in the Sheaves" also made a wonderful impression. In the beginning of the service it was announced that 31,112 delegates, representing every state, territory, and province in North America, had registered at Washington. Many others present did not register.

All applause was stilled throughout the rest of this service and the services in the other tents. A period of silent prayer preceded the preaching of the sermon by Rev. James I. Vance, D.D., of Nashville, whose subject was " The New Faith of the Old Gospel."

Sermon by Rev. James I. Vance, D.D., Nashville, Tenn.

TEXT.— May we know what this new doctrine, whereof thou speakest, is ? — *Acts xvii. 19.*

What is true religion? Christianity makes a distinct and unique contribution to the solution of that problem. Religion is as old as the race and older, but there is that in the Gospel of Jesus Christ which is ever new. We speak of the " old, old story ; " we sing of the " old-time religion ; " we read of " the faith once delivered to the saints ; " but the fact is there is that in the Gospel which never grows old, and which to the men of every generation will go down under no other caption than " the new."

Worship is no new thing. Men have always worshipped something, somehow. Prayer is not new. Reverence, adoration, faith in the hereafter, is as old as the race. But as Paul preached Jesus Christ in Athens, the scholarly men said, " Here is something brand new, something that has never before suggested itself to the thought of the world in connection with religion; something out of the ordinary and commonplace." They were philosophers who said this; not twilight mystics, but men of profound thought, before the majesty of whose intellectual greatness the world still bows, and in whose presence certain agnostics of our day, who strut across the stage, squeaking themselves hoarse with " We don't know ; we hope so, but we don't know," seem but pigmies.

These philosophers of the Epicureans and Stoics, struck with the originality of Paul's faith, gathered around him and said, " May we know what this *new* doctrine, whereof thou speakest, is ? "

The Gospel is not novel, but new. This characteristic of his teachings Christ emphasized again and again. He approached man's religious life from new standpoints, punctured spiritual delusions, and upheaved effete customs. A common phrase on his lips was, " Ye have heard how it hath been said by them of old times, but I say unto you — " He spake as never man spake. Jesus was the greatest iconoclast that ever lived; and these people who boil with indignation in their frenzied hostility to everything that is new would have been found in the company that tried to cry down our Lord into silence.

The new in a doctrine is not always its damnation. It is well enough to revere the Fathers and to respect the way the thing has always been done. Still, the world can never get to anything better along that track. Suppose the Fathers had always acted on the principle that they must do the thing the way it always had been done? To-night we should be back in the year one. The best way is not the way it always has been done, but the way it never has been done ; and the world has moved out into light only because every age has had some great souls whose faces were turned toward the morning.

The new in Christianity has ever been that which was hard to accept. We naturally read our customs, prejudices, and experiences into everything about us. Hence, when Apostolic Christianity preached its doctrines to surrounding Paganism and Judaism, the tendency was for the environment to project its preconceived opinions of religion into the new faith. The result was that very early Christianity was corrupted. Pagan feast-days found their way into the Christian calendar, Judaistic rites fastened themselves upon the Christian cult. There was a paganized Christianity, or a Christianized paganism. In so far as Christianity has failed, its failure has been due to the failure to apprehend and lift up into importance those celestial marks by which Jesus Christ has differentiated his Gospel from every other religion under heaven.

These marks are the " new faiths " of the old Gospel, and together they constitute the sum total of true religion.

What is true religion? What are its fundamental characteristics? It touches three realms in the individual life: first, that of the consciousness; second, that of conduct; third, that of destiny. What is true religion in its contact with the inner life? What is true religion in its influence upon conduct? What is true religion in its conception of destiny? Dr. James Stalker has given this admirable summary of the religion for young men. He says, " Let it be not a creed, but an experience; not a restraint, but an inspiration; not an insurance for the next, but a programme for the present, world."

I do not see why we should have a different religion for the old and for the young, one sort of religion for men and another for women. God's salvation is one, a quality of life rather than a form of character, and identically the same for all, always. He has never saved but in one way. Therefore what is good religion for young men is good religion for all men, for all sexes, for all classes, everywhere.

Nevertheless, I think Dr. Stalker's admirable summary states but one side of the truth. I should rather put it this way: True religion is not only a creed, but an experience; not only a restraint, but an inspiration; not only an insurance for the next, but a programme for the present, world.

In the realm of consciousness, Christianity is not only a creed, but an experience. In the realm of conduct, Christianity is not only a restraint, but an inspiration. In the realm of destiny, Christianity is not only an insurance for the next, but a programme for the present, world. These are the new faiths of the old Gospel.

True religion is not only a creed, but an experience.

It is certainly a creed. Think of having a religion without a creed! Think of trying to believe, and having nothing to believe in! You might as well try to nourish an elephant with syllabub, or hang a planet on a moonbeam, as to have a religion without a creed. Creeds are to religion what the bones are to the body, what scaffolding is to a house. They are not life, but they are essential to life; and a vast deal of the minimizing of creeds that is indulged in nowadays is either palpable absurdity or sheer ecclesiastical demagoguery.

But creeds are nothing new. The world has always had its creeds — not so good, to be sure, in the quality of the truths embodied as the creeds of Christianity; but admirable, nevertheless. The dearth of the world has never been a dearth of abstract truth. The main trouble has been that the truth has been a thing apart from the life.

Christ teaches that a creed is worth nothing by itself. It must be incarnated. It must be clothed with flesh and blood. The place to keep it is not on a parchment page or a library shelf, but in the life. That is the glorious thing about the person of Jesus. He is divine truth clothed in flesh and blood. He is heaven's creed incarnated.

We must do vastly more than hold our creeds. We must experience them. When Nicodemus came to Christ to inquire the way of life, Jesus said, " Nicodemus, you must be born again. You are a teacher of the Jews, and are familiar with religion as a system. It must become your life."

To the woman at the well in Samaria, he said, " Whosoever drinketh of the water that I shall give him shall never thirst, but the water that I shall give him shall be in him a well of water springing up into everlasting life." What are we to understand by that central and cardinal fact of the new dispensation — the indwelling of the Holy Ghost in the believer's life — if it be not that our creeds are to become our experience, and our truths to pulsate with our life-beat?

Here is the mistake which many of us have made. We have deemed it sufficient to stop with an orthodox subscription. The Church has had too much of the spirit of a North Carolina elder, who was denouncing evangelists as unpresbyterian; and when asked whether the evangelists were not saving souls, replied, " Yes, brethren; but for God's sake, let's save them according to the constitution."

We have substituted ecclesiastical machinery for Holy Ghost energy. We have mistaken pleasurable emotions and approval of pious efforts for regenerated life. There is many a man who will applaud to the echo Daniel's allegiance to God, but who will not make the first effort to live Daniel's life. That is not Christianity; it is only baptized paganism. You can't make a lawyer out of a ream of legal cap and a copy of the State code. You can't make a physician out of a box of pills and a case of surgical instruments. You can't make a merchant out of a show-window and a full-page advertisement in the Sunday morning papers. Neither can you make a saint out of the Shorter Catechism and the Prayer-Book.

True religion is an experience. It is God in the life. It is not so much copying after Christ as it is having Christ formed within you, the hope of glory. The denominational name is not the great thing. The experience is the same for all churches. What makes one a child of God in the Presbyterian Church is precisely the same as that which makes him God's child in the Baptist, Methodist, or Episcopal Church. It is the experience of God's life. The trouble too often is that we lift our denominationalism into undue importance. Men come into contact with our ordinances and forms, and are made churchmen. We need Christians rather than churchmen; and it were as easy for a boy to become an astronomer by looking through a telescope as for one to become God's child by subscribing to a creed.

Wanted: A religion that is not only a creed but an experience, a religion that incarnates its convictions until its truths pulsate with the heart-throb of its own being.

True religion is not only a restraint, but an inspiration.

It is certainly restraint. It is manifestly a poor religion that does not put fetters on vice and curb the unholy appetites within us. The Gospel frowns down on all that is sinful, saying to every disciple, " Abhor that which is evil, cleave to that which is good." Calvary is not in conflict with Sinai. Christ came not to destroy, but to fulfil the law.

> " In vain we call old notions fudge,
>   And bend our conscience to our dealing ;
> The Ten Commandments will not budge,
>   And stealing *will* continue stealing."

But there are numbers who stop here. Their piety exhausts itself with a restraint. They regard religion as a pruning-knife whose only mission is to lop off their excesses and debaucheries. If you ask them what it means to be a Christian, they will tell you that it means not to do so and so. They dwell much on what they must surrender. It is a dreary prospect that confronts them,—sacrifice, self-denial, Puritanism. Christ moved on away beyond that. He substituted the " Thou shalt" for the " Thou shalt not." He taught that religion was to be a restraint, to be sure, but a restraint because it had become a glorious inspiration. He put a spring in the step and a song in the heart of all those who follow him, when he said, " If ye *love* me, keep my commandments." Here is a black abyss of awful danger, and yonder is a man running from it with all his might. You do not need to build a barrier to keep him from toppling over the brink into that black pit of horrors. His safety is in that which speeds him in the other direction. There are Christians who crawl as near to the brink of the non-permissable as possible, and who think that the Gospel's mission is to exercise some sort of restraint that will keep them from falling quite over. The true Christian needs no such restraint. His face fronts away from evil. He is running Godward with all his might. His inspiration is his restraint.

I do not believe that religion was ever intended to be an incubus to life. We have trouble enough without making our faith an additional burden. The Gospel is intended to help us front life's duties with courage, endure its misfortunes with serenity, surmount its obstacles with hope, and achieve its victories with humility. What an unspeakable blunder to quench all this with the dismal creed that one's piety is as potent as it is sombre, and that glory and gloom are synonymous !

Away with all such. The religion that God gives is an inspiration. He curbs the evil by enabling us to fall in love with the good. The religion that would capture the world must be an inspiration. The faith of those heroic souls whose sacrifices and martyrdoms have glorified the history of the Church has been not merely a restraint, but an inspiration. The men and women who this hour, in far distant heathen lands, amid privation and persecution, proclaim the unsearchable riches of Jesus Christ, have for the sustenance of their souls not a dismal restraint, but a glorious inspiration. While Parliaments and Senates, while statesmen and sovereigns, have let a year and a half go by in discussing what shall be done to stop the atrocities of the brutal Turk and minister to the pitiable sufferings of stricken Armenia, a woman more than seventy years of age, with a red cross on her breast, has crossed the seas and mountain wilderness, carrying bread and love to the starving thousands of that smitten land. God bless Clara Barton! Hers is not a religion of restraint, but of unconquerable inspiration.

Fellow Endeavorers, if your religion is to bless the world it must quit thinking of what it needs to sacrifice. It must be song, not dirge. There must be some magnetism, some glory-crown, upon it that will transform its very defeats into victories. It is said that a brave British officer led his regiment through the darkness of the night, over a dreary trackless waste, guided only by one bright star, on which he kept his eye steadily fixed. In the gray dawn of the next morning, when the battle was joined, he was the first to fall, mortally wounded. As his superior officer leaned over him, the dying man's brow was mantled with a blush of pride, as he said, "Did n't I guide them straight, sir?"

May we see the star, my brothers. May the glorious hope with which God dowers his children shine out so bright on the sky yonder that it shall be our guide through all the wilderness and night of this lifetime. Then what matters it if death does come in the morning. It will be given us to look up into the face of him who is the great Captain of our Salvation, and say, "Did n't I guide them straight?"

Wanted: A religion that is not only a restraint, but an inspiration; a restraint because it is an inspiration.

True religion is not only an insurance for the next, but a programme for the present, world.

It is certainly an insurance for the next world. Think of a religion without a hereafter! It is like a kingdom without a monarch, or a nation without citizens, or a ship without a sea on which to sail. Think of religion without the supernatural! It is stark idiocy. A good woman in Nashville, where I live, has a sceptical husband. He is troubled about the supernatural; can not believe in the supernatural. Some time ago she went to one of our pastors, and, telling him of her husband's spiritual difficulties, asked him to preach a special sermon on "The Supernatural." He consented, and laid himself out in the construction of an elaborate discourse that would annihilate the most pugnacious scepticism of the supernatural. The Sabbath morning came for the delivery of this masterly piece of pulpit apologetics, and the good woman was there early, and with her infidel husband occupied a conspicuous seat in a front pew. Hardly had the text been announced and the preacher well begun his introduction when his sceptical auditor dropped his head and started for the land of Nod. He slumbered soundly through the entire sermon, awaking only to catch the flashes of the closing pyrotechnics in the preacher's peroration. The minister left his pulpit that day a sadder but a wiser man, convinced that the only effect of his sermon had been to make a supernatural fool of himself in attempting to discuss religion with a man who began by denying the existence of the supernatural, without which there can be no religion.

But religion is not all supernatural and hereafter. It is a mistake to suppose that the Gospel is only a scheme by which to dodge hell, or a contrivance by which to get into heaven. Selfishness is none the less damnable because it gets itself baptized with the name of religion. True religion is vastly more than insurance against fire in the world to come on the one hand, or an endowment policy for the hereafter, on the other.

It is chiefly a programme for the present world. Christ taught this unmistakably. He said something about the hereafter, to be sure, but only enough to assure us that it is there, and that the way to attain the best there is to be and do the best here. When we are converted we are started out on service.

We are not to be so much concerned about getting up to heaven as with getting heaven down to earth. All that Christ had to say to the woman taken in adultery was, " Go, and sin no more." When Zaccheus was converted, instead of regaling his religious imagination with visions of the bliss of paradise, he gave half his goods to the poor, and to all whom he had defrauded he restored fourfold. No wonder the people began to ask whether the end of the world was at hand. If a few conversions like that were to take place here in Washington, we would begin to suspect that the millennium was just over the hill-top.

Wanted : A religion that is not only an insurance for the next, but a programme for the present, world; that goes about doing good now; that can exchange its surplus for a trowel and melt its dogmas into deeds; that founds asylums and hospitals, visits the sick, comforts the disheartened, clothes the naked, and that by thus making this life worth while, makes heaven a surer heritage.

The new faiths of the old Gospel! Let our religion be all of this and it will need no further defence. We have various kinds of evidences for the divine origin of the Christian religion,—prophecies, miracles, providences, evidences external and internal. It seems to me there should be something in the Gospel itself to certify its divinity. The sun does not need to prove that it shines. It just shines. So, if Christianity is of divine origin, there should be that within it that would ray out the divinity; and there is. Let the Gospel be itself and it will need no other apologetics.

Ninety-nine hundredths of all the attacks made by infidelity are directed against a caricature of Christianity. Men have gone down into their prejudices and preconceived opinions, and brought up a conception which they have called the Gospel, and they have attacked that.

Infidelity has taken it for granted that Christianity is only a creed, a formula of words, a dry, dead dogma, and it has pitched into that. Perhaps it has rendered service of some value in exposing mental frauds and heaping sarcasm on the pharisaism that professes more than it puts in practice. Christ himself has done as much.

But wait till the creed becomes an experience, wait till the truth takes hold of the life, substituting base passions, transforming character, begetting higher ideals; then infidelity's guns are spiked. Let the sceptic himself get an experience of God in his own life, let him form a personal acquaintance with the Almighty, and he will get a conviction of the reality of religion which all the devils of doubt can not quench. Infidelity has taken it for granted that religion is only a restraint, and it has ridiculed the endless forms, the petty rules, the prayers and liturgies, the sacraments and vestments, with which the mortal would fain fit himself for immortality. But wait till a man's religion becomes an inspiration. Watch it lifting him out of selfishness and vice, and sending him out to do the best and most self-sacrificing things for the world. Infidelity has no ridicule for that, and its shaft falls harmless from an unnerved hand.

Again, infidelity has taken it for granted that the Gospel is only an insurance for the world to come. It has denounced the *a fortiori* God who brings creatures into existence to be damned; or after he has done his utmost, can only keep a certain proportion of them out of the torments of hell-fire. It has branded as infamous the God who, sitting safe in some distant heaven, sates his greed for adoration on the prayers of his victims, while humanity writhes in the throes of innumerable ills.

But wait till it gets a better conception of God. Wait till infidelity sees divinity, in the person of Jesus Christ, coming down into the lost world to carry out a programme of infinite sympathy and transcendent relief for suffering brothers and sisters. Infidelity can not criticise that God. Then wait till men and women baptized with the Christ-Spirit go about the same blessed ministry, reaching out helping hands to all around them, and finding God in the pauper at their door and the consumptive in their hospital. That Gospel is not infamous; it is divine! It needs no trumpet blast to announce it, for itself is its sufficient vindication.

You say you can not believe in the hereafter. It is far more important that you believe in the now and the here.

These are the new faiths of the old Gospel. They clothe Calvary with perennial rejuvenescence. This is the sort of religion for which this Christian Endeavor movement among the youth of militant Christendom stands. We do not make creeds; we try to be the creed. We do formulate rules that shall act as barriers to keep us from falling into the devil's domains, but we try to get so far over on God's territory that no barrier shall ever be needed. We have a blessed hope for that life beyond death's shadow, but we believe it is to them who by patient continuance in well-doing seek for immortality that the gates of light swing large and free. We believe that the things which unite us are greater than the things which divide us, and so we stretch hands electric with the fellowship of grace across denominational walls, and salute one another in the new faiths of the old Gospel,— not only a creed, but an experience; not only a restraint, but an inspiration; not only an insurance for the next, but a programme for the present, world.

With that experience surging within us, with that conduct making seraphic every ministry, and with that destiny arching its glory across our pathway day by day may we go back to our churches and homes from this place where we have seen the Lord.

We shall need him to go with us. He himself is the Gospel. He is the way, the truth, and the life. He is the life, our experience. He is the truth, our inspiration. He is the way, our example as we try day by day to make religion a programme for this present world.

Don't you see what it all comes to at last? The "new faiths of the old Gospel" means, not the dead Christ, but the Christ of Galilee and Bethlehem and Calvary alive in you and me who walk the earth to-day.

There is an old Indian legend that once the Great Spirit visited his people, and, before he went away, promised to return again. That they might recognize him on his return, he left his image on the stone face of the mountain. It is said that one old Indian gazed constantly upon the stone face by day, dreamed of it by night, and looked often and anxiously into the faces of his brothers and sisters to see if he could distinguish its lineaments there. At last, after the nation had been purified by peace, they looked into the old prophet's face and discovered that all unconsciously it had been transformed into the likeness of the Great Spirit, who had returned and become incarnate in his rapt follower.

Only a stumbling story of a heathen people, but it is the parable of Christ and his disciple. May we long for his coming with such intense yearning that directly we shall be what we would see, and until the old, old story of Samaria and Gennesaret, of Capernaum and Bethsaida, and of the Christ who glorified these holy places with his blessed presence shall live anew in the faiths of us who try to follow him.

The hymn "Scatter Sunshine" was sung, and then Mr. Shaw began the consecration service with a brief but earnest address urging all his hearers to take Jesus Christ into their lives and live as he would have them live.

Then each state, territory, and foreign land represented in the Convention was called upon, and one delegate from each arose to his turn and responded by a verse of Scripture, or of a hymn, or by a word of greeting and love, renewing vows of loyalty to the Saviour. In a number of instances the whole delegation arose and recited the chosen text in unison, or sang the verse.

It was a most beautiful and impressive service, and a spirit of deep reverence pervaded the whole vast assemblage. At the close four verses of the hymn "Just As I Am" were sung softly, sweetly, as a prayer.

Then came the Mizpah benediction, the hymn "God Be with You Till We Meet Again," and the last meeting at Tent Williston was a thing of the past.

Tent Endeavor.

Tent Endeavor held the largest crowd in its short but eventful experience the closing night. The throngs were early entering its openings, and long before the hour for the meeting to begin arrived the streamers were a-tremble with the vibration of the songs poured out beneath them. Half a dozen different hymns were being sung simultaneously in different sections of the audience, and yet no inharmonious results were observable. In the seating of the delegates the representatives of the various States were grouped together, the various State delegations having been divided into three parts, so that each could be represented in all of the three tents, where such important exercises were to be held. When the regular praise service began the singers who had been following their own leaders joined right heartily, under the baton of Mr. Excell, and after " Keep Step with the Master " was rendered a grand chorus outpoured, "All Hail the Power of Jesus' Name."

The presiding officer, Secretary John Willis Baer, announced that Rev. F. W. Gunsaulus, D.D., of Chicago, who was expected to have delivered the sermon, was unavoidably absent. He read a telegram announcing that death in Dr. Gunsaulus's church prevented his attendance, and a great chorus of regretful exclamations arose, but quickly changed to pleasurable applause when Rev. Dr. Wm. Patterson, of Toronto, Can., was announced to take the noted Chicago preacher's place. Mr. Excell sang, by request, "Let a Little Sunshine In." There was singing by the Hampton Octette. Again the Endeavorers were treated to the peculiar singing heard only among Southern negroes. Now plaintive as a wail, now joyful as a pæan, the voices of the boys arose in quaint unison, and there was no one in the audience, probably, who was not touched or impressed by the singing. The devotional exercises were conducted by Rev. Thomas Marshall, D.D., of Chicago, Ill., closing with a strong and impressive prayer. Mr. Baer, in a few complimentary words about the choir, announced that it would sing the anthem, "Awake the Song." The music was rendered in a truly splendid manner, and the applause was so great that the anthem was repeated. There was more applause when Mr. Baer announced that the composer of the anthem was Mr. Excell.

That popular Canadian trustee, Rev. William Patterson, then preached the sermon. He was received with a glorious Chautauqua salute. His eloquent sermon was suggested by the " prophesying upon dry bones " of Ezekiel, and was an earnest presentation of the power we all can gain through brave and entire obedience to the Spirit. " It is better to be a man," said he, " than to be an angel. We can do a work that angels can not do. We can know things that angels desire to look into ; for how eagerly the angels would descend into the slums, if it were permitted them, to lift up the fallen ! "

After Mr. Excell's impressive.singing of " It Pays To Serve Jesus," Mr. Baer introduced the consecration meeting.

The State responses were much as in Tent Washington. After Florida's reply Dr. Hoyt offered fervent prayer for all Endeavorers at home, that the spirit of the great Convention might come upon them. Maine, where the pledge was born, reasserted her allegiance to its promises. By raising their hands, all in the great congregation joined Maine in her vow, and Dr. Muir sealed the vow with prayer. Pennsylvania's magnificent pledge for work along all lines of Christian Endeavor was also adopted by rising, Rev. J. M. Lowden offering prayer.

And in the closing minutes, when the Holy Spirit seemed resting on every heart, Mr. Baer called upon all to join him, prayerfully,—with full resolve, if at all,— in a personal promise, before the end of the year to speak to at least one soul out of Christ, and to try to bring him to a knowledge of the Saviour's love. To this high purpose nearly all the assembly rose. Dr. Power, of Washington, prayed for God's blessing on the great endeavor, Mizpah was pronounced, and with Mr. Patterson's benediction the blessed service was at an end.

Tent Washington.

It was Tent Washington that saw the greatest of all the great meetings,— a crowd that stretched out into the White Lot beyond the walls of the tent ; large state and provincial delegations, and many foreign representatives. Rev. Dr. McKim, of Washington, and Rev. A. L. Geggie, of Truro, N. S., conducted the opening devotional exercises. The spiritual song service, and Dr. Clark's impressive opening words, helped to prepare the vast congregation for Bishop Baldwin's message of power, and for the covenant time that ensued. " Ye shall receive power " (Acts i. 8) was the text of the sermon preached by Rt. Rev. M. S. Baldwin, of London, Ont., Lord Bishop of Huron.

Sermon by Rt. Rev. M. S. Baldwin, D.D., Huron, Ont.

My Dear Christian Friends : — I understand that this is a consecration service, and the text I have therefore chosen is one which speaks of power. It is from the first chapter of the Acts of the Apostles, eighth verse :

" But I shall receive power, after that the Holy Ghost is come upon thee : and ye shall be my witnesses both in Jerusalem, and Judæa, and in Samaria, and unto the ends of the earth."

When we look up on a starry night upon the sky it seems as if the stars are scattered in rich profusion, without order and without symmetry; but the astronomer tells us that on the contrary all those bodies move in the most exquisite harmony, and have so moved for ages past. It is just thus with the Word of God. There seems to be a great many books, a great many subjects and themes, but the Bible contains but three histories. Now the three histories which it contains are as follows : the history of Israel, the history of the Church of God, and the history of the governmental nations of the earth. Now these three histories move around one common centre, and that common centre is the stone Jesus Christ, the stone which the builders refused but which God has made the corner and glorious stone of Christ. Now let us observe that those three histories revolve around that one centre. Thus Israel to-day stumbles upon that stone of Christ Jesus, and Israel in her synagogue is saying, The Messiah has not come, because Israel stumbles upon this glorious stone. Then we come to the Church of Christ, and it is built upon this stone, and the Church's one foundation, Jesus Christ, our Lord; and when we come to the governmental nations of the earth we find that the stone which is cut out with hands is that stone which will destroy all human authority, overturn all power, and constitute that one stone, the solitary earth, and that stone is Jesus Christ, so that to-day we find that all lines in the Bible converge upon that one glorious Being, one majestic object, and that object our Lord, Jesus Christ. Now, bearing this in mind, let us come to ask, What is power? Now just as in the Bible there is one centre, so we find that God in the Holy Ghost has come to magnify that one centre, that the whole work which he does upon earth, and in the Church of the living God, is to exalt Jesus Christ, to uplift him, to make him Lord of all; and therefore when we go into the pulpit and on the platform with some other object before us, to endorse this Church, to uplift this community, to teach this science, to advance this theory, God, the Holy Ghost, can not and will not help that work, and it must pass with the weakness which it deserves. But I will say to all Christian workers that the first thought to bear in mind is this: that God the Holy Ghost has given to those consecrated men, and to those women whose lives, whose voices, whose beings, God and the Holy Ghost can use to the personal exaltation of Jesus Christ our Lord. Bear this in mind. Let me ask you in the next place to notice how it is he works. Let us look at the first dispensation, the dispensation of the Father. It was the time of preparation, the time of growth, of expansion. Then came the short dispensation of the Son, our Saviour, Jesus Christ. That was short, but it never was intended to be permanent, and I would ask you to notice that however desirable our Lord's personal acquaintance might have been it taught them that there was something better, something even better than his own dear holy presence.

And what is the distinguishing characteristic of the dispensation in which we are now living? It is summed up in this sentence: "God was in you." It is this idea that alone dominates. In that first dispensation God was above; in the second he was by the man's side; in the third dispensation God is within us. So that a man who is holy is a man in whom God, the Holy Ghost, dwells in power, and it is only when we grasp this truth that we grasp what power means. It is God, dear friends, swelling within you. Now in the next place, let me ask you if you observe how he manifests himself? There was only one building ever erected which was without windows, at least intended for man, and that was the Tabernacle, in the first instance, and the Temple in the second. Now when we came to the Tabernacle, we found, as we studied the Word of God, that there were absolutely no side lines, no windows, no piercings in the wall, no light from the roof, no light anywhere from the outside, but you came into a room that was still bright, and that brightness came from the Jews called the Minorah, that is, the seven bright candlesticks, and that was the light of the sanctuary. Now let me say that in the Church of the living God there ought to be no windows; we ought to receive no light from the windows. I wish to be distinctly understood here. In the ancient Tabernacle, the high priest and the priest did not learn from Israel. They did not learn God's efforts from the nation at large; they learned it from the light of God himself, for the Holy One of Israel was afire. Now when we come to the Church of the living God to-day, we find people coming and saying you want business principles. I wish to say that business principles are the ruin of the Church of Christ. We want no business principles if the Church is to do the work of God and to be mighty, by the pure, the blessed, theme that comes from the truth itself. How often is it that some grand church, perhaps, with a huge congregation, has fallen into debt, or perhaps broken down from some cause or another, and there is a great gathering of people, and some one stands up and he says to them, " Well, you must introduce business principles if you wish to succeed;" and he suggests a larger organ, a greater choir, and a more splendid building, and this is the outside light. These are the windows that men put into the fabric, but which are unhallowed in the sight of God, which, let me say, that power will come when the Church kneels down and discards all human teaching and against the teaching of the Holy Ghost. What is needed is a deeper piety, a profounder grasp of the truth that is in Jesus, and then members will receive power after that the Holy Ghost has come upon them.

Again, let me ask you to notice in the next place how that blessed Spirit works in regard to the individual. We shall receive power. Now power is never given except for activity. God gives nothing to man who is going to idle, to waste, or to squander time. The arm that is slung is not the arm to be used, and God, the Holy Ghost, never comes except to help that great Church of God, and he never comes to help us except as we are going forth to teach the language, to gather and prepare the sheaves against the coming of the Lord and Saviour, Jesus Christ. A regiment that is lying in barracks wants no ammunition for the war; it is in the day of battle, it is for the campaign, and it is for the day of trial he needs to be armed with all the necessary adjuncts for successful fight; and so it is that the ideal Church will rest and rot under the sun, but the weak, as far as regards human oversight, will grow strong, and that is putting forth its power for the conquest of the world and to gather souls against the coming of the Lord Jesus Christ. Now I would ask you to notice, Christians, how he watches us individually. I hear sometimes Christians say, "We want to get more into the world, we want to become more detached from the things of time and of tradition, and it is this that our consecration meeting is for." Let me say, dear friends, that the only way we can become detached is by becoming attached to the Lord Jesus Christ. You can not hold together the world until you are made one with the Lord Jesus Christ, and therefore growth in Christ. Becoming detached from the world is by the process of growing in union, in oneness, in the blessed perfectness in the Lord Jesus Christ. Let us ask ourselves how does the winter go; how does it come to us and how does it go?

And I would ask you, in the last place, to observe that which is the work of God, the Holy Ghost. He has to give us a power to do three things, and if you will look at those three you will see they are just what the Lord taught. They are, first, to teach us to deny ourselves, to take up our cross and follow the Lord Jesus Christ. Now, people say, " Well, we do deny ourselves." Here is a man who says, "I will give up tobacco;" another man says he will give up wine; another man says he will give up some luxury; but that is not denying ourselves, that is denying ourselves the use of tobacco, the use of wine, the use of luxury. But how did Peter deny our Lord? Why he cursed and he swore, and he said, " I do not know the man." Now our Lord would have us deny ourselves and say we do not know ourselves, that we are willing just to go where he pleases. We are to deny ourselves, and say, " Not my will, but thine, to be done." Look at those two Moravian missionaries who went to the Lazar-House of South Africa; they went to the leper-house there and said, " We wish to go and preach to your lepers." " Well," they said, " you can not enter here because you would take the infection with you." " But," they said, " we are anxious to go." " Well," they said, " if you go to the lepers you must stay with them." They said, " For how long?" " Well," they said, " until the leprosy blanches your own cheek and you lay down and die as lepers yourselves;" and they looked out on that great world, and then they looked up at the Lord Jesus Christ, and they said, " For that, O Lord Jesus Christ, we will go." And they went there and preached the blood of the Lord Jesus Christ, and told it to dying lepers, from year to year, until the leprosy palsied their arms and made white their cheeks, and at last laid them low in the lepers' grave. Yes, that is denying ourselves, and we ought to take up the Lord's cross, our cross. We are to take up the cross he gives us, not his cross, because his cross was dying for a lost world, but the cross he gives us, and follow him. Young people of the Christian Endeavor, are you ready to follow the Lord Jesus Christ? Look at the depth from which he came to the height to which he rose. Dear members of the Christian Endeavor, follow Jesus, and the Lord God, the Holy Ghost, will strengthen you. He says, "My grace is sufficient for that, for my strength will be made perfect in your weakness," and when he comes it will be to anoint you to be prophet and to be king for the sake of the Lord Jesus Christ.

The world is dying all about you; opportunities lie on every side; there is a multitude of voices saying to you everywhere, "Go, for the fields are wide and the harvest rich," and I wish to say however weak, however feeble, however helpless, you may be, God will give you power as you go forth in the name of the Lord Jesus Christ. And let me conclude by saying this is a message that you have to tell,— tell the lost, tell the sick,— that the blood of Jesus Christ cleanses from all sins. Tell the lost that God says, "Come and let us read together, though your sins be as scarlet, they shall be as white as snow; though they be red like crimson they shall be as wool."

The doctrine of substitution is the Gospel of Jesus Christ. When Barabbus came out he said, no doubt, to himself, "Am I afraid, am I afraid?" and people gathered about him and said, "Barabbus, you are afraid," and he said, "Who made me afraid?" And they said, "You see that lone man there, that lone man of whom all Israel has heard, who went about doing good, Barabbus, he is to die in thy stead and be crucified in thy room." Young man, tell it to the world about you, and God will bless this Gospel,—"that God so loved the world that he gave his only begotten Son, that whosoever believeth in him should not perish but have everlasting life." There are some to whom the Lord will say at the last, "Come, ye blessed, receive the kingdom prepared for you;" some that he will bid sit on his throne; some upon whose heads he will put crowns; and some that shall reign as kings in heaven forever — and who are they? Not the young men and young women, the rich, the great, or the honorable of the world, but those dear servants of his that uplifted the banner of Jesus Christ to the world.

"Saved by Grace" appropriately sang the chorus after the sermon. Dr. Clark then took charge of the meeting, urging that the delegates let nothing come between them and God.

Remarks of President Francis E. Clark, D.D.

And now, dear friends, we come to this hour that we have been looking to for so many days, this crowning hour. I always come to it myself, when it is my duty to lead the consecration meeting, with trembling. And I say, "Who is sufficient for these things?" I fear that I may get in the way, that something or somebody may get between us and God. I fear that some words may not be spoken to his glory. Yet, I do not know that we need have these fears, for I think that this may be of all services the most simple, the most natural, as it is the most sweet. We have come to-night to the close of the Convention. We have been preparing for it during all these days; surely we are ready for it now. There are but three things for us to do. I believe that a true consecration meeting must have an upward look, if it would be a sincere consecration meeting. If we are looking at each other, or thinking of each other; if we are thinking of an eloquent address, or what somebody is to say, it will not be sincere in our heart that we can give our word and devotion. But if first of all we look up to God — O friends, that is it, look up to God, and I pray you in these opening moments look up to him, for the presence of God is here this evening. He is looking at us; we may look up into his very face to-night. For a moment, in the stillness of this hour, look up into God's face. It demands something else, it seems to me; it demands not only an upward look, but an attentive ear. It demands that we ask the question, "Lord, what wilt thou have me to do?" We can not consecrate ourselves until we have made that plea and asked that question, —"Lord, what wilt thou have me to do?" O friends, there is something for each one; why is it that you have come here? The registration committee tells us that there are between 30,000 and 40,000 Endeavorers in town. Do not think of the masses, but think of yourselves; why are you here? How does it happen that out of the million of Endeavorers in America you are here, you are one; what does it mean, this high privilege? You have come here, one out of a hundred, one out of a thousand, perhaps, from your section. Why is it? In order that you may hear God speak, and that you may take home the message. You come with a tremendous responsibility, the weight of responsibility that rests upon you who can come to such convention and such a consecration meeting. You have something to hear; you have a message given to you; you have something to take home, or you are recreant to your high trust and to your high privilege. Christian Endeavorers, listen, listen if you would consecrate yourselves. What has God to say to you? What have you to say to God? Ask the question, "What wilt thou have me to do?" and now listen for an answer. And one other thing is to obey when you have prayed. Oh, did you not hear in that moment of silence some word? Did you not think of some new thing at home, of something for your church, for your pastor, for your weekly reports to your meeting, for your Sunday school, for some associate member, for some who have not come to Christ? Did you not hear God speak to you and give you a message for some one, tell you some thing?

And then the remaining thing is to go and do. We have heard, we have sung, we have talked together, we have inspired each other's hearts, we have lifted up our eyes, we have listened with open ears, and now go and do! Do you remember what Dr. Bonner says about the apostles as he imagines them talking together on their way to Galilee? He said to them, "I go into Galilee; meet me there," and they walked along on that long journey to meet Christ in Galilee, and Dr. Bonner imagines them talking together, and Peter says — what more can he say? — "He has told us of his love. He has said, 'I call you no longer servants, but friends.' He has given us his love." "Yes," says John, "and not only that, but he has told us of the peace which he gives, the peace which surpasseth the understanding; what more is there that he can give?" "Yes," says James, "not only has he given us peace and love, but he has given us joy." And they wonder what our Lord has to say to them that he has not said to them, and they go to Galilee, and he meets them there and he says to them — what? Nothing about peace, nothing about joy, nothing about love. He has said all these things, but there is a more imperative message and a more important message for them just then; he says, "Go, go, go into all the world and preach my Gospel to every creature." So, Christian Endeavorers, he has been talking to us about peace, joy, and love, the sweet thought that surpasseth understanding, the love which is his to give, the joy which has made our hearts swell in this, the most spiritual of all the conventions that the Christian Endeavor Society has perhaps ever held. And now there is something more. In this closing consecration meeting he comes to us with another voice. We go to our homes. Some of us leave in an hour's time, and the most of us to-morrow, and the message is, "Go, go, go, Christian Endeavorers; you have heard of peace, joy, and love, all of these things have come to you in the Convention, and now go and preach my Gospel, and do my will." O Endeavorers, in this consecration hour, in this closing blessed service, as you look up and as you listen, will you hear? Will you obey? Will you go? Will you go and do his will? God grant it; God grant it. Go and do his will. God grant it.

In hushed and reverent tones "Just As I Am" was sung, and the united prayer was offered aloud in concert, "Create within me a clean heart, O God, and renew a right spirit within me." "O God, open thou my lips and my mouth shall show forth thy praise."

So was introduced the summoning of the hosts to the altar of their vows. South Carolina, the first State called, declares the Lord its rock and fortress. Wisconsin in an original poem proclaims "Forward" its watchword. West Virginia. a goodly delegation, quotes Paul's, "I press " as its motto, and sings, "We 're Marching Upward to Zion." "Washington for Christ!" "I can do all things through Christ," cries the next State. Virginia, a solid delegation near the rear of the tent, takes as its own the motto, "This one thing I do." "I can not be everywhere, I can be somewhere; I can not do everything, I can do something; what I can do I ought to do, and by the grace of God I will," is the beautiful vow recorded by Vermont. Utah follows with a word of Scripture, Texas sings a verse of its noble State song, and then Tennessee arises and expresses its gratitude to God for his answer to prayer in giving it Nashville, '98. The State's familiar and impressive response, "Where He Leads Me, I Will Follow," is sung with fine feeling. "South Dakota for Christ" follows, with the motto, " Not to be ministered unto, but to minister." In excellent unison Rhode Island quotes a verse from the Psalms, and Pennsylvania's multitude arise and pledge themselves to remain true to their covenant obligations,— devotion to Christ, church loyalty, soul-winning, missionary extension, good citizenship, and Christian fellowship. Oregon's one delegate vows "This one thing," and Ohio, a great company, says of the Lord that he is their strength, their refuge, their fortress. North Dakota sweetly sings, " My Life, My Love, I Give to Thee." New York's large delegation quotes the Convention motto, "Not by might, nor by power," and New Mexico sings, "Nearer, my God, to Thee." The orange and black of the New Jersey flags are upraised as the host of delegates sing softly, " My Jesus, I Love Thee. '

The home friends and the Endeavorers the world around, who could not share the Convention's blessings, are remembered in special prayer, and the roll-call is continued. New Hampshire, which re-affirms the pledge, Nevada, Nebraska, Montana, Missouri, Mississippi, Minnesota, and Michigan are called, and most of them quote Holy Writ as consecration vows, and Missouri adds a verse of "Missouri for Christ." A special consecration hymn, written for this Convention, is sung by Massachusetts to the tune of the Portuguese Hymn. "The love of Christ constraineth" Maryland, and she thrills the vast concourse of people by her "Maryland, My Maryland." Maine repeats the first clause of the pledge; Louisiana is "for Christ and the Church;" Kentucky sings its beautiful State hymn, to the tune " My Old Kentucky Home." Another State song, "Iowa for Christ," succeeds, and Indiana proclaims its Endeavorers ambassadors for Christ. Illinois's State president speaks a few sentences, and the delegation sings, " My Faith Looks Up to Thee."

Idaho and Georgia have Scriptural vows, and Florida avers that "the fairest of our flowers are lives of noble endeavor; our sweetest fruits, their deeds of loving service ; and our brightest sunshine, that which streams into our souls from the Sun of Righteousness." "Florida for Christ!" Eight Floating Society Endeavorers find God in "the uttermost parts of the sea," and sing prayerfully, "Jesus, Saviour, Pilot Me." This prompts the Convention to unite in special prayer for sailors and all upon the deep waters.

" For me to live is Christ," says Delaware. Connecticut would present its bodies as living sacrifices. Colorado can do all things through Christ, and would lift up the Saviour. Canada's united and robust delegation responds in vigorous tones with the first two verses of the twelfth chapter of Romans. California's young people, realizing their especial responsibilities for next year, look to the Lord, who says, " I will keep." "Arkansas for Christian Endeavor" cries one of the smaller delegations, which then sings " My Faith Looks Up to Thee." The associate members at this point are remembered in prayer. Arizona next responds with a faithful saying, John v. 4, and the last State, Alabama, takes as its own the ambition that Paul records in 2 Cor. v. 9. Afterward a soldier spoke the desire of the Christian Endeavorers in the army.

What follows graphically portrays the universal fellowship, and moved all hearts. Foreign lands were asked for a consecration sentiment. Mexico is the first to respond. Great Britain follows, impressively quoting the Saviour's prayer "that they all may be one." Australia has a message from the Book, and Persia declares that "the ends of the earth shall see the salvation of God." A thrill of emotion passes over the meeting at Turkey's significant response, given by an Armenian : "Who shall separate us from the love of Christ? shall tribulation, or distress, or persecution, or famine, or nakedness, or peril, or sword? Nay, in all these things we are more than conquerors through him that loved us."

A native Chinaman speaks for the delegation from China, " Let all the people praise thee." Japan prays to be consecrated to the Lord's service; Liberia sends a written response; Germany answers in the tongue of the fatherland; and Africa, with missionary zeal, says, " Let the old pray and give; let the young prepare and go." The District of Columbia, the Convention's hosts, came next, with the song by the chorus and other Convention workers, " My Life, My Love, I Give to Thee."

Thus end the voluntary responses. The sense of sacredness and nearness to the Master that has pervaded the meeting is increased, and the verses that Dr. Clark afterward gives are repeated with fervor. To the choir he suggests, " I will sing unto the Lord as long as I live." To the clergymen, the shepherds of the Christian Endeavor flock, is given the Scripture, " Make me to understand the way of thy precepts ; so shall I talk of thy wondrous works."

Are the young men in the Church? Behold the multitude that next rises, and let your heart take courage. Thousands of bright, strong, manly young men get up and quote, " I have written unto you, young men, because ye are strong, and the Word of God abideth in you, and ye have overcome the wicked one." A still greater mass of people arise when the young women are requested to stand and testify, " A woman that feareth the Lord, she shall be praised."

There are yet other pledges, and the service grows in intensity. The active members of the Society promise, " I will never forget thy precepts, for with them thou hast quickened me." In response to the appeal to "all who love the Lord Christ," nearly the entire company recites, " Lord, thou art the strength of my life ; of whom shall I be afraid ? " In tender tones Dr. Clark asks that the associate members unite in the song that all are reverently to sing, " Nearer, my God, to Thee."

The last moments have come. Every one is standing. As a final, complete, and comprehensive covenant, the thousands upraise their right hands — what a sight it is ! — and repeat the first clause of the pledge, holding their hands aloft while a prayer of consecration is offered. How many associate members take this vow for the first time only the watching angels know. The gavel strikes the platform railing in token of the adjournment of the Fifteenth International Christian Endeavor Convention. " The Lord watch between me and thee, when we are absent one from another " is repeated, and with " At the Cross " on their lips and in their souls, the delegates go out into the night, with hearts enlarged and purposeful.

EVANGELISTIC MEETINGS.

"Not by might, nor by power, but by my spirit, saith the Lord of hosts," was the District of Columbia consecration verse at Boston last year. Relying upon the principle contained in that verse, and upon the Holy Spirit, for constant direction and results, the work was undertaken and carried on.

Through correspondence with presidents and secretaries of local unions, leaders for evangelistic meetings were appointed, and companies organized several weeks before the Convention. In order to equip themselves for the work these bands held meetings for prayer and consultation before starting, and on the way to Washington. By far the most effective work was done by those bands whose leaders had time to learn their place of assignment and acquaint their workers with the nature of the service expected of them. While not at all underrating the labor of others, the preparation for the campaign the Chicago, New York City, and New Jersey bands rendered was especially valuable. Meetings of remarkable power were held by these workers at the new post-office building, Central Power-station, jail, workhouse, and in the "Division," the scarlet plague spot of Washington. All of the bands that filled their appointments did nobly, as visible results clearly show. Over three hundred were personally dealt with; one hundred and sixty-nine requested prayers for themselves; eighty-one manifested deep concern for their souls; and twenty-seven professed to give themselves to Jesus. (These figures do not include the large Monday meetings at Central Union Mission, the leaders of which did not report.) But neither statistics nor time will reveal all the good done. In all there were eighty-three meetings held, mostly in open air. The audiences numbered from twenty to two thousand, aggregating twenty-five thousand. Inside meetings were held at homes and hospitals, jail, workhouse, chapels, missions, in two Sunday schools, and in four churches on Sunday evening, taking the place of the regular evening service. There were three Gospel temperance meetings held by the Rev. W. P. Ferguson. The leader's reports indicate that the Holy Spirit was present in power at nearly every one of these meetings.

From one mission chapel came the report, "Thirteen requests for prayer; many outside quietly listening," from another, "Several gave themselves in full surrender to God." From the two Sunday schools and four churches good reports have been received. From the jail and workhouse the report is, "Most wonderful meeting we ever attended. The prisoners cried aloud for mercy, and testified to the saving power of Jesus. Tracts and Testaments were given; thirty requests for prayer."

From the Division work the report was "One meeting; power of God wonderfully manifested." Another, "Nineteen requests for prayer; five professed surrender; nine names and addresses of anxious ones secured." Another, "Thirty requests for prayer; nineteen seekers' cards signed." Still another, "Very peculiar meeting; hand-to-hand work by women with women and men with men. Fully one hundred persons spoken to and plead with; fifteen requests for prayer; two seekers spoke." At one of these Division meetings (which were held from ten to twelve o'clock at night, using the Gospel wagon); "a young lady worker noticed a young man standing in the crowd while 'Sunshine' was being sung, apparently interested. The leader was directed by her to him. He was prayed with there, and at the hotel where these workers were stopping. He gave himself to Christ, and later went down into the Division, where he was well known, and gave his testimony. He is of good family, and holds a responsible position in a large business house." At the new post-office there were several gangs of men, one gang composed of Catholics. When the meeting began, this gang, or their boss, turned on steam to disturb the service; but every time he did that the Endeavorers struck up a hymn, and finally they tired him out and the meeting ended in "good cheer and hand-shaking all around."

On one of the bicycle runs, a party took refuge from a shower in the 14th Street car-barns, and while waiting for the rain to subside held a praise service.

Miss Deborah K. Knox, of Pawtucket, R. I., who led the meetings at Bethany Chapel, besides doing valuable personal work, distributed a large number of tracts.

The New Jersey Endeavorers held a meeting at the Newsboys' Home, which will result in the formation of a Junior Society there.

Rev. E. D. Bailey, of the Central Union Mission, writes: "The evangelistic services at the Mission were among the best of the Convention. The testimonies of Mission converts and Christian Endeavorers mingled constituted a service which for strength and effectiveness is rarely ever exceeded. Each service was larger in attendance than the preceding, the large auditorium being filled. The Gospel wagons were used each evening, their services culminating in the service at Market Space at six o'clock, Sunday P. M., where an immense throng, estimated at three thousand, listened attentively, and joined in a most thrilling Gospel service. The enthusiasm broke all bounds and manifested itself at every turn of the service." The superintendent at the new post-office says, " The meetings held here by the Christian Endeavorers were very satisfactory. I have only words of commendation respecting them."

THE BIBLE STUDIES.

One of the most practically helpful parts of the crowded Convention programme was the series of Bible studies conducted by President G. S. Burroughs, D.D., of Crawfordsville, Ind. The large New York Avenue Presbyterian Church was crowded daily, before the morning sessions. Note-books were to be seen everywhere, and were liberally used to supplement the excellent syllabi printed in the programme.

President Burroughs is a clear, dignified, attractive speaker, and held close attention from beginning to end. Each day a single book of the Bible was studied,—"Amos, the Prophet of Righteousness," "Hosea, the Prophet of Love," "Galatians, Glad News of Freedom," "First Corinthians, Practical Christianity." These were chosen as illustrations of the method of Bible-study the leader advocated,—the study of whole books at a time, especially of the key books; and all the hundreds of Endeavorers that took this valuable course will be far better Bible students hereafter.

SEEKING GOD EARLY.

In a Convention where the deepening of the spiritual life was made the prominent topic, the early morning prayer meetings, three in number daily, naturally held a most important place. Unity of purpose was given by assigning on the programme a special topic for each morning. These topics were drawn from different clauses of the pledge, after the first day, when the subject was " Prayer for the Convention." As at Boston, much inspiration was gained, and the thought of the hour was made more definite and practical by reports from those that had been engaged in evangelistic work on the day before. A good variety was to be noted in the ways in which the different meetings were conducted. One would be made by the leader largely a Bible-reading, the passages having been assigned to different ones before the opening of the meeting. Thus these gatherings were helpful both because of their spiritual uplift and because of their suggestions of new methods.

On Friday there was an innovation that proved to be well worth repeating. It was but one of the signs of the growing interest in Junior work, and was an early morning meeting for Juniors. Led by two Juniors and attended by others, it attracted a large number of those engaged in Junior work. An excellent chalk-talk and one or two short addresses were given, and many took part in the prayers and testimonies.

RESOLUTIONS OF THE BOARD OF TRUSTEES AND OFFICERS OF THE UNITED SOCIETY OF CHRISTIAN ENDEAVOR.

Resolved. That the heartiest thanks of the Trustees of the United Society of Christian Endeavor and of the entire Convention are most certainly due and are hereby most gladly expressed:

First. To the Capital City of Washington, for its welcome, metropolitan and national in every way.

Second. To the painstaking, persistent, to the least and last thing, attentive, and splendid Committee of '96.

Third. To the enthusiastic and admirable preparation and service of Colonel Bright, Sergeant-at-Arms, United States Senate, and to the Capitol police.

Fourth. To the United States Marine Band, for its surpassing music, both on the stand and in the parade.

Fifth. To the police of the city of Washington, for their constant courtesy, care, and unrelaxing attention.

Sixth. To the great and wonderful Washington Christian Endeavor choir —never was there a choir so large, better trained, readier in various service. The harmonious songs on the Capitol steps, like the sound of many waters — who that heard can ever forget that wonderful sound and scene ?

Seventh. To the press, for every possible attention and for such full and accurate reports.

Eighth. To the Government of the United States, for its use of the White Lot, and for the liberty of gathering at the east front of the Capitol.

Ninth. To Col. John M. Wilson, Superintendent of Public Buildings and Grounds, for his invaluable aid in the arrangement for the places of meeting.

Tenth. Nor in any wise should most grateful thanks be omitted to the beautiful and thoughtful attention and service of those on whom the convenience of the members of the Convention was most dependent, the motor-men, drivers, and conductors of the street railroads of Washington.

NUMBER OF SOCIETIES, JULY, 1896.

UNITED STATES.

	Young People's.	Junior.	Interme-diate.	Mothers'.	Senior.	Total.
Alabama	107	22				129
Alaska Territory	4					4.
Arizona Territory	17	3				20
Arkansas	122	29				151
California	779	442	11		1	1.233
Colorado	220	100				320
Connecticut	528	192	5		1	726
Delaware	70	30				100
District of Columbia	77	56				133
Florida	166	44				210
Georgia	144	20				164
Idaho	37	14				51
Illinois	1,802	836	17	21	4	2,680
Indiana	1,352	498	11			1,861
Indian Territory	38	8				46
Iowa	1,302	468	1	1	1	1,773
Kansas	982	349	2	11		1,344
Kentucky	337	82	2			421
Louisiana	62	13				75
Maine	610	170	4			784
Maryland	365	107		1		473
Massachusetts	917	461	9			1,387
Michigan	914	318	3	1		1,236
Minnesota	589	314	5		1	909
Mississippi	42	6				48
Missouri	846	379	2		1	1,228
Montana	47	22				69
Nebraska	541	214	2	1	1	759
Nevada	9	6				15
New Hampshire	302	103			3	408
New Jersey	778	390				1,168
New Mexico Territory	28	7				35
New York	2,971	1,104	5		1	4.081
North Carolina	222	45				267
North Dakota	113	23				136
Ohio	2,311	716	11	3	1	3.042
Oklahoma Territory	137	26	1			164
Oregon	304	134	1			440
Pennsylvania	3,273	1,224	8	7	3	4 515
Rhode Island	145	65				210
South Carolina	64	10	1			75
South Dakota	209	65		1		275
Tennessee	349	121	1			471
Texas	408	174	3			585
Utah	45	26			1	72
Vermont	327	124	1		1	453
Virginia	178	22				200
Washington	232	94	4			330
West Virginia	225	50				275
Wisconsin	539	237	4			780
Wyoming	19	6				25
	26,203	9.969	114	47	21	36,354

CANADA.

	Young People's.	Junior.	Parents'.	Mothers'.	Total.
Alberta	12	2			14
Assiniboia	47	7			54
British Columbia	38	5			43
Manitoba	117	21			138
New Brunswick	152	12			164
Newfoundland	5				5
Nova Scotia	394	42			436
Ontario	1,817	261		1	2,079
Prince Edward Island	63	2			65
Quebec	224	58	2		284
Saskatchewan	5				5
Total,	2,879	410	2	1	3,292

FOREIGN.

	Young People's.	Junior.	Intermediate.	Senior.	Total.
Africa	33	5			38
Asiatic Turkey	1	1			2
Australia	1,850	150		4	2,004
Austria	2				2
Belgium	1				1
Bermuda	6				6
Brazil	2	1			3
Burmah	14				14
Chili	6				6
Colombia	1				1
China	36	4			40
Egypt	1	1			2
England and Wales	3,062	245	1		3,308
France	66				66
Germany	18				18
Guatemala	1				1
Hawaiian Islands	6	3			9
Holland	1				1
India	117	11			128
Ireland	52	6			58
Italy	2				2
Japan	63	3			66
Labrador	1				1
Laos	10				10
Madagascar	93				93
Mexico	55	7			62
Norway	4				4
Persia	3	1			4
Samoa	10				10
Scotland	300	15			315
South Sea Islands	2				2
Spain	4	1			5
Siam	1				1
Switzerland	7				7
Syria	3				3
Sweden	1				1
Turkey	33	8			41
Upper Hebrides	1				1
West Indies	60	3			63
Total,	5,929	465	1	4	6,399

RECAPITULATION.

	Young People's.	Junior.	Interme-diate.	Mothers'.	Senior.	Parents'.	Total.
United States	26,203	9,969	114	47	21		36,354
Canada	2,879	410		1		2	3,292
Foreign	5,929	465	1		4		6,399
Floating Societies . .							80
							46,125

INDEX.

OFFICERS

www.ingramcontent.com/pod-product-compliance
Lightning Source LLC
La Vergne TN
LVHW091247080426
835510LV00007B/149